I0348797

TANTRA

TANTRA

LIBERATION IN THE WORLD

Prabhuji

TANTRA
LIBERATION IN THE WORLD
BY PRABHUJI

Copyright © 2023
First edition

Printed in Round Top, New York, United States

All rights reserved. None of the information contained in this book may be reproduced, republished, or re-disseminated in any manner or form without the prior written consent of the publisher.

Published by Prabhuji Mission
Website: prabhuji.net

Avadhutashram
PO Box 900
Cairo, NY, 12413
USA

Painting on the cover by Prabhuji:
"Night"
Acrylic on canvas, New York
Canvas Size: 20" x 20"

Library of Congress Control Number: 2021906563
ISBN-13: 978-1-945894-36-7

Contents

Preface 1
Introduction 5

Section 1: Tantric Vision

Chapter 1 – The essence of the Tantric vision 9

Chapter 2 – The foundations of Tantra 17
Meanings of the term Tantra 17
Tantric metaphysics 22
Two parallel revelations: Vedic and Tantric 23

Chapter 3 – Śiva–Śakti: The non-dual Tantric polarity 33
Shaivism 37
The *tri-mūrti* or "trinity" 41
The names of Śiva 42
The qualities of Śiva 46
Manifestations of Śiva 48
Śiva as pure subjectivity 48
Śiva as Nirguṇa-brahman 49
Śiva as Saguṇa-brahman 49
Śiva as individual souls 51
Śiva as an enlightened being 52
Śiva as the Vedic deity Rudra 52
Śiva as our authentic nature 53
Shaktism 54

Section 2: Development of Tantra

Chapter 1 – The origin and development of the Tantric revelation 61
The pre-Tantric *Śaiva Ati-mārga* or "the supreme or direct path" 63
The *Śaiva Mantra-mārga* or "the path of the mantra" 64
The *Śakta Kula-mārga* or "the path of the clans" 66
The Non-dual *Trika* Kashmir Shaivism 68

The *Vaiṣṇava Pāñca-rātra* ... 70
The influence of Tantra on other religions ... 71
Tantra today ... 73

CHAPTER 2 – THE *ATI-MĀRGA* OR "THE DIRECT PATH" ... 83
Initiated and uninitiated *Śaivas* ... 83
Śaiva Ati-mārga ... 87
1. *Pāśu-pata* or *pāñcārthika* ... 89
2. *Lākula, Kālā-mukha* or *Mahā-vratins* ... 117
3 *Kāpālika* or *Soma-siddhānta* ... 127

CHAPTER 3 – THE *MANTRA-MĀRGA* OR "THE PATH OF MANTRAS" ... 147
Two movements: devotional and Tantric ... 147
The emergence of the Tantric revelation ... 148
Saiddhāntika and non-*Saiddhāntika* ... 150
1. *Saiddhāntika* – The *Śaiva-siddhānta Āgamas* ... 155
The different stages of *Śaiva-siddhānta* literature ... 157
I. Early *siddhānta* ... 157
II. The Tamil devotional poets ... 158
III. Sanskrit *siddhānta* ... 159
IV. Systematic theologians in the Tamil language ... 160
V. The systematization of devotional *Śaiva-siddhānta* ... 160
2. Non *Saiddhāntika* – The *Bhairava Tantras* ... 162
2.1 The *Mantra-pīṭha* ... 163
2.2 The *Vidyā-pīṭha* ... 166
2.2.1 The *Vāma Tantras* (left Tantras) or the *Guhya Tantras* (secret Tantras) ... 167
2.2.2 The *Yāmala Tantras* or "Union Tantras" ... 168
2.2.3. The *Śakti Tantras* or "Energy Tantras" ... 173
2.2.3.1 The *Śakti Tantras* – The *Trika* ... 174
2.2.3.2 The *Śakti Tantras* – Kālī ... 186
2.3 Amṛteśvara-bhairava and Amṛta-lakṣmī ... 193

CHAPTER 4 – THE KULA-MĀRGA OR "THE KAULA PATH" ... 199
Āmnāyas or "transmissions" ... 215
1. *Pūrvāmnāya* or "eastern transmission": Īśāna Face ... 219
2. *Uttarāmnāya* or "northern transmission": Sadyo-jāta Face ... 224
3. *Paścimāmnāya* or "western transmission": Tat-puruṣa Face ... 234

4. *Dakṣiṇāmnāya* or "southern transmission": Aghora Face 240
5. *Anuttarāmnāya* or "supreme transmission" 243
6. *Ūrdhvāmnāya* or "superior transmission": Vāma-deva Face 251

CHAPTER 5 – KASHMIR'S *TRIKA* SHAIVISM 261
Circumstances of emergence... 262
Chronology.. 263
The exegetical writers 263
General characteristics of the *Trika*.. 264
The arrival of Islam 266
Abhinava-gupta: The brightest star in Kashmir's sky 267
The four schools of Kashmir Shaivism 273
1. The *Kaula Trika* school 273
The *Trika* or "the triple principle" 278
Trika philosophy 279
2. The *Pratyabhijñā* school 282
3. The *Krama* school 283
4. The *Spanda* school 285
The literature of Kashmir Shaivism 285
The thirty-six *tattvas* or "categories of existence" 286
Śuddha-tattvas or "pure categories of existence" 288
Śuddhāśuddha-tattvas or "pure-impure categories of existence" 291
Aśuddha-tattvas or "impure categories"....................................... 292
The three *antaḥ-karaṇas* or "internal organs" 292
The *pañca-jñānendriyas* or "five cognitive organs" 292
The *pañca-karmendriyas* or "five organs of action" 293
The *pañca-tanmātras* or "five subtle elements" 293
The *pañca-mahā-bhūtas* or "five great elements" 293
Śuddhādhvā-tattvas or "pure elements" 294

CHAPTER 6 – TANTRIC VAISHNAVISM 299
The *Vaiṣṇava Āgamas* 314
Pāñca-rātra 314
Vaikhānasa...315
Bengali *Kṛṣṇa-bhakti*...316
Sahajiyās 317

Chapter 7 – Later Tantric sects 321
Liṅgāyata or *Vīra* Shaivism 321
The founders prior to Basava 323
The vision of *Vīra* Shaivism 323
Ṣaṭ-sthala-siddhānta 326
Nātha-sampradāya or *Nātha-siddha-siddhānta* 327

Section 3: Tantric Scriptures

Chapter 1 – Agamic or Tantric Literature 333
The relationship with the Vedas 334
Oral tradition 335
The subject matter of the *Āgamas* 337
Mantra, yantra, and Tantra 338
The sections of the *Āgamas* 349
Classifying the canon 350

Chapter 2 – The *Śaiva Tantras* 355
The *Śaiva* literature: Vedic, Puranic, and Agamic 355
The revelation of the *Śaiva* scriptures 357
The emanations of the *Āgamas* from Sada-śiva 368
1. Early Classification of the *Śaiva Āgamas*: five currents (*srotas*) 372
1.1 The upper current: *Śaiva-siddhānta Āgamas* (Tantras) 374
1.2 The northern current: *Vāma Tantras* 376
1.3 The southern current: *Dakṣiṇa Tantras* 378
1.4 The eastern current: *Gāruḍa Tantras* 380
1.5 The western current: *Bhūta Tantras* 383
2. Later classifications of the canon 384
2.1. The three traditions: central (*madhyama*), left (*vāma*), and right (*dakṣiṇa*) 384
2.2. *Saiddhāntika* (*Siddhānta Tantras*) and *non-Saiddhāntika* (*Bhairava Tantras*) 387
2.3. *Mantra-pīṭha* and *Vidyā-piṭha* 388

Chapter 3 – The *Śākta tantras* 389
3.1 The *Bhairava Tantras* 390
3.2 The *Kaula Tantras* 397

Chapter 4 – The *Vaiṣṇava Tantras* 399
4.1 The *Pāñca-rātra* 399

4.2 The *Vaikhānasa Āgamas* 403

CHAPTER 5 – THE *SAURYA TANTRAS* 405

CHAPTER 6 – THE *GĀṆAPATYA TANTRAS* 407

CHAPTER 7 – HIERARCHIES OF THE REVEALED SCRIPTURES 409

SECTION 4: TANTRIC PRACTICE

CHAPTER 1 – THE TANTRIC VISION OF THE HUMAN BODY 415
Three bodies or *śarīras* 421
The astral body or *liṅga-śarīra* 422
Prāṇa or "vital energy" 425
Types of *prāṇa* 427
The evolution of *prāṇa* 428
The *nāḍīs* or "energy channels" 429
The ten main *nāḍīs* 431
Other important *nāḍīs* 434
The difference between *kuṇḍalinī-śakti* and *prāṇa-śakti* 440
Chakras, *marmas*, and *granthis* 446
Chakras or "energy centers" 446
The *marmas* or "vital points" 450
The *granthis* or "knots" 458

CHAPTER 2 – QUALIFICATIONS AND STAGES FOR TANTRIC PRACTICE 461
Qualifications for Tantra yoga practice 461
Stages of Tantric *sādhana* 464

CHAPTER 3 – ESSENTIAL ELEMENTS OF TANTRIC *SĀDHANA* 467
Accepting a guru 467
Initiation or *dīkṣā* 468
Bhūta-śuddhi or "bodily purification" 471
Nyāsa or "mental purification" 472
Yantras 473
Mantras 474
Japa 475
Bhāva or "disposition" 477

Chapter 4 – Types of Tantric *Sādhana* 491
Sādhana according to the *guṇas* 491
Pañca-ma-kāra according to levels.... 492
Types of Tantric *sādhana* in the *Śrī-vidyā* tradition 497
Samayācāra sādhana.... 497
Dakṣiṇācāra sādhana.... 497
Vāmācara sādhana 498
Miśra sādhana 498
Kaulācāra sādhana.... 499

Chapter 5 – Tantric ritualism.... 503
Pūjā or "devotional ritual".... 504
Dīkṣā or "initiation".... 504
Other rituals.... 508
Worship of the *liṅga* and the *yonī*.... 509

Epilogue - Tantra and sexuality 519

APPENDICES
Sanskrit pronunciation guide....523
About Prabhuji....531
About the Prabhuji Mission....541
About the Avadhutashram 543
The Retroprogressive Path.... 545
Prabhuji today....547

ॐ अज्ञानतिमिरान्धस्य ज्ञानाञ्जनशलाकया ।
चक्षुरुन्मीलितं येन तस्मै श्रीगुरवे नमः ॥

oṁ ajñāna-timirāndhasya
jñānāñjana-śalākayā
cakṣur unmīlitaṁ yena
tasmai śrī-gurave namaḥ

Salutations unto that holy Guru who, applying the ointment [medicine] of [spiritual] knowledge, removes the darkness of ignorance of the blinded ones [unenlightened] and opens their eyes.

This book is dedicated, with deep gratitude and eternal respect, to the holy lotus feet of my beloved masters His Divine Grace Avadhūta Śrī Brahmānanda Bābājī Mahārāja (Guru Mahārāja) and His Divine Grace Bhakti-kavi Atulānanda Ācārya Mahārāja (Gurudeva).

Preface

The story of my life is nothing more than a long journey, from what I believed myself to be to what I truly am. It is an authentic inner and outer pilgrimage. It is a tale of transcending what is personal and universal, partial and total, illusory and real, apparent and true. My life is a flight beyond what is temporary and eternal, darkness and light, humanity and divinity. This story is not public but profoundly private and intimate.

Only what begins, ends; only what starts, finishes. One who lives in the present is neither born nor dies, because what has no beginning has no end.

I am a disciple of a seer, an enlightened being, and somebody who is nobody. I was initiated in my spiritual childhood by the moonlight. A seagull who loved flying more than anything else in life inspired me. In love with the impossible, I crossed the universe obsessed with a star. I have walked infinite paths, following the footsteps of those who could see.

Like the ocean that longs for water, I sought my home within my own house.

I am a simple intermediary who shares his experience with others. I am not a guide, coach, teacher, instructor, educator, psychologist, enlightener, pedagogue, evangelist, rabbi, *posek halacha*, healer, therapist, satsangist, psychic, leader, medium, savior, or guru. I am only a traveler whom you can ask for directions. I will gladly show you a place where everything calms upon arrival, a place beyond the sun and the stars, beyond your desires and longings, beyond time and space, beyond concepts and conclusions, and beyond everything that you believe you are or imagine that you will be.

I am just a whim or perhaps a joke from the sky and the only mistake of my beloved spiritual masters.

Aware of the abyss that separates revelation and our works, we live in a frustrated attempt to faithfully express the mystery of the spirit.

I paint sighs, hopes, silences, aspirations, and melancholies, inner landscapes, and sunsets of the soul.

I am a painter of the indescribable, inexpressible, and indefinable of our depths. Or maybe I just write colors and paint words.

Since childhood, little windows of paper captivated my attention; through them, I visited places, met people, and made friends. Those tiny *maṇḍalas* were my true elementary school, high school, and college. Like skilled teachers, these yantras have guided me through contemplation, attention, concentration, observation, and meditation.

Like a physician studies the human body, or a lawyer studies laws, I have dedicated my entire life to the study of myself. I can say with certainty that I know what resides and lives in this heart.

It is not my intention to convince anyone of anything. I do not offer theology or philosophy, nor do I preach or teach, I simply think out loud. The echo of these words may lead you to the infinite space of peace, silence, love, existence, consciousness, and absolute bliss.

Do not search for me. Search for yourself. You do not need me or anyone else, because the only thing that really matters is you. What you yearn for lies within you, as what you are, here and now.

I am not a merchant of rehashed information, nor do I intend to do business with my spirituality. I do not teach beliefs or philosophies. I only speak about what I see and just share what I know.

Avoid fame, for true glory is not based on public opinion but on what you really are. What matters is not what others think of you, but your own appreciation of who you are.

Choose bliss over success, life over reputation, and wisdom over information. If you succeed, you will know not only admiration but also true envy. However, jealousy is mediocrity's tribute to talent and an open acceptance of one's own inferiority.

I advise you to fly freely and never be afraid of making mistakes. Learn the art of transforming your mistakes into lessons. Never blame others for your faults: remember that taking complete responsibility for your life is a sign of maturity. When you fly, you learn that what matters is not touching the sky but the courage to spread your wings. The higher you rise, the smaller and less significant the world looks. As you walk, sooner or later you will understand that every search begins and ends in you.

Your unconditional well-wisher,
Prabhuji

Introduction

Tantra refers to a very diverse corpus of scriptures, techniques, rites, and teachings. It is hard to define because of this wisdom's multifaceted mystical nature. Nobody knows its age with certainty, but like the Vedas, it is considered eternal. It was cultivated and practiced in areas where Brahmanism was less influential, such as northwestern India, Bengal and Assam in the east, and Andhra in the south. Subsequently, Tantrism expanded, influencing not only Buddhism and Jainism, but each and every major religion of the world.

Although many in the West have become familiar with the term *tantra*, few know its true meaning. The West has largely ignored the ancestral religious and spiritual systems of India that present an order of values different from its own. Since it is one of the traditions least studied by Western scholars, it has been misinterpreted and even condemned.

This complex existential phenomenon cannot merely be described by words since it is not an intellectual philosophy, but instead belongs to the world of experience. Tantra emphasizes practice over beliefs and philosophical theories. Scholars try to define Tantra, but yogis do not require any categorization. *Tāntrikas* resort to philosophy only when it is essential to explain their worldview logically and clarify the theological and metaphysical meanings of their practices. In the end, the main intention of Tantra is self-knowledge.

Until we develop enough sensitivity, we will not be able to grasp Tantra. However, we can say without a doubt that getting closer to Tantric sensual spirituality makes us more authentic and real. Tantra leads us to discover deep aspects of our existence that lie dormant or repressed; it guides us to the revelation of our inherent potential that is hidden deep within us.

SECTION I

Tantric Vision

Chapter 1

The essence of the Tantric vision

Tantra is a transcendental revelation with a completely original view of humans, the world, and life. We must delve into its fascinating essence to fully comprehend this religious and spiritual phenomenon. Many consider it to be a rebellion against society or institutionalized religion. However, Tantra is not interested in treating the symptoms. Instead it focuses on the root cause of the disease: human conditioning.

In order to understand the Tantric vision, it is indispensable to take in its subversive and reactionary tenor. Its foundations are based on the absolute unity of life. Its metaphysics is largely Advaitic, but the emphasis on the Self is replaced with *śakti*, "the divine energy." Tantra does not divide reality into sin and virtue or the sacred and profane, but sees these opposites as integral polarities of a single whole. It does not see any essential difference between spiritual and material dimensions, but includes both. Tantra does not conceive life as a set of conflicts but as a totality. Rather than rejecting what is material, it strives to sublimate it. Instead of condemning sin, it aspires to spiritualize it. It sees no struggle between the human and the Divine, but rather harmonious transcendence. It argues that being human is not an obstacle to accessing the Divine, but an inevitable step on the path. Rather than a hindrance, our humanity is a phase of our evolutionary development.

Tantra works in harmony with nature, not against it. The Divine is no longer humanity's adversary and becomes its aspiration. The struggle between the human and the Divine ends, giving way to the yearning of the part for the whole. Tantra does not divide life into material and spiritual, but sees both aspects as two polarities of the same reality. Since they include each other, we must sublimate what is inferior, not destroy it. We should not escape from what is low, but elevate it. We stand before a process of spiritualization of the material, divinization of what we consider to be sinful.

When we separate the profane from the sacred, we create conflict. Life encompasses both matter and spirit, body and soul. Existence palpitates in the profane as well as in the sacred. To embark on the path of Tantra, we must abandon duality. Sex is not inferior to worship; eating is not inferior to praying. They are different expressions of the one unique life, different manifestations of the same reality.

An attitude of acceptance is natural for a metaphysics that sees a single nature underlying everything and everyone. There is no room for disapproval and censorship in the Tantric vision. It would be absurd to condemn a seed for not being a tree. If we crush the seed, we will destroy its potential to become a tree. The seed is a necessary stage in the evolutionary process. Whoever judges the mundane seed rejects the sacred tree; whoever condemns the human denies God.

Tantra is the path of unconditional acceptance par excellence. It begins with accepting the egoic inner movement and ends with recognizing our true nature. It begins by acknowledging what we believe we are and concludes by embracing what we really are. If we denounce the egoic state, we block access to our divine nature. No development is possible without admitting our reality. Human nature cannot be transcended if it is rejected and ignored. The more we repress things, the more our attraction toward them increases, because denial intensifies temptation. Any kind of condemnation, negation, or rejection detains and paralyzes us. Negating the mind produces mental paralysis; denying sensitivity atrophies the faculty of comprehension. Human nature will continue to act—desiring, entreating, and demanding—but it will be insensitive and devoid of awareness.

Understanding stems from observation without resisting, ignoring, repressing, or rejecting. Only as a witness of actions can comprehension be born. It is impossible to know that which is ignored, rejected, or repulsed. Blind repression causes stagnation and leads to obsession. You will walk at night and not appreciate the beauty of the stars. You will pass through the world without knowing its mystery. You will go through life without really living. You will move within your humanity, but guilt and repression will blur the clarity that observation can grant.

Tantra does not advise separating what is from what should be. Its teachings do not portray a conflict between who we are and what we are expected to be. Nor do they permit distancing the mundane from the Divine, the low from the high, the material from the spiritual. Tantra does not hold any repressive attitudes that promise transcendence at the cost of suffocating our own energies. Instead of halting passion with a warlike affectation, it encourages us to wisely utilize the energy that abides in our desires. The Tantric vision is peaceful and devoid of aggression. *Ahiṁsā*, or "nonviolence," lies at its foundation. It is not hostile toward any aspect of the human phenomenon. Tantra's message is one of unconditional acceptance, free of antagonism.

A *Tāntrika* lovingly interacts with the energy hidden behind desires. Our attitude toward cravings, passions, yearnings, and ambitions will eventually influence the way we relate to ourselves. Unconditional acceptance creates faith and self-confidence, while condemnation only produces a guilt complex.

Tantra does not judge our human energies as harmful or evil, but advises us to accept them as simple natural forces. If they are used against us, we will get hurt. But channeled toward our goal, they will benefit us, just as atomic energy is neither useful nor harmful. Depending on how it is used, it can power a city or destroy it. When applied wisely, it is incredibly useful; when misused, it is terribly destructive. Unfortunately, humanity often uses the power of desire immaturely, which leads to degradation. Tantra suggests developing an awareness of desires to understand their origins and phenomenology. Without exploring desire, it is impossible to evolve and transcend it. Tantra suggests consciously surrendering to desires and passions in order to transcend them, that is, consciously observing without being overpowered or dragged down. You will discover that you can use the power of desires to advance, without identifying with their direction. Desires can be transcended without aggressive struggle. In Tantra, confronting passion would violate the vow of ahimsa: while it may not involve violence against others, it is certainly violent toward ourselves.

The Tantric commandment is to renounce all effort to control. It invites us to abandon ourselves to desire instead of trying to dominate it. Tantra tells us to let ourselves be carried away and lose control, because in this surrender the mind and its conditioning are overcome.

It is a question of going beyond the mind and its content without opposing it. Only by getting lost in an unresisting forfeit of control will we awaken to the timeless unity of consciousness.

The mind has been programmed to dominate, never relinquish control, and never go beyond the limits set by its conditioning. The mind wants to adopt the role of controller and doer of whatever happens to it. Years ago, men were taught not to cry and women to laugh in moderation. While it is not easy to stay within these boundaries, it is almost impossible to consciously transgress them. For example, dressing modestly may be uncomfortable, but it is easier than undressing in public. According to the Tantric vision, emancipation lies beyond the limits of the mind, and true liberation is the abandonment of our mental prison. Only when passion is allowed to flow naturally, without any mental manipulation, does authentic freedom become possible.

Tantra teaches that the meditative state is not superior to the ordinary one. Meditations are not classified as good or bad. Tantra does not separate consciousness from unconsciousness, nor does it see conflict between them. It knows that even those who declare themselves unconscious do so from an awareness of their unconsciousness. It does not exclude the material, nor does it advocate what is commonly termed "spiritual." Rather, it invites us to accept the heights and the depths, the sublime and the degraded, the light of day and the darkness of night. It does not condemn darkness nor pursue light. By observing the opposites, we perceive their temporality. Only if we manage to enjoy both without becoming attached to either of them, will we experience that our authenticity transcends them.

Tantra does not recommend hurrying to rid ourselves of our humanity in order to attain divinity. Nor does it advise running away from this world to reach the beyond. It does not encourage us to reject the earthly in favor of the heavenly, for it is not a system that separates "this" from "that." When trying to reach our divine nature, it is a mistake to shake off our humanity without experiencing it in totality. We should not wage war against the egoic phenomenon before we understand it. Once we comprehend it, we will see that it is only a simple illusion, a fantasy completely devoid of substance. Perhaps then we will realize that the fight against the ego is meaningless, and that maybe we never even had an ego in the first place.

The Tantric vision favors a loving acceptance of who we are. When desire is sublimated, it becomes the key that unlocks the chains. The mundane ceases to be an obstacle and becomes the very path to transcendence. The body is no longer a barrier but a way forward. Instead of being the soul's enemy, our carnality becomes the bridge to divinity. The body no longer conflicts with the spirit and once again becomes the temple where God resides. Then we realize that the body, or *śarīra*, allows the Self to perceive itself.

Desires are nourished by the future and can only exist in our fantasies. Since desires live in tomorrow, they make us sacrifice the present moment for an imaginary goal. But if we establish ourselves in the now, our desires naturally evaporate. Desire is not eliminated through blind repression, but by being present.

Generally, the life of a traditional believer unfolds as a conflict between the sacred and the profane.

However, the Tantric attitude does not allow such conflicts between sin and virtue, because both are seen as polarities of the same phenomenon. Accepting that the origin of creation is divine, Tantra does not view anything or anyone as profane. Since God is the source of the universe, everything is sacred. Vice and virtue, sin and holiness, all share the same divine origin.

Historically, Tantra has been condemned for its revolutionary and transgressive attitude. It is no surprise that religious orthodoxy would reject a spiritual tradition that sees no differences in caste, social status, or gender. Ancient sects such as *Pāśu-pata*, *Kālā-mukha*, *Kāpālika* as well as the *Trika* and *Kālī* cults were used to being humiliated, discredited, and ridiculed. In their efforts to get rid of social conditioning, they intentionally encouraged society to reject them. The followers of the Tantric tradition were independent spiritual aspirants who were only loyal to the Truth. Their conclusions, practices, ethics, and morality were not tied to any specific religious movement. Since Tantric tradition was enriched by traditions both from within and outside Vedic beliefs, the orthodoxy doubted its integrity. Hence the Tantric tradition had to hide its teachings.

Any human being with a sincere interest can be initiated and become a true disciple. Tantra is one of the few spiritual traditions free of chauvinism. In most religions, a male presence is required to perform certain rites, and women have no access to privileged positions. But in the Tantric tradition, especially *vāmācāra*, a woman's presence is vital for its most elevated *sādhana*. This attitude stems from the very roots of the Tantric view that no human being is entirely male or female, as both masculinity and femininity reside within everyone. Dormant femininity is present within every man, while unconscious masculinity lies in the depths of every woman. The awakening of consciousness involves a meeting of the two. A man who has not yet awakened his feminine aspect looks for a woman outside of himself; a woman who is not yet aware of her masculine aspect looks for it externally. This superficial search for the opposite sex is only the first stage of inner inquiry. The Tantric path aims at full integration. Any effort by only a man or only a woman is incomplete; it is necessary to create harmony between the two poles.

The Tantric vision guides us on a search for our true nature, for the essence of what we are, for liberation from everything and everyone, including ourselves. At the highest levels, every attachment is transcended, even the attachment to detachment and the desire to transcend desires. As its name *tan*, or "expansion," suggests, Tantra indicates an expansion at the level of consciousness.

Tantra is often wrongly perceived as a way to increase sexual pleasure. Some see it as justification for debauchery and promiscuity. Although sex is part of Tantric *sādhana*, this is a preparatory practice and not the goal. Tantra includes sex because it is clearly impossible to reach elevated levels if we ignore the basic ones. However, Tantra perceives sex as vital energy and not mere sensual gratification.

It does not see sex only as a physical act but as life itself: the entire universe vibrates sexually, full of vital energy. While the ascetic path suggests calming or extinguishing this inner fire, the Tantric path ignites and redirects it to the source.

The beauty that we perceive in the animal world is largely due to sexuality. Birds' enchanting plumage and delightful songs are sexual calls. Tantra perceives sexuality even in the cosmos and identifies certain celestial bodies as masculine or feminine. The Moon is feminine, the Sun masculine, and planet Earth is our mother. Life unfolds within the magnetic field created by the male and female poles. The universe is manifested because of this sexual polarity.

On the Tantric path, sincerity and humility are essential in accepting our limitations. If we try to go beyond our capabilities, we will not remove the veils that cover our true nature but instead add new ones. Although Kālī can help us by breaking our chains, she may also end up destroying us if we do not consider our limitations.

Passion used wisely can bring us closer to our true nature. Aspirants should endeavor to properly channel it toward the ideal. They must be willing to use any legitimate means to manage and direct this energy toward enlightenment. In order to do this, it is essential to not only act appropriately but to adopt a proper attitude. Conventional morality is imposed upon people by society; Tantric morality is born within each individual. Ordinary morality is mechanical because it is part of human conditioning. Tantric morality comes from within; it is the fruit of consciousness.

More important than our actions is the attitude that motivates them. The same action can free one person and enslave another, depending on the intention. There is a story about two friends who traveled from their village to the city. While walking around, they saw a brothel across from a temple. One decided to visit the deities in the temple, and the other went to the brothel. The friend in the brothel was surrounded by beautiful women and drank liquor but suffered from remorse. He could not help thinking he had made the wrong decision and should be meditating in front of the temple altar. Meanwhile, the friend in the temple regretted that he had not followed his friend to the brothel. He tried to meditate but could not stop thinking about the beautiful women. So the friend who went to the brothel got the spiritual benefits of the one who attended the temple. And the friend who went to the temple was actually in the brothel. What counts is the attitude and consciousness that lie behind our actions rather than the actions themselves.

CHAPTER 2

THE FOUNDATIONS OF TANTRA

Meanings of the term Tantra

Many mistakenly believe Tantra to be cheap literature about magic and spells. Quite the contrary, it is a sophisticated religious and spiritual system that leads its followers to enlightenment through the cultivation of inner power.

The famous Tantric master Rāma-kaṇṭha, who lived around 950–1000 CE, defined Tantra as follows:

> तन्त्रं च परापरपुरुषार्थाधिकारिणं विशिष्टसंस्कार प्रतिपादन पूर्वकमीश्वराराधनाय नियतविधिनिषेधं तदाज्ञात्मकं वाक्यजातम् ।
>
> *tantraṁ ca parāpara-puruṣārthādhikāriṇaṁ viśiṣṭa-saṁskāra pratipādana pūrvakam īśvarārādhanāya niyata vidhi niṣedhaṁ tadājñātmakaṁ vākya-jātam.*
>
> A Tantra is a body of divinely revealed teachings that explain the requirements and obstacles in the practice of worshipping the Divine; it also describes the initiation and purification ceremonies needed for Tantric practice. These lessons are taught to those who are qualified to pursue the highest and lowest goals of human existence. (Rāma-kaṇṭha's commentary on the *Sārdha-triśati-kālottara*, 1.1)

The Sanskrit word *tantra* has been understood in many ways: a philosophical conclusion, a branch of the Vedas, a set of duties (*iti kartavyatā*), a composition (*prabandha*), a specific text (*śāstra* or *śāstra-viśeṣa*), and so on.

These are some of the main meanings:

Philosophical conclusion, or *siddhānta*: Kātyāyana and Patañjali, who can be considered Pāṇini's successors in the field of Sanskrit grammar, use the word *tantra* to describe a methodology of study or a school of a discipline. According to the *Amara-kośa* dictionary, the word *tantra* means "the main subject or part," but does not refer to a specific religious text or sect. Some people believe the Tantras were still unknown when the *Amara-kośa* dictionary was compiled, so the term had a different meaning at the time.

In some contexts, the term *tantra* refers to a *darśana*, or "orthodox metaphysical school." We find expressions such as *Kāpila Tantra* and *Gautama Tantra* for the schools of Kāpila and Gautama, respectively. Bhāskararāya called the *Mīmāṁsā* system *Jaiminīya Tantra.*

Finally, Bhaṭṭoji refers to the *Mīmāṁsā* and Vedanta systems as *Pūrva Tantra* and *Uttara Tantra* in his book *Tantrādhikāri-nirṇaya.*

***Śāstra*, or *śāstra-viśeṣa*:** The word *tantra* often refers to specific texts, or *śāstras*, as seen in this verse from the *Mahābhārata*:

कौसल्ये धर्मतन्त्रं त्वां यद्ब्रवीमि निबोध तत् ॥

kausalye dharma-tantraṁ tvāṁ
yad bravīmi nibodha tat

O Kausalya, I am narrating the *Dharma-Tantra* (*Dharma-Śāstra*) to you, listen to me.

(*Mahābhārata*, "*Ādi-parva*," 114.72b)

In the *Artha-śāstra* scripture of Kauṭilya, *Adhikaraṇa* (chapter) 15 is entitled *Tantra-yukti*, which means "canons of propositions or principles of the exposition of a *śāstra*."

Śaṅkarācārya also used the term *tantra* in his book *Śārīraka-bhāṣya* to refer to a list of *śāstras*, which includes *smṛtis*.

In Pāṇini's *Mahā-bhāṣya* and Kumārila Bhaṭṭa's *Vārttika*, the term *sarva-tantraḥ* means "one who has studied all the Tantras"; *dvi-tantraḥ* refers to "one who has studied two Tantras."

Governing: Sometimes we see the term *tantra* used to mean "governing, attending, or taking care". For example, in the *Abhijñāna-śākuntalam* (5.5), Kāli-dāsa used this expression:

प्रजाः प्रजाः स्वा इव तन्त्रयित्वा ।

prajāḥ prajāḥ svā iva tantrayitvā.

Having governed the people like his own children [...].

(*Abhijñāna-śākuntalam*, 5.5)

Weaving: The word *tantra* also means "weaving." Just like the term *yoga*, or "union," which refers to the act of harmonizing, merging, or uniting, *weaving* suggests that everything we experience is interconnected. People, objects, and situations we perceive represent a much larger reality than the one we see with the naked eye.

Loom: The Vedas use the term *tantra* to refer to a loom (*Ṛg Veda* 10.71.9, *Atharva Veda* 10.7.42, *Taittirīya Brāhmaṇa* 11.5.5.3). We see this usage in the following verse, which condemns the attitude of some *Brāhmaṇas*:

इमे ये नार्वाङ्न परश्चरन्ति न ब्राह्मणासो न सुतेकरासः ।
त एते वाचमभिपद्य पापया सिरीस्तन्त्रं तन्वते अप्रजज्ञयः ॥

ime ye nārvāṅna paraś caranti
na brāhmaṇāso na sutekarāsaḥ
ta ete vācam abhipadya pāpayā
sirīs tantraṁ tanvate aprajajñayaḥ

Those who neither step back nor move forward, who are neither *Brāhmaṇas* nor preparers of libations and have sinfully reached *Vāk* (speech, recitation), spin out their thread in ignorance like spinners.

(*Ṛg Veda*, 10.71.9)

The *Amara-kośa* dictionary follows the *Ṛg Veda* tradition of translating *tantra* as "weaving."

Body: Some scholars trace the word *tantra* from *tanu*, or "body," because Tantra pays special attention to the body.

Reduce: According to the *paṇḍit* H. P. Śāstrī, *tantra* means "to shorten or abbreviate" and refers to the process of reducing or compressing.

Procedure: The *Āpastamba-śrauta Sūtra* uses the term *tantra* to mean "a procedure consisting of many parts," while the *Śāṅkhāyana-śrauta Sūtra* refers to the term *tantra* as "that which is done once but serves the purpose of many actions."

Save: Other scholars believe that the term *tantra* comes from the root *trai*, meaning "to save," because it saves its followers. The following verse uses this meaning:

तनोति विपुलानर्थांस्तत्त्वमन्त्र समाश्रितान् ।
त्राणं च कुरुते यस्मात्तन्त्रमित्यभिधीयते ॥

tanoti vipulān arthāṁs
tattva-mantra-samāśritān
trāṇaṁ ca kurute yasmāt
tantram ity abhidhīyate

That which expounds many meanings, addresses the Truth and its mantras, and has the power to rescue us from danger, is called *tantra*, for it saves us.

(*Pūrva-kāmikā Āgama*, 1.29)

According to this definition, Tantra is a wisdom that protects or saves. Through *sādhana*, it protects *Tāntrikas* from falling into the clutches of illusion and keeps them focused on the ultimate reality. It also protects them from physical and mental diseases and in some cases even works as therapy. For example, hatha yoga has a rich variety of psychophysiological practices.

We cannot ignore the Tantric roots of Hindu medicine. The *Śabda-kalpa-druma* Sanskrit dictionary references *tantra* as medicine and a doctrine. That is, Tantra saves the *Tāntrika* both through knowledge and therapy, which suggests an intimate union between mind and body.

Expansion and liberation: Other sources remind us that the term *tantra* is composed of two verb roots: *tan* (*tanoti*), or "to expand or extend," and *tra* (*trāyate*), or "to rescue or protect," suggesting the release of something held in captivity. Hence Tantra implies an expansion at the level of awareness and liberation in the energetic aspect, specifically of the *kuṇḍalinī-śakti*, or "the creative divine energy," which lies dormant in the first chakra. *Kuṇḍalinī* is *śakti* within the human being and represents the evolution of the goddess who animates everything in the universe. The above mentioned *Kāmikā Āgama*, as well as the *Ajita-mahā-tantra* use this meaning:

तनोति विपुलानर्थांस्तत्त्वमन्त्रसमाश्रितान् ।
त्राणं च कुरुते पुंसां तेन तन्त्रमिति स्मृतम् ॥

tanoti vipulān ārthaṁs
tatva-mantra samāśritān
trāṇaṁ ca kurute puṁsāṁ
tena tantram iti smṛtam

> Because it expands (*tanoti*) on many profound topics, especially those related to the principles of reality (*tattva*) and sacred mantras, and because it bestows liberation (*trāṇaṁ*) to humans, it is named *Tantra*.
>
> (*Ajita-maha-tantra,* 1.115)

***Tattva* and mantra:** *Tattva* means "cosmic principles" or "categories of existence." Mantra is the cosmic sound. This indicates that the main subject matter of Tantra is knowledge of *tattva* and mantra. This wisdom carries a grace that bestows self-realization.

Spiritual and material: The *Śabda-kalpa-druma-kośa* dictionary refers to *tantra* as a science that deals with the creation and dissolution of the universe, the duties of the four *varṇas* (social castes) and *āśramas* (stages of life), and six supernatural powers: destroying enemies with magical ceremonies (*māraṇa*), eradicating (*uccāṭana*), subjugating (*vaśī-karaṇa*), immobilizing (*stambhana*), pacifying (*śānti*), and provoking fights (*vidveṣaṇa*). This definition makes it clear that Tantra is not exclusively spiritual wisdom disconnected from the earthly and mundane. Tantra's materialistic spiritualism is suggested by the Monier-Williams dictionary, which defines Tantra as follows:

> A class of works teaching magical and mystical formularies and said to deal with five subjects, (1) the creation and (2) the destruction of the world, (3) the worship of the gods, (4) the attainment of all objects, especially of six superhuman faculties, (5) the four modes of union with the supreme spirit by meditation.

This definition makes it clear that the goals of Tantra include the achievement of dharma (duty), *artha* (wealth), *kāma* (desire), and *mokṣa* (liberation). Tantrism does not reject this world in exchange for a spiritual goal; it includes both.

Tantric metaphysics

Tantra has penetrated all cultures around the world in one way or another, but only in Hinduism it has played a relatively important role. Although it emphasizes practice over theory and hypothetical belief, it is based on a very solid metaphysics. To manifest our hidden divine potential, we must first become aware it exists. For this purpose, Tantra provides a metaphysical system that has influenced the main traditions of Hinduism: Shaivism, Vaishnavism, and Shaktism. The central topics of Tantric metaphysics are ultimate reality, the universe, the individual being, and liberation.

1. Ultimate reality is eternal, unlimited, omniscient, omnipresent, and infinite. It is the origin and source of the universe, and is both immanent and transcendent. Each tradition calls it by a

different name: in the *Pāśu-pata* school it is *Pati*, or "the Lord" and in the *Śaiva-siddhānta* it is *kāraṇa*, or "cause." Vaishnavism calls it *Para-brahman* and Shaktism calls it Śakti. Both Kashmir Shaivism and Shaktism consider that consciousness, or *cit*, is synonymous with ultimate reality.

2. The universe originates from the One; however, it seems divided due to the three modes of nature, or *guṇas*: *sattva*, *rajas*, and *tamas*. The cosmic manifestation is the result of imbalance between these modes. The *Pāśu-pata* system teaches that the creation of the objective universe is not a result of an effort but a game; Vaishnavism says it is a pastime (*līlā*).
3. Individual being: Tantra recognizes the intimate micro–macro relationship between the universe and the individual being, or the "I" and the "not I." As an integral part of the cosmos, the human body is composed of the same three *guṇas*, which are closely related to the *pañca-mahā-bhūtas*, or "five essential elements," of *prakṛti*. Our physical and mental health depends on the balance between the *guṇas*. The universe is a manifestation of consciousness, which resides in the body of every individual as life energy, or *prāṇa*. This single life energy is classified into five functions. Harmony between the functions results in psychophysiological health, while imbalance causes disease.
4. Liberation: Tantric metaphysics explains human bondage and how to transcend it. Besides imparting knowledge as a means of liberation, it gives importance to *sādhana*, which creates a favorable situation for receiving divine grace. It is possible to overcome and renounce desires, but not before one becomes aware of them by trying to satisfy them. Instead of escaping desires, Tantra directs us to explore and face them.

Two parallel revelations: Vedic and Tantric

We find two parallel revelations within Hinduism: the *Vaidika* (Vedic) and the *Tāntrika* (Tantric). Rather than contradicting each other, these are two approaches to the same Truth. The first is Brahmanical and is based on the Vedas, while the second is based on the *Āgamas*—sacred Tantric texts considered to be divine revelations and the very voice of God, or *āpta-vākya*.

Tantra's sacred wisdom was preserved through chains of disciplic succession, or *paramparās*, which originated with the Tantric deities. This distinguishes Tantric lineages from Vedic and *Smṛti* ones. The Tantric seers, or *ṛṣis*, transmitted their transcendental experience for the benefit of humanity.

The Vedic religion includes a dharmically permissive path, called *pravṛtti-mārga* or *bhoga*, and another path of absolute renunciation, called *nivṛtti-mārga* or *tyāga*. It also includes a path of action aimed at the proper functioning of society (*karma-kāṇḍa*) and a path of knowledge that leads to renunciation and enlightenment (*jñāna-kāṇḍa*).

Tantra wisely harmonizes *pravṛtti* and *nivṛtti* by bringing enlightenment closer to those who have not adopted the path of renunciation. It opts to accept nature instead of withdrawing from it to avoid its difficulties. Tantric *sādhana* comprises both *bhoga*, or "enjoyment," and *tyāga*, or "renunciation." We could say that in Tantra, *bhoga* is only superficial since it includes *tyāga*. In this way, Tantric *sādhana* includes elements of enjoyment of *karma-kāṇḍa*, as well as those of renunciation with the knowledge and understanding of *jñāna-kāṇḍa*.

Generally, the Vedic tradition considers sensual enjoyment an obstacle on the path to liberation. But on the Tantric path, enjoyment is directed toward enlightenment. Tantra does not see *mokṣa* as an objective of human life, or *puruṣārtha*, but aspires to liberation in life, or *jīvan-mukti*.

As Patañjali Maharṣi indicates in his *Yoga Sūtra*:

प्रकाशक्रियास्थितिशीलं भूतेन्द्रियात्मकं भोगापवर्गार्थं दृश्यम् ॥

prakāśa-kriyā sthiti śīlaṁ
bhūtendriyātmakaṁ
bhogāpavargārtham dṛśyam

> Nature, its three qualities, and the derived categories—the elements and the senses—exist for the enjoyment and the liberation of those who see.
>
> (*Yoga Sūtra*, 2.18)

Thus, Tantra is a path of liberation that offers a fusion between *pravṛtti*, or "the positive use of material conditions," and *nivṛtti*, or "the renunciation of material conditions." Since it harmonizes pleasure and renunciation, Tantra can transform *bhoga* (sensual enjoyment) into yoga (union), as this verse states:

योगी चन्नैव भोगी स्याद्भोगी चेन्नैव योगवित् ।
भौगयोगात्मकं कौलं तस्मात्सर्वाधिकं प्रिये ॥

yogī cen naiva bhogī syād
bhogī cen naiva yoga-vit
bhoga-yogātmakaṁ kaulaṁ
tasmāt sarvādhikaṁ priye

> O beloved, [in other traditions it is said that] whoever is a yogi is not a *bhogī* (a sensual person), and one who is a *bhogī* cannot become a knower of yoga. The *Kula* system has both mundane enjoyment and yoga, therefore it is superior.
>
> (*Kulārṇava Tantra*, 2.23)

Thus, *bhoga* is not enjoyed for its own sake but for the sake of yoga, or "union with ultimate reality."

भोगो योगायते साक्षात्पातकं सुकृतायते ।
मोक्षायते च संसारः कुलधर्मे कुलेश्वरि ॥

bhogo yogāyate sākṣāt
pātakaṁ sukṛtāyate
mokṣāyate ca saṁsārḥ
kula-dharme kuleśvari

> O Kuleśvarī, in *Kula-dharma*, the mundane pleasures (*bhoga*) are indeed transformed into yoga, sin becomes merit, and the world becomes a state of liberation.
>
> (*Kulārṇava Tantra*, 2.24)

For Tantra, everything is divine. It accepts the diverse aspects of our reality and tries to purify them. It does not reject this world for the next one, nor does it renounce happiness here for happiness in the hereafter, as expressed in this verse:

नान्यः पन्था मुक्तिहेतुरिहामुत्र सुखाप्तये ।
यथा तन्त्रोदितो मार्गो मोक्षाय च सुखाय च ॥

nānyaḥ panthā mukti-hetur
ihāmutra sukhāptaye
yathā tantrodito mārgo
mokṣāya ca sukhāya ca

> There is no other path like that of Tantra, which is the cause of liberation and realization of happiness, both in this world and the next.
>
> (*Mahā-nirvāṇa Tantra*, 2.20)

In the search for the whole, Tantra does not reject the part. Its holistic wisdom invites us to discover the "macro" by observing the "micro," the eternal through the temporal, the One through diversity, the ocean through a drop of water, the whole through the individual. It finds the transcendental within this world.

Many Tantric practices include Vedic elements. Even scriptures such as the *Kulārṇava Tantra* do not consider Tantra separate from the *Vaidika-dharma* but instead say that it is the very essence of Vedic religion:

मथित्वा ज्ञानदण्डेन वेदागममहार्णवम् ।
सारज्ञेन मया देवि कुलधर्मः समुद्धृतः ॥

mathitvā jñāna-daṇḍena
vedāgama-mahārṇavam
sāra-jñena mayā devi
kula-dharmaḥ sam-uddhṛtaḥ

O Devī, after churning the great ocean of the Vedas and *Āgamas* with the rod of wisdom, the *Kula-dharma* was extracted by me, the knower of essence.

(*Kulārṇava Tantra*, 2.10)

एतन्येव कुलस्यापि षडङ्गनि भवन्ति हि ।
तस्माद्वेदात्मकं शास्त्रं विद्धि कौलात्मकं प्रिये ॥

etāny eva kulasyāpi
ṣaḍ-aṅgāni bhavanti hi
tasmād vedātmakaṁ śāstraṁ
viddhi kaulātmakaṁ priye

The *Kula-śāstra* also has these six limbs (the six *darśanas* of the Vedas), therefore, O beloved, know the Vedic scriptures to be the non-different than the *Kula-śāstra*.

(*Kulārṇava Tantra*, 2.85)

Bhāskararāya Bhāratī, also called Bhāsurānanda-nātha (1690–1785 CE), was a great master and an undisputed authority on the worship of the Divine Mother in the sect *Śrī-vidyā*. He says that the Tantras include the essence of the Upanishads. Similarly, the famous and respected *Śākta* scripture *Tripurā-rahasya* says:

वैदिकं वैष्णवं शैवं शाक्तं पाशुपतं तथा ।
विज्ञानं सम्यगालोच्य यदेतत्प्रविनिश्चितम् ॥

vaidikaṁ vaiṣṇavaṁ śaivaṁ
śāktaṁ pāśu-pataṁ tathā

vijñānaṁ samyag ālocya
yad etat praviniścitam

This (text) is the concentrated extract of the essence of the Vedic, *Vaiṣṇava*, *Śaiva*, *Śākta*, and *Pāśu-pata* lore taken after a deep study of them all.

(*Tripurā-rahasya*, *jñāna-khaṇḍa*, 1.4)

Kullūka Bhaṭṭa, the great commentator on the Laws of Manu, confirms that both traditions are orthodox and accepted as *śruti* by quoting the *Hārīta Dharma-śāstra*:

श्रुतिश्च द्विविधा वैदिकी तान्त्रिकी च ।

śrutiś ca dvi-vidhā
vaidikī tāntrikī ca

The Vedic and the Tantric [paths] are known as two kinds of *śruti*.

(Kullūka Bhaṭṭa, commentary on the *Manu Smṛti*, 2.1)

Both traditions developed in parallel over many generations and both emphasize the significance of the body. However, Tantra stopped seeing it as a tool for sin and instead accepted it as a microcosm that contains clues to realize the Truth—an attitude very conducive to the development of such systems as hatha yoga.

The great master of Kashmir Shaivism, Abhinava-gupta, explained these differences in his book *Tantrāloka*:

यदार्षे पातहेतूक्तं तदस्मिन्वामशास्सने ।
आशुसिद्ध्यै यतः सर्वमार्ष मयोदरस्थितम् ॥

yad ārṣe pāta-hetūktaṁ
tad asmin vāma-śāsane
āśu-siddhayai yataḥ sarvam
ārṣa māyodara-sthitam

> That which according to the Veda is a source of sin on the account of its leading to the womb of delusion, according to the doctrine of the left leads directly to liberation.
>
> (*Tantrāloka*, 37.5 and 37.10b–11a)

Many might be surprised to learn that practices such as hatha yoga postures and *prāṇāyāma* owe much more to Tantra than to the Vedic tradition. We find many characteristic elements of Tantra in the temples, mythology, yoga, medicine, rituals, and ceremonies of *Sanātana-dharma*. Some even refer to the Tantric scriptures as the fifth Veda, that is to say, a transcendental revelation that continues the teachings of the traditional four sacred Vedas.

While we can distinguish between the Tantric and Vedic traditions, we cannot separate Tantra from Hinduism. It would be incorrect to consider the Tantric tradition a religion outside Hinduism, which is impregnated with Tantric elements to such an extent that it would be impossible to imagine it without Tantra. Without Tantra, Hinduism would not have gurus, initiations, hatha yoga, deities, or altars. The Tantric tradition could be defined as a way of experiencing Hinduism.

The main traditions of Hinduism were all influenced by Tantra; however, Tantra found no fertile soil to develop within orthodox systems controlled by Brahmanism. We could say that Tantric ideas and practices survived but without any vitamins to renew themselves. Only Shaktism offered favorable conditions for them to flourish. As a heterodox and flexible religion, Tantra spread among the castes considered inferior within the *varṇāśrama* system. These castes became impregnated with popular cult and worship, its beliefs and ceremonies.

Lord Kṛṣṇa indicates this in the *Bhāgavata Purāṇa*:

वैदिकस्तान्त्रिको मिश्र इति मे त्रिविधो मखः ।
त्रयाणामीप्सितेनैव विधिना मां समर्चरेत् ॥

vaidikas tāntriko miśra
iti me tri-vidho makhaḥ

trayāṇām īpsitena iva
vidhinā māṁ sam-arcaret

> One must worship me diligently, choosing one of the three ways I accept sacrifices: the Vedic, the Tantric, or the mixed one.
>
> (*Bhāgavata Purāṇa*, 11.27.7)

The mixed way (*miśra*) refers to Hinduism, where we find a mixture of Tantric and Vedic elements. The *miśra* is an organic unity, a Vedic–Tantric religion.

There is controversy among scholars about the origin of the Tantric tradition since some of its occult practices oppose the Vedas, including the *cīnācāra* practices mentioned in the *Yonī Tantra*, *Kumārī Tantra*, *Niruttara Tantra*, and *Gupta-sādhana Tantra*. Based on this, most scholars think that the religion of the Tantras differs from that of the Vedas and therefore is not Vedic.

The truth is that the practices taught by the Tantras can be divided into *āstika*, or "Vedic," and *nāstika*, or "non-Vedic." The two traditions do not, in fact, differ in philosophy, only in practice. That is to say, the differences between them are more about the attitude and practice than the philosophical essence of their teachings.

In Vedic worship, *yajñas* take place in mostly open spaces without deities or shrines. Tantric worship recommends *pūjās*, ceremonies performed in temples to deities or icons. However, this does not necessarily mean that Tantric *Āgamas* and the Vedas oppose each other.

The scholar Teun Goudriaan defined Tantrism as "the systematic search for salvation or spiritual excellence through the implementation and cultivation of the bipolar and bisexual divinity within the body itself." He also listed a number of key elements of Tantric *sādhana*:

- The use of mantras and *maṇḍalas*, or "sacred diagrams."
- Visualization and worship of deities.
- Distinctive initiation ceremonies.
- Yogic practices involving the subtle body.

Tantric traditions of all affiliations, Buddhist or Hindu, are characterized by a strong focus on meditation and ritual. The French scholar Jean Filliozat defined Tantrism as "merely the ritual and technical part of Hinduism." With time, the powerful Tantric practice supplanted the ancient Vedic ritual system, giving birth to the Vedic–Tantric integration that today we call *Hinduism*.

CHAPTER 3

ŚIVA–ŚAKTI: THE NON-DUAL TANTRIC POLARITY

At the foundation of Tantra there lies a mystical paradox: a pure undivided consciousness called Brahman, which is apparently divided, giving rise to a polarity. I emphasize the word *apparently* because this duality is not real. We perceive life through this illusory polarity: he and she, positive and negative, yin and yang, day and night, life and death, static and dynamic, this and that. The relativity we experience stems from the continuous, harmonious, and balanced relationship between these extremes. They seem opposed but are in fact complementary.

In the sacred Bhagavad Gita, Lord Kṛṣṇa refers to himself as a masculine–feminine polarity:

पिताहमस्य जगतो माता धाता पितामहः ।
वेद्यं पवित्रमोङ्कार ऋक्साम यजुरेव च ॥

pitāham asya jagato
mātā dhātā pitāmahaḥ
vedyaṁ pavitram-oṁkāra
ṛk-sāma-yajur eva ca

I am the father and the mother of this universe, the support and the grandfather. I am that which deserves to be known; I am the purifier and the syllable *Oṁ*. I am the Vedas: *Ṛg*, *Sāma*, and *Yajur*.

(Bhagavad Gita, 9.17)

Just like electricity, life requires two opposite poles. If we want pleasure, pain is inevitable. This is a dialectic polarity in which both extremes attract and repel each other. Neither can exist alone since both feed off each other. Our capacity for suffering is proportional to our capacity for happiness. Hence if we try to eradicate sadness, we will also diminish joy.

Many religious traditions ask us to repress the negative pole and cultivate only the positive one. Tantra, on the other hand, gives up trying to eradicate one in favor of the other because destroying the negative would also destroy the positive. Tantra advises us to only invest time and energy in increasing the positive, while consciously giving the negative its place. When both coexist harmoniously, the negative acquires the quality and the perfume of the positive. When the positive absorbs the negative, it does not destroy it but sublimates it. Anger becomes free of selfishness. Indignation grows wise. Passion becomes beautiful.

Tantra aims for the ultimate reality, where all conflicts disappear and are revealed to be complementary. In Tantric sublimation, the positive expresses itself in its infinity until the negative disappears. The immensity of the Divine can absorb the mundane. Just as light dispels darkness, falsehood vanishes into the Truth and "what is" makes every absence disappear. Tantra tells us not to fear the negative but to let it have a place within the positive. It lets illusion be part of the real, because in the end, only what is real will remain.

This path can create the conditions for us to become aware that we are immersed in this divine game of relativity. Tantra invites us to undertake an exciting exploration, free of the repressive and condemnatory attitude so characteristic of other religions. Tantra assures us that the opposites are reconciled in the original source.

According to the Tantric vision, the original source of the objective universe is a single absolute principle called Śiva–Śakti, or the consciousness–energy principle. The apparent separation of the cosmic manifestation is present in every human being. Therefore, we constantly strive to return to the original unity from which the apparent emerged. We find it difficult to grasp the idea of two opposite principles interacting harmoniously. Perceiving ourselves only as parts, we think we are limited, and this keeps us in a state of constant dissatisfaction. The egoic phenomenon stems from this partial self-perception. We believe we are disconnected from everything and everyone. As long as that fracture persists, we will continue to live as parts and perceive life from a partial perspective. It is impossible to realize the Absolute if our fragmentary experience shows us a world of opposites.

In the *Skanda Purāṇa*, Lord Indra asks Lord Viṣṇu about the ability of Brahman to unfold as a masculine–feminine polarity. Lord Viṣṇu replies that both poles are involved in the process of creation and that they are inseparable, like gold from a jewel or water from the ocean. Śiva tells Pārvatī:

पाथोधिपोऽहं वीचिस्त्वं प्रकृतिस्त्वं पुमानहम् ॥
विद्यात्वंवेदितव्योऽहंवात्त्वमार्थोऽपिपार्वती ।
ईश्वरोऽहंमदंशाऽसित्वयैवाज्ञास्वरूपया ॥
सृष्टिस्थित्युपसंहारविधानानुग्रहेश्वरे ।
न भेदोऽतस्त्वया कार्यः पृथग्जनवदावयोः ॥

pāthodhipo 'haṁ vīcis tvaṁ
prakṛtis tvaṁ pumān aham

vidyā tvaṁ veditavyo 'haṁ
vāk tvam artho 'pi pārvatī
īśvaro 'haṁ mad aṁśā 'si
tvayaivājñā svarūpayā

sṛṣṭi sthity upasaṁhāra
vidhānānugraheśvare
na bhedo 'tas tvayā kāryaḥ
pṛthag-janavad āvayoḥ

You are the wave and I am the ocean. You are Prakṛti and I am Puruṣa. You are knowledge and I am the knowable. O Pārvatī, you are the word and I am its meaning. I am the supreme Lord and you, by the virtue of being order

> incarnate, are a part of me, O Goddess, you are competent to create, sustain, annihilate, duly arrange, and bless. Hence you must not entertain any difference between us as ordinary unenlightened people do.
>
> (*Skanda Purāṇa*, 1.3.21.15b–17)

This subjective polarity is called Puruṣa and Prakṛti, or Śiva and Śakti. On the unmanifested plane, both aspects exist only as potentiality and are indistinguishable. At the level of subjective duality, Śiva is the unmanifested, whereas Śakti is the manifested. Śiva is consciousness and Śakti is Śiva's dynamic aspect. This polarity refers not only to the universal expression, but also manifests itself at the individual and microcosmic level. When this inseparable polarity manifests itself in an organism, one of the poles predominates, depending on the evolutionary level of the organism.

The *Skanda Purāṇa* also mentions that Pārvatī, the beloved consort of Lord Śiva, wanted to merge with him forever. Śiva then manifested as Ardhanārīśvara, an androgynous manifestation of Śiva and Pārvatī, half male and half female. The male half represents Śiva and the female half the Devī, Pārvatī, or Umā. Ardhanārīśvara is the unity of the masculine–feminine polarity of Śiva–Śakti, or Puruṣa–Prakṛti. The following verse describes the merge:

इत्युक्त्वेशो निषण्णस्तांपार्श्वदेशेन्यवेशयत् ।
गौरीं स्वकीय एवाङ्गे गूहमानामिव ह्रिया ।
अङ्गद्वयंतयोरैक्यमगात्प्रेम्णा च लीनयोः ।
अर्थद्वयमिवाऽह्नाय सन्निकर्षोपलम्भतः ।

ity uktveśo niṣaṇṇas tāṁ
pārśva-deśe nyaveśayat
gaurīṁ svakīya evāṅge
gūhamānām iva hriyā

aṅga-dvayaṁ tayor aikyam
agāt-premṇā ca līnayoḥ
artha-dvayam ivā 'hnāya
sannikarṣopalambhataḥ

> After saying this, Īśa (Śiva) sat down and made her (Pārvatī) sit at his side. He made Gaurī (Pārvatī) hide inside him as if out of bashfulness. When they lovingly merged into each other, the two bodies were united as one.
>
> (*Skanda Purāṇa*, 1.3.21.21a–c)

The great poet Kāli-dāsa beautifully described this relation in the beginning of his epic *Raghu-vaṁśa*:

वागर्थाविव संपृक्तौ वागर्थप्रतिपत्तये ।
जगतः पितरौ वन्दे पार्वतीपरमेश्वरौ ॥

vāg-arthāviva sampṛktau
vāg-artha pratipattaye
jagataḥ pitarau vande
pārvatī-parameśvarau

> I salute the progenitors of the universe, Pārvatī and Parameśvara, who are as inseparable as the word and its meaning, for achieving articulation and understanding.
>
> (Mahā-kavi Kāli-dāsa, *Raghu-vaṁśa*, 1.1)

This relative world is an expression of this polarity: Śiva is the supreme static paternal power, while Śakti is the dynamic power of Mother Nature. In Vedic yoga, Puruṣa is the central focus. However, in Tantra, Śakti is the dominant active power in the universe. Tantra directs us toward harmony between nature, or Śakti, and the spiritual principle, or Śiva; between the subject *aham* (I am) and the object *idam* (this).

Shaivism

The Tantric tradition was born out of devotion to Śiva. To understand the context in which Tantra revelation emerged, we need to delve into the fundamental principles of Shaivism.

Shaivism is the path of devotion to Lord Śiva. This ancient tradition has given Hinduism some of its most profound teachings. Śiva is omnipresent, omnipotent, omniscient, independent, immortal, causeless, and eternally pure. Time does not limit him. He is infinite intelligence and bliss and the incarnation of *tamas*, or "centrifugal inertia." He is known both in his personal aspect with qualities, and in his impersonal aspect devoid of attributes, or Brahman itself. He is both transcendent and immanent. He transcends the cosmic manifestation and at the same time resides in the heart of every living being.

In the *Śiva Purāṇa* (*Vidyeśvara Saṁhitā*), Brahmā and Viṣṇu praise Lord Śiva:

ब्रह्माच्युतावूचतुः
नमो निष्कलरूपाय नमो निष्कलतेजसे ।
नमः सकलनाथाय नमस्ते सकलात्मने ॥
नमः प्रणववाच्याय नमः प्रणवलिंगिने ।
नमः सृष्ट्यादिकर्त्रे च नमः पञ्चमुखायते ॥
पचब्रह्मस्वरूपाय पञ्च कृत्यायते नमः ।
आत्मने ब्रह्मणे तुभ्यमनन्तगुणशक्तये ॥
सकलाकलरूपाय शंभवे गुरवे नमः ।
इति स्तुत्वा गुरुं पद्यैर्ब्रह्मा विष्णुश्च नेमतुः ॥

brahmācyutāvūcatuḥ-

namo niṣkala-rūpāya
namo niṣkala-tejase
namaḥ sakala-nāthāya
namaste sakalātmane

namaḥ praṇava-vācyāya
namaḥ praṇava-liṅgine
namaḥ sṛṣṭy ādi kartre ca
namaḥ pañca-mukhāyate

pañca-brahma-svarūpāya
pañca-kṛtyāyate namaḥ

ātmane brahmane tubhyam
ananta-guṇa-śaktaye

sakalākala-rūpāya
śaṁbhāve gurave namaḥ
iti stutvā guruṁ padyair
brahmā viṣṇuś ca nematuḥ

Brahmā and Viṣṇu said: salutations to you of the bodiless form. Salutations to you of the formless luster. Salutations to you, the lord of everything. Salutations to you, the soul of everything. Salutations to you stated by the *Praṇava* (*Oṁ*). Salutations to you, symbolized by *Praṇava* (*Oṁ*). Salutations to you, the author of creation, and so on. Salutations to you of five faces. Salutations to you, identical to the Pañca-brahma form. Salutations to you of five-fold functions. Salutations to you, the Ātman, the Brahman, of endless attributes and power. Salutations to Śiva, the preceptor with both embodied and bodiless forms.

(*Śiva Purāṇa*, 1.10.28–31)

The *Śiva-mahimnaḥ Stotra* states:

महेशान्नापरो देवो महिम्नो नापरा स्तुतिः ।
अघोरान्नापरो मन्त्रो नास्ति तत्त्वं गुरोः परम् ॥

maheśān nāparo devo
mahimno nāparā stutiḥ
aghorān nāparo mantro
nāsti tattvaṁ guroḥ param

There is no god higher than Śiva. There is no hymn better than a hymn to the greatness of Śiva. There is no mantra more powerful than the name Śiva. There is no higher knowledge than the true nature of the guru.

(*Śiva-mahimnaḥ Stotra*, 35)

According to the *Śaiva* tradition, Tantric wisdom comes from Lord Śiva himself, who is called Mahā-kaula, or "the great *Tāntrika*." The treatise on spirituality and Tantra called *Paraśurāma-kalpa-sūtra* says that Śiva is the supreme master:

भगवान्परमशिवभट्टारकः श्रुत्याद्यष्टादशविद्याः सर्वाणि दर्शनानि लीलया तत्तदवस्थाऽऽपन्नः प्रणीय, संविन्मय्या भगवत्या भैरव्या स्वात्माभिन्नया पृष्टः पञ्चभिः मुखैः पञ्चाम्नायान् परमार्थसारभूतान् प्रणिनाय ॥

bhagavān parama-śiva bhaṭṭārakaḥ śruty ādi aṣṭā-daśa vidyāḥ sarvāni darśanāni līlayā tat tad avasthā "pannaḥ praṇīya, samvinmayyā bhagavatyā bhairavyā svātmābhinnayā pṛstaḥ pañcabhiḥ mukhaiḥ pañcāmnāyan paramārtha sārabhūtān praṇināya.

Lord Parama-śiva Bhaṭṭāraka teaches Pārvatī eighteen *vidyās* including the Vedas, which are all the branches of philosophy with a focus on logic. Bhairava has five mouths, which symbolize the five essential ways to improve the lives of others.
(*Paraśurāma-kalpa Sūtra*, *sūtra* 2)

In Hinduism, all aspects of God have corresponding Śaktis, or feminine consorts. Mahādeva shared his divine teachings in different Tantras in the form of dialogues with his consort, the Devī, in her manifestation as Pārvatī.

कैलासशिखरासीनंदेवदेवंजगद्गुरुम् ।
पृच्छति सामहादेवी ब्रूहिज्ञानंमहेश्वरम् ॥

kailāsa śikharāsīnam
deva-devaṁ jagad-gurum
pṛcchati sā mahādevī
brūhi jñānaṁ maheśvaram

On top of Mount Kailash, Mahā-devī asked *Jagat-guru*, Lord Śiva, "O Maheśvara, be so good as to reveal the wisdom to me."
(*Jñāna-saṅkalinī Tantra*, 1)

The *tri-mūrti* or "trinity"

नमस्त्रिमूर्तये तुभ्यं प्राक्सृष्टेः केवलात्मने ।
गुणत्रयविभागाय पश्चाद्भेदमुपेयुषे ॥

namas tri-mūrtaye tubhyaṁ
prāk-sṛṣṭeḥ kevalātmane
guṇa-traya-vibhāgāya
paścād-bhedam upeyuṣe

Salutations to you of three forms, the one soul before the creation of the world, who afterward divided yourself into the three *guṇas* (*sattva*, *rajas*, and *tamas*) and manifested a variety (of forms).

(*Kumāra-sambhava*, 2.4)

According to Hinduism, the cosmic functions of creation, maintenance, and destruction are performed by Brahmā, Viṣṇu, and Rudra (also called Śiva), respectively. They make up the *tri-mūrti*, a trinity that represents birth, growth, and death. God is called Brahmā when he creates, Viṣṇu when he sustains the creation, and Śiva when he annihilates. These are not different gods but aspects of one reality: a single God with three different functions.

In the Hindu pantheon, Śiva is a member of this triad. However, Shaivism sees in Śiva the ultimate reality and the supreme deity that includes both Brahmā and Viṣṇu; he alone is the cause of the creation, maintenance, and dissolution of the universe.

We can see this view reflected in the way Skanda is approaching Lord Śiva (Śrī-kaṇṭha) in the beginning of the *Śuddhākhya Tantra*:

देवदेव जगन्नाथ सर्वज्ञ त्रिपुरान्तक ।
स्थित्युत्पत्तिलयेशान प्रणतार्तिहर प्रभो ॥

deva-deva jagan-nātha
sarva-jña tri-purāntaka

sthity-utpatti-layeśāna
praṇatārti-hara prabho

> O God of gods, Lord of the worlds, omniscient, destroyer of the three forts, Lord of preservation, emanation, and destruction, dispeller of your devotees' sorrows, allmighty.
> (*Śuddhākhya Tantra*, 1.3)

From the smallest insects to the greatest gods, all beings are born and dissolved in Śiva, the supreme deity. His sacred mantra is *oṁ-kāra*, or "the sacred mantra *Oṁ*." *Oṁ* is composed of the sounds A, U, M that represent the *tri-mūrti*, indicating that Śiva performs the three basic functions of the cosmic manifestation.

Śiva destroys the universe. But every death leads to rebirth. The end of the caterpillar is the beginning of the butterfly. A seed dies as a flower is born. The cosmic manifestation rests in Śiva until he regenerates it in the next cycle of creation. Therefore, although Śiva destroys, he is also the creator Brahmā and the maintainer Viṣṇu. The stories of the *Purāṇas* narrate how Śiva manifests from the forehead of a furious Viṣṇu or from a *Brāhmaṇa* eager for progeny.

Both *Śāktas* and *Tāntrikas* worship Satī, the divine wife of Śiva, who committed suicide after her father insulted her husband in his absence. Śiva later married Pārvatī, who is the reincarnation of Satī and is also known as Durgā, Dākṣāyaṇī, Kālī, Umā, and Bhavānī.

The names of Śiva

In Sanskrit, the name Śiva means "auspicious, favorable, prosperous, or benevolent." According to Śaṅkarācārya, Śiva means "pure" or "he who purifies by the mere mention of his name."

निस्त्रैगुण्यतया शुद्धत्वाच्छिव ।

nistrai-guṇyatayā śuddhatvāt śiva

Śiva: pure, free of the three qualities.
(Śaṅkarācārya, *Viśṇu-sahasra-nāma Bhāṣya*, verse 17)

नाममात्रदग्धसर्वपाप ते नमः शिवाय ।

nāma-mātra-dagdha-sarva-pāpa te namaḥ śivāya

Salutations to Śiva, the utterance of whose name burns all sins.
(Śaṅkarācārya, *Śiva-pañcākṣara-nakṣatra-mālā*, verse 5)

The *Śuddhākhya Tantra* also describes this:

शुद्धत्वात्शिवमुद्दिष्टं ।

śuddhatvāt śivam uddiṣṭaṁ

He is called Śiva because of his purity.
(*Śuddhākhya Tantra*, 1.20a)

The Sanskrit commentary (*tika*) on this verse, which was written by an unknown author, elaborates:

शुद्धत्वात् शिवमिति शुद्धत्वात् स्वभावतोऽनादिकृत्वा मोहमदरागविषादशोषवैचित्त्य हर्षकाख्यस्सप्तविधमलशक्तिकारणाभावात् मलशून्यत्वात् शुद्धम् । स्वतन्त्रतया स भगवानात्मनां सृष्ट्यादिना मलपरिपाकं विधाय दीक्षादिव्यापारेण परापरमोक्षं प्रयच्छति च इति शुद्धम् । तस्मात् शुद्धत्वात् विशुद्धिकारणत्वाच्च शिवम् । ये चान्ये परापर-मोक्षभाजस्तिष्ठन्ति ते सर्वेऽपि तत्प्रसादात् ध्वस्तकलुषाः । ये चान्ये मुमुक्षवः तानपि स एव शिवं भवति तानपि स एव मोच्यति ।

śuddhatvāt śivam iti. śuddhatvāt svabhāvato 'nādi kṛtvā moha-mada-rāga-viṣāda-śoṣa-vaicittya-harṣakākhya-sapta-vidha-mala-śakti-kāraṇābhāvāt mala-śūnyatvāt śuddham. svatantratayā sa bhagavān

> *ātmanām sṛṣty-adinā mala-paripākaṁ vidhāya dīkṣādi-vyāpāreṇa parāpara-mokṣaṁ prayacchati ca iti śuddham. tasmāt śuddhatvāt viśuddhi-kāraṇatvāc ca śivam. ye cānye parāpara-mokṣa-bhājas tiṣṭhanti te sarve 'pi tat prasādāt dhvasta-kaluṣāḥ. ye cānye mumukṣavaḥ tān api sa eva śivaṁ bhavati tān api sa eva mocayati.*
>
> "Because of his purity, he is called Śiva (*śuddhatvāt śivam*)": "Because of his purity," that is, he is free of impurity naturally and eternally. He is pure because he lacks the causes of the seven powers of impurity (*mala-śakti*), which are: delusion, intoxication, passion, depression, desiccation, mental disorder, and excitement. This Lord is pure, because after accomplishing the evolution of impurity (*mala*) through [the process of] emanation, etc., he independently grants the souls superior and inferior liberation, through the process [that begins with] initiation (*dīksā*). He is Śiva (pure), since he is both pure and the cause of purity. All other (souls), who enjoy superior or inferior liberation, have overcome their impurity by his grace. And, additionally, he releases other souls who desire liberation, therefore, he is Śiva, (pure), only due to purity.
>
> (*Śuddhākhya-tantra-ṭika* on verse 1.20)

The Vedas call him Rudra, or "the terrible one," because he is a destructive deity. However, Hinduism prefers to euphemistically call him Śiva.

The *Śiva Purāṇa* (chapter 69) and the *Mahābhārata* ("*Anuśāsana-parva*," chapter 17) mention 10,008 names of Lord Śiva. These are the best-known ones:

- Mahā-deva, or "the great God."
- Maheśa, or "the great Lord."
- Mahā-kāla, or "the great time."
- Tri-locana and Tryambaka, or "three-eyed."
- Tri-purāri, or "the enemy of Tripura."
- Kāma-ghna, or "the murderer of Kāma-deva (the god of desire)."

- Śambhu, or "the bestower of happiness."
- Nīla-kaṇṭha, or "blue throat."
- Aghora, or "non-terrible one."
- Bhāgavata, or "the Divine."
- Candra-śekhara, or "having a crescent moon."
- Gaṅgā-dhara, or "the carrier of the Ganges."
- Girīśa, or "the Lord of the mountain."
- Paśu-pati, or "the Lord of the beasts (living beings)."
- Jaṭā-dhara, or "the one with matted hair."
- Mṛtyuñ-jaya, or "the conqueror of death."
- Ugra, or "the fierce one."
- Viśva-nātha, or "the Lord of the universe."

Śiva as the supreme guru is called Dakṣiṇā-mūrti. He is also called Śaṅkara, which means "the doer of good," and Hara, or "the remover of evil." Another of his names is Tri-netreśvara, or "the Lord with three eyes." His third eye is situated in the middle of his forehead and denotes the ability to see beyond the apparent and superficial. The sacred scriptures say that it is the eye of wisdom, capable of burning both demons and sins.

Śiva is also known as Soma-sundara, or "as beautiful as the moon." The moon (*soma*) represents the power of sacrificial offerings. The moon of the fifth day (*pañcamī*) on his head represents his control over time.

The name Nīla-kaṇṭha means "blue throat." His throat turned blue after drinking the poison *kālakūṭa*, generated by the gods when they churned the Ocean of Milk to obtain the nectar of immortality. The poison did not affect him, because his consort Pārvatī tied a cobra around his neck, which kept the poison in his throat. Therefore, the cobra around his throat represents both immortality and *kuṇḍalinī*.

The qualities of Śiva

जटाजूटमध्ये स्फुरद्गाङ्गवारिं ।

jaṭājūṭa-madhye sphurad-gānga-vārim

I meditate on him, from whose matted hair flow the holy waters of the great Ganges River.

(Śaṅkarācārya, *Veda-sāra Śiva-stava*, 1.3)

Śiva resides in his divine abode on Mount Kailash. His wavy hair reminds us that he is Vāyu, or "the wind god," who is the breath of life in every living being. His matted hair, or *jaṭā*, is arranged in a pointed bun over his forehead. In the hole of the bun, the sacred river Ganges materializes and rebounds. Śiva intercepts it in its eternal fall from the heavenly planets to prevent it from engulfing the Earth with its power. The Ganges River symbolizes fertility and Śiva's creative aspect.

भवं भास्वरं भस्मना भूषिताङ्गं ।

bhavaṁ bhāsvaram bhasmanā bhūṣitāṅgaṁ

I meditate on him, who is existence itself shining like the underlying consciousness, and whose body is adorned with sacred ashes.

(Śaṅkarācārya, *Veda-sāra Śiva-stava*, 3.3)

Like his devotees, Śiva covers his grayish-blue skin with *bhasma*, or "crematory ashes," to remind us that life, at its core, is death. In his hand, he holds a *ḍamaru*, or "small drum," which represents the origin of speech that generates all forms of expression.

प्रभो शूलपाणे विभो विश्वनाथ ।

prabho śūla-pāṇe vibho viśva-nātha

O Lord (Prabhu), the one with a trident in his hand (*śula-pāṇi*), the all-pervading one (*vibhu*), the Lord of the universe (Viśva-nātha).

(Śaṅkarācārya, *Veda-sāra Śiva-stava*, 9.1)

Śiva carries a *triśūla*, or "trident," as a symbol of his three functions as the creator, sustainer, and destroyer–regenerator. The trident in his hand shows that he has full control of these three functions as well as time itself: past, present, and future. His necklace of skulls represents the extinction and regeneration of human beings.

विभुं विश्वनाथं विभूत्यङ्गभूषम् ।

vibhuṁ viśva-nāthaṁ vibhūty aṅga-bhūṣam

[I praise that Lord] who is the all-pervading Lord of the universe (Viśva-nātha) and whose body is adorned with sacred ashes (*vibhūti*).

(Śaṅkarācārya, *Veda-sāra Śiva-stava*, 2.2)

The three lines on Śiva's forehead are made with sacred ashes called *vibhūti*. As ash is what remains from fire, *vibhūti* represents the purity of our authentic nature that remains after impurities (*malas*) and subtle desires (*vāsanās*) have been burned. Hence *vibhūti* is considered a form of Śiva.

व्याघ्राजिनाम्बरधराय मनोहराय ।

vyāghrājināmbara-dharāya mano-harāya

[Salutations to that Śiva] who looks captivating [to his devotees] as he wears the tiger skin.

(Śaṅkarācārya, *Śivāṣṭaka*, 4.3)

Śiva wears a tiger skin because the tiger is the vehicle of the goddess Śakti. This represents his supremacy over all energies and powers. He also wears an elephant and a deer skin. The elephant stands for pride; the deer stands for the mind. Śiva is the conqueror of both.

Lord Śiva has three sons: Ayyappa, Gaṇeśa, and Skanda, also known as Kārtikeya, the god of war. Ayyappa was born of Mohinī, a female incarnation of Viṣṇu that killed the demon Bhasmāsura. Gaṇeśa and Kārtikeya are the sons of Pārvatī. Gaṇeśa commands the *pramathas*, Śiva's supernatural servants and troops, or *gaṇas*.

Manifestations of Śiva

Śiva as pure subjectivity

> **यदिदंविभवात्मकं भूवनजातमुक्तं गर्भी कृतानन्त विचित्रभोक्तृभोग्यं, तत्र यदनुगतं महाप्रकाशरूपं तत्महासामान्यकल्पं परमशिवरूपम् ।**
>
> *yad idaṁ vibhavātmakaṁ bhuvana-jāta muktaṁ garbhī-kṛtānanta vicitra-bhoktṛ-bhogyaṁ, tatra yad anugataṁ mahā-prakāśa-rūpaṁ tat-mahā-sāmānya-kalpaṁ parama-śiva-rūpam.*
>
> Parama-śiva is the single absolute reality, which contains and covers all existence. It is just like the common essence of the entire phenomenal existence, and had been termed as Parama-śiva, the absolute God.
>
> (Abhinava-gupta, *Tantra-sāra*, 8.1)

From the absolute perspective of Parama-śiva, all that exists is *aham*, or "I am." In this state of pure subjectivity, the initial creative activity of Parama-śiva begins. Two categories begin to become distinct within "I am": the "I" as Śiva or the Self, and the "am" as Śakti or the awareness of the existence of the Self. Śiva is pure subjectivity, or pure "I," devoid of any vestige of "this" or "that." Within Kashmir Shaivism, it is called *aham*, or "beingness." This principle is distinct from *ahaṅkāra*, or "the egoic phenomenon," which manifests itself at a later stage of the evolutionary process of the cosmic manifestation.

Śiva as Nirguṇa-brahman

As his *nirguṇa* aspect, or "the aspect devoid of qualities," Śiva is the transcendental reality, or Brahman itself without any qualities or attributes: the ultimate mystery mentioned throughout Upanishadic literature.

अद्वैतं परमानन्दं शिवं याति तु कैवलम् ॥

advaitaṁ paramānandaṁ śivaṁ yāti tu kaivalam

> In reality, everything is Śiva, *Advaita*, the One absolute. There is no difference of any kind.
>
> (*Kaivalya Upanishad*, 47)

Tantric literature uses the term Śiva to refer to God, the ultimate reality, also called Parama-śiva, Sadā-śiva, or Parameśvara. Parama-śiva, the supreme consciousness, is the ultimate recipient and knower. He is the support, abode, and foundation of the whole universe. He transcends space, time, and causality. He does not dwell in any particular place, because everything and everyone lie within him.

His nature is defined as *sac-cid-ānanda*, or "absolute existence, consciousness, and bliss." Sat, or "existence," does not mean that Parama-śiva exists, but that he is existence itself. *Cit* (*caitanya* or *parasaṁvid*), or "consciousness," does not imply that he is conscious of something or someone, but that he is consciousness itself. *Ānanda* means "bliss," but it is not a mere dualist happiness or absence of sadness, it is absolute bliss.

Śiva as Saguṇa-brahman

As his *saguṇa* aspect, or "aspect with qualities," Śiva is the cosmic Lord of the manifested universe. Called Maheśvara, this supreme awakened Being is in charge of the activities of creation, maintenance, destruction, concealment, and liberation.

चितिः स्वतन्त्रा विश्वसिद्धिहेतुः ॥

citiḥ svatantrā viśva-siddhi-hetuḥ

Consciousness (*citiḥ*), in its freedom (*svatantrā*), brings about the manifestation, maintenance, and dissolution (*siddhi*) of the universe (*viśva*).

(*Pratyabhijñā-hṛdayam* by Kṣema-rāja, *sūtra* 1)

He fulfills these functions through his five supreme powers:

1. *Cic-chakti* (*cit-śakti*), or "divine consciousness."
2. *Ānanda-śakti*, or "absolute bliss."
3. *Icchā-śakti*, or "divine will."
4. *Jñāna-śakti*, or "divine omniscience."
5. *Kriyā-śakti*, or "power to manifest."

Through his dynamic power, or *śakti*, he projects the objective universe upon himself, as a reflection in the mirror. Creation is the conscious dream of Śiva, an alternative reality that is neither real nor illusory. Śiva creates the reality of names and forms in which he hides himself as the *jīvas*, or "individual souls."

In the *Śiva Purāṇa*, Śiva tells Brahmā and Viṣṇu:

अहमेव परं ब्रह्म मत्वरूपं कलाकलम् ।
ब्रह्मत्वादिश्वाहं कृत्यं मेनुग्रहादिकम् ॥

aham eva paraṁ brahma
mat svarūpaṁ kalākalam
brahmatvād īśvaraś cāhaṁ
kṛtyaṁ menugrahādikam

I am the supreme Brahman. My form is both manifested and unmanifested in view of my brahma-hood and *īśvaratva*. My duty is blessing, and so on.

(*Śiva Purāṇa*, 1.9.36)

अनुग्रहाद्यं सर्गांतं जगत्कृत्यं च पङ्कजम् ॥
ईशत्वादेव मे नित्यं न मदन्यस्य कस्यचित् ।

anugrāhādyaṁ sargām taṁ
jagat-kṛtyaṁ ca paṅkajam
īśvatvād eva me nityaṁ
na mad anyasya kasyacit

There are five activities in the universe, beginning with the grace of revealing (*anugraha*) and ending with creation (*sarga*). Therefore, these activities devolve on me and not on anyone else, because I am Īśa.

(*Śiva Purāṇa*, 1.9.38b–39a)

Śiva as individual souls

जीवः शिवः शिवो जीवः स जीवः केवलः शिवः ।
तुषेण बद्धो व्रीहिः स्यात्तुषाभावेन तण्डुलः ॥
एवं बद्धस्तथा जीवः कर्मनाशो सदाशिवः ।
पाशबद्धस्तथा जीवः पाशमुक्तः सदाशिवः ॥

jīvaḥ śivaḥ śivo jīvaḥ
sa jīvaḥ kevalaḥ śivaḥ
tuṣeṇa baddho vrīhiḥ syāt
tuṣā-bhāvena taṇḍulaḥ

evaṁ baddhas tathā jīvaḥ
karma-nāśo sadā-śivaḥ
pāśa-baddhas tathā jīvaḥ
pāśa-muktaḥ sadā-śivaḥ

> *Jīva* (the soul) is Śiva. Śiva is *jīva*. That *jīva* is Śiva alone. Bound by husk, it is paddy; freed from husk, it is rice. In the same way, *jīva* is bound [by karma]. If karma perishes, (*jīva*) is Sadā-Śiva. So as long as *jīva* is bound by the bonds of karma, he is *jīva*. If freed from its bonds, then he is Sadā-śiva.
>
> (*Skanda Upanishad*, 6–7)

Individual souls, or *jīva*s, are Śiva in his illusory aspect. An individual soul is Śiva covered by impurities, but his essence is unaffected. The *jīva*s and Śiva are one reality. When the veil of ignorance is removed through grace, or *anugraha*, the *jīva* is liberated. It realizes its authentic nature as Śiva the same way a wave discovers that it is not separated from the sea.

Śiva as an enlightened being

Śiva assumes different incarnations to restore order on the manifested plane. These enlightened and awakened beings are part of the *Śaiva* pantheon. These are manifestations of the transcendental that appear in different phases of the creative process to execute the will of Śiva. His best known incarnations are Dakṣiṇā-mūrti, Tāṇḍava-mūrti, Bhairava, Vīra-bhadra, Ardha-nārīśvara, Bhikṣāṭana-mūrti, Hanumān, Caṇḍikeśvara, and Mahā-kaleśvara. Some *Śaiva* schools believe that Śiva is perfect, as well as his creation. Therefore, they believe that these incarnations are highly evolved souls that descend to the physical plane to fulfill certain tasks in service to Śiva.

Śiva as the Vedic deity Rudra

Vedic priests recognized that Rudra was worshipped by the native traditions of India as Śiva. Thus, the Vedic deity Rudra and Śiva became synonymous because both refer to the same deity. The god Rudra is mentioned for the first time in the *Ṛg Veda*, which praises him in three of its hymns and considers him 'the most powerful among the powerful'. Rudra means 'the roar' and is a fierce and destructive deity associated with wind, rain, thunder, and hunting. The hymn

10.92 refers to two aspects of Rudra: one wild, aggressive, and cruel (Rudra), and the other peaceful (Śiva). Smritic literature reveals a great diversity of aspects of Śiva. In his aspect of the destroyer Rudra, he is closer to the nature of Śakti. Śiva is the lord of the yogis, or Yogeśvara. He is also called Kulaśekhara, or 'the Lord of the *Kaulas*'.

Śiva as our authentic nature

अहं निर्विकल्पो निराकाररूपो विभूत्वाच्च सर्वत्र सर्वेन्द्रियाणाम् ।
न चासङ्गतं नैव मुक्तिर्न मेयः चिदानन्दरूपः शिवोऽहं शिवोऽहम् ॥

ahaṁ nirvikalpo nirākāra-rūpo
vibhūtvāc ca sarvatra sarvendriyāṇām
na cāsaṅgataṁ naiva muktir na meyaḥ
cid-ānanda-rūpaḥ śivo 'haṁ śivo 'ham

> I am changeless, formless, and I envelop everything. Untouched by senses, I am omnipresent. Unfathomable, I am beyond freedom. I am the embodiment of knowledge and bliss. I am Śiva, I am Śiva.
>
> (Śaṅkarācārya, *Nirvāṇa-ṣaṭkam*, 6)

More than just a being, Śiva is our true nature, what we really are. Śiva as Rudra is destructive because he symbolizes the destruction of the egoic phenomenon and all that comes with it. Spiritual life is destructive since it is not designed to give us something but to purify us of everything. Nothing is missing; we just have an erroneous conclusion about our reality. All fierce and voracious deities symbolize the imminent destruction of the personal in favor of realizing the universal. This destruction does not imply destroying the personal but rather transcending it.

Shaktism

Shaktism is a religious and spiritual system entirely dedicated to the worship of God's feminine aspect. Literally, the term *śākta* in Sanskrit means "related to *śakti*," "the doctrine of power" or "the goddess doctrine." This branch of Hinduism focuses on the worship of Śakti, or Mahā-devī, whose devotees are called *Śāktas*.

The differences between Shaktism and Tantric Shaktism are minimal. Tantric Shaktism considers divinity to be a polarity of two complementary aspects: Śiva and Śakti. Śiva is the transcendental masculine aspect of the Absolute. Śakti is the power, the energy, or the divine cosmic force. In the absence of dynamic divine femininity, the male God is inactive and impersonal and, therefore, plays a secondary role. Constantly active, Śakti creates, maintains, and dissolves in the eternal divine dance with Śiva. God is incomplete in the absence of his feminine partner, as stated by Śaṅkarācārya:

शिवः शक्त्या युक्तो यदि भवति शक्तः प्रभवितुं
न चेदेवं देवो न खलु कुशलः स्पन्दितुमपि ।
अतस्त्वामाराध्यां हरिहरविरिञ्चादिभिरपि
प्रणन्तुं स्तोतुं वा कथमकृतपुण्यः प्रभवति ॥

śivaḥ śaktyā yukto yadi bhavati śaktaḥ prabhavituṁ
na ced evaṁ devo na khalu kuśalaḥ spanditum api
atas tvām ārādhyāṁ hari-hara viriñcādibhir api
praṇantuṁ stotuṁ vā katham akṛta-puṇyaḥ prabhavati

If Śiva is united with Śakti, he can be powerful. If not, Lord Śiva is unable to even move. If this is so, how dare someone without merit salute or praise you? O goddess who is worthy of being adored even by Hari, Hara, Viriñca, and others.

(*Saundarya-laharī*, 1.1)

Shaktism is less well-known in the West but has had a strong influence on all Hindu traditions. The Divine Mother of the universe is not only worshipped by *Śākta* devotees. Her worship has spread both to Shaivism and Vaishnavism to the extent that all male manifestations in the Hindu pantheon have *śaktis* represented by female consorts. Shaktism cannot be cataloged as either monist or dualist, since it transcends and embraces both. The absolute reality is both immanent and transcendent. It transcends matter but does not deny it, since matter is its real manifestation.

The universal dimension of the Divine Mother is beautifully described in the *Devī-māhātmyam*:

या देवी सर्वभूतेषु मातृरूपेण संस्थिता ।
नमस्तस्यै नमस्तस्यै नमस्तस्यै नमो नमः ॥

yā devī sarva-bhūteṣu
mātṛ-rūpeṇa saṁsthitā
namas tasyai namas tasyai
namas tasyai namo namaḥ

I offer my most humble and respectful obeisance to the Devī, who resides as the mother in every living being.

(*Devī-māhātmyam*, 5.71–73)

Tantric Shaktism is based on the idea that the objective universe we perceive and experience is a manifestation of the divine energy of the goddess, who creates and maintains the cosmos and its creatures. All mothers are considered direct manifestations of the Divine Mother, as stated in this verse:

विद्याः समस्तास्तव देवि भेदाः
स्त्रियः समस्ताः सकला जगत्सु ।

vidyāḥ samastās tava devi bhedāḥ
striyaḥ samastāḥ sakalā jagatsu

O Devī, all types of knowledge are your different forms, all the women of the world are your different manifestations.

(*Devī-māhātmyam*, 11.6a)

According to the Tantric scriptures, creative power is especially expressed in the sensuality of human beings and in their quest for the reintegration of both genders. It is the universal manifesting itself in the individual dimension, the absolute in the relative.

In essence, Tantra involves both the intention and the practical means to stimulate the powers of nature. Hence it is intimately connected to the worship of Śakti as nature's vital energy.

Śākta Tantra focuses on mantras, *bījas*, *mudrās*, and *nyāsas*. While the highest ideal of Tantric Shaivism and Vaishnavism is liberation, Tantric Shaktism aspires further, to control the powers of nature and acquire knowledge of the cosmos. Without disregarding *mokṣa*, or "liberation," it does not stop there. Its goal is to realize our oneness with the entire universe and merge with the goddess.

Everything perceivable in the objective world is an expression of Śakti. Every physical, mental, emotional, and energetic manifestation is Śakti, which comes from Śiva, the substratum. The system of chakras, or "energy centers," is consciousness, or Śiva, projecting himself from Śakti. She is called by different names in her multiple aspects. She is *prāṇa* when referring to organizing and developing matter in its great variety of life forms. She is *kuṇḍalinī* when referring to the dormant power that lies in everything and can be awakened through Tantric practice. She is called Kālī when she dissolves the cosmic manifestation and draws it back to her womb at the end of each *yuga*.

She is Pārvatī, the consort of Śiva. She is the primary power, or Ādya, the universal Mother. She is Īśvarī, the consort of Īśvara, the Lord of the universe. She is Avidyā-rūpiṇī, or "the form of ignorance," because individuality emanates from her. She is also Vidyā-rūpiṇī, or "the form of knowledge," since she is the means to remove the bonds that prevent us from being liberated.

The *Kulārṇava Tantra* says, "that which makes us fall can help us rise." Śakti is every individual's mind, which can both enslave and liberate. She is *māyā*, the creator of illusion, since her power prevents us from perceiving reality as it is. Likewise, the perception of objective reality is possible through the power of Śakti, whereas self-perception is possible through Śiva. The power and manifestation of

Śakti is infinite, and hence she is venerated in countless forms.

The phenomenal world is merely consciousness perceived as multiplicity through the veil of illusion, or *māyā*. Although we distinguish names and forms that change in time and space, they do not represent a real change or transformation in the nature of consciousness. The phenomenal universe manifests through the power of Śakti, while Śiva remains unchanged.

Tantra considers the material universe to be a form or expression of the Whole. It does not question the reality of what is manifested or unmanifested. It accepts both as different expressions of the same reality. It invites us to use the body and everything around us to realize what lies beyond.

Enlightenment means transcending the illusory curtain of *māyā-śakti*. Tantra's ultimate ideal is to go beyond all illusory duality. To this end, this path seeks involution by reversing the process of the cosmic manifestation and returning to the original union of Śiva and Śakti.

In the supreme experience, the reality of pure consciousness emerges, free from the transcendental subjective duality of Śiva and Śakti. In enlightenment, there is only Brahman, "the One without a second." The Śiva–śakti poles merge, as we see depicted in the erotic Tantric sculptures where they are united in a state devoid of separation. Only the divine couple keeps the secret that two are capable of being one, without ceasing to be two.

SECTION II

Development of Tantra

CHAPTER 1

THE ORIGIN AND DEVELOPMENT OF THE TANTRIC REVELATION

Within the essence of every human being dwells the yearning to understand what lies beyond the earthly plane. Many spiritual paths have attitudes similar to that of Tantra. We can find Tantric elements in the ritualism of the most diverse traditions, even in modern indigenous tribes on different continents. In order to achieve altered states of consciousness, many cultures in Latin America use rituals similar to the *Kaula* that involve amulets, white or black magic, the practice of sex, drugs, alcoholic drinks, and the mystical powers of certain words or mantras. Even in the mysticism of Semitic religions, we can find Tantric features. The Tantric spirit can be traced to the origins of religion as a phenomenon.

The history of Tantra is the tale of fervent spiritual seekers willing to sacrifice their social status in order to find Truth. Instead of their benevolent and compassionate gods, they opted to worship the fierce goddesses that would not settle for anything less than the heads of their own devotees. The receivers of this revelation forsook a prosperous and tranquil life to undertake an esoteric path guided by enlightened gurus. Attempting to reconstruct the mosaic of Tantra's development, we follow the long-gone footprints of the brave souls who were not satisfied with the paradise promised by conventional religion and, with a deep spiritual nonconformity, looked for paths that could lead them to ultimate liberation.

To reconstruct Tantra's history, we have to draw on the few clues not erased by time or by the woeful destruction brought about by religiously intolerant conquerors. These foreigners could not appreciate the divine miracle that took place in ancient India.

Instead, they thought that the images of erotic *yoginīs* reflected a culture of exhibitionism and sin. They could not see that they had come not only to a distant land, but to a future time; they encountered a culture with such advanced moral and spiritual values that it would take years for the West to understand.

We should bear in mind that the Tantric revelation is much older than its literature. At first, it was transmitted orally from master to disciple. However, these lines of succession were often broken and, unfortunately, the revelations have not reached us intact. The data are scarce and scholars have to work hard to reconstruct the chain of historical events. We are deeply indebted to them for collecting the pieces of this puzzle and helping us to form a fuller picture of the way the Tantric miracle unfolded. Although this book presents a coherent succession of facts, revelations, writings, and sects, information is often insufficient. New evidence that sheds light on these traditions is constantly emerging.

The clues that we have are inscriptions carved on temple walls, poorly preserved manuscripts on palm leaves, and references to lost texts in much later commentaries. We also know of some sects because their names, appearance, and customs are described in theater scripts that have ascetic or religious characters.

Although we start with the historical context of Tantra, we will focus on the truths revealed to those fervent seers whom divinity gave ladders to return to their origin. We will first present a summary and then elaborate on the main Tantric traditions in the following chapters.

At the beginning of the first millennium of the Common Era, Vedic Brahmanism was well established in India. The Vedic revelation is eternal and its beginnings are lost to history. Historians estimate that it began around 2000 BCE. At the time, priests performed elaborate public rituals called *śrauta*, or "belonging to *śruti*," in accordance with the *Brāhmaṇa* section of the Vedas. These rituals involved worshipping elements of nature such as fire and rivers, offering sacrifices to heroic gods such as Indra, and singing the hymns of the *Ṛg Veda* to praise them. They also included rituals for the moon called Soma, animal sacrifices, and seasonal offerings. Believers would pray for wealth, prosperity, progeny, longevity, and a chance to pass into the celestial world of the ancestors at the moment of death. The *varṇāśrama* system of the Vedic society reserved the highest knowledge for the Brahmanical cast. Only *Brāhmaṇas* educated in the oral tradition were qualified to conduct these ceremonies.

Between 200 and 400 CE, the worship of the Vedic god Rudra gained popularity. The *Śvetāśvatara Upanishad*, which was put into writing sometime between 400 and 200 BCE, was the first text that systematized *Śaiva* philosophy. It revealed that the Vedic god Rudra was the transcendent supreme Being and the creator, preserver, and destroyer of the cosmic manifestation. The god Śiva was identified as Rudra and raised in the Vedic pantheon to the supreme Self. The path of Shaivism centered on bhakti yoga and devotional practices: offering service to Śiva, remembering him at all times, and listening to the stories about him. These practices developed into traditions of worshipping Śiva between 200 BCE and 100 CE. The religion of Puranic Shaivism developed during the reign of the Gupta dynasty. The *Purāṇas* were written down between the sixth and eleventh centuries CE. Many *Brāhmaṇas* increased the popularity of this tradition by orally spreading Puranic stories about Śiva throughout India.

The pre-Tantric *Śaiva Ati-mārga* or "the supreme or direct path"

Between the second and fifth centuries CE, an ascetic devotional tradition developed what was later called the *Ati-mārga*, or "the supreme or direct path." Lay followers of Śiva who aspired for final liberation, or *mokṣa*, requested initiation and adhered to an ascetic life of extreme penance. The later Tantric sects adopted these practices, and therefore, the *Śaiva Ati-mārga* is thought to be the origin of the Tantric tradition. It is believed to have developed in western India and then expanded to Orissa in the east, Tamil Nadu in the south, and Kashmir in the north.

There are three predominant Ati-margic sects, which will be described in more detail in later chapters: *Pāñcārthika Pāśu-patas*,

Lākulas (*Kāla-mukhas*), and *Kāpālikas* (also called *Mahā-vratas* and *Soma-siddhāntas*). In the beginning, only members of the lower castes were admitted, but later, the sublime goal of liberation began to attract educated *Brāhmaṇas* and they also chose an ascetic life. Their *sādhana* was antinomian and anti-Brahmanical in nature. They practiced meditative absorption in the deity, lived on cremation grounds, and consumed impure substances such as meat and alcohol. In their eagerness to transcend social conditioning, they adopted external symbols and transgressive behaviors rejected by society. They lived on alms and ate from cups made of human skulls. They worshipped the masculine aspect of Śiva in his ferocious Bhairava manifestation, which is associated with annihilation.

The *Śaiva Mantra-mārga* or "the path of the mantra"

Around the fifth century CE, the first sects that can be considered Tantric formed within a tradition called the *Mantra-mārga*, or "the path of the mantra." The earliest evidence of the *Mantra-mārga* is the *Niśvāsa-mūla* scripture, from between 450 and 550 CE. Over the next few centuries, this tradition spread throughout India. It inherited many of the practices adopted by the *Lākulas* and the *Kāpālikas*. Unlike the "direct" path to liberation proposed by the *Ati-mārga*, the *Mantra-mārga* suggested using the experience of celestial pleasures (*bhoga*) and mastery of nature through supernatural powers (*siddhis*) to reach *mokṣa*.

The ascetic life, considered to be the essential means to obtain liberation, was replaced by ritual practice. Hence now married people of all castes could be initiated and aspire to maximum realization in this life. Even women were accepted, although only as passive beneficiaries of initiation.

The *Mantra-mārga* inherited meditation and asceticism from the *Ati-mārga*, but emphasized rituals and mantras, especially in the initiation ritual. The *dīkṣā* ceremony was very elaborate, and Śiva himself acted through the guru, who was his consecrated representative. Only the guru was allowed to perform the ritual, during which Śiva destroyed the bonds of the souls mature enough for liberation.

This tradition included two branches: the *saiddhāntika*, which means "related to an established truth," and the non-*Saiddhāntika*. The former was more conservative. It followed the purity rules of Brahmanism, respected the caste system, and focused on public rituals for the benefit of society. The latter eliminated class differences and incorporated cults that took place in private, benefited only the participants, and included the consumption of prohibited substances.

With the intention of preserving the Brahmanical socio-religious order, the *Saiddhāntikas* eliminated the countercultural elements of their predecessors and adhered to the offerings and practices that were accepted by the established criteria for purity. In contrast, the non-*Saiddhāntika Śākta-śaiva* systems maintained *Ati-mārga* practices. The more *Śākta* the sect was, the more transgressive elements it incorporated. Orthodox Vedic followers rejected Tantric texts, but *Tāntrikas* did incorporate Vedic ideas and considered the *Āgamas* to be a later and more refined revelation. This attitude made Hinduism a living and dynamic faith.

Unlike Semitic traditions, where the original word is the ultimate authority, Hinduism sees religion as a living organism that evolves over time, incorporating new revelations suitable for the period, circumstances, goals, and inclinations of different types of people. Thus, the *Tāntrikas* granted greater authority to their own texts. They believed that the original tradition should be respected, but if a contradiction arose, the newer revelation was considered higher and more relevant.

The Vedic vision marks a division between matter and spirit; therefore, the body is considered an obstacle to purity. Instead, the Tantric approach emphasizes the immanent aspect of God and sees divinity in the cosmic manifestation. Since the body is a sacred temple, its components are not impure but magnificent instruments for attaining liberation in life, or *jīvan-mukti*.

The *Saiddhāntika* philosophy was dualist and worshipped the benevolent Sadā-śiva. Although his consort Umā also appeared in the pantheon, worship was still directed toward the masculine aspect. The non-*Saiddhāntika* tradition was monist, and as we shall see later, it had two branches: the *Mantra-pīṭha*, which worshipped

Bhairava, Śiva's fierce masculine aspect, and the *Vidyā-pīṭha*, which worshipped the female divinity.

The *Śakta Kula-mārga* or "the path of the clans"

Around the ninth century CE, the *Kaula* lineage originated with the legendary Macchanda-nātha (or Matsyendra-nātha), who reformed the earlier *yoginīs* cult, that are female semi-divine entities. By refining the rituals and eliminating the mortuary elements, he made it popular beyond cremation grounds. Matsyendra made the *Kāpālika* ritual accessible to married people. The *Kaula* path aspired to unite the male and female deities within one's own body. It outlined a copulation ritual between a man and a woman that would reconstruct the union of Śiva and his wife Śakti.

The Tantric sects of the *Mantra-mārga*, especially those of the *Vidyā-pīṭha* branch, influenced by the powerful *Kaula* rituals, gave rise to the *Kula-mārga* sects. This fusion of Tantra and *Kaula* was called *Kula-mārga*, or "the path of the clans." This name seems to refer to the clans (*kula*) of *yoginīs* in which the initiated male adept, or *vīra* (hero), sought to be accepted. Their orientation was predominantly *Śākta* and worship centered on the Devī. However, the *Śaiva* and *Śākta* traditions have always overlapped and it is difficult to separate them.

Kaula adepts aspired for *kaulika* power (*siddhi*) that would allow them to become one with the universal consciousness in a physical body. Like the *Mantra-mārga*, the *Kula-mārga* offered liberation, but its means had more in common with the practices of the *Ati-mārga Kāpālikas*. Scholars suggest that the *Kula-mārga* developed directly out of the *Kāpālika* sect and preserved its distinctive features, but in a more intensified and pure way. *Kaulas* showed respect to the Brahmanical tradition as the source from which the revelation emerged, but considered it to be a path that could not grant liberation. Once aspirants gained access to the *Kaula's* esoteric practices and literature, they still had to respect Brahmanism as valid for the uninitiated.

It is difficult to identify the beginnings of the *Kula-mārga*, but the available evidence suggests that it reached its greatest popularity in the ninth century CE or perhaps even a century earlier. Between the ninth and twelfth centuries CE, this path was very well established in Kashmir, in northern India.

Its practice included two types of rituals: one guided by the *Śākta*-oriented texts from the *Mantra-mārga* and another considered superior, based on its own texts called the *Kula-śāstras*. Instead of the elaborate ritual and the long process of initiation involving oblations (*hautrī-dīkṣā*), these latter texts introduced the initiation through the induction of possession (*āveśa*) by the goddess and the consumption of sacramental substances (*caru-prāśanam*, *vīra-pāna*). Secret and mystical cults reserved for initiates included sexual intercourse with a consecrated consort (*dūtī*), blood sacrifices, and collective orgiastic rites. However, like the non-*Saiddhāntikas* of the *Mantra-mārga*, *Kaula* adepts also gave importance to public rituals for the protection of society and the state.

The *Kula-mārga* was a widely inclusive path. It welcomed serious seekers, ascetics, and married people of all castes, including the so-called untouchables. It accepted women, who were encouraged to practice and even become gurus. It argued that the notion of castes did not come from nature but was a cultural construct, and therefore, should be ignored. Those who showed signs of discrimination were expelled from the group.

The attitude toward the female deities that characterized the *Vidyā-pīṭha Tantras* continued to develop on this "final path" of Tantric practice. The goddess took center stage over her male consorts and was even worshipped alone. This path was rich in erotic and transgressive practices intended to break taboos and social norms to overcome the mind and achieve liberation. The *Kaula* sacrifice (*yajña*) became an internal act. In fact, any effort to evoke the supreme reality was considered a sacrifice. However, adepts also performed simple rituals in sacred places as to not exclude the external aspect of the sacrifice.

According to early Tantras such as *Kubjikā-mata*, *Ciñciṇī-mata-sāra-samuccaya*, and *Manthāna-bhairava*, the *Kula-mārga* includes four sub-traditions (*āmnāyas*) that emanated from the faces of Sadā-śiva and were named after the cardinal directions. The eastern transmission, called *Pūrvāmnāya*, focused on the worship of Kuleśvara and Kuleśvarī and gave birth to the *Kaula Trika* tradition with a triad of goddesses: Parā, Parāparā, and Aparā. The northern transmission, *Uttarāmnāya*, venerated different manifestations of the fierce goddess Kālī and gave birth to the *Kaula-krama* tradition, which was the only one to worship the female goddess exclusively. The western transmission, *Paścimāmnāya*, had the hunchback goddess Kubjikā as its central deity. The southern transmission, *Dakṣiṇāmnāya*, focused on the beautiful and benevolent goddess Kāmeśvarī, and later gave birth to the worship of Tripura-sundarī.

Later scriptures, such as the *Sat-sahasrika-saṁhitā* and *Kulārṇava Tantra*, describe additional transmissions such as the *Anuttarāmnāya*, also called *Śrī-vidyā*, which worships the goddess Tripura Sundarī. Below, we elaborate on the six different *āmnāyas*.

The Non-dual *Trika* Kashmir Shaivism

Kula-mārga followers were mostly illiterate and were more interested in practice than philosophy. However, toward the beginning of the tenth century CE, the Tantric sects, especially the *Trika* and the *Krama*, began to incorporate highly educated initiates. These brilliant and refined aesthetes began to elaborate a vast body of commentaries on their sects' scriptures. While the *Āgamas* were considered divine revelations received either from Śiva or from the Devī, these exegeses came from human authors. Since they were enlightened, their words contained the vibration of their direct experience. Hence these texts were the most accurate explanations of reality and were revered as much as the revelation itself.

These brilliant masters ushered *Śaiva* Tantra into a golden age. Erotic and transgressive practices were transferred to the inner world of the practitioner. They saw the ferocious goddesses as expressions of the different energies of the mind and the human body, and the mortuary symbols came to represent the death of the ego.

These exegetes gave sophisticated expressions to the transgressive elements of *Śaiva* Tantra. They purified the shocking aspects of the cult of the goddesses and reinterpreted the external elements as symbols of inner spiritual experience. Since they were refined aesthetes, they believed the highest state of consciousness was aesthetic rapture: a transcendental perception of beauty in the embodied existence. In this way, they interpreted the mortuary practices as part of the divine totality. Supposed impurities were treated as facets of the inclusive beauty of existence.

In the tenth century CE, the *Śaiva* Tantra scene was dominated by two diametrically opposed schools: the non-dual *Śākta* traditions, mainly the *Trika* and the *Krama*, and the dual *Śaiva-siddhānta* movement that was part of the *Saiddhāntika Mantra-mārga*. The non-dual *Trika* school of Kashmir Shaivism integrated some elements of transgressive traditions and some orthodox elements from the *Śaiva-siddhānta*. In this new non-dual tradition, transgressive elements were internalized so they were less offensive to the orthodoxy, and the movement became popular throughout India.

This school became known in the West as Kashmir Shaivism because the commentators on the scriptures were mostly from this part of northern India. However, this modern term does not aptly describe this school, because it was not limited to this region. The names given to it in its own time included *Pratyabhijñā-darśana* (the school of recognition) and *Trika-śāsana* (the triad system). This sophisticated philosophical system combined elements of four schools, which will be later described in more detail: *Pratyabhijñā*, *Kula*, *Krama*, and *Spanda*.

The soteriological goal of *Trika* initiates was to merge their individual consciousness with the transcendental consciousness. The daily ritual was very demanding as it followed the pattern of the *Śaiva-siddhānta*. The *sādhana* included forms of logical practice called *upāya* as well as *kuṇḍalinī-yoga*. Initiates used mantras to purify their bodies, visualized mental rituals in which Śiva's trident penetrated their bodies, and performed external worship with a symbolic diagram called a *maṇḍala*. They worshipped forms of Śiva and the goddess Kālī. The sect accepted men and women of all castes. Initiates, in fact, formed a single "caste": lovers of God.

The *Vaiṣṇava Pāñca-rātra*

Vaishnavism, also called Bhagavatism, was already well established in India when *Śaiva* Tantrism began to flourish. It had the support of kings, especially between the fourth and seventh centuries CE. Vaishnavism, like Shaivism, was born from the depths of the Vedic revelation. It is a path that from its very foundation was based on devotion to a personal God (bhakti) called Viṣṇu, Kṛṣṇa, Vāsudeva, or Nārāyaṇa. Within Vaishnavism, there are many schools, lineages, and sects, each centered on a different incarnation of Viṣṇu.

During the second half of the first millennium, Tantric Shaivism was gaining popularity and followers. The Tantric view of the body, the acceptance of all castes, its soteriological goals, and the sophisticated system of rituals and mantras attracted many followers. The *Vaiṣṇava* tradition, on the other hand, was more committed to the devotional aspect of Vedic practice and, therefore, was less receptive to the emerging Tantric attitude. However, the winds of the Tantric revelation reached the *Vaiṣṇava Pāñca-rātra* sect that worshipped Nārāyaṇa, although today it no longer identifies itself as Tantric. The influence of Tantrism on this tradition gave rise to new scriptures known collectively as *Pāñca-rātra Āgamas*, which were probably composed in the vicinity of Kashmir. It is difficult to estimate when this revelation was put into writing, but it may have been between the eighth and fourteenth centuries CE.

The *Pāñca-rātra* literature comprises Agamic scriptures in Sanskrit that glorify Lord Viṣṇu and his consort Lakṣmī as the supreme divine couple. Its content derives from the *Mantra-mārga Śaiva* canon but takes a more moderate and orthodox tone. Around the middle of the ninth century CE, the *Pāñca-rātra* ritual system was reformed according to *Śaiva Mantra-mārga Saiddhāntika* models that were very popular at the time. The *Pāñca-rātra* tradition claims to have had a canon of 108 texts revealed by Viṣṇu in his Vāsudeva or Nārāyaṇa form, most of which are apparently lost.

Pāñca-rātra means five (*pañca*) nights (*rātra*). There are many explanations of the name of this school. One of the most accepted states that the daily routine of its followers was divided into five parts:

temple attendance for the morning ritual (*abhigamana*), acquisition of materials necessary for worship (*upādāna*), deity worship (*ijyā*), the study of scriptures (*svādhyāya*), and meditation on divinity (*yoga*). The goal of this fivefold practice was to reach the glorious and supreme feet of Viṣṇu. When the *jīva*s experience God, they seem to merge into him but still maintain a subtle distinction.

Vaishnavism incorporated the worship of God's feminine aspect as the consort of Lord Viṣṇu. In turn, Shaivism adapted some transgressive elements of Vaishnavism, such as the cult of Narasiṁha. The Tantric *Pāñca-rātra* scriptures were adopted as the official worship manuals in later *Vaiṣṇava* schools, beginning with Rāmānujācārya.

In addition to the *Vaiṣṇava Pāñca-rātra*, other *Vaiṣṇava* sects were also influenced by Tantra. It is worth mentioning the *Vaikhānasa* sect, which produced its own *Āgamas*.

Between the fifteenth and nineteenth centuries CE, the Bengal region was the scene of a Tantric renaissance, especially within Brahmanical circles.

These later sects combined the worship of Kṛṣṇa and the fearful goddess Kālī, who assumed the aspect of a protective mother. From the sixteenth century CE, the bhakti tradition *Sahajiyā* adopted Hindu and Buddhist Tantric practices within the theological framework of Vaishnavism, which included venerating the love of the divine couple Kṛṣṇa and Rādhā through sexual rituals among devotees.

The influence of Tantra on other religions

Tantra has had a significant influence on the development of other Indian religions, such as Jainism and Buddhism. We will mention them only briefly since our focus is on the development of Tantra within Hinduism.

Buddhist Tantric traditions began to develop in the mid-seventh century CE. In *Mahāyāna* Buddhism, there had already been a growing interest in magic and mystical powers for several centuries. Around the fifth century CE, Buddhists composed several works that included magic formulas (*dhāraṇī*) and explanations of the rites they performed to accomplish worldly goals. It is no coincidence that this was also the central theme of the *Śaiva Tantras*, written at the same time. Around the eighth century CE, more sophisticated Buddhist Tantric traditions emerged that included practices of union with the deity and secret methods for rapidly attaining Buddhahood. These traditions focused on the scriptures that were later classified as *Yoga*, *Mahā-yoga*, and *Yoginī Tantras*. The Buddhist *Yoginī Tantras* worshipped female goddesses known as *yoginīs* or *ḍākinīs* and suggested antinomian practices inspired by the scriptures of the *Vidyā-pīṭha* branch of the Śaiva *Mantra-mārga*. This new Tantric literature was considered the highest because it taught the yogic practices of "the stage of perfection." It included the manipulation of the subtle body, which is composed of *prāṇas* (vital energies), *bindu* (semen), *nāḍīs* (subtle channels), and chakras (energy centers). These new Tibetan traditions affirmed that the ability to manipulate the subtle body through yogic practices was a requirement to become fully awakened.

This new Tantric Buddhism spread rapidly within India and beyond. It reached Tibet during the eighth century CE and then southeastern Asia. Both the Hindu and Buddhist Tantric traditions influenced other religions, such as Jainism, Islam, and Sikhism in Southern Asia and Taoism and Shintō in Eastern Asia. Tibet's Bön tradition was completely transformed by Tantric Buddhism.

The *Saura* tradition of Hinduism, which focused on the Sun god Sūrya, produced several Tantric texts, such as the *Saura Saṁhitā*, which was also known as the *Saura Tantra*. Very few copies of this work have survived. The *Saura* tradition went into decline during the medieval period and became part of Shaivism; *pūjās* to Sūrya were added before the worship of Śiva.

Jainism was also influenced by Tantra, and its secondary texts mention the existence of a substantial corpus of Tantras based on the Sūrya tradition that developed in western India. Unfortunately, these manuscripts have not survived. Currently, Jainism does not identify itself as Tantric, but several Jain authors describe meditations and Tantric rituals in texts from 800 CE. Tantra aroused much interest among the Jainas, but they censored some elements that were contrary to their tradition, such as rituals that involved sex or violence. Jainas began to worship goddesses from the *Mantra-mārga Śaiva* tradition. The worship of these goddesses was adapted to the moral rules of Jainism: rituals were limited to vegetarian offerings and excluded animal sacrifices.

Tantra today

The majority of Tantric sects are no longer living traditions. We only have some scriptures and stories of glorious times when elevated souls visited our planet and revealed the secrets of these paths to liberation. However, Tantric colors will always paint the spiritual landscape of modern Hinduism. Within Hinduism, we can no longer demarcate the differences between the Vedic and Tantric traditions. Both melted together until all boundaries were erased. What would Hinduism be without chakras, mantras, and deities?

The classical Tantra period culminated around 1200 CE. Unfortunately, this was followed by centuries of Muslim occupation that abruptly interrupted the fascinating Tantric miracle. Deprived of state support, *Śaiva* Tantric institutions, temples, and monasteries were dismantled. The torch of Tantra was passed to sects with less formal structures, influenced by the *Kaula* lineages. Married people, who used to finance Tantric traditions, stopped following these practices. The revelation was now in the hands of ascetics. These nomadic *sādhus*, generally illiterate, did not document many of their yogic discoveries: they were more concerned with practice and austerities than philosophy.

In the postclassical period beginning around 1300 CE, Tantra went through a series of transformations. Tantric practices were incorporated into hatha yoga traditions, which would later become the inspiration for modern yoga systems that today enrich the lives of millions of people in India and the West. The influences of Tantra on hatha yoga could fill an entire book. Today, scholars are looking for further evidence about the origins of hatha yoga to understand the factors that influenced its development. New texts are being translated into English for the first time, shedding more light on its unknown aspects.

First of all, it is necessary to clarify that Patañjali is not the founder of hatha yoga, as many believe. There is no direct historical connection between the pre-Tantric yoga presented by Patañjali and the much later hatha yoga system. Patañjali (c. 100 CE) was a sage and native of Kashmir who followed the *Sāṁkhya* system. He compiled a series of aphorisms, the *Yoga Sūtra*, which describe an eight-limbed yoga method called *aṣṭaṅga*. It is a system of raja yoga that culminates in *samādhi*. Its third member is asana and fourth is *prāṇāyāma*; therefore, Patañjali is considered the founder of what would later be called hatha yoga. However, since this was a system of meditation, Patañjali described a comfortable and static sitting posture suitable for practicing meditation. His intention was different from that of later hatha yogis, who used various bodily postures as part of their retroprogressive process.

Tantric sects adopted *Aṣṭaṅga-yoga* and mentioned its name in various scriptures. However, they only incorporated the practical side, because the philosophy behind the *Yoga Sūtra* is *Sāṁkhya* dualism that divides matter and spirit. *Tāntrikas* embraced this meditative practice but retained their own monist philosophy of unity and divinity of matter. Kashmir Shaivism adopted the twenty-five *tattvas* of *Sāṁkhya* and completed its description of reality with eleven more *tattvas*, which are described later. The ashtanga system was enriched with so many Tantric elements that it would be more correct to say that hatha yoga originated in Tantra.

After the twelfth century CE, a new tradition arose. It originated from the *Kula-mārga* and would later be called *Nātha-sampradāya*. Its adepts claimed to be descendants of Gorakṣa-nātha, who can in fact be considered the father of hatha yoga. His master was the legendary Matsyendra-nātha, who spread the *Kula-mārga* during the current age of Kali. Gorakṣa-nātha wrote down the hatha yoga tradition, which until then was only transmitted orally among ascetics. In his teachings, he included *Kaula* material on the cults of Tripura-sundarī and Kubjikā.

He used *kaula* terminology and concepts but tended to reject external *Kaula* and transformed it into an internal practice. In this new "domesticated" synthesis, transgressive practices, such as the consumption of sexual fluids, were internalized as visualization techniques. In this way, members of conventional Brahmanical society could experience their true identity as Bhairava without violating the conformist norms of the high castes.

Works such as the *Jayad-ratha Yāmala* and *Netra Tantra* began to transform the *pīṭhas* (mounds) and circular temples of *yoginīs* into a system of chakras (circles) of goddesses. In the following centuries, in works such as the *Kubjikā-mata Tantra* and *Rudra Yāmala*, these became the standard system in hatha yoga of six chakras plus one. The entire process was incorporated into the practitioners' bodies, instead of the external offering of bodily components or the semen during sexual relations with *yoginīs*. By situating the *śakti* entirely inside the body, the chakra system allowed them to sublimate the sexual ritual into a visualization practice. Over time, the multiple goddesses and *yoginīs* were brought together into a single Śakti called *Kuṇḍalinī*. This female energy sleeps in the lower abdomen with her mouth on a subtle *liṅga*. Awakened by breath control and other techniques, she elevates through the *suṣumṇā-nāḍī* and the chakras to join the masculine Śiva in the cranial vault. This union culminates the process of involution and expands the practitioner's consciousness.

With the advent of hatha yoga, as recorded in works such as the *Gorakṣa-śataka* and *Viveka-mārtaṇḍa* (twelfth century CE, attributed to Gorakṣa-nātha), these practices were further transformed. Yogis autonomously embodied both poles of Tantric sexuality. They manipulated thc flow of masculine (white as semen) and feminine (red as menstrual blood) liquids by controlling their breathing channels: female (*iḍā*, lunar) and male (*piṅgalā*, solar). Through internal hydraulics and thermodynamics, they elevated these liquids to the cranial vault to fill it with semen (*bindu*). The *bindu* became nectar and gave them supernatural powers (*siddhis*) and immortality (*amṛta*).

These yogic transformations of the body had completely lost all traces of the Tantric practice of the *yoginīs*. They probably gave rise to a new group of practices, first recorded in the tenth century CE, that use the body as a laboratory. Hindu alchemists visualized how the semen of Bhairava (Śiva) and the uterine blood of Bhairavī (Śakti) reached the male–female union within their own bodies. The main classical texts of hatha yoga explain that the goal of practicing asanas is to raise the latent power of the goddess Kuṇḍalinī. They present the system of chakras and subtle anatomy inherited from Tantra.

Nowadays, academic interest in these esoteric traditions helps us rediscover these treasures, restore the image of Tantra, and reconstruct its history.

Tradition	*Śaiva Ati-mārga*	*Śaiva Mantra-mārga*	*Śākta Kula-mārga*	Non-dual *Trika* Kashmir Shaivism	*Vaiṣṇava Pāñca-rātra*
Name Translation	The supreme or direct path.	The path of the mantra.	The path of the clans.	It has also other names, such as *Praty-abhijñā-darśana* (the school of recognition), *Trika-śāsana* (the system of the triad).	The Vaishnavism of the five (*pañca*) nights (*rātra*).
First evidence	Between the second and fifth centuries CE.	The *Niśvāsa-mūla* text from 450–550 CE.	The ninth century CE.	The early tenth century CE.	Between the eighth and fourteenth centuries CE.
Sects	1. *Pāñcārthikas* or *Pāśu-patas* 2. *Lākulas* or *Kāla-mukhas* 3. *Kāpālikas* or *Soma-siddhāntas*	1. *Saiddhāntika* 2. Non-*Saiddhāntika*	1. *Pūrvāmnāya* 2. *Dakṣiṇāmnāya* 3. *Paścimāmnāya* 4. *Uttarāmnāya*	1. *Praty-abhijñā* 2. *Kula* 3. *Krama* 4. *Spanda*	1. *Vaiṣṇava Pāñca-rātra* 2. *Bhakti-sahajiyā*
Location	Western India; expanded east to Orissa, south to Tamil Nadu, and north to Kashmir.	Spread throughout India during the second half of the first millennium CE.	Kashmir	Kashmir	Kashmir and then Bengal.

Tradition	*Śaiva Ati-mārga*	*Śaiva Mantra-mārga*	*Śākta Kula-mārga*	Non-dual *Trika* Kashmir Shaivism	*Vaiṣṇava Pāñca-rātra*
Description and development	Pre-Tantric sects. Among the lay followers of Śiva, those with higher spiritual aspirations were initiated and adopted an ascetic life of extreme penance.	First Tantric sects. They inherited many practices from the second and third sects of the *Ati-mārga*.	Their means had more in common with the practices of the third sect of the *Ati-mārga*.	It combined the practices of the *Kula-mārga* with *Śaiva-siddhānta* ritualism.	The winds of Tantric revelation reached the *Vaiṣṇava Pāñca-rātra* sect, which worshipped Nārāyaṇa.
Goal	Final liberation, or *mokṣa*.	Liberation (*mokṣa*) through the experience of celestial pleasures (*bhoga*) and the mastery of nature through supernatural powers (*siddhis*).	Identification with the universal consciousness in the physical body through the *Kaulika* power (*siddhis*).	The soteriological objective of the *Trika* initiate was to merge the individual consciousness with the transcendental consciousness.	To reach the glorious and supreme feet of Viṣṇu.
Practice	Their practices were antinomian and anti-Brahmanical in nature. They practiced meditative absorption in the deity.	The *Mantra-mārga* inherited meditation and asceticism, but emphasized ritual and mantras, especially the initiation ritual.	Erotic and transgressive practices with the aim of breaking taboos and manners imposed by society.	Logical practices called *upāyas* and *kuṇḍalini-yoga*.	Fivefold practice: *abhigamana*, *upādāna*, *ijyā*, *svādhyāya*, and *yoga*.

Tradition	*Śaiva Ati-mārga*	*Śaiva Mantra-mārga*	*Śākta Kula-mārga*	Non-dual *Trika* Kashmir Shaivism	*Vaiṣṇava Pāñca-rātra*
Deity	Bhairava, the ferocious masculine manifestation of Śiva, associated with annihilation.	*Saiddhāntikas: Sadā-śiva.* Non-*saiddhāntikas:* Bhairava and female divinity Bhairavī.	Śiva in union with his wife Śakti.	Forms of Śiva and the goddess Kālī.	Viṣṇu, Kṛṣṇa, Vāsudeva, or Nārāyaṇa and their female consorts.
Members	Educated *Brāhmaṇas* who chose an ascetic life. Almost exclusively male *Brāhmaṇas.*	Married people of all castes. All castes could be initiated and aspire to the maximum realization in this life. They accepted women, although only as passive beneficiaries of initiation.	Serious seekers, ascetics or married people of all castes. Both men and women. Women were encouraged to practice and even to assume the role of the guru.	Men and women of all castes. Initiates formed a single "caste": lovers of God.	Men and women of all castes as well as converts from other religions. Bhakti is an inclusive movement that accepts members of all classes. The *Sahajiyā* sect even accepted Buddhist scriptures.
Ritual	Rituals on cremation grounds. Offerings and consumption of substances that were impure according to Brahmanism.	*Saiddhāntikas*: offerings and practices according to established purity rules. Non-*saiddhāntikas*: Atimargic rituals with sexual intercourse and the consumption of meat and alcohol.	Two types of rituals: those based on the *Mantra-mārga* and more elevated rituals based on the *Kula-śāstras.*	The *Kaula* sacrifice (*yajña*) became an internal act.	Devotional rituals with the Tantric spirit performed for Viṣṇu and his consort.

Diagram and Timeline of the Tantric Revelation

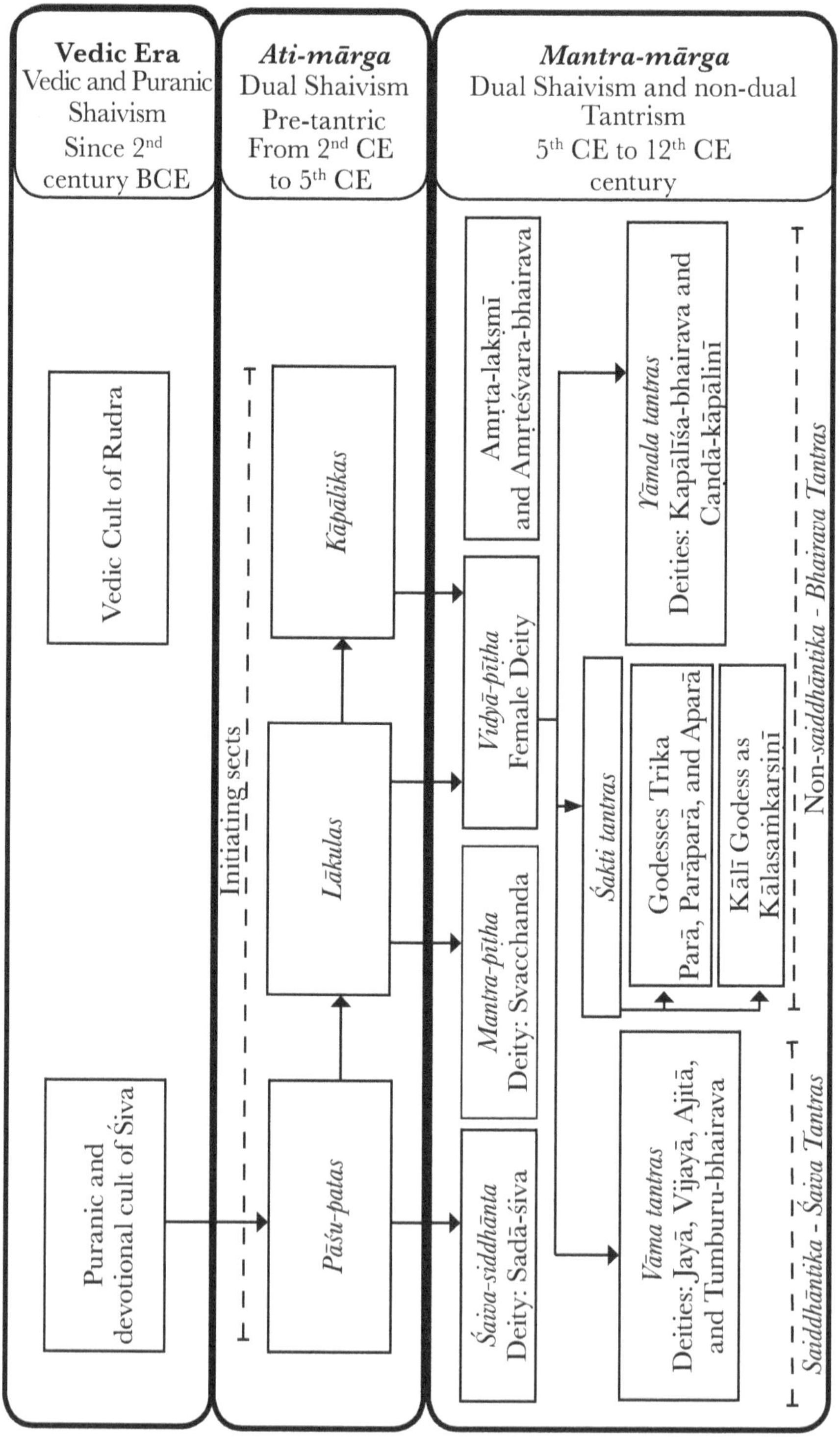

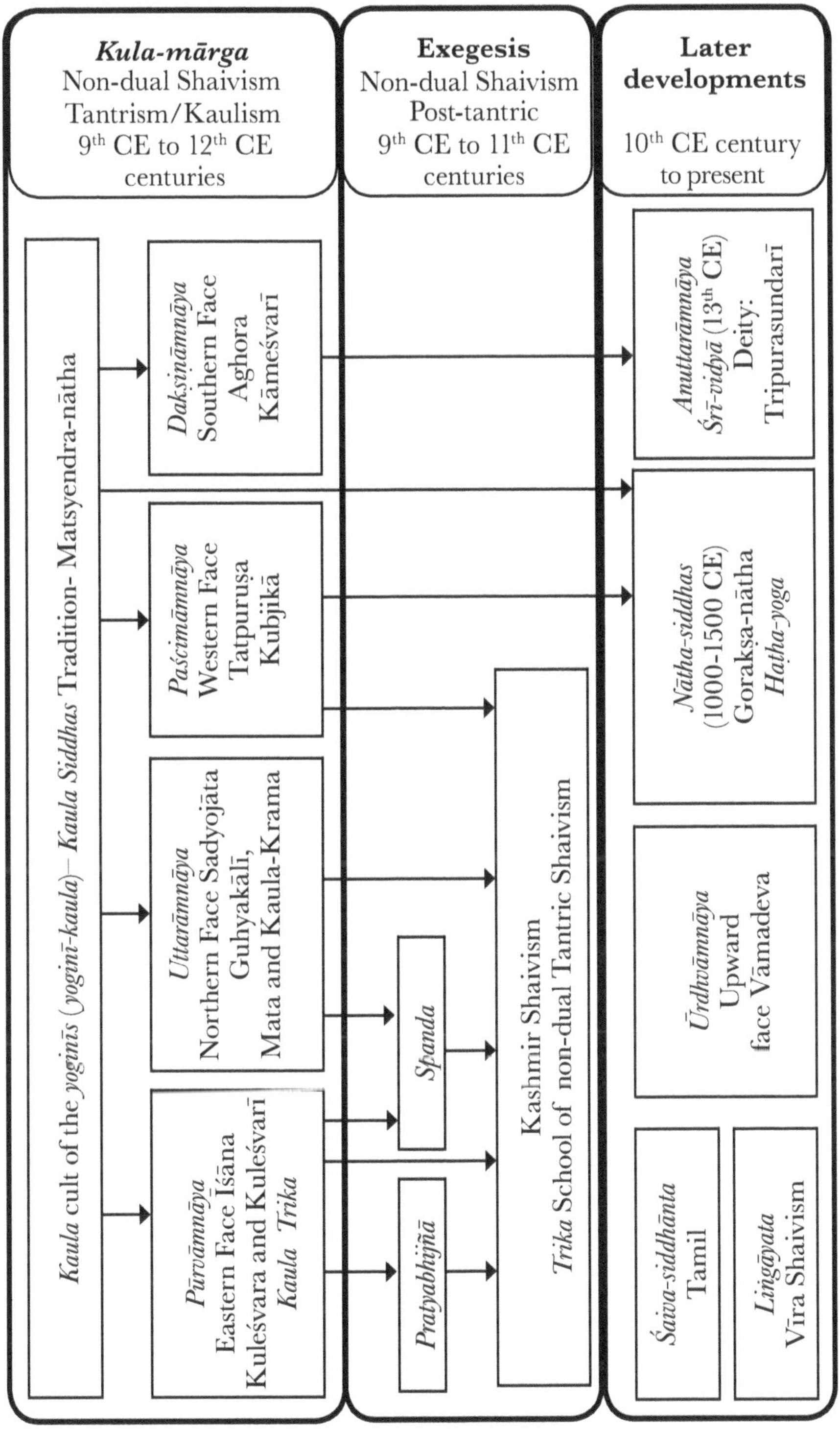

Kula-mārga
Non-dual Shaivism
Tantrism/Kaulism
9th CE to 12th CE centuries
Exegesis
Non-dual Shaivism
Post-tantric
9th CE to 11th CE centuries
Later developments
10th CE century to present
Kaula cult of the yoginīs (yoginī-kaula)– Kaula Siddhas Tradition- Matsyendra-nātha
Dakṣiṇāmnāya
Southern Face
Aghora
Kāmeśvarī
Paścimāmnāya
Western Face
Tatpuruṣa
Kubjikā
Uttarāmnāya
Northern Face Sadyojāta
Guhyakālī,
Mata and Kaula-Krama
Pūrvāmnāya
Eastern Face Īśāna
Kuleśvara and Kuleśvarī
Kaula Trika
Spanda
Pratyabhijñā
Kashmir Shaivism
Trika School of non-dual Tantric Shaivism
Anuttarāmnāya
Śrī-vidyā (13th CE)
Deity:
Tripurasundarī
Nātha-siddhas
(1000-1500 CE)
Gorakṣa-nātha
Haṭha-yoga
Ūrdhvāmnāya
Upward
face Vāmadeva
Śaiva-siddhānta
Tamil
Liṅgāyata
Vīra Shaivism

Chapter 2

The *Ati-Mārga* or "the direct path"

The earliest evidence of the *Śaiva* tradition is from the second century BCE. Although there were no organized sects or schools, we have evidence that Lord Śiva was worshipped as well as the names of his devotees. By the fifth century CE, Shaivism had clearly emerged as the dominant tradition in India and even southeast Asia, after which a great variety of traditions developed.

During the Gupta dynasty (320–500 CE), Puranic literature became popular throughout the Indian subcontinent. Based on these texts, various forms of Brahmanical worship developed, called *Smārta* or *Paurāṇika*. By the time the Gupta dynasty declined, *Smārta* worship had been well-established. At this point, India saw significant growth in esoteric cults. Some elements of these cults were absorbed by Brahmanical worship. However, most followers of the orthodoxy rejected the new systems, considering them to be a threat to Vedic purity. As a result, Śiva followers were divided into two groups: the initiated and the uninitiated.

Initiated and uninitiated *Śaivas*

Uninitiated *Śaivas* adhered to the *varṇāśrama* system. These were married *Brāhmaṇas* who worshipped orthodox forms of Lord Śiva and followed domestic rites, which included Puranic *pūjā* with Vedic mantras. In contrast, the earliest initiated adepts opted for an ascetic life and were formally initiated into one of the *Śaiva* sects. These initiated *Brāhmaṇas* committed to a life of complete celibacy.

The first evidence of initiated devotees is from the *Pāśu-pata* lineage in 450–550 CE. *Pāśu-patas* considered the ascetic life to be higher than the four stages of the *āśrama* system. They called this fifth stage *siddhāśrama*, or "the perfected *āśrama*." Unlike later schools and sects, *Pāśu-patas* did not reject the *vaidika* tradition; instead they saw their own teachings as its culmination.

Initiation was reserved for *sādhakas* with high aspirations who were ready for sacrifice and surrender. After being initiated, they were granted access to Tantric literature and esoteric practices that were prohibited for the uninitiated.

There was never any competition between the two groups, because initiation was considered a more elevated step in approaching the transcendental. Uninitiated *Śaivas* focused primarily on bhakti yoga, the path of devotion to Lord Śiva, while initiates emphasized the Yogic path. From Tantric Shaivism a great diversity of sects and practices emerged. Left-hand *sādhana* was transgressive because it included sexual rituals and the consumption of meat and alcohol. Right-hand practices focused on mantras, yantras, and rituals. Over time, left-hand practices were internalized, proposing an inner awakening of our own feminine and masculine aspects.

The *Śiva-dharma* is based on a broad literary canon. Its scriptures offer information and guidance for the path of devotion to Lord Śiva. The main works are the *Umā-maheśvara-saṁvāda*, *Śiva Upanishad*, *Śiva-dharma-saṅgraha*, *Vṛṣa-sāra-saṅgraha*, *Lalita-vistara*, *Uttarottara-mahā-saṁvāda*, *Dharma-putrikā*, and *Śiva-dharmottara*. It is also based on certain *Purāṇas*, especially the *Skanda Purāṇa*, as well as *Liṅga Purāṇa*, *Śiva Purāṇa*, *Vāyu Purāṇa*, *Devī Purāṇa*, and a large number of short compositions. Only initiates also had access to the Tantras. These esoteric writings were revealed by Śiva to benefit an elite within the *Śaiva* community. They are classified as *Śaiva Tantras*, *Rudra Tantras*, *Bhairava Tantras*, and all the later *Kula-mārga* scriptures.

The *Śaiva* devotional path favored the worship of the Vedic Śiva, called Rudra. Other Tantric paths cultivated devotion to furious aspects of Śiva, such as Bhairava. Sects with a *Śākta* inclination focused their devotion on the feminine aspect of divinity.

Although all the sects were devotional in nature, their rituals differed. Puranic Shaivism was inclined toward public ritualism in temples. Tantric initiates preferred private practice at home or in a guru's residence. Their rituals were more internal and required fewer material elements. For Tantric followers, having a small *liṅga* or a *Rudrākṣa-mālā* was enough.

The daily routine of the *Śaiva-bhaktas* involved the family and included temple attendance to celebrate the many festivals, as recommended in the sacred scriptures. They donated at least one third of their income for the maintenance of the community and the construction of temples. Initiated disciples, on the other hand, resided for extended periods in their guru's home. In this way, they had the opportunity to interact with their master in a more intimate way and apply teachings to their daily lives. They received constant instruction and spiritual education as well as intense practice. Such closeness allowed the disciples to vibrate in tune with the master's presence, until they achieved a communion impossible to reach from a distance.

Disciples who opted for marriage resided in their own homes but often visited their master's house to attend organized meetings called *sat-saṅgas*, or "encounters with the Truth." Only formally initiated disciples could attend these meetings. They usually consisted of a ritual, a lecture by the guru, and finally a celebration. On the other hand, *Kaula sat-saṅgas*, called *melāpas*, were more sensual and even reaching orgiastic situations. In such *melāpas*, cultural barriers and social taboos were transcended in an attempt to overcome psychological conditioning. The intention was to expand consciousness in order to perceive the sacred in the objective world.

Although both groups were devoted to Lord Śiva, they differed in their aspirations. Secular *Śaivas* sought success and security, both in this world and the afterlife, where they longed to arrive to the paradise of their worshipped deity, which they called *Śiva-loka* or *Rudra-loka*. However, it was clear to them that after the merits accumulated on the earthly plane were exhausted, they would have to accept earthly incarnations again. On the other hand, although initiated disciples attained mystical powers (*siddhis*), such as *śānti* (relief from afflictions) and *abhicāra* (destruction of enemies), their main yearning was *mokṣa* (liberation) from worldly dissatisfaction.

	Uninitiated *Śaivas*	Initiated *Śaivas*
Initiation	Uninitiated *Śaiva* devotees were known as *Śiva-bhaktas* or *upāsakas*. They practiced the devotional *Śaiva* tradition but had no access to Tantric practices.	Śiva's followers with higher spiritual aspirations were initiated and obtained access to esoteric literature reserved for initiates.
First evidence	Between the second century BCE and the fourth century CE.	This probably began with the *Pāśu-pata* lineage that began around the second century CE.
Practice	Devotional discipline, or bhakti yoga. Unwavering devotion to God. Practices: service to Śiva, remembering him at all times, and listening to stories about him.	They focused more on ritual and yogic knowledge. Their *sādhana* varied from antinomian practices that included sexual rituals and the consumption of meat and alcohol to practices that focused on mantras, yantras, and rituals.
Literature	The main literature of secular Shaivism is the *Śaiva-dharma*, which means "the religion of Śiva" and teaches how to live according to his principles.	*Shaiva Tantras, Rudra Tantras, Bhairava Tantras,* and all the later literature developed within the *Kula-mārga* framework.
Deity	The Vedic deity Rudra.	Bhairava, Śiva's furious aspect. Later sects worshipped the feminine aspect of divinity as well.
Rituals	The world of public worship and the celebration of festivals.	Private rituals at home or in the house of the guru. Tantric practice was more internal and did not require many material items.
Lifestyle	Generally, they lived a married life, attended the temple, celebrated the many festivals, and donated a third of their income.	The first sects led an ascetic life. In later Tantric sects, married people were also initiated.
Goal	Success and security in this life and after death; they aspired to ascend to the paradise of the deity they worshipped (*Śiva-loka, Rudra-loka*).	Supernatural powers (*siddhis*), but mainly liberation (*mokṣa*) from the cycle of births and deaths.

Śaiva Ati-mārga

Ati-mārga means "the highest or the direct path" and refers to the pre-Tantric *Śaiva* sects. There are those who translate this term as "those off the path" because many of its practices clashed with Vedic tradition. There is evidence that this tradition existed at least four centuries before Tantric Shaivism was systematized. Various theories have been proposed concerning the beginnings and origins of Tantric revelation. In light of the evidence, it is undeniable that the *Ati-mārga* paved the way for Tantrism. There is no other tradition as similar to Tantra in terms of doctrine and culture. Both traditions clearly share the same source and origin.

The following elements are present in both the Tantric and Ati-margic sects: 1) yogic *sādhana* as a means to access *mokṣa*; 2) transgressive practices incompatible with orthodox religion, society, and conventional morality; and 3) a system of elevation through different levels of reality until achieving sameness with divinity. Other common themes are the aspiration to transcend the egoic phenomenon, attachment to the physical body, and fear of death. They both use *Brahma-mantras*, see the body as a microcosm of the sacred universe, and worship Bhairava, which is the most popular deity in the Tantric tradition.

However, the *Ati-mārga* is considered a different revelation because it differs with Tantra on several essential points. For example, *Ati-mārga* sects accepted only men, asceticism was mandatory, and most sects demanded a vow of celibacy. They considered obtaining mystical powers to be a mundane goal and aspired only for *mokṣa*.

The *Ati-mārga* tradition included three main sects: *Pāśu-pata*, or *Pāñcārthika*; *Lākula*, sometimes called *Kāla-mukha* or *Mahā-vrata*; and *Kāpālika*, or *Soma-siddhānta*.

Yamunācārya (early tenth century CE), the great *Viśiṣṭādvaita* master, in his work *Āgama-prāmāṇya*, established the *Vaiṣṇava Pañca-rātra Āgamas* as an authoritative means of knowledge. He mentioned four *Śaiva* groups following the *Śaiva Tantras*, which are the three main *Ati-mārga* sects; the fourth is perhaps the lay *Śaivas*.

यथा माहेश्वरे तन्त्रे विरुद्धं बहु जल्पितम् ।
चतुर्विधा हि तत्सिद्धचर्यामार्गानुसारिणः ॥
यथा कापालिकाः कालामुखाः पाशुपतास्तथा ।
शैवास्तत्र च कापालं मतमेवं प्रचक्षते ॥

yathā māheśvare tantre
viruddhaṁ bahu jalpitam
catur-vidhā hi tat siddha
caryā-mārgānusāriṇaḥ

yathā kāpālikāḥ kālā-
mukhāḥ pāśupatās tathā
śaivās tatra ca kāpālam
matam evaṁ pracakṣate

For there are four kinds of followers of the way of life set forth by the *Maheśvara Tantras*: *Kāpālikas*, *Kāla-mukhas*, *Pāśu-patas*, and *Śaivas* (perhaps referring to *Śaiva Siddhāntas* of the *Mantra-mārga*).
(*Āgama-prāmāṇya*, 83)

तानि च शास्त्राणि पञ्चविधानि लौकिकम्, वैदिकम्, आध्यात्मिकम्, अतिमार्गम्, मान्त्रं चेति । ...अतिमार्गं तु शास्त्रं रुद्रप्रणीतानि पाशुपत-कापालमहाव्रतानि ।

tāni ca śāstrāṇi pañca-vidhāni— laukikaṁ, vaidikam, ādhyātmikam, ati-mārgam, māntraṁ ceti.
...ati-mārgaṁ tu śāstraṁ rudra-praṇītāni pāśupata-kāpāla-mahā-vratāni.

And there are five kinds of teachings. These are: *Laukika*, *Vaidika*, *Ādhyātmika*, *Ati-mārga*, and *Mantra-mārga*… As for the teachings of the *Ati-mārga*, they are the [three bodies of teachings] promulgated by Rudra called the *Pāśu-pata*, the *Kāpālika*, and the *Mahā-vrata* (*Lākula/Kāla-mukha*).
(*Siddhānta-prakāśikā* of Sarvātma-śambhu,
chapter 2, "*pañca-vidhāni śāstrāṇi*")

लौकिकं वैदिकं चैव तथाऽध्यात्मिकं एव च॥
अतिमार्गं च मन्त्राख्यं तन्त्रमेतदनेकधा।

laukikaṁ vaidikaṁ caiva
tathā 'dhyātmikaṁ eva ca
ati-mārgaṁ ca mantrākhyaṁ
tantram etad anekadhā

Laukika, *Vaidika*, *Adhyātmika*, *Ati-mārga*, and *Mantra-mārga*—in this way the (*Śaiva*) revelation became manifold.
(*Kāmika Āgama*, 1.17b–18a)

1. *Pāśu-pata* or *pāñcārthika*

अतिमार्गत्रयमुच्यते । [तत्र] पाशुपतशास्त्रेण तु प्रतिपाद्यमानोऽर्थः—आत्मानो बहवो व्यापका नित्याः कार्यकारणसंयोग जातास्तु परस्परभिन्नाश्च । एतेषामाणवमलं नास्ति । मायामलेन कर्मपाशेन च सांसारिकाः सुखदुःखान्यनुभवन्ति । वैराग्योत्पत्तौ शास्त्रोक्तक्रमेण दीक्षिते परमेश्वरस्य ज्ञानगुणः संक्रान्तो भवति । पुत्रेषु कुटुम्बधुरं निधाय संन्यासवन्त इव आत्मसु ज्ञानं संक्रमय्य ईश्वरः स्वाधिकारादुपरतो भवति ।

ati-mārga-trayam ucyate. [tatra] pāśupata-śāstreṇa tu pratipādyamāno 'rthaḥ— ātmāno bahavo vyāpakā nityāḥ kārya-kāraṇa-saṁyoga jātāstu paraspara-bhinnaś ca. eteṣām āṇava-malaṁ nāsti. māyā-malena karma-pāśena ca sāṁsārikāḥ sukha-duḥkhāny anubhavanti. vairāgyotpattau śāstrokta-krameṇa dīkṣite parameśvarasya jñāna-guṇaḥ saṁkrānto bhavati. putreṣu kuṭumba-dhuraṁ nidhāya saṁnyāsavanta iva ātmasu jñānaṁ saṁkramayya īśvaraḥ svādhikārād uparato bhavati.

There are said to be three types of *Ati-mārga*. Of these, one is *Paśu-pata-śāstra*, which suggests this: Ātman (the Self) is infinite, omnipresent, and eternal. These (qualities of Ātman) are different from each other due to the conjunction of cause and effect. There is no *āṇava-mala* (impurity that

> arises due to illusion) in this (Self). Since mortals are bound by impurity of illusion and impurity of actions, they experience happiness and sorrow. After renunciation (*vairagya*), *jñāna-guṇa* (quality of knowledge) of Parameśvara is transformed to the seeker (*jīvātma*), according to the order described in the scriptures (*śāstras*). When a seeker, after giving away his responsibilities of the family burden to his son, and taking renunciation, Parameśvara bestows his *jñāna-guṇa* and authority on him, and then the seeker becomes dispassionate on his own.
>
> (*Siddhānta-prakāśikā* of Sarvātma-śambhu, *ati-mārga-traye pāśupata-śāstram*)

The first ascetic *Śaiva* monks belonged to the *Pāśu-pata* sect. These spiritual giants flourished in the turbulence of India during the second century CE. Having renounced their past and without possessions, they wandered without a fixed course, carrying iron tridents and heavy maces. Their appearance was repugnant to the followers of the *Vaidika-dharma*, who were extremely sensitive to the difference between pure and impure, sacred and profane, conventional and transgressive, moral and immoral.

These ascetics wandered wearing deer skins and were smeared with ashes. Their oily locks were tied in buns and their hearts were filled with intense devotion. They saw their beloved Śiva behind the variety of names and forms.

They were benign wizards and passionate devotees of Śiva who were more concerned with inner purity than superficial appearances. They aroused public contempt but they knew that their gain was not in this temporary world. Rejecting public recognition, they longed for appreciation only from divinity. They traveled the roads of the world with a deep aspiration to transcend human conditioning. In order to access the transcendental, they uprooted themselves from the earthly.

This path was like acid for the egoic phenomenon of its practitioners, who aspired to receive *kāruṇya*, or "the compassionate grace," of Lord Śiva. Freedom from social approval was a way to counteract psychological conditioning and get closer to the transcendental, or the beloved Lord Śiva. These fervent seekers gave up their pride, public respect, and vanity in exchange for something this world could not give them.

More preoccupied with liberation from *saṁsāra* than public relationships, they reserved preaching for initiates worthy of the revelation. Hence the information we have about them comes mainly from their detractors. In order to objectively reconstruct the path of these *sādhus*, we must critically examine this information and filter out the disapproving views of society and commentators.

Members

Originally, *Pāśu-patas* were *Śaiva* devotees alienated from the Vedic society, which was dominated by orthodox Brahmanism. However, the sect slowly gained popularity within the Brahmanical community. Gradually, a large number of *Brāhmaṇas*, eager to worship Śiva in complete renunciation, began to join this movement. At some point, Sadguru Lakulīśa, who was a reformer by nature, accepted members only from the three highest castes: *Brāhmaṇas*, *Kṣatriyas*, and *Vaiśyas*.

Then, in an effort to harmonize with Vedic orthodoxy, the sect began to admit only male *Brāhmaṇas* who were willing to abandon their social position to follow an ascetic life.

The *Pāśu-pata Sūtra* states as follows:

अनेन विधिना रुद्रसमीपं गत्वा ॥

anena vidhinā rudra-samīpaṁ gatvā.

Moving closer to Rudra with this behavior.

(*Pāśu-pata Sūtra*, 4.19)

न कश्चिद्ब्राह्मणः पुनरावर्तते ॥

na kaścid brāhmaṇaḥ punar āvartate

No *Brāhmaṇa* returns to the world.

(*Pāśu-pata Sūtra*, 4.20)

The great commentator Kauṇḍinya explains in his *Pañcārtha-bhāṣya*:

आह— अत्रैवं विध्याचरणं समीपगमनं च कस्योपदिश्यते? । उच्यते— न तीर्थयात्रादिधर्मवत् सर्वेषाम् । किन्तु संस्कारवद्ब्राह्मणस्यैव ।
यस्मादाह—
न कश्चिद्ब्राह्मणः पुनरावर्तते ॥
...गृहस्थो ब्रह्मचारी वानप्रस्थो भिक्षुरेकवेदो द्विवेदस्त्रिवेदश्चतुर्वेदो गायत्रीमात्रसारो वानेन विधिना रुद्रसमीपं प्राप्तः सन्न कश्चिद्ब्राह्मणः पुनरावर्तत इत्यर्थः । ब्राह्मणग्रहणं ब्राह्मण्यावधारणार्थं ब्राह्मण एव नान्य इत्यर्थः ।

āha– atraivaṁ vidhyā-caraṇaṁ samīpa-gamanaṁ ca kasyopadiśyate? ucyate – na tīrtha-yātrādi-dharmavat sarveṣām. kintu saṁskāra-vad brāhmaṇasyaiva.
yasmād āha–
na kaścid brāhmaṇaḥ punar āvartate.
…gṛhastho brahmacārī vānaprastho bhikṣur eka-vedo dvi-vedas tri-vedaś catur-vedo gāyatrī-mātra-sāro vānena vidhinā rudra-samipaṁ prāptaḥ san na kaścid brāhmaṇaḥ punar āvartata ity arthaḥ. brāhmaṇa-grahaṇaṁ brāhmaṇy āvadhāraṇārthaṁ brāhmaṇa eva nānya ity arthaḥ.

Now, for whom is advised this practice of following rules of conduct and moving closer to Rudra? The answer is: it is not like the meritorious act of going to places of pilgrimage, which is for everyone. Rather, it is like the sacred sacrament only for a *Brāhmaṇa*. Because he says: "No *Brāhmaṇa* returns to the world (*na kaścid brāhmaṇaḥ punar āvartate*)."

…. No *Brāhmaṇa*, head of household, student, hermit, or ascetic who reads one, two, three, or four Vedas, or who is confined only to the *gāyatrī*, returns to the cycle of death and rebirth (*saṁsāra*) if he comes closer to Rudra through this conduct. The term *brāhmaṇa*, used here, is to restrict to *brāhmaṇas*, he is only the *brāhmaṇa* alone and no one else.

(*Pañcārtha-bhāṣya* of Śrī Kauṇḍinya on *Pāśu-pata Sūtra*, 4.20)

According to Vedic tradition, the life of a *Brāhmaṇa* is divided into four stages, or *āśramas*: *brahmacārī*, *gṛhastha*, *vānaprastha*, and *sannyāsa*. *Brahmacārī* is the stage of a celibate student. *Gṛhastha* is the stage of a married head of household. *Vānaprastha* is the stage in which two married people renounce the world together and live in the forest. *Sannyāsa* is a life as a renounced monk. All candidates were eligible for the *Pāśu-pata* membership at any stage of life. To be accepted as a *Pāśu-pata* meant transcending the orthodox Brahmanical classification and reach the fifth stage called *siddhāśrama*, or "the perfected stage." Unlike other Tantric sects, the *Pāśu-patas* did not completely reject the basic values of the Vedic tradition. Their teachings were not meant to deny the Vedic path, but to perfect it and transcend all suffering. They considered their message to be the most refined version of the Vedic revelation. Śrī Kauṇḍinya wrote in his *Pañcārtha-bhāṣya* commentary that *Pāśu-pata* yogis "must pretend to be madmen or beggars, cover their body with dirt, and grow their beards, nails, and hair and not take care of their body. They detach themselves from the classes (*varṇas*) and the stages of life (*āśramas*) and attain the power of being dispassionate."

प्रेतवच्चरेत् ॥

preta-vac caret

He should wander like a dead person.

(*Pāśu-pata Sūtra*, 3.11)

Kauṇḍinya explains this verse:

अत्र पुरुषाख्यः प्रेतः न मृताख्यः । कस्मात्? । आचरणोपदेशात् । वदिति किञ्चिदुपमा । उन्मत्तसदृशदरिद्रपुरुषस्नातमलदिग्धाङ्गेन रूढश्मश्रुनखरोम-धारिणा सर्वसंस्कारवर्जितेन भवितव्यम् । अतो वर्णाश्रमव्युच्छेदो वैराग्योत्साहश्च जायते ।

प्रयोजननिष्पत्तिश्च भवति अवमानादि । चरेदित्याज्ञामधिकुरुते। धर्मार्जने नियोगे च । संशयान्यत्वाच्चापुनरुक्तोऽयं चरशब्दो द्रष्टव्यः ॥

atra puruṣākhyaḥ pretaḥ, na mṛtākhyaḥ. kasmāt? ācaraṇopadeśāt. vad iti kiñcid upamā. unmatta-sadṛśa-daridra-puruṣa-snāta-mala-digdhāṅgena rūḍha-śmaśru-nakha-roma-dhāriṇā sarva-saṁskāra-varjitena bhavitavyam. ato varṇāśrama-vyucchedo vairāgyotsāhaś ca jāyate. prayojana-niṣpattiś ca bhavati avamānādi. cared ity ājñām adhikurute. dharmārjane niyoge ca. saṁśayānyatvāc cāpunar ukto 'yaṁ cara-śabdo draṣṭavyaḥ.

Preta or "dead": The term *preta* (dead) means a particular type of man, not a dead person. Why? Because it gives advice for this lifestyle.

Vat or "like": This means a degree of similarity. His body should be smeared with ashes and soiled with dirt like a poor man or a lunatic, he should have a beard, long fingernails, as well as body hair, and he should get rid of all refinements. In this way he begins to dissociate himself from the classes (*varṇas*), life stages (*āśramas*), and interest in aversion. Insults etc., will be the achievement of the goal.

Caret or "he should move": The word *caret* is a command to acquire merit and commitment.

(*Pañcārtha-bhāṣya* of Kauṇḍinya on *Pāśu-pata Sūtra*, 3.11)

Name of the sect

Pāśu-patas carefully followed their devotional practices in the worship of Rudra or Śiva as Paśu-pati, or "the Lord of the beasts," the sect's namesake. This name comprises *Paśu*, which means "beast or animal," and *Pati*, which means "master or lord." When they are born, all creatures are conditioned by their karma and sensual desire. The conditioned soul is called *pāśu*. Śiva is considered Paśu-pati, or "the master and lord of the beasts," to whom everyone returns. Only Paśu-pati waits at the end of the path. A fully enlightened being is beyond the level of instinct. The *jīvan-mukta*, or "person liberated in life," can be considered the master and sovereign of bestial inclinations.

Yāmunācārya, while explaining the doctrine of the *Pāśu-patas*, gives a short explanation of their name:

> जीवाः पशव उच्यन्ते तेषामधिपतिश्शिवः ।
>
> *jīvāḥ paśava ucyante teṣām adhipatiś śivaḥ.*
>
> Individual souls (*jīvas*) are called *paśus*, (cattle, beasts), and their overlord (*adhi-pati*) is Śiva.
>
> (Yāmunācārya, *Āgama-prāmāṇya*, passage 84)

Masters

The *Pāśu-pata* sect was born of Lord Śiva himself, who revealed his teachings to a group of wise seers, or *maharṣis*. Around 200 CE, Lakulīśa was born, an *avatar* of Śiva, *sad-guru*, and undisputed leader of the sect. His accession took place in what is now Gujarat. He was a disciple of Śrīkaṇṭha and a contemporary of Patañjali Maharṣi. Lakulīśa's impact on Paśupatism was so profound that after his death, the system was called *Lakulīśa Pāśu-pata*. According to tradition, Lakulīśa, or "Lord of the mace," was a hermit *Brāhmaṇa* who died and was resurrected by Lord Paśu-pati himself, who penetrated his body to deliver the *Pāśu-pata-dharma* to humanity. The village where this miracle happened was called Kāyāvarohaṇa, or "to enter the body of another," and the miracle is still celebrated there with great festivities. In this village, two stone inscriptions were found that honor the names of Lakulīśa's four main disciples: Kuśika, Gārgya, Maitreya, and Kauruṣa. The *Liṅga Purāṇa* describes him as the twenty-eighth incarnation of Lord Śiva:

Bhagavān Śiva said:

> तदा षष्टेन चांशेन कृष्णः पुरुषसत्तमः ।
> वसुदेवाद्यदुश्रेष्ठो वासुदेवो भविष्यति ॥

tadā ṣaṣṭena cāṁśena
kṛṣṇaḥ puruṣa-sattamaḥ
vasudevād yadu-śreṣṭho
vāsudevo bhaviṣyati

In the twenty-eighth age of Dvāpara, Kṛṣṇa, Vāsudeva, the best among men and the best among the Yadu dynasty will be born as the son of Vasudeva.

तदाप्यहं भविष्यामि योगात्मा योगमायया ।
लोकविस्मयनार्थाय ब्रह्मचारि शरीरकः ॥

tadāpy ahaṁ bhaviṣyāmi
yogātmā yoga-māyayā
loka-vismayanārthāya
brahmacāri śarīrakaḥ

Then I [Śiva] shall also be born with the body of a *Brahmacārī* and the soul of a yogi by the means of *yoga-māya*, to the great surprise of the worlds.

शमशाने मृतमुत्सृष्टं दृष्ट्वा कायमनाथकम् ।
ब्राह्मणानां हितार्थाय प्रविष्टो योगमायया ॥

śamaśāne mṛtam utsṛṣṭaṁ
dṛṣṭvā kāyam anāthakam
brāhmaṇānāṁ hitārthāya
praviṣṭo yoga-māyayā

On seeing a dead body forsaken in the cremation ground, I shall enter it and make it free from ailments by means of *yoga-māya*.

दिव्यां मेरुगुहां पुण्यां त्वया सार्धं च विष्णुना ।
भविष्यामि तदा ब्रह्मंल्लकुली नाम नामतः ॥

divyāṁ meru-guhāṁ puṇyāṁ
tvayā sārdhaṁ ca viṣṇunā
bhaviṣyāmi tadā brahmaṁl
lakulī nāma nāmataḥ

Then, in the divine and meritorious cave of Meru, along with you and Viṣṇu, O Brahmā, I will become embodied and shall be named Lakulī.

कायावतार इत्येवं सिद्धक्षेत्रं च वै तदा ।
भविष्यति सुविख्यातं यावद्भूमिर्धरिष्यति ॥

kāyāvatāra ity evaṁ
siddha-kṣetraṁ ca vai tadā
bhaviṣyati suvikhyātaṁ
yāvad bhūmir dhariṣyati

[My] physical incarnation and the holy *siddha-kṣetra* (the place of my incarnation) will be greatly renowned as long as the earth exists.

(*Liṅga Purāṇa*, 1.24.126–130)

The *Liṅga Purāṇa* considers him to be the last *avatar* who expounded the yoga system. Lakulīśa descended to restore the forgotten practices of Tantra and hatha yoga and to present the dual cosmology of *Sāṁkhya*.

सिंहं मृगाणां वृषभं गवां च मृगाधिपानां शरभं चकार ।
सेनाधिपानां गुहमप्रमेयं श्रुतिस्मृतीनां लकुलीशमीशम् ॥

siṁhaṁ mṛgāṇāṁ vṛṣabhaṁ gavāṁ ca
mṛgādhipānāṁ śarabhaṁ cakāra
senādhipānāṁ guham aprameyaṁ
śruti-smṛtīnāṁ lakulīśam īśam

He (Lord Brahmā) made the lion, the lord of animals; the bull, the lord of the cattle, and Śarabha (the fabulous eight-footed beast), the lord of lions; the incomprehensible Guha, the lord of all commanders and Lakulīśa, the lord of *śrutis* and *smṛtis.*

(*Liṅga Purāṇa*, 1.58.13)

आचन्द्रतारकं ज्ञानं ततो लब्ध्वा विमुच्यते ।
यः कुर्याद्देवदेवेशं सर्वज्ञं लकुलीश्वरम् ॥
वृतं शिष्यप्रशिष्यैश्च व्याख्यानोद्यतपाणिनम् ।
कृत्वा भक्त्या प्रतिष्ठाप्य शिवलोकं स गच्छति ॥
भुक्त्वा तु विपुलास्तत्र भोगान् युगशतं नरः ।
ज्ञानयोगं समासाद्य तत्रैव च विमुच्यते ॥
पूर्वदेवामराणां च यत्स्थानं सकलेप्सितम् ।
कृतमुद्रस्य देवस्य चिताभस्मानुलेपिनः ॥
त्रिपुण्ड्रधारिणस्तेषां शिरो मालाधरस्य च ।
ब्रह्मणः केशकेनैकम् उपवीतं च बिभ्रतः ॥
बिभ्रतो वामहस्तेन कपालं ब्रह्मणो वरम् ।
विष्णोः कलेवरं चैव बिभ्रतः परमेष्ठिनः ॥

ācandra-tārakaṁ jñānaṁ
tato labdhvā vimucyate
yaḥ kuryād deva-deveśaṁ
sarva-jñaṁ lakulīśvaram

vetan śisya-praśisyaiś ca
vyākhyānodyata pāṇinam
kṛtvā bhaktyā pratiṣṭhāpya
śiva-lokaṁ sa gacchati

bhuktvā tu vipulās tatra
bhogān yugaśataṁ naraḥ
jñāna-yogaṁ samāsādya
tatraiva ca vimucyate

pūrvad evāmarāṇāṁ ca
yat sthānaṁ sakalepsitam
kṛta mudrasya devasya
citā bhasmānulepinaḥ

tri-puṇḍra-dhāriṇas teṣāṁ
śiro mālā-dharasya ca
brahmaṇaḥ keśakenaikam
upavītaṁ ca bibhrataḥ

bibhrato vāma-hastena
kapālaṁ brahmaṇo varam
viṣṇoḥ kalevaraṁ caiva
bibhrataḥ parameṣṭhinaḥ

He who makes an idol of the omniscient lord of the chiefs of *Devas*, Lakulīśvara, who is surrounded by disciples, and their disciples, and who has lifted his hand in expounding the principles and then installs it with devotion, goes to the world of Śiva.

His abode is liked by all *devas* and *asuras*. By making an idol of the lord as follows and by installing it, one is liberated from the ocean of worldly existence. The lord makes gestures. He has the ashes from the funeral pyre for his unguent, he has the triple mark of Tripuṇḍra, he wears a garland made of skulls, and he wears a single sacred thread constituted by the hairs of Brahmā; with his left hand he holds the excellent skull of Brahmā; as Parameśvara he adopts the body of Viṣṇu.

(*Liṅga Purāṇa*, 1.76.38–43)

The *Mahābhārata* states that the son of Lord Brahmā himself descended to teach the *Pāśu-pata* system. There are inscriptions from the tenth and thirteenth centuries CE that mention the great master Lakulīn or Lakulīśa, considered by his followers to be an incarnation of Lord Śiva.

In the *Tantrāloka*, Abhinava-gupta states that Lakula is one of two authorities on the Śiva doctrine:

एतद्विपर्ययाद्ग्राह्यमवश्यं शिवशासनम् ।
द्वावाप्तौ तत्र च श्रीमच्छ्रीकण्ठलकुलेश्वरौ ॥

etad viparyayād grāhyam
avaśyaṁ śiva-śāsanam
dvāvāptau tatra ca śrīmac
chrīkaṇṭha-lakukeśvarau

> The two ultimate authorities of the *Śiva-śāsana* (the doctrine of Śiva) are called Śrīkaṇṭha and Lakuleśvara.
>
> (*Tantrāloka*, 37.14)

Some think that Lakulīśa joined the existing sect of *Pāśu-pata*; others think he founded it. He brought with him the revelation of Śiva, with his own teachings and reforms. He seems to have been the first to put the doctrine into writing in the *Pāśu-pata Sūtra*, which was lost for centuries and miraculously rediscovered in 1930 CE. This work illuminated some of the mysteries of this sect, from which Tantra would later develop.

Chronology and geographic location

The earliest evidence of the *Pāñcārthika* or *Pāśu-pata* tradition dates back to 380 CE. This is the date of the inscription on the pilaster of Mathura that mentions a lineage of several generations, suggesting that the tradition originated in roughly the second century CE. A Chinese traveler named Hiuen Tsiang toured the Indian subcontinent in the seventh century CE and wrote a travel journal that has been preserved to this day. According to his notes, he saw a myriad of *Pāśu-patas* in Varanasi.

During the eighth century CE, the *Pāśu-pata* tradition expanded to Nepal. The famous Paśu-pati-nātha temple was erected there and is still the main pilgrimage center. There are inscriptions about Lakulīśa in temples, mostly located in the western regions of India where the sect originated, but also as far as Orissa in the east, Kashmir in the north, and Tamil Nadu in the south. At its zenith in the middle ages, the sect expanded to western, northwestern, and southeastern India, where it received royal patronage. In the fifteenth century CE, its influence retracted to Gujarat, Nepal, and the Himalayas.

Main scriptures

The oldest mention of the *Pāśu-pata* sect appears in the *Mahābhārata*, which says that its doctrine was spread by Śrī-kaṇṭha, the master of Lakulīśa. Unfortunately, earlier *Pāśu-pata* literature has not survived. The main scripture seems to have been the *Pāśu-pata Sūtra*, which is attributed to the venerable Lakulīśa even though his name does not appear in the text or its commentaries. This scripture formalizes several previous canons and explains the doctrine's basic theology. Around the fourth century CE, Saint Kauṇḍinya wrote two commentaries on the *Pāśu-pata Sūtra*: the *Pañcārtha-bhāṣya* and the *Mṛgendra Āgama*. The *Pāśu-pata Sūtra* and *Pañcārtha-bhāṣya* were rediscovered in 1930 CE. Other important scriptures include the *Gaṇakārikā* and its commentary *Rāśikara-bhāṣya*.

Initiation

Pāñcārthika or *pāñcārthika-dīkṣā* was a ritual that gave access to religious practices and esoteric revelations. Initiates accepted a vow called *pāśu-pata-vrata*, or "the *Pāśu-pata* vow," which required following the practices for life. Those who reached the *ācārya* level had to initiate and guide new *sādhakas* but could not accept priestly positions in temples. Like most later Tantric schools, *Pāśu-patas* believed that Rudra himself sowed in the aspirant's heart the desire to be initiated and to undertake the ascetic life of total surrender. It was the master's task to recognize a *sādhaka's* sincerity and the signs of divine intention, called *śakti-pāta*, or "the descent of divine energy." Unfortunately, the scarce literature that has survived does not offer detailed descriptions of the initiation ceremony.

व्यक्ताव्यक्तं जयच्छेदो निष्ठा चैवेह पञ्चमी ।
द्रव्यं कालः क्रिया मूर्त्तिः गुरुश्चैवेह पञ्चमः ॥

vyaktāvyaktaṁ jayac chedo
niṣṭhā caiveha pañcamī
dravyaṁ kālaḥ kriyā mūrttiḥ
guruś caiveha pañcamaḥ

The five requisites for initiation into the *Pāśu-pata* system are *dravya* (substance), *kāla* (time), *kriyā* (consecration of the image and of the disciple), *mūrti* (the place just south of Śiva's image), and a guru that leads one to spiritual success. (*Gaṇa Kārikā*, 5)

The *Rāśikara-bhāṣya* commentary on the *Gaṇa-kārikā* indicates that the practical details of the *pāñcārthika-dīkṣā* are mentioned in the *Saṁskāra Kārikā*, which is a lost text. The *Kauṇḍinya* commentary on *Pāśu-pata Sūtra* states that aspirants should fast for three days as part of a purification process. The sacred initiation ceremony was divided into three stages. First, aspirants had to stand in front of the right face of the deity of Lord Mahā-deva (*Daksiṇasyam mūrti*) and smear their bodies with ashes that had been charged with the five *Brahma-mantras*. Second, the marks of their natal socio-religious identity (*utpatti-liṅga*) were eliminated. Third, they were given the five *Brahma-mantras* of the sect (*mantra-śravaṇam*).

Each *Brahma-mantra* emanated from one of Śiva's five faces. These mantras are recited in both Vedic and Tantric traditions. The best known is Rudra's *gāyatrī-mantra*:

ॐ तत्पुरुषाय विद्महे महादेवाय धीमहि तन्नो रुद्रः प्रचोदयात् ॥

oṁ
tat puruṣāya vidmahe
mahā-devāya dhīmahi
tanno rudraḥ pracodayāt

Oṁ. Let us invoke the three spheres: earth (*bhūr*), wind (*bhuvaḥ*), and fire (*svāhā*). *Aum*. Let us invoke the superlative (*tad*), masculine (*puruṣa*), and omniscient Lord (*vidmahe*). Let us meditate and concentrate on (*pracodayāt*) the supreme (*mahā*) Lord (*devāya*). Let us ask Śiva (Rudra) to give us inspiration and guidance (*pracodayāt*) on our spiritual path.

Rituals and practices

The purpose of *Pāñcārthika* rituals was to obtain merit. Unlike in Vedic rituals, adepts danced and sang in front of the deity of Lord Śiva or the *Śiva-liṅga*. Above all, Pashupatism was an ascetic path that rejected dialectical logic and viewed *sādhana* as a means to be worthy of Lord Śiva's mercy (*kāruṇya*). Spiritual practices were reserved exclusively for the initiated. They began with a strict code of restrictions (*yamas*) and observances (*niyamas*), which included celibacy (*brahmacarya*), nonviolence (*ahiṁsā*), and austerities or asceticism (*tapas*). Other practices were *pūjās*, penances, repetition of Śiva's names, smearing the body with sacred ashes, and expressing passionate love for Śiva. The scriptures clearly define five stages.

In the first stage, renounced monks resided in a temple of Śiva. They had to cover their bodies with ashes three times a day, worship the deity through dances and devotional songs, meditate on the five *Brahma-mantras* of the *Yajur Veda*, and repeat the mantra Om. Important components of the practice were laughing out loud, shaking the body, and meditating.

In the second stage, they had to leave the temple and live incognito in regular society. They performed scandalous acts to deliberately invite public censorship: they would babble, snort, walk like a cripple, talk nonsense, and make wild or provocative gestures. In this way, they purified themselves of the need to be accepted by the public and in their own subconscious, established that only Lord Śiva's love is sufficient. Since the aspiration was to free adepts from mental conditioning, these attitudes assured social rejection. These *Brāhmaṇas*, so respected in their secular lives, were freed from the ties to human society that were instilled in them since birth.

Pāśu-patas knew that someone who was firm in virtue and capable of accepting every insult with equanimity was well-established along the path of asceticism. They provoked the contempt of passers-by, believing that by being despised, they would receive the good merit of their detractors and, in turn, transmit their own bad karma to them. This was a sophisticated system of karmic purification.

In the third stage, *Pāśu-patas* retreated to a remote cave in a solitary place to meditate and repeat the *Brahma-mantras* and thus achieve perpetual closeness to Śiva.

In the fourth stage, having reached the uninterrupted consciousness of Rudra, they left their hermitages and moved to cremation grounds. At this stage, they stopped begging for food and fed themselves only on what they could find there.

The fifth stage was to neglect the needs of the body until death. Upon leaving the body, by the divine grace of Rudra, *Pāśu-patas* directly experienced the infusion of Rudra's divine qualities.

Doctrine

Pāśu-patas were monotheists, and as such, they worshipped Lord Śiva as the only God. Their pantheon was exclusively masculine. The feminine aspect of divinity, revealed by later Tantric sects, was not part of the *Ati-mārga* tradition. Prior to Lakulīśa, *Pāśu-pata* philosophy was dualist. Although we do not have any texts older than the *Pāśu-pata Sūtra*, many scholars have concluded, based on previous commentators, that *Pāśu-patas* saw Śiva as the efficient but not the material cause of the universe. It was Lakulīśa who, by revealing Śiva as the material cause, transformed dualism into *bhedābheda*, or "dualism with non-dualism." As stated by the *Kauṇḍinya-bhāṣya* and mentioned by Śaṅkarācārya in his commentaries on the *Brahma Sūtra* (2.2.37), the *Pāśu-patas* recognized these five basic categories of existence: *kāraṇa* (the cause), *kārya* (effect), yoga (union as a state of consciousness), *vidhi* (prescriptions, norms, and ceremonies), and *duḥkhānta* (the end of suffering and pain, liberation).

एवमेते पञ्च पदार्थाः कार्यकारणयोगविधिदुःखान्ताः समासविस्तरविभाग-
विशेषोपसंहार निगमनतश्च व्याख्याताः ।

evam ete pañca padārthāḥ kārya-kāraṇa-yoga-vidhi-duḥkhāntāḥ samāsa-vistara-vibhāga-viśeṣopasaṁhāra nigamanataś ca vyākhyātāḥ.

Thus, these five categories are explained: *kārya*, *kāraṇa*, *yoga*, *vidhi*, and *duḥkhānta*, in summary and in detail, classified and specialized, with terminations and with conclusions.

(*Pañcārtha-bhāṣya* of Śrī Kauṇḍinya, 5.47)

I. *Kāraṇa*, or "cause": This refers to the primordial Īśvara, or Maheśvara, as the original cause of all causes and the original cause of all creation and annihilation. He is identified by the name Pati, which denotes his infinite knowledge and power.

अत्र भव इति विद्याकलापशूनाम् एव ग्रहणम् । तस्योत्पत्तिकर्ता भगवानित्यतो भवोद्भव इति । अत्रोत्पादकानुग्राहकतिरोभावकधर्मि कारणम्, उत्पाद्यानुग्राह्यतिरोभाव्यधर्मि कार्यमित्येतत् कार्यकारणयोर्लक्षणम् । एतस्मिन्कारणे प्रपत्त्यादि क्रमोपयोगि द्रष्टव्यम् ॥

atra bhava iti vidyā-kalā-paśūnām eva grahaṇam. tasyotpatti kartā bhagavān ity ato bhavodbhava iti. atrotpādakānugrāhaka-tirobhāvaka-dharmi kāraṇam, utpādyānugrāhya-tirobhāvya-dharmi kāryam ity etat kārya-kāraṇayor lakṣaṇam. etasmin kāraṇe prapatty ādi kramopayogi draṣṭavyam.

Here *bhava* means the created world: *vidyā*, *kalā*, and *paśu*. God is the source of *bhava* and is called *bhavodbhava*. Here the cause (*kāraṇa*) has the power of producing, preserving, and dissolving while the effect (*kārya*) has the quality of being produced, preserved, and dissolved. This is the distinction between *kāraṇa* and *kārya*. We should consider the gradual course of approaching this cause (with a spirit of self-surrender and so on).

(*Pañcārtha-bhāṣya* of Śrī Kauṇḍinya, 1.44)

क्रीडावानेव स भगवान्विद्याकलापशुसंज्ञकं त्रिविधमपि कार्यमुत्पादयन् अनुगृह्णाति तिरोभावयति चेत्यतो देवः ॥

krīḍāvān eva sa bhagavān vidyā-kalā-paśu-saṁjñakaṁ tri-vidham api kāryam utpādayan anugṛhṇāti tirobhāvayati cet yato devaḥ.

That Lord is a player. He produces, changes, and dissolves three types of *kāryas*: *vidyā*, *kalā*, and *paśu*, and hence he is called *Deva*.
(*Pañcārtha-bhāṣya* of Śrī Kauṇḍinya, 2.2)

II. *Kārya*, or "effect": This refers to everything that depends on the cause. It includes *vidyā* (knowledge, cognition, or animation), *kalā* (the known, inert, or inanimate: organs), and *paśu* (the knower, the living, or the animated: individual souls).

(1) Cognition (*vidyā*): Cognition is a property of the individual (*paśu*) and is of two types:

(1.1) Ignorance (*abodha*: lack of understanding).

(1.2) Knowledge (*bodha*: understanding). There are two types of *bodha*:

(1.2.1) *Viveka-pravṛtti* (with discernment): It takes place when the cognitive power (*citta*) receives knowledge from a valid source. In this way, a *paśu* (conscious being) through *citta* (cognitive power) and with the help of *caitanya* (consciousness) becomes aware (*cetayate*) of the surrounding environment.

(1.2.2) *Aviveka-pravṛtti* (without discernment): This is knowledge, but without the ability to reflect, understand, or be aware.

(2) *Kalā* (the inert): The organs themselves are inert and depend on the cognitive individual to function. There are two types:

(2.1) Effects: There are 10 types of *kalā* effects: *pañca-tan-mātras* (the five subtle elements) and *pañca-mahā-bhūtas* (the five great elements).

(2.2) Causes. There are thirteen *kalā* causes: *pañca-karmendriyas* (the five organs of action), *pañca-jñānendriyas* (the five cognitive organs), and three *antaḥ-karaṇas* (internal organs): *buddhi* (intelligence), *ahaṅkāra* (ego), and *manas* (mind), whose functions are determination of the will, consciousness of the self, and formation of a plan, respectively.

(3) *Paśu* (living being) is the one who has individualism (*paśutva*). There are two types:

(3.1) *Sañjana*: Embodied and has senses.

(3.2) *Nirañjana*: Has no body or senses.

III. Yoga, or "union": It is the union of the soul (*ātma*) with God (Īśvara).

योगी ॥

yogī

One who has united himself with Maheśvara.

(*Pāśu-pata Sūtra*, 5.2)

अत्र योगो नाम – आत्मेश्वरसंयोगो योगः प्रत्येतव्यः ।

atra yogo nāma – ātmeśvara-saṁyogo yogaḥ praty etavyaḥ.

Here, *yoga* means a stable union of the soul and God.

(*Pañcārtha-bhāṣya* of Śrī Kauṇḍinya on *Pāśu-pata Sūtra*, 5.2)

There are two types of yoga:

- *Kriyātmaka*: Active yoga, which refers to *sādhana*.
- *Kriyoparama*: Also known as *saṁvid-gati*; it refers to the cessation of all activity.

According to this system, yoga is the realization of *paramaiśvarya*, or "the supreme power," accompanied by *duḥkhānta*, or "cessation of pain and suffering."

IV. *Vidhi*, or "prescriptions": It refers to a function oriented to dharma and *artha* that is divided into vows (*vrata*) and means (*dvāras*).

यद्येवं विधिः कस्मात्? विधायकत्वाद्विधिः । उपायोपेयभावाच्च । विधिमिति कर्म ।

yady evaṁ vidhiḥ kasmāt? vidhāyakatvād vidhiḥ. upāyopeya-bhāvāc ca. vidhim iti karma.

If so, why is called *vidhi?* Because it joins and suggests the idea of a means and an end. *Vidhim* is used in the action sense.
(*Pañcārtha-bhāṣya* of Śrī Kauṇḍinya on *Pāśu-pata Sūtra,* 1.1)

Vows (*vrata*) include *Bhasma-snāna-śayyā* (bathing and lying in ashes) and *upahāra* (jubilation), which has six components:

1. *Hasita*, or "roaring with laughter."
2. *Gīta*, or "singing." This means glorifying Lord Śiva by singing hymns.
3. *Nṛtya*, or "dancing," following the guidance and indications of the *Nātya-śāstra*.
4. *Huḍūp-kāra*, or "twisting the tongue and emitting the *huḍūp* sound with a bull-like bellow."
5. *Japa*, or "repetition of mantras."
6. *Namaskāra*, or "offering respectful obeisance."

The means (*dvāras*) include:

7. *Krāthana*, or "pretending to be asleep."
8. *Spandana*, or "trembling of the extremities."
9. *Mandana*, or "limping."
10. *Śṛṅgāraṇa*, or "erotic movements."
11. *Avitat-kāraṇa*, or "carrying out an action criticized by society."
12. *Avitad-bhāsaṇa*, or "talking nonsense like an ignorant person."

V. *Duḥkhānta*, or "the end of suffering," that is, the final liberation, the destruction of misery, the elevation of spirit, and the attainment of full powers of knowledge (*dṛk-śakti*) and action (*kriyā-śakti*).

अप्रमादी गच्छेद्दुःखानामन्तमीशप्रसादात् ॥

apramādī gacched duḥkhānām antam īśa-prasādāt

He who is careful gets the end of sorrows by the grace of Īśa (Śiva).

(*Pāśu-pata Sūtra*, 5.40)

एवं कुर्वन्सर्वज्ञोऽस्यासंमोहं ज्ञापयति ।

evaṁ kurvan sarvajño 'syāsaṁmohaṁ jñāpayati

Thus doing, the person becomes omniscient and this reflects one's consciousness.

(*Pañcārtha-bhāṣya* of Śrī Kauṇḍinya on *Pāśu-pata Sūtra*, 5.40)

अत्र येषां साधिकारत्वादनतिप्रसन्नस्तेषामशिवत्वं दृष्ट्वा दुःखान्तं गतेषु च शिवत्वं दृष्ट्वा आह— शिवो मे अस्तु इति ।

atra yeṣāṁ sādhikāratvād anati-prasannas teṣām aśivatvaṁ dṛṣṭvā duḥkhāntaṁ gateṣu ca śivatvaṁ dṛṣṭvā āha— śivo me astu iti.

And those who have gone to the end of sorrows have attained the God (Śiva).

(*Pañcārtha-bhāṣya* of Śrī Kauṇḍinya on *Pāśu-pata Sūtra*, 5.45)

A *Pāśu-pata* is freed from all suffering, which the sacred scriptures divide into three types:

दुःखानाम् इत्यत्र प्रसिद्धानि दुःखान्याध्यात्मिकाधिभौतिकाधिदैविकानि ।

duḥkhānām ity atra prasiddhāni duḥkhāny ādhyātmikādhi-bhautikādhi-daivikāni.

The term *duḥkhānām* refers to the well-known sorrows: personal, natural, and supernatural.

(*Pañcārtha-bhāṣya* of Śrī Kauṇḍinya on *Pāśu-pata Sūtra*, 5.40)

1. *Adhyātmika* (human): This refers to physical discomforts and bodily diseases that arise from mental and psychological disorders caused by laziness, jealousy, envy, greed, anger, fury, hatred, and so on.
2. *Adhibhautika* (cosmic): This refers to afflictions that come from the *pañca-bhūtas*, or "the five basic elements of nature," and the interaction of the three *guṇas*, or "the three modes of material nature." It also includes discomforts and afflictions caused by other entities, such as envious people, microorganisms, reptiles, beasts, and humans.
3. *Adhidaivika* (divine): This is suffering caused by the "supernatural" (although in the end, everything is natural), as well as by the anger of gods (devas) or powerful superior beings, and by ignoring the principles of religion.

The soul not only stops suffering but also attains supreme lordship (*pāramaiśvarya*), which is composed of *dṛk-śakti* (also called *jñāna-śakti*, the power of consciousness or knowledge) and *kriyā-śakti* (the power of action).

अत्र प्रमादशब्दोऽनागतानवधानगतत्वं पारतन्त्रयं च ख्यापयतीत्यर्थः । तदङ्कुरप रिरक्षणवदनागतकालप्रतीकारकरणेन चैवायम् अप्रमादिशब्दो द्रष्टव्यः । तस्माद् युक्तेनैवाप्रमादिना स्थेयम् । तथा वर्तमानेन माहेश्वरमैश्वर्यं प्राप्तमेवेत्युक्तम् ।

atra pramāda-śabdo 'nāgatān avadhānagatatvaṁ pāratantrayaṁ ca khyāpayatīty arthaḥ. tad aṅkura-parirakṣaṇa-vadanāgata-kāla-pratīkāra-karaṇena caivāyam apramādi-śabdo draṣṭavyaḥ. tasmād yuktenaivāpramādinā stheyam. tathā vartamānena māheśvaram aiśvaryaṁ prāptam evety uktam.

Here the word *pramāda* indicates carelessness about future events and dependence on others (i.e., sense-objects).

Hence one should stand solely united and worry-free. And it is said that, by remaining so, one gets the excellence of Maheśvara.

(*Pañcārtha-bhāṣya* of Śrī Kauṇḍinya on *Pāśu-pata Sūtra*, 5.40)

सिद्धः, गच्छेद्दुःखानामन्तम् (अध्याय ५, सूत्र २०, ३९) इत्येवमाद्यो विभागः । ज्ञानशक्तिः क्रियाशक्तिश्च । तत्र ज्ञानशक्तिः मनोजवित्वाद्या ।

siddhaḥ, gacched duḥkhānām antam (adhyāya 5, sūtra 20, 39) ity evam ādyo vibhāgaḥ. jñāna-śaktiḥ kriyā-śaktiś ca. tatra jñāna-śaktiḥ mano-javitvād yā.

And the *sādhaka* goes beyond all sorrows (5.20,39), etc. This constitutes the following classification (of the process of yoga): the power of knowledge (*jñāna-śakti*) and the power of action (*kriyā-śakti*), The power of knowledge is hearing, etc. The power of action is becoming speedy like the mind, etc.

(*Pañcārtha-bhāṣya* of Śrī Kauṇḍinya on *Pāśu-pata Sūtra*, 5.47)

Dṛk-śakti has five components: 1) *Darśana*, or "the knowledge of everything susceptible to sight and to the subtle touch," that is to say, distant and close, 2) *Śravaṇa*, or "the knowledge of every *śabda* (sound)," 3) *Manana*, or "the knowledge of all thoughts," 4) *Vijñāna*, or "the knowledge of the meaning of literature (*śāstra*)," and 5) *Sarvajñatva*, or "the knowledge of all *tattvas* (categories of existence) in regard to everything mentioned or not mentioned, summarized or detailed."

Kriyā-śakti has three components: 1) *Mano-javita*, or "moving at the speed of the mind," 2) *Kāma-rūpitva*, or "the power to exercise control in any way," 3) *Vikaraṇa-dharmitva*, or "the power to do or know something without the help of the senses."

The end of pain can be *anātmaka* or *sātmaka*. *Anātmaka* is the complete cessation of all pain and suffering. *Sātmaka* is the realization of the power that resides in *dṛk-śakti*.

It is said that the Lord is *vāg-viśuddha*, that is, he has no relation to anything that can be expressed in words. The Lord transcends language. Language comes from the mind; when speaking, we are verbalizing ideas, concepts, and conclusions. The transcendental state is beyond the mind. Therefore, ascetics must see the Divine as amorphous and meditate on it as *niṣkala*, or "without form." By separating themselves from the worldly experiences of forms and names and fixing their attention on Śiva, they experience *niṣkriya*, or "the supreme spirit." They then transcend pain and suffering.

वाग्विशुद्धः ॥

vāg-viśuddhaḥ

Completely free of words.

(*Pāśu-pata Sūtra*, 5.27)

अत्रापि वाग्विशुद्ध इत्यपि भगवतो नामधेयम् । न अमी इत्यन्यो भगवान् । स यथा ह्यथो हित्वा वाणीं मनसा सह रूपरसगन्धविद्यापुरुषादिपरो निष्कलो ध्येयः ।
यस्मादुक्तम्—
"आकृतिमपि परिहृत्य ध्यानं नित्यं परे रुद्रे ।
येन प्राप्तं योगे मुहूर्तमपि तत्परो योगः ॥"
परमयोगः इत्यर्थः ।

atrāpi vāg-viśuddha ity api bhagavato nāmadheyam. na amī ity anyo bhagavān. sa yathā hy atho hitvā vāṇīṁ manasā saha rūpa-rasa-gandha-vidyā-puruṣādi-paro niṣkalo dhyeyaḥ.
yasmād uktam—
"ākṛtim api parihṛtya dhyānaṁ nityaṁ pare rudre
yena prāptaṁ yoge muhūrtam api tat paro yogaḥ".
parama-yogaḥ ity arthaḥ.

In this *sūtra*, *vāg-viśuddhaḥ* (completely free of words)is another name of the Lord. God is other than "those" (i.e., he does not have qualities and attributes). He should be meditated upon in his formless aspect (*niṣkala*), unassociated with anything that can be expressed by speech, beyond the range of mind, and not related to form, taste, smell, knowledge, *puruṣa*, and so on. Because it is said: "That is the highest yoga, by which union, one attains the [state of a] continuous meditation upon the Supreme Rudra, even for a moment, avoiding even a form." This means that this is the ultimate yoga.

(*Pañcārtha-bhāṣya* of Śrī Kauṇḍinya on *Pāśu-pata Sūtra*, 5.27)

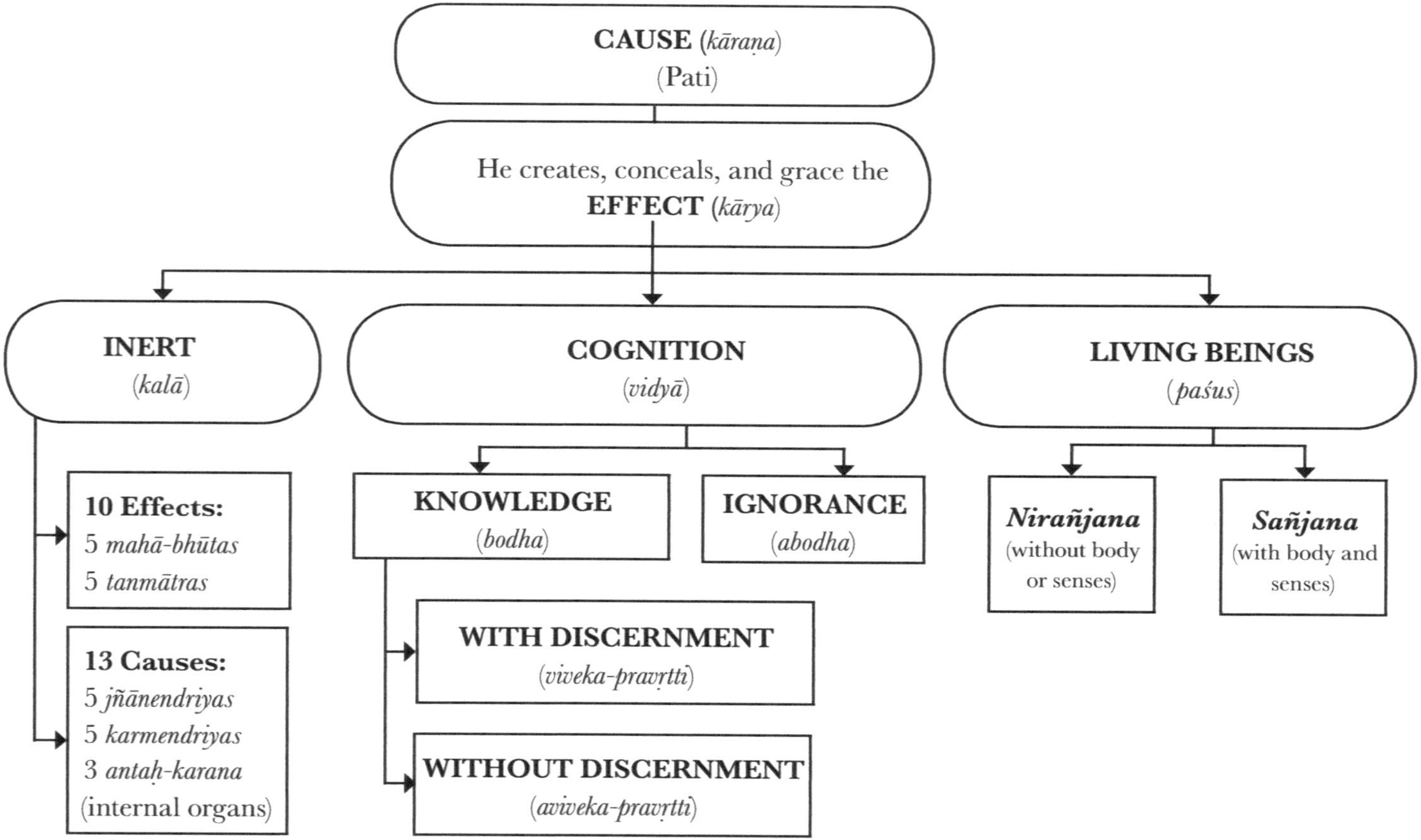
CAUSE (kāraṇa)
(Pati)
He creates, conceals, and grace the
EFFECT (kārya)
INERT
(kalā)
COGNITION
(vidyā)
LIVING BEINGS
(paśus)
10 Effects:
5 mahā-bhūtas
5 tanmātras
13 Causes:
5 jñānendriyas
5 karmendriyas
3 antaḥ-karana
(internal organs)
KNOWLEDGE
(bodha)
IGNORANCE
(abodha)
WITH DISCERNMENT
(viveka-pravṛtti)
WITHOUT DISCERNMENT
(aviveka-pravṛtti)
Nirañjana
(without body
or senses)
Sañjana
(with body and
senses)

Final goal

According to *Pāśu-pata*, when we open our eyes in this world, we see pain and suffering. The soul (*paśu*) cannot approach Śiva (*Pati*) because of its bonds (*pāśa*). This path invites us to learn about, understand, and become aware of these bonds in order to eventually transcend them. Its message is that God can change the destiny of human beings according to his own will, independent of an individual's karma. Even so, *Pāśu-patas* must work to awaken the grace of Śiva by following observances (*vrata*) and spiritual practice (*sādhana*).

अप्रमादी गच्छेद्दुःखानामन्तमीशप्रसादात् ॥

apramādī gacched duḥkhānām antam īśa-prasādāt

> By the grace of Īśa (Śiva or Paśu-pati) one who is not careless will attain the end of all suffering.
>
> (*Pāśu-pata Sūtra*, 5.40)

Pāśu-patas aspired to Rudra's divine omniscience and omnipotence that they would attain at the moment of death. In its liberated state (*sāyujya*), the soul approaches God but does not disappear completely. Liberation is not the fusion of God and the soul, but a state free of all suffering (*duḥkhānta*).

पाशुपताः सङ्क्रान्त्या साम्यमुपगच्छन्ति । तथा हि— कस्तूरिकाद्यामोदः पटादाविवेश्वरस्यं सार्वज्ञ्यादिकं मुक्तपुरुषे सङ्क्रामति । तस्माच्छिवगुण-सङ्क्रान्त्या साम्यमिति ॥

pāśupatāḥ saṅkrāntyā sāmyam upagacchanti. tathā hi– kastūrikādy āmodaḥ paṭādāviveśvarasyaṁ sārva-jñyādikaṁ mukta-puruṣe saṅkrāmati. tasmāc chiva-guṇa-saṅkrāntyā sāmyam iti.

> The *Pāśu-patas* accept *Śiva-sāmya* (as *mokṣa*) through a transfer of the qualities of Śiva, such as omniscience, to released souls, in the same way that the scent of *kastūrikā*, and so on, is

transferred to cloth. Through the transfer of Śiva's qualities, there is *Śiva-sāmya*.

(*Śaiva-paribhāṣā* of *Śivāgra-yogin*, 5.31)

In the *Āgama-prāmāṇya*, Yāmunācārya summarizes the entire *Pāśupata* philosophy in the following way:

तत्रैषा पाशुपतप्रक्रीया-
जीवाः पशव उच्यन्ते तेषामधिपतिश्शिवः ।
स तेषामुपकाराय पञ्चाध्यायीमचीक्लृपत् ॥
तत्र पञ्चपदार्थास्तु व्याख्याताः कारणादयः ।
कारणं कार्यं विधिर्योगो दुःखान्त इति ।
उपादानं निमित्तं च व्याख्यातं कारणं द्विधा ।
निमित्तकारणं रुद्रः, तत्कला कारणान्तरम् ॥
मह्यन्तं महदादि कार्यमुदितं, तद्वद्विधिर्गीयते गूढाचारमुख स्मशान भसित स्नानावसानः, परः।
'योगो' धारणमुच्यते हृदि धियाम् ओंकारपूर्वं, तथा
'दुःखान्तो' हि मतो ऽपवर्ग इति ते पञ्चापि संकीर्तिताः ॥
आत्यन्तिकी दुःखनिवृत्तिः 'दुःखान्त' शब्देनोक्ता । तामेव निश्शेषवैशेषिकात्मगुणोच्छेदलक्षणां मुक्तिं मन्यन्ते । इयमेव च ईश्वरकल्पना शैवानामन्येषां च ।

tatra īṣā pāśu-pata-prakrīyā-

jīvāḥ paśava ucyante teṣām adhipatiś śivaḥ
sa teṣām upakārāya pañcādhyāyīm acīklṛpat

tatra pañca-padārthās tu vyākhyātāḥ kāraṇādayaḥ
kāraṇaṁ kāryaṁ vidhir yogo duḥkhānta iti
upādānaṁ nimittaṁ ca vyākhyātaṁ kāraṇaṁ dvidhā
nimitta-kāraṇaṁ rudraḥ, tat-kalā kāraṇāntaram

mahy antaṁ mahad ādi kāryam uditaṁ, tad vat vidhir gīyate
gūḍhācāra-mukha smaśāna bhasita-snānāvasānaḥ, paraḥ.
'yogo' dhāraṇam ucyate hṛdi dhiyām oṁ-kāra-pūrvaṁ, tathā
'duḥkhānto' hi mato 'pavarga iti te pañcāpi saṁkīrtitāḥ.

ātyantikī duḥkha-nivṛttiḥ 'duḥkhānta' śabdenoktā. tām eva niśśeṣa-vaiśeṣikātma-guṇoccheda-lakśaṇāṁ muktiṁ manyante. iyam eva ca īśvara-kalpanā śaivānām anyeṣāṁ ca.

The *Pāśu-pata* system is as follows: there are individual souls called *paśus* (cattle) and their overlord Śiva (the Lord of cattle). To assist the souls, Śiva composed the *pañcādhyāyī*. It explains the five categories: cause, effect, prescriptions, yoga, and the cessation of misery. There are two kinds of cause, material and instrumental. Rudra is the instrumental cause and a sixteenth part of him is the material cause. The effect comprises all the elements from *mahat* (the great principle) to *pṛthivī* (earth). The prescription mostly includes a number of rites, secret practices, bathing, lying in ashes, and so on. Yoga is said to be concentration, chanting the mantra *Oṁ*, and so on. The cessation of misery is to be liberated. The five categories are thus numbered. The term 'cessation of misery' means total and final cessation of misery. The system says that this cessation or release is defined by the annihilation of all the qualities of the differential soul.

(*Āgama-prāmāṇya* of Yāmunācārya, 84, "*Siddhānte matāntara-parīkṣā*," "*pāśupata-mata-paripādanam*")

2. *Lākula, Kālā-mukha* or *Mahā-vratins*

While the *Pāśu-pata* sect continued to grow in popularity, spread throughout India, receive support from secular *Śaivas*, and initiate more and more *Brāhmaṇas*, something happened that would help Tantra blossom further. A group of initiates, later called *Lākulas* or *Kālā-mukhas*, took the ascetic practices to a more demanding level. They accepted the doctrines of the *Pāśu-pata Sūtra* but were more extreme in rejecting Vedic prescriptions. As they wandered through cremation grounds and places of pilgrimage, the public watched them with disgust. These brave spirits turned their backs on social acceptance and moved toward transcendence. Within this temporal and ephemeral diversity, they aspired only for the One without a second, Śiva.

The *Purāṇas* narrate how Lord Brahmā felt attracted to his own daughter. As punishment, Śiva, in his aspect of Bhairava, cut off Brahmā's fifth head with his thumbnail and the skull stuck to his hand. The only possible atonement for a *brahma-hatya* (killing of *brāhmaṇas*) was to take the *mahā-vrata* vow, or "the great penance," that consists of begging naked, carrying the skull of the victim.

ब्रह्मोवाच-
तदा निरपराधस्य शिरश्छिन्नं त्वया मम ॥
तस्माच्छापसमायुक्तः कपाली त्वं भविष्यसि ।
ब्रह्महन्याकुलो भूत्पारचरतीर्थानि भूतले ॥

brahmovāca-
tadā niraparādhasya śiraś chinnaṁ tvayā mama

tasmāc chāpa-samāyuktaḥ kapālī tvaṁ bhaviṣyasi
brahma-hanyākulo bhūt pāracara-tīrthāni bhūtale

Then Brahmā said: "You have beheaded me without any fault, and through my curse you shall bear a skull as the badge of the sin of inflicting injury on a *Brahmaṇa* and you will roam about in the sacred places."

(*Matsya Purāṇa*, 183.85–86)

Bhairava descended to Earth and after much wandering, managed to atone for his crime when he arrived in Varanasi. The place where Śiva was liberated from the sin of killing a *Brāhmaṇa* was called *kapāla-mocana-tīrtha* (liberated from the skull).

The *mahā-vrata* is detailed in law books, or *Dharma-śāstras*: the sentence for a person who has unintentionally killed a *Brāhmaṇa* priest is to live outside Vedic society for twelve years. To atone for the crime, the murderer must carry the skull of the victim mounted on a stick (*khaṭvāṅga*), beg with a bowl made out of a skull, wear a garland of human bones, cover the body with the ashes of the dead, and have matted hair or a shaved head.

वने पर्णकुटीं कृत्वा वसेत् । त्रिषवणं स्नायात् । स्वकर्म चाचक्षाणो ग्रामे ग्रामे भैक्षमाचरेत् । तृणशायी च स्यात् । एतन्महाव्रतम् । ब्राह्मणं हत्वा द्वादश-संवत्सरं कुर्यात् ।

...

सर्वेषु शवशिरो ध्वजी स्यात् ।

vane parṇa-kuṭīṁ kṛtvā vaset. triśa-vaṇaṁ snāyāt. sva-karma cācakṣāno grāme grāme bhaikṣam-ācaret. tṛṇa-śāyī ca syāt. etan mahā-vratam. brāhmaṇam hatvā dvādaśa-saṁvatsaraṁ kuryāt.

...

sarveṣu śava-śiro dhvajī syāt.

Let a man make a hut of leaves in a forest and dwell in it, let him bathe (and perform his prayers) three times a day, let him collect alms, going from one village to another and proclaim his own deeds, and let him sleep on the grass. This is called *mahā-vrata* (great observance). He who has unintentionally killed a *Brāhmaṇa* must perform this for twelve years. He who performs any of these penances must carry the skull of the murdered person like a flag on his stick.

(*Viṣṇu-smṛti*, 50,1–6 and 15)

The *Lākulas* took Bhairava's punishment upon themselves and adopted *mahā-vrata*, paying for a sin that they had not committed, only to be in tune with Lord Śiva. These *sādhus*, innocent of all crime, voluntarily adopted this vow in their search for transcendence. As *Brāhmaṇas*, they chose to descend from the highest social position to the most deplorable in an act of intense spiritual passion. They undertook a "direct path" (*Ati-mārga*) toward inner purity.

Following the fate of Bhairava, *Lākulas* ended their pilgrimage in Varanasi and thus atoned for their sins. They did not long for anything in the world other than liberation. Instead of defending their reputation, they sought to cleanse themselves of accumulated karma and transcend suffering. They believed that if twelve years of *mahā-vrata* cleansed the karma for killing a *Brāhmaṇa*, the purifying effect of this *vrata* should be immeasurable.

On the relative plane, everything is temporary. Our visit to the world is short and painful. Instead of ignoring this harsh reality by looking for security and success, the *Lākulas* chose to confront it by being present in every moment and turning their backs on the supposed happiness the world offers. Instead of the ashes of cow dung, they chose the ashes of incinerated corpses; instead of a cotton thread, they made thread from the hair of corpses. Their home was the cremation grounds, where everyone arrives sooner or later. They have accepted the reality from which everyone tries to escape by chasing fleeting pleasures. These spiritual giants chose to live with the truth constantly in front of their eyes.

Lākulas founded temples and monasteries in modern Karnataka and other places on the Indian subcontinent. Like *Pāśu-patas*, they were victims of condemnation, discredit, and insults. Their teachings and practices drew many detractors.

Unfortunately, their writings have disappeared, so we know their philosophy only indirectly. If these spiritual revolutionaries gained some esteem from a few open-minded groups, it was because of their courage, sincerity, and a spiritual path without concessions. This appreciation is reflected in an inscription carved in one of their temples, dated to 1162 CE:

> This is a place dedicated to the observances of the saints of Śiva who perpetually led the lives of celibate religious *brahmacārīs*, a place for the silent study of the four Vedas, ... *yoga-śāstras*, and other types of learning; a place where food is always given to the poor, to the defenseless ... to musicians and troubadours whose duty is to awaken their masters with music and songs ... and to mendicant monks and all beggars, ... a place where many sick and homeless people are sheltered and treated, a safe place for all living beings.

Members

The great majority of this sect's members were *Brāhmaṇas* who chose to live as murderers of *Brāhmaṇas*. These elevated spiritual seekers led the life of criminals, confident that anyone degraded in the apparent world is elevated in the real world. Through this penance, *Lākulas*, innocent of all crime, achieved a great elevation and liberation from mental conditioning. Saints and sages remained united in harmony with their Lord Śiva by accompanying him in his penance.

Name of the sect

This sect has different names. One of the most popular ones is *Lākula*, derived from Sad-guru Lakulīśa. They are also called *Kālā-mukhas*, or "black faces," because they painted a black mark on their foreheads as a sign of renunciation. Other scholars maintain that the *Kālā-mukhas* were a subdivision within the *Lākula* sect. The *Kālā-mukhas* are known for the large number of inscriptions in southern India that date between the ninth and the thirteenth centuries CE.

Chronology and geographic location

Lākulas can be considered religious reformers who were able to establish a strong social structure. Their sect developed on the great Deccan Plateau of southern India in the first few centuries CE and reached its peak between 600 and 1000 CE. Its first monasteries were established in Mysore. There were subdivisions within the *Lākula* sect, such as *Śakti-pariṣad* and *Siṁha-pariṣad*. The *sādhus* who followed *Śakti-pariṣad* wandered around a wider area, and those who followed *Siṁha-pariṣad* were mainly in the districts of Dharwar and Shimoga. Scholars think that the later *Vīra-śaiva* school evolved from this sect and eventually replaced the *Lākulas* in the thirteenth century CE, apparently using their temples and ashrams.

Main scriptures

Lākula religious literature has not survived, so the details of its practices and philosophy are unclear. The scarce information we have is from mentions in other texts and inscriptions in the sect's ancient temples. It is known that *Lākulas* accepted the authority of the *Pāśu-pata Sūtra* revealed by Śiva and added it to their own scriptures, *Pramāṇas*, although we have only its title and a brief quotation. *Lākulas* followed the *Pāśu-pata* path, sacred literature, mantras, and practices, but added a more austere *sādhana*. *Lākula* teachings served as a bridge and transition between the *Pāśu-patas* and Agamic Shaivism.

Initiation

The *Lākula* initiation was the essential requirement to be accepted into the *mahā-vrata* practice. The officiant begans the initiation (*dīkṣā*) by installing the five *Brahma-mantras* in the body of the aspirant. Then, the vows (*vratas*) were recited and the knowledge of the eleven-level cosmic hierarchy (*prakriyā*) was revealed. During the involutive process, the ascetic ascended the ladder of the worlds of Rudras until attaining liberation (*bhuvanādhvā*). Then the officiant meditated on this hierarchy and initiated the candidate through "the descent of the word *atha*" (*atha-śabda-nipātah*). Through its descent, the initiate was liberated (*vimucyate*). *Pāśu-pata* initiation was essentially a rite of passage that authorized the practice of the vows, but for the *Lākulas*, as well as for the later Agamic Shaivism, the rite conferred liberation (*ātma-samskāraḥ*). It was consummated at the moment of death, as long as the initiate completed the process of asceticism and gnosis of the cosmic hierarchy. Visualizing the ascension by the ladder of principles (*tattvas*) or worlds, the *Lākula* crossed the barrier (*granthi*) and accessed the spiritual world.

Rituals and Practices

Lākulas did not include *hautrī-dīkṣā* in their rituals, which is an initiation performed by placing offerings in a consecrated fire. The Agamic systems initiated married people and instructed them to satisfy their deities with mantras and offerings placed in the fire. But *Lākulas* were ascetics who lived outside of society, and their rituals did not include fire.

This was the first sect to practice *mahā-vrata*, or "the observance of the great vow," also called *kapāla-vrata* (the observance of the skull), *lokātita-vrata* (the observance that transcends the world), and *mahā-pāśu-pata-vrata* (the great observance of the *Pāśu-pata*). The *Yoga Sūtra* of Patañjali prescribes five abstentions (*yamas*): ahimsa (nonviolence), *satya* (truthfulness), *asteya* (nonstealing), *brahmacarya* (celibacy, restraint of the senses), and *aparigraha* (detachment). Together, they are called *mahā-vrata*, or "great penance." Since we know that the *Pāśu-patas* practiced the *yamas*, some scholars argue that the *Lākulas' mahā-vrata* was the same as the *yamas* and not the penance described in the *Dharma-śāstras*.

The *Niśvāsa-mukha-tattva-saṁhitā*, which is an introductory part of the earliest surviving *Śaiva Tantra* called *Niśvāsa-tattva-saṁhitā*, describes the *sādhana* of the *Lākulas* as follows:

अत्याश्रमव्रतं ख्यातं लोकातीतञ्च मे शृणु ॥
आलब्धः पञ्चभिर्गुह्यैर्दीक्षितश्चैव सो भ्रमेत् ।
खट्वाङ्गी च कपाली च स जटी मुण्डमेव वा ॥
बालयज्ञोपवीती च शिरोमुण्डैश्च मण्डितः ।
कौपीनवासो भस्माङ्गी दिव्याभरण भूषितः ॥
जगद्रुद्रमयम्मत्वा रुद्रभक्ति दृढव्रतः ।
सर्वादस्सर्वचेष्टश्च रुद्रध्यानपरायणः ॥
रुद्रं मुक्त्वा न चान्यो ऽस्ति त्राता मे देवतम्परम् ।
विदित्वैकादशाध्वानं निर्विशङ्कः समाचरेत् ॥

atyāśrama-vrataṁ khyātaṁ
lokātītañ ca me śṛṇu

ālabdhaḥ pañcabhir guhyair
ddīkṣitaś caiva so bhramet
khaṭvāṅgī ca kapālī ca
sa jaṭī muṇḍam eva vā

bāla-yajñopavītī ca
śiro muṇḍaiś ca maṇḍitaḥ
kaupīna-vāso bhasmāṅgī
divyābharaṇa bhūṣitaḥ

jagad-rudra-mayam matvā
rudra-bhakti dṛḍha-vrataḥ
sarvādas sarva-ceṣṭaś ca
rudra-dhyāna-parāyaṇaḥ

rudraṁ muktvā na cānyo 'sti
trātā me devatam param
viditvaikādaśādhvānaṁ
nirviśaṅkaḥ samācaret

Hear now the *Lokātīta*. Touched with the five *Brahma-mantras*, the initiated should wander, carrying a skull staff (*khaṭvāṅga*) and [an alms-bowl fashioned from] a human skull (*kapālam*). He should have matted locks (*sajaṭaḥ*) or shave his head (*muṇḍaḥ*). He should wear a sacred thread (*yajñopavītam*) made from the hair [of the dead], and he should adorn himself with a chaplet fashioned from human skull bones. He may wear nothing but a strip of cloth to cover his private parts. He must smear himself with ashes and decorate himself with celestial ornaments. Seeing all things as Rudra in essence, he should hold firmly to his observance as Rudra's devotee. He may eat and drink anything. No action is forbidden to him. He should remain immersed in contemplation of Rudra, thinking 'None but Rudra can save me. He is the supreme deity.' Provided that he has first understood the [*Lākula*] cosmic hierarchy of eleven [levels], he should practice this observance, remaining free of all inhibition (*nirviśaṅkaḥ*).

(*Niśvāsa-mukha-tattva-saṁhitā,* 4.88b–92)

Lākulas were adorned with human bones: a necklace, earrings, wristbands or bracelets, and a jewel in the hair (*śikhā-maṇi*). The four bone ornaments and the sacred thread were called the *pañca-mudrā* (the five emblems). Ashes were added as a sixth element.

These ascetics distanced themselves still further from the conventional Vedic notions of ritual purity. They intensified their level of impurity but without discarding celibacy, as later *Kāpālikas* did. Part of their *sādhana* consisted of bathing in the ashes of cremated corpses, swallowing those ashes, and consuming alcoholic beverages as a worship of Rudra. Although their practices were opposed to orthodoxy, they considered themselves to be an integral part of the Vedic tradition.

The vows (*vratas*) of the *Lākulas* were closely related to the five-step *sādhana* of the *Pāśu-patas* described in the *Pāśu-pata-śāstra*. *Lākula* practice excluded the third of these five steps:

1. The manifested stage (*vyakta*): Sedentary practice.
2. The unmanifested stage (*avyakta*): Wandering in society provoking contempt (*dveṣa-utpādaya*).
3. The stage of victory (*jaya*): Retreating to a cave or deserted house. This was not part of *Lākula* practice.
4. The cutting stage (*cheda*): Moving to cremation grounds.
5. The completion stage (*niṣṭhā*): Abandoning the body through yogic suicide.

The *Ati-mārga* sects had a monotheistic devotion to Lord Śiva. Some of them believed that there were many divine manifestations—inferior incarnations of Śiva called Rudras—who dominated different dimensions of reality. Meditation on this cosmology and its hierarchical levels of existence was a central *Lākula sādhana*. When leaving the body, the knowledge of each plane would be useful in accessing the dimension of Śiva's reality. Later Agamic Shaivism elaborated on this: while the ascent through the Rudra worlds (*bhuvanādhvā*) was preserved in the *Śaiva* Agamic texts, it applied only to initiation rituals. In practice, yogic ascents were experienced directly and not in the context of rituals. In addition, the *Rudravratas* moved away from the hierarchy of Rudras as lords of worlds (*bhuvaneśa*) to the hierarchy of principles or levels of reality (*tattvas*). Visualizations were either totally impersonal or of deities other than Rudras, both male and female.

Teachings

Lākulas worshipped Lord Śiva in his ferocious Bhairava aspect. To a large extent, they followed *Sāṁkhya* philosophy and denied the independence of the soul. They believed that agency belonged exclusively to *prakṛti*. *Paśus*, or individual beings, included not only the uninitiated but also the initiated while still in the body and even the various Rudra souls who govern the levels of the cosmic hierarchy (*prakriyādhvā*).

The cosmic hierarchy is divided into two parts: a lower and impure universe (*aśuddho-mārga*) and a higher and pure universe (*śuddho-mārga*). A great barrier called *granthi* separates these two. Only initiation and the subsequent cultivation of gnosis and observance allowed *Lākulas* to transcend and reach the pure universes.

Final goal

Liberation grants the soul divine omniscience (*jñāna-śakti*) but not omnipotence (*kriyā-śakti*), since all souls are bound or dominated (*paśavaḥ*). If liberated beings were omnipotent like God, they could disagree with him about the order of creation and as a result, there would be no creation. In all *Śaiva* systems, liberated souls adopt the qualities of God, but according to the *Lākulas*, liberated souls only acquire omniscience and only Śiva is omnipotent.

God is beyond the universe and encompasses everything with his omniscience. He is the only one who has the ability to activate his creation in order to allow the souls under his control to incarnate themselves, act, and be affected by their actions. Before liberation, humans are inactive but conscious, since consciousness is an innate quality. In the state of liberation, all the factors that limit consciousness disappear and the soul becomes omniscient yet remains inactive.

शिवसांयामपि न मोक्षः । तच्च साम्यां उत्पत्तिसङ्क्रान्ति-समावेशाभिव्यक्तिभिश्चतुर्धा सम्भवति । तत्र महाव्रतिनः उत्पत्त्या साम्यमुपगच्छन्ति । तथा हि— मुक्तौ ताविच्छवसाम्यमस्ति । तच्च सर्वज्ञत्वादिरूपम् । तच्च तदैवोत्पद्यते । अन्यथा पूर्वमपि तत्प्रसङ्गात् । तस्माच्छिवगुणसदृशगुणोत्पत्त्यैव शिवसाम्यमिति ॥

śiva-sāṁyām api na mokṣaḥ. tac ca sāmyāṁ utpatti-saṅkrānti-samāveśābhivyaktibhiś caturdhā sambhavati. tatra mahā-vratinaḥ utpattyā sāmyam upagacchanti. tathā hi— muktau tāvac chiva-sāmyam asti. tac ca sarva-jñatvādi-rūpam. tac ca tadaivotpadyate. anyathā pūrvam api tat prasaṅgāt. tasmāc chiva-guṇa-sadṛśa-guṇotpatyaiva śiva-sāmyam iti.

> The sameness with Śiva (*Śiva-sāṁya*) is also not liberation (*mokṣa*). This sameness occurs in four ways: through origination, transfer, possession, or emergence. Of these [four ways], the *mahā-vratins* hold that sameness with Śiva (*Śiva-sāṁya*) occurs through origination. It is as follows: in liberation, there is sameness in the form of Śiva's qualities (omniscience, omnipotence, and omnipresence), which originates only then. Otherwise, there would be the contingence of its occurrence even earlier. Therefore, sameness with Śiva occurs only through the origination of qualities similar to Śiva's.
>
> (The *Śaiva-paribhāśa* of Śivāgrayogin, 5.32)

3. *Kāpālika* or *Soma-siddhānta*

Kāpālikas, or "skull-bearers," were the ascetic pilgrims of the third sect within the *Ati-mārga*. They were the link between pre-Tantric Shaivism and the emerging Tantric revelation. This sect pioneered antinomian practices and doctrines that would flourish in later Tantric sects. These passionate souls went even further in their efforts to free themselves from social conditioning. While *Pāśu-patas* and *Lākulas* were strict celibates, *Kāpālikas* wanted to completely overcome the dualities of pure–impure and holy–profane, so they incorporated practices that included sexual rituals and the consumption of forbidden substances such as meat and wine.

Covered with the ashes of the dead, decorated with human bones, and carrying a skull staff (*khaṭvāṅga*), these ascetics roamed the cremation grounds. Conscious of temporal reality, they dedicated their lives to overcoming the fear of death. They had a disgusting appearance but the innocent eyes of those who had accepted the vow of truthfulness for life. With the purest aspirations, they assumed the appearance that contaminated others, even those who just looked at them. They lived in the forests and only entered villages to beg for food with skull bowls.

This sect's texts have not been preserved. We know a bit about them only from contemporary theater plays that describe *Kapālika* protagonists. For example, from the satiric play *Matta-vilāsa Prahasana* of the King of Pallava named Mahendra Varman we know that *Kāpālikas* gave away their possessions (*saṁvibhāga*) and only kept a loincloth (*kaupīna*) and some sacred objects (*bhairavas*) such as a human skull (*kapāla*) to eat and drink, earrings, a snake skin as a Brahman thread, a *ḍamaru* drum, a *mṛdaṅga*, and a larger drum called a *kāhala*. The play is mocking the *Kāpālika* putting on his lips such words:

> कपाली— प्रिये! पश्य पश्य । एष सुरापणो यज्ञवाट विभूतिमनुकरोति । अत्रहि ध्वजस्तम्भो यूपः, सुरा सोमः, शौण्ड ऋत्विजः, चपकाश्चमसाः शूल्यमांसप्रभृय उपदंशा हविर्विशेषाः मत्तवचनानि यजूंषि, गीतानि सामानि, उदङ्काः स्रुवाः, तर्पोऽग्निः, सुरापणाधिपतिर्यजमानः ।
>
> *kapālī— priye! paśya paśya. eṣa surāpaṇo yajña-vāṭa vibhūtim anukaroti. atra hi dhvaja-stambho yūpaḥ, surā somaḥ, śauṇḍa ṛtvijaḥ' capakāś camasāḥ śūlya-māṁsa-prabhṛya upadaṁśā havir viśeṣāḥ matta-vacanāni yajūṁṣi, gītāni sāmāni, udaṅkāḥ sruvāḥ, tarpo 'gniḥ, surāpaṇādhipatir yajamānaḥ.*
>
> *Kāpālika* (to his woman): Look, look my dear, this liquor shop emulates the grace of a sacrificial ground. Here the signpost forms the sacrificial post. Liquor is the *Soma* juice, drunkards the priests, cups the bowls, condiments like roasted meats the oblations, talks of the intoxicated the *Yajur* mantras, their songs the *Soma* hymns, leathern bags the sacrificial ladles thirst the fire, and the keeper of the shop the patron of the sacrifice.
>
> (*Matta-vilāsa Prahasana*)

Although these were serious seekers of transcendence, the public saw them as simple hedonists dedicated to pleasing the senses. The *sādhus* knew that the best way to overcome pride was to choose the highest and most direct path to God while being accused of giving into the enjoyment of the world. The truth is that the public was not aware of the soteriological reasons for their practices. The sexual ritual was a recreation of the intimate relationship between Śiva and his wife, the goddess Pārvatī or Umā. The happiness of this union is compared to the bliss of liberation, or *mokṣa*. Tantric adepts would recreate this divine blessing in their own acts of ritual sex. The later scripture *Kulārṇava Tantra* reveals some of these secrets:

सुरा शक्तिः शिवो मांसं तद्भोक्ता भैरवः स्वयम् ।
तयोरैक्यसमुत्पन्न आनन्दो मोक्ष उच्यते ॥
आनन्दं ब्रह्मणो रूपं तच्च देहे व्यवस्थितम् ।
तस्याभिव्यञ्जकं मद्यं योगिभिस्तेन पीयते ॥

surā śaktiḥ śivo māṁsaṁ
tad bhoktā bhairavaḥ svayam
tayor aikya-samutpanna
ānando mokṣa ucyate

ānandaṁ brahmaṇo rūpaṁ
tac ca dehe vyavasthitam
tasyābhivyañjakaṁ madyaṁ
yogibhis tena pīyate

Wine (*surā*) is Śakti, flesh (*māṁsa*) is Śiva. The enjoyer of both is Bhairava himself. The pleasure arising from their union [Śiva and Śakti's] is called *mokṣa*. This pleasure, which is the form (*rūpa*) of Brahman, resides in the body [of the worshipper]. Wine makes it manifest. This is why yogis drink wine.

(*Kulārṇava Tantra*, 5.79–80)

Ārya Kṣemīśvara, the author of the Sanskrit play called *Caṇḍa-kauśika*, describes the wisdom and the true aspirations of these ascetics.

Act 4 of his drama takes place in a cremation ground, when Dharma, the god of righteousness, appears disguised as a *Kāpālika*, in front of King Hariścandra. When the King sees the ascetic, he describes him in the following way:

खट्वाङ्गधृग्भस्मकृताङ्गरागो नरास्थिभूषोज्ज्वलरम्यकान्तिः ।
कपालपाणिर्नृकरङ्कमौलिराभाति साक्षादिव भूतनाथः ॥

khaṭvāṅga-dhṛg-bhasma-kṛtāṅga-rāgo
narāsthi-bhūṣojjvala-ramya-kāntiḥ
kapāla-pāṇir nṛkaraṅka-maulir
ābhāti sākṣād iva bhūta-nāthaḥ

Holding a staff with a skull at the top, anointed with ashes, possessed of charming loveliness made bright by the adornment of human bones, and bearing a skull in the hand and a human skeleton on the head, he appears as if he is Śiva himself in person.

(*Caṇḍa-kauśika*, act 4, verse 25)

The *Kāpālika* then speaks:

अयाचितोपस्थित भैक्ष्य वृत्तिर्निवृत्त-पञ्चेन्द्रियनिस्तरङ्गः ।
व्यतीत्य संसारमहाश्मशानं चरामि बिभत्समिदं श्मशानम् ॥
(विचिन्त्य)। स्थाने स खलु रुद्रो भगवान् महाव्रतं चचार । परः किलायं प्रकर्षः
कामचारिणाम् ।
किन्तु भैक्ष्याद्वैतं तपौद्वैतं क्रियाद्वैतं च तत्परम् ।
सुलभं सर्वमेवैतदात्माद्वैतं तु दुर्लभम् ॥

ayācitopasthita bhaiksya vṛttir
nivṛtta-pañcendriya nistaraṅguḥ
vyatītya saṁsāra-mahā-śmaśānaṁ
carāmi bibhatsam idaṁ śmaśānam

(vicintya). sthāne sa khalu rudro bhagavān mahā-vrataṁ cacāra. paraḥ kilāyaṁ prakarṣaḥ kāma-cāriṇām.

kintu bhaiksyādvaitaṁ tapaudvaitaṁ kriyādvaitaṁ ca tatparam
sulabhaṁ sarvam evaitad ātmādvaitaṁ tu durlabham

Living on such alms which given without asking for them and calmed by the restraint of the five senses, passing beyond the great cremation ground of transmigratory existence (*saṁsāra*) now I roam this disgusting cremation ground.

> [Reflecting]. It is quite suitable that divine Rudra performed the great vow (*mahā-vrata*). Supreme indeed is this excellence of [those who] roam at will. But, being exclusively devoted to alms alone, penance alone, and rites alone, all these are easily obtainable. But the realization of the Self is a state that is difficult to obtain.
>
> (*Caṇḍa-kauśika*, act 4, 26–27)

Similar to *Caṇḍa-kausika*, the drama *Mālatī-mādhava*, by the famous writer Bhavabhūti, gives a central role to the *Kāpālikas*. The fifth scene of this play also occurs in a crematorium, where the *Kāpālika* woman named Kapāla-kuṇḍalā and her master Aghora-ghaṇṭa are performing *pūjā*.

Kapāla-kuṇḍalā enters the scene. After offering glories to Lord Śiva, Śakti-nātha, she describes herself:

नित्यं न्यस्तषडङ्गचक्रनिहितं हृत्पद्ममध्योदितं
पश्यन्ती शिवरूपिणं लयवशादात्मानमभ्यागता ।
नाडीनामुदयक्रमेण जगतः पञ्चामृताकर्षणा-
दप्राप्तोत्पतनश्रमा विघटयन्त्यग्रे नभोम्भोमुचः ॥
अपि च ।
उल्लोलस्खलितकपालकण्ठमाला-
सङ्घट्टक्वणितकरालकिङ्कणीकः ।
पर्यस्तं मयि रमणीयडामरत्वं
संधत्ते गगनतलप्रयाणवेगः ॥
तथा हि ।
विष्वग्वृत्तिर्जटानां प्रचलति निबिडग्रन्थिनद्धोपि भारः
संस्कारक्वणदीर्घं पटु रटति कृतावृत्तिखट्वाङ्गघण्टा ।
उर्ध्वं धूनेति वायुर्विवृतशवशिरः श्रेणिकुञ्जेषु गुञ्ज-
न्नुत्तालः किङ्किणीनामनवरतरणत्कारहेतुः पताकाम् ॥

nityaṁ nyasta-ṣaḍaṅga-cakra-nihitaṁ hṛt-padma-madyoditaṁ
paśyantī śiva-rūpiṇaṁ laya-vaśād ātmānam abhyāgatā
nāḍīnām udaya-krameṇa jagataḥ pañcāmṛtākarṣaṇād
aprāptotpatana-śramā vighaṭayanty agre nabhombho-mucaḥ

api ca-
ullola skhalita kapāla-kaṇṭha-mālā
saṅghaṭṭa kvaṇita karāla-kiṅkaṇīkaḥ
paryaptaṁ mayi ramaṇīyaḍamaratvaṁ
saṁdhatte gagana-tala-prayāṇa-vegaḥ

tathā hi-
viṣvag-vṛttir-jaṭānāṁ pracalati nibiḍa-granthinaddhopi bhāraḥ
saṁskāra-kvāṇa-dīrghaṁ paṭu raṭati kṛtā-vṛtti khaṭvāṅga-ghaṇṭā
urdhvaṁ dhūneti vāyur vivṛta-śava-śiraḥ śreṇi-kuñjeṣu guñjan
nuttālaḥ kiṅkiṇī-nāma-navarata-raṇat-kāra-hetuḥ patākām

> Freed from all perishable bonds, I view the eternal soul embodied as the God, forced by my spells to tread the mystic labyrinth, and rise in splendor throned upon my heart. Hence through the many channeled veins I draw, the grosser elements of this mortal body, and soar unwearied through the air, dividing the water-shedding clouds. Horrendous honors await me on my flight. The hollow skulls that hung from my neck emit fierce music as they clash together or strike the trembling plates that gird my loins. My long, braided locks flow loose at my sides.; upon my ponderous staff, the string of bells, light waving to and from, jangles incessantly; my banner floats upborne upon the wailing breeze, whose tone is deepened by the echoes it awakes amidst the caverns of each fleshless skull, that hangs in dread array around me.
>
> (*Mālatī-mādhava*, act 5)

One of the most informative plays, in terms of details about the *Kāpālikas*, is the Vedantic allegoric drama *Prabodha-candrodaya* by Kṛṣṇa Miśra.

In this allegorical plot, a *Kāpalika* named Soma-siddhānta plays an important role. Although, like the *Matta-vilāsa*, this play presents an ascetic somewhat comically, there are still many details and descriptions that can help us understand the *Kāpālikas* and their spiritual approach.

For example, in act 3, Soma-siddhānta enters, praising his own virtues in the following way:

नरास्थिमालाकृतचारुभूषणः
श्मशानवासी नृकपालभोजनः ।
पश्यामि योगाञ्जनशुद्धचक्षुषा
जगन्मिथो भिन्नमभिन्नमीश्वरात् ॥

narāsthi-mālā-kṛta-cāru-bhūṣaṇaḥ
śmśāna-vāsī nṛ-kapāla-bhojanaḥ
paśyāmi yogāñjana-śuddha-cakṣuṣā
jagan-mitho bhinnam-abhinnam īśvarāt

My beautiful ornaments are made from garlands of human bones. I live in the cremation ground and eat my food from a human skull. With eyes that are purified by the ointment of yoga, I view the world as simultaneously separate and not separate from God (Īśvara).

(*Prabodha-candrodaya*, act 3, verse 12)

The Jain monk, who is present in the scene along with a Buddhist monk, is approaching the *Kāpālika*:

क एष कापालिकं व्रतं पुरुषो धारयति? तदेनमपि पृच्छामि । अरेरे कापालिक, नरास्थिमण्डमालाधारक, कीदृशस्तव धर्मः कीदृशस्तव मोक्षः?

ka eṣa kāpālikaṁ vrataṁ puruṣo dhārayati? tad enam api pṛcchāmi arere kāpālika, narāsthi-maṇḍa-mala-dhāraka, kīdṛśas tava dharmaḥ kīdṛśas tava mokṣaḥ?

Who is this man following the *Kāpālikā* way of life? I shall also ask him,
"O *Kāpālika*, wearing the garland of human bones and skulls! What kind of religion is yours and what is the nature of your liberation?"

(*Prabodha-candrodaya*, act 3, verse 13)

Finally, the Jain monk asks the *Kāpālika* again what the nature of happiness and liberation is, according to his religion.

The *Kāpālika* replies:

श्रृणु—
दृष्टं क्वापि सुखं विना न विषयैरानन्दबोधोज्झिता
जीवस्य शितिरेव मुक्तिरुपलावस्था कथं प्रार्थ्यते ।
पार्वत्याः प्रतिरूपया दयितया सानन्दमालिङ्गितो
मुक्तः क्रीडति चन्द्रचूडवपुरित्यूचे मृडानिपतिः ॥

śṛṇu-
dṛṣṭaṁ kvāpi sukhaṁ vinā na viṣayair ānanda-bodhojjhitā
jīvasya śitir eva muktir upalāvasthā kathaṁ prārthyate
pārvatyāḥ pratirūpayā dayitayā sānandam āliṅgito
muktaḥ krīḍati candra-cūḍa-vapur ity ūce mṛḍāni-patiḥ

Listen! Happiness cannot be seen anywhere without objects of pleasure. If liberation is a state of the self without the experience of pleasure, how can a state equal to that of a stone be desired? Mṛḍānīpati (Śiva) has said that the liberated one having a body [equal to that of Śiva whose body is decorated] with the crest-ornament of the moon, enjoys the pleasant embrace of his beloved who is an image of Pārvatī.
(*Prabodha-candrodaya*, act 3, verse 16)

Members

The *Pāśu-pata* and *Lākula* sects only accepted men and preferably *Brāhmaṇas*. However, *Kāpālikas* showed the first sparks of freedom from class and gender, which would develop later in the Tantric sects. Both men and women could be initiated and there were no distinctions based on caste or social order. As we just mentioned above, we find descriptions of a *Kapālika* woman called Deva-somā in the work *Matta-vilāsa*, written by the Pallava king Mahendra Varman at the beginning of the seventh century CE in Tamil Nadu.

In this work, the *Kāpālika* Satya-soma is accompanied by the lovely Deva-somā, his sexual partner who attracts the lustful glances of the other protagonists, such as a Buddhist monk and an ascetic *Pāśupata*. Satya-soma and Deva-somā enjoy meat, which they receive as alms in the skull bowls, and drink liquor from the same vessel.

Name of the sect

The term *kapāla* means "skull," and *kāpālika* means "man of the skull." The sect is also known as *Soma-siddhānta*, which means "doctrine of nectar." *Soma-siddhānta* seems to be the *Kāpālika* metaphysical system mentioned in different texts and inscriptions, although explanations of its principles have not survived. In the *Jayad-ratha Yāmala* (3.35.33), we see the combination *soma-jana-kāpāli*, or "*Kāpālika* of the town of Soma." They were also called *Mahā-vratīs* because they took *mahā-vrata* vows (great penance).

Chronology and geographic location

This tradition seems to have originated in southern India in the first centuries CE. The astronomer and mathematician Varāha-mihira, who lived in Ujjain in approximately 500–575 CE, repeatedly refers to *Kāpālikas*. Hence they must have been well-established in the sixth century CE. Many later Sanskrit texts also refer to them.

A mention in the *Maitrī Upanishad*, probably composed in late first millennium BCE, could suggest that *Kāpālikas* can be traced back to the Upanishadic period:

> कषायकुण्डलिनः कापालिनः... परिस्थातुमिच्छन्ति ।
>
> *kaṣāya-kuṇḍalinaḥ kāpālinaḥ... paristhātum icchanti.*
>
> And moreover, there are others who desire to appear with the red robe, earrings, and skulls.
>
> (*Maitrī Upanishad*, 7.8)

Main scriptures

More than a doctrine, the *Kāpālika* sect was a monastic order. As no text has survived, its doctrines and foundations are reconstructed from indirect references. However, we have to read these documents with care because the order was criticized and ridiculed. There are also inscriptions that record donations to or from *Kāpālikas*.

Initiation

Like all esoteric *Śaiva* sects, initiation was required to access the teachings and vows such as *mahā-vrata*. We have no details of the initiation ritual (*dīkṣā*), but it is speculated that, like in prior and later Tantric sects, *Kāpālikas* believed that initiation conferred liberation, which was consummated upon leaving the physical body.

Rituals and Practices

Like *Lākulas*, *Kāpālikas* took the *mahā-vrata* vow. Rāmānujācārya describes the *Kāpālika* worship in his commentary on the *Brahma Sūtra* (*Śrī-bhāṣya*):

यथाहुः कापालाः ।
मुद्रिकाषट्कतत्वज्ञाः परमुद्राविशारदः ।
भगासनस्थमात्मनं ध्यात्वा निर्वाणमुच्छति ॥
कण्टिका रुचकं चैव कुण्डलं च शिखामणिः ।
भस्म यज्ञोपवीतं च मुद्राषटकं प्रचक्षते ॥
आभिर्मुद्रितदेहस्तु न भूयः इह जायते ।

yathāhuḥ kāpālāḥ-
mudrikā-ṣaṭka-tatva-jñāḥ
para-mudrā-viśāradaḥ
bhagāsana-stham ātmanaṁ
dhyātvā nirvāṇam ucchati

kaṇṭikā rucakaṁ caiva
kuṇḍalaṁ ca śikhā-maṇiḥ
bhasma yajñopavītaṁ ca
mudrā-ṣaṭakaṁ pracakṣate

ābhir mudrita-dehas tu
na bhūyaḥ iha jāyate

> The *Kāpālikas* declare: 'One who knows the essence of the six *mudrās* (*mudrikā-ṣaṭka*), who is proficient in the highest *mudrā* (*paramudrā-viśarada*), and who meditates on the Self as seated in the female vulva (*bhagāsana-stha*) attains *nirvāṇa*.' They define the six *mudrās* as the *kaṇṭhikā* (necklace), the *rucaka* (a neck ornament), the *kuṇḍala* (earing), the *śikhāmaṇi* (crest-jewel), ashes, and the sacred thread. A person bearing these *mudrās* is not born again in this world.
> (*Brahma Sūtra Śrī-bhāṣya* by Rāmānujācārya, 2.2.35)

Yāmunācārya indicates that they also carried two secondary emblems (*upa-mudrās*): a skull (*kapāla*) and a mace (*khaṭvāṅga*).

They did not follow food restrictions, since they consumed meat and even leftovers from strangers. From the Brahmanical point of view, they were considered impure to such an extent that a *Brāhmaṇa* who was touched by a *Kāpālika* had to take a ritual purification bath.

They worshipped Bhairava, who demanded both propitiation and imitation from his devotees. Propitiation was performed through animal and probably human sacrifices. Imitation was performed through the ritual recreation of Bhairava's mythological feats. *Mahā-vrata* was both propitiation and imitation that recreated the penance of Śiva. In communion rituals, the devotee joined divinity through food, drink, sex, or mental ecstasy. To access these rituals, the devotees had to be purified by propitiatory acts.

This sect began the practice of the five M's (*pañca-ma-kāra*), which later became popular among the left-hand Tantric traditions. This ritual included five elements that were prohibited by the Vedas and whose names began with the letter m: *madya* (liquor), *māṁsa* (meat), *matsya* (fish), *mudrā* (dry grain), and *maithuna* (sexual relations). The female sexual partner is usually described as a woman of a low caste who is not the male adept's wife. However, such behavior took place in the context of a controlled ritual, not as a simple hedonistic enjoyment. In the play *Vidyā-pariṇayana* of Ānanda-rāya Makhī, a

Soma-siddhānta Kāpālika explains that the use of wine and meat is recommended by his own scriptures:

> वयं यथा भैरवागमानुरोधेन वेदप्रामाण्यवादिनो वेदविरुद्धमधुमांसादि-निषेवणाभिर्वेदबाह्यतया पाषण्डेषु गण्यामहे तद्वदिमेऽपि पाञ्चरात्रागमानुरोधेन वेदप्रामाण्यवादिनो वेदविरुद्धैराचारैः पाषण्डा एव ।
>
> *vayaṁ yathā bhairavāgamānurodhena veda-prāmāṇya-vādino veda-viruddha-madhu-māṁsādi niṣevaṇābhir veda-bāhyatayā pāṣaṇḍeṣu gaṇyāmahe tad vad ime 'pi pāñcarātrāgamānurodhena veda-prāmāṇya-vādino veda-viruddhair ācāraiḥ pāṣaṇḍā eva.*
>
> We are considered heretics because we deviate from the Veda with addiction to wine (*madhu*), meat (*māṁsa*), and so on, which are forbidden by the Vedas. But in fact, we respect the authoritative doctrine of the Vedas as long as it is in accordance with the *Bhairava Āgamas*.
>
> (*Vidyā-pariṇayana*, act 4, 33)

The *Kāpālika* Unmana-bhairava, who debated with Śaṅkarācārya, proudly declared that his father and grandfather were liquor-distillers and followed a completely hedonistic code of conduct. In the work *Matta-vilāsa*, the *Kāpālika* also defends wine and women as the path to salvation recommended by Śiva. In the work *Prabodha-candrodaya*, a *Kāpālika* describes wine as the remedy prescribed by Bhairava against (transmigratory) existence.

> कापालिकः : (पीत्वा शेषं भिक्षुक्षपणकयोरर्पयति ।)
> इदं पवित्रममृतं पीयतां भवभेषजम् ।
> पशुपाशसमुच्छेदकारणं भैरवोदितम् ॥
>
> *kāpālikaḥ: (pītvā śeṣaṁ bhikṣu-kṣapaṇakayor arpayati.)*
> *idaṁ pavitram amṛtaṁ*
> *pīyatāṁ bhava-bheṣajam*
> *paśu-pāśa-samuccheda*
> *kāraṇaṁ bhairavoditam*

> *Kāpālika* (drinks the wine and then offers the remaining to the mendicant and Jaina monk):
>
> Drink this pure nectar which is the medicine for worldly existence; Bhairava has said that this is the instrument to remove the bondage of the soul.
>
> (*Prabodha-candrodaya*, act 3, 20)

The Tantric ritual of sexual communion was central to *Kāpālikas*. The participants mentally identified themselves with Śiva and Śakti. In the ecstasy of sexual union, the couple experienced the divine bliss of the union between Śiva and Śakti. In this context, final liberation (*mukti*) meant not only the end of the cycle of births and deaths, but the experience of a perpetual orgasm.

Teachings

Kāpālika faith was based on devotion (bhakti) to a personal god, generally Bhairava, Śiva in his terrifying aspect. Ānanda-giri's biography of Śaṅkarācārya describes an encounter with *Kāpālikas*. Śaṅkarācārya asks them what their observances (*ācāra*) and precepts (*vidhi*) are and they respond:

> स्वामिन्!
> अस्मदाचारः सर्वप्राणिसन्तोषकरः कर्महीनः, कर्मणा न मुक्तिरिति वचनात् ।
> मदुपास्यो भैरव एक एव जगत्कर्ता । ततः प्रलयो भवतीति यो व प्रलयकर्त्ता । स एव स्थित्युत्पत्त्योरपीति ।
> उपसंहारबले नैव नीयतां स उपक्रम इति शास्त्रवृत्तिः उपसंहारबलान्निश्चारित उपक्रामोऽपि चेति शास्त्रवृत्तेः तदंशा एव सर्वे देवाः तत्तदधिकारसम्पन्नाः श्रीमद्भैरवाज्ञां शिरसा धृत्वा तदुक्ति प्रत्यासन्न शक्तयः तत्तत्कार्य्यपराः बभूवुः ।
>
> *svāmin!*
> *asmad ācāraḥ sarva-prāṇi-santoṣa-karaḥ karma-hīnaḥ, karmaṇā na muktir iti vacanāt.*
> *mad upāsyo bhairava eka eva jagat-kartā. tataḥ pralayo bhavatīti yo va pralaya-karttā. sa eva sthity utpattyor apīti.*
> *upasaṁhāra-bale naiva nīyatāṁ sa upakrama iti śāstra-vṛttiḥ*

upasaṁhāra-balān niścārita upakrāmo 'pi ceti śāstra-vṛtteḥ tad aṁśā eva sarve devāḥ tat tad adhikāra-sampannāḥ śrīmad-bhairavājñāṁ śirasā dhṛtvā tad ukti pratyāsanna śaktayaḥ tat tat kāryyaparāḥ babhūvuḥ.

O Swami! our observance, which is free from karma, causes satisfaction to all beings since it is said, 'There is no salvation with (or by means of) karma.' I must worship Bhairava alone, the creator of the world, who then becomes the (cause of) destruction. He who is the cause of destruction is also the cause of preservation and creation. All the gods, each endowed with a particular authority, are merely parts of him. They carry the command of Bhairava on their heads, and their powers, which obey his word, perform a particular duty.
(*Ānanda-giri-viracita Śaṅkara-vijaya*, chapter 23)

Rāmānujācārya and other commentators on the Brahma Sūtra believe that the expression "creator of the world" (*jāgat-kartṛ*) suggests that *Kāpālikas* distinguished between the material and the efficient cause of the universe. In the same biography, Bodholbaṇa Nityānanda and his *Kāpālika* followers further elaborate on their doctrine:

एकोऽपि भैरवो ह्यष्टमूर्त्तिधरः असिताङ्गो रुरुश्चण्डः क्रोधश्चोन्मत्तभैरवः। कापाली भीषणश्चैव संहारश्चाष्ट भैरवाः ॥ इति वचनात् ॥ आसिताङ्गो विष्णुरूपः । रुरुर्ब्रह्मरूपः । चण्डः सूर्यः । क्रोधो रुद्रः । उन्मत्तः इन्द्रः । कापाली चन्द्रः । भीषणोयमः । संहारः स्वयं । एतद् ह्यतिरिक्त देवाः तत्तदंशाः सृष्टिकर्तारः सर्वेऽपि रुद्रांशाः । स्थितिकर्तारः सर्वेऽपि असिताङ्गांशाः । संहारकर्त्तारः सर्वेऽपि क्रोधांशा इति । एवं जगत्सृष्ट्यादिकं कृत्वा प्रलयानन्तरं निज सप्तमूर्त्ति सङ्कोचं कृत्वा एकः शाश्वतः संहारभैरवः परमात्मा वर्त्तते ।

eko 'pi bhairavo hy aṣṭa-mūrtti-dharaḥ asitāṅgo ruruś caṇḍaḥ krodhaś conmatta-bhairavaḥ. kāpālī bhīṣaṇaś caiva saṁhāraś cāṣṭa bhairavāḥ. iti vacanāt. āsitāṅgo viṣṇu-rūpaḥ rurur brahma-rūpaḥ caṇḍaḥ sūryaḥ krodho rudraḥ. unmattaḥ indraḥ kāpālī candraḥ bhīṣaṇo yamaḥ saṁhāraḥ svayaṁ. etad hy atirikta devāḥ tat tad aṁśāḥ sṛṣṭi-kartāraḥ sarve'pi rudrāṁśāḥ. sthiti-kartāraḥ sarve 'pi asitāṅgāṁśāḥ. saṁhāra-karttāraḥ sarve 'pi krodhāṁśā iti. evaṁ jagat-sṛṣṭy ādikaṁ kṛtvā pralayānantaraṁ nija sapta-mūrtti saṅkocaṁ kṛtvā ekaḥ śāśvataḥ saṁhāra-bhairavaḥ paramātmā varttate.

Bhairava has eight major forms: Asitāṅga, Ruru, Caṇḍa, Krodha, Unmatta, Kāpālin, Bhīṣaṇa, and Saṁhāra. The first seven of these belong to the gods Viṣṇu, Brahmā, Sūrya, Rudra, Indra, Candra, and Yama, respectively. The eighth, Saṁhāra-bhairava, is Bhairava himself. The remaining gods are merely his portions and are distinguished as creation-makers (*sṛṣti-kartṛs*), preservation-makers (*sthiti-kartṛs*), and destruction-makers (*saṁhāra-kartṛs*). Taken together, creation-makers are his Rudra portions (Ruru-Brahmā), preservation-makers his Asitāṅga portions (Viṣṇu), and destruction-makers are his Krodha portions (Rudra). *Kāpālikas* conclude: "Thus having caused the creation of the world and so on, and then the dissolution, he contracts seven of his forms, and only the eternal Saṁhāra-bhairava remains, who is the *paramātma*."

(*Ānanda-giri-viracita Śaṅkara-vijaya*, chapter 23)

Final goal

Liberation was achieved when the aspirant was possessed by his beloved deity. The purpose of *Kāpālika* rituals was mystical communion between the worshipper and the worshipped god. Through the *mahā-vrata* vow, ascetics ritually equated with Śiva and obtained some of his divine attributes, especially the eight magical powers (*siddhis*).

कापालिकाः समावेशेन साम्यमुपगच्छन्ति । तथा हि— यथा ग्रहाः पुरुषेष्वाविशन्ति तथेश्वरगुणा मुक्तेष्वाविशन्ति । तस्माच्छिवगुणसमावेशेन साम्यमिति ॥

kāpālikāḥ samāveśena sāmyam upagacchanti. tathā hi—yathā grahāḥ puruṣeṣvāviśanti tatheśvara-guṇā mukteṣvāviśanti. tasmāc chiva-guṇa-samāveśena sāmyam iti.

> The *Kāpālikās* accept *Śiva-sāṁya* (sameness with Śiva) [as *mokṣa*] through possession. It is as follows: as planets possess a person, in the same way, the qualities of God possess liberated souls. Therefore, by the possession of Śiva's qualities, *Śiva-sāṁya* occurs.
>
> (The *Śaiva-paribhāṣa* of Śivāgrayogin, 5.32)

On the mundane plane, devotees gained superhuman magical powers. On the transcendental plane they attained final liberation from transmigratory existence (*mukti*) and lived in a heaven of perpetual sexual happiness. They obtained these blessings through communion rituals or as a gift from the deity for penances and sacrifices.

In chapter 15 of Dhana-pati-sūri's *Ḍiṇḍima* commentary on *Śaṁkara-vijaya* of Mādhava Vidyāraṇya, the *Kāpālika* Unmatta-bhairava explains:

> आनन्दो यो व्यक्तिमायाति सङ्गात्तद्रूपो ऽसौ भैरवो देहपाते ॥ तस्य प्राप्तिर्मोक्ष इत्येव तत्त्वमित्युक्तः ॥
>
> *ānando yo vyaktim āyāti saṅgāt tad rūpo 'sau bhairavo deha-pāte tasya prāptir mokṣa ity eva tattvam ity uktaḥ.*
>
> The bliss that becomes manifest through sexual union is the (true) form of Bhairava. The attainment of (bliss) at death is *mokṣa*. This is the ultimate Truth.
>
> (*Dhana-pati-sūri*, *Ḍiṇḍima* commentary, 15.28, verse 22)

Name	*Pāñcārthika Pāśu-pata*	*Lākulas* or *Kālā-mukhas*	*Kāpālikas* or *Soma-siddhāntas*
Name Translation	They worshipped the Paśupati aspect of Śiva, or "the Lord of the animals."	"Black faces" because they had black marks on their foreheads. The term lākula means "mace" and comes from the name of Satguru Lakulīśa.	The term *kapāla* means "skull," and the word *kāpālika* means "man of the skull."
Description	The oldest Śaiva sect. Renounced ascetic monks devoted to Śiva.	A group of ascetics within the *Pāśu-pata* sect who took the ascetic practices to a more demanding level.	*Kāpālikas* wanted to completely overcome the duality of pure–impure, and incorporated practices that included sexual ritualism and the consumption of forbidden substances such as meat and wine.
Members	They only accepted male *Brāhmaṇas* willing to give up their status for an ascetic life.	*Brāhmaṇas*, ascetic *Pāśu-patas*.	Men and women of all castes.
Masters	Lakulīśa	Lakulīśa	Unknown
Time	Around the second century CE	The first few centuries CE	The first few centuries CE
Location	It originated in western India and expanded to Orissa in the east, Kashmir in the north, and Tamil Nadu in the south.	The sect developed on the great Deccan Plateau of southern India.	It originated in southern India.

Name	*Pāñcārthika Pāśu-pata*	*Lākulas* or *Kālā-mukhas*	*Kāpālikas* or *Soma-siddhāntas*
Goal	Liberation from all suffering (*duḥkhānta*).	Divine omniscience (*jñāna-śakti*) but not omnipotence (*kriyā-śakti*). To reach the pure universes.	To reach final liberation from transmigratory existence (*mukti*) and live in a heaven of perpetual sexual happiness.
Deities	Monotheist. They worshipped Lord Śiva as the only and all-powerful god without a female consort.	*Lākulas* worshipped Lord Śiva in his extreme form of Bhairava, the fierce one.	Devotion (bhakti) and a personal god, usually Bhairava, Śiva's terrifying aspect.
Reality	At first dualism (*dvaita*) and later dualism with non-dualism (*bhedābheda*).	Dualism	Dualism
Scriptures	*Pāśu-pata Sūtra* and its commentary called *Pañcartha-bhāṣya.*	*Pāśu-pata Sūtra* revealed by Śiva, to which they added their own scripture, *Pramāṇas* (authorities).	Their writings have not survived.
Initiation	Initiation rituals gave access to esoteric revelations.	Initiation conferred liberation (*ātma-saṁskāra*), which was consummated at the moment of death, provided the process was completed with asceticism and gnosis of the cosmic hierarchy.	Initiation was a requirement to access the teachings and the vows. We do not know the details of the rituals.

Name	*Pāñcārthika Pāśu-pata*	*Lākulas* or *Kālā-mukhas*	*Kāpālikas* or *Soma-siddhāntas*
Rituals	They did not include fire but danced and sang in front of the deity of Śiva or the *Śiva-liṅga*.	*Lākulas* were ascetics who lived outside of society, and their rituals did not include fire.	Rituals of propitiation, imitation, and union.
Practice	*Yama* (restrictions) and *niyama* (observances), which included *brahmacarya* (celibacy), strict *ahiṁsā* (nonviolence), and *tapas* (austerities or asceticism). Other practices included *pūjā*, penance, repetition of the names of Śiva, anointing with holy ashes, and expressing passionate love for Śiva.	Celibacy. Asceticism. Mahā-vrata, or "the great observance." Extremely austere *sādhana*. Meditation on the cosmic hierarchy.	Asceticism but without celibacy. *Mahā-vrata* vow. The ritual included five elements that are prohibited by the Vedas and whose names begin with the letter m: *madya* (liquor), *māṁsa* (meat), *matsya* (fish), *mudrā* (dry grain), and *maithuna* (sexual relations).
Philosophy	The five categories this system discusses are *kāraṇa* (the cause), *kārya* (effect), yoga (union as a state of consciousness), *vidhi* (prescriptions, norms, and ceremonies), and *duḥkhānta* (the end of suffering and pain, liberation).	This sect adopted the conceptions of the *Sāṁkhya* philosophy. They maintained that souls never act independently. They believed that agency belonged exclusively to *prakṛti*.	Rāmānujācārya suggests that *Kāpālikas* distinguished between the material and efficient cause of the universe.

Chapter 3

The *Mantra-mārga* or "the path of mantras"

Two movements: devotional and Tantric

Ancient Vedic Hinduism was in the hands of the orthodox priestly class. *Brāhmaṇas* had the responsibility of memorizing the Vedic revelation and transmitting it from master to disciple. They had to learn to perform the complex ritual practices explained in the Vedas. These rituals included offerings to the gods in a sacrificial fire (*homa*) and ranged from simple offerings of vegetarian food in small fires in private houses (*gṛhya*) to great solemn public rituals with animal sacrifices (*śrauta*).

During the first millennium CE, new revelations took place within the Vedic tradition that led to remarkable transformations. Two important movements developed: devotional and Tantric. The former was characterized by devotion and the latter by yogic and meditative practices.

The devotional movement performed offering rituals to a single supreme God. Tantric practice, on the other hand, suggested visualizing oneself as a deity and placed more emphasis on the internal process of ritual.

These movements readapted many previous Vedic practices. For example, the Vedic ritual of royal consecration, *rājyasūya*, was transformed into the Tantric rite of *abhiṣeka* initiation. The Vedic *śrauta* sacrificial system began to lose popularity beginning in the fifth century CE as seekers of Truth became more drawn to new ritual systems.

Modern Hinduism is a fusion of Tantric and devotional attitudes that developed during the first millennium CE.

The emergence of the Tantric revelation

Tantra is not a philosophy invented by an imperfect human mind. It is a divine revelation whose origins cannot be located in space and time. The Tantric revelation was transmitted to receptive sages throughout the history of mankind. These masters, in turn, transmitted it orally to their disciples through *paramparās*, or "lines of disciplic succession." When we discuss the historical beginnings of the Tantric phenomenon, we are actually talking about when it was put into writing and organized sects began to follow its doctrines.

Due to the scarcity of historical evidence, the origin of the Tantric tradition is an enigma. Some scholars say that its beginnings are irrevocably shrouded by the mists of time. Others believe that Tantra derives from tribal or Shamanic practices outside of Indian Brahmanism. There have even been attempts to trace it to the age of ancient Hindu sages or the Indus valley civilization. The sparse available evidence suggests that the earliest distinctive Tantric traditions emerged from unorthodox Hindu *Śaivas* around the fifth century CE during the Gupta dynasty (320–550 CE).

The only written information we have is a few manuscripts and inscriptions on temple walls. The oldest known Tantric text is the *Niśvāsa-tattva Saṁhitā* from approximately 450–550 CE. Its name means "the collection of principles exhaled by God." This voluminous text, composed somewhere in northern India, is so extensive and detailed in its cosmology that it was probably based on an earlier oral tradition.

Tantra became popular at a particularly turbulent time in Indian history when the great Gupta Empire had collapsed and numerous small kingdoms were fighting among themselves. The uncertainty was so great that nobody had a secure home or income. In those times, people longed to find ways to strengthen themselves. Tantra filled this need by offering new and more effective methods for transforming one's mind, body, and surroundings. Although Tantra promised worldly benefits to some, what it ultimately offered was the possibility of stabilizing one's inner state, regardless of external circumstances, and ultimately, of achieving liberation.

Furthermore, the predominant orthodox Brahmanical system that followed the strict rules, laws, and regulations of the *Smṛtis*, failed to include the working class. For a family man who worked most of the day to support his wife and children it was practically impossible to devote the same time and energy to his spiritual life as a *Brāhmaṇa* could. Tantra gained popularity because it was a path that was taught by people of one's own social class, suggested simple and less formal worship to deities, offered the guidance of a guru, had a respectful and liberal attitude toward women, and was unconcerned with the *varṇāśrama* caste system. The liberal spirit of the Tantric revelation disregarded patriarchy, etiquette, and the formalities of spiritual matters.

Tantric liberalism helped popularize Tantra among the lower castes from which great masters flourished, such as the five *ādi-siddhas*, as the *Nātha* tradition calls them. For example, both Macchanda-nātha and Gorakṣa-nātha were fishermen, and Hāḍi was a stable sweeper. Tantric masters did not reject members because of their caste or gender. They imparted their teachings to ascetics as well as workers, artisans, and farmers from lower castes.

The *Mantra-mārga* tradition marks the beginning of Tantric Shaivism and dates to approximately 400–800 CE. It continued the transformation begun by the *Ati-mārga* sects. *Mantra-mārga* means "the path of mantras," not only because it uses mantras in ritual and practice, but because it teaches that the step-by-step progression toward liberation occurs through the mastery of *mantra-siddhis*. Unlike the *Ati-mārga*, or "the direct path," the *Mantra-mārga* promulgates a path of *siddhis* (supernatural powers) and *bhoga* (enjoyment); that is, as aspirants obtain supernatural powers, they are elevated to higher levels of existence until they attain liberation.

Mantra-mārga sects began to grant initiation not only to ascetics but also to married people. Men and women of all castes had a chance for liberation. Unlike in *Ati-mārga* sects, the requirement was not ascetic practices but rituals. In the initiation ritual, Śiva destroys the bonds of the soul, and liberation is completed at the time of death. In Tantric Shaivism, the benefits of initiation could be granted to women, the elderly, young children, and monarchs, all of whom could not undertake post-initiatory disciplines. Thus, there were active and inactive initiates. After initiation, inactive adepts had to express their devotion like uninitiated *Śaiva* bhaktas and contribute with monetary donations to the development of the movement. For this reason, many monarchs were attracted to this tradition and gave generous donations (*dakṣiṇā*) that financed the construction of temples and monasteries. As a result, the movement quickly became popular and expanded throughout India. Its adepts founded monasteries (*maṭhas*) and became preceptors of kings (*rāja-gurus*), to whom they offered the benefits of initiation. They consecrated kings with a *Śaiva* version of the Brahmanical ceremony of royal consecration (*rājābhiṣeka*), considered vital for the well-being of the entire society.

In the *Mantra-mārga* tradition, initiation did not symbolize the acceptance of a new religion or lifestyle as it did in the *Ati-mārga* tradition, but implied a true transformation at every level. Traditional *Ati-mārga* initiation marked the beginning of a path of austerities and practices intended to achieve liberation. *Mantra-mārga*, on the other hand, maintained that due to specific mantras carefully pronounced during the initiation ritual by the spiritual master, Śiva cut the bonds that tied the aspirant to the world.

Although *Ati-mārga* had initiation, used mantras, and promoted liberation, these elements were reconfigured in the *Mantra-mārga*: mantras (with the exception of the five *Brahma-mantras*) were not of Vedic origin, initiation became a ritual of transformation, and liberation did not require a long practice of austerities accessible only to men *Brāhmaṇas*. People of all *varṇas* and both genders could transcend suffering and achieve omnipresence and omnipotence. These innovations made the *Mantra-mārga* attractive and many people began to follow this revelation.

Saiddhāntika and non-*Saiddhāntika*

Mantra-mārga bifurcated into two main branches according to the aspect of Śiva that was worshipped: *Saiddhāntika*, or "the followers of established truth," and non-*Saiddhāntika*. The former mainly worshipped the benevolent Sadā-śiva, commonly represented by the *Śiva-liṅga*. The latter venerated the ferocious Bhairava or various configurations of goddesses, culminating in female cults of Kālī.

This bifurcation was inherited from the two branches of *Ati-mārga*. It is believed that the *Saiddhāntika* branch was developed out of the more conservative *Pāśu-pata* tradition, and the non-*Saiddhāntika* branch developed out of the transgressive practices of the *Lākula* and *Kāpālika* traditions.

The non-*Saiddhāntika* branch was divided into two types of lineages:

- ***Mantra-pīṭha*:** Lineages that worshipped with the mantras of male deities and taught the worship of Śiva in his Svacchanda form.
- ***Vidyā-pīṭha*:** Lineages that worshipped with mantras of female deities and taught the worship of Śhakti, the Mother of the Universe.

At the same time, another lineage developed called *Amṛteśvara*. It was an eclectic system that offered specialized rituals suitable for both branches.

Scriptures

The *Śaiva* Tantric revelation was put into writing between 400 and 800 CE. The *śāstras* of divine origin contained valuable spiritual wisdom about rituals (*kriyā*), observances (*cārya*), practices (yoga), and knowledge or gnosis (*jñāna*). The information we have about the *Ati-mārga* is minimal, but fortunately, a vast body of Sanskrit *Mantra-mārga* literature has been preserved:

***Saiddhāntika*:** It is a well-defined and relatively homogeneous canon that constitutes the authority of this tradition; it is composed of 10 *Śaiva Āgamas*, 18 *Rudra Āgamas*, and complementary scriptures.

Non-*Saiddhāntika*: Diverse and numerous writings collectively called *Bhairava Āgamas*, or "the teachings of Bhairava" (*Bhairava-śāstra*). The sixty-four *Āgamas* are classified into:

***Mantra-pīṭha*:** This includes 12,000 mantras in eight main

Āgamas: *Svacchanda*, *Caṇḍa*, *Krodha*, *Unmatta*, *Asita*, *Ruru*, *Jhaṅkara*, and *Kapālīśa*.

Vidyā-pīṭha: This is an extensive corpus. Its main *Āgamas* are *Sarva-vīra-samā-yoga*, *Siddha-yogeśvarī-mata*, *Pañcāmṛta*, *Viśvādya*, *Yoginī-jāla-śaṁvara*, *Vidyā-bheda*, *Śiraś-cheda*, *Mahā-saṁmohana*, *Nayottara*, and *Mahā-raudra*.

Both branches produced hundreds of secondary *Āgamas* (*Upāgamas*), as well as commentaries written by *ācāryas*.

Rituals

Saiddhāntika and non-*Saiddhāntika* rituals are variants of a single system. They differ in the following details:

Saiddhāntika: This is a conservative ritual system that follows the purity rules of the Brahmanical tradition and only makes lacto-vegetarian offerings. It respects the caste separation of ritual participants. Although it was based on the *Ati-mārga*, it discarded the transgressive elements and adapted it to Vedic rules. Ceremonies generally took place in public spaces for the benefit of the whole society. Followers worshipped the masculine aspect of divinity as Sadā-śiva, in the form of *liṅga* or in images on altars, with or without his consort. The feminine aspect was not central but represented the potency (*śakti*) of Śiva. The goddess was a metaphysical abstraction: the creative power of the male deity. Rudra was worshipped without a female consort.

Non-*saiddhāntika*: This ritual system made the transgressive offerings of the *Ati-mārga* more extreme and included liquor, blood, and meat. Worship did not take place in the temple for the benefit of the public, but propitiatory rites were performed by individuals in private for their own benefit. In the non-*Saiddhāntika* branch, there were two traditions, *Mantra-pīṭha* and *Vidyā-pīṭha*:

Mantra-pīṭha: This tradition taught the propitiation cult of Bhairava in his Svacchanda-bhairava aspect. He was seen as a higher form of Śiva and was sometimes depicted standing on Sadā-śiva, which symbolizes superiority. He was worshipped alongside his consort Aghoreśvarī or Bhairavī.

Vidyā-pīṭha: This was a transgressive *Śākta* cult of propitiation centered on the worship of fierce female deities, sometimes depicted with one foot on Bhairava.

Teachings

Saiddhāntika: This doctrine advocates dualism and defines three categories of existence: God, the cosmic manifestation, and individual souls. The *jīva* that is hidden in a material body is qualitatively equal to God but is a separate entity. The soul must seek an authentic guru and accept initiation. Only divine grace can liberate it. Liberation is the full manifestation of the potential of the soul, which achieves its divine qualitative nature but remains separate. This doctrine, although dual, is essentially Tantric since its metaphysics is based on Tantric scriptures, uses Tantric mantras, and developed forms of Tantric yoga.

Non-*Saiddhāntika*: These systems are non-dualist (*Advaita*) and chose a practice that does not distinguish between the sacred and the profane (*advaitācāra*). Since everything is Divinity, nothing is impure.

Although the two branches have philosophical and ontological differences, much of the foundational doctrines are the same. They are inseparably linked through a set of central theological principles, such as the belief in the absolute unity of Śiva–Śakti.

Practice

Saiddhāntika: This tradition was dualist in practice, that is, it preserved the distinction between what is permitted or prohibited according to the Brahmanic *Smṛti*.

Non-*Saiddhāntika*: Powerful spiritual experiences were achieved through the cultivation of sexual rituals and yoga.

Within both branches, liberation (*mukti*) and the enjoyment of supernatural powers (*bhukti*) were achieved through the power of mantras, propitiation, and complex rituals that could only be performed after initiation (*dīkṣā*).

Name	*Saiddhāntika*	Non-*saiddhāntika*
Translation	Followers of established truth.	Non-followers of established truth.
Description	The *Pāśu-pata* tradition was more conservative and subsequently developed into the *Saiddhāntika* tradition.	The Non-*Saiddhāntika* tradition developed from the transgressive practices of the *Lākulas* and *Kāpālikas.*
Chronology	Fifth century CE	Fifth century CE
Location	It originated in Kashmir and later moved to Tamil Nadu, where it merged with the bhakti movement.	Kashmir
Deities	The deity was the benevolent Sadā-śiva, commonly worshipped in the *Śiva-liṅga.* The goddess was a metaphysical abstraction; she was the creative power of the male deity. Rudra was worshipped without a female consort.	The ferocious Bhairava and the goddess.
Doctrine	Dualism in three categories: God, the cosmic manifestation, and individual souls.	Non-dualism.
Scriptures	28 *Śaiva Āgamas* (10 *Śiva* and 18 *Rudra*).	64 *Bhairava Agamas.*
Rituals	Rituals focused on the male aspect of divinity with public rituals and were limited to lacto-vegetarian offerings, in accordance with the Brahmanical purity laws.	Rituals were for both male and female aspects of divinity. Propitiatory private rituals were conducted with offerings of liquor, blood, and meat.
Practice	Power of mantras, propitiation, complex rituals.	Powerful spiritual experiences were achieved through the cultivation of sexual rituals and yoga.

1. *Saiddhāntika* – The *Śaiva-siddhānta Āgamas*

Within *Saiddhāntika*, the *Śaiva-siddhānta* tradition emerged. The meaning of the term *siddhānta* is "final conclusion," so *Śaiva-siddhānta* means "the final conclusion of Shaivism." It refers to a *Śaiva* system that originated in Kashmir, in northern India, and gradually moved to Tamil Nadu, where it has predominated for the last three hundred years. The term comes from Sadyo-jyoti in the ninth century CE, who referred to the tradition in his *Bhoga Kārikā*:

रुरुसिद्धान्तसंसिद्धौ भोगमोक्षौ ससाधनौ ।
वचामि साधकबोधाय लेशतो युक्तिसंस्कृतौ ॥

ruru-siddhānta-saṁsiddhau
bhoga-mokṣau sasādhanau
vacāmi sādhaka-bodhāya
leśato yukti-saṁskṛtau

For the purpose of the adepts, I am briefly describing both mundane experience and liberation, along with their means, as they are described in the teachings of Ruru (*Ruru-siddhānta*) and established through perfect logical argumentation.

(*Bhoga Kārikā*, 2)

And in the *Ratna-traya* of Bhaṭṭa Śrī-kaṇṭha, with the commentary of Aghoraśivācārya, it is explained:

सिद्धान्तशब्दः ... योगरूढ्या शिवप्रणितेषु ।
कामीकादिषु दशाष्टादशसु तन्त्रेषु प्रसिद्धः ॥

siddhānta-śabdaḥ... yoga-rūḍhyā śiva-praṇīteṣu
kāmīkādiṣu daśāṣṭā-daśasu tantreṣu prasiddhaḥ

The term *siddhānta* is used for Shaivism on the basis of eighteen and ten (twenty-eight) Tantras, such as the *Kāmika Āgama*, composed by Śiva.

More than speculative philosophy, the *Śaiva-siddhānta* is a dualist devotional path. Its vision is based on a canon of 28 *Āgamas* (10 *Śaiva Āgamas* and 18 *Rudra Āgamas*). A large part of these *Āgamas* is devoted to descriptions of temples, *liṅgams*, and iconographic forms of gods and goddesses, as well as worship rites.

Its dualist theology maintains a difference between God, individual souls, and the universe that holds souls in captivity. Its liturgy preserves the personal character of the dualist *Āgamas*. The fusion with the southern devotional tradition with 63 *Nāyanārs*, the famous *Śaiva* saints, transformed the *Śaiva-siddhānta* into a Tamil religion. The Tamil culture expressed itself through poetry in *Caṅkam* literature prior to the third century CE.

This system is an integral part of Hinduism because it accepts the Vedas as a divine revelation. Its sacred scriptures are the *Tirumurai* (devotional poems composed by the *Nāyanārs*), the Vedas, the *Śaiva Āgamas*, and the *Siddhānta śāstras*. The *Śaiva-siddhānta* differs from the Vedic worship of Lord Śiva by adhering to the *Āgamas*, which allow all four castes to worship.

According to tradition, the first *Śaiva-siddhānta* master was Kadamba-guhādhivāsī, whose name means "one who resides in the Kadamba cave." This *siddha* master was believed to be an incarnation of Śiva. Kadamba-guhādhivāsī was succeeded by Śaṅkha-maṭhādhipati, or "the superintendent of the Śaṅkha monastery." The successor of Śaṅkha-maṭhādhipati was Tirambipāla, whose name can be translated as "the protector of the Terambi village." The successor of Tirambipāla was Āmardakatīrtha-nātha, or "the Lord of the brightness of Āmardaka." It is a tradition rich in great masters who commented on Tantric texts; a few of the most important masters were Sadyo-joti from Kashmir (seventh century CE), and Bhoja-deva (eleventh century CE) and Aghoraśiva (twelfth century CE) from the south.

From the time of Āmardaka, around 775 CE, the *Śaiva-siddhānta* began to found monastic orders to spread its message. The Āmardaka order was founded by Rudra-śambhu, the Mātta-mayūra order by Purandara, and the Mādhu-mateya order by Pavana-śiva. Using the support of pious kings, such as Cālukya Avani-varman (ninth century

CE), many ascetics dedicated themselves to teaching the system in neighboring kingdoms, especially in the south. Beginning in Mātta-mayūra, they established monasteries in Mahārāṣṭra, Koṅkan, Karnāṭaka, Āndra, and Kerala. The *Śaiva-siddhānta* blossomed wherever it was taught. When Muslims invaded India, the spread of the system was stopped, and other forms of Hinduism became popular. The *Śaiva-siddhānta* survived in Tamil territory, which is why the system adopted a traditional Tamil form.

The different stages of *Śaiva-siddhānta* literature

The history of *Śaiva-siddhānta* literature reflects the evolution of a vision. To understand it better, we can divide the sequence into four stages: early *siddhānta*, the Tamil devotional poets, Sanskrit *siddhānta*, and the Tamil systematic theologians.

At all stages, there never was any doubt that Śiva held the central position; the dilemma was about the right path to him. In the beginning, the path of knowledge was considered the most appropriate. However, over time, devotion was revealed as the path to God.

I. Early *siddhānta*

This period marks the origins of *siddhānta*, which leads us to the *Śaiva Āgamas*. These texts are classified into four groups: pastoralist dualist, lunar, pastoralist monist, and *Śaiva*. The *Śaiva Āgamas* are divided into three groups: *Vāma* (left), *Dakṣiṇa* (right), and *Siddhānta*. *Śaiva-siddhānta* accepts 28 *Āgamas* as authoritative and classifies them into 10 dualist *Śaiva Āgamas* and 18 monist-dualist *Rudra Āgamas*. Each of the *Āgamas* has four *pādas* (feet), or "sections":

1. Knowledge, or *jñāna*: Explanations of metaphysics and epistemology.
2. Ritualism, or *kriyā*: The rules of liturgy.

3. Iconic prescriptions, or *caryā*: Architectural laws and the creation of deities, or *mūrtis*.
4. Discipline, or yoga: Creating the right situation for approaching divinity.

II. The Tamil devotional poets

The stage of devotional poets, the 63 *Nāyanārs*, lasted from the seventh to tenth century CE. At this time the supremacy of knowledge as a means to access God found great resistance from Tamil *bhaktas*, who saw devotion as the only door to Śiva.

One of the main Tamil saints was Tirumūlar Nāyanār, also called Mūlar. He was one of the eight disciples of the master Tirumandi Devar as well as one of the eighteen *siddhars*. His place of residence was a hill called Potiyān. His desire to visit the great master Agastya made him travel to the south. In a village on the banks of the Kāveri River, he ran into a herd of cows that were crying bitterly over the death of their shepherd Mūlan. Tirumūlar felt very sorry for them so he used a mystical power called *parakāya-praveśa* to go into the dead body of the shepherd. Meanwhile, he left his own body hidden inside a hollow tree. The people realized that a profound transformation had occurred in the Mūlan that they knew: the previous person was an ordinary man, while this one was a fully enlightened being. At some point, Tirumūlar realized that his original body had disappeared and he was forced to remain in the shepherd's body.

His most important literary contribution was the *Tirumandhiram*, one of the key texts of the *Śaiva-siddhānta*. He remained in a state of *samādhi* for long periods and wrote only when his state of consciousness permitted. The sage Tirumūlar proposed a monist theism in which everything was Śiva. His work revealed *siddhānta* as a path that included a moral way of living, temple worship, and the inner worship of Lord Śiva through the grace of the spiritual master. It says that after enlightenment, the spiritual body continues its development until the soul emerges in Śiva.

III. Sanskrit *siddhānta*

The period of systematic Sanskrit theologians lasted from the ninth to eleventh century CE. It included the works of Bhoja, Śrī-kumāra, and Aghora-śiva. Śrī-kumāra states in his *Tātparya-dipikā* commentary that Śiva is one and refers to *Pati*, *paśu*, and *pāśa* as one and the same.

Like previous masters, Bhoja, brilliant in the *siddhānta*, does not explain the relationship between the transcendental and the phenomenal, or between Śiva and *paśu* or *pāśa*. The lack of a clear position on this gave rise to the dilemma of *siddhānta*: whether to postulate self-differentiation or emanation in God himself in the form of categories such as the five *tattvas*, or "pure principles," from the *Śaiva-siddhānta* doctrine. Divine self-differentiation would imply a divine self-emptying and the fall of transcendence into the phenomenal, while the absence of self-differentiation meant eliminating the five *tattvas* or relegating them to the unconscious. Harmonizing emanation with *bheda*, or "the theology of difference," has perhaps been the greatest metaphysical problem of this system.

Aghora-śiva, who lived around the year 1100 CE, preferred a theology of difference and established the foundation of the *Śaiva-siddhānta* doctrine. This great figure was from a Āmardaka monastery in Chidambaram and a disciple of Bhaṭṭa Rāmakaṇṭha (1100–1130 CE). He connected the Sanskrit and Tamil traditions. His writings were decisive in establishing the foundation of the doctrine. He saw Śiva as the supreme transcendence, both the *śaktimat* (energetic) and the *śakti* (energy). He included in the *pāśa* category (bond) the first five *tattvas* (categories): *nāda*, *bindu*, *sadā-śiva*, *īśvara*, and *śuddha-vidyā*. That is to say, he affirmed that the universe includes all material and mental phenomena. Aghora-śiva elaborated on the *Śaiva-siddhānta* doctrine, moving it away from its original form that arose in the north. The only thing left to reveal was whether Śiva was accessible through knowledge or devotion.

Aghora-śiva established the foundations of *Śaiva-siddhānta* on an irrefutable theology of difference. Rejecting his postulate would have meant adopting Vedantic monism, which would eliminate *siddhānta* identity.

IV. Systematic theologians in the Tamil language

The period of systematic theologians in the Tamil language occurred between the thirteenth and eighteenth centuries CE. In this period, *siddhānta* opted for Tamil as the language of its theology. It began when the master Aghoraśiva solved the great dilemma of duality versus monism. Doctrines prior to *siddhānta* that appeared to deny the submission of the soul to God, such as *Śiva-samavāda*, lost popularity and were rejected. There was a renewed awakening of pure non-dualism, to such an extent that the Tamil *siddhānta* described itself as *śuddhādvaita*.

Non-dualism implies an inseparable relationship between souls and God, but not the identity of their substance. As part of a return to the Agamic origins, Sanskrit Siddhantists were gradually abandoned. The system of Bādarāyaṇa was held above all other doctrines. This path of devotion expanded in southern India.

V. The systematization of devotional *Śaiva-siddhānta*

We cannot ignore the contribution of Meykaṇḍār, who systematized the devotional *siddhānta* in the first half of the thirteenth century CE. Meykaṇḍa-deva, whose name means "the discoverer of the Truth," was a disciple of Parañjoti-muni. Meykaṇḍār is considered the most important *santānācārya*, a group that included his disciple Aruḷnandi Śivācārya as well as Marai-jñāna Sambandharand and his disciple Umāpati Śivācārya. His methodology is described in a collection of fourteen works known as the *Meykaṇḍa-śāstras*, or "the disciplines of Meykaṇḍa." His first two treatises are the *Tiruvunthiār*, or "the sacred effort of the master," and the *Tirukkalirruppadiar*. His greatest contribution is a Tamil work of twelve verses entitled *Śiva-jñāna-bodham*, or "the understanding of Śiva's knowledge." This is a commentary on twelve *kārikās*, or *sūtras*, from the *Rauravāgama*. It contains the classic explanation of Tamil *Śaiva-siddhānta*. The *Śivajñānabodham* is composed of twelve *sūtras*, divided into four groups of three. The twelve aphorisms of this important work deal with the following topics:

1. Śiva, who brings about the dissolution of the manifested universe, is also its cause.
2. How the universe is recreated.
3. The existence of the soul.
4. The distinction between the soul and the body.
5. Divine help to souls.
6. The real and the unreal.
7. The soul, as neither real nor unreal.
8. How the soul acquires knowledge.
9. The purification of the soul.
10. The purification of the triple contamination.
11. How the soul reaches the holy feet of God.
12. How Śiva, who is beyond the perception of our senses, can be worshipped as something perceivable to our senses.

This work, along with other works of important masters, established the basis of the Meykaṇḍār *sampradāya*, which proposes a pluralistic realism where souls, Śiva, and the cosmic manifestation coexist. It speaks of an eternal dual-unity without beginning or end that has three categories of existence: *Pati* (the supreme divinity), *paśu* (soul), and *pāśa* (cosmic manifestation).

The vision of the sage Meykaṇḍār was further developed by Aruḷnandi (who lived around the year 1253 CE) in his treatise *Śiva-jñāna-siddhiyār*, or "the test of Śiva's knowledge." This text consists of two parts: *supakkam*, or "the proper doctrines," and *parapakkam*, or "the foreign doctrines." *Supakkam* describes the doctrine, while *parapakkam* refutes teachings that conflict with *siddhānta*.

Aruḷnandi's successor, Umāpati (who lived around the year 1306 CE), continued his work with two important treatises: *Śiva-pirakāśam*, or "the light of Śiva," which describes the philosophy, and *Śaṅkalpa-nirākaraṇam*, or "the repudiation of doubts," which refutes teachings opposed to *siddhānta*. Umāpati wrote four other treatises on the subject of grace, a commentary on the *Pauṣkarāgama*, and *Śata-ratna-saṅgraha*, or "the collection of one hundred gems."

This doctrine culminated with two authors: Śivāgra-yogin in the sixteenth century CE and Śiva-jñāna-yogin in the eighteenth century CE. *Śivāgrābhāṣyam*, or "the exposition of Śivāgra," addresses the non-dualism of Śrīkaṇṭha as far as it is consistent with the *siddhānta*'s metaphysics of difference. As we see in his commentary on the *Pauṣkarāgama*, Śivāgra-yogin criticized some of Umāpati's opinions and was not always in total agreement with the previous Tamil *siddhānta* masters. Śivāgra-yogin also wrote *Kriyā-dipikā* (the lamp of actions), *Śaiva-sannyāsa-paddhati* (the Manual of the ascetic *Śaivas*), and *Śivaneri-pirakāśam* (the impact of the illumination of Śiva).

Śiva-jñāna-yogin wrote mainly in Tamil. In works such as the *Cirrurai*, or "the small commentary," and the *Drāviḍa-māpāḍiam*, or "the exhibition of the great Dravidian," he tries to reconcile contradictory points of view among Meykaṇḍār's commentators.

In *Śaiva-siddhānta*, bhakti means service to the Lord and intimate friendship with him. In the text *Bhakti-karma-samuccaya*, the celebrated *Śaiva* master Śrī-kaṇṭha describes bhakti as a path to liberation. He was the first *Śaiva* master to reconcile the Vedic and Agamic traditions.

The *Śaiva-siddhānta* system flourished until the eleventh century CE, when the Muslim invasions began. It has survived to this day in the southern part of the Indian subcontinent and uses Tamil instead of Sanskrit.

2. Non-*Saiddhāntika* – The *Bhairava Tantras*

The *Bhairava Tantras* contain the teachings of Bhairava to his consort. They are classified in different ways. One approach divides the teachings into two categories: *Mantra-pīṭha*, or "the seat of mantras," and *Vidyā-pīṭha*, or "the seat of *vidyās*." Mantra and *vidyā* are synonyms that mean "formulas of sacred sounds" in Sanskrit: mantra is a masculine noun and *vidyā* is feminine. In this context, *Pīṭha* means "corpus." Hence the *Mantra-pīṭha* scriptures focus on the worship of the masculine aspect of divinity and *Vidyā-pīṭha* on the feminine aspect.

The collection *Vidyā-pīṭha Tantras* is subdivided into *Vāma Tantras* (left Tantras), *Yāmala Tantras* (union Tantras), and *Śakti Tantras* (energy Tantras). The *Śakti Tantras* include *Trika Tantras* and texts related to the Kālī cults.

2.1 The *Mantra-pīṭha*

Deities

The *Āgamas* classified as *Mantra-pīṭha* give instructions for worshipping Śiva as Svacchanda-bhairava, or "autonomous Bhairava," known euphemistically as Aghora, or "the non-terrible one." He has eighteen arms and five faces with white complexions, each embodying one of the five *Brahma-mantras*. His appearance is both mischievous and powerful, two qualities that reflect his natural essence of radical autonomy. He stands on the prostrate body of Sadā-śiva, the form worshipped in *Śaiva-siddhānta*, now transcended by this new revelation. Sadā-śiva was worshipped alone, but the *Mantra-pīṭha* doctrine incorporates a female consort as the personification of Śhakti. Bhairavī, or Aghoreśvarī, is surrounded by lower Bhairavas within a circular enclosure in the cremation grounds. She has the same appearance as Svacchanda-bhairava but is still subordinate to him. They are first worshipped together and then he is worshipped alone.

Svacchanda-bhairava, or "autonomous Bhairava"

Teachings

The main text, the *Svacchanda-bhairava Tantra*, offers extensive explanations of Tantric practice and cosmology, but very little information about its philosophy. The traditions of the *Bhairava Tantras* elaborated on the practices of *Kāpālikas*, from whom they originated. Hence the basic form of *Mantra-pīṭha* ascetic observance was *kapāla-vrata*, or *mahā-vrata*. The *Kāpālika* influence on the *Mantra-mārga* is evident in the iconography of the divine couple. Worshipped within a cremation chamber, they are decorated with bone ornaments and carry the skull staff (*khaṭvāṅga*) as in the *Kāpālika* tradition. Svacchanda-bhairava has softer elements that make him a transitional deity between the benevolent God of the *Śaiva-siddhānta* and the *Vidyā-pīṭha* gods, which put more emphasis on the *Kāpālika* appearance. The *Svacchanda-bhairava Tantra* is this cult's authoritative text. It also provides guidance on the rituals for secondary forms of Svacchanda-bhairava, such as Koṭa-rakṣā (the hollow eye) and Vyādhi-bhakṣa (the consumer of diseases), fearsome deities that resemble the Bhairavas from the classic *Kāpālika* tradition.

Since the *Mantra-pīṭha* tradition does not seem to have had a clearly defined philosophy, commentators from other traditions felt comfortable incorporating its ritualistic practices and offered their own interpretation in the light of their doctrines. There are commentaries from the dualist *Saiddhāntikas* and from the non-dualist *Kaulas*. It seems that the non-dualists were more popular, because only their commentary (the *Svacchanda-tantra-uddyota* by Kṣemarāja) has been preserved. Svacchanda-bhairava continued to be worshipped in Kashmir and Nepal until the twentieth century CE.

Scriptures

The sixty-four *Bhairava Tantras* are the main scriptures of this category. From citations in later works we know that there were other significant secondary texts such as the *Aghoreśvarī-svacchanda*, *Dvādaśa-sāhasra*, *Mantra-pīṭha-svacchanda*, and *Rasa-svacchanda*. The *Svacchanda-bhairava Tantra* was evidently the most important, because many copies of this text have survived in different parts of India. Many worship manuals (*paddhatis*) come from this text and it seems to be the source of instructions for the *Saiddhāntika* initiation ritual explained by Bhojadeva in his work *Siddhānta-sāra-paddhati*.

Practice

This tradition incorporated both *Siddhānta* and *Kaula* elements. That is, the cult of the goddess began to emerge, but she was still subordinate to Bhairava. Worship included some slightly transgressive elements, such as wine or rice beer, but they were only offered to the deity and not consumed by adepts.

2.2 The *Vidyā-pīṭha*

The fifteen *Vidyā-pīṭha* scriptures are divided into three subgroups, each representing a higher level of esotericism and feminization: the three *Vāma Tantras* (left Tantras) or *Guhya Tantras* (secret Tantras), the five *Yāmala Tantras* (union Tantras), and the seven *Śakti Tantras* (energy Tantras). The goddesses are more and more prominent. At first they become superior to Bhairava and then completely autonomous, as in cults exclusive to the terrible goddesses (*eka-vīrā*) like Kālī.

In these scriptures, the *Kāpālika* culture of the cremation grounds becomes prominent. Adepts could access deities' powers through initiation and the *Kāpālika* vow. Ascetics were intoxicated with alcohol and spent periods of the night wandering (*niśāṭana*) followed by periods of worship (*pūjā*). In worship, they invoked and satisfied the deities of the *maṇḍala* chosen for their initiation.

They used the insignia of the *Kāpālika* vow: matted hair, ornaments of human bones, smeared ashes of the dead, a sacred thread made of hair from a corpse, a skull staff, a drum (*ḍamaru*), and a skull bowl for alms. Their rituals involved a *dūtī*, a consecrated consort, with whom they produced the sexual fluids that propitiated the deities.

In the *Ati-mārga* and some *Mantra-mārga* sects, the hierarchy of the cosmic levels (*bhuvanādhvā*) was governed by Rudras. Starting with the *Vidyā-pīṭha*, the male hierarchy was replaced by female hierarchy of wild *yoginīs*, who drank blood and were decorated with skulls. They emanated from the heart of the deity and formed an omnipresent network of power (*yoginī-jāla*). They populated this vertical order of the cosmic hierarchy and radiated throughout sacred space, sending consecrated and venerated emanations into seats of power (*pīṭhas*) connected to cremation grounds throughout India.

The *Kāpālikas* of the *Vidyā-pīṭha* sought to merge with *yoginīs* (*yoginī-melaka*) through a process of visionary invocation in which they lured them from heaven, gratified them with offerings of their own blood, and ascended to heaven with them as leaders of their band. The sixty-four *yoginīs* occupied a prominent place in all *Vidyā-pīṭha* traditions. They radiated externally from eight mother goddesses (*mātṛ*): Brāhmī, Māheśvarī, Kaumārī, Vaiṣṇavī, Indrāṇī, Vārāhī, Cāmuṅḍā, and Mahā-lakṣmī. They were divided into eight clans or families (*kulas*) of eight *yoginīs* each. At the time of consecration, adepts sat in front of a *maṇḍala* enthroning these eight Mothers. They went into a trance, and the possessive power of the deity caused their hand to throw a flower on the *maṇḍala*. The area it fell on indicated which Mother they had more affinity with and they joined her family (*kula*). On nights auspicious for their Mother's ritual, devotees had to seek a *yoginī* from their *kula* and offer her worship with the aspiration to receive the Mother's blessing of supernatural powers and occult knowledge.

2.2.1 The *Vāma Tantras* (left Tantras) or the *Guhya Tantras* (secret Tantras)

Description

We do not have much information about this tradition. It seems that its influence was minimal. It emerged from a male-oriented culture and was one of the first traditions to worship female goddesses. In addition, it was one of the first transgressive traditions in which adepts' advancement depended on the degree to which they broke social norms and mental conditioning.

Chronology and geographic location

This tradition spread at the beginning of the Tantric revelation. The Buddhist scholar Dharma-kīrti mentioned it as early as 600 CE.

Before the Tantric culture reached its height, the tradition of the *Vāma Tantras* had already disappeared.

Deities

The sisters Jayā, Vijayā, Ajitā (also called Jayantī), and Aparājitā were the deities of this tradition. They were worshipped alongside their brother Tumburu-bhairava, a form of Lord Śiva with four faces visualized as those of his sisters. The *Vīṇāśikhā Tantra* says that the four goddesses were visualized as white, red, gold, and black, respectively, and their vehicles were a corpse, an owl, a horse, and a flying vehicle. It seems that they were originally worshipped for victory in battle.

Scriptures

Kashmir literary sources mention three *Vāma Tantras*: *Nayottara*, *Mahā-raudra*, and *Mahā-saṁmohana*, but unfortunately, they have not been preserved. The Sdok Kak Thom inscription, made in Cambodia in 1052 CE, adds the *Vīṇāśikha* to the list, indicating that the complete canon of this tradition was composed of four *Vāma* scriptures emanating from the four faces of Tumburu. We can conclude from the inscription that the *Vīṇāśikha* was the last revealed text. From this we can surmise that the *Vīṇāśikha* was the last text to be revealed. It is not mentioned in the *Jayad-ratha Yāmala* and the *Picumata* because it was not yet part of the canon. The *Vīṇāśikha* is the only text that has survived; it is a palm leaf manuscript from the twelfth or thirteenth century CE.

Rituals

The *Vāma Tantras* describe rituals for using magic against enemies and pacifying demons.

2.2.2 The *Yāmala Tantras* or "Union Tantras"

Name

The term *yāmala* means "a couple in union" and generally refers to the union of God with his consort. In this context, *yāmala* acquires a special meaning as the union of mantra and *vidyā*. That is, this tradition unites works with rituals dedicated to both gods (as mantras) and goddesses (as *vidyās*).

Description

On the *Mantra-mārga* spectrum, the *Yāmala* tradition would be to the left of the *Dakṣiṇa* tradition. The female deity was superior to the male one. Compared to other left-hand sects, it had more mortuary images and more transgressive practices in cremation grounds.

Chronology

The sixth-century *Skanda Purāṇa* mentions the *Yāmala* tradition and lists seven *Mātṛ-tantras* with titles that include the word *yāmala*, beginning with the *Brahma Yāmala*. It seems that this tradition did not survive into the classical period of Tantric revelation (900–1100 CE).

Deities

The scriptures give instructions for the cult of Kapālīśa-bhairava, or "the Lord of the skull," and his furious consort Caṇḍā-kāpālinī. Here we see the first signs of Śhakti's superiority and autonomy. In the *Mantra-pītha*, the deities that surrounded Svacchanda-bhairava and Bhairavī in the *maṇḍala* were masculine and solitary. But here, women are superior to their male consorts. Bhairava is the one who grants energy (*śakti-pāta*) to these secondary deities, but he is transcended by Śhakti in the iconography.

Scriptures

According to scriptures such as the *Jayad-ratha Yamala*, this tradition has eight texts. The five main ones are the *Brahma Yāmala*, *Viṣṇu Yāmala*, *Rudra Yāmala*, *Skanda Yāmala*, and *Umā Yāmala*. The remaining three are called by different names in different works. Although all Union Tantras were revealed by Bhairavas, their female consorts had greater autonomy and the retinue surrounding the divine couple was composed of female *yoginīs*.

The *Brahma Yāmala*, also called *Picu-mata* and *Ucchuṣma*, was the most important *Yāmala*, and its 12,000 verses have survived, preserved for centuries on palm leaves. This *Yāmala* descends directly from Lord Śiva through a chain of disciplic succession of several masters. This *paramparā* includes Bhairava, who gave it to Krodha, Kapila, and Pādma. Pādma taught it to Devadatta who in turn passed it on to his fourteen disciples.

इच्छा नामेन सञ्जाता तया बिन्दुः प्रबोधितः ॥
प्रबुद्धस्य ततो बिन्दोर्ज्ञानौघं निष्कलं ततः ।
अभिव्यक्ति महादेवि अकस्मान्मन्त्रविग्रहः ।
ज्ञानसंपूर्णदेहस्तु सदाशिवपदे स्थितः ॥
तस्मत्सदाशिवानुज्ञा ततः सृष्टिरभूत्पुनः ।
हूहुकान्तावधूतस्था तत्त्वमाला स्वभावतः ॥
लोकस्य हितकाम्यायाममृताख्येन सुव्रते ।
निबद्धं तु समासेन ज्ञानौघं विमलात्मकम् ॥

icchā nāmena sañjātā
tayā binduḥ prabodhitaḥ

prabuddhasya tato bindor
jñānaughaṁ niṣkalaṁ tataḥ
abhivyakti mahā-devi
akasmān mantra-vigrahaḥ
jñāna-saṁpūrṇa-dehas tu
sadā-śiva-pade sthitaḥ

tasmat sadā-śivānujñā
tataḥ sṛṣṭir abhūt-punaḥ
hūhu-kāntāvadhūta-sthā
tattva-mālā svabhāvataḥ

lokasya hita-kāmyāyām
amṛtākhyena suvrate
nibaddhaṁ tu samāsena
jñānaughaṁ vimalātmakam

> From the inconceivable Śiva, the supreme Self, arose the supreme Śakti, called *icchā*. By her, *bindu* was awakened. Then, from the awakened *bindu*, [emerged] the undifferentiated mass of scriptural wisdom. From this, O Mahā-devī, suddenly a body of mantras became manifest at the level of the Sadā-śiva [*tattva*], its body completely filled with scriptural wisdom. From this, with the authorization of Sadā-śiva, the creation then took place again, according to its nature, as the series of *tattvas* situated at the [supreme Śakti] *avadhūta* down to [the Rudra] Huhuka.
>
> For the good of the people, O pious lady, the great mass of scriptural wisdom, consisting of the *Vimala*, was set down in abbreviated form under the name *Amṛta*. And the Parāparā God [Sadā-śiva], moreover, presented to Śrī-kanṭha [the scripture], consisting of mantra, doctrine, and ritual, after emerging from the state beyond observances, for having seen both [the pure and impure] paths.
>
> (*Brahma Yāmala*, 1.34b–37)

This *Yāmala* describes rituals and contains a vast collection of magical methods and spells with mantras, mystical diagrams, *mudrās*, and so on. This text has a *Kāpālika* character and develops the antinomian and bloody culture in the *Mantra-mārga*. The *Rudra Yāmala* has one of the first references to the chakras.

It is important to mention three secondary texts: the *Mahā-bhairava-maṅgalā*, *Piṅgalā-mata*, and *Mata-sāra*, which instruct on the worship of the same pantheon as that of the *Picu-mata* but with their own peculiarities. The *Piṅgalā-mata* mentions a great variety of *sādhanas* and refers to two kinds of Tantras: *Kāma-puri* and *Uḍḍiyāṇa*. The center of its *maṇḍala* has Kapalesa, Bhairava, and Caṇḍā-kāpālinī. All the other deities are female, and even the main mantras of worship belong to Caṇḍā-kāpālinī. Her partner's mantras are secondary.

The *Jayad-ratha Yāmala*, a supplement to the *Brahma Yāmala* dedicated to Kālī, has four thousand verses. It mentions many sects such as *Kāla-saṁkarṣaṇī*, *Carcikā*, and *Siddhi-lakṣmī*. The supplementary *Yāmalas* are a step in the evolution of Tantric literature toward a new orientation.

Teachings

The ancient *Yāmala* tradition was mainly directed at power-seeking ascetics. Here we find the Shamanic roots of Tantra: a world of magical powers. Its rituals summoned spiritual powers with skulls and mostly took place on cremation grounds on nights with new moons.

Yāmalas are important because they describe a variety of traditions. They expand the Tantric pantheon and instruct on the worship of new gods and goddesses. The Union Tantras are the main source of information on early *Kaula* ritualism. They include initiations, sexual rituals, esoteric practices, and spiritual possession induced by *yoginīs*. They depict profuse *Kāpālika* imagery and contain secret conversations of the divine couple, *Yāmala*, which is the doctrine's namesake.

Practice

In this tradition's practices, aspirants find themselves alone in the universe with feminine entities. In the rituals, they are surrounded exclusively by *yoginīs* and visualize themselves as full of femininity at all levels.

Rituals

Through rituals and *sādhana*, aspirants seek to expand their consciousness and transcend all duality, which will allow them to realize Bhairava's authentic *Advaita* nature.

> यो ऽसौ अचिन्त्यमित्याहुः शिवः परमकारणः ।
> निःसंज्ञो निर्विकारश्च व्यापी शान्तस्तथैव च ॥
> निःस्वभावो महादेवि क्रियाकारणवर्जितः ।
> निष्कलो निर्विकल्पस्त्वरूपो गुणवर्जितः ॥
> निर्ममो निरहङ्काराद्वैतपदसंस्थितः ।
> योगिनां ध्यानगम्यो ऽसौ ज्ञानरूपो महायशे ॥
> निराचारपदावस्थः संज्ञामात्रः प्रभुः परः ।
> तस्यापराज्योतिरूपं सर्वानुग्रहकारकः ॥
> व्यापी ह्यव्यक्तरूपी चामनस्को महात्मनः ।

yo 'sau acintyam ity āhuḥ śivaḥ parama-kāraṇaḥ
niḥsaṁjño nirvikāraś ca vyāpī śāntas tathaiva ca

niḥsvabhāvo mahādevi kriyā-kāraṇa-varjitaḥ
niṣkalo nirvikalpas tvarūpo guṇa-varjitaḥ

nirmamo nirahaṅkārādvaita-pada-saṁsthitaḥ
yogināṁ dhyāna-gamyo 'sau jñāna-rūpo mahā-yaśe

nirācāra-padāvasthaḥ saṁjñā-mātraḥ prabhuḥ paraḥ
tasyāparā-jyoti-rūpaṁ sarvānugraha-kārakaḥ

vyāpī hy avyakta-rūpī ca amanasko mahātmanaḥ

Śiva, the one who is called *inconceivable*, is the supreme cause, with no name or transformation, pervasive and inactive, with no inherent nature. O Mahādevī! He is devoid of action and cause, undifferentiated, free from conceptualization, form, *guṇas*, notions of "mine" and "I," and is situated in the state of non-duality. He can [only] be approached by yogis through meditation, and his form is wisdom. O woman of great renown, the Supreme Lord only abides in the state beyond activity, consciousness (*saṁjñā*). He, the agent of grace for all, has the form of the supreme effulgence. He is pervasive, has an unmanifested form, and is beyond the mind of great souls.

(*Brahma Yāmala*, 122–126a)

2.2.3. The *Śakti Tantras* or "Energy Tantras"

The *Śakti Tantras*, or "Energy Tantras," are the third collection of the *Vidyā-pīṭha*. The *Jayad-ratha Yāmala* lists this tradition's seven main texts: the *Sarva-vīra-samā-yoga*, *Siddha-yogeśvarī-mata*, *Śiraś-cheda*, *Pañcāmṛta*, *Viśvādya*, *Vidyā-bheda*, and *Yoginī-jāla-śaṁbara*. Only two scriptures have survived: a summarized version of the original

Siddha-yogeśvarī-mata and the *Jayad-ratha Yāmala*, or *Śiraś-cheda*, which at this point only had one part (*ṣaṭkam*). Three more were added later. These Tantras are the authority of the esoteric cults of the goddesses Trika and Kālī, which are described separately.

2.2.3.1 The *Śakti Tantras* – The *Trika*

Name

The sect received the name *Trika*, or "triad," because it worshipped three goddesses: Parā, Parāparā, and Aparā, with or without their Bhairava consorts.

Description

This is one of the sects that practiced social transgression such as accepting women and giving them access to the complete practice. Women could aspire to their own spiritual liberation instead of accumulating their husbands' merits. The oldest text specified that its most powerful mantra was reserved for women and was only transmitted between women.

Geographic location

The *Trika* spread throughout India. It probably started in Mahārāṣṭra and then became established in Orissa. Since its greatest exponent, Abhinava-gupta, is from Kashmir, some believe it originated there.

Deities

The term *trika* refers to a ritual entity rather than a theology.

यावन्त्यः प्रथिताः काश्चिद्योगेश्वर्यो महाबलाः ।
तासां योनिः समाख्याता रुद्रशक्तिर्वरानने ॥
तयैवोद्बलिताः सत्त्वाः क्रीडन्ते ते ऽविशङ्किताः ।
सा परापररूपेण व्याप्य सर्वमिदं स्थिता ॥
योगेश्वरीति विख्याता तस्या मूर्तिस्त्रिधा प्रिये ।

yāvantyaḥ prathitāḥ kāścid yogeśvaryā mahā-balāḥ
tāsāṁ yoniḥ samākhyātā rudra-śaktir varānane

tayaivodbalitāḥ sattvāḥ krīḍante te 'viśaṇkitāḥ
sā parāpara-rūpeṇa vyāpya sarvam idaṁ sthitā

yogeśvarīti vikhyātā tasyā mūrtis tridhā priye

> O beautiful one, the source of all powerful (*mahā-balāḥ*) *yoginīs* in their manifested form, (*prathitāḥ*) is called Rudra-śakti (the Power of Rudra). All creatures are empowered by her. They do their pastimes free of inhibitions, while she pervades the whole universe with her form, transcendental and non-transcendental. She is called Yogeśvari and her form is threefold, O beloved one. Now, I will tell you about these divisions as they exist in this world.
>
> (*Siddha-yogeśvarī-mata*, 2.21–23a)

Parā is the central goddess, who is white, beautiful, and benevolent. She has one face and two hands. One holds a sacred text and the other makes the *cin-mudrā* gesture, which represents self-realization. Parāparā and Aparā are fierce *Kāpālika* deities who carry the skull staff (*khatvāṅga*). Parāparā is on Parā's right and is red; Aparā is on her left and is black.

1. The goddess Parā

Parā has two aspects. In her lower aspect, she is one of the three goddesses; in her higher aspect called Mātṛ-sad-bhāva, or "the essence of the Mothers," she is the sum of the three goddesses. She is the apex of the hierarchy of feminine powers that are part of the cult of *yoginīs*, who are fierce, blood-thirsty female spirits decorated with skulls. Later, the cult was given a mystical interpretation. Mātṛ-sad-bhāva became the essence of sentient beings and the three goddesses became the three fundamental powers of a universe that is only consciousness. Parā was the potency of the subject (*pramātṛ*),

Aparā was the potency of the object (*prameya*), and Parāparā was the realm or cognitive medium (*pramāṇa*) that made the relationship between Parā and Aparā possible. Mātṛ-sad-bhāva was the ultimate unity of these three, which was revealed to worshippers who were liberated from the illusion of duality.

The *Parā-triṁśikā-tātparya-dīpikā* scripture invoked Parā as follows:

अकलङ्कशशाङ्काभा त्र्यक्षा चन्द्रकलावती ।
मुद्रापुस्त लसद्वाहा पातु वः परमा कला ॥

akalaṅka-śaśāṅkābhā
tryakṣā candra-kalāvatī
mudrā-pusta-lasad-vāhā
pātu vaḥ paramā kalā

May the supreme power (Parā) protect you, [who is as brilliantly white] as an unmarked moon, has three eyes, is adorned with the crescent moon [upon her hair], and whose hands are gesturing (*mudrā*) and holding a book.

(*Parā-triṁśikā-tātparya-dīpikā*, 2)

A verse from the *Parā-stuti* hymn of Sahajānanda-nātha describes Parā in the following way:

भक्तजनभेदभञ्जनचिन्मुद्राकलितदक्षपाणितलं ।
पूर्णहन्ताकारणपुस्तकवर्येण रुचिरवामकरम् ॥

bhakta-jana-bheda-bhañjana-cin-mudrākalita-
dakṣa-pāṇi-talaṁ
pūrṇa-hantākāraṇa-pustaka-varyeṇa
rucira-vāma-karam

Her right hand shows the gesture of consciousness, which destroys duality in [the minds of] her devotees, and her left hand displays [a bound manuscript of] the supreme scripture, which is the means of attaining the state [of liberation], the state of the unity that includes everything.

(*Parā-stuti*, *Nityotsava*, 196.5)

Parā is white and is associated with eloquence and learning. These characteristics, as well as the gestures of her hands, indicate that Parā was the Tantric aspect of the goddess Sarasvatī as the incarnation of the word (Vāgīśvarī) or the alphabet (Mātṛkā-sarasvatī, Lipi-devī). In the *Siddha-yogeśvarī-mata* scripture, Parā and Mālinī, the deity of the alphabet, are presented as two aspects of a single absolute word. The worshipper places Parāparā on the left prong of the trident, Aparā on the right, Mālinī in the center, and finally, Parā above Mālinī.

Abhinava-gupta explained that Mālinī and Mātṛka are identical to Parā. Parā is ultimate consciousness, *tattva* number 37, which is unity and totality beyond the 36 *tattvas* that were usually recognized in the *Śaiva* tradition. Parā is the abbreviation of *Parā-vāk*, or "the supreme word," which is the deep structure of reality, that is to say, the organic pattern of consciousness.

The *Trika* practice was a complex and beautiful system of linguistic mysticism: the Sanskrit language is composed of phonemes that are concretions of vibrations of subtle divine energy. They are the basis of thought and the fundamental building blocks of the manifested universe. The separation between words (signifiers) and objects (signified) is apparent since both originate in a single, non-dual matrix of subtle vibration, which is the supreme Word embodied as the goddess Parā.

The goddess Parā

2. Parāparā and Aparā

The icons of Parāparā and Aparā are basically *Kāpālika*. Unfortunately, we have little information about the details of their icons and their symbolic meanings. The *Siddha-yogeśvarī-mata* offers the most complete visual description. Parāparā was described as follows:

दक्षिणे तत्र शूलाग्रे न्यसेद्देवीं परापराम् ।
अष्टात्रिंशांस्तथा वर्णाञ्ज्वलत्पावकसंनिभाम् ॥
कपालमालाभरणां नेत्रत्रितयभासुराम् ।
विद्युज्जिह्वां महाकायां महासर्पविभूषिताम् ॥
विकरालां महादंष्ट्रां महोग्रां भ्रुकुतीक्षणाम् ।
महापन्नगसंवीतां शवमालाविभूषिताम् ॥
महाशवकराम्भोजचारुकर्णावतंसकाम् ।
प्रलयाम्बुदनिर्घोषां ग्रसन्तीमिव चाम्बरम् ॥

dakṣiṇe tatra śūlāgre
nyased devīṁ parāparām
aṣṭā-triṁśāṁs tathā varṇāñ
jvalat pāvaka-saṁnibhām

kapāla-mālābharaṇāṁ
netra-tritaya-bhāsurām
vidyuj-jihvāṁ mahā-kāyāṁ
mahā-sarpa-vibhūṣitām

vikarālāṁ mahā-daṁṣṭrāṁ
mahogrāṁ bhruku-tīkṣaṇām
mahā-pannaga-saṁvītāṁ
śava-mālā-vibhūṣitām

mahā-śava-karāmbhoja-
cāru-karṇāvataṁsakām
pralayāmbuda nirghoṣāṁ
grasantīm iva cāmbaram

> There, on the right prong, one should place the goddess Parāparā, the thirty eight syllables [as a mantra], [red] as blazing fire, wearing a garland of skulls, with three glowing eyes, she sits with a trident and a skull staff in her hands on [the shoulders of Sadā-śiva,] 'the great transcendent one.' Her tongue flickers in and out like lightning. Her gross body is adorned with great serpents. Her mouth yawns wide and has terrible fangs at its corners. Ferocious, with her brow enraged, she wears a sacred thread in the form of a huge snake and is adorned with a chain of human corpses around her neck, with the [severed] hands of a human corpse for lotuses to adorn her ears. Her voice is like the thunder of the clouds at the world's end, and she seems to swallow space itself.
>
> (*Siddha-yogeśvarī-mata*, 6.19–22)

This scripture says that Aparā looks the same but is reddish-black (*kṛṣna-piṅgalā*) instead of red. The *Piṅgalā-mata* instructs how to paint the three goddesses: Parā should be white, Parāparā should be black, and Aparā should be yellow. All three must have three faces, carry a trident, and be seated on lotus thrones.

Parāparā

Aparā

Teachings

The *Trika's* doctrine includes dualism, non-dualism, and a level beyond both. Parā is unity, Parāparā is unity in diversity, and Aparā is diversity. The great master Abhinava-gupta believed that this broad spectrum made the *Trika* the ideal cult to unite the entire tradition of Tantric Shaivism. He adopted the non-dualist version of the ritual, known as the *Kaula Trika*, which is an internalization that is thought to be superior and more esoteric.

Scriptures

The *Siddha-yogeśvarī-mata* is the scripture that teaches the cult of the three goddesses and has survived to the present. This scripture gave birth to the *Mālinī-vijayottara*, which became the basis of the *Śākta Trika* system. The *Mālinī-vijayottara* is part of a larger corpus that includes the *Bhairava-kula*, *Devyā-yāmala*, *Tantra-sad-bhāva*, *Tri-śiro-bhairava*, *Trika-kula-ratna-mālā*, *Trika-sāra*, *Vīrāvalī*, and *Yoga-saṁcāra*.

Three additional scriptures—the *Bīja-bheda*, *Bhairavodyāna*, and *Trika-sārottara*—indicate in their colophons that they are part of the *Siddha-yogeśvarī-mata* tradition.

The *Parā-triṁśikā*, or *Anuttara-triṁśikā*, taught a *Trika* cult called *Anuttara* or *Parā-krama*. It focused on the essence of these teachings and worshipped only Parā. Finally, the scripture *Vijñāna-bhairava* was probably related to the *Trika* cult, although it only included 112 meditations called *nistaraṅgopadeśa*.

Rituals

The three goddesses were worshipped externally with offerings that included alcoholic drinks and red meat. Their thrones were represented by *maṇḍalas*, which could be drawn on the ground as a square of dirt (*sthaṇḍila*), an image painted on cloth (*paṭa*), or a carving on a human skull (*tūra*).

Practice

We find the cult of *yoginīs* in all *Trika* scriptures, especially the network of *yoginīs* (*yogini-jāla*) as the cosmic hierarchy, from the subtlest to the grossest level of the cosmic manifestation. *Trika* ritual aims at liberation by going through the stages of the unfolding of consciousness in the opposite direction: from the grossest to the subtlest level, at which individual consciousness merges with the universal.

The three goddesses Parā, Parāparā, and Aparā are visualized sitting on lotus thrones on the three prongs of a trident. The person meditating imagines that the trident is his or her spine and visualizes the entire map of the sacred reality of 36 *tattvas* within his or her own body. The meditator ascends from the gross elements (*tattvas*) to the nucleus of the goddesses' triad through circuits of lower *yoginīs*. Upon reaching the three lotuses, the universe, space, and time are left behind. At this point, the meditator sees the three powers represented by the three goddesses merging into a single essence at the heart of his or her own consciousness. The meditator rests in the Self and all difference between the worshipper and the worshipped disappears. The three goddesses of the *Trika* are, in fact, expressions of the great goddess Mātṛ-sad-bhāva. This fourth invisible power is the secret doctrine of *Trika* (*trika-rahasya*). Mātṛ-sad-bhāva is the superior or internal nature of Parā. This is the fundamental and eternal nature, the essence of all that is.

Trika meditation

2.2.3.2 The *Śakti Tantras* – Kālī

Name

This section of the *Śakti Tantras* provides instructions on the worship of Kālī as "the destroyer of time" (Kāla-saṁkarṣiṇī). In this extreme left-hand cult, the goddess has supreme autonomy.

Scriptures

The main scripture is the *Jayad-ratha Yāmala Tantra*, also known as the *Śiraś-cheda*. Its 24,000 stanzas describe more than one hundred manifestations of the ferocious goddess Kālī. It is divided into four parts (*ṣaṭkam*) of 6000 verses each. The first part is the oldest and is dedicated exclusively to the worship of Kālī. The later three describe the worship of her numerous esoteric incarnations. These additions probably came from Kashmir and added material related to the posterior tradition called *Kālī-kula* or *Krama*, which we will discuss later.

Deities

1. Kāla-saṁkarṣaṇī

The goddess Kāla-saṁkarṣaṇī is described in the first *ṣaṭkam* of the *Jayad-ratha Yāmala Tantra*. She has five faces of different colors. The front face is black. Her appearance is both beautiful and fierce and she has twenty arms. She holds *Kāpālika* symbols such as the *khaṭvāṅga* (skull staff) and the *muṇḍa* (a decapitated head). A tiger skin smeared with blood covers her body. She stands on the body of Kāla (time) and embraces Bhairava with two arms. They are in the center of concentric circles of goddesses who are surrounded by their guards. A circle of cremation grounds surrounds this *maṇḍala* of goddesses. In an elaborate ritual, the goddesses and guards embrace their consorts. This ritual resembles the *Yāmala* cult of union between Kapālīśa-bhairava and Caṇḍā-kāpālinī; however, Bhairava has been replaced by Kālī and is completely absent from the ritual in the rest of the *ṣaṭkams*. Unlike the beautiful goddesses of the *Yāmala*,

Kālī is shown as a terrifying destroyer. She is the incarnation of the Absolute (*anuttaram*) that devours the ego of her devotees.

In the *Mantra-pīṭha* doctrine, Bhairava stands on Sadā-śiva. In the *Vidyā-pīṭha* doctrine, the goddess stands on Bhairava. With this declaration of superiority, the pantheon becomes completely feminine.

2. Vīrya-kālī

Vīrya-kālī means "Kālī of the fivefold power." The second *ṣaṭkam* describes her in detail. She has six dark faces and is as thin as a dying person. She is surrounded by brilliant light and her hair is on fire. Her body is adorned with necklaces of chopped-off heads and body parts of inferior deities. In her twelve hands she holds musical instruments such as a *ḍamaru* drum and a bell, weapons such as a spiked stick, a sword, and a shield, and *Kāpālika* elements such as a skull staff (*khaṭvāṅga*), a decapitated head, and a bleeding heart.

She rides on the shoulders of the horrific Kālāgni-rudra, "the god of the fire of final destruction." Half of his body is red and the other black, which represents inhalation and exhalation. We see *kuṇḍalinī* principles in this scripture. It explains that when both poles merge along the central axis, the state of supreme consciousness beyond the mind is manifested.

Vīrya-kālī

Teachings

Vīrya-kālī embodies the fivefold power (*vīrya*) that is the essence of all *Vidyā-pīṭha*. Her powers unfold in five phases:

1. *Bhāsā*: She is pure light (*bhāsā*) within the emptiness of Śiva (*śiva-yoma*).
2. *Avatāra*: She becomes embodied (as an *avatar*) as the first step toward manifestation.
3. *Sṛṣṭi*: She emits (*sṛṣṭi*) the content of the cosmic manifestation, which seems to be separate from consciousness.
4. *Kālī-krama*: She reabsorbs the content that she emitted.
5. *Mahā-saṁhādra*: During the great retreat (*mahā-saṁhādra*), she shines once again in her initial state as pure light.

Practice and Rituals

Devotees of Kālī meditate on this sequence (*krama*) to experience it in their own consciousness. They project reality from their own consciousness, reabsorb it, and it returns to its initial state. This cyclic movement is the pulsation of consciousness from moment to moment, and it is the same pulsation that creates and destroys the cosmic manifestation. Devotees visualize Kālī surrounded by blinding light and contemplate her as the deepest vibration (*spanda*) of consciousness.

3. Mahā-kālī

Teachings

The fourth *ṣaṭkam* of the *Jayad-ratha Yāmala Tantra* explains that the final version of the cult is the worship of Mahā-kālī, or "the great Kālī." She is worshipped in a black circle with a vermilion border. A ring of twelve circles surrounds it. Each circle contains a Kālī that has a different name but the same appearance as Mahā-kālī.

In this cult, we see the complete revelation of non-duality. Up to this point, rituals had a hierarchy of the source and its emanations. In contrast, this *maṇḍala* represents the perfect identity in essence (*sāma-rasya*) of the absolute and its manifestations. That is to say, there is no difference between the transcendental state of liberated consciousness (*nirvāṇa*) and its finite projection as the state of transmigratory existence (*saṁsāra*).

Practice and Rituals

The thirteen Kālīs are worshipped externally with orgiastic rites. But these goddesses must be revealed in the internal mystical experience. During sexual union with a *dūtī*, the practitioner experiences the void without ego (*nirahaṅkarā*) through the emptiness of the senses. This system called *Kālī-krama* or *Kālī-kula* connects this cult with the *Krama* that will be discussed later.

Mahā-kālī

4. Kālī-trika cult

The *Trika* and *Kālī* cults influenced each other. The *Jayad-ratha Yāmala Tantra* describes sects that incorporated the *Trika* of Parā, Parāparā, and Aparā. The *Trika* was also influenced by more esoteric cults, and at a later stage it worshipped Kāla-saṁkarṣaṇi above the three goddesses of the trident (*Devyā-yāmala Tantra*). Later, deities who were worshipped in Kālī rituals as incarnations of the phases of cognition were added to the advanced *Trika* ritual. In these rituals, the three goddesses united and emerged as a fourth mystical power. In the location where the goddesses united, the twelve Kālīs of the *Kālī-krama* were placed in a circle.

THE *TRIKA* MANDALA OF THE THREE TRIDENTS

2.3 Amṛteśvara-bhairava and Amṛta-lakṣmī

Name

The deity of this cult was Amṛteśvara, Śiva as the "Lord of the imperishable nectar," alongside his consort Amṛta-lakṣmī. The nature of Amṛteśvara is to grant blessings of nectar to all his devotees.

Description

Although this cult is rooted in the *Mantra-pītha* tradition, it declared itself to be universal and non-sectarian. It had basic rites that could be adapted to both *Saiddhāntika* and non-*Saiddhāntika* contexts. It was an eclectic system that offered specialized rituals applicable to each of the *Mantra-mārga* traditions. It was a domesticated and inoffensive Bhairava cult. Its remarkably flexible rituals made it possible to expand the reach of Tantric *ācāryas* within a Vedic-dominated society.

Chronology and geographic location

The text of this tradition was written between 700 and 850 CE and most likely after 800 CE. This lineage of Tantric Shaivism flourished in Kashmir. Although it did not attract the exclusive devotion of many followers, it was very influential because it was non-sectarian.

Deities

Amṛteśvara is visualized as shining white. He has a face with three wide-open eyes, which represent the three powers that manifest the universe: desire (*icchā-śakti*), knowledge (*jñāna-śakti*), and action (*kriya-śakti*). With two of his four arms, he holds a nectar jar, a symbol of the success he bestows, and a full moon, representing the elimination of fear and the unfolding of the true nature of the Self. With the other two hands, he displays gestures of blessing (*varada-mudrā*) and protection (*abhaya-mudrā*). He is sitting on the lunar disc in the center of a white lotus and is accompanied by his consort Lakṣmī.

Scriptures

This cult's principal divinely revealed scripture is the *Netra Tantra*, which means "the Tantra of the central eye of the Lord." It is also called *Amṛteśa-vidhāna* and *Mṛtyujit*.

Teachings and practice

Amṛteśvara's mantra is *Oṁ Juṁ Saḥ*. The *Netra Tantra* recognizes that all deities are emanations of the divine and indicates that this mantra can be adapted to any form of Divinity one wishes to honor. The mantra of Gaṇeśa, for example, would be *Oṁ Juṁ Saḥ Gaṇeśaya namaḥ*. This scripture also indicates that this mantra can animate deities of ancient lineages that have disappeared and lost potency.

Kṣemarāja, a disciple of Abhinava-gupta, wrote an extensive commentary on the *Netra Tantra* around the eleventh century CE. Following the example of his master, he included many non-dual teachings, such as his interpretation of Amṛteśvara's visualizations. He explains that the macrocosm is reflected as a microcosm in the individual. *Tāntrikas* should visualize the powers of the deity and experience them within themselves. He says that when the *Netra Tantra* instructs us to visualize the Lord of the gods in our own essence, it means that we must contemplate our own form as white and translucent, as the pure and blissful light of unlimited consciousness.

Rituals

The *Netra* teaches the cult of Amṛteśvara-bhairava and Amṛtalakṣmī. It describes a form of worship for use by royal officiants that could be adapted to any Tantric sect.

Amṛteśvara-bhairava and Amṛta-lakṣmī

Name	*Mantra-pīṭha*	*Vāma tantras*	*Yāmala tantras*	*Śakti - Trika*	*Śakti - Kālī*	*Amṛteśvara*
Name Translation	Seat of mantras	Left Tantras	Union Tantras	Triad	Destroyer of time	Lord of the everlasting nectar
Deities	Male deity: Svacchanda-bhairava , or "autonomous Bhairava".	The sisters Jayā, Vijayā, Ajitā, and Aparājitā alongside their brother Tumburu-bhairava.	Kapālīśa-bhairava, or "the Lord of the skull," and his furious consort Caṇḍā-kāpālinī.	Parā, Parāparā, and Aparā.	The goddess Kālasaṁkarsaṇī, Vīrya-kālī, and Mahā-kālī.	Amṛteśvara and his consort Amṛta-lakṣmī.
Scriptures	There were eight Tantras. The principal one was the *Svacchandra-tantra*.	The *Nayottara*, *Mahāsaṁmohana*, and *Mahāraudra*.	There were eight texts. The five main ones were the *Brahma Yāmala*, *Viṣṇu Yāmala*, *Rudra Yāmala*, *Skanda Yāmala*, and *Umā Yāmala*.	The *Siddhayogeśvarīmata* taught the cult of the three goddesses and has survived to the present.	The main scripture was the *Jayadratha Yāmala Tantra*, also known as *Śiraścheda*.	The principal divinely revealed writing was the *Netra Tantra*.
Doctrine	It does not seem to have had a clearly defined philosophy.	It seems that the deities were originally worshipped for victory in battle.	Through rituals and *sādhana*, aspirants sought to expand their consciousness, transcend all duality, and realize their authentic non-dual Bhairava nature.	The *Trika* cult's doctrine included dualism, non-dualism, and a level beyond both. Parā is unity, Parāparā is unity in diversity, and Aparā is diversity.	The Mahā-kālī cult included the complete revelation of non-duality.	The macrocosm is reflected as a microcosm in the individual. Tāntrikas visualized the powers of the deity and experienced them within themselves.

Name	*Mantra-pīṭha*	*Vāma tantras*	*Yāmala tantras*	*Śakti - Trika*	*Śakti - Kālī*	*Amṛteśvara*
Rituals	The cult of the goddess began to emerge, but she was still subordinate to Bhairava.	The *Vāma Tantras* described rituals for using magic against enemies and pacifying demons.	Rituals were directed to power-seeking ascetics. There was a world of magical powers and rituals with skulls that summoned spiritual powers in cremation grounds on nights with new moons.	The three goddesses were worshipped externally with offerings that included alcoholic drinks and red meat. Their thrones were represented by *maṇḍalas*.	The thirteen Kālīs were worshipped externally with orgiastic rites, but these goddesses had to be revealed through internal mystical experiences.	The *Netra* teaches the cult of Amṛteśvara-bhairava and Amṛta-lakṣmī. It describes a form of worship for use by royal officiants that could be adapted to any Tantric sect.
Practice	*Kāpālika* practices.	Transgressive practices to break social norms and mental conditioning.	Different initiations, sexual rituals, esoteric practices, and spiritual possession induced by *yoginīs* with a profuse Kāpālika imagery.	The meditator imagined that the trident was his or her spine and visualized the entire map of the sacred reality of 36 *tattvas* within his or her own body.	During sexual union with a *dūtī*, the practitioner experienced the void without ego (*nirahaṇkarā*) through the emptiness of the senses.	Adepts had to contemplate their own form as white and translucent, as the pure and blissful light of unlimited consciousness.

Chapter 4

The *Kula-mārga* or "the *Kaula* path"

The *Kula-mārga* tradition had a predominantly *Śākta* orientation and consolidated within Tantric Shaivism. *Śaiva* traditions mainly worship the masculine deity; *Śākta* traditions focus on the feminine. However, they have always overlapped and cannot be treated separately. The non-dual traditions present a male deity Śiva in union with his wife Śakti. The aspiration of this involutive path is to realize the union between the two within the human body.

Kula-mārga means "the path of the clans." One of the many explanations of this name is that it comes from the clans (*kulas*) of *yoginīs*. The male adept, or *vīra* (hero), was initiated into the *kaula* to obtain the *kaulika* power (*siddhi*) that would allow him to identify with the universal consciousness in the physical body.

Like the *Mantra-mārga*, the *Kula-mārga* offered liberation, but its approach had more in common with *Kāpālika* practices. Scholars suggest that this path developed directly out of the *Kāpālika* tradition and preserved almost all of its distinctive features in a more intensified and pure way. The followers of the *Kula-mārga* showed respect to the Brahmanical tradition as the source from which the revelation had emerged, but believed it was a path that could not grant liberation. Once members gained access to *Kaula* esoteric practices and literature, they still had to respect Brahmanism as valid for the uninitiated.

It is difficult to precisely date the *Kula-mārga's* beginnings. Current evidence suggests that it peaked in popularity in the ninth century CE, although it may have emerged at least a century earlier. Between the ninth and twelfth centuries CE, this tradition was very well established in Kashmir, in northern India.

This tradition offers two types of rituals: one is guided by *Mantra-mārga* texts that have a *Śākta* orientation, and another, considered superior, is found in the *Kula-mārga's* own texts, called *Kula-śāstras*. Instead of the elaborate initiation ritual that included oblations (*hautrī-dīkṣā*), these texts describe an initiation by inducing possession by the goddess (*āveśa*) and the consumption of sacramental substances (*caru-prāśanam*). The secret and mystical cults reserved for initiates included sexual relations with a consecrated consort (*dūtī*), blood sacrifices, and collective orgiastic rites. However, like in the non-*Saiddhāntika* current of the *Mantra-mārga*, public rituals were also performed for the protection of society and the state.

The *Kula-mārga* path was widely inclusive. It welcomed serious seekers, ascetics, or married people from all castes, including the so-called untouchables. Women were encouraged to practice and even become gurus. *Kaulas* argued that the caste system did not come from nature. Since it is a cultural construct, it should be ignored. Those who discriminated against other members were expelled from the group.

The attitude toward female deities that characterized the *Vidyā-pīṭha* Tantras further developed on this "final path" of *Śaiva* Tantric practice. Goddesses were placed above male consorts and were even worshipped alone. This path was rich in erotic and transgressive practices intended to break taboos and manners imposed by society and thus overcome the mind and achieve liberation. *Kaula* sacrifice (*yajña*) became an internal act. In fact, any effort to evoke supreme reality was considered a sacrifice. However, to not exclude its external aspect, adepts performed simple ceremonies in sacred places.

The *Kula-mārga* is composed of four main sub-traditions. They emanated from the four mouths of Śiva and were named after the cardinal points his faces were oriented toward: *Pūrvāmnāya* (eastern), *Uttarāmnāya* (northern), *Paścimāmnāya* (western), *Dakṣiṇāmnāya* (southern).

Description

The *Kula-mārga's* four traditions all embraced the *Kaula* cult founded by Macchanda-nātha. He was the first guru of the *Navanātha-sampradāya*, a lineage of nine gurus who were believed to have originated from the *ṛṣi* Dattātreya, an incarnation of the Hindu trinity: Brahmā, Viṣṇu, and Śiva. The new ritual system proposed by Kaulism influenced several existing *Mantra-mārga* traditions, which later developed into two versions: *Kaula* and non-*Kaula*. Thus, in certain traditions, aspirants could choose between *tantra-prakriyā* and *kula-prakriyā* initiation.

The original and later Tantra traditions had many differences. Initially, Tantra followed rituals prescribed by the Tantras that purified a hierarchy of *tattvas*, or "worlds," through offerings in a consecrated fire (*hautrī-dīkṣā*). The later *Kaula* proposed an initiation without ritual fire that focused on the essence rather than elaborate external ceremonies. The early Tantric Shaivism of the *Mantra-mārga* was characterized by Śiva worship, controlled ritualism, and a theology centered on transcendence. The *Kaula*, on the other hand, was Shaktism par excellence. It was characterized by transgression centered on Śakti, Shamanic rites of possession, and a theology centered on the immanent. Since the *Kaula* versions of the Tantric sects have survived and the non-*Kaula* forms disappeared, the word *tantra* is popularly used to denote practices that are, in fact, of *Kaula* origin.

Scholars argue that the *Kaula* tradition derived from the ascetic *Kāpālikas*, or *Soma-siddhānta*, of the *Ati-mārga*, and that it retains some of its distinctive characteristics. Actually, a three-stage evolution led to the formation of the *Kula-mārga* path:

1. The *Ati-mārga* sect of *Kāpālikas*: The *Kula* cult began with the practices of the *Kāpālika* ascetics in cremation grounds. They focused on worshipping the terrible aspect of Śiva as Bhairava alongside his consort. They placed special emphasis on the fierce goddess Cāmuṇḍā surrounded by eight Mothers, each with her own clan of *yoginīs*. *Yoginīs* were the retinue of the goddesses and the messengers of esoteric knowledge.

The ascetic culture of the cremation grounds is reflected in the *Kaula* iconography of the divine couple. The goddess Kuleśvarī and the god Kuleśvara were worshipped within a cremation enclosure and were decorated with ornaments made of human bones and skulls. To appease their ferocious deities, *Kāpālika* ascetics offered them blood, meat, alcohol, and sexual fluids. Sexual activity in Vedic society was governed by the *varṇāśrama* code of conduct. *Kāpālikas* broke social taboos by using sexual rites in worship and offering sexual fluids to their deities to obtain supernatural powers (*siddhis*).

While right-hand Tantra, like the *Śaiva-siddhānta*, modeled its religion on the ancient Vedic prototype, the *Kaula* was a left-hand tradition nourished by an equally ancient but more widespread part of Indian religion: a fascinating Shamanic visionary world of the propitiation of nature goddesses and animal-headed *yoginīs*. This cultural background provided a ritual framework that invited rejection and disgust among *Brāhmaṇas*. Ascetic practitioners performed these rituals in terrifying places with mortuary elements, such as human skulls and ashes of the dead. They invoked a group of wild and ferocious goddesses, often imagined as spirits of nature (*apsaras*, *ḍakinīs*, *mātṛs*, *grāhis*, and so on), who were led by a main goddess or Bhairava himself. According to the mythology, if the ritual was successful, the *sādhaka* would be accepted by the goddesses in their clan (*kula*) and would rise to heaven with them to become the leader of their wild band; in other words, he would become Bhairava.

2. The *Kaula* tradition, or Macchanda-nātha's cult of *yoginīs*: The cult of *yoginīs*, like the main initiatory cults of the *Vidyā-pīṭha*, was the specialty of the skull-bearing *Kāpālika* ascetics that withdrew from conventional society. If it were not for the reform of Macchanda-nātha (or Matsyendra-nātha) that probably took place around the ninth century CE, this cult would not have become popular beyond the cremation grounds. Matsyendra reconfigured *Kāpālika* rituals to make them more accessible to married people. This movement within esoteric Shaivism decontaminated *Kāpālika* mysticism and, among other reforms, eliminated some of its mortuary aspects and placed greater emphasis on the erotic element of the cult of *yoginīs*. In this phase, Bhairava was worshipped as Kuleśvara alongside his consort Kuleśvarī and the eight Mothers as the matriarchs of families or clans (*kulas*) of *yoginīs*. In this wild and visionary ritual, the practitioner sought contact (*melāpa*) with *yoginīs* either in disembodied form or embodied in a *dūtī*, or "sexual consort." *Yoginīs* took possession of women and thus were able to more intimately connect with their devotees. The savage and blood-thirsty *yoginīs*

replaced the male hierarchy from the *Mantra-mārga* tradition. They radiated from the heart of the deity and formed an omnipresent network of power (*yoginī-jāla*). They repopulated the ascending order of the *Śaiva* cosmos and radiated throughout sacred space, sending consecrated and venerated emanations into seats of power (*pīṭhas*) tied to cremation grounds throughout the Indian subcontinent.

The ritual's emphasis was less on feeding voracious deities and more on erotic and mystical relationships with them. These feminine deities—often represented as hybrids between humans, animals, birds, and plants—were both divine and demonic, terrible and benign. Humans traditionally worshipped them with blood offerings and animal sacrifices. If they were satisfied by these offerings, they would become embodied as attractive young women in order to gratify their human devotees and grant them supernatural powers (*siddhis*), for example, the ability to fly.

The *Kaula* phase was the domestication and essentialization of the *Kula*. Although scholars consider Kaulism a part of the Tantric tradition, it is, in fact, markedly different from the Tantric sects because it rejects external ritual, both *homa* and *liṅga* worship, and questions the basic meaning and purpose of ritualistic acts.

3. *Kula-mārga*: In the third evolutionary stage, this new revelation transformed some traditions that already existed in the *Mantra-mārga*, especially the *Vidyā-pīṭha*, and gave birth to new, purely *Kaula* traditions. Kaulism was not sectarian, since it did not worship a particular deity. Kuleśvara and Kuleśvarī could be identified with any sectarian deity, and thus, any Tantric cult could be reformulated into a *Kaula* version and reinterpreted in these new terms.

The *Kaula* is a body of techniques for controlling different beings, especially *yoginīs*, who were male practitioners' female ritual consorts.

Kaula practitioners aspired for supernatural powers (*siddhis*), bodily immortality (*jīvan-mukti*), supernatural enjoyment (*bhukti*), and liberation from the cycle of births and deaths (*mukti*). The main tools were:

- Mantras: Phonemes capable of controlling these beings, if pronounced in an appropriate manner and under favorable conditions.
- Possession: Techniques that would allow these beings to act in the body of the practitioners.
- Sacrifices and offerings: Gratifying these beings by offering them the contents of one's own body, which symbolize surrender at the feet of the deity. Sexual fluids were generated and ingested by the participants during rituals.

Kaulism developed into four main systems known as the four transmissions (*āmnāyas*): eastern, western, northern, and southern. Each had its own set of deities, mantras, *maṇḍalas*, and mythical saints. Kaulism was positioned as a higher and more refined version of Tantric practice that replaced meticulous rituals with visionary and subversive ones. Kashmir scholars formulated respectable metaphysics and soteriology based on *Kaula* ritual. They proposed a more subtle and essential version of the path. The Shaktism of this fourfold scheme of *āmnāyas* became very popular after the period of classical Tantra (c. 800–1200 CE). *Kaula* practices have survived, while many purely Tantric practices have gone extinct.

The development of Kaulism

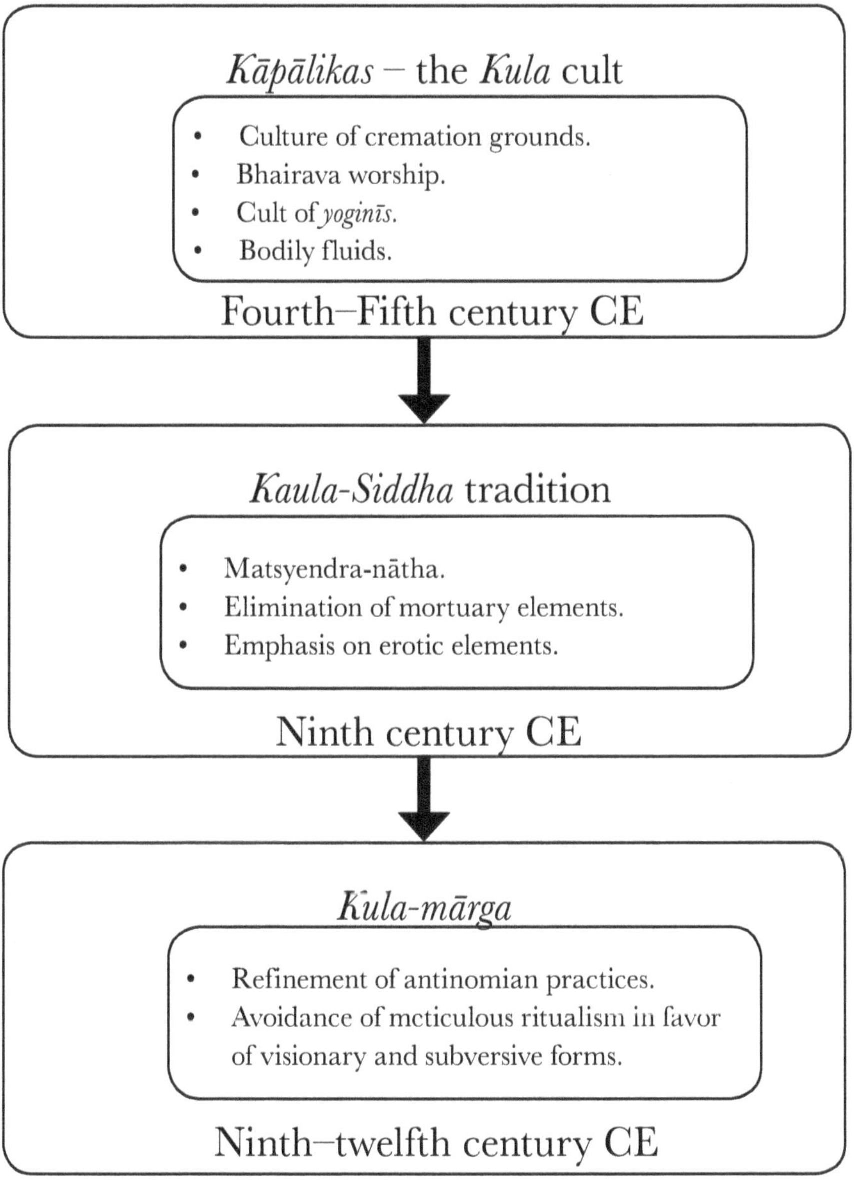
Kāpālikas – the *Kula* cult
• Culture of cremation grounds.
• Bhairava worship.
• Cult of *yoginīs*.
• Bodily fluids.
Fourth–Fifth century CE
Kaula-Siddha tradition
• Matsyendra-nātha.
• Elimination of mortuary elements.
• Emphasis on erotic elements.
Ninth century CE
Kula-mārga
• Refinement of antinomian practices.
• Avoidance of meticulous ritualism in favor of visionary and subversive forms.
Ninth–twelfth century CE

Name

It is not easy to translate *kula* or *kaula*. These terms are synonymous and are used interchangeably, although in this book we call the early stage *Kula* and the later *Kaula*. Literally, *Kula* means an autonomous unit, group, clan, or family. It refers to the cult of the eight mother goddesses and their incarnations in the "clans" of *yoginīs*. At the time of initiation, the adept became possessed (*āveśa*) and threw a flower at the *maṇḍala* that represented the eight clans of *yoginīs*. The place where the flower fell indicated the clan with which his soul had affinity. The adept became part of the selected family (*kula-sāmanyatā*). The powers that the *yoginīs* gave in exchange for the worship were called *kaulikī-siddhiḥ*.

In the later stage, Kaulism introduced a new level of esotericism based on a synonym of the term *Kula: Kaula*. *Kula* also means "body" and refers to the "body of power" (*śakti*), which implies the universe and includes the totality of phenomena. As a theological term, *kula* represents the *śakti*, while *akula* represents Śiva. This cosmic body includes the powers of the eight families of the Mothers. Philosophically, it denotes a unifying transcendental connection to the multiplicity of names and forms of the cosmic manifestation. Another meaning is "a group of people" committed to the practice of this spiritual discipline.

Circumstances of emergence

The chronology of these traditions cannot be determined with much precision, but we can safely say that the *Mantra-mārga* and *Kula-mārga* arose after the *Ati-mārga*. The earliest *Mantra-mārga* text is the *Niśvāsa-mūla* from 450–550 CE. *Mantra-mārga* teachings based on this corpus were established before the eighth century CE. The *Mantra-mārga* and *Kula-mārga* probably reached their apogee between the ninth and the twelfth centuries CE. Unambiguous evidence of the *Kula-mārga's* existence is in the *Hara-vijaya* text, written by Ratnākara of Kashmir at the beginning of the ninth century CE. It is possible that these events were contemporaneous and that the division between Tantra and *Kaula* was geographic, with *Kaula* located in the central strip of Vindhya, and Tantra concentrated in the north and south.

Both the *Kula-mārga* and the *Vidyā-pīṭha* have *Kāpālika* heritage. They pursued the same goals but developed different methodologies. Although they were both anti-Brahmanical in offerings and observances, the *Kaula* domesticated and decontaminated the teachings of the ascetics. Among other changes, the *Kaula* rejected the sectarian prejudice of the pioneering *Kāpālikas* and forbade *kapalā-vrata*. Moreover, it censored all types of external marks of sectarian affiliation, transferring ritual from ascetic living in the forest and cremation grounds to the lifestyle of respectable head of household who practiced at home or in private *Kula* meetings.

In the *Kaula* phase, ritual was intensified to cause sudden enlightenment. *Kaula* initiations (*kula-prakriyā*) shortened the *Mantra-mārga* version (*tantra-prakriyā*): *homa* was eliminated and three elements were added that were central in the *Kaula*: 1) the consumption of transgressive substances, such as consecrated liquor, as a proof of non-dual consciousness, 2) the initiation requirement of aspirants being possessed (*āveśa*) by Bhairava or the goddess, 3) the presence of an enlightened guru who dominates the spiritual stratum and can initiate someone with a glance, without the need for laborious rituals.

Other characteristics of the *Kula-mārga* were the erotic rituals with a female partner (*ādya-yāga*), orgiastic rituals (*vīrā-melāpa*), bloody practices for propitiating ferocious goddesses with animal and perhaps human sacrifices, and the idea that supernatural powers could be achieved by extracting vital fluids of living beings with yogic methods.

Kaula ritual did not belong to any particular sect; it was a methodology that emphasized the essence of ritual. It offered liberation not only for ascetics but for every sincere aspirant, without any distinction based on *varṇa* and *āśrama*. This tradition gained such popularity that over time it came to influence the *Vidyā-pīṭha* traditions, such as the *Trika* cult and the worship of Kālī, leading to new sects that adopted the *Kaula* reform, which we call *Kula-mārga*.

Despite its transgressive elements, the *Kula-mārga* was not only joined by marginal groups. Since these rituals were free of the mortuary elements and the *kāpālikas'* appearance, they attracted the attention of members of royal courts, where a refined and aestheticized version developed.

Deities

The texts of the *Kula-mārga*, also called *Kula-śāsanam* or *Kulāmnāya* (the teachings of *kula*), focused on the propitiation of the goddess Kuleśvarī, alone or alongside Bhairava (Kuleśvara), surrounded by the eight Mothers, and helped by Gaṇeśa and Vaṭuka. The four *yuga-nāthas*, the mythical and perfect gurus (*siddhas*) who spread the tradition in the four ages, were worshipped in an auxiliary cult alongside their consorts (*dūtīs*). The *siddha* of the Age of Kali is Macchanda-nātha, considered to be the founder of Kaulism. He is worshipped alongside his wife Koṅkaṇā and their six non-celibate sons (*rāja-putras*), revered as qualified (*sādhikāra*) to convey the cult of the *Kaula* alongside their consorts. They were the founders of the six lineages (*ovallis*) of Kaulism. At the time of consecration, aspirants were initiated into one of these lineages and received a name with an ending that identified the clan they belonged to. They learned the secret hand signs of the cult (*chommā*) used by members to identify each other. All lineages maintained networks of shelters near sacred sites throughout India for its members and recognized the legitimacy of its visitors through these secret signs.

Over time, rituals were divided into four liturgical systems, each with a distinctive pantheon. The *Ciñciṇī-mata* scripture describes the four systems of *Kaula* ritual, which are called *āmnāyas* (transmissions), one for each cardinal direction. As mentioned above, the eastern transmission (*Pūrvāmnāya*) was the original *Kaula* and worshipped Kuleśvara and Kuleśvarī. It developed out of the *Trika* from the *Mantra-mārga*, which worshipped the three goddesses Parā, Parāparā, and Aparā. The northern transmission (*Uttarāmnāya*) worshipped the goddess Kālī. The western transmission (*Paścimāmnāya*) venerated the goddess Kubjikā, and the southern transmission (*Dakṣiṇāmnāya*) focused on the beautiful goddess Kāmeśvarī, or Tripura-sundarī.

Philosophy and theology

The *Kula-mārga* traditions were non-dualist and believed that divinity was inherent to the manifestation. Instead of denying the world, they saw it as the realm where divinity was fully experienced. The universe was created for the self-realization of humans and it offers liberation to those who favor the Divine. Human beings are able to reveal the mysteries of this pulsating and vibrating universe. The universe is sexual and includes the polarity of Śiva and Śakti. Divinity is generally tied to Śiva; Śakti is its self-manifestation. It is a universe of hierarchical categories of existence (*tattvas*). The higher *tattvas* are closer to the source and reabsorb the lower ones. The Tantric universe is emancipatory and is born of the endless play of divine consciousness. Both gross matter and the human body are intrinsically free. Therefore, these traditions value experience and not only knowledge. Corporeal, practical, and concrete experience is liberating.

Kaula does not divide objects into pure and impure. The determining factor is our perspective. The only impurity is spiritual ignorance; knowledge is intrinsically pure. Nothing is impure if we recognize the supreme consciousness. Self-conscious adepts are not affected by external impurities and use what is reprehensible to achieve transcendence.

Main scriptures

Kula-mārga scriptures include the *Śākta* -orientated *Mantra-mārga* texts such as the *Mālinī-vijayottara* and the three later chapters (*ṣaṭkams*) of the *Jayad-ratha Yāmala*. These traditions had two different cults, one following the *Mantra-mārga* and the other following the *Kula-mārga*, which was considered superior. In addition, the *Kula-mārga* produced its own independent texts (*Kula-śāstras*), such as the *Kula-pañcāśikā*, *Kula-sāra*, *Kulānanda*, *Kaula-jñāna-nirṇaya*, and *Timirodghāta*.

- *Pūrvāmnāya*, the *Trika* school: The *Siddha-yogeśvarī-mata*, *Mālinī-vijayottara Tantra*, and *Śiva Sūtra*.
- *Dakṣiṇāmnāya*, the *Śrī-vidyā* school: The *Vamakeśvarī-mata* (consisting of *Nityā-ṣoḍaśikārṇava* and *Yoginī-hṛdaya*), *Jñānārṇava*, *Paraśurāma-kalpa Sūtra*, *Gāndharva Tantra*, *Tripurā-rahasya*, *Tantra-rāja*, *Prapañca-sāra*, and *Tripurārṇava*.
- *Paścimāmnāya*, the *Kubjikā* school: The *Kubjikā-mata*, *Ṣaṭ-sāhasra-saṁhitā*, *Ciñciṇī-mata-sāra-samuccaya*, and many others.

- *Uttarāmnāya*, which includes the *Krama*, *Kālī*, and *Tārā* schools: The *Krama Āgamas*, *Vātūla-nātha Sūtra*, *Mahā-kāla Saṁhitā*, *Parānanda Sūtra*, *Śakti-saṁgama Tantra*, *Kālī Tantra*, *Niruttara Tantra*, *Bṛhan-nīla Tantra*, *Toḍala Tantra*, *Yoginī Tantra*, *Yonī Tantra*, *Kula-cūḍā-maṇi*, *Mātṛka-bheda Tantra*, *Tārā Tantra*, *Kumārī Tantra*, *Mahā-cīnācāra-krama Tantra*, *Phet-kārīṇī Tantra*, *Nirvāṇa Tantra*, and many others.

Rituals

Kula-mārga practices are based on Tantra and related to the *Siddha* tradition and Shaktism. *Kaula* sects prescribed breaking taboos that limit consciousness and transgressing social customs as a means of liberation.

The *Kaula* originated in the cults of *Kāpālikas*, the inhabitants of the cremation grounds (*śmaśāna*). The *Kula-mārga* initiation was performed through possession (*āveśa*) by the goddess and consumption of sacramental substances that were considered impure (*caru-prāśanam*). When male adepts were possessed by a female deity, they obtained supernatural powers (*siddhis*).

Kaula sacrifice (*yajña*) was mainly an internal act. It was not about following certain regulations; rather, every action performed for the purpose of evoking the supreme reality was considered a sacrifice. However, the system would be limited and dual if it prohibited external sacrifice. For this reason, *Kaula* adepts also performed symbolic rituals in certain sacred places according to different ritual instructions.

The *Kaula* cult was very private and, more than anything, secret and mystical. It included sexual relations with consecrated consorts (*dūtīs*), blood sacrifices, and collective orgiastic rites celebrated by assemblies of initiates. However, certain public rituals were also performed for the protection of society and the state.

The cult of the *yoginīs* is of considerable importance in the Tantric literary sources of the *Kaula*. *Yoginīs* were semi-divine mythical beings that possessed human women in order to interact with the male devotees in the *Kaula* sexual ritual. In secular literature, these *yoginīs* were portrayed as powerful and dangerous women whom only brave men would approach or try to seduce. That is why men initiated in the *Kaula* sects were called *vīras*, or "virile heroes." They were also called *siddhas*, or "perfect beings," because they rose to the level of semi-divine beings to be the masculine partners of the *yoginīs* in India's medieval epic mythology.

Kaula revealed that *yoginīs* usually descend on certain nights of the lunar month or the solar year. They choose fearful places called clan seats (*kula-pīṭhas*) such as cremation grounds or remote hilltops (*kula-parvatas*). It was on those nights that female and male initiates met. These meetings were called *melakas*, *melanas*, or *melāpas*, which means "interlacing." During this *Kaula* practice par excellence, women were possessed by *yoginīs* and united with the heroic (*vīra*) or perfect (*siddha*) men in copulation.

Yoginīs descended from heaven to earth to participate in these meetings and merge with their loyal human devotees. But in order to fly, *yoginīs* needed to receive food. They asked for sacrifices of human or animal flesh. However, the most virile devotees, those perfected beings really eager to join the *yoginīs*, were able to offer them a more subtle and powerful source of energy. Through their practice, self-control, and passionate devotion, they offered them the distilled essence of their own bodily constituents: semen (*vīrya*). If the *yoginīs* were satisfied with the offerings, they imparted their grace to the surrendered *siddhas*. With their gallantry, *vīras* managed to seduce the indomitable *yoginīs* and receive their sexual fluids. The sensual and attractive *yoginīs* carried in their bodies the germinal plasma of Divinity that their courtiers longed for. Through the possessed bodies of the young and beautiful human *yoginīs*, these celestial fairies gave their devotees the nectar of the clan (*kulāmṛta*), also called the fluid of the clan (*kuladravyam*) and the essence of the vulva (*yonī-tattva*). When the heavenly *yoginīs* delighted in the semen of their courtiers, they agreed to give them the divine essence.

The *Kaula* tradition explains that the single divinity is externalized as a group of eight great goddesses. Each has her own retinue of eight *yoginīs*. Divinity occupies the center of the clan's *maṇḍala*, or the diagram through which grace flows. The eight mothers (*mātṛkas*) surround divinity, and the sixty-four *yoginīs* occupy the outer circles.

The divine essence of the clan diagram flows naturally in the women initiated into *Kaula*. But men who seek the divine nectar can only receive it through clan initiation and constant interaction with women possessed by *yoginīs*. These women give them the liquid essence of Divinity through sexual or menstrual discharge (*raja-pāna*) that emanates from their "mouths": the vulvas of *yoginīs*.

Through Tantric sex, esoteric knowledge is transmitted through the sexual fluid of the *yoginī's* vulva. She initiates the practitioner into the *Kaula* lineage and gives him the clan's fluid gnosis (*kula-jñāna*) through messages that are transmitted sexually.

In this erotic–mystic practice, *Kaula* practitioners consumed energetic substances in the form of sexual fluids through oral communion or a form of sex called *vajrolī-mudrā* (urethral suction). The *vīra* sucked the organ of his sexual partner and thus absorbed the fluids that gave him a mystical experience and supernatural powers. He could fly and ascend to the celestial strata with the *yoginīs* as the leader of the clan. This experience would be later reinterpreted as the ascension to divine consciousness.

Both the orthodox *Śaiva-siddhānta* traditions and the unorthodox *Kula* maintained that knowledge (*bodha*) and liberation were produced from substances (*drayas*). According to tradition, Matsyendra-nātha was initiated by the yoginis in Kāma-rūpa. He founded the *Yoginī Kaula*, which was the transition from the earlier *kula* of the *kāpālikas* to the later *Kaula* of the *Kula-mārga*. Because of their femininity and their sexual fluids, *yoginīs* could naturally complete what was lacking in the gnosis of the earlier *Kula* centered on masculinity.

In India, there are monumental temples dedicated to the sixty-four goddesses linked to the eight Mothers, which were probably built beginning in the tenth century CE. The celestial *yoginīs*, erotic and attractive, are often shown as hybrids of female human bodies with heads of animals and a rich iconographic symbolism. Their sculptures stand in circles, with the image of the central deity, mostly Bhairava, lying at the center. These temples have no roof, and it is believed that *kaula* practices took place there.

Over time, the *Kaula* revelation was gradually refined and began to put more emphasis on internalized yogic concepts. Consumption of mixed male and female sexual fluids continued to be a practice for those who aspired to obtain supernatural powers. Those who aspired for liberation offered the fluids of orgasm to their deities. With the refinement of this cult, the eight Mothers of the *yoginīs'* clans were linked to the eight constituents of the practitioner's subtle body: sound, touch, sight, taste, smell, volition, reason, and ego. In this way, the devotee became the very temple of his deities. He had to invoke the central deity (Kuleśvara or Kuleśvarī), who projected these Mothers, as his true identity, the transcendental consciousness of eternal bliss.

The *Kāpālikas* of the *Vidyā-pīṭha* sought to merge with the *yoginīs* through a process of visionary invocation, attract them from heaven, gratify them with an offering of their own blood, and ascend with them as their leader. This visionary fantasy was restated in aesthetic terms by *Kaulas* as a mystical experience. The *yoginīs* were in essence their own senses (*karaṇeśvarīs*) and were revealed through bodily sensations.

In texts such as the *Mālinī-vijayottara*, mortuary rituals were replaced by internal yogic practices that involved observing the *śaktis* within the human body. The *Kubjikā-mata*, for example, describes a series of bodily chakras at the locations of five groups of female deities: *devīs* (goddesses), *dūtīs* (consorts), *mātṛs* (mothers), *yoginīs*, and *khecarīs* (travelers from heaven).

Tantric sex, instead of a means to produce fluids to satisfy external deities, became a way of obtaining the experience of orgasm that satisfied the inner deities of the senses (*yoginīs*). It also allowed the central deity (Kuleśvara or Kuleśvarī) to penetrate and expand the consciousness of bliss. In this way, *Kaula* liturgy and rituals became a means to intensify orgasmic experiences.

In general, when intense pleasure is experienced, inner consciousness becomes cloudy and one becomes a victim of desires (*paśu*). However, when one overcomes the identification with the ego, external sources of sensation become subtle and shine within the cognition in their aesthetic forms. Thus, the *yoginīs* of the senses savor the offerings of pleasure as nectar. When they are gratified, they merge with the practitioner's inner transcendental identity, which is the enlightened consciousness of transcendental bliss.

These goddesses, gratified by the bodily fluids offered internally by the practitioner, ascend along his spine to converge in the cranial vault. Here we find the origins of the practice of *khecarī-mudrā*, in which the practitioner internally drinks the nectar, elevated and refined through his practice of hatha yoga, to attain immortality.

The *Kaula* aspires to self-sufficiency and liberation. This path encourages devotees to overcome mental and egoistic limitations and free themselves from external social and cultural preconceptions.

Social conditioning is overcome by dissociating traditional distinctions between pure and impure and being adopted by the guru's spiritual family. Mental freedom is achieved by awakening the *kuṇḍalinī* through the practice of asanas, *prāṇāyāma*, *mudrās*, and mantras. Consciousness is elevated by amplifying and sublimating vital and mental energies. This process culminates in spiritual enlightenment.

Members

In the *Kula-mārga*, women can be priestesses and gurus, initiate disciples, found their own ashrams, and hold religious positions. Although not all female aspirants did this, there were many holy women. The *Kaula* Tantras explain that women are purer sources of transmission to grant sacred revelation. Tantric knowledge must be transmitted through *yoginī-mukha*, "the lips of self-realized *yoginīs* and enlightened women." Many *Āgamas* are dialogues in which the goddess Pārvatī or Bhairavī assumes the role of guru and grants the revelation to Śiva. Numerous texts mention that many *Tāntrikas* received their first inspiration and subsequent initiation from ascetic women or *yoginīs*. Moreover, it is believed that for a doctrine to be valid as a revelation, it must be revealed by a *yoginī*.

Such *yoginīs* also appear in a disembodied form: in dreams or trance-like states. The *Kaula-jñāna-nirṇaya* text speaks of the *Yoginī Kaula* tradition that originated in Assam, northeast India. This tradition was transmitted orally through a line of female ascetics (*siddhas*) who were liberated through *Kaula sādhana*. In the *Krama* sect of Kashmir, the first Tantric ascetics received this knowledge from "the lips of the *yoginīs*." Tantras repeatedly state that female gurus have the authority to initiate (*dīkṣā*) and that their initiations are more effective because they are identical to the supreme goddess.

Tantra gives prominence to the feminine principle and recognizes the ritualistic role of women in *Śākta-dharma*. Many rules did not apply to women, because they were all considered gurus. In some cases, there were fewer restrictions for women than for men. If they simply received the main mantra, they could assume the role of a guru and initiate others by reading the mantra from an authoritative text. Men and women share the same metaphysical and social space. This tradition does not discriminate based on caste or gender in terms of spiritual *sādhana*. The precepts of *Śākta* Tantra are applicable to both men and women. Married and unmarried women, as well as female ascetics, have access to Tantric practice.

Āmnāyas or "transmissions"

The *Kaula* traditions were systematized into *āmnāyas*, or "transmissions," during the eleventh century CE. The term *ānmnāya* refers to specific groups of scriptures within the *Kula Āgamas* that share a common affiliation.

आदित्वात्सर्वमार्गाणां मनोल्लासप्रवर्द्धनात् ।
यज्ञादिधर्महेतुत्वादाम्नाय इति कीर्तितः ॥

āditvāt sarva-mārgāṇāṁ
manollāsa-pravarddhanāt
yajñādi-dharma-hetutvād
āmnāya iti kīrtitaḥ

Because it is the premier (*āditva*) among all paths, because it sets into movement joy in the mind (*manollāsa*), because it is the cause of dharma in the form of sacrifice (*yajña*), and so on, it is called *āmnāya* (transmission).

(*Kulārṇava Tantra*, 17.48)

The original division seems to have included four *āmnāyas*, each one symbolically placed at a compass point. The earliest scriptures named only four *āmnāyas*, sometimes correlated with the four ages (*yugas*). *Paścimāmnāya* is the most relevant *āmnāya* in the current Age of Kali. Later texts mention five, six, or even seven *āmnāyas*. The division of five is equated with the five vital breaths (*prāṇas*), comprising the four original *āmnāyas* and a superior one called *Anuttarāmnāya* (ultimate or supreme tradition). In the division of six, another called *Ūrdhvāmnāya* (superior tradition) is added. Alternatively, the sixth one could be the lower mouth (*Īśāmnāya*), which is the mouth of the *yoginī*.

These sacred doctrines were paths of liberation that could be learned only through the guidance of a self-realized guru. Various *Kaula* sources state that these five traditions flow from the five mouths of Śiva, represented either by the five-headed Sadā-śiva as he is worshipped in the *Śaiva-siddhānta* tradition or by the *pañca-mukha-liṅga*, which is a five-faced phallic image of Śiva. The *Kulārṇava Tantra* states:

मम पञ्चमुखेभ्यश्च पञ्चाम्नायाः समुद्गताः ।
पूर्वश्च पश्चिमश्चैव दक्षिणश्चोत्तरस्तथा ।
ऊर्ध्वाम्नायश्च पञ्चैते मोक्षमार्गाः प्रकीर्त्तिताः ॥

mama pañca-mukhebhyaś ca
pañcāmnāyāḥ samudgatāḥ
pūrvaś ca paścimaś caiva
dakṣiṇaś cottaras tathā
ūrdhvāmnāyaś ca pañcaite
mokṣa-mārgāḥ prakīrttītāḥ

The five *āmnāyas* (transmissions), which are secure paths to liberation, emerged from my five faces looking east, west, south, north, and upward.

(*Kulārṇava Tantra*, 3.7)

Each of Śiva's faces is oriented toward a different cardinal point and reveals one of the five *āmnāya* traditions. The Īśāna face looks east and expresses *Pūrvāmnāya* wisdom. The Aghora face looks south and expresses *Dakṣiṇāmnāya* wisdom. The Tat-puruṣa face looks west and expresses *Paścimāmnāya* wisdom. The Sad-yojāta face looks north and expresses *Uttarāmnāya* wisdom. Finally, the Vāma-deva face looks up and expresses *Ūrdhvāmnāya* wisdom.

Pūrvāmnāya represents creation and offers the path of the mantra to realize divinity. *Uttarāmnāya* symbolizes the grace of God (*anugraha*) and it is the path of pure knowledge. *Paścimāmnāya* represents the destruction of duality and it is the path of karma yoga through which realization can be achieved. *Dakṣiṇāmnāya* represents maintenance and reveals the path of devotion. *Ūrdhvāmnāya* emanates from the face that looks upward and is Śiva himself in his absolute form.

1. The *Pūrvāmnāya* (eastern or previous transmission) worships Kuleśvara and Kuleśvarī and later the *Trika* goddesses Parā, Aparā, and Parāparā.
2. The *Uttarāmnāya* (northern or later transmission) worships the goddess Kālī. It is also known as *Krama*, or "sequence."
3. The *Paścimāmnāya* (western or final transmission) worships the goddess Kubjikā.
4. The *Dakṣiṇāmnāya* (southern transmission) worships the goddess Kāmeśvarī.
5. The *Ūrdhvāmnāya* (upper transmission) worships Ardhanārīśvara, who is half Śiva and half Śakti.

   (a) *Anuttarāmnāya* (final or supreme transmission) is a transmission that evolved out of *Dakṣiṇāmnāya* and gave birth to the Tripura-sundarī cult, believed to include and surpass all *āmnayas*.

   (b) *Īśāmnāya*: Some sources consider that the sixth transmission emanates from the face of Śiva that looks down. It is also interpreted as the lower mouth of the *yoginī*, meaning, her vulva. It refers to the *Kaula* cult of *yoginīs* (*yogini-kaula*), which was the *Kaula Siddhas* tradition founded by Matsyendra-nātha.

The *Kulārṇava Tantra* describes it as follows:

पूर्वाम्नायः सृष्टिरूपः स्थितिरूपश्च दक्षिणः ।
संहारः पश्चिमो देवि उत्तरोऽनुग्रहो भवेत् ॥

pūrvāmnāyaḥ sṛṣṭi-rūpaḥ
sthiti-rūpaś ca dakṣiṇaḥ
saṁhāraḥ paścimo devi
uttaro 'nugraho bhavet

The central truth of *Pūrvāmnāya* is creation (*sṛṣṭi*); that of *Dakṣiṇa* is maintenance (*sthiti*), that of *Paścima* is destruction (*saṁhāra*), and that of *Uttara* is compassion (*anugraha*).

(*Kulārṇava Tantra*, 3.41)

मन्त्रयोगं विदुः पूर्वं भक्तियोगश्च दक्षिणम् ।
पश्चिमं कर्मयोगश्च ज्ञानयोगं तथोत्तरम् ॥

mantra-yogaṁ viduḥ pūrvaṁ
bhakti-yogaś ca dakṣiṇam
paścimaṁ karma-yogaś ca
jñāna-yogaṁ tathottaram

The path of *Pūrva* is mantra yoga, that of *Dakṣiṇa* is bhakti yoga, that of *Paścima* is karma yoga, and that of *Uttara* is *jñāna-yoga.*

(*Kulārṇava Tantra*, 3.42)

उर्ध्वाम्नायस्य चैतानि न सन्ति कुलनायिके ।
साक्षाच्छिवस्वरूपत्वान्न किञ्चित्कर्म विद्यते ॥

urdhvāmnāyasya caitāni
na santi kula-nāyike
sākṣāc chiva svarūpatvān
na kiñcit karma vidyate

O Kula-nāyikā! There are none of these in the *Ūrdhvāmnāya*. Since it is in the exact form of Śiva, it has no karma.

(*Kulārṇava Tantra*, 3.45)

These sects are called transmissions because esoteric knowledge was transmitted through *yoginīs* and gurus. These divisions can be called "systematic genealogies" or "flow charts." The flow of teachings, traditions, and liturgy is transmitted, ultimately, in the form of sublimated sexual fluids, which originate in the supreme deity and emanate through the goddesses and *yoginīs* through the transmission of the clan liquid to its suborders.

Kaula traditions were based on oral transmissions passed secretly from masters to disciples of proven courage, seriousness, and commitment, because only in this way could the tradition be preserved and protected from abuse. Its essence cannot be learned from books. Gurus are not merely sources of information, but they can decipher the codes of the scriptures and explain their subtle meanings. They are vehicles through which the occult power of the teachings is transmitted. With immense grace, the guru initiates souls who are thirsty for liberation and opens the door for them to a new existential condition of liberated souls. Through the master, divinity transmits the teachings that are beyond words.

A transition happens at the moment of initiation, when disciples receive mantras that will accompany them on the path toward self-recognition. The mantras from the scriptures are ineffective unless an enlightened master fills them with vitality through the power of his or her consciousness. Only mantras duly uttered by someone who has activated the hidden energy of his or her own consciousness can transmit that power to others.

1. *Pūrvāmnāya* or "eastern transmission": Īśāna Face

Name

Pūrvāmnāya means "eastern transmission." It is thought to be the closest to the original *Kaula* tradition.

Description

The *Trika* of the *Vidyā-pīṭha* was the first Tantric sect to be influenced by the *Kaula* and gave birth to the *Kaula Trika*. This path cleansed the Tantric practice from elaborated rituals that could distract practitioners from the essence. It condensed the liturgy to make room for the spontaneity of the experience itself (*tan-mayī-bhāva*, *samāveśa*).

Chronology and location

The *Kaula* form of the cult flourished in Kashmir beginning around 900 CE. The exegesis of *Trika* literature, written in Kashmir toward the end of the tenth century CE, describes that there had long been a clear hierarchical distinction between inferior Tantric worship (*tantra-prakriyā*) and the superior *Kaula* tradition (*kaula-prakriyā*).

Kaula Trika literature has not survived, so we know of its existence only from quotations in the exegetic literature from Kashmir. However, there is a reason to believe that this tradition did not originate in Kashmir. Scholars think that there was a previous developmental phase. Quotations from scriptures such as the *Mālinī-vijayottara Tantra* and *Tantra-sad-bhāva Tantra* do not mention the goddess Kālī or Kāla-saṁkarṣiṇi, nor do they present the world as a projection into and from consciousness. This was central in the subsequent development of the *Trika* in Kashmir.

Deities

The *Kaula Trika* tradition worshipped the goddesses Parā, Parāparā, and Aparā. It was strongly influenced by earlier *Krama* traditions.

I. The early period – before 800 CE.

In its beginnings, the *Trika* was a system of rituals to obtain the powers of the goddesses Parā, Parāparā, and Aparā. The eight Mother goddesses and their incarnations in *kulas* (clans) of *yoginīs* were part of this cult. *Yoginīs* were invoked and propitiated with offerings of alcohol, blood, meat, and sexual fluids. Adepts joined one of the eight clans at the time of initiation and then worshipped their clan's *yoginīs* to receive *siddhis* and gnosis.

II. Second phase of development – after 800 CE.

At this stage, the worship of Kālī was incorporated as the transcendental goddess to Parā, Parāparā, and Aparā, who were her emanations. The pantheon from the cognition cycle of *Krama* Shaivism was incorporated later, probably in Kashmir.

III. Third phase of development – starting around 900 CE.

The *Trika* continued its development as part of Kashmir Shaivism. It was influenced by the metaphysics of *Pratyabhijñā* and left behind the visionary world to emphasize internal experience. Instead of performing rituals to receive powers, adepts engaged in rituals of inner contemplation and selfless action. These rituals were secondary and could be set aside to focus on experiencing the essence.

The erotic–mystic *Kaula* cults were reserved for a minority of very advanced followers who were ready for these esoteric practices. Abhinava-gupta advanced the idea that the purpose of interaction with *yoginīs* through *dūtīs* was not the transmission of gnosis through the exchange of sexual fluids but the moment of orgasm itself, which revealed the dynamism of the supreme Being and allowed adepts to experience a glimpse of the joy of consciousness.

In this phase, the cult aimed to unify all *Śaiva* traditions, from the *Śaiva-siddhānta* to the *Bhairava tantras* as well as the *Kaula* and *Krama*.

Scriptures

Many *Trika* scriptures had a *Kaula* orientation. These have not survived, and the only references that we have are quotations of the scriptures in Abhinava-gupta's *Tantrāloka* and Jaya-ratha's commentary. The main scriptures of this *āmnāya* are the *Yoga-saṁcāra*, *Tri-śiro-bhairava*, *Trikasāra*, *Trika-kula-ratna-mālā*, *Bhairava-kula*, and *Vīrāvalī*. There is not much information about the rituals, but the scripture *Virāvalī* describes the highest *Kaula* practice, which emphasized the internal experience of the worshipper.

The *Siddhakhaṇḍa* explains that different scriptures offer deeper wisdom and higher means of liberation. It organizes the following scriptures on an ascending scale:

- *Bhairava tantras*
- *Mālinī-vijayottara*
- *Bhairava-kula*
- *Vīrāvalī*
- *Krama*
- *Manthāna-bhairava*

Teachings

The *Trika* advocated non-dualist idealism within Shaivism.

Rituals

In the *Kaula Trika* cult, the divine *Kaula* couple (Kuleśvara and Kuleśvarī) was drawn or visualized in the center of the *maṇḍala*. They were surrounded by a triangle. The three goddesses Parā, Parāparā, and Aparā occupied the triangle's vertices. This tradition had both external and internal ritual. External ritual was performed on a red cloth spread on the ground, in a circle of vermilion powder with a black border.

The ritual could be offered to the genitals of the *dūtī* or during sex with her. The tradition was then internalized and the deities were worshipped within one's own body as *prāṇa* using a visualization of the nectar of breath. Even more subtle was the *smvidi-pūjā* ritual in which worship takes place only in thought.

Initially, aspirants worshipped the entire *Kaula* pantheon, which was enriched as indicated above. As they reached higher levels of consciousness, they worshipped fewer and fewer deities until they worshipped only Kuleśvara.

An important component of this *āmnāya* was the worship of *yuga-ṇāthas*. The original *Kaula* teachings were transmitted by the founding masters of Kaulism and, therefore, they must be venerated in all *Kaula* cults. Before beginning the ritual, officiants had to be purified by projecting the mantras of Parā and Mālinī onto their bodies in the prescribed manner. Once they were filled with cosmic power, they identified their Bhairava nature. They then offered libations to Bhairava and recognized the energy circles that surrounded them as their own sensory and mental powers. To do this, they drank a mixture of male and female sexual fluids (*kuṇḍa-golaka*) from a previously filled sacrificial jar. In this way, officiants reached a vision of the fullness of their universal nature, brilliantly manifested by the energy of the sacrificial offering. If they wished to see this same fullness manifested in the external world through an overflow of their sensory energies, they proceeded with the external ritual. This began with the worship of the *Kaula* masters in a sacred circle (*maṇḍala*) called *siddha-cakra*, drawn on the ground with colored powders.

There was a triangle that represented the divine matrix (*yonī*). In its center Kuleśvarī resided in a state of excitement in union with Paramānanda-bhairava, from whom *kula* flows, the blissful power of emission (*visarga-śakti*) from which the cosmic order is generated. The *maṇḍala* triangle was worshipped by contemplating the creative flow of bliss in the unity of the universal consciousness. Its microcosmic equivalent is the female sexual organ. This ritual could be performed in elevated states of consciousness or through the static experience of physical orgasm. The goddess emerged from the center of her energies alongside Paramānanda-bhairava. In this way, *kula* emerged, and the worship of the *yuga-nāthas* came to fruition. The *maṇḍala* the *yuga-nāthas* were worshipped in was divided into five sections:

1. The mantras of the *Trika* goddess.
2. The masters of the *Kaula*.
3. The sphere of the Mālinī Wheel, which corresponds to the flow of vital breath.
4. The sphere of the Mātṛkā Wheel, which corresponds to the activity of consciousness.
5. The outer square, which represents the senses.

All together they constituted *kula*, the micro–macrocosmic totality. In the center resided the goddess Kuleśvarī, who could be worshipped in the form of any of the three *Trika* goddesses, alone, or with her male consort Kuleśvara.

Practice

When adepts were initiated in the *Kaula Trika* cult, their spiritual master put them on the path to liberation and removed all obstacles that might appear at various levels of the cosmos. He helped them reach the subtlest level, united them with the supreme deity, equipped them with a divine body, and returned them to the material world as initiates free of all karmic attachments. Unlike the Tantric ritual in which initiates remained passive while offerings were placed in a fire, these initiates entered a trance, had direct experiences of the various levels of the cosmos, and showed signs of being possessed (*āveśa*).

The *Vīrāvalī* scripture explains that *āveśa* is a better method. Initiates would lose control of themselves as the goddess possessed their bodies and consciousness. The *Vīrāvalī* proposed the *sāmarasya* method, in which the master spontaneously merges with the disciple.

Members

Unlike the Tantric version, the *Kaula Trika* mostly attracted married people. Only *Kāpālikas* could follow the demanding and intense Tantric tradition. Kaulism offered a domesticated form of the tradition and welcomed fervent married aspirants, putting more emphasis on divine possession and mystical experiences.

2. *Uttarāmnāya* or "northern transmission": Sadyo-jāta Face

Name

Uttarāmnāya means "the northern transmission," and it emanated from the Sad-yojāta face of Sadā-śiva.

Description

After influencing the *Trika*, the *Kaula* was embraced by the cults of the goddess Kālī from the *Kālī Tantras* of the *Vidyā-pīṭha*. In merging with the *Kaula*, it gave birth to a tradition that became the most extreme in monism, worship of the feminine, inclusion of castes and genders, transgression of social norms, and mortuary symbolism. Unlike the rest of the *Kula-mārga* sects, this tradition did not prohibit *Kāpālika* elements.

What came to be called *Uttarāmnāya* included three doctrines dedicated to the worship of Kālī:

1. *Mata*, or "doctrine": We do not know much about this tradition, since it disappeared without leaving much information. We do know that it originated from the *Jayad-ratha Yāmala* scripture. The *Kaula Mata* worshipped the Kālīs of the *Kālī-krama*. It also worshipped deities with animal faces and numerous heads. Three wonderful deities are found at the center of its pantheon: Trailokya-ḍāmarā (the terrifier of the universe), Mata-cakreśvarī (the goddess of the *mata* circle), and Ghora-ghoratarā (the most terrible of the terrible). The scarce evidence we have is from the *Ciñciṇī-mata-sāra-samuccaya*, which presents two mystical texts of twelve and fifty verses, which are probably related to the mythical gurus Vidyānanda-nātha and Niṣkriyānanda-nātha, respectively.
2. The cult of the goddess Guhya-kālī: It emerged from the *mata* doctrine. She has three faces of the *mata* goddesses Trailokya-ḍāmarā, Mata-cakreśvarī, and Ghora-ghoratarā. Her three-faced and eight-armed form was worshipped as a transcendent unity. She had a dark complexion and danced on the body of Bhairava in the cremation grounds.

Beginning by the tenth century CE, the abstract Kālīs from the *Kālī-krama* took an iconic form in this cult as the retinue of Guhya-kālī. In general, as Tantra evolved, its deities were worshipped less as icons and more as amorphous mystical energies. However, we often see that later developments become less subtle and, instead of continuing this tendency, go back to more concrete forms of deity worship.

The first mention of this cult is found in Vimala-prabodha's *Kālī-kula-kramārcana*. This is a manual that provides instructions on Tantric ritual and reciting mantras. This text and many others from that tradition are preserved in Nepal, where Gukya-kālī was worshipped as the esoteric and fearsome aspect of Guhyeśvari, the main local goddess.

Gukya-kālī

3. *Krama* (sequence) is also called the Great Path (*mahā-naya*), the Great Truth (*mahārtha*), and the Path of the Goddess (*devī-naya*). *Krama* literature has a much more elaborate *Kaula* system of Kālī worship. The pantheon of other sects is concentric, but in the *Krama* it is organized in phases or sequences. Kālī is worshipped as the central deity (Bhagavatī-saṁvid) in a sequence of deities located in a circle around her. These twelve Kālīs embody the successive phases of the cyclic pulse of cognition (*saṁvid*). Dynamic consciousness must be contemplated through sequential worship, following the cyclic ebb and flow of the worshipper's consciousness in the perception of objects. The *Krama* is the sequential display of the phases of consciousness present in every cognition. *Krama* initiates venerated these phases as emanations of Kālī Kāla-saṃkarṣiṇī, the supreme deity of the cult. She is the insatiable void at the heart of consciousness. She can only be accessed by disintegrating the limited ego.

The term *krama* means "progress, gradation, stages, or succession" and refers to the gradual refinement of cognition as a means of liberation. *Krama's* aspiration is development and purification through a series of successive phases from darkness to perfect clarity.

The *Devī-pañca-śatikā* is the most authoritative scripture that describes these four or five phases:

1. Emission (*sṛṣṭi-krama*).
2. Maintenance of the emitted (*sthiti-krama*), also called incarnation (*avatāra-krama*).
3. Retraction of the emitted (*saṁhāra-krama*).
4. The unnamable (*anākhya-krama*), also called the phase of the Kālīs (*kālī-krama*). In this phase, all trace of the preceding process dissolves in the liberated and omnipresent consciousness. This phase is identical to the thirteen (12 + 1) Kālīs of *Mata*. This group of deities is the most constant feature among Kālī cults.

5. The *Krama-sad-bhāva* scripture further elaborates on the tetradic *Krama* tradition and creates the pentadic *Krama*, adding a fifth phase to the four previous ones: Pure Light (*bhāsā-krama*). It worships a system of sixty-four *yoginīs* or *śākinīs* in five phases as the prelude to the worship of the Kālīs of the unnamable.

The *Krama* scriptures present a detailed epistemological analysis of the cognitive experience and define twelve stages of perception, each presided over by one of the Kālī goddesses. The cult of the Kālīs is an important aspect of this tradition. In the cognitive process, our attention shifts from our interior to the perceived object and then returns to the mental recipient that we have created, giving us a certain feeling.

The twelve Kālīs correspond to the twelve movements of cognition. When we observe an object, the sensation travels from our thoughts to the object's place and then returns to our thoughts, resulting in the cognition of the object. We do not perceive the object where it is but in our mind. Perception moves from within us to the object and then returns from the object to our thoughts. These movements are distributed in twelve forms like the twelve Kālīs in the *Krama* system.

THE THIRTEEN KĀLĪS OF THE *KĀLĪ-KRAMA*

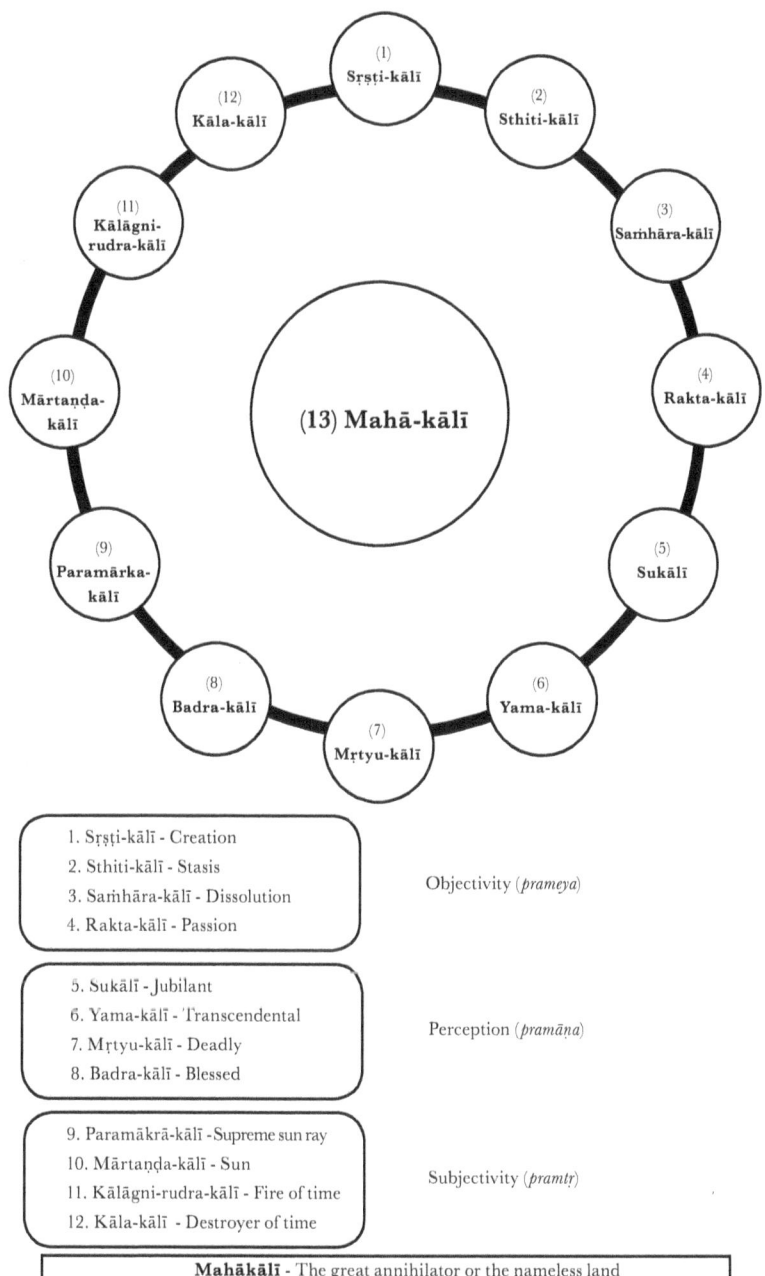

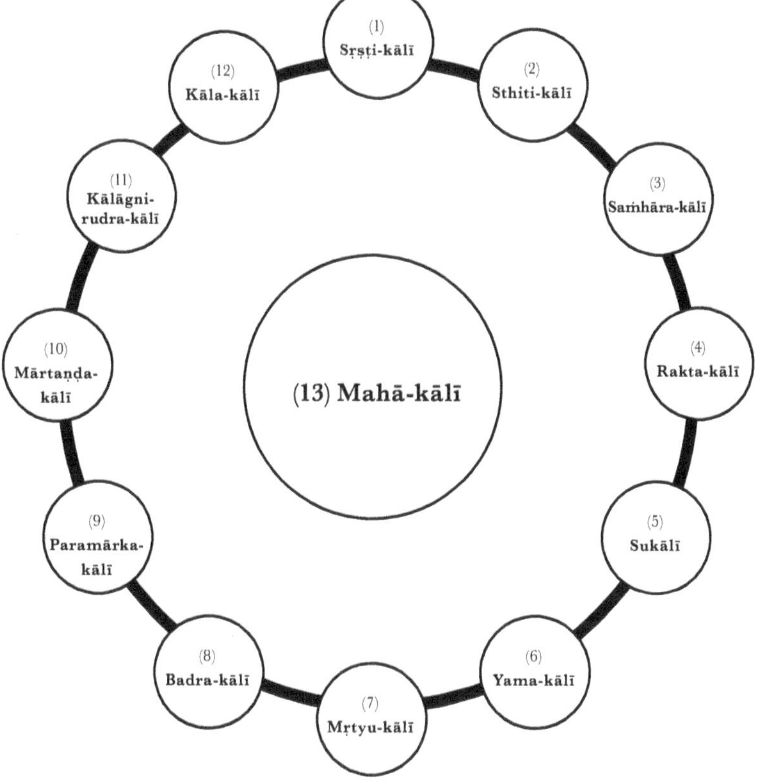

1. Sṛṣṭi-kālī - Creation
2. Sthiti-kālī - Stasis
3. Saṁhāra-kālī - Dissolution
4. Rakta-kālī - Passion

Objectivity (*prameya*)

5. Sukālī - Jubilant
6. Yama-kālī - Transcendental
7. Mṛtyu-kālī - Deadly
8. Badra-kālī - Blessed

Perception (*pramāṇa*)

9. Paramākrā-kālī - Supreme sun ray
10. Mārtaṇḍa-kālī - Sun
11. Kālāgni-rudra-kālī - Fire of time
12. Kāla-kālī - Destroyer of time

Subjectivity (*pramtṛ*)

Mahākālī - The great annihilator or the nameless land
Here, Kālī reabsorbs in herself the limiting states of objectivity (*prameya*), perception (*pramāṇa*), and subjectivity (*pramtṛ*).

Circumstances of its emergence

We see a continuity through the earliest scriptures (the *Bhairava Tantras* and *Vāma Tantras*), the sectarian *Kaula Tantras* of the *Trika* and the *Krama*, and finally to the exegetical works of Kashmir Shaivism. In the middle of the ninth century CE, the mostly anonymous *Trika* and *Krama* scriptures emerged from the hidden world of the *Śaiva Āgamas* to the world of the *śāstras*. For at least 200 years, the discourses of Tantra and *Kaula* remained vitally linked because of the Tantric adepts. They were living sources who revealed the hidden meaning of the *Āgamas*. The *Trika* and *Krama* schools progressively evolved and developed a more refined interpretation of the Tantras' esoteric meaning.

At a certain stage of its development, the *Krama* emerged as a *Kaula* cult and was defined as one of the *āmnāyas*. We do not know whether *Kālī-krama* was known as *Uttarāmnāya* as soon as it emerged, but it certainly was at some point.

In the period of the Kashmir exegetes, elements of these two traditions were unified. However, a permanent division remained between the tetradic and the pentadic *Krama*, derived from the *Devī-pañca-śatikā* and the *Krama-sad-bhāva*, respectively.

Since *Krama* doctrine focuses on essentialization and internalization, it is clearly *Kaula* in nature. In the two scriptures mentioned above, it is the goddess who teaches Bhairava. Here the roles are reversed because Bhairava cannot know the cycle of cognitive power that comprises the self-awareness the goddess embodies.

Chronology and location

The *Krama* can be traced back to the master Durvāsā, who introduced it at the beginning of the Age of Kali. However, Jñāna-netra (also known as Śivānanda-nātha) is considered the founder of the *Krama*, who was initiated at the end of the ninth century CE by Maṅgalā (Kālī) and the goddesses of the cremation grounds in Uḍḍiyāṇa. This distinguished master had three great erudite female disciples: Keyūravatī, Madanikā, and Kalyāṇikā, who continued the lineage by imparting the wisdom to others. Among the many who studied directly from these three female masters, there were notable masters such as Govindarāja, Bhānuka, and Eraka. Govindarāja, in turn, was the master of the great Somānanda. The lineage of Bhānuka included masters such as the great Ujjaṭa and Udbhaṭa. The *Krama's* spiritual lineage had the longest continuity: for five centuries (until the fifteenth century CE), the transmission from masters to disciples (*pāramparā*) continued with fully realized masters.

It is impossible to precisely determine where most Tantras originated. However, in the case of the *Krama*, the scriptures (such as the *Kālikā-kula-pañca-śataka* and *Kālī-kula-krama-sad-bhāva*) and later commentators agree that the revelations took place in Uḍḍiyāṇa, although it may be more myth than fact. This is the seat of northern power (*uttara-pīṭha*), which is located in the Swat Valley (in modern Pakistan), about three hundred kilometers northwest of the Kashmir Valley. This valley appears in the hagiographic histories of Buddhism as the main center from which the traditions of the *Yoginī Tantras* (*Yogānuttara Tantras*) spread.

The *Krama* had a profound influence not only on the *Trika* but also, through the works of Kṣema-rāja, on the understanding of the *Svacchanda*, the *Netra*, and a wide range of *Śaiva* texts aimed at a wider audience.

With the advent of Islam and the subsequent collapse of urban and monastic culture in the region, all traces of the Tantric traditions disappeared.

Scriptures

Many *Krama* texts have survived that were written beginning in the middle of the ninth century CE, both in Sanskrit and in the ancient language of Kashmir.

The northern *āmnāya*, unlike other Tantric revelations, was revealed by the *piṭheśvarīs*, female clans of *yoginīs* called "lovers of the mounds." It was these goddesses who transmitted the revelation to the founding gurus of the lineages, or *Kaula paramparā*. This is the reason the *Śakti Tantras* are considered by Abhinava-gupta and other commentators of his stature to be the most official and significant texts within the *Kaula* revelation.

One of the most important *Kaula Krama* texts is the three later sections (*ṣaṭkas* of 6000 verses each) of the *Jayad-ratha Yāmala*, originally a "Union Tantra." These last three sections are dedicated to the purely *Śākta* cults of Kālī, totally independent of any male consort. Each *ṣaṭka* teaches the propitiation of innumerable forms of divinity, but later the *Tantra-rāja-tantrāvatāra-stotra* (eleventh to twelfth centuries CE) indicated the main deity of each section:

- *Ṣaṭka* 1: Kāla-saṁkarṣaṇī, the main deity of the *Krama*.
- *Ṣaṭka* 2: Siddha-lakṣmī, worshipped to this day in Nepal under the name Siddhi-lakṣmī.
- *Ṣaṭka* 3: Sāra-śakti, venerated as the essence of three *vidyās*.
- *Ṣaṭka* 4: Siddhayogeśvarīmata, a form of Parā from early *Trika*.

Krama literature includes texts of divine origin and from human authors. The revealed texts comprise anonymous works and the *Krama Āgamas*: the *Pañca-śatika*, or *Devī-pañca-śatikā*, *Sārdha-śatika*, *Krama-rahasya*, *Krama-sad-bhāva*, *Kālikā-krama*, and *Krama-siddhi*. The rest of the texts include the non-agamic works such as the *Krama Sūtra*, *Siddha Sūtra*, *Mahā-naya-paddhati*, *Kramadaya*, *Amāvasyā-triṁśikā*, and *Rājikā*.

Rituals

Krama scriptures are considered superior to *Vidyā-pīṭha* scriptures. Although it is true that there are continuities with the *Jayad-ratha Yāmala*, *Krama* worship is more sophisticated in several ways. For example, it includes mantras but replaces the crudest level of material deities with iconic forms. External ritual is greatly simplified and is considered inferior to mental worship, since the order of worship (*pūjā-krama*) is no more than a reflection of the sequence of cognition (*saṁvit-krama*), which is always present.

In the *Kālī-kula-kramārcana*, Vimala-prabodha describes the *Krama* ritual in which male and female adepts are collectively worshipped with offerings of food and drink (*cakra-krīḍā*). The cult sponsor provides a secret phrase (*samaya-chommakam*) to be used by all invited participants to refer to the five *Krama* phases, from emission (*sṛṣṭi*) to radiant light (*bhāsā*).

Teachings

The *Krama* system is both Tantric and *Śaiva* monist. These are some of the characteristics of its doctrine:

- The *Krama* is a Śakti-oriented Tantric system.
- Despite having a firm monist tendency, on a practical level it leans toward monism–dualism.
- Self-realization is not obtained through an ascetic life of aversion but by attaining a synthesis of *bhoga* and *mokṣa*.
- The *Krama* emphasizes the epistemic side of human experience.
- Its philosophy indicates that until transcendence is realized, time has to be understood as real. One rises in succession, step by step. This gradual progress makes the realization firm. Since it deals with successive realization, it recognizes the existence of space and time. Only at the end, and not during the process, does the adept transcend duality and experience a state without time or space.
- *Krama* adepts aspire to *jīvan-mukti*, or "liberation in life."

Practice

The elevation of *kuṇḍalinī-prāṇa* in the *Krama* is described as a progression from one chakra to the next and from one state to next. Its scriptures provide detailed descriptions of the ascension process of *kuṇḍalinī* through each chakra up to *sahasrāra-cakra* at the crown of the head.

This path was rich in *vratas* (vows), mantra *sādhanas*, and esoteric practices. It combined refined and sophisticated philosophical thinking with transgressive practices. It stands out for its intention to make ritual an efficient means of liberation. The fact that more than nine generations of masters achieved liberation by walking this path proves its effectiveness.

Despite challenging the social order, the *Krama* was considered very elevated in Kashmir and Nepal. It attracted highly respected people such as ministers and rulers. Its influence was so great that the *Trika* adopted some of its doctrines. The two schools eventually merged into Abhinava-gupta's Shaivism, an esoteric *Kaula Trika* with a *Krama* essence.

After the tenth century CE, the *Krama* teachings were promulgated under the name *Mahārtha* (the great teaching) or *Mahā-naya* (the great way). In the eleventh and twelfth centuries CE, three texts by different authors transmitted the teachings of the *Mahārtha*, all under the same title, *Illumination of the Great Way* (*Mahā-naya-prakāśa*). The first text, written by Arṇa-siṁha (1050–1075 CE) of the Prabodha lineage, explains how *Krama* worship reflected and embodied the central structures of consciousness itself. The second text contains detailed instructions on an intensive nine-day *Krama* worship training course. It also identifies the natural flow of cognition as the flow of energy within the human body.

3. *Paścimāmnāya* or "western transmission": Tat-puruṣa Face

Name

Paścimāmnāya, or "western transmission," worships the goddess Kubjikā, who is simultaneously tender and fierce. She incorporates features of previous Tantric deities and is often considered an emanation of the goddess Parā, which connects this tradition to the higher *Trika*.

Description

The *Kubjikā-mata Tantra* narrates the origin of the goddess. Śiva Bhairava visited the god of the Himalayas. In those mountains, he met Pārvatī, whom the text calls Kālīka, or "the little Kālī." Deeply attracted to Kālīkā, Bhairava gave her a vision of the universe in flames along with the bliss of the Transmission of Power, or *ājñā*, a vision that leads to awakening. He told her that she would achieve her essential nature, which transcends all qualities. After that he vanished, leaving Kālīkā confused and wondering: "Who am I? What am I doing here?" Then she went west in search of Bhairava. She reached paradise and found a magical rock there. When mounting the stone, she received the Transmission of divine Power. Then the goddess became a female *liṅga*, or a bisexual mix. Thus she experienced bliss with absolute independence. She is represented as hunched while enjoying licking her own vulva; hence her name is Kubjikā, or "the hunchback." Bhairava reappeared and praised her in her bisexual form of a female *liṅga*, awakening Kālīkā from her state of introspection. She then manifested as multifaceted. Kālīkā was ashamed when Bhairava asked her about the Transmission of Power, because she knew that her enlightenment must be externally manifested through conjugal union. The posture she adopted, out of shame, is another reason for her name.

Kubjikā is the personification of *kuṇḍalinī-śakti*, or "the divine power," that lies dormant in every human being. From the union of Śiva and Śakti in *sahasrāra-cakra*, the "immortal ultimate point" is created. The explosion of that point generated the universe. Although the union of Śiva and Śakti is a very high state of consciousness in the Kubjikā tradition, it is believed that the absolute fusion of the two is still higher. This is the state that precedes and follows the emanation of the final point. As in the *Śrī-vidyā* tradition, in its first stage of emanation, the point is manifested outward in the generative *yonī*. It has the shape of a triangle whose vertexes represent desire, knowledge, and action. *Kuṇḍalinī-yoga* originates in *Kubjikā* literature. Later we see the chakra system of this discipline integrated into the literature of hatha yoga.

Krama terminology in the text reveals its influence on this tradition. Like Kālī, Kubjikā is the divine nature behind everyone and everything. The enlightened being perceives everything in this world as an expression of eternal bliss. This ultimate amorphous reality is expressed dynamically, in spite of being the final rest.

Chronology and location

The *Kubjikā* cult was revealed in the western Himalayas, in the tenth century CE, although it quickly spread to Candrapura, the kingdom of Koṅkaṇā. In southern India, an alternative form of the *Kubjikā* cult called *Śāmbhavānanda* developed, in which Kubjikā was worshipped along with her consort Navātma (the one of nine parts). Gradually, the lineage of *Śāmbhavānanda* incorporated the cult *śrī-vidyā* to Tripura-sundarī. This combination was one of the main sources of the hatha yoga system that emerged after the decline of classical Tantra. The *Matsyendra Saṁhitā* (*The Compendium of Matsyendra*), a text from the thirteenth century CE attributed to the *Śāmbhavānanda* line, is a transition between Tantra and hatha yoga. This lineage also influenced the Vedanta–Tantra fusion associated with the Śaṅkarācāryas of Śṛṅgerī and Kāñcī, as reflected in the *Ānanda-laharī* section of the *Saundarya-laharī*.

Deities

Kubjikā is a goddess with immense metaphysical depth and is related to different forms of yoga, especially the wisdom of the movement of vital breath. The *maṇḍala* of the western transmission has a pentatonic structure related to the chakras. Kubjikā is the central deity, who has a dark complexion, six faces, and twelve arms. She is surrounded by serpents and wears ornaments of human bones with a garland of decapitated heads around her neck. She embraces her consort Navātma, who has five faces and ten arms. He is dark-skinned, good-looking, and young. They dance together on a lotus that grows from the navel of Agni, the god of fire. Worshippers of this divine couple visualize the lotus growing from their own cranial opening (*brahma-randhra*) at the top of a shining beam of light that rises from the energy center near the genitals, *svādhiṣṭhāna-cakra*.

Kubjikā

Scriptures

The most important *Kubjikā* texts are the *Kubjikā-mata*, *Ṣaṭ-sāhasra Saṁhitā*, and *Manthāna-bhairava Tantra* of 24,000 verses, all of which also have a pentatonic structure. This structure comprises five energy centers that correspond to *devīs*, *durīs*, *mātṛs*, *yoginīs*, and *khecarīs*, all aligned along the *suṣumṇā-nāḍī* in the astral body. The *Kubjikā-mata* offers an outline of the astral body that hatha yoga teachings will describe in more detail later on. We find something similar in the *Jayad-ratha Yāmala* and the *Netra Tantra*.

Teachings

Paścimāmnāya is said to be the highest Agamic school because it combines the upper *Kaula* and the most refined *Śaiva* doctrines. The *Kaula* revelation is divided into two vitally interconnected categories: *Yoginī-kaula* and *Siddha-kaula*.

Yoginī-kaula was revealed from the mouths of *yoginīs*, who heard the esoteric knowledge from Śiva's lips and kept it within their own line of transmission. The *Kaula-jñāna-nirṇaya* scripture mentions that Matsyendra-nātha was the founder of the *Yoginī-kaula* tradition, associated with the legendary land of Kāma-rūpa, although he himself seems to have belonged to the *siddha* or *siddhāmṛta-kaula*. In certain places, *Paścimamnaya* is considered to be the tradition of *yoginīs* (*yoginī-krama*). This part of the *Kula* doctrine reveals the essence of the *yoginīs'* teachings and conveys the secrets of their oral tradition. The *Paścima* doctrine is also considered to be part of the *Siddha-kaula* and instructs that it should not be revealed to anyone who is not initiated into the *Siddha* school. This is not in fact a contradiction. Kubjikā is the deity who presides over this tradition; she is *kuṇḍalinī*, which is an essential *Yoginī-kaula* teaching. But at its highest level, the *Yoginī-kaula* instructs that the final object of devotion is Śiva, also called Śambhu. He is the home of the Śāmbhava state; he transcends all characterization and grants infinite qualities. In his home, all practice ceases and the yogi accesses the source of all revelations.

The *Kubjikā-mata* tradition is *Śākta*, that is to say, it emphasizes the goddess (Śakti) over Bhairava (Śiva). But in this *Paścimāmnāya* tradition there is also a parallel system known as *Śāmbhava* that emphasizes Navātma (Śiva). There were also masculine *Trika* variants that worshipped the three goddesses (Parā, Parāparā, and Aparā) as the powers of Tri-śiro-bhairava (three-headed Bhairava), and in the *Krama*, in which Manthāna-bhairava occupied the place of the thirteenth Kālī from the *Kālī-krama*. However, the *Śāmbhava* system was the most widespread. It is described in the *Śambhu-nirṇaya Tantra* and post-scriptural literature in southern India, such as the *Śambhu-nirṇaya-dīpikā* of Śivānanda-muni. It was even adapted into the main tradition of the purified *Kaula* that spread throughout southern India.

Among the *Kaula* traditions that come from the sacred places (*pīṭhas*), the *Paścimāmnāya* has the most vital doctrine of the whole *Kaula* tradition, including *Yoginī-kaula*. The *kuṇḍalinī* system that emerged during the second millennium CE first appeared in the *Kubjikā-mata*, the fundamental scripture of the western *Kaula* tradition. The goddess *Kuṇḍalinī* is Kubjikā. Its system of six chakras spread on such a scale that it influenced the cult of *Śrī-vidyā* (Tripura-sundarī) and became part of the hatha yoga system that has survived to the present.

Rituals

The cult of Kubjikā is extensive. She is endowed with all the metaphysical attributes of a supreme deity and an absolute being. Kubjikā is also a very esoteric goddess. Her cult was kept secret for centuries by her initiates in the Kathmandu valley.

Navātma, also called Naveśvara or Navaka, was worshipped as a solitary hero (*eka-vīrā*). The divine couple (Navātma and Kubjikā) assumed six forms (*yāmalas*) to preside over the six energy centers along the *suṣumṇā-nāḍī*, which correspond to the five elements (earth, water, fire, air, and ether) and the mind (*manas*). This tradition was a form of later *Kaula* that incorporated the worship of *siddha* founders such as Matsyendra-nātha.

Practice

The system of the six chakras characterizes *Kubjikā-mata* yogic rituals. Like all *Kaula* traditions, *Paścimāmnāya* is considered a secret oral transmission. Masters only taught to those who showed sincerity and commitment to the path and, due to their spiritual advancement, were not at risk of abusing the revelation.

This school places special emphasis on the importance of the master. It is also known as *Gurvāmnāya*, or "the tradition of the guru," from whose mouth emanates spiritual knowledge and the power of the mantra. The guru is the Lord of the *Paścimāmnāya*; he or she is much more than a source of information or a decoder of the scriptures. The hidden teachings are transmitted through masters, and only they can open the door for disciples to a new dimension of existence through initiation. The grace of the deity is embodied in the master. Serious disciples will be able to become enlightened, like the master, and thus perpetuate the transmission of the teachings.

The main practice is the repetition of mantras. Tantric practices cannot be learned from the written word. Mantras have no value unless they are uttered by those who have released the hidden power in their own consciousness.

Members

In the *Paścimāmnāya*, like the rest of the *Kaula* traditions, women played a special role. There is a proverb that says: "One should put wisdom in a woman's mouth and take it again from her lips." Women are Tantric consorts (*dūtīs*), who can transmit the revelation and should be shown the same respect as spiritual masters.

4. *Dakṣiṇāmnāya* or "southern transmission": Aghora Face

Name

Dakṣiṇāmnāya, "the southern transmission," is the last of the four *āmnāyas* described in the *Ciñciṇī-mata-sāra-samuccaya*. This *āmnāya* has much in common with the later *Anuttarāmnāya*, which is a stream that emerged from the *Dakṣiṇāmnāya* and presented itself as a superior development.

Description

The southern transmission is a cult of erotic magic that worships the goddess Kāmeśvarī in a *maṇḍala* that includes her consort, the god Kāma-deva, and eleven *nityā* goddesses, whose names are related to sex and romance, for example, Kṣobhinī (the exciter) and Drāvinī (the melting one). Kāma-deva is similar to Eros, the god of sexual attraction in Greek mythology, and Cupid, his Roman equivalent.

The very growth of this *āmnāya* led to its disappearance. This cult of the goddess of erotic pleasure was taken as a prototype by the later *Kaula* cult of the goddess Tripura-sundarī. In the new cult, Kāmeśvarī was worshipped in the *Śrī-cakra* of nine triangles. Kāmeśvarī and Kāma-deva were united in the sexual embrace *kāma-kalā* in the center of the *Śrī-cakra*.

Deities

Kāmeśvarī is a slim maiden with two arms and one face. She has three eyes and slim hips. She shines like a hundred million lightning bolts and yet is still as pleasing to the eye as the rising sun. She is full of passion (*kama*) and descends to the world in the form of a young virgin (*kumāri*), who is the flow of vitality (*śukra-vāhini*). She manifests as *Kaula-yoginī* in a divine, peaceful, and pure form like a translucent crystal. Her place of residence is north of the Mālinī Mountain. Behind the mountain is the bay (*gahvara*) called the Place of the Nightingale, which was inhabited by wild birds, such as ducks and geese. The goddess resided in the cave called the Face of the Moon. Absorbed in meditation, Khecarī, Bhūcari, Siddha, and Śākini also resided in the same bay. Ascetics, *munis*, and *siddhas* practiced austerities there for thousands of years until they reached old age and became liberated. Their gaze was directed upward, toward the Inner Face, until they saw the goddess Śukrā and thus reached the state of divine drunkenness (*ghūrṇyāvasthā*) by virtue of her divine splendor. After the goddess transmitted this divine knowledge, Kāma-deva appeared before her in a divine form and the power of Kāmeśvarī melted him. Kāmeśvarī and Kāma-deva became one and gave rise to the Rudra (*yāmala*) couple. The son born from this union was Kauleśa, who taught this divine knowledge.

Tripura-sundarī

Scriptures

The literature of this tradition must have been vast, but unfortunately, we now only have an incomplete Nepalese manuscript called *Nityā-kaula*.

Teachings

Amṛtānanda-nātha was a commentator who explained the *Śrī-vidyā* doctrine. In the *Saubhāgya-subhodaya*, he relates the four *āmnāyas* to symbolic aspects of the *mantra* called *rāja*, which is one of the main mantras of the *Śrī-vidyā*. This mantra is composed of four syllable-seeds, one from each *āmnāya*. The energy of Kāma-deva is in the syllable-seed of the *dakṣiṇāmnāya*. The *Ciñciṇī-mata-sāra-samuccaya* refers to the other three syllable-seeds, in addition to Tripura, as energies of the goddess Kāmeśvarī. In the *Śrī-vidyā* tradition, these are found in the innermost triangle of the *Śrī-cakra*, leaving no doubt that the *Śrī-vidyā* tradition is *Kaula* in nature.

Rituals

This *āmnāya* revealed the cult of the magic of love that was the origin of the *Śrī-vidyā* or *Anuttarāmnāya*. It was called the *Nityā* cult and its goal was to ensure the affection of one's sexual partner.

5. *Anuttarāmnāya* or "supreme transmission"

Name

The later development of the *Dakṣiṇāmnāya* was called *Anuttarāmnāya*, "the final or supreme tradition," to indicate that it transcends the fourfold division of *Kaula* traditions. This is the *Śrī-vidyā*, or Tripura lineage.

Description

The classical form of this cult was linked to the southern transmission, but it is thought to contain all four *āmnāyas*. From the cult of Kāmeśvarī it adopted the ritual of love, and, in fact, Tripura-sundarī is also called Kāmeśvarī. From Kubjikā theology, it acquired the divinization of passion and of sexual desire that originates in the union of the goddess and Śiva. The doctrine, practice, and philosophy of the *Trika* had a substantial influence on the *Śrī-vidyā*. This influence is clear from the incorporation of the main mantra of the *Trika* goddess Parā (*Sauḥ*) at the center of the *Śrī-vidyā* liturgy, which was preserved as the main Tripura mantra. The *Trika* flourished for a time alongside the *Śrī-vidyā* until it finally disappeared. A further development of the Tripura-sundarī cult was known as the Kālī doctrine (*kālī-mata*) and incorporated versions of the pantheons of these other systems. The *Śrī-vidyā* became very popular and spread throughout India, from Kashmir to Tamil Nadu, eventually eclipsing the traditions that nurtured its development. The liturgy of this new form of Kaulism has survived from the Middle Ages to the present day.

The *Śrī-vidyā* is the only original *Śaiva* Tantra sect that has survived to the present, though in a distilled form. All the transgressive elements of the *Kaula* have been eliminated, but some of its doctrines and rituals remain intact. Conservative *Smarta Brāhmaṇas* from the south incorporated the *Śrī-cakra-pūjā* from the *Śrī-vidyā*. Today we see a Vedanta–Tantra syncretism that is practiced by the Śaṅkarācāryas of Śṛṅgerī and Kāñcī and is expressed, for example, in the *Saundarya-laharī* scripture. Tripura-sundarī is worshipped by Smartas in Tamil Nadu, as well as by part of the population of Kathmandu in Nepal.

Chronology

Without a doubt, Tripura was the last *Kaula* lineage, since none of the canonical accounts found in the other traditions mention it. The *Śrī-vidyā* dates back to the tenth or eleventh century CE and developed out of *Śrī-kula* texts. Of these texts, the *Yoginī-hṛdaya* is particularly important; it was written around the eleventh century CE.

Deities

The main goddess is Tripura-sundarī. Her name means "the beautiful one of the three citadels." She manifests herself as three forms:

1. *Sthūla*, or "gross form." This is her iconographic representation as Lalitā Tripura-sundarī, a 16-year-old girl who has just developed her sexual energy. Her breasts are exposed and in the later version she wears a red sari and garlands of red flowers, which symbolize passion. She is beautiful and her skin is reddish. In her four hands she holds an elephant prod (*aṅkuśa*), a rope (*pāśa*), five arrows from the god of love, and a bow made of sugar cane. Her nose rings shine brighter than the stars and her ears are decorated with the rings of the sun and the moon. Her voice is sweeter than the sound of Sarasvatī's veena and her smile is so beautiful that Śiva cannot stop looking at her. She is sitting in the lotus posture on Sadāśiva and on the lower gods Brahmā, Viṣṇu, Rudra, and Īśvara.
2. *Sūkṣma*, or "subtle form." The *Śrī-cakra*, or *Śrī-yantra*, a diagram of nine intertwined triangles that represent the sequence of the emanation and reabsorption of reality, from and to the central point of ultimate reality (*bindu*) that contains them in a non-manifested form.
3. *Atisūkṣma*, or "subtler form." The *Śrī-vidyā* itself, the mantra of the goddess. This mantra is the aural equivalent of the *Śrī-cakra*. The mantra is composed of *Oṁ* and fifteen other syllables. It is also called *ṣoḍaśī* because it has sixteen syllables. The *Śrī-vidyā* mantra is divided into three groups of five syllables, which each express one of the three goddesses whose combined essences form Tripura-sundarī:

   A. *Jñāna-śakti*: The first five syllables express the power of knowledge. They are associated with Vāgīśvarī (the incarnation of the word) and grant liberation.

   B. *Kriyā-śakti*: The second five syllables express the power of action. They are associated with Kāmeśvarī and grant romantic and sexual desires.

   C. *Icchā-śakti*: The third five syllables express the power of will. They are associated with Parā-devī and remove obstacles.

Śrī-vidyā

Scriptures

The main scripture of this tradition is the *Nityā-ṣoḍaśikārṇava*, also called the *Vāmakeśvarī-mata*. The date of the work is uncertain, but we know that it was written before the beginning of the thirteenth century CE, when Jaya-ratha of Kashmir wrote his commentary. For that reason, it is estimated that it was revealed between the tenth and twelfth century CE. This text has five chapters and 400 verses. It deals with the external aspects of Tripura-sundarī worship. It is an unsophisticated text that focuses on the supernatural effects the rituals grants the worshipper, especially the power to control women.

The *Nityā-ṣoḍaśikārṇava*, a *Śrī-vidyā* scripture (*Anuttarāmnāya*), describes the worship of Tripura-sundarī and teaches how to acquire supernatural powers to attract women, which is clearly an influence of the *Dakṣiṇāmnāya*. It also talks about liberation, but as a later idea. Over time, the *Śākta* cult of Tripura-sundarī became the most widespread and has survived to this day. However, the Tripura-sundarī cult does not consider itself as derived from the *Dakṣiṇāmnāya*, but as superior to the four *āmnāyas*.

The second key text of this tradition, the *Yoginī-hṛdaya*, offers deeper insights and explains the coherence between the external elements of the ritual and the metaphysical meaning of the sequence of creation and reabsorption represented by the *Śrī-cakra*. Thus, the text of the ritual, which apparently was related to erotic magic, became a medium for ritualized gnostic contemplation. Judging by the clear influences of the Kashmir exegeses from the *Trika* and *Krama*, it is estimated that the *Yoginī-hṛdaya* was written in southern India after 1050 CE. Amṛtānanda-nātha (1325–1375 CE) wrote the first known commentary in the fourteenth century CE. Lakṣmī-dhara wrote a particularly remarkable commentary between the seventeenth and eighteenth centuries CE.

Teachings

The *Śrī-vidyā* is a Tantric *Śākta* tradition. Its metaphysics is monist and holds that ultimately there is only one reality: the reality of consciousness, which is linked to the goddess Tripura-sundarī. She is manifested in her *Śrī-vidyā* mantra and her sacred *Śrī-cakra* diagram of nine intersecting triangles within a circle. The adepts of the *Śrī-vidyā* seek liberation from the cycle of reincarnation (*saṁsāra*) by merging with the goddess.

The parts of the *Śrī-cakra maṇḍala* with nine intertwined triangles are incarnations of the four *āmnāyas* that nourished it, equated with the four phases (emission, maintenance, retraction, and the unnamable). It is a tetrad derived from the *Krama*, making the *maṇḍala* proof that this cult surpasses all other *Kaula* traditions. There is no doubt about the *Kaula* character of the *Śrī-vidyā* school. The *Nityā-ṣoḍaśikārṇava* says that the form of the *Śrī-cakra* and the *Śrī-vidyā* mantra arose in the waves of the infinite *Kula* ocean. In fact, it is expressly stated that it is *Kula vidyā*, the great knowledge of *yoginīs*.

Rituals

The goddess Tripura is young and beautiful. Her eyes, slightly red from drinking wine, make her the perfect archetype of *Kaula* consorts. Tripura presides over the phases of the cosmic cycles of time. She is *Kula*, the power of the supreme deity. Therefore, the *Yoginī-hṛdaya* recommends that only those who practice *kulācāra* worship her. The *Śrī-vidyā* tradition includes an essential element of every *Kaula* ritual, namely, the worship of the *yuga-nāthas*.

Practice

The *Śrī-cakra* symbolizes the interpenetration of dynamic female energy (*śakti*) and passive male consciousness (Śiva). This diagram is used in rituals and meditation to help practitioners see they are one with the goddess, symbolized by the yantra. Tripura practitioners see the diagram as a dynamic map of reality, a substrate for ritual, and a focal point for meditation.

The guru is essential on this path, since many *Śrī-vidyā* mantras are considered more potent when received from a guru during initiation. It is believed that an aspirant has to be Śiva himself or be in the last birth to obtain the *Śrī-vidyā* mantra, and that one can worship Tripura only if she allows it.

It is believed that the mantras reveal the unity of the deity, the guru, the initiate, and the mantra itself. The first mantra that the initiate receives is the *bala-tripura-sundarī-mantra*, which visualizes the goddess as a little girl. The next mantra is the *pañca-daśī* of fifteen syllables. A higher mantra is the *ṣoḍaśī* of sixteen letters.

The practical benefits of this *sādhana* are physical, mental, and emotional health, which lead to harmonious relationships at home and with the external world. This grants success in all aspects of life. Followers of this sect aspired to achieve both material prosperity and self-realization.

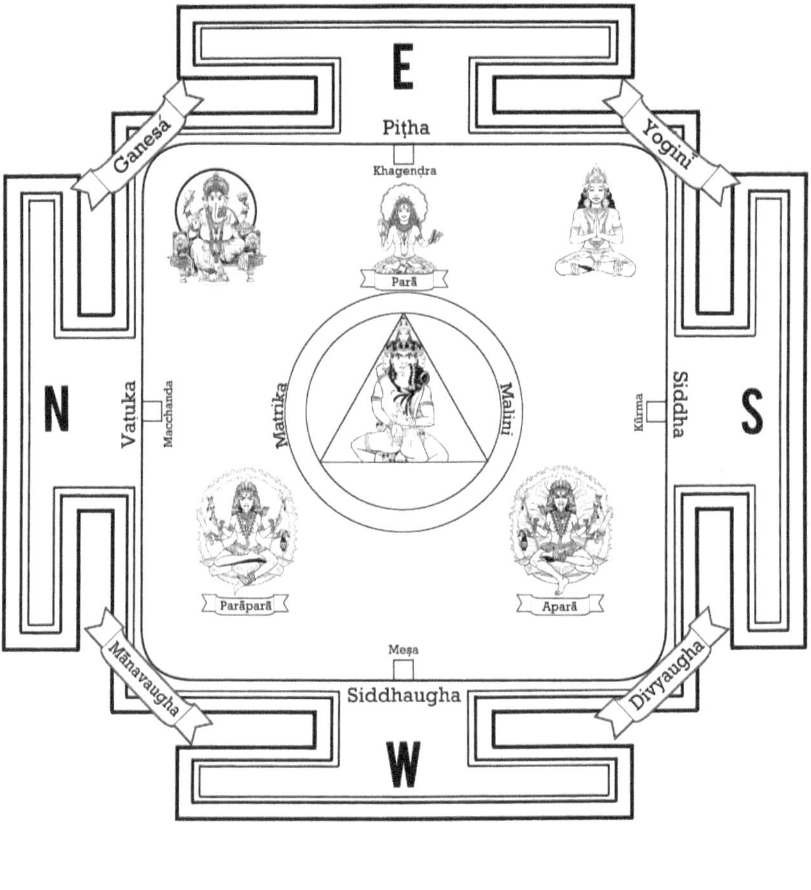
E
Piṭha
Khagenḍra
Ganesá
Yogini
Parā
N
Vaṭuka
Macchanda
Matrika
Malini
Kūrma
Siddha
S
Parāparā
Aparā
Meṣa
Mānavaugha
Siddhaugha
Divyaugha
W

ŚRĪ-CAKRA

6. *Ūrdhvāmnāya* or "superior transmission": Vāma-deva Face

Name

After the twelfth century CE, a new form of *Kaula* emerged called *Ūrdhvāmnāya* (superior tradition). It is said to have emanated from Śiva's Vāma-deva face, which looks upward and declares superiority over the *Śākta* –*Śaiva* forms that preceded it. The *Kulārṇava Tantra* states that the Tantras related to *Ūrdhvāmnāya* are superior to the rest.

ऊर्ध्वत्वात्सर्वधर्माणामूर्ध्वाम्नायः प्रशस्यते ।
ऊर्ध्वं नयत्यधःस्थञ्च ऊर्ध्वाम्नाय इतीरितः ॥
ऊर्ध्वतत्त्वात्कुलेशानि ध्वस्तसंसारसागरात् ।
ऊर्ध्वलोकैक सेव्यत्वादूर्ध्वाम्नाय इति स्मृतः ॥

ūrdhvatvāt sarva-dharmāṇām
ūrdhvāmnāyaḥ praśasyate
ūrdhvam nayaty adhaḥ sthañ ca
ūrdhvāmnāya itīritaḥ

ūrdhva-tattvāt kuleśāni
dhvasta-saṁsāra-sāgarāt
ūrdhva-lokaika sevyatvād
ūrdhvāmnāya iti smṛtaḥ

Because it is the most elevated dharma (*ūrdhva*), the *Ūrdhvāmnāya* is the supreme path. It is called such because it raises those who are below. O Kuleśāni! Its essence is high, it destroys the world's oceans, and the higher worlds wait in its service, hence it is called *Ūrdhvāmnāya*.

(*Kulārṇava Tantra*, 3.17–18)

According to this Tantra, the path is called superior because it is above all religions and elevates those who have not yet reached their maximum potential.

Description

The later *Śākta* literature of southern India includes five or six *āmnāyas* in its classification. However, this *āmnāya* has little in common with the elaborate pantheons and earlier mantra systems. The *Kulārṇava Tantra* describes five *āmnāyas* and indicates that the *Ūrdhvāmnāya* is the highest of all.

सर्वलोकेषु सर्वेभ्यो ह्यहं पूज्यो यथा प्रिये ।
अम्नायेषु च सर्वेषु उर्ध्वाम्नायस्तथा शिवे ॥

sarva-lokeṣu sarvebhyo
hy ahaṁ pūjyo yathā priye
amnāyeṣu ca sarveṣu
urdhvāmnāyas tathā śive

Just as all the worlds and people adore me above all, similarly, O Śiva! *Ūrdhvāmnāya* is to be cherished above all other *āmnāyas*.
(*Kulārṇava Tantra*, 3.20)

The *Ūrdhvāmnāya* transmission is considered a direct path to becoming Śiva himself. Moreover, it is said that one will hear about *Ūrdhvāmnāya* only if it is one's last birth and one's Karmic debt is about to be paid.

This *āmnāya* can only be learned from a self-realized guru. With the mere initiation into this tradition, liberation is assured. Practitioners receive blessings, and the place where they live becomes filled with prosperity. A mere theoretical study of the *Kaula-dharma* texts cannot help readers understand the subject. It is a secret doctrine, and only worshippers who follow their guru's instructions can adequately understand its most difficult practical aspects.

Deities

This tradition teaches a simplified worship of Ardha-nārīśvara, a deity who is half Śiva and half Śakti. The god who presides over the *Ūrdhvāmnāya* is Śiva, and the mantra is our own breath. When we breathe, we pronounce the mantra *Haṁsa*. *Ha* means Śiva, *m* refers to *aham*, or "I am," and *sa* means Śakti. The subtle meaning of *haṁsa* is "I am both Śiva and Śakti." *Haṁsa* is not a mantra but the subtle sound of the breath: *ha* synchronizes with the exhalation and *sa* with the inhalation. Both Śiva and Śakti come together to form the universe. Without Śakti, creation is not possible.

Main scriptures

Śiva teaches Pārvatī the *Ūrdhvāmnāya* doctrine in the *Kulārṇava Tantra.* He tells her that he propagated five transmissions: *Pūrvāmnāya*, *Dakṣiṇāmnāya*, *Paścimāmnāya*, *Uttarāmnāya*, and *Ūrdhvāmnāya*. *Pūrvāmnāya* preaches the path of merit; *Dakṣiṇāmnāya*, bhakti yoga; *Paścimāmnāya*, the philosophy of karma yoga; and *Uttarāmnāya*, *jñāna-yoga*. The *Ūrdhvāmnāya* is above all of them.

मन्त्रयोगं विदुः पूर्वं भक्तियोगश्च दक्षिणम् ।
पश्चिमं कर्मयोगश्च ज्ञानयोगं तथोत्तरम् ॥

mantra-yogaṁ viduḥ pūrvaṁ
bhakti-yogañ ca dakṣiṇam
paścimaṁ karma-yogañ ca
jñāna-yogaṁ tathottaram

> The path of *Pūrva* is mantra yoga, of *Dakṣiṇa* is bhakti yoga, of *Paścima* is karma yoga, and of *Uttara* is *jñāna-yoga*.
> (*Kulārṇava Tantra*, 3.42)

Teachings

From each of his four faces, Śiva reveals a group of goddesses. If the adept properly worships and recites the mantras of these goddesses, Śiva and Śakti are revealed. It is beneficial to follow any of these four *āmnāyas* with discipline and sincerity. However, for liberation, the grace of Śiva is important. *Ūrdhvāmnāya* is the direct form of Śiva himself and, therefore, it is considered highly secret.

The *Kulārṇava Tantra* states that no one can learn the *Ūrdhvāmnāya* transmission from studying the Vedas, *śāstras*, or *Purāṇas*, by religious practices, or with mantras or herbs, but only from the lips of the guru and by his or her grace. Thus, this Tantra warns *sādhakas* that the master's grace is necessary to access the secret Tantric knowledge.

न वेदैर्नागमैः शास्त्रैर्न पुराणैः सुविस्तरैः ।
न यज्ञैर्न तपोभिर्वा न तीर्थव्रतकोटिभिः ॥
नान्यैरुपायैर्देवेशि मन्त्रौषधिपुरः सरैः ।
आम्नायो ज्ञायते चोर्द्धः श्रीमद्गुरुमुखं विना ॥

na vedair nāgamaiḥ śāstrair
na purāṇaiḥ suvistaraiḥ
na yajñair na tapobhir vā
na tīrtha-vrata-koṭibhiḥ

nānyair upāyair deveśi
mantrauṣadhi-puraḥ-saraiḥ
āmnāyo jñāyate corddhvaḥ
śrīmad-guru-mukhaṁ vinā

Neither through Vedas, *Āgamas*, *śāstras*, or *Purāṇas*, however exhaustive they may be, nor through sacrifices, austerities, or a million pilgrimages, nor even through mantras and herbs, can one know about the *Ūrdhvāmnāya*. It can be known only from the mouth of a guru.

(*Kulārṇava Tantra*, 3.28–29)

Furthermore, since *Ūrdhvāmnāya* is an incarnation of Śiva, or the supreme Being, there is no karma in it. Therefore, those who want to reach salvation the easiest way should follow only this path.

Practice

The deity Ardha-nārīśvara is a variant of the *Trika* goddess Parā. This fusion is also seen in the mantras *prāsāda-parā* (*Hsauṁ*) and *parā-prāsāda* (*Shauṁ*), which are combinations of the mantra of Parā (*Sauḥ*), the *Trika* supreme goddess, with *Prāsāda* (*Hauṁ*), Śiva's mantra from the *Saiddhāntika* tradition. However, beyond the mantra, there is no discernible connection with the *Trika*.

After describing the greatness of *Ūrdhvāmnāya*, the *Kulārṇava Tantra* discusses the *Śrī-prāsāda-parā* or *parā-prasāda* mantra. Śiva tells Pārvatī that this mantra presides over the doctrine of *Ūrdhvāmnāya*. Since it is the embodiment of Śiva and Śakti, this mantra can help *sādhakas* achieve their true nature.

श्रीप्रासादपरामन्त्रमूर्ध्वाम्नायमधिष्ठितम् ।
आवयोः परमाकारं यो वेत्ति स स्वयं शिवः ॥

śrī-prāsāda-parā-mantram
ūrdhvāmnāyam adhiṣṭhitam
āvayoḥ paramākāraṁ
yo vetti sa svayaṁ śivaḥ

The *Śrī-prāsāda-parā* is the mantra presiding over the *Ūrdhvāmnāya*. This mantra is the complete form of us both [Śiva and Śakti]. Thus, one who knows it is Śiva himself.

(*Kulārṇava Tantra*, 3.49)

Śiva explains that all creation recites the mantra when it inhales and exhales in the form of *Haṁ* and *Sa*:

शिवादिक्रिमि पर्यन्तं प्राणिनां प्राणवर्त्मना ।
निश्वासोच्छ्वासरूपेण मन्त्रोऽयं वर्तते प्रिये ॥

śivādi-krimi paryantaṁ
prāṇināṁ prāṇa-vartmanā
niśvāsocchvāsa-rūpeṇa
mantro 'yaṁ vartate priye

From Śiva to a tiniest worm, all the organisms keep on repeating this mantra in the form of expiration and inspiration of breath.

(*Kulārṇava Tantra*, 3.50)

The Tantra describes the extraordinary power of this mantra and says that it imparts all things coveted by a human being, including *svarga* (paradise) and *mokṣa* (liberation). It states that all creation remains present in this mantra and provides several analogies: just as wind is invariably present in a fan, a bud in a seed, oil in a sesame seed, heat in fire, light in the sun, and so on.

पराप्रासादमन्त्रेण स्यूतमेतच्चराचरम् ।
अभिन्नं तत्त्वतो देवि तालवृन्ते यथानिलः ॥
बीजेऽङ्कुरस् तिले तैलम् अग्नावुष्णं रवौ प्रभा ।
चन्द्रे ज्योत्सनाऽनलः काष्ठे पुष्पे गन्धो जले द्रवः ॥

parā-prāsāda-mantreṇa
syūtam etac carācaram
abhinnaṁ tattvato devi
tāla vṛnte yathānilaḥ

bīje 'ṅkuras tile tailam
agnāvuṣṇaṁ ravau prabhā
candre jyotsanā 'nalaḥ kāṣṭhe
puṣpe gandho jale dravaḥ

The entire mobile and immobile creation is pervaded by the mantra *parā-prāsāda*. Essentially, the two are inseparable, just like air in a fan, sprouts in a seed, oil in a sesame seeds, heat in fire, light in the sun, moonlight in the moon, fire in wood, fragrance in flowers, and moisture in water.

(*Kulārṇava Tantra*, 3.52–53)

The *Kulārṇava Tantra* further describes the efficacy of *prāsāda-parā*: *japa* performed with this mantra turns a *paśu* (an ordinary creature) into Paśu-pati, or Lord Śiva. It says that the mantra duly uttered by a *sādhaka* gives the supreme knowledge that all creation is nothing but the manifestation or the dual force: Śiva and Śakti.

Name	*Pūrvāmnāya* *Kaula Trika*	*Uttarāmnāya* *Kaula Krama*	*Paścimāmnāya* Kubjikā	*Dakṣiṇāmnāya* Kāmeśvarī	*Anuttarāmnāya*	*Ūrdhvāmnāya*
Translation	The eastern transmission	The northern transmission	The western transmission	The southern transmission	The final transmission	The supreme transmission
Face	Īśāna	Sadyo-jāta	Tat-puruṣa	Aghora	None	Vāma-deva
Chronology	Beginning around 900 CE in Kashmir.	From the ninth to the fifteenth century CE.	Revealed in the tenth century CE.	Around the ninth or tenth century CE.	The tenth or eleventh century CE.	After the twelfth century CE.
Deities	Kuleśvarī and Kuleśvara. Also Parā, Parāparā, and Aparā - Kālasaṃkarṣaṇī.	*Kālīs* of the *kālī-krama* (*Mata*), *Gukyakālī*, Kālasaṃkarṣaṇī.	The goddess Kubjikā and her consort Navātma.	Kāmeśvarī, the goddess of erotic love.	Tripura-sundarī.	Ardhanārīśvara, a deity that is half Śiva and half Śakti.
Scriptures	The *Yogasaṁcāra*, *Triśiro-bhairava*, *Trikasāra*, *Trikakularatnamālā*, *Bhairavakula*, and *Vīrāvalī*.	The *Jayadratha Yāmala* (the three later *ṣaṭkas*).	The *Kubjikāmata*, *Saṭsāhasra Samhita*, and *Manthāna-bhairava*.	*Nityā-kaula*	*Nityā-ṣoḍaśikārṇava*	*Kulārṇava Tantra*

Name	*Pūrvāmnāya* *Kaula Trika*	*Uttarāmnāya* *Kaula Krama*	*Paścimāmnāya* Kubjikā	*Dakṣiṇāmnāya* Kāmeśvarī	*Anuttarāmnāya*	*Ūrdhvāmnāya*
Doctrine	Non-dualist idealism within Shaivism.	The *Krama* is both Tantric and *Śaiva* monist.	*Śākta* tradition. There is also a parallel system known as *Śāmbhava* that emphasizes Navātma (Śiva).	*Śākta Kaula* tradition.	Tantric *Śākta* monist tradition.	The direct form of Śiva himself; it was kept secret for this reason.
Rituals	External and internal worship.	The external ritual is simplified. Mental worship of the sequence of cognition.	The divine couple (Navātma and Kubjikā) assume six forms (*yāmalas*) to preside over the chakras. It incorporated the worship of the *siddha* founders.	The cult of the magic of erotic love that worships the goddess Kāmeśvarī in a *maṇḍala*, alongside her consort Kāma-deva and eleven *nityā* goddesses.	Worship of Tripura-sundarī, the *yuga-nāthas*, and the *Śrī-cakra*.	Simplified worship of Ardhanārīśvara.
Practice	Divine possession (*āveśa*) and fusion with the guru.	*Vratas* (vows), mantra, and *kuṇḍalinī*.	*Kuṇḍalinī-yoga*, *guru-yoga*, and mantra repetition.	Nityā cult.	Meditation and worship of the *Śrī-cakra* yantra.	The *prasāda-parā* mantra.

Chapter 5

Kashmir's *Trika* Shaivism

In the fertile valley of Kashmir in northwestern India, beings walked with their eyes lifted to the snowy peaks of the Himalayas. Their aspiration was to climb to spiritual heights and discover the mystery of being alive and aware. A breathtaking natural setting, a temperate climate, beautiful lakes, and the meditative silence of the valley provided an ideal environment for reflection that gave birth to the most refined philosophical schools in India. The *Vaiṣṇava*, *Śaiva*, *Śākta*, and *Saura* traditions flourished here as well as some Buddhist schools.

Kashmir borders the Swat and Chitral valleys in Gilgit, a region once crossed by the Silk Road. This route was established by China in the first century CE to export silk to other countries and led to an exchange of goods and culture between Asia, Europe, and Africa. Thus, while the rest of the Hindu continent remained disconnected from the world's advancements, the travelers of the Silk Road contributed to the multiculturalism of Kashmir.

During the High Middle Ages, the main city called Śrīnagara (the Blessed City or the City of the goddess), located on the shores of a large lake, was the valley's exquisite capital. Small kingdoms promoted religious, cultural, artistic, scientific, and philosophical development. In addition to religious studies, secular fields flourished, for example Sanskrit literature and sciences such as mathematics, astronomy, and medicine.

Kashmir was a famous center of learning among Buddhists and Hindus alike. Scholars traveled to the valley to be trained in Sanskrit disciplines and enrich themselves with other philosophical perspectives. Beginning in the fourth century CE, Buddhist monks started from here on their journeys along the Silk Road as they spread their philosophies in central Asia. It is believed that even the renowned Śaṅkarācārya, the highest exponent of *Advaita* Vedanta, climbed the 5000 feet to Kashmir in order to plant the seeds of monism that would soon germinate as non-dual *Śaiva* schools.

Circumstances of emergence

The Tantric revelation flourished in Kashmir. It reached such a scope that it spread throughout India and infiltrated all aspects of religion on the subcontinent.

Due to the openness of the *Kula-mārga* sects, many illiterate seekers found spiritual refuge on this path. Toward the end of the ninth century CE, the movement also began to attract highly educated and refined aesthetes, many of whom were connected to royal courts.

Although they found a detailed guide for practice and ritual in the Agamic literature, its theology and philosophy were not clearly presented. Many rituals emphasized magic and some included practices that were offensive to educated society. The Tantras were mostly interpreted in a superficial and dualist manner. Moreover, the Tantric corpus was scattered and inconsistent.

Inspired by scriptures, scholars and self-realized *Śaiva* masters created a coherent and elegant system of thought. They wrote commentaries on the Tantric scriptures and gave them new interpretations while still respecting the veracity and validity of the revelation. They wrote texts that gave greater philosophical sophistication and respectability to the *Kula-mārga* sects, especially the *Trika* and the *Krama*. Since many of them were fully realized, their words vibrated with the power of their own experience. Their writings came to be respected as equivalent to the scriptures because they described reality according to the most direct vision of consciousness.

Chronology

Kashmir Shaivism is a *Śaiva* school but it has its own spirit and orientation. It flourished from the eighth to the end of the twelfth century CE. It was born out of the depths of the Tantric revelation and enriched by the teachings of non-dual *Śaiva* masters who lived in the valley.

It is believed that during the fourth century CE, three types of Tantra began to emerge, each presenting a different explanation of the nature of reality. The theology of the first ten *Śaiva Āgamas* was purely dualist (*bheda*). Next, the eighteen *Rudra Āgamas* appeared with a monist–dualist perspective (*bhedābheda*). Finally, the sixty-four *Bhairava Āgamas* were monist (*abheda*) and the most refined.

The evolution of *Śaiva* philosophical thought from dualism to non-dualism culminated in Kashmir's *Trika* Shaivism. The geniuses of the *Trika* believed that just as nature is subject to an evolutionary process, the receptivity of human beings also evolves and this allows them to channel increasingly secret levels of divine revelation. They managed to organize the scattered and seemingly contradictory Tantric canon into a congruent system that can be considered a *darśana*.

The brilliant Abhinava-gupta synthesized these seemingly contradictory perspectives under the umbrella of *Trika* Shaivism in Kashmir. He showed them to be different evolutionary stages of divine revelation and complementary visions that could help people at different levels realize reality.

The exegetical writers

The exegetical monist writers who were initiated on the path of the *Kaula* explained the philosophy and theology behind the esoteric teachings that Śiva taught Śakti. These brilliant thinkers and self-realized beings presented a domesticated version of the *Kaula* that attracted people from high castes. In this way, the Tantric revelation came out of the cremation grounds and expanded to include even members of royal courts. Over time, it became popular throughout India and grew into one of the most sophisticated monist schools.

They presented the canon as a hierarchical development of the revelation. They did not exclude antinomian practices but kept them secret and allowed them only to the most advanced *Tāntrikas*. In this way, they combined metaphysical thinking with spiritual practice, even in its most esoteric form.

Vasu-gupta (c. 875–925 CE) took the first steps of monist Shaivism. According to tradition, he had a dream of Śiva instructing him to go to a mountain and remove a rock. Vasu-gupta did so and discovered texts inscribed on a stone that imparted the teachings of *Śaiva* monism. This scripture came to be called the *Śiva Sūtra* and was the keystone of monism, revealed by Śiva himself.

Other principal authors of *Śaiva* monist texts were Somānanda (c. 900–950 CE), who wrote the *Śiva-dṛṣṭi* (*The Vision of Śiva*), and his disciple Utpala-deva (c. 925–975 CE), an influential philosopher, theologian, and the author of the *Īśvara-pratyabhijñā Kārikā* (*Verses on the Recognition of the Lord*). He was the master of Lakṣmaṇa-gupta, who was in turn the master of the most brilliant of all the exegetes, Abhinava-gupta (c. 950–1025 CE). The words of these exegetes were venerated as sacred because they gave a clear vision of reality, described by those who had the direct experience of consciousness.

General characteristics of the *Trika*

Kashmir Shaivism was the later development of the eastern *Kula-mārga* transmission known as the *Trika* (triple). The name *Trika* derives from several triads that have both philosophical and esoteric importance.

The exegetical writers of Kashmir did not take the Shamanic rites literally but reinterpreted the antinomian elements of *kaula* rituals as aspects of inner spiritual experience.

They argued that the fierce goddesses are, in fact, energies of the human mind. The senses are dominated by these goddesses, and when a ritual is performed for them, they feel satisfied and reward the

Tāntrika with blissful consciousness. The mortuary symbols represent the death of the ego. When the ego is overcome, external objects shine within consciousness like flavors of pure aesthetic experience.

This was a process of refining controversial practice into a gnoseological system based on the aesthetics of vision and hearing. This system reserved the most esoteric and transgressive practices for advanced *Tāntrikas*. It was a religion of dissimulation. The following aphorism sums up the new attitude:

अन्तःशाक्ता बहिः शैवाः सभायां वैष्णवा मताः ।
नानावेषधराः कौलाः विचरन्ति महीतले ॥

antaḥ-śāktā bahiḥ śaivāḥ
sabhāyāṁ vaiṣṇavā matāḥ
nānāveṣa-dharāḥ kaulāḥ
vicaranti mahī-tale

> In private, *Śāktas*, in public, *Śaivas*, among the people, V*aiṣṇavas*; with various external appearances, *Kaulas* spread across the earth.
>
> (*Yonī Tantra*, 4.20)

For these great aesthetes, the highest state of consciousness was *camat-kāra*, or "aesthetic rapture," which is the experience of wonder in the face of the beauty of embodied existence. Everything must be included in the beauty of existence. There is no separation between pure and impure if we recognize the divinity that underlies the entire cosmic manifestation. Tantric art born out of this vision presents images of ferocious yet benevolent deities.

It is believed that these brilliant masters were enriched with the sophisticated monist philosophy of Śaṅkarācārya's *Advaita* Vedanta, Bhartṛhari's *Śabda* Absolutism, and *Mahāyāna* Buddhist Absolutism that was very popular in the region. Kashmir philosophers shaped *Śaiva* Absolutism following the methodology of these systems.

Trika monism holds that the Lord, the individual soul, and the universe are not separate ontologies but identical to pure consciousness (*cit*). The material universe is a vibration of consciousness and souls are manifestations of the one reality. Initiates aspire to merge their individual consciousness with the absolute consciousness of Śiva, who becomes Kālī in the esoteric heart of *Tāntrikas*.

The theoreticians of the exegetic stage made an innovative reinterpretation of existing Tantric theology and integrated aesthetics and linguistics. They argued that the absolute divinity communicates with the human microcosm through a stream of phosphorescent light and as a succession of the vibrating phonemes of the Sanskrit language. The universe is created by a divine outpouring of light and sound. Hence Tantric practitioners can identify their divine nature by connecting to these light photons and sound phonemes through meditation.

Trika sādhana includes elaborate daily rituals, *kuṇḍalinī-yoga*, and logical practices called *upāyas* (methods). Through the repetition of mantras, mental rituals, visualizations, and the worship of external symbolic diagrams (*maṇḍalas*), adepts become purified and realize their true divine identity.

The arrival of Islam

The *Śaiva* exegetes came to spread light and wisdom in the valley, but unfortunately, bloodshed soon followed. The Muslim invasion at the end of the thirteenth century CE put an end to this miracle. Temples were destroyed, spiritual leaders killed, and sacred scriptures burned, many of them lost forever.

Nowadays, Kashmir is one of the world's most troubled regions. It is at the center of confrontation between Muslims and Hindus, witness to horrendous crimes, and a base for militant groups.

Its blue lakes are tainted with bloodshed driven by hatred, greed, and religious intolerance. The mountains that witnessed glorious times pray for humans to awaken from the nightmare of oblivion and for divinity to again descend into the valley.

With the arrival of Islam, the institutional base of *Śaiva Tantra* was dismantled because its adepts no longer had the state support.

As with most esoteric sects, those that practiced in informal settings without an organized clerical structure survived in secret. Tantra began as a practice of ascetics, then was dominated by heads of households during the classical period (800–1200 CE), and under Muslim and Mughal rule, preserving it again fell to ascetic yogis. However, since these *sādhus* were mostly illiterate, the metaphysical apogee of the exegetes did not continue and they did not record their teachings and revelations.

In the post-classical period, *Kaula* practices were internalized and domesticated even more and finally merged with hatha yoga.

Abhinava-gupta: The brightest star in Kashmir's sky

It is an exceptional event when a soul of Abhinava-gupta's magnitude descends to earth. His brilliant intellect, love for art, openness to all paths, and passion for life show what human beings can become when they express their divine potential. Like a busy bee, he collected pollen from all the flowers of the valley and transformed it into the sweetest honey ever produced by Mother India.

Although there were geniuses both before and after him, there is no doubt that Abhinava-gupta was the brightest star in the sky of Kashmir.

At the end of the first millennium, he brought the lamp of wisdom to illuminate the dark Tantras.

It is estimated that he lived from 950 to 1016 or 1025 CE. He was a *mahā-siddha*, a brilliant scholar, a great philosopher, an esoteric mystic, a fervent devotee, and a refined aesthete. His influence on Hindu music, poetry, and drama is remarkable. His multifaceted personality influenced the culture of India and the destiny of the Tantric revelation.

Ancestors

Abhinava-gupta's mother was called Vimalā and she was a very pious and devout woman. His father Narasiṁha-gupta was a dedicated devotee of Maheśvara and a great Sanskrit scholar. We know that his grandfather was called Varāha-gupta and that his ancestor Atri-gupta came to Kashmir from Madhya-deśa in the eighth century CE, invited by King Lalitāditya.

Vimalā died when he was just two years old and this early loss probably propelled him to a life of detachment and spirituality. Alongside his brother Manoratha and his sister Ambā, he was raised by his father, who was his first guru and taught him Sanskrit, grammar, logic, and literature.

Birth and childhood

Abhinava-gupta had a consecrated birth. His parents were advanced Tantric practitioners who conceived him during a *Kaula* ritual. In this secret ritual, a *yoginī* (initiated woman) and a *siddha* (initiated man) join in copulation and induce each other a spiritual awakening through the intensity of their love. In the orgasmic state, they unite on physical, mental, and astral planes and then are absorbed in the consciousness of the Self. Once merged, they become the supreme couple of Śiva and Śakti. This *Kaula* sacrifice is reserved only for those who can identify their nature as Bhairava and Bhairavī, even during sexual union. It is believed that a soul that is conceived during the ritual is a *yoginībhū* (born of a *yoginī*) and, therefore, has an extraordinary intellect and an exceptional vocation for liberation.

Spiritual masters

His insatiable thirst for knowledge led Abhinava-gupta to drink from all the wells of wisdom in Kashmir. He studied with Buddhists, *Vaiṣṇavas*, *Śaiva-siddhānta* dualists, and Tantric scholars. He was initiated by more than fifteen gurus, mystics, philosophers, and scholars.

At an early age, Abhinava-gupta was initiated into the *Krama* lineage by Bhuti-rāja, his father's guru, who was a disciple of the renowned Cakra-bhānu. Bhuti-rāja taught Abhinava-gupta the *Dvaitādvaita* (dualist monist) Tantras and initiated him into the esoteric *pañcākṣarī* mantra. He studied the *Dvaita* (dualist) Tantras of *Śaiva-siddhānta* with Vāma-nātha, and the *Advaita* (non-dualist) Tantras with Lakṣmaṇa-gupta, including the *Krama*, *Trika*, and *Pratyabhijñā*. But it was Śambhu-nātha who taught him the *Kaula* tradition and granted him final liberation.

Kaula initiation

Śambhu-nātha was the one who finally quenched his spiritual thirst. This *Kaula* master came from the sacred pilgrimage site (*śakti-pīṭha*) called Jālandhara, in Punjab. He was an expert in the *Trika* and *Kaula Trika* traditions. It is said that the wife of Śambhu-nātha was the sexual partner (*dūtī*, or "conduit") of Abhinava-gupta in the *kaula* initiation ritual. She transmitted *śakti* to him that was sublimated in his heart and then in his consciousness. This descent of grace (*śakti-pāta*) led him to his final awakening. While the *Kaula* initiation is the quickest and most effective, it is reserved for those who have overcome mental limitations and purified their hearts.

Abhinava considered Śambhū-nātha to be his *sad-guru* and praised him above all others. He compared him to the sun for his ability to dispel darkness and to the moon that shines on the ocean of *Trika* knowledge. Following his request and guidance, Abhinava composed the *Tantrāloka*, an invaluable legacy of Tantric glory.

Literary heritage

The scriptural treasure that Abhinava-gupta left us is vast. During his long and intense life, he wrote more than 35 texts on philosophy, theology, devotional poetry, aesthetics, rituals, and yoga practices, as well as brilliant commentaries on Tantric scriptures. But there can be no doubt that his magnum opus, which secured him a glorious place in the history of Kashmir Shaivism, was the *Tantrāloka*, or "Light on the Tantras." This is an encyclopedic treatise divided into twelve volumes that explains all the philosophical and practical aspects of the *Kaula* and the *Trika*.

Abhinava-gupta's literary evolution can be divided into three periods, each with their own writings.

In the first period, he wrote about the *Krama*, or "the school of gradation." The *Krama* was his first love. When his mind was restless, he found shelter in the esoteric system of the twelve Kālīs, who represent the evolutionary stages of the flow of *śakti*. He wrote the *Krama Stotra* (Gradation Hymn) and then composed a commentary on this work called *Krama-keli* (Gradation Frolicking). At this time, he also wrote a commentary on the *Mālinī-vijayottara Tantra*, the most authoritative Agamic text of the *Trika* sect, called *Pūrva-pañcikā* (Antecedent Pentad). These three works are now lost.

Although the *Krama* fascinated him, it did not quench his thirst and he was drawn to explore the mysterious Kaulism. He composed the *Bhairava-stava* (Praise to the Tremendous God) and two commentaries on the *Parā-triṁśikā* called *Vivṛti* and *Vivaraṇa*.

Later, he felt it was important to write a text for those who could not grasp the subtle philosophical concepts of the *Trika*. He composed the *Bodha-pañcadaśikā* (*Fifteen Verses on Enlightenment*), which explains the basic monist aspects of *Trika* Shaivism.

In the second period, Abhinava-gupta expressed his passion for aesthetics. The most important text of this period is a commentary on the *Nāṭya-śāstra* (*Treatise on Dance*), which expounds the theory of *rasas* that has inspired Hindu art for centuries. The work *Abhinava-bhāratī* (*New Eloquence*) connects art with spirituality and the experience of relishing (*rasa*) with the realization of the Self. He also wrote a commentary on the *Dhvany-āloka* (*Light of Suggestion*) called *Dhvay-āloka-locana* (*The Illumination of the Light of Suggestion*), and composed *Kāvya-kautuka-vivaraṇa* (*Exposition of the Wonder of Poetry*), now lost.

In his third literary period, Abhinava-gupta devoted himself completely to analyzing and presenting the main theological subjects of the *Trika*. He wrote the *Gītārtha-saṅgraha* (*Compendium on the Gītā*), a *Trika* interpretation of the Bhagavad Gita. He intended to show that the *Trika* does not contradict the principles taught in the Gita, which are respected by all schools of Hinduism.

He also wrote two important philosophical commentaries, one short and one long, on Uptala-deva's *Īśvara-pratyabhijñā Kārikā* (*Verses on the recognition of the Lord*). In his works *Bṛhad-vimarśinī* (*The Short Examination*) and *Laghu-vimarśinī* (*The Great Examination*), he gave the *Trika* a firm metaphysical position.

However, all these wonderful writings are incomparable with the depth, brilliance, and scope of his masterpiece, which was also written in this period: the *Tantrāloka*. In this encyclopedic treatise, the *Trika* is integrated and presented in a unified and coherent manner. Its pages include details of all branches of thought and, in particular, delve into the practice of the *Trika*. His brilliant disciples, Kṣema-rāja and Maheśvarānanda, continued his literary work with their own commentaries on this text.

Personality and way of life

Abhinava-gupta's thirst for knowledge was exceptional. His curiosity for discovering the mystery of life had no social or religious boundaries. He studied almost every branch of knowledge available at the time, including Jainism, Buddhism, and various Tantric traditions. His unique combination of aesthetic theory and non-dualist metaphysics gave Hindu Tantra a new direction. His originality has the air of someone who does not copy others but experiences his own individuality. That is why his name is so appropriate: Abhinava-gupta means "new" in Sanskrit, and this unique being always renewed himself by exploring new directions.

Abhinava-gupta was a writer and master who lived to the fullest the message he taught to his followers. His life was long and intense. For more than thirty years, he studied hard and traveled throughout Kashmir to learn from different teachers. He finally settled in a house that was effectively an ashram. He lived with his relatives and disciples, who gave him the peace and support he needed to dedicate himself to writing. Surrounded by disciples, teachers, and family, he had all the support and conditions for his genius to manifest. He remained single but probably not celibate, because the *Kaula* ritual was part of his *sādhana*. He was not an ascetic monk, nor did he assume the obligations of a householder, which would have distracted him from his spiritual searching and writing.

No one knows how his life ended. Tradition tells that he entered a cave with twelve hundred disciples and never returned. The cave still exists today and is believed to be a tunnel to the spiritual world.

Disciples

Abhinava-gupta had both admirable masters and fully realized disciples. He was able to receive the torch of wisdom, fuel its fire during his life, and pass it on to the next generation. His most prominent disciple was Kṣemarāja, who extensively explained his master's teachings and, following his example, continued to synthesize the various branches of *Trika* thought. Maheśvarānanda was central to clarifying Abhinava's syncretic approach.

Contribution

Abhinava-gupta's main contribution was to synthesize the hundreds of Tantric texts that were scattered and taught separately in different sects. They shared terms, subjects, and practices, but they did not have a coherent or systematic doctrine. Toward the end of the tenth century CE, he composed his magnum opus called the *Tantrāloka* (Light on the Tantras). It was a work that showed that all the Tantric sects share a unique vision of reality (*darśana*).

The language of the Tantras was mostly symbolic and sometimes unintelligible. Abhinava gave extensive explanations of the Tantric symbolism, without which we could not have accessed the revelation. When he wrote his exegesis, the entire Tantric corpus was intact. But over time, most of the scriptures were lost, and we only know of their existence and content thanks to works like these, which quote many of their verses. He not only illuminated the Tantras but also saved many of them from oblivion.

This master of syncretism integrated *Trika* thought with the ideas of the *Spanda*, *Kaula*, *Krama*, and *Pratyabhijñā* schools that were in vogue in Kashmir, giving birth to the most complete and profound philosophy.

The *Pratyabhijñā* school emphasizes the knowledge of reality (*jñāna*) and maintains that self-realization is achieved by recognizing the unity of the Self with all beings through universal love. Abhinava-gupta used the concept of *Pratyabhijñā* to connect Kashmir Shaivism's various schools.

The *Spanda* school focuses on the dynamic aspect of consciousness called *spanda* or *kriyā*. It shows how the realization of the Self can be achieved in action when activity becomes spontaneous and conscious. Abhinava-gupta pointed out that *spanda* is Śakti, the natural dynamism of Śiva, and therefore an integral part of him. *Pratyabhijñā*, being the knowledge of the Self, cannot be separated from *spanda*.

The *Krama* school emphasizes successive steps. It explains that since Śiva manifested the world of names and forms sequentially, we should use these sequences to meet with the Self in the same progression. Abhinava-gupta sees the *Krama* within the *Pratyabhijñā* because the aim of uniting with the Self is the same; the only difference is in the means. Hence it is also possible to reach Śiva through the successive steps taught by this school.

The *Kaula* school emphasizes the unity of Śiva and Śakti. It suggests a *sādhana* that includes the copulation of a man and a woman to embody this unity and realize higher consciousness. It follows the path of the left hand that includes the practice of the five Ms (*pañca-ma-kāra*). The *Kula* also aspires to self-realization (*pratyabhijñā*) and proposes a powerful and effective method that helps us rise above the duality of the sacred and the profane. As sexual energy is sublimated, universal love begins to flow, which is the path to liberation according to the *Pratyabhijñā* school.

These four schools found refuge under the umbrella of *Pratyabhijñā*. The genius Abhinava-gupta explained and developed these ideas for the benefit of the most serious seekers of Truth.

The four schools of Kashmir Shaivism

1. The *Kaula Trika* school

In his *Tantrāloka* (chapter 36), Abhinava-gupta recalls how Agamic tradition describes that after the importance of the *Śaiva Āgamas* had diminished, they were revealed again by Lord Śiva in his form Śrī-kaṇṭha. On Mount Kailash, he transmitted the revelation directly to the sage Durvāsā. Since Durvāsā could not find qualified disciples to receive the teachings, he created three perfect sons and called them Āmardaka, Śrīnātha, and Tṛyambaka. He taught each one of them one type of *Āgamas*: the 10 dualist *Śaiva Āgamas*, the 18 dualist-non-dualist *Rudra Āgamas*, and the sixty-four non-dualist *Bhairava Āgamas*, respectively.

Try-ambaka had a daughter named Ardha-try-ambakā, which means "half Try-ambaka." She started the lineage of the *Kaula*, also called *Adhyuṣṭa-pīṭha* (the tradition of three and a half).

Abhinava-gupta wanted to learn these four traditions and tells us who taught him each one. Vāma-nātha, a descendant of Eraka-vara, taught him the dualist tradition; a descendant of Bhūti-rāja taught him the dualist-non-dualist tradition; Lakṣmaṇa-gupta, a disciple of the great Utpala-deva, taught him the non-dualist tradition that goes back to Try-ambaka. Finally, Śambhu-nātha, a descendant of Somadeva, taught him the *Kaula* tradition.

The wisdom of the *Kaula* was forgotten over time, but at the beginning of the fifth century CE, Macchanda-nātha (Lord of the fish) reintroduced it to Kashmir. He revived this esoteric cult and taught it to his disciple Gorakṣa-nātha, the founder of the hatha yoga system. By the ninth century CE, the teachings had become distorted, and the master Sumati-nātha reestablished original Kaulism. Soma-nātha continued his lineage and Śambhu-nātha was his disciple. The great Abhinava-gupta received the treasure of the *Kaula* from his venerated master Śambhu-nātha.

Until the arrival of Abhinava-gupta, Kaulism did not receive as much attention in Kashmir as the *Spanda* and *Pratyabhijñā* schools. Since Abhinava-gupta achieved final liberation through *Kaula*, it was expected that he would give Kaulism the privileged place it deserved. Most texts on the *Kaula* tradition have been lost. If it were not for Abhinava-gupta's extensive explanations, we would have very little information about its rituals.

The terms *kula* and *kaula* seem to be synonymous in many contexts, but Abhinava-gupta explains the difference. The *kula* is the path that comes from the *Kāpālika* ascetics of the *Ati-mārga*, who wore mortuary insignia and performed the extreme practices of cremation grounds. The *Kaula* was a reform of the *Kula*, adapted for heads of household. Abhinava-gupta places the *Trika* at the top of the hierarchy, above both the *Kula* and the *Kaula*.

The original *Kula* cult, called the Cult of the *Yoginīs*, could be carried out only by those who had renounced life in society and lived in forests and cremation grounds. The *Kaula* reform revealed by Macchanda-nātha emphasized internal experience rather than the extreme sacrifices of the *Kula*. Heads of household were able to incorporate the *Kaula* into their practices and enrich themselves with its powerful effect. This domesticated ritual was considered as effective as the *Kāpālikas'*, although it was simpler and internal. The version of the *Kaula* adapted by Kashmir Shaivism was considered the essence of Tantric practice.

From a spiritual perspective, it is understandable that the public saw the *Kaula* as a dangerous path. Its rituals touch the delicate boundary between using the energy of desire for liberation and simply satisfying sensual desires. Fully aware of this risk, the *Kaula* insisted on initiation from an authentic guru for the most advanced practices. These rituals and practices have mostly been kept secret for generations. The *Kula-yāga* (Kula sacrifice) is not for the masses but for very elevated souls, as explained by Abhinava-gupta in the *Tantrāloka*:

अथ समुचिताधिकारिणमुद्दिश्य रहस्य उच्यते ऽत्र विधिः ।

atha samucitādhikāriṇaṁ uddiśya
rahasya ucyate 'tra vidhiḥ

Next, the secret ritual, which is intended for those who are properly qualified, will be described.

(*Tantrāloka*, 29.1a)

अथ सर्वाप्युपासेयं कुलप्रक्रिय योच्यते ।
तथा धाराधिरूढेषु गुरुशिष्येषु योचिता ॥

atha sarvāpy upāseyaṁ
kula-prakriyayā ucyate
tathā dhārādhirūḍheṣu
guru-śisyeṣu yocitā

Now, the entire preceding ritual is described according to *Kula* procedure, which is appropriate for the most advanced gurus and disciples.

(*Tantrāloka*, 29.1b–2a)

Unfortunately, charlatans have discredited the *Kula-yāga* by often misusing it for the sake of sensual pleasure and undermining its sacred nature. Likewise, Western culture has misunderstood its true essence. Tantric practices are not simply sexual relations for sensual enjoyment. *Kaula* sex is part of a sacred ritual, inspired by the quest for fusion with Śiva, or enlightenment. According to the *Krama* and *Kaula* schools, the woman is not a means of carnal enjoyment but the embodiment of Śakti, a true goddess.

Although Tantric sexual practices are the most controversial part of this path, it has much more to contribute to the sincere seeker. The *Kula* lineage is closely related to the *Siddha* and *Nātha* traditions.

Since the *Kula* emphasizes practice and experience, texts were not that important and its literature is limitedf. Some of the main works are the *Siddha-yogeśvarī-mata Tantra*, *Rudra-yāmala Tantra*, *Kulārṇava Tantra*, *Jñānārṇava*, *Nityā-ṣoḍaśikārṇava*, *Svacchanda Tantra*, *Netra Tantra*, *Tantra-rāja Tantra*, and *Kālī-kula*. These *Kula* teachings are the foundation of Abhinava-gupta's *Tantrāloka* and *Tantra-sāra*.

The *Kaula* system emphasizes how to live on the material plane while preserving universal consciousness, which is our true nature. It speaks of an ascent and descent: when we rise, we realize our nature, and when we descend, we recognize that we have the same essence as the entire cosmos. The *Kaula* does not suggest escaping from the world but living fully in it.

The *Kaula* reform influenced existing Tantric sects and gave birth to new traditions that adopted the Agamic revelation and applied the *Kaula* techniques. Each transmission of this later stage called *Kula-mārga* had its own set of deities, mantras, *maṇḍalas*, and so on. As described in chapter 8, the four main ones were:

1. *Pūrvāmnāya*, or "eastern transmission," whose main deity is Kuleśvarī.
2. *Uttarāmnāya*, or "northern transmission," whose main deity is Kālīkā, that is, the twelve Kālīs.
3. *Paścimāmnāya*, or "western transmission," whose main deity is Kubjikā.
4. *Dakṣiṇāmnāya*, or "southern transmission," whose main deity is Kāmeśvarī, or Tripura-sundarī.

The *Pūrvāmnāya* sect originated in the *Trika* sect *Vidyā-pīṭha*. It was the first to be influenced by Kaulism. Here we see how the *Trika* bifurcated into two sects: a Tantric one that practiced only Agamic rituals (*tantra-prakriyā*) and a reformed one that incorporated *Kaula* rituals (*kula-prakriyā*). Abhinava considered *kula-prakriyā* to be superior to *tantra-prakriyā*. The *Kaula Trika* took the essence of Tantric practice but set aside elaborate rituals that distracted practitioners from the spiritual essence. This reform was well-established in Kashmir by around 800 CE.

Kashmir Shaivism is, in fact, the later development of the *Pūrvāmnāya* (*Kaula Trika*), which was enriched by the *Uttarāmnāya* (*Krama*), incorporated the *kuṇḍalinī* wisdom revealed by the *Paścimāmnāya*, and finally, absorbed the monist philosophies that arose in Kashmir, namely, the *Spanda* and the *Pratyabhijñā*. It also took elements and practices from the *Śaiva-siddhānta*.

In its first stage, the *Trika* was a Tantric sect. In its second stage, it was influenced by the *Kaula* and split off as the *Kaula Trika* sect. In the third stage, which we call Kashmir Shaivism, it was enriched by the influence of Vasu-gupta (c. 825–875 CE), who revealed the *Śiva Sūtra* and founded the *Spanda* school. This school proposes that ultimate reality is a vibration (*spanda*), which manifests itself both in the transcendent state of consciousness and in its immanent state, that is, in the external world. Liberation consists in realizing the *spanda* as our own essence.

Next, the great sage Somānanda (c. 900–950 CE) revealed the *Śiva-dṛṣṭi*, a seminal work of what would later be called the *Pratyabhijñā* school. He developed the *Spanda* philosophy of the school that Vasugupta started. Next, Utpaladeva (c. 925–975 CE), a disciple of Somānanda, developed a classical formulation of the school in his book *Īśvara-pratyabhijñā Sūtra*, the namesake of *Pratyabhijñā*, the school of recognition.

Abhinava realized that the *Kaula* and the *Pratyabhijñā* were complementary, so he integrated them into a single tradition. The *Pratyabhijñā* provided Kashmir Shaivism with a metaphysical and philosophical framework and taught how to recognize our own nature and reside in the transcendental state of consciousness. *Kaula* practice guides us to realize the totality of the universe in a single atom. Every part contains the entire universe. We must rise from the closest reality to the highest, and thus experience the nature of the Self also on this plane. It shows the way to realize the presence of the Self, Śiva, and see Śiva in the grossest *tattva* of matter. In this way, everything is integrated into a non-dual whole, which the Kashmir Shaivism calls Parama-śiva. *Sādhana* is a process of first ascending and then descending to realize that the true nature of the Self is both omnipresent and immanent.

Abhinava-gupta describes *Trika sādhana* in the *Tantrāloka*. It consists of a daily *Śaiva-siddhānta* ritual, yogic *sādhana*, and a method called *upāya* that includes the practice of *kuṇḍalinī-yoga*.

The *Trika* or "the triple principle"

Kashmir Shaivism is often called the *Trika*. Historically, the term *trika* had a specialized meaning, but it has become synonymous with the non-dual Kashmir Shaivism as a whole. *Trika* means "three," and this type of Shaivism is called the *Trika* because it is full of triads, such as the three *Trika* goddesses: Parā (non-dual), Aparā (dual), and Parāparā (unity in duality), which represent the three levels of reality.

Different systems of Hinduism delve into the three fundamental principles: the nature of the divine Self, the soul, and the cosmic manifestation. Each school gives them different names. Vedanta calls them Brahman (Īśvara), *ātman* (*jīva*), and *jagat* (*māyā*). Kashmir Shaivism calls them Śiva, Śakti, and *aṇu* or *Pati*, *paśu*, and *pāśa*.

It is also called the *Trika* because its main authority is the triad of three *Āgamas*: *Siddha*, *Nāmaka*, and *Mālinī*. It is also based on three philosophies: *bheda* (dualism), *bhedābheda* (dualism with non-dualism), and *abheda* (non-dualism).

According to modern scholars, it was called the *Trika* because its original book, the Śiva *Sūtra*, is divided into three sections. It could also be because of the three sections in *Śaiva* literature: Śiva, Rudra, and Bhairava or the names of its first three teachers: Āmardaka, Śrī-nātha, and Try-ambaka. The name *Trika* could also have been related to its three branches: *Try-ambaka*, *Spanda*, and *Pratyabhijñā*.

Trika philosophy

According to Kashmir Shaivism, the universe is one, but it appears to be multiple because of karmic dispositions and the perception that there are different individuals. The single universe shows itself full of consciousness only to those who have transcended empirical boundaries. Wisdom appears only with the disappearance of ignorance. Everything is Śiva for those who receive *anugraha*, or "divine grace," and free themselves from illusion (*māyā*) and karma.

According to this school, *Pati* is Para-śiva, or "the ultimate principle, consciousness, or God." As noted in the *Pratyabhijñā-hṛdaya*:

> श्रीमत्परमशिवस्य पुनः वीश्वोत्तीर्ण-वीश्वात्मक-परमानन्दमय-प्रकाशैकघनस्य एवंविधमेव शिवादि-धरण्यन्तमखिलमभेदेनैव स्फुरति, न तु वस्तुतः अन्यत् कि ञ्चित्ग्राह्यं ग्राहकं वा ।
>
> *śrīmat parama-śivasya punaḥ vīśvottīrṇa-vīśvātmaka-paramānanda-maya-prakāśaika-ghanasya evaṁ-vidham eva śivādi-dharaṇyantam akhilam abhedena eva sphurati, na tu vastutaḥ anyat kiñcit grāhyam grāhakaṁ vā.*
>
> He is both immanent in the universe and transcends it. The universe is the very manifestation of God within himself. Of all [36] *tattvas* (principles, categories), from the *tattva* of Śiva to the *pṛthvī*, are within him. He is luminous, illuminating, and full of joy.
>
> (*Pratyabhijñā-hṛdaya*, 3, commentary)

Vimarśa, or *śakti*, is the power of Śiva that allows him to create and destroy, which Kṣemarāja mentions in his well-known *Parā-prāveśikā*:

> यदि निर्विमर्शः स्यादनीश्वरो जडश्च प्रसज्येत ।
>
> *yadi nir-vimarśaḥ syād anīśvaro jaḍaś ca prasajyeta.*

> If Śiva lacked *vimarśa*, he would be impotent and inert.
>
> (*Parā-prāveśikā* by Kṣema-rāja, 2)

It is important to clarify that *vimarśa*, or *śakti*, is not part of Śiva; instead, both are one: Śiva is *śakti* and vice versa, as stated by Somānanda in the *Śiva-dṛṣṭi*:

न शिवः शक्तिरहितो न शक्तिर्व्यतिरेकिणी ॥
शक्तिशक्ति मतोर्भेदः शैवे जातु न वर्ण्यते ।

na śivaḥ śakti-rahitao
na śaktir vyatirekiṇī
śakti-śakti mator bhedaḥ
śaive jātu na varṇyate

> Never has Śiva been stripped of *śakti* or vice versa. *Śaivas* do not recognize any difference between *śakti*, or 'power,' and the possessor of Śakti.
>
> (*Śiva-dṛṣṭi*, 3.2b–3a)

By the power of *vilaya* (dissolution) or *tirodhāna* (concealment), the *Parameśvara* (supreme Being) is reflected as *cit* (consciousness) in innumerable *paśus* (individual souls). *Tirodhāna* power is the cause of concealment, while *anugraha* is the power of grace that leads to liberation.

The powers of Śiva are infinite. However, Abhinava-gupta lists the most important ones in his famous work *Tantra-sāra*:

तत्र परमेश्वरः पञ्चभिः शक्तिभिः निर्भर इत्युक्तम् स स्वातन्त्र्यात् शाक्तिं तांताम् मुख्यतया प्रकटयन् पञ्चधा तिष्ठति । चित्प्रधान्ये शिवतत्त्वम्, आनन्दप्रधान्ये शक्तितत्त्वम्, इच्छाप्राधान्ये सदाशिवतत्त्वम्, इच्छाया हि ज्ञानक्रिययोः साम्यरूपाभ्य् उपगमात्मकत्वात्, ज्ञानशक्तिप्राधान्ये ईश्वरतत्त्वम्, क्रियाशक्तिप्राधन्ये विद्यातत्त्वम् इति ।

tatra parameśvaraḥ pañcabhiḥ śaktibhiḥ nirbhara ity uktam, sa svātantryāt śāktiṁ tāṁ tām mukhyatayā prakaṭayan pañcadhā tiṣṭhati.

cit-pradhānye śiva-tattvam, ānanda-pradhānye śakti-tattvam, icchā-prādhānye sadā-śiva-tattvam icchāyā hi jñāna-kriyayoḥ sāmya-rūpābhy upagamātmakatvāt, jñāna-śakti-prādhānye īśvara-tattvam, kriyā-śakti-prādhanye vidyā-tattvam iti.

It has already been explained that the Lord's perfection consists in his possession of five powers (*śaktis*). While the Lord is manifesting any [one] of his individual *śaktis*, his principal *śakti* remains shining in five different ways. When the power of consciousness becomes predominant, it is called the Śiva principle (*śiva-tattva*). Similarly, when [the power of] bliss (*ānanda-śakti*) becomes predominant, it is known as the Śakti principle (*śakti-tattva*). When, on the other hand, [the power of] will (*icchā-śakti*) becomes predominant, this is the Sadā-śiva principle. It is because of the dominance of the [power of] will that a balanced state of *jñāna* and *kriyā* exists in the Sadā-śiva principle (*sadā-śiva-tattva*). When the [power of] knowledge (*jñāna-śakti*) becomes dominant, this is the Īśvara principle, and when the power of action (*kriyā-śakti*) becomes dominant, this principle is known as pure knowledge (*śuddha-vidyā*).

(*Tantra-sāra*, chapter 8)

To summarize, the powers are:

1. *Cit*: The power of self-disclosure.
2. *Ānanda*: Absolute bliss, or the freedom to be or do everything.
3. *Icchā*: The willpower to be or create everything without obstacles.
4. *Jñāna*: The divine omniscient power.
5. *Kriyā*: The power to create everything by and from himself.

Somānanda explains it in his *Śiva-dṛṣṭi* in the following way:

योगिनामिच्छया यद्वन्नानारूपोत्पत्तिता ।
तथा भगवदिच्छैव तथात्वेन प्रजायते ।

yogināṁ icchayā yadvan nānārūpotpattitā
tathā bhagavad-icchaiva tathātvena prajāyate

> Just as a yogi is capable of creating something without a material cause, or *upādāna*, so does the willpower of Śiva.
> (*Śiva-dṛṣṭi*, 1.44a, 45a)

2. The *Pratyabhijñā* school

Pratyabhijñā means "to recognize," and it refers to the recognition of the Self, our authentic nature. The *Pratyabhijñā* school, or *Pratyabhijñā-darśana*, does not speak of *upāyas*, or "means to attain or obtain the Self." It is a system that guides without techniques or practices because we already are what we want to be and are where we aspire to be.

Understanding the Self is not about knowing but recognizing. Enlightenment is the experience of who we really are; it is to return to the place we have never left. But this recognition is not mental, otherwise it would be a mere projection from our memory.

According to this school, enlightenment means becoming aware that we have always been enlightened. The Lord is eternally close to us and within us as ourselves, though we are not aware of this. Therefore, it is not a matter of remembering something that we knew and forgot, but of recognizing what we already are.

Recognition is an awakening to the reality that whatever our state is, it is part of absolute consciousness. That is to say, absolute consciousness is not the apex of our evolution but includes our current state, even if we call it ordinary. When we recognize this, we begin to see others as enlightened beings who have not yet noticed their true reality.

According to an ancient Hindu custom, parents choose spouses for their children. Often these commitments are made before the children know each other. Imagine a young woman who has not met her fiancé. She often goes to a shop where he works, without knowing that he is her future husband. Even though she sees him often, she does not pay much attention to him. When her parents inform her that he will be her husband, she recognizes her husband in the shopkeeper. Although she was eager to meet him, she actually knew him for a long time. Likewise, the recognition of our authentic nature is realizing that we have always known what we thought we did not know.

This system flourished at the beginning of *Kali-yuga*. Its wisdom was falling in oblivion, until the eighth century CE, when Somānanda revived it in his famous *Śiva-dṛṣṭi*. His disciple Utpala-deva continued the work of his master and organized the fundamental philosophical principles in his famous work *Īśvara-pratyabhijñā* (The Recognition of the Lord). He was followed by his disciple Lakṣmaṇa-gupta, the guru of the great master Abhinava-gupta, who clearly explained the *Pratyabhijñā-darśana*.

3. The *Krama* school

Kashmir Shaivism scriptures call this school *Krama-śasana*, *Krama-darśana*, or *Krama-naya*. The term *krama* means "progress, gradation, stages, or succession" and refers to the gradual refinement of the idea as a means to liberation. That is to say, the *Krama* aims for a successive process of development and purification from darkness, through different states, to perfect clarity.

The *Krama* offers a detailed epistemological analysis of the cognitive experience, defining twelve stages of perception, each presided over by one of the Kālī goddesses. The worship of the Kālīs is an important aspect of this school. In the cognitive process, our attention shifts from our interior to the perceived object, to return again to the mental container that we have created and that gives us a certain sensation. In other words, we never experience the object in the place where it is located, but inside ourselves.

The *Krama* includes detailed descriptions of the ascent of *kuṇḍalinī* through each of the energy centers until it reaches the *sahasrāra-cakra* at the crown of the head.

Since the *Krama* suggests a progressive development, it has special interest in the concepts of time and space. While the *Kula* and

Pratyabhijñā schools focus on the reality that transcends space and time, this school believes such a reality is only relevant at the end of the process, not during it.

The *Krama* system is both Tantric and monist *Śaiva* and constitutes the emergence of the *Śākta* trend within Kashmir Shaivism. That is to say, it is a synthesis of Tantrism and Shaktism based on monist Shaivism.

While some do not see any substantial difference between the *Krama* and the *Kula*, it is clear that the *Krama* is its own school. While it certainly has much in common with both the *Pratyabhijñā* and the *Kula* schools, the *Krama* possesses a great intrinsic value that makes it independent. Even though it is an integral part of Kashmir Shaivism, there is clear evidence of its philosophical, historical, and even geographical independence.

As we mentioned earlier in this book, the *Krama* school goes back to the master Durvāsā, who introduced it at the beginning of the age of Kali. However, its founder is considered to be Śivānanda-nātha, who reinstated it in Kashmir at the end of the seventh century CE. This distinguished master had three very scholarly female disciples: Keyūravatī, Madanikā, and Kalyāṇikā. They continued the lineage by imparting this wisdom. Among the many who studied directly under these three female masters, there were disciples of high stature such as Govinda-rāja, Bhānuka, and Eraka. Govinda-rāja, in turn, was the master of the great Somānanda. Bhānuka also began a lineage of masters, including great ones such as Ujjaṭa and Udbhaṭa.

4. The *Spanda* school

The word *spanda* means "movement or vibration" and refers to the original creative and intelligent pulse of the universe that expresses itself in the dynamism of every life form. It is the first wave of Śakti that originates from Śiva at the beginning of the creation process. It is a vibrating wave of activity that is expressed naturally and spontaneously. Thus, Śiva is the reality that includes everything and is expressed through its inherently infinite movement.

This school teaches that existence necessarily implies movement and life cannot lack dynamism. It evaluates movement in all states of consciousness, even in deep sleep. At the individual level, *spanda* is consciousness expressed through thought, with the purpose of manifesting itself as creative and intelligent actions.

All human beings directly experience *spanda* as an impulse to act according to their most inner desires, following the natural rhythm of their body. Thus, this school encourages conscious connection to *spanda* through practices such as hatha yoga.

These teachings are found in the *Vijñāna-bhairava Tantra*, the *Svacchanda Tantra*, and in the sixth chapter of the *Tantrāloka*. This school was introduced by Vasu-gupta in Kashmir at the beginning of the eighth century CE. This distinguished master is the author of both the *Śiva Sūtra* and the *Spanda Kārikās*. Many commentaries on these *kārikās* were written; the most notable ones are the *Spanda-vṛtti* of Kallaṭa Bhaṭṭa, the *Vivṛtti* of Rāmakaṇṭha, and the *Spanda Kārikā* of Kṣema-rāja.

The literature of Kashmir Shaivism

The literature of Kashmir Shaivism is divided into three groups: *Āgama-śāstra*, *Spanda-śāstra*, and *Pratyabhijñā-śāstra*.

The first group includes the *Āgamas*, which are considered to be divinely revealed texts and are as important as the Vedas. According to Śaṅkarācārya's *Saundarya-laharī*, there are sixty-four *Āgamas* and their main topics are knowledge (*jñāna*) and practices (*kriyā*). This group includes Vasu-gupta's *Śiva Sūtra*.

The second group includes the *Spanda-śāstra* or *Spānda Kārikās*. The word *spanda* means "vibration," but in this context it can be translated as "the divine creative pulse." These texts delve into the philosophical principles of the *Śiva Sūtra* and are even thought to be its continuation. The main texts in this category are the *Spanda Sūtra* by Vasu-gupta and the *Spanda-sūtra-vṛtti* by Kallaṭa, the main disciple of Vasu-gupta. Masters such as Vasu-gupta, Kallaṭa Bhaṭṭa, Somānanda, Utpala-deva, Abhinava-gupta, and Kṣema-rāja did not transmit intellectual knowledge in texts, but instead shared their own transcendental experiences.

Finally, the *Pratyabhijñā-śāstras* are closely related to Agamic literature since they are based on the *Śaiva Tantras*. *Pratyabhijñā* means "recognition," and states that the *jīvātman*, or "the individual soul," is Śiva. The soul mistakenly identifies itself with *śarīra*, or "body," because it has forgotten its authentic divine nature. *Śivo 'haṁ*, or "the realization of one's authentic nature as Śiva," is called *pratyabhijñā*. The *Pratyabhijñā-śāstras*, also called *Manana-śāstra* or *Vicāra-śāstra*, comment on the fundamental principles of the school. Its main texts are the *Śiva-dṛṣṭi* by Somānanda-nātha (875–925 CE) and the *Pratyabhijñā Kārikā* by Utpala-deva (900–950 CE), one of his disciples.

Without a doubt, Abhinava-gupta (950–1025 CE) was the most brilliant of the masters. His commentary on Uptala's *Pratyabhijñā-kārikās*, as well as his own works *Tantrāloka* and *Paramārtha-sāra* have ensured him a glorious place in the history of Kashmir Shaivism.

Finally, we cannot fail to mention the great literary contribution of Kṣema-rāja (975–1025 CE), Bhāskara, and Varada-rāja.

The thirty-six *tattvas* or "categories of existence"

According to Kashmir Shaivism, God is not the external creator of the universe: he transforms himself into the creation. The manifestation of the universe is a movement of materialization of the spirit. With the elevation of *kuṇḍalinī*, the direction is reversed and the spiritualization of matter begins. The *tattvas*, or "categories or principles of existence," correspond to the different states that consciousness adopts in the objectifying process until it expresses itself as the material universe. In the opposite direction, the *tattvas* are the steps that consciousness traverses as it returns to its original state. In order to grasp the true meaning of the awakening, ascent, and descent of *kuṇḍalinī-śakti*, it is essential to understand the thirty-six *tattvas*.

Although the early Sankhya school addressed this issue, it only postulated the twenty-five impure *tattvas*. Without a doubt, Kashmir

Shaivism is the path of Hinduism that has most lucidly investigated and explained the complexity of the *tattvas*, by defining an additional five pure and six pure-impure *tattvas*.

Reality is solely consciousness. Consciousness does not create a separate universe, rather it objectifies itself. When consciousness vibrates in multiple frequencies, it manifests as diverse categories, but there is no substantial differences between them. Thus, the evolutionary process moves from the subtle to the dense, from unity toward multiplicity. When *kuṇḍalinī* rises, consciousness involutes and is reabsorbed back into itself. Its direction reverses from solidity toward subtlety.

The human being is a tiny universe or a microcosm: the process that happens within a person also occurs macroscopically, as is noted in this verse:

चितिसंकोचात्मा चेतनोऽपि संकुचितविश्वमयः ॥

citi-saṅkocātmā cetano 'pi saṅkucita viśva-mayaḥ

> Even the individual, whose nature is consciousness in a contracted state, embodies the universe in a contracted form.
>
> (*Pratyabhijñā-hṛdayam*, 4)

In our embodied state, we are contractions of the universe. The descent of *kuṇḍalinī-śakti* is the universal process of manifesting the individual. The ascent of *kuṇḍalinī-śakti* begins a process of involution that leads to the dissolution (*laya*) of the individual; hence, *kuṇḍalinī-yoga* is also called *laya-yoga*, or "yoga of dissolution."

Śakti is a power that is capable of revealing or concealing the Self. Cosmic manifestation is a process that camouflages consciousness as *śakti* descends, whereas its ascent is the return of consciousness back into itself. The awakening and elevation of *kuṇḍalinī* is a process in which *śakti* gradually reabsorbs the many *tattvas* until its final fusion with Śiva in *sahasrāra-cakra*.

Śiva or *Parama-śiva*, the Supreme Consciousness, is the perceiver and ultimate knower. He is the support, dwelling, home, and basis of the entire universe. He transcends time, space, and causality. He does not reside in any particular place because he lies both inside and outside everything and everyone. Since the universe is his manifestation, he cannot be categorized within the structure of the *tattvas*.

चितिः स्वतन्त्रा विश्वसिद्धिहेतुः ॥

citiḥ svatantrā viśva-siddhi-hetuḥ

Consciousness, in its freedom, brings about the attainment of the universe.

(*Pratyabhijñā-hṛdayam*, 1)

The study of the *tattvas* involves learning the process of creation. As she descends, Śakti covers the indivisible consciousness and shows it as relative duality. When she ascends, Śakti gradually reveals the single consciousness. In other words, in her descent, Śakti materializes herself, concealing the Absolute, which she reveals in her ascent.

The thirty-six *tattvas* are divided into three groups: pure (*śuddha*), pure-impure (*śuddhāśuddha*), and impure (*aśuddha*).

Śuddha-tattvas or "pure categories of existence"

1. *Śiva-tattva*: This is the initial creative movement of Parama-śiva. In the subjective state of purity—from the absolute point of view of Parama-śiva—everything that exists is *aham*, or "I am." Two categories begin to differentiate within "I am": the "I" as Śiva or the Self and the "am" as Śakti, the awareness of his existence.
2. *Śakti-tattva*: While Śiva is the internal aspect of consciousness, Śakti is the external one. Both are interdependent and inseparable, like wetness to water or heat to fire. *Śakti-tattva* and *śiva-tattva* are an eternal reality of pure subjectivity that does not admit duality. Śiva and Śakti are powers that appear to be separate but are actually two different aspects of Parama-

śiva. Śakti is the creative aspect of Brahman, the dynamism of consciousness. In their union, Śiva and Śakti are the pure subjective experience of *aham*, "I am." Śakti is the mirror in which Śiva observes his own reflection, creating the subjective polarity. Therefore, from *śakti-tattva*, consciousness projects itself in a subjective polarity giving raise to *idam*, or "That." This is stated in the following verse:

सा जयति शक्तिराद्या निजसुखमयनित्यनिरूपमाकारा ।
भाविचराचरबीजं शिवरूपविमर्शनिर्मलादर्शः ॥

sā jayati śaktir ādyā
nija-sukha-maya-nitya-nirūpam ākārā
bhāvi-carācara-bījaṁ
śiva-rūpa-vimarśa-nirmalādarśaḥ

She, the primordial Śakti, who exceeds all and who, in her own true nature, is eternal and limitless bliss, is the seed (*bīja*) of all the moving and motionless things that are to be, and is the pure mirror in which Śiva experiences himself.

(*Kāma-kalā-vilāsa*, 2)

3. *Sadā-śiva* or *sadākhya-tattva*: *Sadā-śiva* emerges from Śiva-Śakti as the first principle of the cosmic manifestation. From the pure subjectivity of "I am" (*aham*) arises "That" (*idam*), which is the root and origin of objectivity, the counterpart of subjectivity. In *Sadā-śiva*, the emphasis is more on *aham* than *idam*.
4. *Īśvara-tattva*: *Iśvara* is the Lordship principle that emerges from the pure subjectivity of *idam-aham*, "That is me," with a clear emphasis on the objectivity or *idam*. For Śiva, the cosmic manifestation is unreal as a dual-objective phenomenon, but it is real as his own expansion or continuation. The difference between the experiences of *Sadā-śiva* and *Īśvara* are remarkably subtle: the realization in both *tattvas* is practically the same, although less refined in *Īśvara*. The experience of "I am that" or "I am this universe" is that of *Sadā-śiva*, while in *īśvara-tattva*,

the realization is that "this universe is my own expansion." The great saint and philosopher Utpala-deva refers to *īśvara-tattva* in the following way:

सर्वो ममायं विभव इत्येवं परिजानतः ।
विश्वात्मनो विकल्पानां प्रसरे ऽपि महेशता ॥

sarvo mamāyaṁ vibhava
ity evaṁ parijānataḥ
viśvātmano vikalpānāṁ
prasare 'pi maheśatā

One who knows that all this glory of manifestation is mine [belongs to the spirit], one who realizes that the entire cosmos is the Self, possesses Lordship even when the *vikalpas* (thought constructs) have their play.

(*Īśvara-pratyabhijñā-kārikā*, 4.1.12)

5. *Śuddha-vidyā-tattva*, or "pure wisdom": In this state, both the subjective and objective aspects of consciousness acquire the same clarity. There is instability and imbalance because sometimes *aham-idam* predominates and at other times it is reversed, *idam-aham*. In *śuddha-vidyā*, unity and multiplicity are shown as identical expressions of transcendental consciousness. This *tattva* is the last of the pure categories without differentiation. In *śuddha-vidyā*, it is the power of action (*kriyā-śakti*) that prevails, since it is from here that the categories carry impurities that allow the manifestation of consciousness.

Śuddhāśuddha-tattvas or "pure-impure categories of existence"

6. *Māyā*, or "illusion": Contraction, relativity, duality, and limitation begin here. The experience of the Divine is hidden behind the veil of forgetfulness that *māyā* covers the Self with. While experience of the *śuddha-tattvas* is inclusive, *māyā* separates *idam* from *aham*. *Māyā* excludes one from the

other, creating the dual cognitive state of subject and object. From *māyā*, the *pañca-kañcukas*, or "five limiting powers," are born. These are five subtle, limiting powers through which consciousness voluntarily restricts its attributes and creates the conditions for a limited existence. The *kañcukas* are the following five *tattvas*: *kalā*, *vidyā*, *rāga*, *kāla*, and *niyati* (power, knowledge, desire, time, and space). Each *kañcuka* restricts one of Śiva's divine powers: *cit*, *ānanda*, *icchā*, *jñāna*, and *kriyā* (consciousness, bliss, will, knowledge, and action).

7. *Kalā-kañcuka*, or "limitation of power": This *tattva* reduces divine omnipotence, or the divine power of action (*kriyā-śakti*), to limited action.
8. *Vidyā-kañcuka*, or "limitation of knowledge": This *tattva* reduces divine omniscience, or the power of wisdom (*jñāna-śakti*), to limited knowledge about a particular topic or field.
9. *Rāga-kañcuka*, or "limitation of desire": This *tattva* reduces divine plenitude, or divine willpower (*iccha-śakti*), through the false impression of deficiency, which induces desires and a constant search for something or someone in order to regain plenitude.
10. *Kāla-kañcuka*, or "limitation of time": This *tattva* reduces the divine power of eternal bliss (*ānanda-śakti*) to an internal perception of time. It refers to psychological or internal time rather than that of clocks or calendars, which is measured in minutes, hours, or years.
11. *Niyati-kañcuka*, or "limitation of space": This *tattva* reduces divine omnipresence, or the power of consciousness (*cic-chakti*), to an illusory impression of residing in a specific place.

Aśuddha-tattvas or "impure categories"

12. Puruṣa: *Māyā* limits universal consciousness and reduces it to individual subjects. According to Kashmir Shaivism, just as Śakti becomes *prakṛti*, Śiva becomes the individual principle, that is to say, the soul (*jīva*). *Ahaṅkāra* is the subjective aspect of the ego; its experience when facing the universe is "I am not that."

13. *Prakṛti*: It is nature, from which the three modes known as *guṇas* flow: *sattva* (goodness), *rajas* (passion), and *tamas* (ignorance). Just as Puruṣa comes from Śiva, the origin of *prakṛti* is Śakti. Prakṛti refers to our external or superficial reality, while Puruṣa is our subjective internal world.

The three *antaḥ-karaṇas* or "internal organs"

Here, thought is born and developed.

14. *Buddhi*, or "the intellect": Its function is to evaluate, rationalize, accept, or reject what the *manas* (mind) perceives through the senses. Buddhi analyzes, reflects, determines, discriminates, and decides the nature of what is perceived.
15. *Ahaṅkāra*, or "the ego": This is the limiting "I" in its objective aspect. This phenomenon leads to take what is being experienced personally and to relate experiences to itself.
16. *Manas*, or "the mind": *Manas* sees, feels, hears, touches, and constantly conveys impressions to the subconscious mind. It is a product of *ahaṅkāra*, "the ego."

The *panca-jñānendriyas* or "five cognitive organs"

Objective reality is perceived through the five cognitive organs.

17. Ears (*śrotra*) for hearing (*śravaṇendriya*).
18. Skin (*tvak*) for touching (*sparsendriya*).
19. Eyes (*cakṣu*) for seeing (*cakṣurindriya*).
20. Tongue (*rasanā*) for tasting (*rasanendriya*).
21. Nose (*ghrāṇa*) for smelling (*ghrāṇendriya*).

The *pañca-karmendriyas* or "five organs of action"

22. Mouth (*vāk*) for speech (*vāg-indriya*).
23. Hands (*pāṇi*) for handling (*hastendriya*).
24. Feet (*pāda*) for locomotion (*pādendriya*).

25. Anus (*pāyu*) for excretion (*pāyvindriya*).
26. Genitals (*upastha*) for reproduction (*upasthendriya*).

The *pañca-tanmātras* or "five subtle elements"

27. *Śabda*, or "sound": It stems from ether, or *ākāśa-mahā-bhūta.*
28. *Sparśa*, or "touch": Its origin is air, or *vāyu-mahā-bhūta.*
29. *Rūpa*, or "form or color": Its origin is fire, or *tejas-mahā-bhūta.*
30. *Rasa*, or "taste": It stems from the element of water, or *jala-mahā-bhūta.*
31. *Gandha*, or "smell": It stems from the element of earth, or *pṛthivī-mahā-bhūta.*

The *panca-tanmātras* are the dwelling places of our senses (hearing, touch, sight, taste, and smell). They are the subtle principles that precede them.

The *pañca-mahā-bhūtas* or "five great elements"

The last five *tattvas* are the most dense and solid. The entire universe of names and forms rests upon them. The five *mahā-bhūtas* are under the control of the three modes of nature. Our physical body is a combination of these *pañca-mahā-bhūtas*, therefore, each one of them has certain characteristics that affect us individually. They are responsible for various functions in the human body and for tissues and fluids. The five great elements are the following:

32. *Ākāśa*, "ether or ethereality": This provides the necessary space for the other four to exist. This element is under the control of *sattva*. This *tattva* dominates the area from the throat up to the elevated planes of the astral body.
33. *Vāyu*, "air or airiness": This element is under the control of *sattva* and *rajas*. It dominates the region that extends from the heart up to the throat. *Vāyu-tattva* is activated after *tejas-tattva.*

34. *Tejas*, or "fire": This element is under the control of *rajas* and dominates the region from the navel up to the heart, where digestion happens. Fire receives its energy from *ākāśa.*
35. *Āpas*, "water or liquidity": This element is under the control of *rajas* and *tamas*. It controls the region from the hips to the navel.
36. *Pṛthivī*, "earth or solidity": This element is under the control of *tamas*. It is the base and foundation of our dense body. *Kuṇḍalinī* rests in solidity and density.

Śuddhādhvā-tattvas or "pure elements"

The first five categories are called *śuddhādhvā-tattvas*, or "pure categories." In order to understand this category, it is necessary to clarify that for Kashmir Shaivism, purity is related to the integrating experience of yoga, which means "union." It is a concept that has been brilliantly explained by Abhinava-gupta in his famous *Tantrāloka*:

मृतदेहेऽथ देहोत्थे या चाशुद्धिः प्रकीर्तिता ।
अन्यत्र नेति बुध्यन्तामशुद्धं संविदश्च्युतम् ॥
संवित्तादात्म्यमापन्नं सर्वं शुद्धमतः स्थितम् ।

mṛta-dehe 'tha dehotthe
yā cāśuddhiḥ prakīrtitā
anyatra neti buddhyantāṁ
aśuddhaṁ saṁvidaś cyutam

saṁvit tādātmyam āpannaṁ
sarvaṁ śuddham ataḥ sthitam

The impurity that the Veda attributes to a corpse and to the bodily secretions is well known and is not found anywhere else. According to the point of view of the faculty of reason, all that is separated from consciousness is impure. On the other hand, all that reaches identity with consciousness is pure.

श्रीमद्वीरावलौ चोक्तं शुद्ध्यशुद्धिनिरूपणे ॥

śrīmad vīrāvalau coktaṁ
śuddhy aśuddhi-nirūpaṇe

Regarding the determination of pure and impure, the *Vīrāvali-tantra* says:

सर्वेषां वाहको जीवो नास्ति किञ्चिदजीवकम् ।
यत्किञ्चिज्जीवरहितमशुद्धं तद्विजानत ॥

sarveṣāṁ vāhako jīvo
nāsti kiñcid ajīvakam
yat kiñcij jīva-rahitam
aśuddhaṁ tad vijānata

Life (*jīva*) is what animates everything. Nothing exists in the absence of life. All that is deprived of life should be considered impure.

तस्माद्यत्संविदो नाति दूरे तच्छुद्धिमावहेत् ।
अविकल्पेन भावेन मुनयोऽपि तथा भवन् ॥
लोकसंरक्षणार्थं तु तत्तत्त्वं तैः प्रगोपितम् ।

tasmād yat saṁvido nāti
dūre tac cuddhi māvahet
avikalpena bhāvena
munayo 'pi tathā bhavan

loka-saṁrakṣaṇārthaṁ tu
tat tattvaṁ taiḥ pragopitam

Therefore, all that is near consciousness bestows purity. This is also believed by mystics who are indifferent to the duality between pure and impure. In order to protect the world, they have kept this reality (*tattva*) secret.

(*Tantrāloka*, 4.240–244a)

Impurity is separation, difference, division, and duality. We purify ourselves to the extent that we perceive our existence as an integral part of the Whole. To perceive ourselves as disconnected from life and existence gives rise to all impurities. Impurity originates in ignorance, while purity originates in wisdom.

The *śuddhādhvā-tattvas* are the fruit of *Śaiva* sages' efforts to describe consciousness. Śiva stays in the purest subjectivity that transcends the subject-object duality. The *śuddhādhvā-tattvas* include five different categories, which are five aspects of the same consciousness. They are projections of the five main *śaktis* of the Absolute:

- *Cic-chakti* (*cit-śakti*), or "divine consciousness," projects *śiva-tattva.*
- *Ānanda-śakti*, or "absolute bliss," projects *śakti-tattva.*
- *Icchā-śakti*, or "divine will," projects *sadā-śiva-tattva.*
- *Jñāna-śakti*, or "the divine omniscient power," projects *īśvara-tattva.*
- *Kriyā-śakti*, or "manifesting power," projects *śuddha-vidyā-tattva.*

The state of *śuddhādhvā* is the divine experience of Śiva. It is a purely subjective perception, which transcends the subject-object duality. The ordinary experience of ego comprises a subject and an object. However, Śiva does not experience the universe as something distant and separate, but as an extension or projection of himself. Any experience of pure subjectivity of Śiva in the state of *śuddhādhvā* can be summarized in the word *aham*, or "I am." *Aham* is the *dhāma*, or "dwelling or abode," of all categories, just as "I am" is the basis and foundation of any individual life. The word *aham* refers to the sole subject that perceives the objective, while *idam*, or "that," is the subject's own projection.

Experience in the ordinary state of ego and perception in the *śuddhādhvā* state are radically different. The former is based upon the dual and relative subject-object platform, while the latter is a subjective experience. The egoic experience resembles a dream-like state that, in spite of being projected by dreamers, is objectivized by them. That is to say, dreamers perceive the world of dreams as separate and different from themselves. On the contrary, when we stand before a mirror, we have no doubt that the reflection is ours.

This is like the pure subjective consciousness of *śuddhādhvā*. The reflection is not perceived as a separate object disconnected from the subject. It is a subjective perception because the figure in the reflection is me. Similarly, Śiva projects the universe from himself as *idam*, fully conscious that it is his own projection and, therefore, an integral part of himself. This consciousness of absolute unity is the experience of pure subjectivity that transcends duality, despite the presence of *idam* in each and every one of the *śuddhādhvā* categories.

The 36 *tattvas*

Śuddha Pure	1.	*Śiva-tattva*	
	2.	*Śakti-tattva*	
	3.	*Sadāśiva*	
	4.	*Īśvara-tattva*	
	5.	*Śuddha-vidyā-tattva*	
Śuddhāśuddha Pure-impure	6.	*Māyā*	
	7.	*Kalā-kañcuka*: limitation of power	*Pañca-kañcukas* The five limiting powers
	8.	*Vidyā-kañcuka*: limitation of knowledge	
	9.	*Rāga-kañcuka*: limitation of desire	
	10.	*Kāla-kañcuka*: limitation of time	
	11.	*Niyati-kañcuka*: limitation of space	
Aśuddha Impure	12.	Puruṣa	
	13.	*Prakṛti*	
	14.	*Buddhi*: intelect	*Antaḥ-karaṇas* Internal organs
	15.	*Ahaṅkāra*: ego	
	16.	*Manas*: mind	
	17.	*Śravaṇendriya*: hearing	*Pañca-jñānendriyas* The five cognitive organs
	18.	*Sparsendriya*: touching	
	19.	*Cakṣurindriya*: seeing	
	20.	*Rasanendriya*: tasting	
	21.	*Ghrāṇendriya*: smelling	
	22.	*Vāg-indriya*: speech	*Pañca-karmendriyas* The five organs of action
	23.	*Hastendriya*: handling	
	24.	*Pādendriya*: locomotion	
	25.	*Pāyvindriya*: excretion	
	26.	*Upastha*: reproduction	
	27.	*Śabda*: sound	*Pañca-tanmātras* The five subtle elements
	28.	*Sparśa*: touch	
	29.	*Rūpa*: form or color	
	30.	*Rasa*: taste	
	31.	*Gandha*: smell	
	32.	*Ākāśa*: ether or ethereality	*Pañca-mahā-bhūtas* The five great elements
	33.	*Vāyu*: air or airiness	
	34.	*Tejas*: fire	
	35.	*Āpas*: water or liquidity	
	36.	*Pṛthivī*: earth or solidity	

Chapter 6

Tantric Vaishnavism

Vaishnavism is a major branch of Hinduism characterized by an exclusive devotion to Viṣṇu or his incarnations. The word *vaiṣṇava* means "related to Viṣṇu." *Vaiṣṇava* devotees see Viṣṇu as the supreme and only God. In addition to Shaivism, Shaktism, and Smartism, it is one of the main branches of Hinduism, and it has the largest number of followers. Within Vaishnavism, there are a number of schools, lineages, and sects, each focused on one of Viṣṇu's incarnations.

Rāma and Kṛṣṇa are the greatest focus of devotion, whom their devotees consider to be the supreme God. Rāma is tied to greater solemnity, while Kṛṣṇa offers a relationship that has a spirit of intimacy.

The corpus of *Vaiṣṇava* sacred scriptures includes the Upanishads, the *Brahma Sūtra*, the *Rāmāyaṇa*, and the *Mahābhārata*, which includes the Bhagavad Gita. Its religious aspect comes from the *Purāṇas*—especially the *Viṣṇu Purāṇa*—the *Vaiṣṇava Āgamas*, and the *Nālāyira-divya-prabandham* in Tamil.

Vaishnavism, like Shaivism, was born from the depths of the Vedic revelation. It is centered in India, but in the last few decades it has spread to the West. It can be considered one of the most beautiful notes within the *Sanātana-dharma* symphony.

Many generations of saints, sages, and enlightened *Vaiṣṇavas* have contributed to the development and evolution of the Viṣṇu cult. Slowly, the transcendental experiences and insights of new generations of seers have led to the development of theologies and rituals different from the rest of the Hindu sects. Over millennia, an incomparable literary treasure has been built up. It includes works that offer guidance from a purely *dvaita* vision to the most refined *advaita*. A variety of sacred texts lead us from a dualist conception to an abstract experience of God, as we see in the *Bhāgavata Purāṇa*:

वदन्ति तत्तत्त्वविदस्तत्त्वं यज्ज्ञानमद्वयम् ।
ब्रह्मेति परमात्मेति भगवानिति शब्द्यते ॥

vadanti tat tattva-vidas
tattvaṁ yaj jñānam advayam
brahmeti paramātmeti
bhagavān iti śabdyate

The wise ones who have realized the absolute Truth call this non-dual Brahman, Paramātmā, or Bhagavān.

(*Bhāgavata Purāṇa*, 1.2.11)

The first mention of the term *Vaiṣṇava* in the scriptures is found in the great epic *Mahābhārata*:

अष्टादशपुराणानां श्रवणाद्यत्फलं भवेत् ।
तत्फलं समवाप्नोति वैष्णवो नात्र संशयः ॥

aṣṭā-daśa-purāṇānāṁ
śravaṇād yat phalaṁ bhavet
tat phalaṁ samavāpnoti
vaiṣṇavo nātra saṁśayaḥ

The merit a Vaishnava obtaines by listening to the 18 *Purāṇas* might be obtained by listening to the *Mahābhārata* alone. There is no doubt about this.

(*Mahābhārata*, 18.6.97)

Vaishnavism's very roots are based on bhakti, or "devotion," to a personal God called Viṣṇu, Kṛṣṇa, Vāsudeva, or Nārāyaṇa. Tantra enriches Vaishnavism with the worship of the feminine aspect of God, the consort of Lord Viṣṇu. Early *Āḷvār* literature identifies Lakṣmī as the female aspect of Lord Viṣṇu. *Āḷvārs* were holy poets who embraced bhakti to Viṣṇu. They lived in southern India between the fifth and tenth centuries CE.

Devotional songs written in Tamil by the *Āḷvārs* mention the *gopīs*, or "cowherd girls," the devotees of Lord Kṛṣṇa. They are closely related to Śrīmatī Rādhārāṇī, the eternal feminine principle associated with Lord Kṛṣṇa as his *hlādinī-śakti*, or "pleasure-giving energy." The daughter of Periyāḷvār called Andal or Kodai experienced *rāgānugā-bhakti* and considered herself to be one of Kṛṣṇa's *gopīs*.

In the *Viṣṇu Purāṇa*, there are references to the feminine principle as Mahā-lakṣmī, the consort of Lord Viṣṇu. In the *Mārkaṇḍeya Purāṇa*, there are paragraphs that describe the goddess as Viṣṇu-māyā, the *śakti* of Lord Viṣṇu, and Nārāyaṇī, the consort of Nārāyaṇa. The *Lakṣmī Tantra* presents a different type of *Vaiṣṇava Ati-mārga* that includes left-hand practices (*vāmācāra*).

Vaishnavism was undoubtedly influenced by the Tantric tradition. Rāmānujācārya and Madhvācārya recognized Śakti as Lakṣmī, while Nimbārka, Vallabha, and Caitanya saw her as Rādhā.

Rādhā was revealed for the first time in the beautiful poems of *Āḷvār* Andal. Her presence was foreshadowed in the *Bhāgavata Purāṇa*. In the *Rādhā-prakaraṇa* section of the *Ujjvala Nīlamaṇi*, Rūpa Gosvāmī states that Śrīmatī Rādhārāṇī is *hlādinī-śakti*, the greatest of all *śaktis*, so he refers to Rādhā as Mahā-śakti. Of course, she resembles the Mahā-śakti venerated in Tantra. Jīva Gosvāmī himself, in his commentary on the *Brahma Saṁhitā*, quotes a verse from the *Sammohana Tantra* on Rādhā.

Many modern scholars see the divine couple of Vaishnavism as another version of Tantra's Śiva–Śakti. The relationship between Śrī Śrī Rādhā and Kṛṣṇa was given special attention in Jaya-deva's *Gītā-govinda*, in the *Brahma-vivarta Purāṇa*, and in the poetry of Vidyā-pati and Caṇḍī-dāsa. This treatment comes from the Tantric *Vaiṣṇava-sahajiyā* sect, which Jayadeva says he followed. There are even scholars who are inclined to call Śrī Caitanya a *sahajiyā*. They suggest that Śrī Caitanya had a Tantric relationship with Ṣāṭhī, the daughter of Sārva-bhauma Bhaṭṭācārya. This is why Amogha, the husband of Ṣāṭhī, became angry with Śrī Caitanya when he visited Sārva-bhauma Bhaṭṭācārya's home to accept *prasādam*.

হেনকালে 'অমোঘ,' – ভট্টাচার্যের জামাতা ।
কুলীন, নিন্দক তেঞ্হো ষাঠীকন্যার ভর্তা ॥

hena-kāle 'amogha,' — bhaṭṭācāryera jāmātā
kulīna, nindaka teṅho ṣāṭhī-kanyāra bhartā

At this time Bhaṭṭācārya had a son-in-law named Amogha, who was the husband of his daughter Ṣāṭhī. Although he was born to an aristocratic Brahman family, Amogha was a great faultfinder and blasphemer.

ভোজন দেখিতে চাহে, আসিতে না পারে ।
লাঠিহাতে ভট্টাচার্য আছেন দুয়ারে ॥

bhojana dekhite cāhe, āsite nā pāre
lāṭhi-hāte bhaṭṭācārya āchena duyāre

Amogha wanted to see Śrī Caitanya Mahā-prabhu eat, but he was not allowed to enter. Indeed, Bhaṭṭācārya guarded the threshold of his house with a stick in his hand.

তেঞ্হো যদি প্রসাদ দিতে হৈলা আনমন ।
অমোঘ আসি' অন্ন দেখি' করয়ে নিন্দন ॥

teṅho yadi prasāda dite hailā āna-mana
amogha āsi' anna dekhi' karaye nindana

However, as soon as Bhaṭṭācārya began distributing *prasādam* and was a little inattentive, Amogha came in. Seeing the quantity of food, he began to blaspheme.

এই অন্নে তৃপ্ত হয় দশ বার জন ।
একেলা সন্ন্যাসী করে এতেক ভক্ষণ! ॥

ei anne tṛpta haya daśa bāra jana
ekelā sannyāsī kare eteka bhakṣaṇa!

This much food is sufficient to satisfy ten or twelve men, but this *sannyāsī* is eating it all by himself!

শুনিতেই ভট্টাচার্য উলটি' চাহিল ।
তাঙ্র অবধান দেখি' অমোঘ পলাইল ॥

śunitei bhaṭṭācārya ulaṭi' cāhila
tāṅra avadhāna dekhi' amogha palāila

As soon as Amogha said this, Sārvabhauma Bhaṭṭācārya turned his eyes upon him. Seeing Bhaṭṭācārya's mood, Amogha immediately left.
(*Śrī Caitanya-caritāmṛta*, "*Madhya-līlā*," 15.245–249)

Vaiṣṇava theology was especially influenced by Tantra in Bengal and Orissa. The Tantric goddess Ekānaṁśā was revealed to be the consort of Lord Kṛṣṇa. In the Ananta-vāsudeva temple in Bhuvaneshwar, she is placed between Kṛṣṇa and Balarāma. In the famous temple of Jaganath Puri, she is depicted as Subhadrā and placed between Jagannātha and Balarāma.

The *śakti* doctrine occupies such an important place in the *Vaiṣṇava* scripture *Lakṣmī Tantra* that even *Śāktas* consider it sacred.

In the *Vivarta-vilāsa*, Ākiñcana-dāsa lists the Tantric partners of *Vaiṣṇava* aspirants.

One sign of Tantra's influence on Vaishnavism is the connection and relationship between the ten *avatars* of Viṣṇu and the ten Tantric *Mahā-vidyās*. A statement to this effect appears in the *Guhyātiguhya Tantra*:

कृष्णमूर्तिः कालिका स्याद्रामममूर्तिस्तु तारिणी ।
छिन्नमस्ता नृसिंहः स्याद्वामनो भूवनेश्वरी ॥
जामदग्न्याः सुन्दरी स्यान्मीनो धूमावनी भवेत् ।
वगला कूर्ममूर्तिः स्याद्बलभद्रश्च भैरवी ॥
महालक्ष्मीर्भवेद्बुद्धो दुर्गा स्याद्कल्किरूपिणी ।
स्वयं भगवती काली कृष्णस्तु भगवान्स्वयम् ॥

kṛṣṇa-mūrtiḥ kālikā syād
rāma-mūrtis tu tāriṇī
chinnamastā nṛsiṁhaḥ syād
vāmano bhūvaneśvarī

jāmadagnāḥ sundarī syān
mīno dhūmāvanī bhavet
vagalā kūrma-mūrtiḥ syād
balabhadraś ca bhairavī

mahā-lakṣmīr bhaved buddho
durgā syād kalki-rūpiṇī
svayaṁ bhagavatī kālī
kṛṣṇas tu bhagavān svayam

> Kālī is the *mūrti* of Kṛṣṇa, and Tāriṇī is the *mūrti* of Rāma. Chinnamastā is Lord Nṛsiṁha and Bhūvaneśvarī is Vāmana Deva. Vagalā is the *mūrti* of Kūrma Avatār and Bhairavī of Baladeva. Mahā-lakṣmī is Lord Buddha and Durgā is a form of Kalki. The very self of the goddess Kālī is Kṛṣṇa, who is Bhagavān.
>
> (*Guhyātiguhya Tantra*)

The Tantric tradition refers to the body as the dwelling place of God. It considers the energy centers (chakras) to be the abodes of either Śakti (*śakti-dhama*) or Śiva (*śiva-dhama*). Similarly, certain *Vaiṣṇava Saṁhitās* refer to Mathura and Vrindavana as dwellings of God. In some *Purāṇas*, Gokula is described as the abode of God in the shape of a lotus of thousand petals. According to Tantra, it is a thousand-petalled lotus called *sahasrāra-padma* that is located at the crown of the head.

We see a very close relationship between the *Pāñca-rātras* and the *Śākta Tantras*. It is well known that the *Śākta Tantras* refer to the omnipresent Ādya-śakti as *yonī*, or "vulva," a symbol of the divine energy of procreation that gives rise to everything. The *Ahir-budhnya Saṁhitā* (59.7) also refers to Lakṣmī as *yonī*.

Even the *Bhāgavata Purāṇa* recognizes the authority of Tantra in matters of worship, initiation, and so on.

पाद्योपस्पर्शार्हणादीनुपचारान् प्रकल्पयेत् ।
धर्मादिभिश्च नवभिः कल्पयित्वासनं मम ॥

पद्ममष्टदलं तत्र कर्णिकाकेसरोज्ज्वलम् ।
उभाभ्यां वेदतन्त्राभ्यां मह्यं तूभयसिद्धये ॥

pādyopasparśārhaṇādīn
upacārān prakalpayet
dharmādibhiś ca navabhiḥ
kalpayitvāsanaṁ mama

padmam aṣṭa-dalaṁ tatra
karṇikā-kesarojjvalam
ubhābhyāṁ veda-tantrābhyāṁ
mahyaṁ tūbhaya-siddhaye

Worshippers should first imagine my seat to be decorated with the personified deities of religion, knowledge, renunciation, and opulence as well as my nine spiritual energies. They should think of the Lord's seat as an eight-petalled lotus, effulgent from the saffron filaments inside its spiral shape. Then, following the regulations of both the Vedas and the Tantras, they should offer me water to wash my feet, water to wash my mouth, *arghya*, and other items of worship. Through this process they achieve both material enjoyment and liberation.

(*Bhāgavata Purāṇa*, 11.27.25–26)

श्रीशौनक उवाच-
अथेममर्थं पृच्छामो भवन्तं बहुवित्तमम् ।
समस्ततन्त्रराद्धान्ते भवान्भागवत तत्त्ववित् ॥

śrī-śaunaka uvāca
athemam arthaṁ pṛcchāmo
bhavantaṁ bahu-vittamam
samasta-tantra-rāddhānte
bhavān bhāgavata tattva-vit

Śrī Śaunaka said: O Sūta, you are the best of learned men and a great devotee of the supreme Lord. So we now inquire from you about the definitive conclusion of all Tantric scriptures.

(*Bhāgavata Purāṇa*, 12.11.1)

एवं क्रियायोगपथैः पुमान् वैदिकतान्त्रिकैः ।
अर्चन्नुभयतः सिद्धिं मत्तो विन्दत्यभीप्सिताम् ॥

evaṁ kriyā-yoga-pathaiḥ
pumān vaidika-tāntrikaiḥ
arcann ubhayataḥ siddhiṁ
matto vindaty abhīpsitām

By worshipping me through the various methods prescribed in the Vedas and Tantras, one will gain from me the desired perfection in both this life and the next.

(*Bhāgavata Purāṇa*, 11.27.49)

सूत उवाच-
नमस्कृत्य गुरून् वक्ष्ये विभूतीर्वैष्णवीरपि ।
याः प्रोक्ता वेदतन्त्राभ्यामाचार्यैः पद्मजादिभिः ॥

sūta uvāca
namaskṛtya gurūn vakṣye
vibhūtīr vaiṣṇavīr api
yāḥ proktā veda-tantrābhyām
ācāryaiḥ padmajādibhiḥ

Sūta Gosvāmī said: offering obeisances to my spiritual masters, I shall repeat to you the description of the opulence of Lord Viṣṇu given in the Vedas and Tantras by great authorities, beginning from the lotus-born Brahma.

(*Bhāgavata Purāṇa*, 12.11.4)

य आशु हृदयग्रन्थिं निर्जिहीर्षुः परात्मनः ।
विधिनोपचरेद् देवं तन्त्रोक्तेन च केशवम् ॥

ya āśu hṛdaya-granthiṁ
nirjihīrṣuḥ parātmanaḥ
vidhinopacared devaṁ
tantroktena ca keśavam

One who desires to quickly cut the knot of false ego, which binds the spirit soul, should worship the supreme Lord, Keśava, following the regulations in Vedic scriptures such as the Tantras.

(*Bhāgavata Purāṇa*, 11.3.47)

तं तदा पुरुषं मर्त्या महाराजोपलक्षणम् ।
यजन्ति वेदतन्त्राभ्यां परं जिज्ञासवो नृप ॥

taṁ tadā puruṣaṁ martyā
mahā-rājopalakṣaṇam
yajanti veda-tantrābhyāṁ
paraṁ jijñāsavo nṛpa

My dear King, in Dvāpara-yuga people who desire to know God, who is the supreme enjoyer, worship him in the mood of honoring a great king, following the prescriptions of both the Vedas and Tantras.

(*Bhāgavata Purāṇa*, 11.5.28)

In the following verses, we can see the Tantric attitude of Viṣṇu's *avatar*, Dattātreya, described in one of the main *Purāṇas*:

दत्तात्रेयो ऽपि विषयान्योगस्थो ददृशो हरिः ॥

dattātreyo 'pi viṣayān
yoga-stho dadṛśo hariḥ

Being Viṣṇu, Dattātreya also enjoyed the objects of the senses while engaged in profound meditation.

(*Mārkaṇḍeya Purāṇa*, 17.15)

मुनिपुत्रवृतो योगी दत्तात्रेयो ऽप्यसङ्गिताम् ।
आभीप्समानः सरसि निममज्ज चिरं प्रभुः ॥
तथापि तं महात्मानमतीव प्रियदर्शनम् ।
तत्यर्जुन कुमारास्ते सरसस्तीरमाश्रताः ॥

muni-putravṛto yogī
dattātreyo 'py asaṅgitām
ābhīpsamānaḥ sarasi
nimamajja ciraṁ prabhuḥ

tathāpi taṁ mahātmānam
atīva priya-darśanam
tat tyajur na kumārās te
sarasas tīra saṁśritāḥ

Surrounded by the sons of *munis*, the lordly yogi Dattātreya, who wanted to be free of all attachments, immersed himself in a lake for a long time. These young men stayed at the edge of the lake and did not forsake him, who was magnanimous and exceedingly benevolent.

(*Mārkaṇḍeya Purāṇa*, 17.17–18)

दिव्ये वर्षशते पूर्णे यदा ते न त्यजन्ति तम् ।
तत्प्रीत्या सरसस्तीरं सर्वे मुनिकुमारकाः ॥
ततो दिव्याम्बरधरां चारुपीननितम्बिनीम् ।
नारीमादाय कल्याणीमुत्ततार जलान्मुनिः ॥
स्त्रीसन्निकर्षाद्यद्येते परित्यक्ष्यन्ति मामिति ।
मुनिपुत्रास्ततोऽसङ्गी स्थास्यामीति विचिन्तयन् ॥
तथापि तं मुनिसुता न त्यजन्ति यदा मुनिम् ।
ततः सह तया नार्य्या मद्यपानमथापिबत् ॥

divye varṣa-śate pūrṇe
yadā te na tyajanti tam
tat prītyā sarasas tīraṁ
sarve muni-kumārakāḥ

tato divyāmbara-dharāṁ
cāru-pīna nitmbinīm
nārīm ādāya kalyāṇīm
uttatāra jalān muniḥ

strī-san-nikarṣād yad yete
parityaksyanti mām iti
munī-putrās tato 'saṅgī
sthāsyāmīti vicintayan

tathāpi taṁ muni-sūtā
na tyajanti yadā munim
tataḥ saha tayā nāryyā
madya-pānam athāpibat

Although a hundred heavenly years had passed, those young *munis* remained on the bank of the lake out of affection for him. Then the *muni*, taking his noble wife clothed in heavenly clothes, beautiful and plump in form, emerged from water, thinking that those sons of *munis* would forsake him because of the presence of a woman, and he would finally become free from all attachments. (*Mārkaṇḍeya Purāṇa*, 17.19–22)

सुरापानरतं ते न सभार्य्यां तत्यजुस्ततः ।
गीतवाद्यादिवनिता भोगसंसर्गदूषितम् ॥
मन्यमाना महात्मानं पीतासव - सविक्रियम् ।
नावाप दोषं योगीशो वारुणीं स पिबन्नपि ॥

surā-pāna-ratam te na

sabhāryyāṁ tatyajus tataḥ
gīta-vādyādi-vanitā
bhoga-saṁsarga dūṣitam

manya-mānā mahātmānaṁ
pītāsava savikriyam
nāvāpa doṣaṁ yogī so
vāruṇīṁ sa pibann api

When he saw that the sons of the *munis* did not abandon him nevertheless, he drank intoxicating liquors in the company of his wife. Although he was absorbed in drinking in the company of his wife, and although he was rendered impure by his addiction to singing, musical instruments, and so on, as well as by sexual intercourse with his wife, they still did not abandon him, believing him to be a great soul that was unattached to religious rites.

(*Mārkaṇḍeya Purāṇa*, 17.23–24)

अन्तावसायिवेश्मान्तर्मातरिश्वा वसन्निव ॥
सुरां पिबन्सपत्नीकस्तपस्तेपे स योगवित् ।
योगीश्वरश्चिन्त्यमानो योगिभिर्मुक्तिकाङ्क्षिभिः ॥

antāvasāyivesmāntar
mātariśvā vasann iva

surāṁ piban sapatīkas
tapas-tepe sa yogavit
yogīśvaraś cintya-māno
yogibhir muktikāṅgibhiḥ

The lord of yogis, although he drinks alcoholic beverages, he does not commit faults. Dwelling like Mātariśvan within the abodes of *caṇḍalas*, consuming strong drinks, the lord of the yogis, skilled in yoga, in the presence of his wife, performed austerities, being meditated on by yogis who longed for liberation from worldly existence.

(*Mārkaṇḍeya Purāṇa*, 17.25)

गर्ग उवाच-
इत्युक्तास्ते तदा जग्मुर्दत्तात्रेयाश्रमं सुराः ।
ददृशुश्च महात्मानं तं ते लक्ष्म्या समन्वितम् ॥
उद्गीयमानं गन्धर्वैः सुरापानरतं मुनिम् ।
ते तस्य गत्वा प्रणतिमवदन्साध्यसाधनम् ॥

garga uvāca
ity uktās te tadā jagmur
dattātreyāśramaṁ surāḥ
dadṛśuś ca mahātmānaṁ
taṁ te lakṣmyā samanvitam

udgīyamānaṁ gandharvaiḥ
surā-pāna-rataṁ munim
te tasya gatvā praṇatim
avadan sādhya-sādhanam

Garga said: "Thus exhorted, the gods then went to Dattātreya's hermitage and saw the *muni* with an elevated soul, helped by Lakṣmī, glorified by Gandharvas, and engrossed in consuming alcoholic beverages."

(*Mārkaṇḍeya Purāṇa*, 18.22–23)

दत्तात्रेय उवाच-
मद्यासक्तोऽहमुच्छिष्टो न चैवाहं जितेन्द्रियः ।
कथमिच्छथ मत्तो ऽपि देवाः शत्रुपराभवम् ॥

dattātreya uvāca-
madyāsakto 'ham ucchiṣṭo
na caivāhaṁ jitendriyaḥ
katham icchatha matto 'pi

devāḥ śatru-parābhavam

Dattātreya said: "I am drinking a strong drink, I have remnants of food in my mouth, and I do not control my senses. How is it, O gods, that you seek victory over your enemies through me?"

(*Mārkaṇḍeya Purāṇa*, 18.28)

देवा ऊचुः-
अनघस्त्वं जगन्नाथ न लेपस्तव विद्यते ।
विद्याक्षालनशुद्धान्तर्निविष्टज्ञानदीधिते ॥

devā ūcuḥ-
anaghas tvaṁ jagan-nātha
na lepas tava vidyate
vidyākṣālana śuddhāntar
niviṣṭa-jñāna dīdhite

The gods said: "You are sinless, O lord of the world; you are immaculate, the light of wisdom has penetrated your heart, which has been purified by the ablution of learning."

(*Mārkaṇḍeya Purāṇa*, 18.29)

दत्तात्रेय उवाच-
सत्यमेतत्सुरा विद्या ममास्ति समदर्शिनः ।
अस्यास्तु योषितः सङ्गादहमुच्छिष्टतां गतः ॥
स्त्रीसम्भोगो हि दोषाय सातत्येनोपसेवितः ।
एवमुक्तास्ततो देवाः पुनर्वचनमब्रुवन् ॥

dattātreya uvāca-
satyam etat surā vidyā
mamāsti sama-darśinaḥ
asyāstu yoṣitaḥ saṅgād
aham ucchiṣṭatāṁ gataḥ

strī-sambhogo hi doṣāya
sā tat yenopasevitaḥ
evam uktās tato devāḥ
punar vacanam abruvan

Dattātreya said: "This is true, O gods! I have impartial knowledge, but because I have been with this woman and have eaten, I am now impure. And because I am with women, I continue to follow depraved tendencies." In response, the gods spoke again:

(*Mārkaṇḍeya Purāṇa*, 18.30–31)

देवा ऊचुः ।
अनघेयं द्विजश्रेष्ठ जगन्माता न दुष्यते ।
यथा सुमाला सूर्यस्य द्विजचण्डालसङ्गिनी ॥

devā ūcuḥ-
anagheyaṁ dvija-śreṣṭha
jagan-mātā na duṣyate
yathā sumālā sūryasya
dvija-caṇḍāla-saṅginī

O sinless *Brāhmaṇa*! This woman is the Mother of the world; she is not depraved but as pure as the sun's halo of rays, which touches the twice-born and the *caṇḍala* alike.

(*Mārkaṇḍeya Purāna*, 18.32)

The *Vaiṣṇava Āgamas*

The V*aiṣṇava Āgamas*, also called *Saṁhitās*, accept the varied incarnations of Lord Viṣṇu as the supreme divinity. They relegate the rest of the deities to a secondary position. They depict conversations between Viṣṇu and his consort Lakṣmī. There are hundreds of

Vaiṣṇava Āgamas. The Tantric *Vaiṣṇava* tradition is divided into two sects, *Pāñca-rātra* and *Vaikhānasa*, which have many ritual differences. For example, *Pāñca-rātra* tradition accepts every human being without distinction, but *Vaikhānasa* only accepts those born in the Brahmanical caste.

Pāñca-rātra

Pāñca-rātra is a *Vaiṣṇava* system that originated in the Himalayas. There are different explanations for its name. One of the most accepted ones says that it comes from the five-part daily routine of its followers:

1. *Abhigamana*: Attend temple for morning worship.
2. *Upādāna*: Acquire materials required for worship.
3. *Ijyā*: Worship the deity.
4. *Svādhyāya*: Study revealed scriptures.
5. Yoga: Meditate on Divinity.

According to Rāmānujācārya, Brahman is Viṣṇu who manifests in five different forms (the *Pāñca-rātra* categories): *vibhava, antaryāmin, arcā, vyūha*, and *para*. *Vibhava* means "divine descent"; it is the thirty-nine incarnations (*avatār*) and emanations (*prādur-bhāva*). *Antaryāmin* means "the internal controller that dwells in all beings and guides their destinies." *Arcā* is the form worshipped in the temple. *Vyūhas* are the four emanations: Vāsudeva, Saṅkarṣaṇa, Pradyumna, and Aniruddha. *Para* is the transcendental or supreme form.

The *Pāñca-rātra* schools trace their origins to the *Ekāyana Veda*, thought to be the source of the other Vedas, and the *Vaikhānasa* school traces its beginnings to the *Aukheya* recension of the *Kṛṣṇa Yajur Veda*. These two lineages come from Nārāyaṇa and Vikhānasa, who learnt from Viṣṇu and Brahmā, respectively.

The *Phenapa* sages, or "foam drinkers," were the first to practice *Ekāntika-dharma*, which is the exclusive worship of Viṣṇu. These great *munis* resided in the foam of the milk ocean and were frightened by the gods. According to the *Mahābhārata*, the *Phenapas* also drank the foam of the remnants of the nectar drunk by Brahmā himself.

These sages imparted the knowledge to Vikhānasa, who in turn taught it to Soma, Marīci, and Bhṛgu. This dharma was lost but reappeared when Soma taught it to Brahmā, who passed it on to Rudra. Rudra imparted it to the Vālakhilyas, and Saṁkarṣaṇa transmitted it to Nārada.

The Tantric revival in Bengal took place between the fifteenth and nineteenth centuries CE. Since it harmonized Tantra with Brahmanical Hinduism, it became very popular in orthodox circles. This path is the perfect combination of devotion to Kṛṣṇa and veneration of Kālī.

The *Pāñca-rātra* school has four means of attaining liberation from the cycle of repeated births and deaths: *jñāna*, *caryā*, *kriyā*, and yoga. *Jñāna* is the knowledge of ultimate reality, or Bhagavan. *Kriyā* and *caryā* refer to the worship of the universal Self at home and in the temple. Yoga refers to meditating on divinity.

Vaikhānasa

The *Vaikhānasa* sect worships Viṣṇu as the supreme Lord. The name comes from its founder, the sage Vikhānasa. His followers were mostly *Brāhmaṇas* of the *Taittirīya Śākhā* of the *Kṛṣṇa Yajur Veda*, and the *Vaikhānasa-kalpa Sūtra*. They were monotheists but leaned toward the non-dual Vedanta, or *Advaita*.

According to this tradition, Vikhānasa was an incarnation of Lord Brahmā. Lord Viṣṇu personally taught him the mysteries of proper worship. Hence these scriptures, like the *Pāñca-rātras*, are considered divine revelations. Most *Vaikhānasa* literature deals with the correct execution of worship and rituals. *Vaikhānasas* see worship in the temple as a continuation of the Vedic fire sacrifice.

The *Vaikhānasa Āgamas* descended directly from Viṣṇu. However, they are called *Vaikhānasa* because Vikhānasa gave them to mankind through the *Maharṣis*, his four disciples: Atri, Marīci, Kaśyapa, and Bhṛgu. He taught them the worship to Viṣṇu following the *paramparā* system. Vikhānasa wrote two treatises: the *Vaikhānasa Kalpa Sūtra* and the *Daivika Sūtra*. The more important is undoubtedly the *Vaikhānasa-kalpa Sūtra*, which has thirty-two chapters and prescribes the veneration of Lord Viṣṇu, both at home and in the temple. The sections on knowledge are very brief.

The texts describe the five aspects of Viṣṇu: Viṣṇu, Puruṣa, Satya, Acyuta, and Aniruddha. Viṣnu is the supreme almighty Lord. Puruṣa is the principle of life. *Satya* is the static aspect of the Divine. Acyuta is the immutable aspect that does not change. Aniruddha is the irreducible aspect. According to the *Marīci Saṁhitās*, the realization of the highest ideal is through worship.

Bengali *Kṛṣṇa-bhakti*

The bhakti movement was founded by Śrī Caitanya (1486–1527 CE) in the sixteenth century CE and is called Gauḍīya Vaishnavism. The name *Gauḍīya* refers to the *Gauḍa* region, which is Bengal.

Although Śrī Caitanya was originally initiated into the *Madhva* tradition, he later developed his own system with a different theology. At first, Caitanya's tradition was similar to that of his contemporary Vallabhācarya. It preached devotion to the divine couple Kṛṣṇa and Rādhā. The fundamental principle was passionate devotion to Kṛṣṇa in the city of Vraja. For this kind of Vaishnavism, bhakti does not mean only love and devotion, but also service to the supreme Lord. In the *Bhakti-rasāmṛta-sindhu*, quoting a verse from the *Nārada Pāñca-rātra*, Rūpa Gosvāmī defines bhakti as follows:

सर्वोपाधिविनिर्मुक्तं तत्परत्वेन निर्मलम् ।
हृषीकेण हृषीकेशसेवनं भक्तिरुच्यते ॥

sarvopādhi-vinirmuktaṁ
tatparatvena nirmalam
hṛṣīkeṇa hṛṣīkeśa-
sevanaṁ bhaktir ucyate

> Bhakti means engaging all our senses in the service of the Lord, the master of all the senses. When the spirit soul renders service unto the supreme, there are two side effects: one is freed from all material designations, and one's senses are purified simply by being employed in the service of the Lord.
>
> (*Bhakti-rasāmṛta-sindhu*, 1.1.12)

Śrī Caitanya's tradition has succeeded in widely disseminating the worship of His Lordships Śrī Śrī Rādhā and Kṛṣṇa, the divine couple of Vrindavana, not only in India but in the whole world.

Sahajiyās

Sahajiyā is a form of bhakti-Tantric Vaishnavism that originated in Bengal and comprised several Tantric lineages. The term *sahaja* means "born together, spontaneous, or innate." In this fascinating tradition, Tantra is mixed with devotion. The origins of this esoteric movement, like that of many other Tantric traditions, are lost in the darkness of time.

Bhakti is expressed in the worship of the divine couple, Śrī Śrī Rādhā and Kṛṣṇa, through rites and sexual practices that physically emulate the divine love of the transcendental couple. Sahajism sees the intimate relationship between Śrīmatī Rādhārāṇī and Kṛṣṇa as a metaphor for the eternal relationship between the soul and God. Practices consist in daring efforts to physically emulate these divine activities. The intention is to transcend the mundane and superficial conception of sex and discover it to be a divine experience. These Tantric practices could be thought of as an attempt to sublimate sex from the human to the transcendental plane.

Condemned and rejected by orthodoxy and society in general, they kept their *sādhana* secret for generations. Public reaction has led them to be very discrete and go underground. Their authors developed *sandhyā-bhāṣā*, an esoteric and enigmatic writing style that substitutes terminology and disguises texts to maintain discretion in teachings and practices. The content of these works is only accessible to initiates.

Esoteric practices such as *gaṇācāra*, or "a group in circle," have remained within small circles. This practice consists in a dance that reproduces the *rāsa-līlā* of Lord Kṛṣṇa with the *gopīs* described in the *Bhāgavata Purāṇa*. It is a non-dual ritual of communion with divinity.

This tradition developed out of Śrī Caitanya's *Gauḍīya* Vaishnavism and offered its own vision to texts such as the *Bhāgavata Purāṇa* and the *Śrī Caitanya-caritāmṛta* by Kṛṣṇa-dāsa Kavirāja Gosvāmī. It was a new interpretation of Caitanya's Krishnaism and his *gosvāmīs* of Vrindavana. This is clear from the *Sahajiyā* commentaries by Ākiñcana-dāsa (born c. 1625 CE) on the *Caitanya-caritāmṛta* in his famous *Vivarta-vilāsa*. He states that the *Gauḍīya* line of disciplic succession passed from Kṛṣṇa-dāsa Kavirāja to his disciple Mukunda-dāsa. He and his disciples are the authors of the most significant *sahajiyā* literary works.

The *Nigūḍhārtha-prakāśāvalī* (c. 1650 CE) states that the four most important texts produced by Mukunda-dāsa's lineage are his *Amṛta-ratnāvalī*, Prema-dāsa's *Ānanda-bhairava*, Mathura-dāsa's *Amṛta-rasāvalī*, and Yugalera dāsa's *Āgama-sāra*. These texts expound the *Sahajiyā* vision and give us access to the school's esoteric teachings. The *Sahajiyā* interpretations of *Gauḍīya* literature facilitated the development of a devotional Tantra, subsequently leading to the communities of *Kartabhajas* and *Bauls*. Within the *Sahajiyā* movement, there is a division between the *dakṣiṇācāras*, or "followers of the right hand," and the *vāmācāras*, or "followers of the left hand." Both lines practice *pañca-ma-kāra*, but the *dakṣiṇācāras* follow it symbolically while the *vāmācāras* do so literally. For *vāmācāras*, the spiritual search is intimately related to sensual experience. Sexuality is accepted as a legitimate means of accessing higher levels of consciousness.

Regarding its literature, we know of the existence of numerous *Sahajiyā* manuscripts at the Baṅgīya-sāhitya-pariṣad library at the University of Calcutta. Many other manuscripts are housed at the Asian Society of Calcutta. For the most part, *Sahajiyā* poems were written by poets such as Caṇḍī-dāsa (born 1408 CE), who was the most prolific, as well as Vidyā-pati, Rūpa, Sanātana, Vṛndāvana-dāsa, Kṛṣṇadāsa Kavirāja, Narahari, Narottama, Locana, and Caitanya-dāsa, among others. Additionally, there is Sahajism in the poetry of the *mahā-siddha* Saraha from the eighth century CE.

CHAPTER 7

LATER TANTRIC SECTS

Liṅgāyata or *Vīra* Shaivism

Vīra Shaivism is also called Lingayatism. The followers of this sect are called *liṅgāyatas*, a term derived from *liṅga-vantha*, which in the Kannada language means "one who wears a *liṅga*." It is a sect of Shaivism that spread in the Karnataka region of southern India.

There are two opinions about the founders of the sect. The first says that it originated from the five sages: Revaṇa-siddha, Maruḷa-siddha, Ekorāma, Paṇḍitārādhya, and Viśvārādhya. The second says the sect was founded by Basava (1134–1196 CE), also known as Basavaṇṇa. He was a great spiritual master nicknamed *Viśva-guru*, or "universal master," because of the openness and universality of his teachings. He was not only a religious person and mystic, but also an important social reformer who fought for gender equality, abolishing the caste system, and labor rights. He held the important office of Prime Minister under King Bijjala, who reigned from 1157 to 1167 CE.

In 1160 CE, Basava founded a movement called Śūnya-siṁhāsana in Kalyāṇī, located in the district of Bidār in Karnataka. More than an institution, this was a meeting place for great saints and mystics of the time.

Basava never wrote a systematic treatise on *Vīra* Shaivism. However, his famous work *Vacana Sāhitya* reveals his devotion to Kūḍala-saṅgama-devā, or Śiva.

ವಚನದಲ್‌ಲಿ ನಾಮಾಮೃತ ತುಮ್‌ಬಿ
ನಯನದಲ್‌ಲಿ ನಿಮ್‌ಮ ಮೂರುತಿ ತುಮ್‌ಬಿ
ಮನದಲ್‌ಲಿ ನಿಮ್‌ಮ ನೆನಹು ತುಮ್‌ಬಿ
ಕಿವಿಯಲ್‌ಲಿ ನಿಮ್‌ಮ ಕೀರುತಿ ತುಮ್‌ಬಿ
ಕೂಡಲ ಸಂಗಮ ದೇವಾ
ನಿಮ್‌ಮ ಚರಣಕಮಲದೊಳಗಾನು ತುಮ್‌ಬಿ

vacanadalli nāmāmṛta tumbi
nayanadalli nimma mūruti tumbi
manadalli nimma nenahu tumbi
kiviyalli nimma kīruti tumbi
kūḍala saṅgama devā
nimma caraṇa-kamala-doḷagānu tumbi

The words uttered [by me] are full of the nectar of [your holy] name! My eyes are enriched with the vision of your form! My mind is full of your thoughts! My ears are full of your glory! O Lord Kūḍala Saṅgama, at your lotus feet, I am like a bee!

(*Vachana Sāhitya* by Basava, *vacana* 1)

ನೀರಿಗೆ ನೈದಿಲೆ ಶೃಙ್‌ಗಾರ
ಸಮುದ್‌ರಕೆ ತೆರೆಯೆ ಶೃಙ್‌ಗಾರ
ನಾರಿಗೆ ಗುಣವೆ ಶೃಙ್‌ಗಾರ
ಗಗನಕೆ ಚಂದ್‌ರಮ ಶೃಙ್‌ಗಾರ
ನಮ್‌ಮ ಕೂಡಲ ಸಂಗನ ಶರಣರ
ನೊಸಲಿಗೆ ವಿಭೂತಿಯೆ ಶೃಙ್‌ಗಾರ

nīrige naidile śṛṅgāra
samudrake tereye śṛṅgāra
naarige guṇave śṛṅgāra
gaganake candrama śṛṅgāra
namma kūṇḍala saṅgana śaraṇara
nosalige vibhūtiye śṛṅgāra

The charm is for water lilies in a pond. The charm is for the ocean tide. The charm is for the female character. The charm

is for the moon in the sky. The charm is for the sacred ash in the forehead of the devotees of the Lord Kūḍala-saṅgama.
(*Vachana Sāhitya* by Basava, *vacana* 2)

The founders prior to Basava

As mentioned above, there are different opinions on the origins of this sect. Not all followers of *Vīra* Shaivism accept master Basava as its founder. Others think he was a later reformer of the system and that the founders were five holy and wise *ācāryas* born from different *Śiva-liṅgas*. Revana-siddha was born from *Someśa-liṅga* in Kollipak, Maruḷa-siddha from *Siddheśa-liṅga* in Ujjain, Bellari district, Karnataka, Ekorāma from *Śrī-sailya-mallikārjuna-liṅga* of the Kurnool district in Andhra Pradesh, Paṇḍitārādhya from the *Rāma-nātha-liṅga* of Kedār-nāth in Uttar Pradesh, and Viśvārādhya from *Viśveśvara-liṅga* in Vārāṇasī in Uttar Pradesh. Revana-siddha, the first of these great sages, founded a *maṭha* in Bale Honnur, in Chikkamanglur, Karnataka.

The vision of *Vīra* Shaivism

To systematically study this sect prior to Basava, we must look at the *Śrī-kara Bhāṣya*, a commentary on the *Brahma Sūtra* by Śrīpati Pandit. This text very clearly states that Agamic *Vīra* Shaivism had a wide Brahmanical support.

This sect is called *Liṅgāyata* because it places so much importance on the *Śiva-liṅga*. Its initiates receive a *liṅga* directly from a master and it is carried as a purifying object their entire lives. The *jīva* cannot manifest its divine nature, because it is covered by the three kinds of impurities, or *malas*: *āṇava-mala* (the impurity of limited agency), *karma-mala* (the impurity of limited action), and *māyīya-mala* (the impurity that creates diversity).

In order to transcend these impurities, one must accept initiation, or *dīkṣā*, from an authentic spiritual master. This sect does not differentiate between genders, and both men and women have a right to *dīkṣā*. In the initiation ceremony, the guru worships a small *liṅga* and then places it around the initiate's neck like a necklace. Finally, the master initiates the disciple into the sacred mantra *Oṁ namaḥ śivāya*.

The basic principles of *Vīra* Shaivism are:

1. The supreme God is Śiva.
2. The main symbol of God is the *Śiva-liṅga*.
3. The formula for liberation is the mantra *Oṁ namaḥ śivāya*.
4. The main code of conduct is the practice of the *pañcācāras*, or "five disciplines."
5. After initiation, disciples must protect themselves with the *aṣṭāvaraṇas*, or "eight covers or shields."

The *pañcācāras* are:

1. *Liṅgācāra*: To worship the *liṅga* received from the guru during initiation every day.
2. *Sadācāra*: To make a living from a decent job and to help preachers and the poor.
3. *Śivācāra*: To associate with all *liṅgāyatas* as if they were Lord Śiva himself.
4. *Bhṛtyācāra*: To cultivate humility toward both Lord Śiva and his devotees.
5. *Gaṇācāra*: To zealously keep religious principles. To protest against the lack of respect for religion. To not accept cruelty to animals.

The *aṣṭāvaraṇas* (covers or shields) are:

1. Guru: Faith and respect toward the spiritual master.
2. *Liṅga*: Treating the sacred *liṅga* with great reverence, respect, and devotion.
3. *Jaṅgama*: Respect for ascetics and mendicants.
4. *Pādodaka*: Purifying oneself by drinking or splashing oneself with the water the master has used to wash his or her feet or bathe.

5. *Prasāda*: Accepting food remnants that have been sanctified through worship.
6. *Brasma*: Covering the forehead and body with sacred ashes, or *vibhūti*.
7. *Rudrākṣa*: Having a *rudrākṣa-mālā* for *japa* and wearing it around the neck like a necklace.
8. Mantra: Repeating the holy mantra *Oṁ namaḥ śivāya* according to the guidance and directions of the spiritual master.

The philosophy of *Vīra* Shaivism is called *Śakti-viśiṣṭādvaita*, a version of qualified non-dualism that accepts both the difference and the non-difference between Brahman and its *śakti*. God is to creative energy as the sun is to light and the fire is to heat. As Brahman is always fully aware of its energy, *viśiṣtatva* implies only *vimarśa*, or "self-consciousness," of the inherent power. Brahman creates, maintains, and dissolves the universe through its power, or *śakti*. This is why the name of the sect is *Śakti-viśiṣṭādvaita*.

In *Vīra* Shaivism, the devotional path culminates in complete absorption in Śiva. Śrī-pati Paṇḍit recommends *śravaṇa*, or "listening to the glories of Lord Śiva," repeating his holy name, meditating, and studying the *Āgamas* in order to realize the sweet nature of Śiva.

Khaṇḍobā, Birobā, and Nāikbā are different aspects of Lord Śiva that are worshipped by many people in India.

Although Śiva and the cosmic power are one, Śiva is transcendental to his creation, which is not illusory but real. God is both the efficient and material cause. After liberation, the soul attains undifferentiated union with Śiva. The goal of life is to realize the union of Śiva and the soul. The *sādhana ṣaṭ-sthala* is a gradual path with six devotional stages:

1. Bhakti, or "devotion."
2. *Maheśa*, or "disinterested service."
3. *Prasāda*, or "the eager search for divine grace."
4. *Prāṇa-liṅga*, or "the experience that everyone is essentially Śiva."
5. *Śaraṇa*, or "taking refuge in Śiva."
6. *Aikya*, or "fusion with Śiva."

Each stage brings the aspirant closer to the final fusion with God, like a river that merges with the ocean.

The initiation ceremony of the *Vīra Śaiva* sect is called *liṅga-dīkṣā*. During this ritual, the aspirant commits to worship the personal *Śiva-liṅga* every day. The sect emphasizes the equality of all members, regardless of caste or gender. *Vīra* Shaivism is alive today and strong in southern India, especially in Karnataka.

Ṣaṭ-sthala-siddhānta

In *Vīra* Shaivism, Brahman is called *sthala*, or "space," because Brahman is as infinite as space. Another meaning of the Sanskrit term *sthala* is "where the universe emerges, evolves, is maintained, and dissolves." According to the *ṣaṭ-sthala-siddhānta* doctrine, God is divided into *liṅga* and *aṅga*. The first aspect refers to God himself, and the second to the *jīva*, or "the individual soul."

Liṅga is divided into three types:

1. *Prāṇa-liṅga*: Reality as perceived by thought.
2. *Bhāva-liṅga*: Reality as the pure Self that can only be perceived through inner intuition.
3. *Iṣṭa-liṅga*: The absolute reality beyond space and time.

Aṅga is divided into three stages:

1. *Tyāgāṅga*: When an individual soul overcomes the illusion or false notion of the cycle of births and rebirths.
2. *Bhogāṅga*: When the soul enjoys the world through the grace of Śiva.
3. *Yogāṅga*: When the soul attains the bliss of union with Śiva.

Jīvas are called *tyāgāṅgas* after renouncing all attachment to the mundane and earthly. After purification, they become *bhogāṅgas* and experience the divine presence, or *prāṇa-liṅga*, within themselves and enjoy the world through the grace of Śiva. In still more advanced states, they become *yogāṅgas*. They experience God as *bhāva-liṅgas* when they see themselves as one with him, and as *Iṣṭa-liṅgas* when they merge with him.

Vīra Shaivism has contributed a long list of masters to Hinduism such as Allama Prabhu and Canna-basavaṇṇa and elevated holy women such as Akka Mahā-devī. There is no doubt that its philosophy has enriched Hinduism.

Nātha-sampradāya or *Nātha-siddha-siddhānta*

Nātha-siddha-siddhānta is a type of *bhedābheda* monism that sees Śiva as both transcendent and immanent and as both the efficient and material cause of the universe.

The *Nātha-siddha-siddhānta* sect was founded by Matsyendra-nātha (c. 800–1000 CE) and was spread by his disciple Gorakṣa-nātha (c. 950 CE). Currently, most *nātha* ritualism is based on the *Śrī-vidyā* tradition and shares its central deities: Bālā-sundarī and Tripura-sundarī.

Gorakṣa-nātha is the author of the *Siddhānta-paddhati*, one of the first works that mention hatha yoga. In this text (2.33), he affirms that asana means to be firmly located in the consciousness of the Self and that its *lakṣaṇa*, or "symptom," means being focused on the object of meditation.

The *Kula-mārga* contains the origins of hatha yoga, also called *haṭha-vidyā*. The origins of the *Kaula* tradition lie in the revelation transmitted by the clans of divine *yoginīs* to enlightened masters. This transmission was perpetuated in detail by the *Maṇḍala-kaula*. Matsyendra-nātha is the *siddhācārya* of the *Kaula* tradition, or the *Kaula-yoginī* school. On the basis of the teachings received from his master, Gorakṣa-nātha began the *nātha* yogic lineage also called the *nātha-sampradāya*. According to the *Kaula-jñāna-nirnaya*, Matsyendra-nātha received the *Kaula* revelations directly from the divine *yoginīs* in the *pīṭha* of Kāma-rūpa. Of his twelve sons, the six who chose not to be celibate founded the six *ovallis*, or "initiatory lineages." These lineages founded hundreds of monasteries all over India, through which the *yoginī-pañjara* was disseminated to the general public. This network of monasteries had a central body as its authority. This led to a process of internalization of the Tantric ascetic practices that allowed access even to Brahmanical circles. This made it possible for *Brāhmaṇas* to worship Bhairava without violating the social norms of their caste. The internalization eliminated external ritual and kept it as a verbal practice. This process internalized both *yoginīs* and *śaktis* to the astral plane.

Texts such as the *Jayad-ratha Yāmala* and *Netra Tantra* refer to the *pīṭhas* and circular temples that hint at energy centers, or chakras. It is the *Kubjikā-mata* and *Rudra Yāmala* scriptures that reveal these as the system of seven chakras. The *Yoga-kuṇḍalinī Upanishad* mentions the names of the six chakras:

1. *Mūlādhāra-cakra*, or "root chakra": The area between the anus and the genitals.
2. *Svādhiṣṭhāna-cakra*, or "sacral chakra": The umbilical region, next to the navel.
3. *Maṇipūra-cakra*, or "solar plexus chakra": The top of the stomach, next to the spleen.
4. *Anāhata-cakra*, or "heart chakra": In the center of the chest, next to the sternum.
5. *Viśuddha-cakra*, or "throat chakra": At the level of the throat.
6. *Ājñā-cakra*, or "third eye chakra": Between the eyebrows.

The names of the chakras reappear in the *Yoga-tattva Upanishad* from the fifteenth century CE.

Instead of making bodily offerings such as semen in sexual rituals to *yoginīs*, this practice was internalized to be experienced meditatively within the human being.

This process allowed a sublimation of sexual energy through contemplative practices. The diversity of goddesses was revealed as the divine *śakti*, which lies dormant in her expression as *kuṇḍalinī* in *mūlādhāra-cakra*. With practice, *kuṇḍalinī* rises through the chakras to attain masculinity and unite with Śiva in *sahasrāra-cakra*, or "crown chakra." This union becomes the awakening to the reality of consciousness.

Works like the *Gorakṣa-śataka* and *Viveka-mārtaṇḍa* by Gorakṣa-nātha reveal that menstrual blood symbolizes *kuṇḍalinī*'s flow and semen is the masculine polarity. Yogis manipulate the polarity through *prāṇa* with breathing techniques that use female *nāḍīs* such as *iḍā* and masculine ones such as *piṅgalā*. *Iḍā* is the left side, white and cold, associated with the Gaṅga River. *Piṅgalā* is the right side, red and hot, representing the sun and associated with the Yamuna River. *Iḍā* ends in the left nostril and *piṅgalā* in the right. Yogis raise fluids and energy through breathing in order to elevate the semen until it fills the cranial vault and then transform it into the nectar of immortality, which also grants *siddhis* (mystical powers). This is *rasāyana*, or "yogic alchemy," which suggests using the aspirant's own body as a laboratory for sublimation. Gradually, the hatha yoga system became independent of Tantra and continued its own development.

Gorakṣa-nātha systematized hatha yoga and transmitted it to his disciples. The *Nātha* masters, in turn, transmitted it to their disciples through the *paramparā* system.

Some of the most outstanding masters in this rich tradition were Śābarānanda, Minanātha, Bileśaya, Bhairava, Manthāna, and Kāka-caṇḍīśvara. Its lines of disciplic succession were organized into nine paths with different inclinations. Some were for pilgrims and others involved a contemplative life at a monastery. These monasteries served as refuges for pilgrims. The *nāthas* were identified as *siddhas* and were greatly appreciated and respected by the public.

One of the earliest definitions of the term *haṭha* is found in the *Yogabīja*, which refers to *ha* as sun, *ṭha* as moon, and *haṭha yoga* as the union of both. It is essential to remember that practices like hatha yoga were transmitted orally from master to disciple. It would be a mistake to make conclusions about this psychophysiological system based only on its literature.

It should be noted that hatha yoga as it is known today in the West is considerably different from the way it was understood and practiced at first. It is a fact that its modern understanding and practice is far from the classical and traditional method. The intention of many early yogis was to elevate and conserve what they considered the essence of life energy, identified with semen, or *bindu*. Its feminine equivalent was menstrual flow, or *rajas*. It was considered wasted if allowed to descend from *sahasrāra-cakra* to exhaustion.

Asceticism and austerity in these groups were for the preservation and sublimation of vital energy. For these ascetics, hatha yoga was for preservation, either through inverted postures or breathing techniques, or *prāṇāyāma*.

The *Kaula*, with its awakening and elevation of *kuṇḍalinī* through the system of chakras, overshadowed the *bindu* system.

The ideal of hatha yoga is the search for a variety of earthly benefits such as physical health and *siddhis* as well as transcendental ones such as enlightenment. Keeping the body healthy is important on this path to enlightenment. Hatha yoga can also lead to *siddhis* such as *kāla-vañcana* (cheating time, or cheating death), *utkrānti* (casting off one's body at will), and *parakāya-praveśana* (entering another's body). From the beginning, there were warnings that mystical powers could be obstacles for attaining the ultimate benefit: *mukti*, or "liberation." However, some texts, generally of *Kaula* origin, offer guidance to achieve these powers.

The system of hatha yoga was enriched by the legacy of Shaivism, Vaishnavism, Tantrism, and even Buddhism.

SECTION III

Tantric Scriptures

Chapter 1

Agamic or Tantric Literature

The *Āgamas* are a large collection of profound sectarian texts written in Sanskrit that maintain a Vedic perspective. They are considered to have emanated directly from the Lord's breath. They have been preserved through the chain of disciplic succession.

The term *āgama* refers to scriptures that impart spiritual wisdom in a traditional and well-structured way. According to Tantra, this wisdom is eternal, or *sanātana*, and one with the supreme reality. Its transcendental nature makes it ungraspable for the human intellect.

The word *āgama* means "what has come to us" and it has been used in different contexts. It can refer to a doctrine or a collection of traditional doctrines as well as texts on the sacrifices of Shaivism, Vaishnavism, Shaktism, Jainism, or Buddhism. The *Mahā-nirvāṇa Tantra* explains further the etymology of this word:

आचारकथनाद्दिव्यगतिप्राप्तिनिदानतः ।
महात्मतत्त्वकथनादागमः कथितः प्रिये ॥

ācāra-kathanād divya-
gati-prāpti-nidānataḥ
mahātma-tattva-kathanād
āgamaḥ kathitaḥ priye

Because it narrates of the course of conduct (*ācāra*) with an aim of arriving at the godly goal (*divya-gati*), because it speaks of the Truth of the great souls (*mahātmas*), it is, O my beloved, called *āgama*.

(*Mahā-nirvāṇa Tantra*, 17.43)

Agamic writings are an extremely important part of the treasure of Hindu literature. They are similar to the *Purāṇas*. They include profound and beautiful dialogues between the goddess and Lord Śiva, who alternate between the roles of the one who inquires and the one who replies, the one who teaches and the one who learns.

For the Tantric sages of antiquity, it was important to keep the revealed wisdom far from the ignorant masses. But they also wanted to preserve the teachings for future generations of Truth seekers, so they had to record this wisdom in writing. The dilemma of whether to keep it in secret or write it down led to the creation of the symbolic language *sandhyā-bhāṣā*. It is intelligible to everyone but contains certain terms and expressions that only initiates understand.

Tantra has been preserved with great discretion throughout the generations because it does not fit social conventions. Tantra is not for the masses, the public, or society. If we talk about religion or enlightenment as an experience, we are in the realm of the individual. The spiritual experience is a phenomenon that manifests only in the individual, never in the collective.

The relationship with the Vedas

The eternal wisdom descends in two forms: *Nigama-śāstra* (Vedic) and *Āgama-śāstra* (Tantric).

The *Āgamas* are the main authority of the Tantric schools; they are considered the essence of the Vedas and the only practical guide for *Kali-yuga*, or "the iron age." Although Tantra respects the Vedic texts, it considers them inapplicable without Agamic knowledge.

The *Āgamas* are the most accredited source on yoga and the basis for many aspects of Hinduism, especially in the post-Vedic era. Spiritually, they are as important as the Vedas. In the hierarchy of sacred literature, the Tantras are fourth after the *Śruti*, *Smṛti*, and *Purāṇas*.

According to the Tantric teachings, different scriptures are recommended for each era, or *yuga*: the *Śruti* for *Satya-yuga* the *Smṛti* for *Tretā-yuga*, and the *Purāṇas* for *Dvāpara-yuga*. Tantric scriptures are recommended for our present age, *Kali-yuga*. It is a time of decadence, darkness, and ignorance when humans live in a state of profound identification with the body. As stated in the *Mahā-nirvāṇa Tantra*:

श्रुतिस्मृतिपुराणादौ मयैवोक्त पुरा शिवे ।
आगमोक्तविधनेन कलौ देवान्यजेत्सुधीः ॥

śruti-smṛti-purāṇādau
mayaivokta purā śive
āgamokta-vidhānena
kalau devān yajet sudhīḥ

O Śiva, I have already stated in the *Śruti*, *Smṛti*, and *Purāṇas* that in *Kali-yuga*, reasonable people should worship the deities according to the methods envisioned by the *Āgamas*.
(*Mahā-nirvāṇa Tantra*, 2.8)

Oral tradition

The Tantric tradition existed long before it was written down, so it is impossible to determine its age based on the scriptures. In the beginning, this wisdom was only transmitted orally. Like the Vedas, it is a revelation that descended to humanity through the *paramparā* system, or "the chain of disciplic succession."

It is unclear when the Tantric teachings were written down. An early testimony of written Tantras is found in the Kādambarī, the great Sanskrit novel by the legendary storyteller Bāṇa-bhaṭṭa, who lived around the first half of the seventh century CE. Bāṇa describes an old *Śaiva* ascetic from southern India:

धूमरक्तालक्तकाक्षरतालपत्रकुहकतन्त्रमन्त्रपुस्तिकासंग्राहिणा जीर्णमहापाशुपतोपदे
शलिखितमहाकालमतेनाविर्भूतनिधिवादव्याधिनासंजातधातुवादवायुना ।

dhūma-raktālaktakākṣara-tāla-patra-kuhaka-tantra-mantra-pustikā-saṁgrāhiṇā jīrṇa-mahā-pāśupatopadeśa-likhita-mahā-kāla-matenāvirbhūta-nidhi-vāda-vyādhinā-saṁjāta dhātu-vāda-vāyunā.

> He had collected manuscripts with magical spells [or information] about jugglery, mystical mantras, and yantras [written] on palm leaves in letters drawn with red lac and fumigated with [incense] smoke. He wrote down the doctrine of the worship of Mahā-kāla according to the instructions of an elderly follower of Paśu-pati. (Baṇa's *Kadambarī*, part 2, edited by P.V Kane, 1913, pp 68–9)

Although there are many *Āgamas*, what is known as Tantric knowledge is in fact the body of oral teachings personally passed down from master to disciple. Still, studying Tantric scriptures gives us a deeper understanding.

In Tantra, it is impossible to replace the guru with the written word. A book cannot substitute for the guidance and personal instructions of a spiritual master.

न च विद्यागुरोस्तुल्यानातीर्थंनचदेवताः ।
गुरोस्तुल्यंनवैकोऽपियद्दृष्टं परमं पदं ॥

na ca vidyā guros tulyaṁ
na tīrthaṁ na ca devatāḥ
guros tulyaṁ na vai ko 'pi
yad dṛṣṭaṁ paramam padam

> There is no learning (knowledge), no holy place nor gods or goddesses that are equal to a guru who has realized the Absolute.
>
> (*Jñāna-saṅkalinī Tantra*, 93)

Tantric practices were mostly secret, as explained by the well-known professor S. K. Ramachandra Rao in his work *The Āgama Encyclopaedia* (page 72): "But they were aware of the Tantric prejudices against exposure, since Tantra is essentially a mystical and secret matter, strictly speaking, an interaction between the practitioner and the master."

This statement is supported by countless verses within the tantras, for example this one from the *Jñāna-saṅkalinī Tantra*:

यस्यकस्य न दातव्यंब्रह्मज्ञानंसुगोपितं ।
यस्यकस्यापिभक्तस्य सद्गुरुस्तस्य धीयते ॥

yasya kasya na dātavyam
brahma-jñānaṁ sugopitam
yasya kasyāpi bhaktasya
sad-gurus tasya dīyate

> The well-kept secret of *Brahma-jñāna* (knowledge of the Absolute) should not be revealed to everyone. It should only be given by the *sad-guru* to the devotees.
>
> (*Jñāna-saṅkalinī Tantra*, 95)

After much persecution, the Tantric masters of India decided to hide the wisdom and left only small fragments on hatha and *kuṇḍalinī -yoga* as public knowledge. They were forced to return to their original method of secretly preserving the wisdom through the lines of disciplic succession. Away from the condemnation of ignorant and worldly moralists, the transcendental teachings continued to be transmitted in an extremely intimate and secretive way. The Tantric tradition was restricted to the individual and renounced any attempt to publicly seek followers. The lack of support from society made it difficult to preserve the Tantric literary heritage. Later texts mention lost manuscripts, many of which we know only by name. There is no doubt that of the philosophical and religious literature of India, Tantric writings are the least understood.

The subject matter of the *Āgamas*

The *āgamas* cover a wide range of topics. Because their knowledge is not purely intellectual or theoretical, they insist on the importance of the direct experience. The *Āgamas* can be considered manuals or guides for practical methods. Among the main topics we find:

1. Philosophy, or *siddhānta*.
2. Cosmogony, or *sṛṣṭi*: The principles of creation, maintenance, and dissolution of the universe.
3. Theology, or *Brahma-jñāna*.
4. Mystical linguistics, or mantras.
5. Mystical diagrams, or yantras.
6. Seals and gestures, or *mudrās*.
7. Spiritual methodology, or *yoga*: Different types of meditation and techniques for liberation and union with the deity.
8. Architecture and sculpture, or *śilpa*.
9. Consecration of temples, or *pratiṣṭhā*, and the principles of selecting an appropriate place to build a temple.
10. Initiation, or *dīkṣā*.
11. Social conduct, or *dharma*.
12. Sacraments and domestic observations, or *saṁskāras*.
13. Rituals of worship, or *arcana*: Ceremonies and rites (*vidhi* and *karma*) and of public worship (*pūjā*) in the temple and in the privacy of the home.
14. Public festivals, or *utsava*.
15. Practical occultism, or *indra-jāla*.
16. Expiations and penances, or *prāyaś-citta*.
17. Deities, or *devatā*: Consecration of images and the principles of choosing materials to carve deities.
18. Knowledge about mystical powers, or *siddhis*.

Mantra, *yantra*, and Tantra

Mantra, yantra, and Tantra are some of the main topics within the Agamic literature.

Mantra: It is the sound aspect of a divine form, so it is not different from the *iṣṭa-devatā* itself. It is the basis for yantra and Tantra. A mantra is a powerful mystical energy contained in a specific sound structure, which is a transcendental vibration that encapsulates a power capable of freeing our mind from the clutches of illusion.

मननात्तत्त्वरूपस्य देवस्यामिततेजसः ।
त्रायते सर्वभयतस्तस्मान्मन्त्र इतीरितः ॥

mananāt tattva-rūpasya
devasyāmita-tejasaḥ
trāyate sarva-bhayatas
tasmān mantra itīritaḥ

Through meditation (*manana*) on the luminous deity who is the form of Truth, it saves (*trāyate*) us from all fear; therefore, it is called *mantra*.

(*Kulārṇava Tantra*, 17.54)

मननं सर्ववेदित्वं त्राणं संसार्यनुग्रहः ।
मननत्राण धर्मित्वान्मन्त्र इत्यभिधीयते ॥

mananaṁ sarva-veditvaṁ
trāṇaṁ saṁsāry anugrahaḥ
manana-trāṇa dharmitvān
mantra ity abhidhīyate

The term *manana* means attaining the capacity to know everything. The term *trāṇa* means bestowing grace on those enmeshed in a worldly life. Since it possesses the power to yield *manana* and *trāna*, it is called *mantra*.

(*Kāmika Āgama*, 1.2.2)

शरीरं त्रिविधं प्राहुर्भौतिकं च मनोमयम् ।
परं ज्ञानमयं नित्यं यदनाशि निरन्तरम् ॥
मुद्रां भौतिकमित्याहुर्यन्त्रं विद्धि मनोमयम् ।
मन्त्रं ज्ञानमयं विद्धि एवं त्रिधा वपुर्भवेत् ॥

śarīraṁ tri-vidhaṁ prāhur
bhautikaṁ ca mano-mayam
paraṁ jñāna-mayam nityaṁ

yad anāśi nirantaram

mudrāṁ bhautikam ity āhur
yantraṁ viddhi mano-mayam
mantraṁ jñāna-mayaṁ viddhi
evaṁ tridhā vapur bhavet

Devī is said to have three permanent bodies: physical, mental, and transcendental knowledge. *Mudrā* is said to be the physical body, yantra is known as the mental body, and mantra is represented by transcendental knowledge. Thus, the body has three forms.

(*Gandharva Tantra*, 5.39–40)

For the mantra to be effective, it must be installed in a disciple by a spiritual master through *dīkṣā*. Mantras are a great help for meditation. The wisdom of mantras has been preserved through generations with great discretion to prevent it from being used for destructive purposes. A mantra is not just a sequence of sounds; through its repetition it is possible to experience the radiation of psychic energy, or *cic-chakti*.

निरोधं मध्यमे स्थने कुर्वीत क्षणमात्रकम् ।
पश्यते तत्र चिच्छक्तिं तुटिमात्रामखण्डिताम् ॥
तदेव परमं तत्त्वं तस्माज्ज्ञातमिदं जगत् ।
स एव मन्त्रदेहस्तु सिद्धयोगीश्वरीमते ॥
तेनैवालिङ्गिता मन्त्राः सर्वसिद्धिफलप्रदाः ।

nirodhaṁ madhyame sthāne
kurvīta kṣaṇa-mātrakam
paśyate tatra cic-chaktiṁ
tuṭi-mātram akhaṇḍitām

tad eva paramaṁ tattvaṁ
tasmāj jātam idaṁ jagat
sa eva mantra-dehas tu

siddha-yogīśvarī-mate

tenaivāliṅgitā mantrāḥ
sarva-siddhi-phala-pradāḥ

One ought to take a stoppage in the midway for a moment. Here, one sees the force of consciousness in its entirety as a flash. This force is the highest reality. This is the highest principle from which the whole universe is born. According to the perspective in *Siddha-yogeśvarī*, it is the body of mantras. All mantras are embraced by that force, yielding the fruits of all *siddhis*.

(*Mālinī-vijayottara Tantra*, 18.37–39a)

सर्वे वर्णात्मका मन्त्रास्ते च शक्त्यात्मकाः प्रिये ।
शक्तिस्तु मातृका ज्ञेया सा च ज्ञेया शिवात्मिका ॥

sarve varṇātmakā mantrās
te ca śakty-ātmakāḥ priye
śaktis tu mātṛkā jñeyā
sā ca jñeyā śivātmikā

O dear one, all mantras consist of letters. The letters are of the form of *śakti*. That *śakti* should be known as *mātṛkā*, and *mātṛkā* should be known as the very form of Śiva.

(*Śrī-tantra-sad-bhāva*, 3.130)

नास्ति मन्त्रैर्विना कश्चित्सर्वं स्थावर जङ्गमम् ।
यावन्तः ये च ते सत्वाः मन्त्राधिष्ठित विग्रहाः ॥

nāsti mantrair vinā kaścit
sarvaṁ sthāvara jaṅgamam
yāvantaḥ ye ca te satvāḥ
mantrādhiṣṭhita vigrahāḥ

> All living beings and inert things have the active presence of mantras. All souls that exist as breathing entities, in fact, possess the forms, activated by their respective mantras.
>
> (*Sarva-jñānottara Āgama*, 6.4)

Mantras are classified according to the number of syllables they contain. The *Nityā Tantra* gives them the following names:

- *Piṇḍa*: One-syllable mantras.
- *Kartarī*: Mantras with two syllables.
- *Bīja*: Mantras with three to nine syllables. The term *bīja* is also used for monosyllabic mantras.
- Mantra: Mantras containing between ten and twenty syllables.
- *Mālā-mantra*: Mantras with more than twenty syllables.

Masculine mantras (*puṁ*) end in *huṁ* or *pnaṭ*. Feminine ones (*strī*) end in *vaṣaṭ* or *svāhā*. Neuter ones (*napuṁsaka* or *klība*) end in *namaḥ*.

मातृकावर्णभेदेभ्यः सर्वे मन्त्राः प्रजज्ञिरे ।
मन्त्रविद्याविभागेन त्रिविधा मन्त्रजातयः ॥
पुंस्त्रीनपुंसकात्मानो मन्त्राः सर्वे समीरिताः ।
मन्त्राः पुंदेवता ज्ञेया विद्याः स्त्रीदेवताः स्मृताः ॥
पुंमन्त्रा हुंफडन्ताः स्युर्द्विठान्ताश्च स्त्रियो मताः ।
नपुंसका नमोऽन्ताः स्युरित्युक्ता मनवस्त्रिधा ॥

mātṛkā-varṇa-bhedebhyaḥ
sarve mantrāḥ prajajñire
mantra-vidyā-vibhāgena
tri-vidhā mantra-jātayaḥ

puṁ-strī-napuṁsakātmāno
mantrāḥ sarve samīritāḥ
mantrāḥ puṁ-devatā jñeyā
vidyāḥ strī-devatāḥ smṛtāḥ

puṁ-mantrā huṁ phaḍ-antāḥ syur
dviṭhāntāś ca striyo matāḥ
napuṁsakā namo 'ntāḥ syur
ity uktā manavas-tridhā

All mantras emanated according to the classification of *mātṛkā* letters. The mantras were divided into three kinds in *mantra-vidyā*. Those kinds are: *puṁ-devatā* (male gods) mantras, *strī-devatā* (female goddesses) mantras, and *napuṁsaka-devatā* (neutral gods) mantras. *Strī-devatā* mantras are known by the name *vidyā-mantras*. *Puṁ* mantras end with *huṁ* and *phaṭ*. *Strī-mantras* end with *svāhā* and *visarga*, and *napuṁsaka-mantras* end with *namaḥ*.

(*Śāradā-tilaka Tantra*, 2.57–59)

Bhaṭṭa Raghava, in his commentary to the *Śāradā-tilaka Tantra*, mentions a quote from the *Prayoga-sāra* by Devabhadra:

वषड्फडताः पुंलिङ्गा वौषट्स्वाहान्तगाः स्त्रियः ।
नपुंसका हुँ नामोऽन्ता इति मन्त्रास्त्रिधा स्मृताः ॥
तारेणाप्यनुमीयन्ते मन्त्राः स्वाद्यन्तमध्यतः ।
प्रत्यासन्नात्मभावेन यथा पुंस्त्रीनपुंसकाः ।
बिन्दुसर्गेन्दुखण्डान्तस्तद्वदेव प्रकीर्त्तिताः ॥

vaṣaṭ-phaḍ-antāḥ puṁ-liṅgā
vauṣaṭ-svāhāntagāḥ striyaḥ
napuṁsakā huṁ nāmo 'ntā
iti mantrās tridhā smṛtāḥ

tāreṇāpy anumīyante
mantrāḥ svādhy anta-madhyataḥ
pratyāsannātma-bhāvena
yathā puṁ-strī-nāpuṁsakāḥ
bindu-sargendu-khaṇḍāntās
tad vad eva prakīrttitāḥ

> Mantras ending with *vaṣaṭ* and *phaṭ* are masculine in gender. Mantras ending with *vauṣaṭ* and *svāhā* are feminine, and those ending with *huṁ* and *namaḥ* are neuter. In this way, mantras are divided into three categories. Mantras pronounced with a high pitch and end with the letter *ṁ* are masculine. Those with a similar tone at the beginning, middle, and end and have the suffix *visarga* are feminine mantras. Those with a soft tone that are repeated again and again and end with the nasal sound *candra-bindu* are known as neuter gender mantras.
>
> (*Prayoga-sāra*, as quoted by Bhaṭṭa Raghava)

Mantras are also classified as *siddha-mantras* (perfected mantras) or *kāmya-mantras* (mantras related to desires). *Siddha-mantras* such as *Oṁ namo nārāyaṇāya* and *Oṁ namaḥ śivāya* are effective even if not received directly from a spiritual master. *Kāmya-mantras* work only if they have been received from a master. They help overcome difficulties in different areas of life.

There are also solar mantras (*saura* or *āgneya*) related to the right *nāḍī* called *piṅgalā* and lunar mantras (*cāndra* or *saumya*) related to the left *nāḍī* called *iḍā*. This division is closely connected to the gender division mentioned above. The first group generally includes mantras that contain the syllable *oṁ*, the sound *ra* and *ha*. All other mantras are considered lunar and are associated with peace.

आग्नेया मनवः सौम्या भूयिष्टेन्द्वमृताक्षराः ॥
आग्नेयाः संप्रबुध्यन्ते प्राणे चरति दक्षिणे ।
भागेऽन्यस्मिन्स्थिते प्राणे सौम्या बोधं प्रयान्ति च ॥
नाडीद्वयं गते प्राणे सर्वे बोधं प्रयान्ति च ।
प्रयच्छन्ति फलं सर्वे प्रबुद्धा मन्त्रिणां सदा ॥

āgneyā manavaḥ saumyā
bhūyiṣṭendvamṛtākṣarāḥ

āgneyāḥ saṁprabudhyante
prāṇe carati dakṣiṇe

bhāge 'nyasmin sthite prāṇe
saumyā bodhaṁ prayanti ca

nāḍī-dvayaṁ gate prāṇe
sarve bodhaṁ prayānti ca
prayacchanti phalaṁ sarve
prabuddhā mantriṇāṁ sadā

> *Āgneya* mantras (mantras related to Agni) have more 'nectar letters' (*Ra, Oṁ*, and *Ha*); and the *saumya* mantras (related to Soma) have more *Sa* and *Va*. When the vital air (*prāṇa-vāyu*) moves through the right side of the body, *āgneya* letters awake and when it moves through the left side, *saumya* letters awake. If *prāṇa-vāyu* moves in both *nāḍīs*, both *āgneya* and *saumya* emanate. Both benefit the worshipper.
>
> (*Śāradā-tilāka Tantra*, 2.61b–63)

Solar mantras are especially effective during the day and lunar ones at night. The *praṇava*, or the mantra *Oṁ*, is the most important of all. *Bījākṣras*, or *bīja-mantras* (seed mantras), as the name implies, are the seeds of sound that contain the invoked deity. They are used in five parts (*pañcāṅga*) of practice: worship (*pūjā*), repetition of the mantra (*japa*), offerings (*tarpaṇa*), fire rituals (*homa*), and propitiation (*samārādhana*). All *bīja-mantras* have the potential to transform *sādhakas* because they are intimately connected to the chakras.

Generally, a mantra is effective if it is received directly from a master who has achieved the benefit of that mantra. Initiation into a mantra must take place at an auspicious time for the *sādhaka*. Only the master can choose the right place and time.

At the initial stages, aspirants worship the deities of Viṣṇu, Śiva, or the Devī. At more advanced levels, these images are replaced by yantras. This transition from the deity to the yantra represents a step from the gross to the subtle. Each yantra has its corresponding mantra, which is an even subtler manifestation of the deity. The form of the yantra and the sound of the mantra are combined to invoke different aspects of divinity. Both stimulate meditation, help us tune into the universe, and generate an expansive movement of consciousness.

Yantra: Generally, this term is translated as "machine, tool, instrument, artifact, apparatus, or symbol." These are geometric shapes that represent different aspects of divinity. These diagrams can be engraved in copper, silver, or gold plates or be drawn on the leaf of a *bhūrja* (birch tree). Devotees treat them with the same respect and devotion as the aspect of God they represent. Visualizing yantras helps transcend the dual plane.

शरीरमिव जीवस्य दीपस्य स्नेहवत् प्रिये ।
सर्वेषामपि देवनां तथायन्त्रं प्रतिष्ठितम् ॥

śarīram iva jīvasya
dīpasya snehavat priye
sarveṣām api devānāṁ
tathā yantraṁ pratiṣṭhitam

Like the body for the soul and oil for a lamp, the yantra is the seat of all deities.

(*Kulārṇava Tantra*, 6.87)

Yam means "control" and *tra* "protect." Yantras are diagrams charged with mystical energy that protect us by helping us control the six passions. They are powerful instruments capable of awakening different powers and energy circuits in the *sādhaka*.

कामक्रोधादिदोषोत्थसर्वदुःखनियन्त्रणात् ।
यन्त्रमित्याहुरेतस्मिन्देवः प्रीणाति पूजितः ॥

kāma-krodhādi doṣottha
sarva-duḥkha niyantraṇāt
yantram ity āhur etasmin
devaḥ prīṇāti pūjitaḥ

> Because it controls all the pains that arise due to *kāma*, *krodha*, and so on (the six impurities: desire, anger, greed, pride, attachment, and jealousy), it is called *yantra*. The deity is pleased when is worshipped in the yantra.
>
> (*Kulārṇava Tantra*, 6.86)

For a yantra to be effective and suitable for worship, it must be properly consecrated. In rituals, yantras are used for six different purposes, or *ṣaṭ-karmas*:

1. To control, or *vaśī-karaṇa*.
2. To immobilize, or *stambhana*.
3. To evoke hatred, or *vidveṣaṇa*.
4. To expel, or *uccāṭana*.
5. To murder, or *māraṇa*.
6. To bestow peace and nourishment, or *śāntika-pauṣṭika*.

Dhāraṇa-yantras are worn around the neck or arms. If it comes in contact with a contaminated object or a corpse, the yantra loses its power. Some of the most important yantras and their effects are:

- Gaṇeśa yantra: For wealth and prosperity.
- Hanuman yantra: To acquire strength and safety in travel.
- Bhadrakālī yantra: For knowledge, strength, and health.
- Sudarśana yantra: To relieve illnesses and drive away malignant spirits.
- Subrahmaṇya yantra: For exorcism or expelling demons.
- Cāmuṇḍā yantra: To kill enemies.
- Śarabha yantra: To heal epilepsy.

Just as there are many mantras to meditate on, there are also many yantra meditations. If *sādhakas* wish to access the profound wisdom contained in these sacred diagrams, they must seek the guidance of a spiritual master. There are also yantras for specific deities or aspects of divinity.

During worship ceremonies and rituals, it is customary to draw a yantra on the ground. For a deity installation ceremony (*prāṇa-pratiṣṭhā*), yantras can be engraved on a metal plate. Yantras are a link between the gross and the subtle. Like the mantras, they are only effective if aspirants infuse them with vital energy through the power of concentration. In reality, aspirants are worshipping their own vital energy infused into the yantra.

According to *Śākta* Tantra, the universe is a manifestation or expression of energy, though a common person may be not aware of this. That which is worshipped cannot be inferior to the worshipper and, therefore, vital energy must be infused into the object of worship by the worshipper. This process is carried out with the help of *mantra-japa* (meditative repetition of divine names), and the other four limbs of *puraś-caraṇa* (five-limbed worship practice).

पूजा त्रैकालिकी नित्यं जपस्तर्पणमेव च ।
होमो ब्राह्मणभुक्तिश्च पुरश्चरणमुच्यते ॥

pūjā trai-kālikī nityaṁ
japas tarpaṇam eva ca
homo brāhmaṇa-bhuktiś ca
puraś-caraṇam ucyate

Daily *pūjā* at three prescribed hours, regular *japa*, *tarpaṇa* (offering water), *homa* (sacrificial fire), and feeding the *Brāhmaṇas* are the five-fold worship called *puraś-caraṇa*.

(*Kulārṇava Tantra*, 15.8)

पार्वत्युवाच-
विना यन्त्रेण चेत्पूजा देवता न प्रसीदति ।
तस्मात्कथय देवेश यन्त्रमस्या मनोहरम् ॥
यस्य दर्शनमात्रेण दारिद्र्यं नश्यति ध्रुवम् ।

pārvaty uvāca-
vinā yantreṇa cet pūjā

devatā na prasīdati
tasmāt kathaya deveśa
yantram asyā manoharam

yasya darśana-mātreṇa
dāridryṁ naśyati dhruvam

Pārvatī said: 'If worship is done without a yantra, the deity is not pleased. Therefore, O lord, please tell me about the beautiful yantra, which by mere looking at it, poverty is surely extinguished.

(*Gandharva Tantra,* 5.1–2a)

Tantra: This is the aspirants' practical manual: a combination of mantra, philosophy, and yogic methodology for spiritual evolution. Tantra includes the philosophy and practical methods for reorienting and channeling energies. It has a central place in the *Āgamas*. Generally, the practices are called *Tantra*, while *Tantra-Śāstras* are texts that unite practice and theory. The *Tantra-śāstra* is also called *Pratyakṣa-śāstra* (the wisdom of real experience), *Sādhana-śāstra* (the wisdom of spiritual practice), and *Upāsanā-śāstra* (the wisdom of worship).

The sections of the *Āgamas*

ज्ञानं क्रिया च चर्या च योगश्चेति सुरेश्वरि ।
चतुष्पादः समाख्यातो मम धर्मस्सनातनः ॥

jñānaṁ kriyā ca caryā ca
yogaś ceti sureśvari
catuṣ pādaḥ samākhyāto
mama dharmas sanātanaḥ

O goddess, my eternal dharma is fourfold: *jñāna*, *kriyā*, *caryā*, and yoga.

(*Śiva Purāṇa*, "*Vāyavīya Saṁhitā*", 2.10.30)

In general, *Āgamas* are divided into four sections called *pādas*, or "feet," which calls to mind a table that needs four legs to be stable. The sections are called *jñāna-pāda*, *yoga-pāda*, *kriyā-pāda*, and *caryā-pāda*.

Jñāna-pāda: This section describes the Tantric worldview. It offers extensive knowledge about the nature of the universe, the cause of the phenomenal world, the dissolution of creation, the eternal and transitory principles of nature, the nature of the Self, the philosophy of captivity, and liberation. It gives an in-depth explanation of the principles *Pati*, *paśu*, and *pāśa* (Lord, bounded souls, and bondage).

Yoga-pāda: The second section explains yoga's eight primary components and six auxiliary ones. It deals with the practical means of attaining the experience of knowledge described in the *jñāna-pāda*. It describes how to merge the personal and the universal. Through certain methods, it is possible to attain purification at all levels. This is not only a question of achieving the transcendental experience, but of transforming ourselves into instruments of the Divine. The *sādhana* presented here includes the internal aspect (*antaraṅga*) and the external one (*bahiraṅga*). *Tantra-śāstra* places special emphasis on three types of yoga: *laya*, *kuṇḍalinī*, and mantra.

Kriyā-pāda: This section deals with the proper ways to plan cities and villages, make icons, and organize festivals. It also instructs on religious subjects, such as temple architecture, home rituals, temple ceremonies, expiations, pilgrimages, and worship.

Caryā-pāda: The last section deals with codes of conduct, and rules and regulations for initiation, or *dīkṣā*. It also explains the rites for the ancestors, worship, rituals, festivals, and expiations.

Classifying the canon

Relatively few *Āgamas* have survived. Some of them contain lists of numerous works that have been lost. Thanks to these lists, we know that the Tantric corpus was very vast and only a small portion has been preserved. Most of the earliest texts have disappeared, and only a few extant texts have been translated from Sanskrit.

The word *āgama* refers to the entire Tantric canon, but each tradition has a different generic term for its own texts. The *Śaiva* texts are called *Āgamas* (traditions); the *Vaiṣṇava* texts, *Saṁhitās* (collections); and the *Śākta* texts, Tantras (treatises or doctrines). But since Tantra is a part of the *Āgama*, the terms are often used interchangeably. It is not easy to delineate the boundaries between *Śaiva* and *Śākta* Agamic literature, because the two traditions are very similar, both in their spiritual vision and in their *sādhana*.

Each of the main branches of Hinduism has its own *Āgamas*:

1. *Śaiva Tantra*: Śiva is the supreme master.
2. *Vaiṣṇava Tantra*: Nārāyaṇa is the main deity.
3. *Saurya Tantra*: Sūrya, the Sun is the primordial force.
4. *Gāṇapatya Tantra*: Gaṇeśa is the main deity.
5. *Śākta Tantra*: Śakti is the supreme deity.

There are other Tantric scriptures that belong to the Buddhist and the Jaina traditions.

The *Āgamas* are divine revelations. Therefore, the *Śaivas* believe they were revealed by Śiva, the *Vaiṣṇavas* by Viṣṇu, and the *Śāktas* by the Devī. In the *Śaiva* texts, Śiva takes the role of teacher and answers questions from the goddess, which is why they are called *Āgamas*. In the *Śākta* texts, called *Nigamas*, Śakti instructs Śiva. In the *Vaiṣṇava* texts, the dialogue is between Viṣṇu and Lakṣmī.

सत्कथालापमात्रञ्च न तेषां मनसि क्वचित् ।
त्वया कृतानि तन्त्राणि जीवोद्धरणहेतवे ॥
निगमागमजातानि भुक्तिमुक्तिकराणि च ।
देवीनां यत्र देवानां मन्त्रयन्त्रादिसाधनम् ॥

sat-kathālāpa-mātraṁ ca
na teṣāṁ manasi kvacit
tvayā kṛtāni tantrāṇi
jīvoddharaṇa-hetave

nigamāgama-jātāni
bhukti-mukti-karāṇi ca
devīnāṁ yatra devānāṁ
mantra-yantrādi sādhanam

There has never been a thought in their minds of having a conversation about the Truth. The Tantras, which have arisen from the *Nigamas* and *Āgamas* and contain mantras, yantras, etc., of the gods and goddesses, have been composed by you for the salvation of the embodied souls, and offer both enjoyment and liberation.

(*Mahā-nirvāṇa Tantra*, 1.50–51)

There are numerous ways to classify the canon, and particular sects have created their own classifications. The *Sammohana Tantra* mentions twenty-two types of *Āgamas*, including *Cin-āgama* (*Śākta*), *Pāśu-pata* (*Śaiva*), *Pāñca-rātra* (*Vaiṣṇava*), *Kāpālika*, *Bhairava*, *Aghora*, *Jaina*, and *Bauddha*, each with its respective Tantras and *Upatantras* (minor Tantras), as we see in this list:

1. ***Śaiva Tantras*:** 32 Tantras, 325 *Upatantras*, 10 *Saṁhitās*, 5 *Arṇavas*, 2 *Yāmalas*, 3 *Ḍāmaras*, 1 *Uddāla*, 2 *Uḍḍīśas*, 8 *Kalpas*, 8 *Upasaṁkhyās*, 2 *Cūḍā-maṇis*, 2 *Cintā-maṇis*, and 2 *Vimarśinīs*.
2. ***Śaiva-śākta Tantras*:** 64 Tantras, 327 *Upatantras*, 8 *Yāmalas*, 4 *Ḍāmaras*, 2 *Kalpa-latās*, and several *Saṁhitās*, *Cūḍā-maṇis* (100), *Arṇavas*, *Purāṇas*, *Upavedas*, *Kakṣa-puṭas*, *Vimarśinīs*, and *Cintā-maṇis*.
3. ***Vaiṣṇava Tantras*:** 75 Tantras, 205 *Upatantras*, 20 *Kalpas*, 8 *Saṁhitās*, 1 *Arṇavaka*, 5 *Kakṣa-puṭas*, 8 *Cūḍā-maṇis*, 2 *Cintā-maṇis*, 2 *Uḍḍīśas*, 2 *Ḍāmaras*, 1 *Yāmala*, 5 *Purāṇas*, 3 *Tattva-bodha-vimarśinīs*, and 2 *Amṛtas* (*Tarpaṇa*).
4. ***Saura Tantras*:** 30 Tantras, 96 *Upatantras*, 4 *Saṁhitās*, 2 *Upasaṁhitās*, 5 *Purāṇas*, 10 *Kalpas*, 2 *Kakṣa-puṭis*, 3 *Tattvas*, 3 *Vimarśinīs*, 3 *Cūḍā-maṇis*, 2 *Ḍāmaras*, 2 *Yāmalas*, 5 *Uddālas*, 2 *Avatāras*, 2 *Uḍḍīśas*, 3 *Amṛtas*, 3 *Darpaṇas*, and 3 *Kalpas*.

5. ***Gāṇapatya Tantras*:** 50 Tantras, 25 *Upatantras*, 2 *Purāṇas*, 3 *Sāgaras*, 3 *Darpaṇas*, 5 *Amṛtas*, 9 *Kalpakās*, 3 *Kakṣa-puṭis*, 2 *Vimarśinīs*, 2 *Tattvas*, 2 *Uḍḍīśas*, 3 *Cūḍā-maṇis*, 3 *Cintā-maṇis*, 1 *Ḍāmara*, 1 *Candra Yāmala*, and 8 *Pāñca-rātras*.
6. ***Bauddha Tantras*:** 5 *Avataraṇakas*, 5 *Suktas*, 2 *Cintā-maṇis*, 9 *Purāṇas*, 3 *Upasaṁkhyas*, 2 *Kakṣa-puṭis*, 3 *Kalpa-drumas*, 2 *Kāma-dhenus*, 3 *Sabhāvas*, and 5 *Tattvas*.

Another way to classify the *Āgamas* is by place of origin. This assigns sixty-four texts to each group and refers to each region according to the means of transportation used there: *Viṣṇu-krāntā* (The region of Viṣṇu - northeast), *Ratha-krāntā* (Wagon region- northwest), *Aśva-krāntā* or *Gaja-krāntā* (horse or elephant region - south).

The Tantric texts are also divided into true (*sad-āgama*) and false (*asad-āgama*). The worship of the former is in accordance with tradition, while the latter is not.

The *Āgamas* can also be classified into *āstika* (Vedic) and *nāstika* (non-Vedic). According to their main deity, the *āstika Tantras* are further subdivided into *Vaiṣṇava*, *Śaiva*, *Saura*, *Gāṇapatya*, and *Śākta*. The *Śākta Tantras* are classified into ten groups according to the names of the ten *Mahā-vidyās* goddesses. The *nāstika* Tantras belong to Buddhism and Jainism.

There are many other ways to categorize the *Āgamas*, for example:

- *Srotas* (traditions).
- *Pīṭhas* (collections).
- *Guṇas* (modes of nature: *sattva*, *rajas*, and *tamas*).
- *Kalpas* (mythological eras: *Vārāha-kalpa*, *Kāla-kalpa*, and so on).
- Attitudes explained in the *Brahma Yāmala*: *Dakṣiṇa* (right), *Vāma* (left), and *Madhyama* (central).

CHAPTER 2

THE *ŚAIVA TANTRAS*

The *Śaiva* literature: Vedic, Puranic, and Agamic

The accredited scriptures of lay Shaivism are the fourteen *Śaiva* Upanishads and the six *Śaiva Purāṇas*. The absolute position of Śiva as the supreme Self is established on the authority of the six *Śaiva Purāṇas*: *Liṅga Purāṇa*, *Śiva Purāṇa*, *Skanda Purāṇa*, *Matsya Purāṇa*, *Kūrma Purāṇa*, and *Brahmāṇḍa Purāṇa*. The most important are the *Liṅga Purāṇa* and the *Śiva Purāṇa*, which are both rich in general matters as well as *Śaiva* material. They contain information on the duties of different castes, teachings about *Dharma Śāstra* and astrology, details about the installation of *liṅgas* in *Śaiva* temples, and descriptions of Śiva's form and nature. The fourteen Upanishads deal principally with *Śaiva* theology. They discuss the symbolism, clothing, rituals, and paraphernalia of the *Śaiva* cult.

Vedic scriptures: The *Ṛg Veda* praises Śiva under the name Rudra. The fourteen minor Upanishads classified as *Śaiva* are the *Kaivalya*, *Atharva-śiras*, *Atharva-śikhā*, *Bṛhaj-jābāla*, *Kālāgni-rudra*, *Dakṣiṇā-mūrti*, *Śarabha*, *Akṣa-mālikā*, *Rudra-hṛdaya*, *Bhasma-jābāla*, *Rudrākṣa-jābāla*, *Gaṇapati*, *Pañca-brahma*, and *Jābāli*. While the *Ṛg Veda* professes theistic absolutism, the Upanishads present Śiva as the metaphysical Brahman.

एको हि रुद्रो न द्वितीयाय तस्थुर्य इमाँल्लोकानीशत ईशनीभिः ।
प्रत्यङ्नास्तिष्ठति सञ्चुकोचान्तकाले संसृज्य विश्वा भुवनानि गोपाः ॥

eko hi rudro na dvitīyāya tasthur
ya imān llokān īśata īśanībhiḥ

pratyaṅ-janās tiṣṭhati sañcukocānta-kāle
saṁsṛjya viśvā bhuvanāni gopāḥ

> He who protects and controls the worlds by his own powers, Rudra, is indeed only one. There is no one beside him who can make him the second. O men, he is present inside the hearts of all beings. After projecting and maintaining all the worlds, he finally draws them into himself.
>
> (*Śvetāśvatara Upanishad,* 3.2)

Some Vedic texts use the term *Rudra* to refer to the supreme goal and the essence of everything. Others include sections dealing with the symbolism of the rituals, deities, and clothing of the *Śaiva* cult.

Puranic scriptures: These texts continue the Vedic *Śaiva* tradition. After the revelation of the *Purāṇas*, Shaivism began to establish itself as the main Hindu tradition. Its beliefs ranged from devotional dualist theism (Śiva bhakti) appropriate for married people, to the monist theism, especially suitable for ascetic renunciates dedicated to yoga and meditation. Although the *Purāṇas* were saturated with non-orthodox *Śaiva* material, they belonged to the framework of Vedic orthodoxy, or Smarta, and condemned Tantric systems that threatened Vedic purity. The *Kūrma Purāṇa*, for example, condemns the *Pāśu-pata* sect and gives authority to the *Atharva-śiras Upanishad*, a late Upanishad containing *Śaiva* material. The orthodox *Śaivas*, also called *Maheśvaras*, were not initiated. They simply worshipped Śiva with Vedic domestic rites prescribed by the *varṇāśrama-dharma,* such as Puranic *pūjās* and Vedic mantras. Their aspiration was to be taken to Śiva's paradise (*Śiva-loka*) at the time of death.

***Āgamas*, or Tantras:** Only *Śaivas* who were initiated into the Tantric tradition had access to the revelation of the *Āgamas*. The aspirants chose between two branches: the *Ati-mārga* (the direct or higher path), which used meditation, and the *Mantra-mārga* (the path of the mantras) dedicated to the recitation of mantras. The *Mantra-mārga* was subdivided into two traditions: *Saiddhāntika* (orthodox), based on 28 *Āgamas* (18 *Rudra Āgamas* and 10 *Śaiva Āgamas*), and non-*Saiddhāntika* (non-orthodox with *Śākta* inclination), based on 64 *Bhairava Āgamas*.

These scriptures teach three views of reality: dualism (18 *Rudra Āgamas*), qualified monism (10 *Śaiva Āgamas*), and monism (64 *Bhairava Āgamas*).

The revelation of the *Śaiva* scriptures

According to the theology adopted by Smarta Hinduism, which is based on the *Purāṇas*, Lord Śiva is a member of the *tri-mūrti* (divine trinity): Śiva destroys, Brahmā creates, and Viṣṇu preserves. However, in the cosmology of the *Śaiva Āgamas*, these three cosmic activities are all performed by Śiva. He also performs two more activities related to souls. The fourth is the concealment of grace (*tirodhāna-śakti*), through which he limits our consciousness and conceals reality to allow us to evolve. The fifth is revelation (*anugraha-śakti*), through which Lord Śiva liberates us from illusion and grants us the realization of our true nature as inseparable parts of God.

सर्वमेतत्स एवेशस्तस्मादन्यन्न विद्यते ।

sarvam etat sa eveśas
tasmād anyan na vidyate

> This Lord (Śiva) is all that exists (Everything that exists is Lord Śiva only). There is nothing different from him.
>
> (*Ajita Tantra*, 2.13a)

On the other hand, according to the *Śaiva-siddhānta* philosophy, Lord Śiva is one and includes everything and everyone but manifests himself in three forms:

1. Without form (*niṣkala*). Śiva is the absolute reality: Para-śiva.
2. Formed–formless (*sakala-niṣkala*). Śiva is pure consciousness: Parā-śakti or Sadā-śiva.
3. With form (*sakala*). Śiva is personal: Parameśvara or Maheśa.

शिवं सदाशिवं चैव महेशं च त्रिधा स्मृतम् ।
शिवतत्त्वं महासेन निष्कळं त्विति कीर्तितम् ॥
सकलं निष्कलं चैव सादाख्यमिति चोच्यते ।
महेशं सकलं विद्यात्त्रिविधास्ते भवन्ति वै ॥

śivaṁ sadā-śivaṁ caiva
maheśaṁ ca tridhā smṛtam
śiva-tattvaṁ mahā-sena
niṣkalaṁ tviti kīrtitam

sakalaṁ niṣkalaṁ caiva
sādākhyam iti cocyate
maheśaṁ sakalaṁ vidyāt
tri-vidhās te bhavanti vai

Śiva is revealed as being of three kinds: Śiva, Sadā-śiva, and Maheśa. O Mahā-sena, the entity Śiva is well known as *niṣkala* (without form). Sadā-śiva is said to be the *sādākhya, sakala and niṣkala* (with and without form). One should know Maheśa as *sakala* (with form). These are the three varieties.
(*Vātula-śuddhākhya Tantra,* 1.15–16)

Śiva is the supreme consciousness with the effulgence of trillions and trillions of suns. If his fullness manifested directly, worlds would be incinerated. Therefore, his presence descends gradually through expansions, which are his inseparable parts but with less effulgence.

The *Viṣṇu-dharmottara Purāṇa* explain this principle beautifully:

अतो भगवतानेन स्वेच्छया तत्प्रदर्शितम् ।
प्रादुर्भावेष्वथाकारं तं दिशन्ति दिवौकसः ॥
एतस्मात्कारणात्पूजा साकारस्य विधीयते ।

ato bhagavatānena
svecchayā tat pradarśitam
prādurbhāveṣvathākāraṁ
taṁ diśanti divaukasaḥ

etasmāt kāraṇāt pūjā
sākārasya vidhīyate

Because the invisible condition is understood with great difficulty by corporeal beings, the supreme Lord, through his own will, he has shown his [form] in various manifestations, which is also pointed out by the gods. For this reason, the supreme Lord is worshipped with form.

(*Viṣṇu-dharmottara Purāṇa*, 3.46.5–6a)

The formed–formless Sadā-śiva is the aspect of Śiva that performs the five cosmic functions: creating, preserving, destructing, concealing, and revealing. For this purpose, he has five aspects that are called Pañca-brahmas, "five great lords": Īśāna, Tat-puruṣa, Aghora, Vāma-deva, and Sadyo-jāta.

The *Viṣṇu-dharmottara Purāṇa* describes:

सद्योजातं वामदेवमघोरं च महाभुज ।
तथा तत्पुरुषं ज्ञेयमीशानं पञ्चमं मुखम् ॥

sadyo-jātaṁ vāmadevam
aghoraṁ ca mahā-bhuja
tathā tat-puruṣaṁ jñeyam
īśānaṁ pañcamaṁ mukham

Mārkaṇḍeya said: "O strong-armed one, Sadyo-jāta, Vāmadeva, Aghora and Tat-puruṣa should be known [as the four faces of Śiva], and the fifth face is [Īśāna]."

(*Viṣṇu-dharmottara Purāṇa*, 3.48.1)

The absolute reality, Para-śiva, has no form, but it is known as Sadā-śiva when it is represented in the Śiva-liṅga. This non-iconic *mūrti* represents the formed-formless (*sakala-niṣkala*) aspect of God. It rests on a pedestal that symbolizes Śakti. The five Lords are visualized in the *Śiva-liṅga*. Their faces are actually carved on some *liṅgas*.

लिङ्गोत्पत्तिं ततो वक्ष्ये शृणु वारिजलोचन ।
पुरुषस्य तु यच्चिह्नं पुरुषव्यक्तिकारणम् ॥
सदाशिवस्य तल्लिङ्गं शिवलिङ्गमिति स्मृतम् ।

liṅgotpattiṁ tato vakṣye
śṛṇu vāri-ja-locana
puruṣasya tu yac cihnaṁ
puruṣa-vyakti-kāraṇam

sadā-śivasya tal liṅgaṁ
śiva-liṅgam iti smṛtam

Next, I will tell you about the birth process of the *liṅga*. Listen, O lotus-eyed one, that which is the sign of the soul, that is to say, a cause of the soul's manifestation; such a sign for Sadā-śiva is traditionally known as *Śiva-liṅga*.

(*Ajita Tantra*, 3.1–2a)

The supreme Lord Para-śiva performs the cosmic activities within the realm of pure *māyā* through his form of Lord Sadā-śiva (or Pañca-brahma). Since Sadā-śiva exists on the causal plane, he cannot be directly involved with the impure *māyā* that reigns on the astral and physical planes. Therefore, he creates five delegated (*adhiṣṭhita*) Lords: Brahma, Viṣṇu, Rudra, Maheśvara, and Sadā-śiva (different from the great Sadā-śiva). Pañca-brahma supervises their activities.

Sadā-śiva is formed–formless (*sakala-niṣkala*); however, on the subtle level on which Sadā-śiva exists, he does not have a form and is only the seeds or potentialities of sound. Thus, his body is made up of five mantras, collectively known as the Pañca-brahma.

It is explained in the *Ajita Tantra*:

इत्यवेत्य स देवेशः शिवः सर्वान्तरस्थितः ॥
लोकानुग्राहको भूत्वा जन्तूनां भुक्तिमुक्तिदः ।
पञ्चब्रह्मतनुः साक्षात्स शिवोऽभूत्सदाशिवः ॥

ity avetya sa deveśaḥ
śivaḥ sarvāntara-sthitaḥ

lokānugrāhako bhūtvā
jantūnāṁ bhukti-mukti-daḥ
pañca-brahma-tanuḥ sākṣāt
sa śivo 'bhūt sadā-śivaḥ

Being aware of that [of the limitations of those with little knowledge for perceiving him without a form], this Lord of gods, Śiva, who is within everything, who extends his grace to all and gives creatures elevated joy and liberation, this Śiva became Sadā-śiva, whose body is manifested as the Pañca-brahma.

(*Ajita Tantra*, 2.31b–32)

And the *Mṛgendra Āgama* also describes:

मूलाद्यसम्भवाच्छाक्तं वपुर्नैतादृशं प्रभोः ।
तद्वपुः पञ्चभिर्मन्त्रैः पञ्चकृत्योपयोगिभिः ॥
ईशतत्पुरुषाघोर वामाजैर्मस्तकादिकम् ।

mūlādy asambhavāc chāktaṁ
vapur naitādṛśaṁ prabhoḥ
tad vapuḥ pañcabhir mantraiḥ
pañca-kṛtyopayogibhiḥ
īśa-tat-puruṣāghora
vāmājair mastakādikam

Since the Supreme Lord is free from body-creating seeds such as impurity (*mala*), karma and so on, his body is not like our own bodies. His body is only made of the very nature of Śakti. Śiva's body comprises five mantras so it is instrumentally useful in performing the five cosmic functions. With these five mantras, the head and other parts of Śiva's body are designed. The five mantras are Īśana, Tat-puruṣa, Aghora, Vāma, and Sadyo-jāta.

(*Mṛgendra Āgama*, 3.8)

Devotees communicate with the five Lords through five mantras called *Pañca-brahma-mantras*, which are formulas of homage to these five entities. At the time of initiation, the guru installs these mantras in the body of the aspirants and gives them a spiritual body. They unite with Śiva by meditating (*dhyāna*) on the image of the five heads oriented in five directions.

The *Pañca-brahma-mantras* are found in the *Taittirīya Āraṇyaka* (10.17–21) and also appear in the *Mahā-narāyaṇa Upanishad* (17.1–5).

Sadā-śiva

The *Āgamas* describe the five Lords in the following way:

1. Sadyo-jāta: His name means "gives birth quickly" because he is the origin of birth. Śiva creates Sadyo-jāta and entrusts him with the manifestation of all nature. Sadyo-jāta creates the universe through his delegate, Lord Brahmā. He faces west. He is related to the sphere of earth (*pṛthivī-maṇḍala*), and his syllable of the *pañcākṣara* mantra is *Na*. The scriptures describe him as young and attractive, of white complexion, smeared with sandalwood paste, and decorated with white flowers. One hand makes the gesture *varada-mudrā* (granting desires gesture) and the other the *abhaya-mudrā* (fear-not gesture).

The Sadyo-jāta mantra in the *Pañca-brahma-mantras*:

सद्योजातं प्रपद्यामि सद्योजाताय वै नमः ।
भवे भवे नातिभवे भजस्व मां भवोद्भवाय नमः ॥

sadyo-jātaṁ prapadyāmi
sadyo-jātāya vai namo namaḥ
bhave bhave nātibhave bhajasva
māṁ bhavodbhavāya namaḥ

I totally and repeatedly submit my mind, words, and body to Lord Sadyo-jāta, who manifests himself and instantaneously creates bodies and worlds, who appears to devotees in the forms contemplated by them and yet transcends the forms he takes, and who has a retinue of deities formed of millions of mantras. May he make my form like his.
(*Mahā-narāyaṇa Upanishad*, 17.1 and *Taittirīya Āraṇyaka*, 10.17)

2. Vāma-deva: His name means "charming or delightful." He is the aspect of Śiva that preserves through his delegate, Lord Viṣṇu. He faces north. He is related to the sphere of water (*jala-maṇḍala*) and his syllable of the *pañcākṣara* mantra is *Ma*. The scriptures describe him as reddish in complexion, good-

looking, and aristocratic, dressed in fine clothes with a turban and garlands of flowers. In his hands, he holds a sword and a shield.

The Vāma-deva mantra in the *Pañca-brahma-mantras*:

वामदेवाय नमो ज्येष्ठाय नमः
श्रेष्ठाय नमो रुद्राय नमः
कालाय नमः कलविकरणाय नमो
बलविकरणाय नमो बलप्रमथनाय नमः
सर्वभूतदमनाय नमो मनोन्मनाय नमः ॥

vāma-devāya namo jyeṣṭhāya namaḥ
śreṣṭhāya namo rudrāya namaḥ
kālāya namaḥ kala-vikaraṇāya namo
bala-vikaraṇāya namo bala-pramathanāya namaḥ
sarva-bhūta damanāya namo
manonmanāya namaḥ

Salutations to the luminous Lord Vāma-deva who sportively creates everything. Salutations to the one who is eternally the eldest, transcending the great cycles of time. Salutations to him whose lordship excels all other gods. Salutations to him who removes the sufferings of all living beings. Salutations to him who is eternal time. Salutations to him who puts into operation the divisions of time and keeps the worlds in order. Salutations to him who, being the source of strength, strengthens the auspicious forces. Salutations to him who, being the bearer of strength, withdraws the strength of inauspicious forces and extirpates them. Salutations to him who guides all souls to finally reach him.
(*Mahā-narāyaṇa Upanishad*, 17.2 and *Taittirīya Āraṇyaka*, 10.18)

3. Aghora: His name means "not terrifying." He is the aspect of Śiva that destroys through his delegate, Lord Rudra. He faces south. He is related to the sphere of fire (*agni-maṇḍala*) and his

syllable of the *pañcākṣara* mantra is *Śi*. The scriptures describe him as terrifying and decorated with mortuary elements. His complexion is the color of a dark cloud; he wears a crown with a half moon and a beautiful pendant. Although he is adorned with snakes, scorpions, and garlands of skulls, his expression is benevolent. His four left hands hold a fire, *khaṭvāṅga* (bone), a shield, and a rope. The four right hands hold a trident, an ax, a sword, and a staff.

The Aghora mantra in the *Pañca-brahma-mantras*:

अघोरेभ्योऽथ घोरेभ्यो घोर घोरतरेभ्यः ।
सर्वतः सर्व सर्वेभ्यो नमस्ते अस्तु रुद्ररूपेभ्यः ॥

aghorebhyo 'tha ghorebhyo
ghora ghoretarebhyaḥ
sarvataḥ sarva-sarvebhyo
namaste astu rudra-rūpebhyaḥ

Salutations to Lord Śiva Aghora who manifests himself in countless benign forms, in frightful and terrifying forms, and to all those countless forms of Rudra. Salutations to all these manifestations of Lord Śiva.
(*Mahā-narāyaṇa Upanishad*, 17.3 and *Taittirīya Āraṇyaka*, 10.19)

4. Tat-puruṣa: His name means "supreme soul." He is the aspect of Śiva that conceals from the souls their true nature through his delegate, Lord Maheśvara. He looks east. He is related to the sphere of air (*vāyu-maṇḍala*), and his syllable of the *pañcākṣara* mantra is *Va*. The scriptures describe him with a golden complexion and wearing silk yellow robes. He wears a crown decorated with a crescent moon. In one hand he carries a string of pearls and in the other, a trident.

The Tat-puruṣa mantra in the *Pañca-brahma-mantras*:

तत्पुरुषाय विद्महे महादेवाय धीमहि ।
तन्नो रुद्रः प्रचोदयात् ॥

tat-puruṣāya vidmahe
mahā-devāya dhīmahi
tan no rudraḥ pracodayāt

As guided by my guru, I realize the form of Śiva known as Tat-puruṣa. I meditate with pure mind and refined intellect on the great illuminator. Let Tat-puruṣa, who cuts asunder the limiting bonds of the souls and by this act comes to be known as Rudra, guide, enlighten, and strengthen my organs of knowledge and action and my internal faculties.
(*Mahā-narāyaṇa Upanishad*, 17.4 and *Taittirīya Āraṇyaka*, 10.20)

5. Īśāna: His name means "ruler." He is the aspect of Śiva that gives the revelation through his delegate, Lord Sadā-śiva (different from the Sada-śiva who is a general name for all the five faces). He looks upward. He is related to the sphere of ether (*ākāśa-maṇḍala*), and his syllable of the *pañcākṣara* mantra is *Ya*, the final part of the mantra *Namaḥ Śivāya*. The scriptures describe him as benevolent, as having three eyes, and wearing a crown with a half-moon. One of his hands holds a trident, another a mālā, and the other two make the gestures of *abhaya-mudrā* (fear-not gesture) and *dhyāna-mudrā* (meditation gesture).

The Īśāna Mantra in the *Pañca-brahma mantras*:

ईशानस्सर्वविद्यानामीश्वर सर्वभूतानां ब्रह्माधिपतिः ।
ब्रह्मणोऽधिपतिर्ब्रह्मा शिवो मे अस्तु सदाशिवोम् ॥

īśānas sarva-vidyānām
īśvaras sarva-bhūtānām
brahmādhipatiḥ
brahmaṇo 'dhipatir
brahmā śivo me astu sadā-śivoṁ

Iśāna is the supreme Lord and revealer of all knowledge and spiritual disciplines, the nourisher and controller of all living beings, the directing Lord of Sadā-śiva, the guiding and directing authority for the eight Vidyīśvaras, the directors of Brahmā, Viṣṇu, and others; may he be present in this *Śiva-liṅga*. Through this benign presence, let there be absolute purity and auspiciousness in me. *Oṁ*. (*Mahā-narāyaṇa Upanishad*, 17.5 and *Taittirīya Āraṇyaka*, 10.21)

The emanations of the *Āgamas* from Sada-śiva

सृष्टिकाले महेशानः पुरुषार्थ प्रसिद्धये ।
विधत्ते विमलं ज्ञानं पञ्चश्रोतोऽभिलक्षितम् ॥

sṛṣṭi-kāle maheśānaḥ
puruṣārtha prasiddhaye
vidhatte vimalaṁ jñānaṁ
pañca-śroto 'bhilakṣitam

At the time of creation, Lord Śiva, in order to enable the souls to gain worldly enjoyments, revealed pure knowledge (*Āgama*) through his five faces in the form of five scriptural streams.

(*Mṛgendra Āgama*, "*Vidyā-pāda*," 1.21)

Para-śiva is inaccessible to the senses, speech, and mind. In the realm of *māyā*, he communicates through Sadā-śiva, who resides in the *Śiva-liṅga* and is the object of worship and the transmitter of the Tantric scriptures. From his faces, Sadā-śiva reveals different traditions for the benefit of souls trapped in ignorance. His five faces utter the scriptures at different stages of the revelation.

सद्योवाम महाघोर पुरुषेशान मूर्तयः ॥
प्रत्येकं पञ्चवक्त्रास्स्युः तैरुक्तं लौकिकादिकम् ।
पञ्चविंशति भेदेन स्रोतोभेदः प्रकीर्तितः ॥

sadyo-vāma mahā-ghora
puruṣeśāna mūrtayaḥ

praty ekaṁ pañca-vaktras syuḥ
tair uktaṁ laukikādikaṁ
pañca-viṁśati bhedena
sroto bhedaḥ prakīrtitaḥ

There are five faces: Sadyo-jāta, Vāma-deva, Aghora, Tatpuruṣa, and Īśāna. Each face appears as five faces. The *Laukika* and *Vaidika* scriptures were revealed by these five faces. Each face revealed five different scriptures. Thus, there was the revelation of twenty-five different (types of) scriptures.
(*Kāmika Āgama*, 1.18b–19)

एष्वेवान्तर्गतं वक्तुं वाङ्मयं वस्तुवाचकम् ।
तेष्वेव मन्त्रतन्त्राख्यं सदाशिव मुखोद्गतम् ॥
सिद्धान्तं गारुडं वामं भूततन्त्रं च भैरवम् ।
उर्ध्वं पूर्वं कुबेरास्य याम्यवक्त्राद्यथाक्रमम् ॥

eṣvevāntar-gataṁ vaktuṁ
vāṅ-mayaṁ vastu-vācakam
teṣveva mantra-tantrākhyaṁ
sadā-śiva mukhodgataṁ

siddhāntaṁ gāruḍaṁ vāmaṁ
bhūta-tantraṁ ca bhairavam
ūrdva pūrva kuberāsya
yāmya-vaktrād-yathā-kramam

In order to clearly express the nature of the one who remains concealed at the exact core of the word, scriptures such as the mantras and the Tantras flowed out from the Sadyojāta face. The Tantras known as Siddhānta, Gāruḍa, Vāma, Bhūta, and Bhairava flowed out, respectively, from the top face (Ūrdva), the east face (Pūrva or Iśāna), the south face (Kubera or Tat-puruṣa), the left face (Vāma), and the right face (Yāmya or Aghora), in that order.

(*Kāmika Āgama,* 1.20–21)

Face	Sadyo-jāta	Vāma-deva	Aghora	Tat-puruṣa	Īśāna
Name translation	Gives birth quickly	Charming or delightful	Not terrifying	Supreme soul	Ruler
Cardinal direction	West	North	South	East	Upward
Direction	Behind	Left	Right	Front	Above
Color	Pearl white	Red	Dark blue	Golden yellow	Crystalline
Element	Earth	Water	Fire	Air	Ether
Power	Creation (*sṛṣṭi*)	Maintenance (*sthiti*)	Dissolution (*saṁhāra*)	Covering grace (*tirodhāna*)	Revealing grace (*anugraha*)
Delegated Lords	Brahma	Viṣṇu	Rudra	Maheśvara	Sadā-śiva
Syllable of the mantra *pañcākṣara*	*Na*	*Ma*	*Śi*	*Va*	*Ya*
Śāstras	*Ṛg Veda*	*Yajur Veda*	*Sāma Veda*	*Atharva Veda*	*Āgamas*
Teachings	*Laukika-vijñāna* - Worldly Knowledge	*Vaidika* – Vedic teachings	*Adhyātmika* - Teachings of the supreme being	*Atimārga* - The elevated path	*Mantramārga* - The path of the mantras
Mantramārga	*Bhūta Tantras*	*Vāma Tantras*	*Bhairava Tantras*	*Gāruḍa Tantras*	*Siddhānta Tantras*
Kulamārga (mouths=*śaktis*)	*Paścimāmnāya*	*Uttarāmnāya*	*Dakṣiṇāmnāya*	*Pūrvāmnāya*	*Ūrdhvāmnāya* / *Anuttarāmnāya*

1. Early Classification of the *Śaiva* *Āgamas*: five currents (*srotas*)

The division of the *Śaiva* corpus is discussed in various scriptures, such as *Kāmika Āgama* and *Ajita Tantra*. However, they do not completely agree and use different names for the same texts. They tend to give their own tradition a higher place in the hierarchy. Therefore, it is an extremely complex task to classify the canon.

We will present some of the classifications that are mentioned in different sources.

One of the earliest and most comprehensive classifications of the *Śaiva* cannon divides the revelation into five currents (*pañca-srotas*) emanating from the five faces of Sadā-śiva. Although each tradition worships its own deities, these cults are similar in essence and can be said to be aspects of a single ritual system. Next, we will discuss each in more detail. It may be noted that this classification was replaced in later scriptures by another classification: the *pīṭhas*, which we will also describe later.

THE FIVE TRADITIONS (*ĀMNĀYAS*) OR CURRENTS (*SROTAS*) THAT EMANATED FROM SADĀ-ŚIVA

Īśāna: Upward face
Siddhānta Tantras

Vāma-deva: Nortern face
Vāma Tantras

Sadyo-jāta: Western Face
Bhūta Tantras

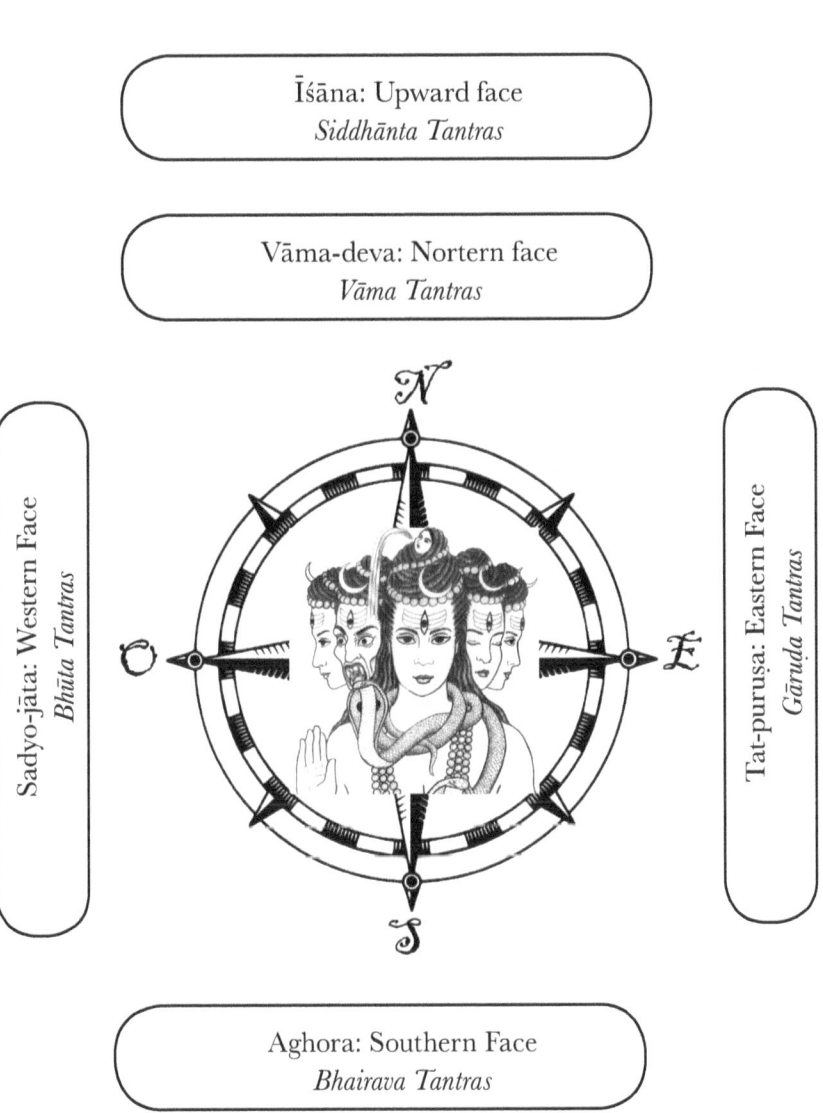

Tat-puruṣa: Eastern Face
Gāruḍa Tantras

Aghora: Southern Face
Bhairava Tantras

1.1 The upper current: *Śaiva-siddhānta Āgamas* (Tantras)

ईशानवक्त्रादूर्ध्वस्थाज्ज्ञानं यत्कामिकादिकम् ।
दशाष्टादश भेदेन शिवरूद्रावतारकैः ॥

īśāna-vaktrād ūrdhva-sthāj
jñānaṁ yat kāmikādikaṁ
daśāṣṭā-daśa bhedena
śiva-rudrāvatārakaiḥ

From the Īśana face, facing upwards, scriptures such as the *Kāmika* and others were revealed in two different streams of ten and eighteen scriptures, which belong to the forms of Śiva and Rudra, respectively.

(*Kāmika Āgama,* 1.1.22)

From the upper face, named Īśāna, emanate the *Śaiva-siddhānta* scriptures, which are divided into two sub-canons: the 10 *Śiva-bhedas* and the 18 *Rudra-bhedas*. Since Īśāna is the aspect of Śiva that grants *anugraha*, or "revelatory grace," this classification suggests that the *Śaiva-siddhānta* canon is superior. Its writings are in harmony with the established orthodoxy. The benevolent Sadāśiva is worshipped in his gentle five-faced and ten-armed form, without a female consort. The offerings are lactovegetarian and exclude alcoholic beverages.

There are different ways of classifying the *Śaiva-siddhānta* schools. According to one of them, the 10 *Śiva-bhedas* represent the school of *Advaita* (monism) and the 18 *Rudra-bhedas*, the school of *Viśiṣṭādvaita* (qualified monism). In addition, the *Śiva-bhedas* emphasize knowledge, while the *Rudra-bhedas* give priority to religious practices.

The 10 *Śiva-bhedas* are:

1. *Kāmika* with 3 *Upāgamas*.
2. *Yogaja* with 5 *Upāgamas*.
3. *Cintya* with 6 *Upāgamas*.

4. *Kāraṇa* with 7 *Upāgamas*.
5. *Ajita* with 4 *Upāgamas*.
6. *Dīpta* with 9 *Upāgamas*.
7. *Sūkṣma* with 1 *Upāgama*.
8. *Sāhasraka* with 10 *Upāgamas*.
9. *Aṁśumat* with 12 *Upāgamas*.
10. *Supra-bedham*.

The 18 *Rudra-bhedas* are:

1. *Vijaya* with 8 *Upāgamas*.
2. *Niḥśvāsa* with 8 *Upāgamas*.
3. *Svayaṁbhuva* with 3 *Upāgamas*.
4. *Anala* with 1 *Upāgama*.
5. *Vīra* with 13 *Upāgamas*.
6. *Raurava* with 6 *Upāgamas*.
7. *Mukuṭa* with 2 *Upāgamas*.
8. *Vimala* with 16 *Upāgamas*.
9. *Candra-jñāna* (or *Candra-hāsa*) with 14 *Upāgamas*.
10. *Mukha-biṁba* (or *Biṁba*) with 15 *Upāgamas*.
11. *Prodgīta* (or *Udgīta*) with 16 *Upāgamas*.
12. *Śarvokta* with 5 *Upāgamas*.
13. *Lalitā* with 3 *Upāgamas*.
14. *Pārameśvara* with 7 *Upāgamas*.
15. *Siddha* with 4 *Upāgamas*.
16. *Kiraṇa* with 9 *Upāgamas*.
17. *Santāna* with 7 *Upāgamas*.
18. *Vātula* (or *Pārahitā*) with 12 *Upāgamas*.

Although the *Śaiva-siddhānta* scriptures were originally addressed to ascetics seeking mystical powers, they were readapted over time to serve as a *sādhana* guide for the *Māheśvaras*, or the *Śaiva-gṛhasthas* (heads of household), who made up the majority of the adepts. In the beginning, the practice was private. However, starting in the eleventh century CE, it expanded to become intricate public worship in temples.

Between the eighth and tenth centuries CE, *Brāhmaṇas* from Kashmir wrote commentaries, or *paddhatis*, on the Agamic writings to facilitate understanding of the revelation. The best-known authors were Ugra-jyoti, Sadyo-jyoti, Rāma-kaṇṭha, Vidyā-kaṇṭha, Vibhūti-kaṇṭha, Śrī-kaṇṭha, Nīla-kaṇṭha, Soma-śambhu, Īśāna-śambhu, Hṛdaya-śiva, Brahma-śiva, Vairāgya-śiva, Jñāna-śambhu, Trilocana-śiva, Varuṇa-śiva, Īśāna-śiva, and Aghora-śiva. Almost all the commentaries on the *Śaiva* literature of the *Mantra-mārga* have been preserved.

Among the most important texts are the *Kāmika Āgama* and *Mṛgendra Āgama* as well as the commentary *Soma-śambhu Paddhati*.

1.2 The northern current: *Vāma Tantras*

नयसूत्रादि भेदेन वामं वामाद्विनिर्गतम् ।
चतुर्विंशति संख्याकं अवतीर्णं शिवाज्ञया ॥

naya-sūtrādi bhedena
vāmaṁ vāmād vinirgatam
catur-viṁśati saṁkhyākaṁ
avatīrṇaṁ śivājñayā

The *Vāma Tantra* with its variations such as *Naya Sūtra* and others, came out from the Vāma face according to the *vāma* direction (left side) given by Śiva; their number is twenty-four.
(*Kāmika Āgama*, 1.1.25b–26a)

From the northern face, called Vāma-deva, emanated the *Vāma Tantras*, which teach the worship of four sisters (Jayā, Vijayā, Ajitā, and Aparājitā) and their brother Tumburu.

Vāma-deva is the most feminine of Sadā-śiva's faces. The scriptures revealed by this face emphasize the worship of the goddess and teach how to obtain mystical powers (*siddhis*) and perform magical rites to defeat enemies and pacify evil spirits. In the early *pañca-srotas* classification, the *Vāma Tantras* included scriptures that explained the cult of Tumburu, a four-faced form of Śiva, and of his four consort sisters (*catur-bhaginī*), whose names denote victory and invincibility. Over time, this tradition faded away and many *Śākta* scriptures emerged. They were categorized as *Vidyā-pīṭha* instead of *Vāma* texts, according to the new *pīṭha* model described below. In this way, the *Vidyā-pīṭha* category effectively replaced *Vāma*.

The 24 *Vāma Tantras* are:

1. *Naya*
2. *Nayottara*
3. *Mūka*
4. *Mohana*
5. *Mohanāmṛta*
6. *Kara-pūjā-vidhāna*
7. *Vīṇā*
8. *Jayā*
9. *Vijayā*
10. *Ajitā*
11. *Aparājitā*
12. *Siddha-nityodayā*
13. *Jyeṣṭhā*
14. *Cintāmaṇī-mahodaya*
15. *Kuhaka*
16. *Kāma-dhenu-kadambaka*
17. *Ānanda*
18. *Rudra*
19. *Bhadra*
20. *Kiṁkara*
21. *Ananta-vijaya*
22. *Bhokta*
23. *Daurvāsa*
24. *Bīja-bheda*

1.3 The southern current: *Dakṣiṇa Tantras*

द्विविधं तन्त्रमुद्भूतं भैरवं दक्षिणास्यतः ।
असिताङ्गादिभिर्भूमौ कथितं तदनेकधा ॥

dvi-vidhaṁ tantram udbhūtaṁ
bhairavaṁ dakṣiṇāsyataḥ
asitāṅgādibhir bhūmau
kathitaṁ tad anekadhā

The *Bhairava Tantra* was revealed by the south face (Aghora) to be of two different categories. They were later revealed in this world in the name of Asitāṅga and other Bhairavas in many different ways.

(*Kāmika Āgama,* 1.1.27)

From the southern face, called Aghora, emanated the *Dakṣiṇa Tantras*, which teach how to worship the fearful Bhairava manifestations of Śiva and the goddess:

- Svacchanda-bhairava and his consort Aghoreśvarī, or Bhairavī.
- Kapālīśa-bhairava and his consort Aghorī, or Caṇḍā-kāpālinī.
- The triad of the goddesses Parā, Parāparā, and Aparā, with or without their Bhairava consorts.
- Kāla-saṁkarṣaṇī and other manifestations of the goddess Kālī.

The *Dakṣiṇa Tantras* were revealed by Aghora, Sadā-śiva's fiercest aspect. These texts focus mainly on the worship of Bhairava with mortuary images. In the later *pīṭhas* classification scheme, this category was effectively replaced by the *Mantra-pīṭha*.

The *Pratiṣṭhā-lakṣaṇa-sāra-samuccaya* scripture by Vairocana (ninth century CE) presents a list of the canon that follows the *pañca-srotas* division and includes 28 *Siddhānta Āgamas*, 28 *Gāruḍa Tantras*, 20 *Bhūta*

Tantras, 24 *Vāma Tantras*, and 32 *Dakṣiṇa Tantras*. It should be noted that the *Vāma* and the *Dakṣiṇa Tantras* should total 64, so eight *Tantras* are missing.

Additionally, among the *Dakṣiṇa Tantras*, other scriptures are mentioned such as the *Siddha-yogeśvarī-mata*, a *Trika* text dedicated to the goddess, and the *Yoginī-jāla-śaṁvara*, a text about the Mothers and the *yoginīs*. This shows that the *pañca-srotas* classification was not a very accurate grouping of Bhairava texts. For this reason, it was later replaced by the *pīṭhas* classification, which will be explained below.

The 32 *Dakṣiṇa Tantras* are:

1. *Svacchanda-bhairava*
2. *Caṇḍa-bhairava*
3. *Krodha-bhairava*
4. *Unmatta-bhairava*
5. *Asitāṅga-bhairava*
6. *Ruru-bhairava*
7. *Kapālīśa*
8. *Samuccaya*
9. *Ghora*
10. *Ghoṣaṇa*
11. *Ghora*
12. *Niśā-saṅcāra*
13. *Durmukha*
14. *Bhīmāṅga*
15. *Ḍāmara-rāva*
16. *Bhīma*
17. *Vetāla-mardana*
18. *Ucchuṣma*
19. *Vāma*
20. *Kapāla*
21. *Bhairava*
22. *Puṣpa*
23. *Advaya*
24. *Tri-śira*
25. *Eka-pāda*

26. *Siddha-yogīśvara*
27. *Pañcāmṛta*
28. *Prapañca*
29. *Yoginī-jāla-śaṁvara*
30. *Viśva-vikaṇṭha*
31. *Jhaṅkāra*
32. *Tilakodyāna-bhairava*

1.4 The eastern current: *Gāruḍa Tantras*

संख्यया गारुडं तद्वत्पूर्वं वक्राद्विनिर्गतम् ॥
सावित्र्याद्यं च सिद्ध्यर्थमुक्तं तदवतारकैः ।

saṁkhyayā gāruḍaṁ tad vat
pūrva vaktrād vinirgatam
sāvitry ādyaṁ ca siddhy artham
uktaṁ tad avatārakaiḥ

In the same count, the *Gāruḍa Tantra* came out of the east face (Tat-puruṣa). During the subsequent transmissions, these were revealed in order to accomplish fulfilment in *Sāvitri* and other mantras.

(*Kāmika Āgama,* 1.1.24b–25a)

From the eastern face, called Tat-puruṣa, emanated the *Gāruḍa Tantras*. They revealed therapeutic procedures and cure for snake bites. The *Gāruḍa Tantras* and *Bhūta Tantras* disappeared at an early stage of the Tantric revelation. They were omitted by the non-*Saiddhāntika* systems, probably because they were considered a lesser revelation.

The *Gāruḍa Tantras* take their name from Garuḍa, the celestial bird who is the enemy of snakes and poison. They contained magical procedures to control snakes. The rituals evoked mythical serpents (*nāgas*), which, according to this tradition, were responsible for bringing rain to protect the crops.

For example, the *Kriyā-kāla-guṇottara* begins with Karttikeya approaching the Īśvara in the following way:

विविधं मे श्रुतं तन्त्रं लोके अश्चर्यकारकम् ।
सिद्धिमुक्तिप्रदं सर्वं त्वयोक्तं परमेश्वर ॥
न श्रुतं गारुडं किञ्चित्सद्यःप्रत्ययकारकम् ।
तमाचक्ष्व सुरश्रेष्ठ मम भक्तस्य शङ्कर ॥
लक्षणं नागजातीनां गर्भोत्पत्तिमशेषतः ।
रूपकं सर्वनागानां व्यन्तराणां च जातकम् ॥

vividhaṁ me śrutaṁ tantraṁ
loke āścarya-kārakam
siddhi-mukti-pradaṁ sarvaṁ
tvayoktaṁ parameśvara

na śrutaṁ gāruḍaṁ kiñcit
sadyaḥ pratyaya-kārakam
tam ācakṣva sura-śreṣṭha
mama bhaktasya śaṅkara

lakṣaṇaṁ nāga-jātīnāṁ
garbhotpattim aśeṣataḥ
rūpakaṁ sarva-nāgānāṁ
vyantarāṇāṁ ca jātakam

Kārtikeya said: "O Parameśvara, I have heard everything you have spoken about the various Tantras that produce miracles in the world of humans and grant magical powers and liberation. But O Śaṅkara, I have never heard of Gāruḍaṁ, which produces immediate proof of efficacy. O, the best of gods, please tell me, your devotee, without omitting any detail, the classification of the types of serpents, the birth of their young, the traits of all serpents, and the class of indistinct types."

(*Kriyā-kāla-guṇottara*, 1.2–4)

Different sources contain extensive lists of texts, but almost none have survived. The only two preserved texts (*Tvaritā-mūla Sūtra* and *Tvaritā-jñāna-kalpa*) were found in Nepalese manuscripts on palm leaves and claim to be part of the 11,000 verse *Trottala Tantra*, a text cited by the scholar Kṣema-rāja.

The *Kriyā-kāla-guṇottara* text has also survived, and although it is not included in the canonical accounts, there is a clear evidence that it contains material from the *Gāruḍa Tantras* and *Bhūta Tantras*; it was quoted by Kṣema-rāja in his *Netroddyota*. We also find quotations from these scriptures in other *Śaiva* scriptural sources, especially in the *Jayad-ratha Yāmala*.

The 28 *Gāruḍa Tantras* are:

1. *Hara*
2. *Huṁkāra*
3. *Bindu-sāra*
4. *Kālāmṛta*
5. *Deva-trāsa*
6. *Sutrāsa*
7. *Śābara*
8. *Kāla-śābara*
9. *Pakṣi-rāja*
10. *Śikhā-yoga*
11. *Śikhā-sāra*
12. *Śikhāmṛta*
13. *Pañca-bhūta*
14. *Vibhāga*
15. *Sūlya-bheda-vinirṇaya*
16. *Kāla-kāṣṭha*
17. *Kālāṅga*
18. *Kāla-kūṭa*
19. *Paṭa-druma*
20. *Kamboja*
21. *Kambala*
22. *Kuṁkuma*
23. *Kāla-kuṇḍa*

24. *Kaṭāhaka*
25. *Suvarṇa-rekhā*
26. *Sugrīvā*
27. *Totalā* (or Trottala)
28. *Totalattarā* (or *Trottalottara*)

1.5 The western current: *Bhūta Tantras*

कौलादि विंशत्संख्यातं भूततन्त्रं तु सद्यतः ॥

kaulādi viṁśat-saṁkhyātaṁ
bhūta-tantraṁ tu sadyataḥ

Twenty scriptures, *Kaula* and others, collectively known as the *Bhūta Tantra*, came of the Sadyo-jāta face.
(*Kāmika Āgama*, 1.1.26b)

From the western face, called Sadyo-jāta, emanated the *Bhūta Tantras*. They teach exorcism rituals to free oneself from spirits and non-corporeal entities, such as *bhūtas*, *pretas*, *piśācas*, and so on. The *Gāruḍa* and *Bhūta Tantras* invoke angry forms of Rudra, such as Aghora, Krodheśvara, Lohaka, Nīla-kaṇṭḥa, Jvareśvara, Khaḍga-rāvaṇa, and Deva-trāsa.

It is believed that the *Bhūta Tantras* come from *Soma-siddhānta* sources (*Śaiva Ati-mārga* sect, also called *Kāpālikas*).

None of the *Bhūta Tantras* survived to this day. The only one that is mentioned in other scriptures is the *Caṇḍāsi-dhāra Tantra.*

The 20 *Bhūta Tantras* are:

1. *Hālāhala*
2. *Haya-grīva*
3. *Karakoṭa*
4. *Kaṭaṅka*
5. *Karkoṭa*
6. *Maṇḍamā*

7. *Kaṅkoṭa*
8. *Khaḍga-rāvaṇa*
9. *Caṇḍāsi-dhāra*
10. *Huṅkāra*
11. *Hāhākāra*
12. *Śivārava*
13. *Ghorāṭṭahāsa*
14. *Ucchiṣṭa*
15. *Ghurghura*
16. *Duṣṭa-trāsaka*
17. *Vimala*
18. *Vikaṭa*
19. *Mahoṭkata*
20. *Yama-ghaṇṭa*

2. Later classifications of the canon

2.1. The three traditions: central (*madhyama*), left (*vāma*), and right (*dakṣiṇa*)

The non-*Saiddhantika* scripture *Picu-mata* (or *Brahma Yāmala*) modifies the *Pañca-srotas* classification and places the non-*Saiddhāntika* traditions above the *Saiddhāntika* ones. It classifies the *Śaiva* scriptures according to an ascending hierarchy of three main traditions emanating from the three powers of the deity:

1. *Madhyama* (central): *Siddhānta Tantras.*
2. *Vāma* (left): *Vāma Tantras.*
3. *Dakṣiṇa* (right): *Bhairava Tantras.*

Agamic literature is subdivided into *Vāma* and *Dakṣiṇa*. The former category consists of texts that advocate drinking alcohol, consuming meat, and having sex, while the latter leaves out these practices. *Śaiva* schools such as *Kāpālikas*, *Kālā-mukhas*, and *Aghoras* as well as many *Śākta* lines belong to *Vāma*.

These categories are compared to rice preparation. *Siddhānta* resembles removing the shells from the grains (*tuṣa*). *Vāma* is the cleaning of the grains to eliminate the bran (*kambūka*). Lastly, *Dakṣiṇa* is cooking pure white grains.

ज्ञानौघः परमो यस्तु त्रिभिः स्रोतैर्विनिर्गतः ॥
वामदक्षिणमध्यस्थो नानाभेदव्यवस्थितः ।

jñānaughaḥ paramo yas tu
tribhiḥ srotair vinirgataḥ

vāma-dakṣiṇa-madhya-stho
nānā-bheda-vyavasthitaḥ

The supreme mass of scriptural wisdom emerges forth in three streams, situated on the left, right, and middle (of Sadā-śiva) with manifold divisions.

(*Brahma Yāmala*, 38.16b–17a)

The *Brahma Yāmala* further divides the *Dakṣiṇa Tantras* to four divisions or *pīṭhas* according to the main subject which they are dealing with:

1. *Mudrā-pīṭha*: *mudrās.*
2. *Maṇḍala-pīṭha*: *maṇḍalas.*
3. *Mantra-pīṭha*: *mantras.*
4. *Vidyā-pīṭha*: philosophical knowledge.

दक्षिणेण तु वक्रेण दक्षिणास्त्रोतसम्भवम् ॥
चतुष्पीठप्रभेदेन शुद्धाशुद्धविभेदितम् ।
पृच्छकाश्रयभेदेन बहुधा संव्यवस्थितम् ॥
विद्याश्रितानि यानि स्युर्विद्यापीठं वरानने ।
मन्त्राश्रितानि यानि स्युर्मन्त्रपीठं तथैव च ॥
मुद्राश्रितानि यानि स्युर्मुद्रापीठं तु सुव्रते ।
मण्डलापीठकानि स्युर्मण्डलं पीठमुच्यते ॥
विनिर्गतानि तन्त्रानि क्रियाभेदेन चैव हि ।

dakṣiṇena tu vaktreṇa
dakṣiṇā-srota sambhavam

catuṣ-pīṭha-prabhedena
śuddhāśuddha-vibheditam
pṛcchakāśraya-bhedena
bahudhā saṁvyavasthitam

vidyāśritāni yāni syur
vidyā-pīṭhaṁ varānane
mantrāśritāni yāni syur
mantra-pīṭhaṁ tathaiva ca

mudrāśritāni yāni syur
mūdrā-pīṭhaṁ tu suvrate
maṇḍalā-pīṭhakāni syur
maṇḍalaṁ pīṭham ucyate

vinirgatāni tantrāṇi
kriyā-bhedena caiva hi

> From (Sadā-śiva's) right face, the *dakṣiṇā-srotas* arise, divided into the pure and impure, with a division of four *pīṭhas*, according to speakers and listeners. Those based upon *vidyā-mantras* comprise the *Vidyā-pīṭha*, O fair woman, and likewise, those based on mantras comprise the *Mantra-pīṭha*. Those based on *mudrās* comprise the *Mudrā-pīṭha*, O pious woman. Those that belong to the seat of *maṇḍalas* are called the *Maṇḍala-pīṭha*. In this way, the Tantras emerged, which have ritual differences (*kriyā-bheda*).
>
> (*Brahma Yāmala*, 38.29b–33a)

This classification excludes the *Gāruḍa Tantras* and *Bhūta Tantras*, as well as other Tantric systems, such as the *Vaiṣṇava Pāñca-rātra*, and places them in the lower tradition (*adhaḥ-srotaḥ*).

2.2. *Saiddhāntika* (*Siddhānta Tantras*) and non-*Saiddhāntika* (*Bhairava Tantras*)

Over time, the cults of the *Vāma Tantras*, *Bhūta Tantras*, and *Gāruḍa Tantras* became gradually less influential, and the *Śākta–Śaiva* worship described in the *Dakṣiṇa Tantras* gained popularity. With this change, a new classification emerged that absorbed the *Vāma* within the *Dakṣiṇa* and presented the canon as a simple division between *Saiddhāntika* and non-*Saiddhāntika* scriptures.

The *Saiddhāntika* system, or "the followers of established truth," emanates from the Īśāna face that looks upward, suggesting its superiority. Its writings follow the truth established by the orthodoxy. Its central deity is Sadā-śiva, the benevolent form of Śiva that performs the five cosmic functions through the Pañca-brahmas. Its offerings follow the Vedic purity codes. In this category we find 28 *Siddhānta* scriptures: 10 Śiva *Tantras* and 18 *Rudra Tantras*.

Among the major *Saiddhāntika Tantras* we find the following: *Ananta-vijaya, Kāmika, Sārdha-tri-śikha, Sapta-śatika-kālottara, kiraṇa, Nandikeśvara-mata, Niśvāsa, Bhārgava, Mṛgendra, Raurava, Lalita*, and *Sarva-jñānottara.*

The non-*Saiddhāntika* system, or "that which does not follow the established truth," emanates from the four remaining faces of Sadā-śiva that look toward the cardinal directions. The texts describe cults with *Śākta–Śaiva* orientations and fiercer deities. They often include mortuary elements of the *Ati-mārga* cremation practices, such as offerings of meat, alcohol, and bodily substances.

Among the major *Non-saiddhāntika Tantras* we find the following: *Svacchanda, Ānanda-bhairava, Kula-cūḍāmaṇi, Khecarī-mata, Gupta, Guhya, Nandi-śikha, Picu-mata, Bhairava Yāmala, Mālinī-vijayottara, Siddha-yogeśvarī-mata, Skanda-yāmala,* and *Jayad-ratha Yāmala.*

2.3. *Mantra-pīṭha* and *Vidyā-piṭha*

The classification into *pīṭhas* (collections or mounds) accepts the division of *Saiddhāntika* and non-*Saiddhāntika* and subdivides the latter into *Mantra-pīṭha* and *Vidyā-pīṭha*. The *Mantra-pīṭha* includes texts centered on the cult of the male Bhairava aspect, while the *Vidyā-pīṭha* includes those centered on the goddess. This *Śākta*-oriented classification excludes the *Bhūta Tantras* and *Gāruḍa Tantras*. Colophons of the *Vidyā-pīṭha* texts usually indicate that they belong to the *Vidyā-pīṭha* within the *Bhairava-srota* (Bhairava tradition), a term that identifies non-*Saiddhāntika* scriptures.

The *Vidyā-pīṭha* scriptures teach the highest level of esoteric practice and are associated with Tantric goddesses who are superior to their male consorts or completely autonomous. The 15 *Vidyā-pīṭha* scriptures are subdivided into three groups, each representing a higher level of esotericism and feminization:

- 3 *Vāma Tantras* (Left *Tantras*) or *Guhya Tantras* (Secret Tantras).
- 5 *Yāmala Tantras* (Union Tantras).
- 7 *Śakti Tantras* (Energy Tantras).

Chapter 3

The *Śākta Tantras*

The Hindu *Śākta* traditions worship different manifestations of the goddess (Devī) and consider her to be the supreme deity. Shaktism includes both devotional and Tantric traditions. The best known *sādhana* is mostly devotional but incorporates some rituals and contemplative practices that originate in Tantra.

The *Śākta* tradition is closely related to the *Śaiva* tradition and they clearly overlap. Both worship the bipolar divinity that manifests within the practitioner's own body. This divinity is typically conceived of as a male deity (Śiva or Viṣṇu) in union with his consort, Śakti. Tantra traditions are classified as *Śaiva* or *Śākta* based only on their emphasis.

However, there was also an independent *Śākta* tradition throughout South Asia that was not related to Shaivism. In the old Vedic pantheon, there are only a few female deities. But in the *Purāṇas*, we see that the worship of the goddess grows. The early *Devī-māhātmya* scripture presents numerous manifestations of the Mother as the supreme creative deity. This text was composed around the sixth century CE, at the same time as the *Vidyā-pīṭha Tantras* were becoming popular in Tantric circles.

The sixty-four *Bhairava Āgamas* are considered *Śaiva*, but they include the scriptures classified as *Vidyā-pīṭha*, in which we see the birth of the *Śākta* revelation. It would then flourish further at the stage of the *Kula-mārga* with the *Kaula Tantras*.

The *Kaula Tantras* were the foundation of the *Śākta* tradition. One of the main *Śākta* transmissions was *Dakṣiṇāmnāya*, which worshipped the beautiful and erotic goddess Śrī (Śrī-kula). From this cult, the *Śrī-vidyā* was born, a right-hand orthodox tradition that has become popular in southern India and remains alive today.

The *Uttarāmnāya* and *Pūrvāmnāya* transmissions, for their part, gave rise to the Tantras of the clan of the ferocious goddess Kālī. Kālī is still worshipped in eastern and southern India and remains one of the best known and beloved Hindu goddesses, despite her frightening aspect. She is one of the 10 *Mahā-vidyās*, a group of 10 goddesses whose worship is still very popular in Bengal.

3.1 The *Bhairava Tantras*

Bhairava means "terrifying." The syllables of the name are *bha*, which stands for *bharaṇa*, or "maintenance"; *ra* for *ravaṇa*, or "withdrawal"; and *va* for *vamana*, or "creation of the universe." This is the most powerful form of Śiva, a furious deity with a wide-open mouth, long tusks, and big eyes. He carries a *kapāla* (skull bowl), a decapitated head, and a *khaṭvāṅga* (skull staff). His multiple hands hold various weapons. The iconography of Bhairava is closely related to the ascetics, whose aspiration for *siddhis* led them to perform various sexual, magical, and funerary rituals. The *Bhairava Tantras* contain teachings that Bhairava imparts to his consort. Each Bhairava is accompanied by his respective Śakti.

The *Rudra Yāmala* quotes a manual of worship to Vaṭuka-bhairava, or Bhairava as a little boy. It also mentions his mantra: *hrīṁ vaṭukāya āpad-uddhāraṇam kuru kuru vam vaṭukāya hrīṁ oṁ svāhā.*

The large number of Tantric works are classified by the *Vārāhī Tantra* as *Āgama*, *Yāmala*, or *Tantra*.

The *Āgamas* deal with seven main topics:

1. The creation process.
2. Dissolution of the universe.
3. Worship of a particular deity.
4. *Sādhana-kriyā*, or "spiritual discipline."
5. *Puraścaraṇa*, or "initiation ritual."
6. *Dhyāna-yoga*, or "meditation system.
7. *Ṣaṭ-karma*, or "a group of six rites," which include a propitiatory ritual to pacify (*śānti*), a ritual to subdue, one to control, one

to appease (*vaśī-karana*), a meditative rite (*manana*), and one to remove negative energies (*uccāṭana*).

The *Yāmalas* treat eight distinctive topics:

1. *Sṛṣṭi*, or "the story of creation."
2. The positions of the planets.
3. *Nitya-kṛtya pratipādana*, or "daily ritual."
4. *Krama*, or "evolution."
5. *Sūtras*, or "aphorisms."
6. *Varṇa-bheda*, or "the distinction between *varṇas*."
7. *Jāti-bheda*, or "the distinction between castes."
8. Obligations and duties of different *āśramas*.

We can identify Tantras by 24 signs, some of which have been already mentioned. Here is the list of eight additional ones:

1. Presentation of the mantras.
2. Sacred diagrams, or yantras.
3. Descriptions of different gods and goddesses.
4. *Tīrthas*, or "holy places of pilgrimage."
5. *Vratas*, or "fasts or vows."
6. Demarcation lines between the profane and the sacred.
7. Description of the *rāja-dharma* (the duties of the king) and the *vyavahāra* (conduct) of the ordinary man.
8. *Adhyātma-varṇanam*, or "description of wisdom."

It should be noted that although the *Vārāhī Tantra* mentions certain distinctive characteristics of Tantric literature, not all of them are present in all Tantric texts. What characterizes all Tantric literature is its emphasis on *sādhana-kriyā*, or *kriyā-yoga*, as well as the abundance of esoteric elements and mantras.

The *Vāmakeśvarī-mata* mentions the following sixty-four *Bhairava Tantras*:

भगवन्सर्वमन्त्राश्च भवता मे प्रकाशिताः ।
चतुष्षष्टिस्तु तन्त्राणि मातृणामुत्तमानि तु ॥

महामाया शम्बरं च योगिनी जालशम्बरम् ।
तत्त्वशम्बरकं देव भैरवाष्टकमेव च ॥
बहुरूपाष्टकं ज्ञानं यामलाष्टकमेव च ।
चन्द्रज्ञानं वासुकिं च महासम्मोहनं तथा ॥
महोच्छुष्मं महादेव वाथुलं च नयोत्तरम् ।
हृद्भेदं मातृभेदं च गुह्यतन्त्रं च कामिकम् ॥
कलापादं कालसारं तथाऽन्यत्कुब्जिकामतम् ।
नयोत्तरं च वीणाद्यं त्रोतुलं भ्रोतुलोत्तरम् ॥
पञ्चामृतं रूपभेदं भूतोड्डामरमेव च ।
कुलसारं कुलोड्डीशं कुलचूडामणिं तथा ॥
सर्वज्ञानोत्तरं देव महापिचुमतं तथा ।
महालक्ष्मीमतं देव सिद्धयोगीश्वरीमतम् ॥
कुरूपिकामतं देवरूपिकामतमेव च ।
सर्ववीरमतं देव विमलामतमेवच ॥
अरुणेशं मोदनेशं विशुद्धेश्वरमेव च ।
एवमेतानि शास्त्राणि तथाऽन्यान्यपि कोटिशः ॥
भवतोक्तानि मे देव सर्वज्ञानमयानि च ।
विद्याः षोडश देवेश सूचिता न प्रकाशिताः ॥

bhagavan sarva-mantrāś ca
bhavatā me prakāśitāḥ
catuṣ-ṣaṣṭis tu tantrāṇi
matṛṇam uttamāni tu

mahā-māyā śambaraṁ ca
yoginī jāla-śambaram
tattva-śambarakaṁ deva
bhairavāṣṭakam eva ca

bahu-rūpāṣṭakaṁ jñānaṁ
yāmalāṣṭakam eva ca
candra-jñānāṁ vāsukiṁ ca
mahā-sammohanaṁ tathā

mahocchuṣmaṁ mahā-deva
vāthulaṁ ca nayottaram

hṛd-bhedaṁ mātṛ-bhedaṁ ca
guhya-tantraṁ ca kāmikam

kalā-pādaṁ kāla-sāraṁ
tathā 'nyat kubjikā matam
nayottaraṁ ca vīṇādyaṁ
trotulaṁ bhrotulottaram

pañcāmṛtam rūpa-bhedaṁ
bhūtoḍḍāmaram eva ca
kula-sāraṁ kuloḍḍīśaṁ
kula-cūḍāmaṇiṁ tathā

sarva-jñānottaraṁ deva
mahā-picu-mataṁ tathā
mahā-lakṣmī-mataṁ deva
siddha-yogīśvarī-matam

kurūpikā-mataṁ deva
rūpikā-matam eva ca
sarva-vīramataṁ deva
vimalā-matam eva ca

arūṇeśaṁ modaneśaṁ
viśuddheśvaram eva ca
evam etāni śāstrāṇi
tathā 'nyāny api koṭiśaḥ

bhavatoktāni me deva
sarva-jñāna mayāni ca
vidyāḥ ṣoḍaśa deveśa
sūcitā na prakāśitāḥ

> Devī said: sixty-four Tantras were revealed to me with the essence of the words: the *Mahā-māyā*, *Śambara*, *Yoginī*, *Jala-śambara*, *Tattva Śambara*, the eight *Bhairavas*, the eight *Bahu-rūpās*, the *Jñāna*, the eight *Yāmalas*, the *Candra-jñāna*, the *Vāsuki*, *Mahā-Sammohana*, *Māha-Ucchuṣma*, *Vāthula*, *Māyā-uttara*, *Hṛd-bheda*, *Mātṛ-bheda*, *Guhya-tantra*, *Kāmika*, *Kāla-pāda*, *Kāla-sāra*, *Kubjikā-mata*, *Vātula-uttara*, *Viṇā*, *Trotula*, *Bhrātula-uttara*, *Pañācamṛta*, *Rūpa-bheda*, *Bhūta-uddāmara*, *Kula-sāra*, *Kuloddīśa*, *Kula-cūḍāmaṇi*, *Sarva-jña-uttara*, *Mahā-picu-mata*, *Mahā-lakṣmī-mata*, *Siddha-yogīśvarī-mata*, *Kurūpikā-mata*, *Rūpikā-mata*, *Sarva-vīra-mata*, *Vimalā-mata*, *Aruṇeśa*, *Modaneśa*, *Viśuddeśvara*; all these *śāstras* have been revealed to me, along with ten million more, which are the body of wisdom.
>
> (*Vāmakeśvari-mata*, 1.13–22)

Among the sixty-four *Bhairava Tantras*, the most prominent is the *Svacchanda-bhairava Tantra* (sixth to tenth century CE), which teaches the cult of Svacchanda-bhairava, a mild form of Bhairava. His consort is Aghoreśvarī, the most venerated Tantric deity in Kashmir. The scripture *Śrī Bahu-rūpa-garbha Stotra* reveals that his mantra is *Oṁ aghorebhyo 'tha ghorebhyo ghora-ghoratarebhyaś ca sarvataḥ śarva namaste rudra-rūpebhyaḥ Oṁ*. Like most Tantric mantras, this one has a great variety of meanings. In the iconography, Svacchanda-bhairava is depicted sitting astride the prostrate body of Sadā-śiva, the supreme deity of the *Śaiva-siddhānta*. This posture symbolizes the superiority of his cult.

The sixty-four *Bhairava Tantras* are grouped into eight categories, each presided over by a main Bhairava. These eight *Aṣṭāṅga Bhairavas* dominate the eight directions of the universe. All Bhairavas are subordinate to Mahā-kāla-bhairava Svarṇa, also known as Kāla-bhairava, the supreme controller of time. His consort is Bhairavī, the terrible aspect of Pārvatī or Kālī. The names of the scriptures vary in different descriptions of the canon. The eight Bhairavas are:

1. *Asitāṅga-bhairava*
2. *Ruru-bhairava*

3. *Caṇḍa-bhairava*
4. *Krodha-bhairava*
5. *Unmatta-bhairava*
6. *Kapāla-bhairava*
7. *Bhīśaṇa-bhairava*
8. *Saṁhāra-bhairava*

I. *BHAIRAVA* DIVISION

1. *Svacchanda-bhairava*
2. *Caṇḍa-bhairava*
3. *Krodha-bhairava*
4. *Unmatta-bhairava*
5. *Asita-bhairava*
6. *Ruru-bhairava*
7. *Jhaṅkāra-bhairava*
8. *Kapālīśa-bhairava*

II. *YĀMALA* DIVISION

9. *Brahma Yāmala*
10. *Rudra Yāmala*
11. *Viṣṇu Yāmala*
12. *Skanda Yāmala*
13. *Gautamīya Yāmala*
14. *Atharvā Yāmala*
15. *Vetāla Yāmala*
16. *Ruru Yāmala*

III. *MATA-TANTRA* DIVISION

17. *Raktā-mata*
18. *Peṭikā-mata*
19. *Bhāruṇḍī-mata*
20. *Iḍā-mata*
21. *Piṅgalā-mata*
22. *Nīlakeśī-mata*
23. *Śāmbarā-mata*
24. *Utphullā-mata*

IV. *MAṄGALĀ* DIVISION

25. *Bhairava-maṅgalā*
26. *Candra-garbha-maṅgalā*
27. *Śānti-maṅgalā*
28. *Sumaṅgalā*
29. *Sarva-maṅgalā*
30. *Vijayā-maṅgalā*
31. *Ugra-maṅgalā*
32. *Sad-bhāva-maṅgalā*

V. *CHAKRA* DIVISION

33. *Svara-cakra* (*Mantra-*)
34. *Varna-cakra*
35. *Nāḍī-cakra* (*Śakti*)
36. *Guhya-cakra* (*Kalā*)
37. *Kāla-cakra* (*Bindu*)
38. *Saura-cakra* (*Nāda*)
39. *Āgneya-cakra*
40. *Somaja-cakra*

VI. *ŚIKHĀ* DIVISION

41. *Śaukrī*
42. *Mandā* (*vīṇa-śkhā*)
43. *Mahocchuṣmā*
44. *Bhairavī* (*Svarascheda*)
45. *Śaṁbarī* (*Ḍāmara*)
46. *Prapañcaki*
47. *Mātṛ-bhedī*
48. *Rudra-kālī*

VI. *BAHU-RŪPĀ* DIVISION

49. *Andhakī*
50. *Ruru-bhedā*
51. *Śaṅkhā*
52. *Śūlinī*
53. *Karṇa-moṭī*
54. *Ṭaṅkī*
55. *Jvālinī*
56. *Mātṛ-rodhinī*

VI. *VAG-ĪSA* DIVISION

57. *Siddhā*
58. *Citrā*
59. *Hṛllekhā*
60. *Bhairavī*
61. *Kadaṁbikā*
62. *Haṁsinī*-(*Candra-lekhā*)
63. *Haṁsa-mālā*
64. *Candra-koṭi*

Although it was not included in the *Mantra-pīṭha* classification, it is worth mentioning the *Netra Tantra* scripture (700–850 CE) that teaches the cult of Amṛteśvara-bhairava and his consort Amṛta-lakṣmī. It includes instructions on how to protect kings and *Brāhmaṇas*. The fact that it also deals with other royal issues suggests that Tantric techniques were integrated in kings' courts.

3.2 The *Kaula Tantras*

The *Śaiva Āgamas* use the term *srotas* (traditions, lineages) to refer to the major groups of scriptures organized according to the cardinal directions. Similarly, the term *āmnāya* (transmission) is used to classify the *Kula Āgamas*. Each *āmnāya* is formed by a set of Tantras that share an affiliation with a single tradition. Each of Sadā-śiva's faces is oriented toward a different cardinal direction and reveals one of the five *āmnāya* traditions described in the Tantric scriptures. These scriptures have different names: *Kulāmnāya*, *Kula Tantras*, *Kaula Āgamas*, *Kula-śāstras,* and *Kula-śāsana* (the teachings of *Kula*).

These scriptures were predominantly *Śākta*. Although they shared many teachings with the *Mantra-mārga*, they also propagated other methods influenced by the *Kaula* tradition, whose offerings and observances were anti-Brahmanical in nature. These traditions offered two types of worship to their deities: the *Mantra-mārga* taught by the *Vidyā-pīṭha* scriptures and the new cult revealed in the *Kula Śāstras*, which was considered higher.

The *Kula Śāstras* eliminated the elaborate cult and the long process of initiation and introduced initiation through possession (*āveśa*) by the goddess, the consumption of sacramental substances considered impure by the Hindu orthodoxy, blood sacrifices, ritualized sexual relations with a consecrated consort (*dūtī*), and collective orgiastic rites practiced within the *kaula* (a select group of advanced initiates).

These texts teach the propitiation of the goddess Kuleśvarī, with or without Bhairava (Kuleśvara), surrounded by a retinue of the eight Mothers. The ritual also includes Gaṇeśa and Vaṭuka. In addition, these texts are characterized by the auxiliary worship of the four *siddhas* (*yuga-nāthas*), who taught the tradition in four different ages with their consorts. Macchanda-nātha and Koṅkaṇā are the *siddhas* of the present age of Kali and are worshipped along with their six princely sons, *rāja-putras*, and their respective consorts.

Over time, the liturgical systems were modified and the deities Kuleśvara and Kuleśvarī adopted different identities. The *Kaula Āgamas* were divided into *āmnāyas* (transmissions). The number of *āmnāyas* indicated in the Tantras varies depending on the scripture (four, five, or six). These are the *āmnāyas* and their main Tantras:

1. *Pūrvāmnāya* (eastern or previous transmission): It worships the *Trika* goddesses Parā, Aparā, and Parāparā. Its main scriptures are the *Siddha-yogeśvarī-mata*, *Mālinī-vijayottara Tantra*, and *Śiva Sūtra*.
2. *Uttarāmnāya* (northern or later transmission): It worships the goddess Kālī. It is also known as *Krama*, or "sequence." Its main scriptures are the *Krama Āgamas, Vātūla-nātha Sūtra, Mahā-kāla Saṁhitā, Parānanda Sūtra, Śakti-saṅgama Tantra, Kālī Tantra, Niruttara Tantra, Bṛhan-nīla Tantra, Toḍala Tantra, Yoginī Tantra, Yonī Tantra, Kula-cūḍā-maṇi, Mātṛka-bheda Tantra, Tārā Tantra, Kumārī Tantra, Mahā-cinācāra-krama Tantra, Phet-kāriṇī Tantra,* and *Nirvāṇa Tantra,* among many others.
3. *Paścimāmnāya* (western or final transmission): It worships the goddess Kubjikā. Its main scriptures are the *Kubjikā-mata, Ṣaṭ-sāhasra Saṁhitā*, and *Ciñciṇī-mata-sāra-samuccaya.*
4. *Dakṣiṇāmnāya* (southern transmission): It worships the goddess Kāmeśvarī. Its main scriptures are the *Vamakeśvarī-mata* (consisting of *Nitya-ṣoḍaśī-karṇava* and *Yoginī-hṛdaya*), *Jñānārṇava, Paraśurāma-kalpa Sūtra, Gāndharva Tantra, Tripurā-rahasya, Tantra-rāja, Prapañca-sāra*, and *Tripurārṇava.*
5. *Ūrdhvāmnāya* (upper transmission): It worships Ardha-nārīśvara, who is half Śiva and half Śakti. Its main scriptures are the *Kulārṇava Tantra* and *Kaula-jñāna-nirṇaya.*
6. *Anuttarāmnāya* (supreme transmission): It worships the beautiful and benevolent goddess Tripura-sundarī. Its main scripture is the *Nityā-ṣoḍaśikārṇava*, also called the *Vāmakeśvarī-mata*.

CHAPTER 4

THE *VAIṢṆAVA TANTRAS*

The *Vaiṣṇava Āgamas*, also called *Saṁhitās*, accept Lord Viṣṇu and his different incarnations as the supreme deity, relegating the rest of the deities to a secondary position. These scriptures portray conversations between Viṣṇu and his consort Lakṣmī. There are hundreds of *Vaiṣṇava Āgamas*, which are classified into two groups: *Pāñca-rātra* and *Vaikhānasa*.

4.1 The *Pāñca-rātra*

The *Pāñca-rātra* literature comprises Agamic *Vaiṣṇava* scriptures written in Sanskrit that glorify Lord Viṣṇu and his consort Lakṣmī as the supreme divinity. The name *Pāñca-rātra* comes from the *Śata-patha Brāhmaṇa* (12.6), which describes how Nārāyaṇa performs a sacrifice for five nights and transforms himself into a transcendent and immanent being. There are those who connect the name *Pāñca-rātra* to the teachings imparted by Vāsudeva in the course of five nights to the five sages: Maunjāyana, Aupagāyana, Śāṇḍilya, Bhāradvāja, and Kāśyapa.

According to the legend, Lord Viṣṇu revealed these sacred texts to Garuḍa, Ananta, Rudra, Brahmāa, and Viṣvaksena.

The first to systematize the *Pāñca-rātra* vision was Śāṇḍilya (c. 100 CE), who composed verses glorifying Nārāyaṇa. Subsequently, the *Pāñca-rātra* was adopted, spread, and popularized by Śrī Rāmānujācārya (eleventh century CE). In the Śrī *Vaiṣṇava* school of Rāmānujācārya, this literature is central.

The seven groups of *Pāñca-rātras* are *Brahma*, *Śaiva*, *Kaumara*, *Vasiṣṭha*, *Kapila*, *Gautamīya*, and *Nāradīya*. The earliest source of information about the *Pāñca-rātras* is the *Nāradīya* section of the *Śānti-parva* of the *Mahābhārata*.

The three most important *Pāñca-rātra* texts are called The Three Jewels, which include the *Sāttvata Saṁhitā*, *Pauṣkara Saṁhitā*, and *Jayākhya Saṁhitā*. Each of these works has a corresponding commentary written in one of the three main *Vaiṣṇava* centers in the south of India. The commentary on the *Pauṣkara Saṁhitā* is the *Parameśvara Saṁhitā* written in Śrī-raṅgam. The commentary on the *Jayākhya Saṁhitā* is the *Pādma Saṁhitā* written in Kanci. The commentary on the *Sāttvata Saṁhitā* is the *Īśvara Saṁhitā* that comes from Melkote.

For both the *Pāñca-rātra* and the *Vaikhānasa* texts, the supreme deity is Viṣṇu, who is always in the company of Lakṣmī. His innumerable qualities are divided into six groups called *ṣaḍ-guṇas*: knowledge, or *jñāna*; virility, or *vīrya*; energy, or *śakti*; splendor, or *tejas*; force, or *bala*; and sovereignty, or *aiśvarya*. He has five different emanations called *para*, *vyūha*, *vibhava*, *antaryāmi*, and *arcā*, each of them having six qualities. *Para* is the transcendental form called Para-vāsudeva, formless and blissful. *Vyūha* is the name of the four forms he divides himself into. These *vyūhas* are Vāsudeva, Saṁkarṣaṇa, Pradyumna, and Aniruddha. Each of these forms serves a certain purpose. Para-vāsudeva is the supreme form. Saṁkarṣaṇa is in charge of destroying the universe and revealing the *dharma* of exclusive devotion (*aikāntika-dharma*). For this purpose, he employs *jñāna* (wisdom) and *bala* (strength). Pradyumna uses *vīrya* and *aiśvarya* to create the world and to preach. Śakti and *tejas* are used by Aniruddha to maintain the created universe and to grant to individuals the results of their actions. These four *vyūhas* are collectively called *Cātur-ātmya*.

The total number of texts that make up the *Pāñca-rātra* literature exceeds two hundred, although not all have been published. Many still exist only as manuscripts. The existence of many is known only because they are mentioned in other texts. Below is a short list of some of the available texts with a brief description of their content:

Jayākhya Saṁhitā: This is one of the most important *Pāñca-rātra* texts. It has detailed information on the creation of the universe, yoga, the correct repetition of mantras (*mantropāsana*), various *Vaiṣṇava* mantras, the fire ritual (*homa*), *dīkṣā* methods, temple worship,

Vaiṣṇava etiquette (*ācāra*), and expiation of sins. This text consists of 33 chapters, or *paṭalas*.

Ahir-budhnya Saṁhitā: This is a great work with 3880 verses divided into 60 chapters. The text deals with the four emanations of the Lord, or *vyūhas*. It also mentions certain rituals to cure diseases and offers descriptions of many important mantras and yantras.

Aniruddha Saṁhitā, or *Aniruddha Saṁhitā Mahopaniṣad*: This work has detailed descriptions of different rituals, *dīkṣās*, expiations of sinful activities (*prāyaścittas*), regulations to be followed in deity installation, and so on. It consists of 34 chapters.

Īśvara Saṁhitā: Dedicated in large part to rituals of worship, this work also describes images, different methods of initiation (*dīkṣā*), meditation techniques, methods related to the repetition of mantras, and glorification of the Yādava Mountain. It consists of 24 chapters.

Hayaśira Saṁhitā: This is a treatise on the rituals for the preparation and installation of deities. It consists of 144 chapters divided into four sections, or *kāṇḍas*: *Pratīṣṭhā-kāṇḍa*, *Saṅkarṣaṇa-kāṇḍa*, *Liṅga-kāṇḍa*, and *Saura-kāṇḍa*.

Kaśyapa Saṁhitā: This is a short text that refers to different kinds of poisons and healing through mantras. It is composed of 12 chapters.

Mahā-sanatkumāra Saṁhitā: This is a great treatise that deals exclusively with worship rituals. It consists of 10,000 verses organized into 40 sections and four chapters.

Pādma Saṁhitā: This text has 31 chapters divided into four sections: *jñāna-pāda*, *yoga-pāda*, *kriyā-pāda*, and *caryā-pāda*. It deals with ritualism and the repetition of mantras.

Parama Saṁhitā: In this book, there is information about the creation of the universe as well as details on the rituals of *dīkṣā* and *arcana*. It also contains information about both karma yoga and *jñāna* yoga. It affirms the superiority of *jñāna* over karma yoga, which it calls the worship of God. The material is divided into 31 chapters.

Pārameśvara Saṁhitā: It contains extensive information about the methods of mantra meditation, sacrifices, rituals, and *prāyaścittas*, or "expiations of sins." It is a relatively short text of 15 chapters.

Viṣṇu-tattva Saṁhitā: It deals with the worship of the deities, purification baths, and the marks that *Vaiṣṇavas* paint on their bodies.

This treatise comprises 39 chapters.

Parāśara Saṁhitā: This is a work dedicated to the repetition of mantras, or *japa*. It comprises eight chapters.

Viṣṇu Saṁhitā: This work is about the ritual of worship. It has a philosophy similar to Sankhya. It has 30 chapters.

Pauṣkara Saṁhitā: This text contains information about deity worship, funerary rituals, and philosophy. It is one of the oldest texts in *Pāñca-rātra* literature. It consists of 43 chapters.

Sudarśana Saṁhitā: This is a treatise that discusses meditation with mantras and atoning for sinful activities. It comprises 41 chapters.

Vihagendra Saṁhitā: It deals with mantra meditation, sacrifices, and the place of *prāṇāyāma* within the prayer ritual. This book has 24 chapters.

Vanrāha-guru Saṁhitā: This is a manual used exclusively for worship.

We see that for the most part, the *Pāñca-rātra* texts have the term *saṁhitā* added to their name. This indicates that they are Vedic in origin. They claim to be derived from the *Ekāyana Śākhā* of the *Śukla Yajur Veda*, which sadly no longer exists.

We read about the *Ekayāna Śakha* in the *Chāndogya Upanishad* when Nārada Muni tells the Sanat-kumāras that he learned this wisdom from the *Ekāyana Śākhā* together with the Veda. For Vaishnavism, *Pāñca-rātra* literature is as accredited as the Vedas. According to the followers of Viṣṇu, the teachings contained in these texts are in perfect harmony with the Vedas and, therefore, are unquestionable. Repeatedly, *Vaiṣṇava* literature refers to them as Vedic literature, granting all of them the same level of authority as the Vedas. Yāmunācārya was commissioned to prove this in his famous work *Āgama Prāmāṇyam*. Similarly, Śrī Vedānta Deśika, in his *Pāñca-rātra-rakṣā*, established that the *Pāñca-rātras* have the same authority as the Vedas.

4.2 The *Vaikhānasa Āgamas*

This term derives from the name of the sage Vikhanas. Numerous texts about *Vaikhānasa Āgama* were written by his disciples Atri, Marīci, Bhṛgu, and Kaśyapa. The surviving texts include the *Samūrtārcanādhikaraṇa* by Atri, *Vimānārcana-kalpa* and *Ānanda Saṁhitā* by Marīci, *Kriyāhikāra* by Bhṛgu, and *Jñāna-kāṇḍa* by Kaśyapa.

The *Vaikhānasa-kalpa Sūtra*, written by Vikhanas, says that only men born in *Vaiṣṇava Brāhmaṇa* families are eligible to worship Lord Viṣṇu in the temple. It preaches the exclusive worship of Viṣṇu only with Vedic mantras.

The *Vaikhānasas* developed the theory of the five aspects of Viṣṇu:

1. Viṣṇu is the omnipresent supreme deity.
2. Puruṣa is the principle of life.
3. Satya is the static aspect of the deity.
4. Acyuta is the immutable aspect.
5. Aniruddha is the irreducible aspect.

In addition, they describe the two presences of Viṣṇu: *niṣkala* is the primitive and indivisible form, and *śakala* is the divisible and mobile form. The goddess Śrī is prakṛti (nature) and the *śakti* (energy) of Viṣṇu. Śrī and Viṣṇu always remain together. She has the form of *mūla-prakṛti*, or "the primordial matter," so she is the cause of any activity of Viṣṇu.

Viṣṇu must be worshipped in four different ways: through the repetition of mantras (*japa*), devotional offerings (*heta*), offerings of flowers (*arcana*), and meditation (*dhyāna*). Deity worship should include the repetition of the corresponding *Vaiṣṇava* mantras, the fire ceremony, and meditation on Viṣṇu. *Vaikhānasa* literature offers detailed information on the construction of temples and carving of deities.

Chapter 5

The *Saurya Tantras*

The *Saurya* cult has practically disappeared, but it is worth mentioning since it was part of the glorious Tantric past.

As a source of heat and light, Sūrya, or "the sun," is one of the main deities mentioned in the Vedas. On some occasions, he is considered to be Savitṛ and Ādityā. Nearly 30 hymns found in the *Ṛg Veda* and the *Atharva Veda* are dedicated to Sūrya (*Ṛg Veda*: 1.50, 115; 10.37, 158, 170, 189; *Atharva Veda*: 2.21; 13.2.3, 4; 19.65, 66, 67). Sūrya is the source of light and heat and reigns over crops and seasons. The old agriculture-based economy gave him a central place.

Seeing all, Sūrya knows everything. Because of their effulgence, both Sūrya and Agni are named Jatadeva, or "the knower of entities." Sūrya's visionary power connects him to Mitra and Varuṇa as he is considered the eye of both. In classical Hinduism, he is the guardian of the cardinal points along with Indra, Agni, Vāyu, and Candrama.

Generally, he carries a lotus flower in each hand and travels through the sky in a beautiful carriage pulled by seven horses or by a single horse with seven heads. Sūrya is compared to a bird that flies through the heavens and is described as the jewel of the sky. He has four hands: three hold a wheel, a conch shell, and a lotus flower. The fourth is in the *mudrā* of protection. His charioteer is Aruṇa, the god of dawn, who carries a whip in his hand. Sūrya is called "the eye of Varuṇa," the god of the Sun and a manifestation of the divine energy of paradise.

The origins of this sect are lost to the annals of history because the sun has always been venerated by different cultures for millennia. Even the most primitive people could feel the power of the Sun, contemplate it with admiration, and identify it as the maintainer of life. Many consider this cult mere worship of nature since they do not understand its deeper meaning. The *Sauras* do not worship the Sun as something physical but as a symbol of the Absolute, or Brahman. The Sun illuminates the solar system, just as Brahman, the supreme illuminator, is the source of all that is seen and hidden, known and unknown. The Sun shows the power of Śakti that operates throughout the universe. It is a symbol of the light of consciousness, or Śiva.

Just as nothing can live without the Sun, nothing can exist without Brahman, which is both the light of consciousness (Śiva) and the power of manifestation and sustenance (Śakti). Sun worship is a clear and beautiful way to venerate the transcendental through a symbol. Within the Smarta tradition, Sūrya is one of the five deities considered different aspects of Brahman. He is mentioned in the sacred *gāyatrī-mantra*.

The Hindu *Saura* tradition flourished in Rajasthan, Gujarat, Madhya Pradesh, Bihar, Jharkhand, and Odisha. There are very few temples dedicated to Sūrya. One of them is the Konark Sun Temple in Odisha, where the rituals revealed in the *Saurya Āgamas* are still performed. In the post-Vedic era, the *Sūrya* tradition was overshadowed by the cults of Śiva, Viṣṇu, and Śakti to the point that it has nearly disappeared.

CHAPTER 6

THE *GĀNAPATYA TANTRAS*

Gaṇeśa is a god beloved throughout India, but there are more followers of this sect in western India. Gaṇeśa is a son of Śiva and Pārvatī and represents the expression of both. Śiva is consciousness and Śakti is the manifestation. Their union, expressed in their child, represents the ability to understand.

Most Hindu rituals begin by invoking the protection of Lord Gaṇeśa. His devotees ask for his help before beginning any important task, since without understanding, they will not be able to achieve anything. The grace of Gaṇeśa allows them to understand and, therefore, succeed in their endeavors.

Traditionally, many Sanskrit scriptures are believed to be written by Gaṇeśa. As he is the god of understanding, this suggests that higher wisdom is necessary for the scriptures to be written and used by spiritual seekers.

To promote understanding, many Tantric texts begin by invoking Lord Gaṇeśa with his mantra *Śrī Gaṇeśāya Namaḥ* or "Reverence to the bliss of Gaṇeśa."

The Tantric system taught in the *Gānapatya Tantras* is simple and direct, yet sublime and profound. By invoking one's own power of understanding personified by Gaṇeśa, one can come to know oneself and attain enlightenment. This path requires a fervent desire to know. The curiosity for the mystery that is born from the heart is expressed in the worship of Gaṇeśa. Today, this sect is no longer an independent Tantric group. It has been absorbed into mainstream Hinduism.

CHAPTER 7

HIERARCHIES OF THE REVEALED SCRIPTURES

In this section we will explore how the *Jayad-ratha Yāmala* scripture explains the hierarchy of revelation and places the *Āgamas* in the general context of the Sanskrit corpus.

In the first part (*ṣaṭka*) of the *Jayad-ratha Yāmala* scripture, the goddess asks Bhairava to present her with the canon of the revealed scriptures. Bhairava explains that all revealed *Śāstras* are classified into four levels:

1. *Sāmānya*: Common and universal.
2. *Sāmānya-viśeṣa*: Common but specialized.
3. *Viśeṣa*: Specialized.
4. *Viśeṣatara*: Extra specialized.

Bhairava goes on to explain that the *Śāstra* evolved progressively in four stages, from general to more specialized. The more specialized the scripture, the greater commitment it requires from its followers. Bhairava explains that this gradation is necessary because it is impossible to teach everything at once. These categories follow both a temporal and a logical progression. Bhairava clarifies that however broad or specialized the writing may be, both human and divinely revealed knowledge refers to the same reality.

THE HIERARCHY OF THE REVEALED SCRIPTURES ACCORDING TO THE *JAYADRATHA YĀMALA*

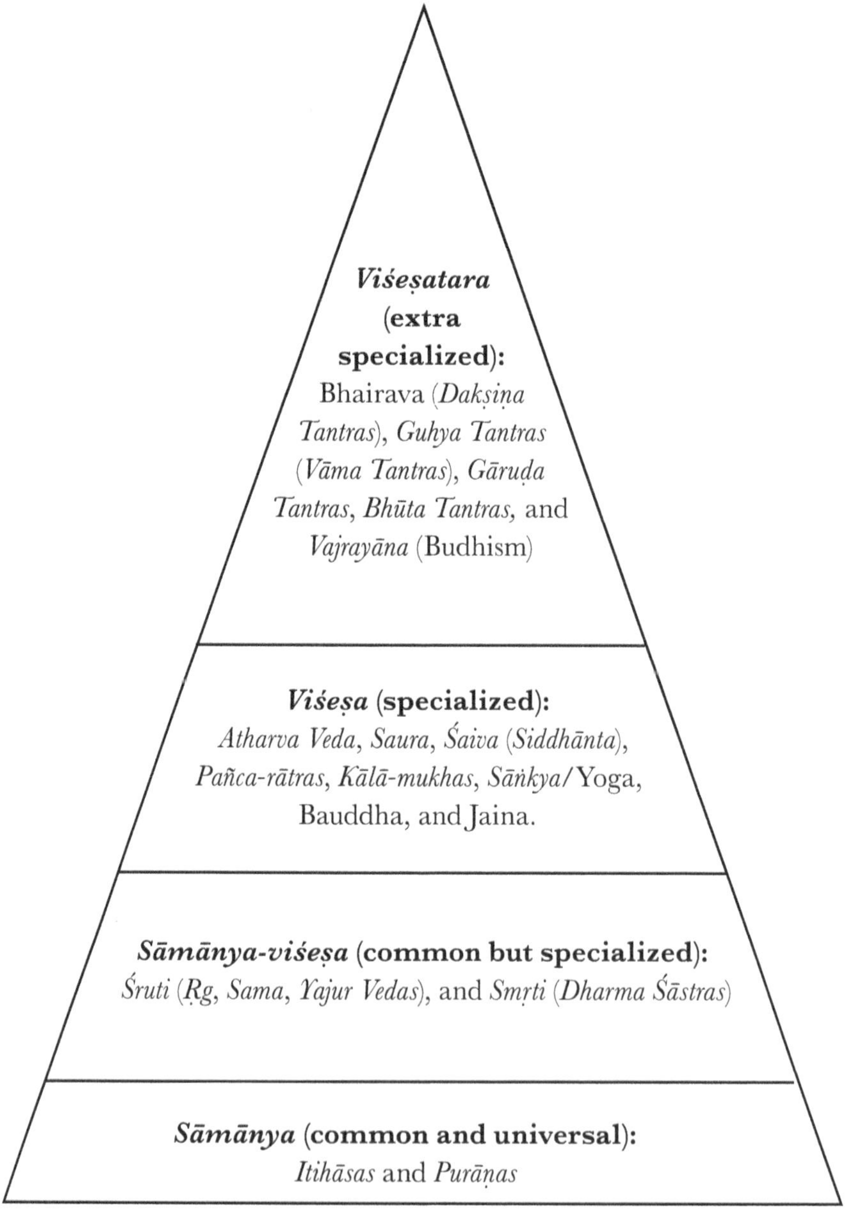

1. *Sāmānya*: This division is inclusive and aimed at the general public. These *Śāstras* enjoy wide popular support and can be studied by people of all castes. Since their scope is very extensive, they are called "common" or "worldly" (*laukika*). They include the *Purāṇas*, literary works (*Kāvya*), the epics *Mahābhārata* and *Rāmāyaṇa* (*Itihāsas*), treatises on mathematics (*gaṇita*), dramaturgy (*nāṭaka*), metrics (*chandas*), and grammar (*śabda*).
2. *Sāmānya-viśeṣa*: This category includes the *Smṛti* (three of the Vedas: *Ṛg*, *Sāma*, and *Yajur*), and among the *Smṛtis*, the *Dharma Śāstra*. *Śūdras* (workers and service providers) could not access these scriptures; that is why they were called "specialized." But they were also considered "common," because it was not required to join a sect in order to study them.
3. *Viśeṣa*: The writings in this category are "particular" because they belong to specific traditions and can be accessed only after taking vows in certain sects. These include the *Atharva Veda*, the *Saura*, the *Siddhānta* part of the *Śaiva* canon, the *Pāñca-rātra* scriptures adopted by the *Vaiṣṇavas*, the *Lākula* and *Vaimala* scriptures of the *Śaiva Ati-mārga*, the *Sāṁkhya* and yoga texts, the *Sahaja-yāna* and *Kala-cakri-yāna* traditions of Buddhism, and the Jaina texts.
4. *Viśeṣatara*: These are the texts of sects dedicated to specific spiritual practices. They are more "particular," because only the person who has taken vows in the initiation can access them. They include the *Bhairava Tantras*: the *Dakṣiṇa Tantras* and *Vāma Tantras* (*Guhya Tantras*), the *Gāruḍa Tantras*, the *Bhūta Tantras*, and the Tantras of *Vajra-yāna* Buddhism. This most select level is for a spiritual elite that accepts the *Śākta* literature as the highest. According to these scriptures, initiation does not imply accepting a different religion, but a radical transformation and access to the most exclusive spiritual level, which can lead to liberation and elevation to the highest platform of the *Śaiva* cosmos. Although these Tantras were rejected by Vedic orthodoxy, their followers included the orthodox system within their own systems as a

lower level of realization and understanding. They saw the revelation as a progressive sequence and placed their own systems at the top of the hierarchy. Tantric *Śaiva* groups regarded their revelations as the esoteric culmination of Vedic orthodoxy.

SECTION IV

Tantric Practice

Chapter 1

The Tantric vision of the human body

In order to understand the Tantric vision, we must grasp the central role the body plays in Tantra metaphysics. On this path, the human body has an unprecedented importance in the history of spirituality. The positive attitude toward the body stems from Tantric metaphysical principles, which argue that the universe is a manifestation of the absolute reality. We live within a field of divine energy and the body is an integral part of that field. The physical configuration of humans is valid, legitimate, and positive at all levels. It is considered to be a very valuable platform for reaching the highest ideal of life.

The cosmos is a real manifestation of the subjective and dynamic aspect of the Absolute. As an integral part of a real universe, the body is clearly not an illusion. It is at once physical, astral, and divine. The same attitude of respect and worship toward the cosmos, stars, mountains, oceans, flowers, and animals is cultivated toward the body, which is the microcosm that allows us to access the reality of the macrocosm.

The human form of life is precious since it possesses self-consciousness and grants the possibility for free will. It allows us to resist conditioning and transcend karma. Without this possibility, we would be stuck as automatons. Having a human body, the soul can identify its authentic nature through the body, as the following verses of the *Kulārṇava Tantra* explain:

सोपानभूतं मोक्षस्य मानुष्यं प्राप्य दुर्लभम् ।
यस्तारयति नात्मानं तस्मात्पापतरोऽत्र कः ॥

sopāna-bhūtaṁ mokṣasya
mānusyaṁ prāpya durlabham
yas tārayati nātmānaṁ
tasmāt pāpataro 'tra kaḥ

After obtaining a human body, which is difficult to obtain and which serves as a ladder to liberation, who is more sinful than one who does not transcend toward the Self?

ततश्चाप्युत्तमं जन्म लब्ध्वा चेन्द्रिय सौष्ठवम् ।
न वेत्त्यात्महितं यस्तु स भवेतात्मघातकः ॥

tataś cāpy uttamaṁ janma
labdhvā cendriya sauṣṭhavam
na vetty ātma-hitaṁ yas tu
sa bhavet ātma-ghātakaḥ

Therefore, upon obtaining the best possible form of life, one who does not recognize his or her own well-being is merely committing suicide.

विना देहेन कस्यापि पुरुषार्थो न विद्यते ।
तस्माद्देहधनं प्राप्य पुण्यकर्माणि साधयेत् ॥

vinā dehena kasyāpi
puruṣārtho na vidyate
tasmād deha-dhanaṁ prāpya
puṇya-karmāṇi sādhayet

How can one come to know the purpose of human life without a human body? Hence having obtained the gift of a human body, one should do meritorious deeds.

रक्षेत्सर्वात्मनात्मानमात्मा सर्वस्य भाजनम् ।
रक्षणे यत्नमातिष्ठेत्यावत्तत्त्वं न पश्यति ॥

rakṣet sarvātmanātmānam
ātmā sarvasya bhājanam
rakṣaṇe yatnam ātiṣṭhet
yāvat tattvaṁ na paśyati

One should completely protect oneself by oneself. One's self is the vessel for everything. One should make an effort to protect oneself. Otherwise the Truth cannot be seen.

पुनर्ग्रामाः पुनः क्षेत्रं पुन वित्तं पुनर्गृहम् ।
पुनः शुभाशुभं कर्म न शरीरं पुनः पुनः ॥

punar grāmāḥ punaḥ kṣetraṁ
puna vittaṁ punar gṛham
punaḥ śubhāśubhaṁ karma
na śarīraṁ punaḥ punaḥ

A village, house, land, money, even auspicious and inauspicious karma can be obtained over and over again, but not a human body.

शरीररक्षणायासः क्रियते सर्वदा जनैः ।
नहीच्चन्ति तनुत्यागमपि कुष्ठादिरो गतः ॥

śarīra-rakṣaṇāyāsaḥ
kriyate sarvadā janaiḥ
nahīccanti tanu-tyāgam
api kuṣṭhādiro gataḥ

People always make an effort to protect the body. They do not wish to abandon the body even when sick with leprosy and other diseases.

तद्गोपितं स्याद्यत्नेन धर्मो ज्ञानार्थमेव च ।
ज्ञानञ्च ध्यानयोगार्थं सोऽचिरात्परिमुच्यते ॥

tad gopitaṁ syād yatnena
dharmo jñānārtham eva ca
jñānañ ca dhyāna-yogārthaṁ
so 'cirāt parim ucyate

For the purpose of attaining knowledge, the virtuous person should make efforts to preserve the body. With knowledge of the yoga of meditation, one will be quickly liberated.

आत्मैव यदि नात्मानमहितेभ्यो निवारयेत् ।
कोऽन्यो हितकरस्तस्मादात्मानं तारयिष्यति ॥

ātmaiva yadi nātmānam
ahitebhyo nivārayet
ko 'nyo hita-karas tasmād
ātmānaṁ tārayiṣyati

If one does not guard against that which is inauspicious, who, with good intentions, will ever cross over to the Self?

इहैव नरक व्याधेश्चिकित्सां न करोति य ।
गत्वा निरौशधं स्थानं व्याधिस्थः किं करिष्यति ॥

ihaiva naraka vyādheś
cikitsāṁ na karoti ya
gatvā nirauśadhaṁ sthānaṁ
vyādhisthaḥ kiṁ kariṣyati

If hellish diseases are not cured while being here on earth, what could one do about a disease when going to a place where there is no remedy?

सुदीप्त भवने को वा कूपं खनति दुर्मतिः ।
यावत्तिष्ठति देहोऽयं तावत्तत्त्वं समभ्यसेत् ॥

sudīpta bhavane ko vā
kūpaṁ khanati durmatiḥ
yāvat tiṣṭhati deho 'yaṁ
tāvat tattvaṁ samabhyaset

What fool starts digging a well when the house is on fire? As long as this body exists, one should cultivate the Truth.

व्याघ्रीवास्ते जरा चायुर्याति भिन्नघटाम्बुवत् ।
निघ्नन्ति रिपुवद्रोगास्तस्माच्छ्रेयः समाचरेत् ॥

vyāghrīvāste jarā cāyur
yāti bhinna-ghaṭāmbuvat
nighnanti ripuvad rogās
tasmāc chreyaḥ samācaret

Old age is like a tigress; life runs out like water from a pot with holes; diseases strike like enemies. Therefore, one should cultivate the highest good now.

यावन्नाश्रयते दुःखं यावन्नायान्ति चापदः ।
यावन्नेन्द्रियवैकल्यं तावच्छ्रेयः समाचरेत् ॥

yāvan nāśrayate duḥkhaṁ
yāvan nāyānti cāpadaḥ
yāvan nendriya-vaikalyaṁ
tāvac chreyaḥ samācaret

One should cultivate the highest good while the senses are not yet frail, suffering is not yet firmly rooted, and adversities have not yet become overwhelming.

(*Kulārṇava Tantra*, 1.16–27)

From the Tantric perspective, the body is not a sack of flesh and bones but embodied consciousness. It is a structure with a nervous system that facilitates elevated expressions of consciousness. One of the Sanskrit terms that refers to the body is *śarīra*, which derives from the verbal stem *śrī*, or "to rest on." That is, the body is the support of the Self to experience the physical plane. The body is a window through which the Whole perceives itself. From this perspective, the body is the temple of God. If the center of bhakti is God, then the center of Tantra is the body. Its importance is such that it is possible to study the entire Tantric phenomenon through human morphology alone.

Kaula reveals that gods inhabit various parts of our organism and animate the senses. These deities are in charge of our physical mobility. A text, probably written by Abhinava-gupta, called the *Deha-stha-devatā-cakra-stotra*, or "the hymn of the circle of deities residing in the body," offers a description of the deities of the *Krama*, one of the *Kaula* traditions. The phenomena that involve the body, from laughter to crying and from dancing to orgasm, are not perceived as personal events but as natural and cosmic. This perspective of the body delineates the difference between Tantric practice and physical activity, between hatha yoga and acrobatics, between *prāṇāyāma* and breathing, between sexual ritualism and ordinary sex, and so on.

The source of human suffering lies not in anatomy but in the mind. The body has never harmed anyone. Human conditioning is not bodily but mental. Many religions have pointed to the body as the origin of human misery. For Tantra, however, suffering originates in mental conditioning. Corporeal and spiritual aspects make up an organic unity. All division between body and soul is mental. *Māyā* is a mental phenomenon and union is only experienced when the mind dissolves. True meditation, authentic prayer, and everything that is divine emerges from the body and never from the mind. The body is truth and authenticity, while the mind is conditioning and illusion.

Every human being has three bodies: physical (*sthūla-śarīra*), astral (*sūkṣma-śarīra*), and causal (*kāraṇa-śarīra*), with five sheaths (*kośas*). Studying the powers and limitations contained in our physical, astral, and causal bodies will help us develop an awareness of our corporeality at all levels.

The physical body is composed of the five basic elements (*pañca-mahā-bhūtas*): ether, air, fire, water, and earth. While asleep, this body is transcended. The astral body is where pleasure and pain are experienced; it is composed of five organs of action (*karmendriyas*), five organs of knowledge (*jñānendriyas*), five vital airs (*prāṇas*), and four internal instruments (*antaḥ-karaṇas*). The causal body is called *kāraṇa-śarīra*, or "seed body," because it stores karma and dominates the development of the other bodies. It is here that we experience joy.

This is the origin of the yogic attitude toward the body. Hatha yoga affects different bodies (*śarīras*) and sheaths (*kośas*). Asanas influence the *sthūla-śarīra*; *prāṇāyāma* and meditation influence the *sūkṣma-śarīra*. Hatha yoga purifies all the bodies and their respective sheaths to allow the manifestation of bliss, which is experienced in the *kāraṇa-śarīra*.

Three bodies or *śarīras*

Humans are multidimensional structures, and their souls are enveloped in many sheaths:

1. The physical gross body, or *sthūla-śarīra*, includes the *anna-maya-kośa*, or "food sheath."
2. The subtle astral body, *liṅga-śarīra* or *sūkṣma-śarīra*, includes three layers: *prāṇa-maya-kośa* (energy sheath), *mano-maya-kośa* (mental sheath), and *vijñāna-maya-kośa* (intellectual sheath).
3. The causal body, or *kāraṇa-śarīra*, includes the blissful sheath called *ānanda-maya-kośa*.

Yoga, like most Eastern medicine practices, speaks of an astral body made of *prāṇa*, in which the *cakras*, or "energy centers," are found and are interconnected by *nāḍīs*, or "energy channels."

The astral and physical bodies are united by a *nāḍī* resembling a silvery thread through which vital energy flows. The physical body dies when this thread is cut, separating from the astral body forever.

The astral body or *liṅga-śarīra*

As mentioned above, we find three different layers (*kośas*) in the *liṅga-śarīra*, each with their own elements:

1. The *prāṇa-maya-kośa* is the energy sheath composed of *nāḍīs* that connect in the chakras. Even though the form of this sheath is subtle, it is very similar to that of the physical body. It is composed of the vital airs (*prāṇas*) and the five organs of action (*karmendriyas*): mouth, hands, feet, anus, and genitals. The *prāṇa* sheath is made up of 72,000 *nāḍīs*, as is indicated in the *Haṭha-yoga-pradīpikā*:

चतुरशीतिपीठेषु सिद्धमेव सदाभ्यसेत् ।
द्वासप्ततिसहस्राणां नाडीनां मलशोधनम् ॥

caturaśīti-pīṭheṣu
siddham eva sadābhyaset
dvāsaptati-sahasrāṇāṁ
nāḍīnāṁ mala-śodhanam

Out of the 84 asanas, *siddhāsana* should always be practiced, because it cleanses the impurities of the 72,000 *nāḍīs*.
(*Haṭha-yoga-pradīpikā*, 1.39)

द्वासप्ततिसहस्राणां नाडीनां मलशोधने ।
कुतः प्रक्षालनोपायः कुण्डल्यभ्यसनादृते ॥

dvāsaptati-sahasrāṇāṁ
nāḍīnāṁ mala-śodhane
kutaḥ prakṣālanopāyaḥ
kuṇḍaly-abhyasanād ṛte

Other than the practice of *kuṇḍalinī*, there is no other way to wash away the impurities of the 72,000 *nāḍīs*.
(*Haṭha-yoga-pradīpikā*, 3.123)

द्वासप्ततिसहस्राणि नाडीद्वाराणि पञ्जरे ।
सुषुम्ना शाम्भवी शक्तिः शेषास्त्वेव निरर्थकाः ॥

dvāsaptati-sahasrāṇi
nāḍī-dvārāṇi pañjare
suṣumnā śāmbhavī śaktiḥ
śeṣās tveva nirarthakāḥ

In the body there are 72,000 *nāḍī* openings. Of these, the *suṣumnā*, which contains the *śāmbhavī-śakti*, is the only important one. The rest are useless.

(*Haṭha-yoga-pradīpikā*, 4.18)

It is also mentioned in the Upanishads:

द्वासप्ततिसहस्राणि प्रतिनाडीषु तैतिलम् ॥

dvāsaptati-sahasrāṇi
pratināḍīṣu taitilam

In each of the 72,000 *nādīs*, there is an oil-like substance.

(*Kṣurikā Upaniṣad*, 17b)

2. The *mano-maya-kośa* is the mental sheath, which consists of the instinctive mind. This mind includes both *manas* (conscious mind) and *citta* (subconscious mind, memory). It is the seat of desires and the sovereign of the organs of cognition and action. It includes the five senses of knowledge, or *jñānendriyas*: nose, tongue, eyes, skin, and ears.

3. The *vijñāna-maya-kośa* is the intellectual sheath, which includes the *ahaṅkāra* (ego) and the *buddhi* (intellect). The former is what we believe ourselves to be, that is to say, the idea of "I" that relates what happens to itself and perceives itself as the doer. The former is the discriminating principle that evaluates and decides.

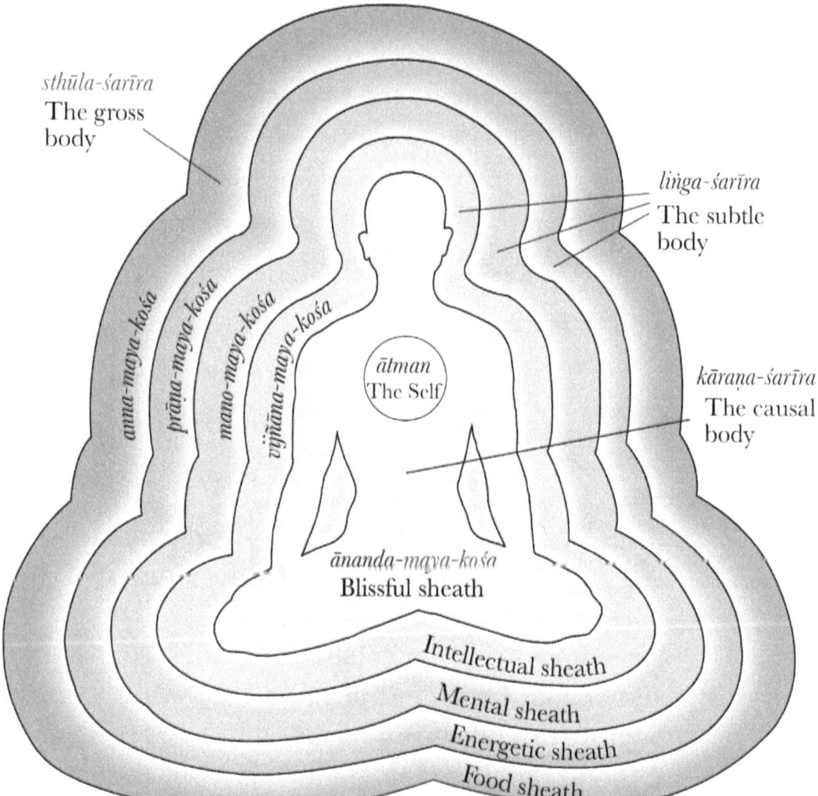

SHEATHS, OR *KOŚAS*

Prāṇa or "vital energy"

The meaning of the Sanskrit word *prāṇa* is "vital energy," but *prāṇa* often refers to breathing because it is the closest expression of it in our physical experience.

Thousands of years ago, the Vedic seers (*ṛṣis*) knew what our Western science has only discovered in the last century: that the solid matter we perceive through our senses is nothing more than energy. The wisdom of *prāṇa* forms an integral part of the Vedas. The ancient *Atharva Veda* has prayers that ask *prāṇa* and *apāna* to protect life from death:

प्राणापानौ मृत्योर्मा पातं स्वाहा ॥

prāṇāpānau mṛtyor mā pātaṁ svāhā

O *prāṇa* and *apāna*, may my life not fall into death (the cycle of births).

(*Atharva Veda*, 2.16.1)

प्राणाय नमो यस्य सर्वमिदं वशे ।
यो भूतः सर्वस्येश्वरो यस्मिन्सर्वं प्रतिष्ठितम् ॥

prāṇāya namo yasya sarvam idaṁ vaśe
yo bhūtaḥ sarvasyeśvaro yasmin sarvaṁ pratiṣṭhitam

Our respectful obeisance to *prāṇa*, which, by controlling the entire universe, has become paramount above all, and upon which all depend.

(*Atharva Veda*, 11.4.1)

The *Chāndogya Upanishad* refers to the vital energy in the following way:

स यदवोचं प्राणं प्रपद्य इति प्राणो वा इदꣳ सर्वं भूतं यदिदं किञ्च तमेव तत्प्रापत्सि ॥

sa yad avocaṁ prāṇaṁ prapadya iti prāṇo vā idaṁ sarvaṁ bhūtaṁ yad idaṁ kiñ ca tam eva tat prāpatsi.

I said, 'I take refuge in *prāṇa*,' because all these beings and everything that exists are in fact *prāṇa*. Therefore, I take refuge only in that.

(*Chāndogya Upaniṣad*, 3.15.4)

Prāṇa is the most subtle form of energy, the fundamental energy unit, so we can say that the cosmos is a manifestation of *prāṇa*. Everything that acts or moves in the universe is an expression of vital energy. The great master and saint of Rishikesh, His Holiness Swami Śivānanda, explains in his important book *The science of prāṇāyāma*: "*Prāṇa* is the sum total of all the energy that manifests in the universe. It is the sum total of all the forces of nature." At the physical level, all capacity to perform work or produce heat is an expression of *prāṇa*. Hence all potential, kinetic, mechanical, caloric, electric, and chemical energy is an expression of *prāṇa*.

Prāṇa is an expression of Brahman, the supreme sustainer of the cosmic manifestation. Life would be impossible without *prāṇa*, as the pranic power makes all the functions of our body possible. It is the original energy of our mental, emotional, and biological faculties: from a thought to a yawn and all the physiological sensations, such as hunger, thirst, cold, and heat. This energy also makes the biological processes of digestion, excretion, and secretion possible. By vibrating at different wavelengths, it carries out involuntary functions, such as those of the immune and circulatory system, as well as sensory activities and bodily movements. It is *prāṇa* that pumps blood from the heart through the blood vessels. Furthermore, it is the power that connects the physical body with the astral body.

Nourishment and breathing are two of the functions that renew *prāṇa* in our bodies. *Prāṇa* is our real food, while its conductors—water, nutrients, vitamins, oxygen, and sunshine—are the vehicles that transport it.

Types of *prāṇa*

Just as electricity can generate cold, movement, light, sound, and heat, *prāṇa* can manifest itself in infinite ways, such as seeing, speaking, feeling, moving, thinking, and so forth.

According to the Sankhya system, *prāṇa* has five major types (*pañca-prāṇas*) and five minor ones (*pañcopa-prāṇas*).The *pañca-prāṇas* are the five main directions in which *prāṇa* circulates. Each fulfills a different function:

1. *Prāṇa*: Circulates in the pectoral area and regulates breathing.
2. *Apāna*: Flows between the anus and the lower abdomen. It cleans and purifies the organism by eliminating urine, semen, and feces.
3. *Samāna*: Flows around the navel and moves in the central part of the body. It governs digestion and stimulates the secretion of gastric juices. It is in charge of the appropriate distribution of nutrients in the body.
4. *Udāna*: Controls the vocal cords and the intake of food and air. It also elevates energy. For this reason, when one is sad or depressed, one must focus on the throat area, where *udāna* circulates.
5. *Vyāna*: Permeates the entire body. It is often called *aura*, since it is the energy that protects the whole surface of the body.

The *pañcopa-prāṇas* are:

1. *Nāga*: Alleviates pressure in the abdominal zone through burping.
2. *Kūrma*: Regulates the size of the iris based on the intensity of light, to facilitate vision. It also controls the movement of the eyelids to protect the eyes from any damage that might be caused by foreign bodies.
3. *Kṛkara*: Causes coughing, to prevent foreign substances from entering the body through the throat or nostrils.

4. *Deva-datta*: Causes yawning and induces sleep.
5. *Dhanañjaya*: Produces phlegm and remains even after the death of the body.

The evolution of *prāṇa*

Brahman is the source from which everything originates, and *prāṇa* is its expression and projection. Therefore, *prāṇa* is not a blind force but an intelligent energy. Brahman is the unmanifested aspect, whereas *prāṇa* is its creative aspect that evolves and assumes a multiplicity of forms. It is the energy that keeps order in the movement of celestial bodies and maintains the ecological balance of our planet. It is in charge of various functions in our body that facilitate life, as described in this passage:

यदिदं किं च जगत्सर्वं प्राण एजति निःसृतम् ।
महद्भयं वज्रमुद्यतं य एतद्विदुरमृतास्ते भवन्ति ॥

yad idaṁ kiñca jagat sarvaṁ
prāṇa ejati niḥsṛtam
mahad-bhayaṁ vajram udyataṁ
ya etad vidur amṛtās te bhavanti

> Everything that exists in this changing world has emerged from *prāṇa* and moves within it, a great terror, like a rigid bolt of lightning. Those who know it achieve immortality.
>
> (*Kaṭha Upaniṣad*, 2.3.2)

Prāṇa evolves and emerges first in the cosmic mind and then in grosser levels as the five basic elements, or *pañca-tattvas*: ether (*ākāśa*), air (*vāyu*), fire (*agni*), water (*āpas*), and earth (*pṛthivī*). This process can be compared to the cooling of water: as temperature drops, water becomes grosser and grosser until it turns into snow or ice. Similarly, in the dynamic process of the concealment of consciousness, the universe is manifested from the subtle to the gross.

Creation occurs at both macrocosmic and microcosmic levels: what takes place in the universe also occurs in every grain of sand and in our own body. The manifestation of the body implies an evolutionary process, a transformation of *prāṇa* from subtle to grosser levels, from hidden to revealed.

1. *Sahasrāra-cakra*: Brahman and its *śakti* lie in the causal plane in perfect union as One, prior to the manifestation of the physical body, in the seventh energy center located at the crown of the head.
2. *Ājñā-cakra*: First, the mind manifests in the sixth center.
3. *Viśuddha-cakra*: Next, ether (*ākāśa*) manifests in the laryngeal plexus.
4. *Anāhata-cakra*: Next, air (*vāyu*) manifests in the cardiac plexus.
5. *Maṇipūra-cakra*: Next, fire (*agni* or *tejas*) manifests in the solar plexus.
6. *Svādhiṣṭhāna-cakra*: Next, water (*ojas* or *āpas*) manifests in the prostatic plexus.
7. *Mūlādhāra-cakra*: Finally, earth (*pṛthivī*) manifests in the sacral plexus. After reaching the earth element, the dynamic aspect of *prāṇa* remains in *mūlādhāra-cakra*, while its static aspect resides in *sahasrāra*.

Vital energy is responsible for evolution. It begins with the five elements and continues its development in the vegetable kingdom and the animal kingdom, up to human beings.

It should be noted that in the process of cosmic manifestation, Brahman and *prāṇa* do not undergo any real change. Only forms and names develop or evolve. Just as the water does not change when it acquires the density of the ice, these changes are superficial changes.

The *nāḍīs* or "energy channels"

Vital energy (*prāṇa-śakti*) and mental energy (*manas-śakti*) do not flow in a disorderly way through our body, but circulate through very well-defined astral paths called *nāḍīs*. The word *nāḍī* is derived from the Sanskrit root *naḍ* meaning "to move." Vital energy flows through these delicate astral channels like blood flows through veins and arteries. Even though we cannot see the *nāḍīs*, they influence the physical body.

The structure of the *nāḍīs* is like a tube or cable with three layers: the exterior layer (*nāḍī*), the intermediate layer (*damani*), and the interior layer (*sira*). There are two types of *nāḍīs*: the conductors of *prāṇa* energy (*prāṇa-vāha-nāḍīs*) and the conductors of mental energy (*mano-vāha-nāḍīs*). Astral channels emanate from the *kanda* and *meḍhra*. The word *kanda* means "root" because it is the origin of all the *nāḍīs*. The *kanda* is shaped like an egg and covered with membranes.

The *Haṭha-yoga-pradīpikā* describes its exact location:

ऊर्ध्वं वितस्तिमात्रं तु विस्तारं चतुरङ्गुलम् ।
मृदुलं धवलं प्रोक्तं वेष्टिताम्बरलक्षणम् ॥

ūrdhvaṁ vitasti-mātraṁ tu
vistāraṁ catur-aṅgulam
mṛdulaṁ dhavalaṁ proktaṁ
veṣṭitāmbara-lakṣaṇam

> The *kanda* is situated above the anus, its length is one palm, and its width is four inches. It is smooth and white, as if it were wrapped in cloth.
>
> (*Haṭha-yoga-pradīpikā*, 3.113)

The *kanda* is located above the first center, specifically in the *granthi-sthāna* (*granthi* means "knot" and *sthāna* means "platform or base"). In this area, the *kanda* connects to the *suṣumṇā-nāḍī*.

The *meḍhra* is found between the first and third chakras, as is indicated in this verse:

ऊर्ध्वं मेढ्रादधो नाभेः कन्दे योनिः खगाण्डवत् ॥
तत्र नाड्यः समुत्पन्नाः सहस्राणां द्विसप्ततिः ।
तेषु नाडीसहस्रेषु द्विसप्ततिरुदाहृता ॥

ūrdhvaṁ meḍhrād adho nābheḥ
kande yoniḥ khagāṇḍavat

tatra nāḍyaḥ samutpannāḥ
sahasrāṇāṁ dvisaptatiḥ
teṣu nāḍī-sahasreṣu
dvisaptatir udāhṛtā

The *meḍhra* is [located] at the top of the base of the perineum and below the navel, which is the point of origin of the *nāḍīs*. It has the shape of an egg and from it 72,000 energy channels emanate. Among these thousands of channels, seventy-two are the most important.

(*Yoga-cūḍāmaṇi Upaniṣad*, 14b–15)

In fact, the place where the *nāḍīs* originate is both the *kanda* and the *meḍhra,* which is the area of the *granthi-sthāna*. They are so close to each other that they are practically in the same place. Remember that we are not referring to solid matter or substance but to the astral plane.

The ten main *nāḍīs*

There are different interpretations of the number of *nāḍīs* in the astral body. According to the *Śiva Saṁhitā* and the *Yoga-cūḍāmaṇi Upaniṣad*, there are ten main *nāḍīs*:

प्रधानाः प्राणवाहिन्यो भूयस्तासु दशस्मृताः ।
इडा च पिङ्गला चैव सुषुम्ना च तृतीयगा ॥
गान्धारी हस्तिजिह्वा च पूषा चैव यशस्विनी ।
अलम्बुसा कुहूश्चैव शङ्खिनी दशमी स्मृता ॥

pradhānāḥ prāṇa-vāhinyo
bhūyas tāsu daśa smṛtāḥ
iḍā ca piṅgalā caiva
suṣumṇā ca tṛtīyagā

gāndhārī hasti-jihvā ca
pūṣā caiva yaśasvinī
alambusā kuhūś caiva
śaṅkhinī daśamī smṛtā

Again, among these [seventy-two], there are ten main *nāḍīs* for the flow of *prāṇa*. These are known as *iḍā* and *piṅgalā*, the third is *suṣumṇā*, the next ones are *gāndhārī*, *hasti-jihvā*, *pūṣā*, *yaśasvinī*, *alambusā*, *kuhū*, and the tenth is *śaṅkhinī*. In this way, they have been mentioned.

(*Yoga-cūḍāmaṇi Upaniṣad*, 16–17)

The same scripture refers to the exact location of the major *nāḍīs*:

एतन्नाडीमहाचक्रं ज्ञातव्यं योगिभिः सदा ।
इडा वामे स्थिता भागे दक्षिणे पिङ्गला स्थिता ॥
सुषुम्ना मध्यदेशे तु गान्धारी वामचक्षुषि ।
दक्षिणे हस्तिजिह्वा च पूषा कर्णे च दक्षिणे ॥
यशस्विनी वामकर्णे चानने चापु अलम्बुसा ।
कुहूश्च लिङ्गदेशे तु मूलस्थाने तु शङ्खिनी ॥

etan nāḍī mahā-cakraṁ
jñātavyaṁ yogibhiḥ sadā
iḍā vāme sthitā bhāge
dakṣiṇe piṅgalā sthitā

suṣumṇā madhya deśe tu
gāndhārī vāma-cakṣuṣi
dakṣiṇe hasti-jihvā ca
pūṣā karṇe ca dakṣiṇe

yaśasvinī vāma-karṇe
cānane cāpu alambusā
kuhūś ca liṅga-deśe tu
mūla-sthāne tu śaṅkhinī

> Yogis should always be aware of this great *nāḍī* complex. *Iḍā* is on the left side and *piṅgalā* on the right. *Suṣumṇā* is in the middle. *Gāndhārī* goes to the left eye and *hasti-jihvā* to the right eye. *Pūṣā* goes to the right ear and *yaśasvinī* to the left ear. *Alambusā* goes to the face. *Kuhū* goes to the genitals and *śaṅkhinī* to the perineum.
>
> (*Yoga-cūḍāmaṇi Upaniṣad*, 18–20)

Suṣumṇā-nāḍī: *Suṣumṇā* is the main *nāḍī* because spiritual energy flows through it and, therefore, it is intimately linked to our progress on the path toward the light. *Suṣumṇā-nāḍī* extends from the first chakra toward *brahma-randhra*. Within *suṣumṇā*, there are three different *nāḍīs*: the most exterior is *vajra-nāḍī*, within that is *chitra-nāḍī*, and in the center is *brahma-nāḍī*, through which *kuṇḍalinī-śakti* ascends toward the seventh chakra.

To the left of *suṣumṇā* is *iḍā-nāḍī*, which channels feminine and lunar energy; it regulates our psychic aspect because it carries mental energy (*manas-śakti*). To the right of *suṣumṇā* is *piṅgalā-nāḍī*, which channels masculine and solar energy; it controls our vital aspect because through it moves *prāṇa-śakti*.

Iḍā-nāḍī and piṅgalā-nāḍī: *Iḍā-nāḍī* flows from the right ovary or testicle to the left nostril. *Piṅgalā-nāḍī* flows from the left ovary or testicle to the right nostril.

Iḍā is connected to the right hemisphere of the brain and thus rules over our intuitions, understandings, and emotions. *Piṅgalā* is connected to the left hemisphere and thus influences language and logical, analytical, and rational thought.

In most human beings, the dominant brain hemisphere alternates every 90 to 180 minutes. Along with the switch, the activity of the *nāḍīs* oscillates so that sometimes *iḍā* predominates and sometimes *piṅgalā*. If *iḍā* predominates, the left nostril will be clearer. If *piṅgalā* prevails, the right nostril will be clearer. The predominant *nāḍī* will activate its nostril, and thus the activity in the nerves associated with it. *Iḍā* is connected to the parasympathetic nervous system, whereas the *piṅgalā* is connected to the sympathetic nervous system. This alternation makes us fluctuate between active and receptive states and between analytical and intuitive states.

Psychologically, the free circulation of *prāṇa* through these two *nāḍīs* is closely tied to the mental activity in the two cerebral hemispheres. *Iḍā* leads to inspiration, while *piṅgalā* makes activity possible. Breathing and activity of these *nāḍīs* are interdependent, thus, by controlling our breathing, we can influence the activity of the *nāḍīs*.

Furthermore, *iḍā-nāḍī* regulates bile, lowers body temperature, and regulates blood pressure. *Piṅgalā-nāḍī* also regulates blood pressure and controls the temperature of the kidneys and the heart.

Other names for *iḍā-nāḍī* are *candra-nāḍī*, *lalanā-nāḍī*, *pitryaṇa*, *śaśi*, *candra-hāra*, and *śītala*. *Piṅgalā-nāḍī* is also known as *surya-nāḍī*.

Gāndhāri-nāḍī: It is under the control of the *piṅgalā*. It flows on the left side of the *iḍā-nāḍī* and goes to the left eye.

Hasti-jihvā-nāḍī: It is under the control of *suṣumṇā*. It flows on the reverse lateral side of *iḍā* and goes to the big toe. It provides vital energy to the nerves that surround the eyes.

Pūṣā-nāḍī and yaśasvinī-nāḍī: *Pūṣā* flows behind the *piṅgalā* toward the right eye. *Yaśasvinī-nāḍī* flows alongside *piṅgalā*, between *pūṣā* and *sarasvatī*. *Yaśasvinī-nāḍī* controls the flow of information in the left ear, whereas *pūṣā-nāḍī* does so in the right ear. The information perceived by the ears is processed by the brain under the control of *suṣumṇā-nāḍī*.

Alambusā-nāḍī: It flows from the anus, terminating in the mouth. It is related to the sense of taste.

Kuhū-nāḍī: It is under the control of *iḍā*. It flows alongside *suṣumṇā-nāḍī* to the nose. It is located near the sexual organs and involved in activating them.

Śaṅkhinī-nāḍī: It is found between the *nāḍīs gāndhārī* and *sarasvatī*. It flows to the side and behind *iḍā-nāḍī* and connects to *mūlādhāra-cakra*. It is located near the kidneys and affects renal functions and urine.

Other important *nāḍīs*

Sarasvatī-nāḍī: It is under the control of *vajra-nāḍī*. It flows to the side of *suṣumṇā-nāḍī* and ends in the mouth.

Payasvinī-nāḍī: It is under the control of *citriṇī-nāḍī*. It flows between *pūṣā* and *sarasvatī nāḍīs*. This *nāḍī* ends at the edge of the right ear and is connected to the gall bladder.

Vāruṇī-nāḍī: It flows between the *yaśasvinī* and *kuhū*. Its functions include maintaining the balance of water in our body and transporting waste.

Śūrya-nāḍī: It flows from the navel toward the space between the eyebrows.

Viśvodarī-nāḍī: It flows between *kuhū* and *hasti-jihvā*. It is connected to *maṇipūra-cakra* and the digestive system.

Important facial *nāḍīs*: *Cakṣu-bhedna, nasikā-bhedna, karṇa-bhedna, tamas, rajas, bṛkuṭi-dhyāna, amṛta-varṣa, divya, mukhar-bindu, tejasvinī, janma-mṛtyur-ganadhākṣa, karma-phala, dikpāla, matṛkā, mūrdha, cakṣu-karṇa, apaṅg, mānya, kṛ-kaṭika, śṛṅgāṭaka, nirama, antar-daha, sam-mukha, naraka-loka,* and *svarga-loka.*

Important *nāḍīs* situated in the shoulders, chest, and stomach: *Madhyama-śayan, sthūla-kriyā, vāk-kriyā, ananta, oṁ-kāra, madhyama-vāca, uṣṭi-viṭalā, prakṛti-puruṣa, pāpa-haraṇa, śipra-bhogī, karmaṇya, pañca-tatva, agni, bhūmi, āpa, ākāśa, vāyu, prāṇa, udāna, vyāna, samāna, apāna, aṅga, kṛ-kāra, kūrma, deva-dūta, dhanañjaya, mihira, rasna, deva-yāna, bhāskara, rudra-rūpa, brahma-randhra, mahā-patha, madhya-mārga, smaśāna, śāmbhavī, śakti-mārga, sūrya, agni-mārga, śasi-lalanā, pitṛ-yāna, candra-hāra, śītala, candra, śipra-gāndhārī, śipra-hasta-jihvā, muhūrartri-kuhu, pitṛ, mātṛ, bhairavī, viśāla, cāmuṇḍā,* and *śirṣa.*

Secondary *nāḍīs* in the palms of the hands and the soles of the feet: *Madhyamā, agni-śūnyā, candra-śūnyā, dhyānā, muktā, vimuktā, śila-oṁ-kārā, śalinā, śiprā, svāhā, śīnā, mādhavī, urvākā, pāvanā, vaidehī, viplakṣā, vimohī, vācā, mukta-bhedā, vaikuṇṭha, rasā-tala, mahā-tala, apratiṣṭha,* and *mahā-bhī.*

Secondary *nāḍīs* in the feet: *Mantrūḍha, dham-samudra, nava-vidyā, sūkṣma-deha, nābhī-sthāna, rakta-samudra, liṅga-sthāna, sāvitrī-candrāṇī,* and *jānu-sthala.*

List of minor *nāḍīs*: *Āṁ, agni, agni-śūnya, agni-mārga, aḥ, ākāśa, alambusā, aṁ, amṛta, ananta, aṅga, antar-daha, apa, apāna, apaṅg, apratiṣṭha, oṁ, baṁ, bhāskara, bhairavī, bhaṁ, bhūmi, brahma-randhra, bṛkuṭi-dhyāna, cakṣu-behdna, cakṣu-karṇa, caṁ, cāmuṇḍa, candra, candra-śūnya, candra-hāra,* *candrāṇī, chaṁ, citriṇī, daṁ, deva-datta, deva-yāna, dham, dhaṁ-samudra, dhanañ-jaya, dhyāna, divya, aiṁ, eṁ, eiṁ, phaṁ, gaṁ, gāndhāri, ghaṁ, haṁ, hasta-jihvā, iṁ, jaṁ, janma-mrityur-ganadhākṣya, jānu-sthala, jhaṁ, jihvā, kaṁ, karma-phalādi-kalpa, karmaṇya, karṇa-bhedna, khaṁ, kṛ-kaṭika, kṛ-kāra, kṣam, kuhu, kūrma, lalanā, laṁ, liṅga-sthāna, lrīṁ, lriṁ, mādhavī, madhyāna-śayana, madhyama-śūnya, madhyama-vaca, madhya-mārga, mahā-patha, mahā-tala, maṁ, mānyā, mātṛkā, mihira, mūrdha, muhuratri-kuhu, mukhar-bindu, mukta-bheda, muktā, nābhī-sthāna, naṁ, ṇaṁ, naraka-loka, nāsikā-bhedna, nava-vidyā, nir-mana, māyan, om-kāra, padavi, paṁ, pañca-tattva, pāpa-haraṇa, pāvana, payasvinī, piṅgala, pitṛ, mātṛ, pitṛ-yāṇa, prakṛti-puruṣa, prāna, pūṣa, rajas, rākā, rakta-samudra, raṁ, rasā-tala, rasna, rīṁ, ṛṣi, rudra-rūpa, saṁ, sa-mana, śāmbhavī, sammukha, śankinī, sarasvatī, śaśi, saumyā, sāvitri, śakti-mārga, śālīna, śaṁ, śīna, śītla, śila, śipra-bhogi, śiprā, śipra-gāndhārī, śipra-hasta-jihvā, śīrṣa, smaśāna, śṛṅgāṭaka, sthūla, sūrya, sūkṣma-deha, suṣumṇa, svāhā, svarga-loka, ṭaṁ, ṭham, tamas, tejasvinī, taṁ, thaṁ, udāna, uṁ, urvāka, ūṁ, vaca, vaidehī, vaikuṇṭha, vajra, vāk-kriya, vaṁ, vāruṇī, vāyu, vimohī, vimukta, viplakṣa, viśāla, viśvodhra, vyāna, yaṁ, yāṁ,* and *yaśasvinī.*

All the astral channels are subordinate, in one way or another, to *suṣumṇā*, because energy rises from *mūlādhāra-cakra* to the cave of Brahman (*brahma-randhra*), which is situated inside the cerebrospinal axis. We read the following:

एवं द्वारं समाश्रित्य तिष्ठन्ते नाडयः क्रमात् ।
इडापिङ्गलासौषुम्नाः प्राणमार्गे च संस्थिताः ॥
सततं प्राणवाहिन्यः सोमसूर्याग्निदेवताः ।
प्राणापानसमानाख्या व्यानोदानौ च वायवः ॥

evaṁ dvāraṁ samāśritya
tiṣṭhante nāḍayaḥ kramāt
iḍā-piṅgalā-sauṣumnāḥ
prāṇa-mārge ca saṁsthitāḥ

satataṁ prāṇa-vāhinyaḥ
soma-sūryāgni-devatāḥ
prāṇāpāna-samānākhyā
vyānodānau ca vāyavaḥ

> Thus these *nāḍīs*, namely *iḍā, piṅgalā*, and *suṣumṇā,* are closely attached to the opening of the paths of *prāṇa*. They are manifestations of the gods Soma (moon), Sūrya (sun), and Agni (fire), respectively, and *prāṇa* moves through them [the three *nāḍīs*]. The *vāyus* (that are moved through the passages) are *prāṇa, apāna*, *samāna*, *vyāna*, and *udāna*.
>
> (*Yoga-cūḍāmaṇi Upaniṣad*, 21–22)

The Vedic sages of antiquity explored the influence of the flow of vital energy through the *nāḍīs* on human health. In a healthy state, *prāṇa* flows in a free and well-balanced manner throughout our body. Energetically, disease is a blockage and disharmony of *prāṇa*, which can have a physical, mental, or emotional origin.

One of the innumerable purposes of hatha yoga postures is to reestablish the circulation of vital energy and overcome energetic obstructions in the *nāḍīs* that can affect our health. Asanas, *prāṇāyāma*, and relaxation allow for the expansion of *prāṇa* as well as its harmonious distribution to all organs and at every level.

For a serious study of the *nāḍīs*, the following accredited books on the subject are recommended: *Jala-darśana Upaniṣad*, *Yoga-cūḍāmaṇi Upaniṣad*, *Yoga-śikha Upaniṣad*, *Gorakṣāṣṭaka*, *Siddha-siddhānta-paddhati*, *Śāṇḍilya Upaniṣad*, and *Ṣaṭ-cakra-nirūpaṇa*. The Upanishads also offer explanations:

> ता वा अस्यैता हिता नाम नाड्यो यथा केशः सहस्रधा भिन्नस्तावताऽणिम्ना तिष्ठन्ति शुक्लस्य नीलस्य पिङ्गलस्य हरितस्य लोहितस्य पूर्णा ।
>
> *tā vā asyaitā hitā nāma nāḍyo yathā keśaḥ sahasradhā bhinnas-tāvatā 'ṇimnā tiṣṭhanti śuklasya nīlasya piṅgalasya haritasya lohitasya pūrṇā.*
>
> In a person, there are nerves called *hita* that are as fine as a hair that has been divided into a thousand parts and they are filled with white, blue, brown, green, and red liquids.
>
> (*Bṛhad-āraṇyaka Upaniṣad*, 4.3.20)

अथ या एता हृदयस्य नाड्यस्ताः पिङ्गलस्याणिम्नस्तिष्ठन्ति शुक्लस्य नीलस्य पीतस्य लोहितस्येत्यसौ वा आदित्यः पिङ्गल एष शुक्ल एष नील एष पीत एष लोहितः ॥

atha yā etā hṛdayasya nāḍyas tāḥ piṅgalasyānimnas- tiṣṭhanti śuklasya nīlasya pītasya lohitasyety asau vā ādityaḥ piṅgala eṣa śukla eṣa nīla eṣa pīta eṣa lohitaḥ.

Now, [from] these arteries (channels) that belong to the heart, arise the finest essences, of the colors reddish brown, white, blue, yellow, and red. The sun is reddish brown, white, blue, yellow, and red.

(*Chāndogya Upaniṣad*, 8.6.1)

तद्यथा महापथातत उभौ ग्रामौ गच्छतीमं चामुं चैवमेवैता आदित्यस्य रश्मय उभौ लोकौ गच्छन्तीमं चामुं चामुष्मादादित्यात्प्रतायन्ते तासु नाडीषु सृप्ता आभ्यो नाडीभ्यः प्रतायन्ते तेऽमुष्मिन्नादित्ये सृप्ताः ॥

tad yathā mahā-pathātata ubhau grāmau gacchatīmaṁ cāmuṁ caivam evaitā ādityasya raśmaya ubhau lokau gacchantīmaṁ cāmuṁ cāmuṣmād ādityāt pratāyante tāsu nāḍīṣu sṛptā ābhyo nāḍībhyaḥ pratāyante te 'muṣminn ādityo sṛptāḥ.

Just as a long and continuous highway passes between two villages, the rays of the sun go between both worlds (*idā* and *piṅgalā*) and the next (*suṣumṇā*). The rays extend from the sun and enter these channels. They extend from these channels and permeate the sun.

(*Chāndogya Upaniṣad*, 8.6.2)

तद्यत्रैतत्सुप्तः समस्तः सम्प्रसन्नः स्वप्नं न विजानात्यासु तदा नाडीषु सृप्तो भवति तं न कश्चन पाप्मा स्पृशति तेजसा हि तदा सम्पन्नो भवति ॥

tad yatraitat suptaḥ samastaḥ samprasannaḥ svapnaṁ na vijānāty āsu tadā nāḍīṣu sṛpto bhavati taṁ na kaścana pāpmā spṛśati tejasā hi tadā sampanno bhavati.

And when one is in complete repose in the forgiving thought of Brahman, one becomes calm and serene, in such a way that one has no dreams, then one enters into [the *ākāśa* of the heart by means of] these arteries. Then, nothing bad can happen to one who has obtained divine enlightenment.

(*Chāndogya Upaniṣad*, 8.6.3)

अथ यत्रैतदबलिमानं नीतो भवति तमभितासीना आहुर्जानासि मां जानासि मामिति स यावदस्माच्छरीरादनुत्क्रान्तो भवति तावज्जानाति ॥

atha yatraitad abalimānaṁ nīto bhavati tam abhitāsīnā āhur jānāsi māṁ jānāsi mām iti sa yāvad asmāc charīrād anutkrānto bhavati tāvaj jānāti.

Now when one is seriously ill, family members who are sitting around say: 'Do you recognize me? Do you recognize me?' He recognizes them until abandoning the body.

(*Chāndogya Upaniṣad*, 8.6.4)

अथ यत्रैतदस्माच्छरीरादुत्क्रामत्यथैतैरेव रश्मिभिरूर्ध्वमाक्रमते स ओमिति वा होद्वा मीयते स यावत्क्षिप्येन्मनस्तावदादित्यं गच्छत्येतद्वै खलु लोकद्वारं विदुषां प्रपदनं निरोधोऽविदुषाम् ॥

atha yatraitad asmāc charīrād utkrāmaty athaitair eva raśmibhir ūrdhvam ākramate sa oṁ iti vā hod vā mīyate sa yāvat kṣipyen manas tāvad ādityaṁ gacchaty etad vai khalu loka-dvāraṁ viduṣāṁ prapadanaṁ nirodho 'viduṣām.

But when the person leaves the body, he goes up by means of these same rays. If he is wise he rises by meditating on *Oṁ*. To the extent that he transcends the mind, he reaches the sun. In fact, the door to the world of Brahman remains open for the sages and closed to the ignorant.

(*Chāndogya Upaniṣad*, 8.6.5)

तदेष श्लोकः । शतं चैका च हृदयस्य नाड्यस्तासां मूर्धानमभिनिःसृतैका ।
तयोर्ध्वमायन्नमृतत्वमेति विष्वङ्ङन्या उत्क्रमणे भवन्त्युत्क्रमणे भवन्ति ॥

tad eṣa ślokaḥ. śataṁ caikā ca hṛdayasya nāḍyas tāsāṁ mūrdhānam abhiniḥsṛtaikā. tayordhvam āyann amṛtatvam eti viṣvaṅṅ anyā utkramaṇe bhavanty ukramaṇe bhavanti.

To confirm this, there is a verse: The heart has 101 arteries; one of these is directed toward the crown of the head. Rising toward it, one reaches immortality. The rest of the arteries are directed in other directions.

(*Chāndogya Upaniṣad*, 8.6.6)

The difference between *kuṇḍalinī-śakti* and *prāṇa-śakti*

Just as water is the common essence of both steam and ice, Brahman is the common essence of *kuṇḍalinī* and *prāṇa*. Both are expressions of the same creative female energy that originates from Brahman. Śakti is called *kuṇḍalinī* when it descends and crosses the abstract boundaries of the causal plane (*kāraṇa-loka*). It is called *prāṇa* when it arrives to the astral plane (*bhuvar-loka*).

Kuṇḍalinī-śakti is higher than *prāṇa-śakti* because it is related to the *ānanda-maya-kośa* (blissful sheath) that is subtler; when the *kuṇḍalinī-śakti* approaches the *vijñāna-maya-kośa* (intellectual sheath), it expresses itself astrally, as *prāṇa-śakti*. The manifestation of *prāṇa-śakti* is perceived physically by the *anna-maya-kośa* (food sheath or physical body). The *prāṇa* is *śakti* in its evolving aspect: from unity toward plurality. On the other hand, *kuṇḍalinī* is *śakti* during involution: from multiplicity toward unity. Kuṇḍalinī is coiled in *mūlādhāra-cakra* and when it awakens, just as a needle is drawn by a powerful magnet, it yearns to reunite with its source. In every *prāṇa* phenomenon, the first energy center (*mūlādhāra-cakra*) will dominate, which is the lowest of all and corresponds to the earth element; whereas in every phenomenon related to *kuṇḍalinī*, the highest center (*sahasrāra-cakra*) will predominate.

Prāṇa descends through *suṣumṇā-nāḍī* in a similar proportion to our formation as egoic entities. The process begins in *sahasrāra-cakra* and descends during our development as human beings and culminates in *mūlādhāra*. Beginning during gestation in our mother's womb, and then continuing as we grow into babies, kids, and adults, *prāṇa* descends as we forget of our essence. Similarly, in reverse, *kuṇḍalinī-śakti* ascends as we wake up to reality.

An awakening of *kuṇḍalinī-śakti* will usually be preceded by an awakening of *prāṇa*. Based on my own experience, the activation of *prāṇa* is an essential and an indispensable prerequisite for awakening *kuṇḍalinī*. Therefore, in the practice of *kuṇḍalinī-yoga*, it is recommended to start with *prāṇāyama*. Many *prāṇāyama* exercises and practices are performed in the physical body (*sthūla-śarīra*) although they influence the astral body (*liṅga-śarīra* or *sūkṣma-śarīra*). The awakening of *kuṇḍalinī*, however, is a phenomenon that begins at the highest levels of the causal body (*kāraṇa-śarīra*) toward the bliss sheath (*ānanda-maya-kośa*).

We can see a significant difference between the ascension of *prāṇa* (*prāṇotthāna*) and an awakening of *kuṇḍalinī*. *Prāṇa* rises on the astral plane from *mūlādhāra-cakra* through *piṅgalā-nāḍī* to the brain and finally disperses. The awakening of *kuṇḍalinī* also begins in *mūlādhāra-cakra*, but at the causal level. Its ascension takes place through the *suṣumṇā-nāḍī* and reaches *sahasrāra-cakra*. While all *prāṇa* awakenings occur on the astral plane and cause pleasant feelings, the ascension of *kuṇḍalinī* is a much more powerful experience because it happens from *kāraṇa-śarīra* to *ānanda-maya-kośa*.

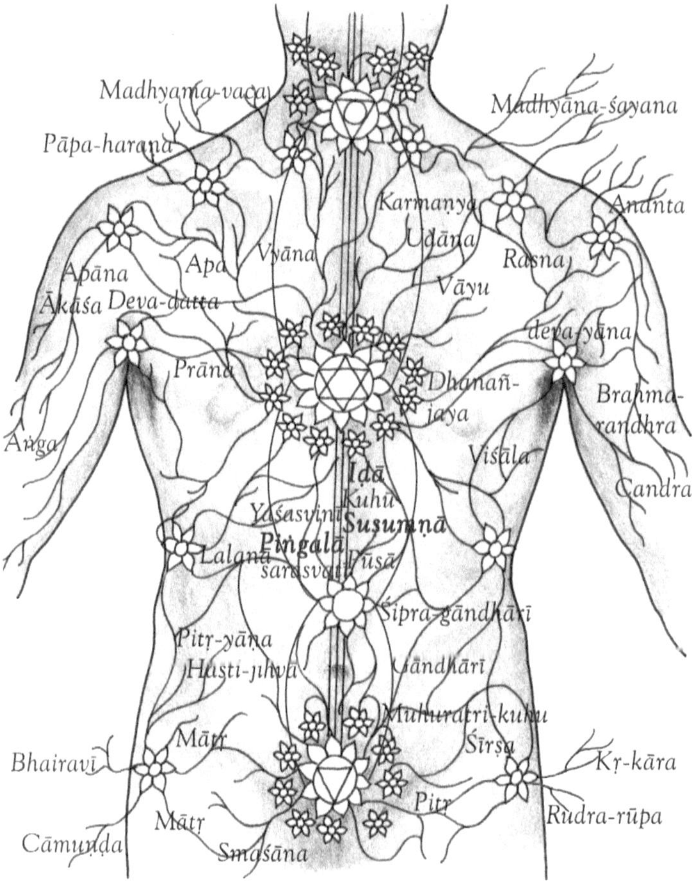

THE *NĀḌĪS* OF THE BODY

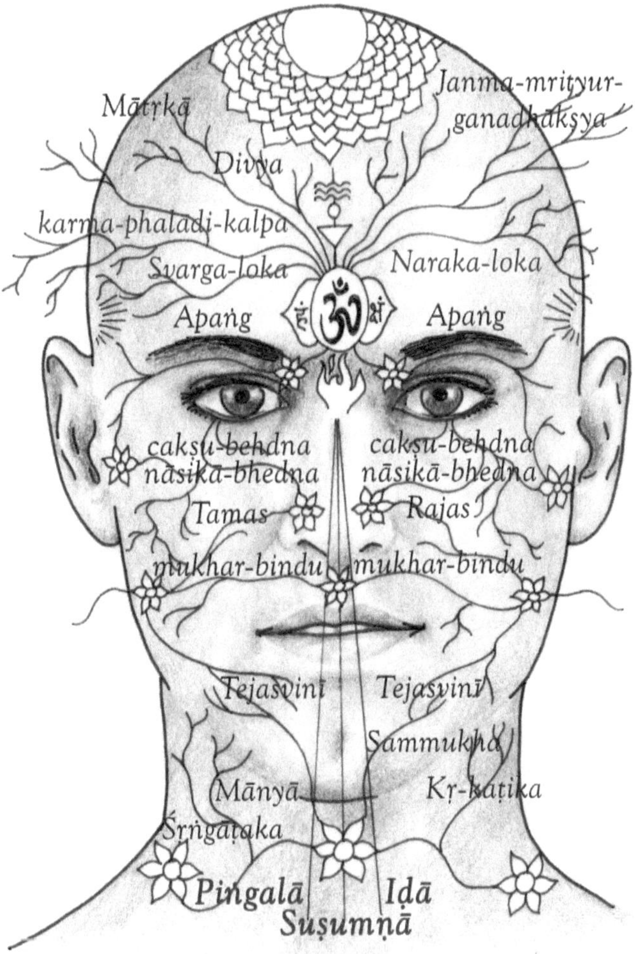

THE *NĀḌĪS* OF THE FACE

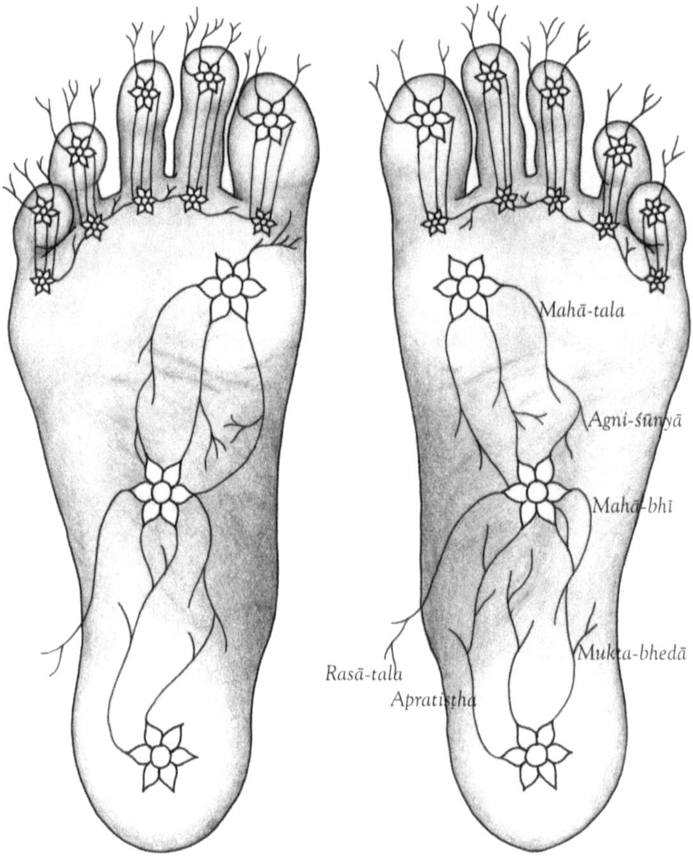

THE *NĀḌĪS* OF THE FEET

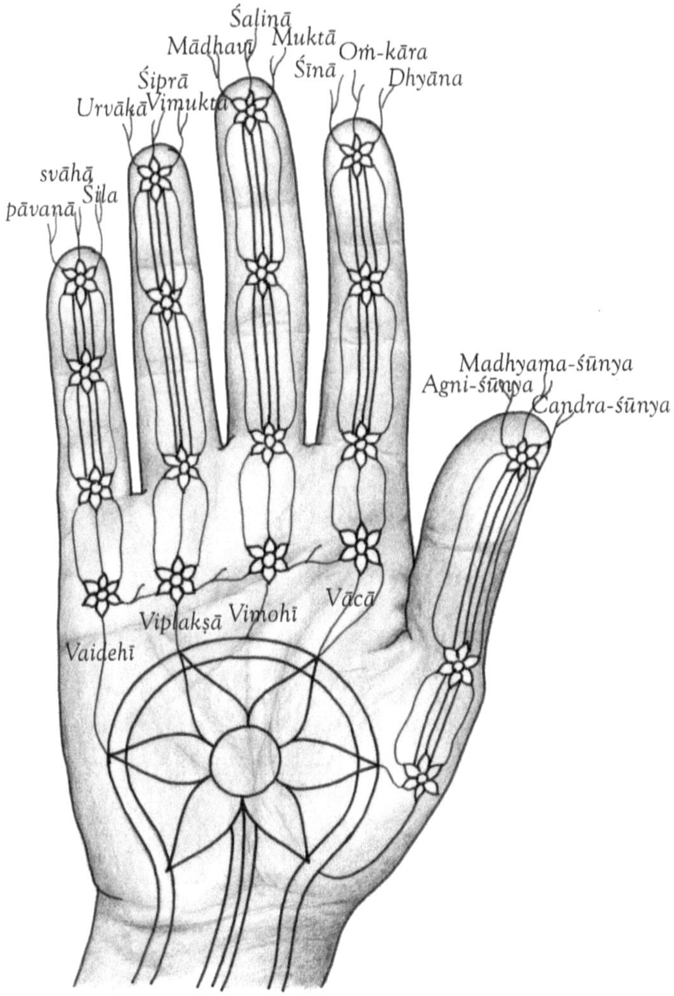

THE *NĀḌĪS* OF THE HANDS

Chakras, *marmas*, and *granthis*

In order to understand the process of *kuṇḍalinī-yoga*, it is essential to acquire at least some basic knowledge of chakras, *marmas*, and *granthis*.

Chakras or "energy centers"

चतुर्दलं स्यादाधारं स्वाधिष्ठानं च षड्दलम् ॥
नाभौ दशदलं पद्मं हृदये द्वादशारकम् ।
षोडशारं विशुद्धाख्यं भ्रूमध्ये द्विदलं तथा ॥
सहस्रदलसङ्ख्यातं ब्रह्मरन्ध्रे महापथि ।

catur-dalaṁ syād ādhāraṁ
svādhiṣṭhānaṁ ca ṣaḍ-dalam

nābhau daśa-dalaṁ padmaṁ
hṛdaye dvādaśārakam
ṣoḍaśāraṁ viśuddhākhyaṁ
bhrū-madhye dvi-dalaṁ tathā

sahasra-dala-saṅkhyātaṁ
brahma-randhre mahā-pathi

It has been said [of the six psychic centers] that *mūlādhāra*, the central base, has four petals. *Svādhiṣṭhāna*, one's center, has six petals. *Maṇipūra*, the center of the navel, has ten petals. *Anāhata*, the heart center, has twelve petals. *Viśuddha*, the center of purification, has sixteen petals, and *bhrū-madhya*, the center of the space between the eyebrows, has two petals. In the great path of the *brahma-randhra* (the opening at the crown of the head) there is a lotus of one thousand petals (*sahasrāra-cakra*).

(*Yoga-cūḍāmaṇi Upaniṣad*, 4b–6a)

The meaning of the Sanskrit word *cakra* is "wheel or disc," which suggests circular movement. The chakras rotate clockwise. They are swirling metaphysical vortexes, transformers of energy both from the astral body, or *liṅga-śarīra*, and toward it. Chakras are functioning normally if they rotate clockwise at the appropriate speed to metabolize the required energy from the infinite ocean of *prāṇa*. The chakras consist of a system of centers of energetic activity. They are intended to receive, assimilate, and transmit vital energies. *Prāṇa* organizes its flow within them. They are the connection between two worlds or realities, the physical and the astral.

There are 88,000 chakras in the astral body. Most are minor and their importance in our energetic system is minimal. There are forty-five important energy centers and of those, only seven are the most relevant. These are *mūlādhāra*, *svādhiṣṭhāna*, *maṇipūra*, *anāhata*, *viśuddha*, *ājñā*, and *sahasrāra*, and they are located along the *suṣumṇā-nāḍī*. In regards to the chakras, the *Atharva Veda* points out:

अष्टाचक्रा नवद्वारा देवानां पूरयोध्या ।
तस्यां हिरण्ययः कोशः स्वर्गो ज्योतिषावृतः ॥

aṣṭā-cakrā nava-dvārā
devānāṁ pūrayodhyā
tasyāṁ hiraṇyayaḥ kośaḥ
svargo jyotiṣāvṛtaḥ

The soul resides in the land of eight chakras and nine gates known as the bright land of the Lords.

(*Atharva Veda*, 10.2.31)

Learning properties and esoteric symbolism of each chakra allows us to focus our attention on each of them. This helps us become deeply aware of the essential nature of each center. The chakras cannot be seen with our physical eyes. However, we can perceive them with our senses in our physical body. They are located along the spinal cord and in the nerve plexuses.

Each one of the energy centers corresponds to a level in the cosmic process of creation and, therefore, it is related to a particular element that gives it certain characteristics and qualities. The relative material reality of names and forms is composed of five basic elements, which are called *pañca-mahā-bhūta* or *pañca-mahā-tattva*. They are the basic states of matter: ether (*ākāśa*), air (*vāyu*), fire (*tejas*), water (*āpas*), and earth (*pṛthivī*). Obviously, these states should not be understood as a mere clump of earth, a glass of water, or the flame of a candle, but in a wider sense that encompasses all their inherent qualities. For example, the heaviness and solidity of earth, the fluidity of water, the light and transforming power of fire, the lightness of air, and so on.

The chakras are a microcosm of creation. Before the cosmic manifestation, only the unified totality exists. The first expression of this unexpressed consciousness is the vibration of the universal Om. From this primordial sound, ether is manifested. When there is activity in the ether, air is formed. From the friction caused by this activity, fire is produced. Then, the liquefaction of fire leads to the manifestation of water, and finally, from solidified water, comes earth.

Each chakra is represented by a yantra (geometric diagram). The vibration of the chakra is indicated with a Sanskrit letter, or *bījākṣara*, in the center of the diagram. A lotus flower with a different number of petals symbolizes the quantity of *nāḍīs* that intersect in the chakra. In each petal, we find the Sanskrit letters that represent the specific vibration of each *nāḍī*. These flowers are open or closed according to a person's particular situation.

Furthermore, each chakra is related to a specific animal, which symbolizes the movement of *prāṇa* in the center. Each center is also related to a specific plane of consciousness; there are different dimensions of existence and forms of life. According to the holy Vedic scriptures, below the earthly plane there are seven *talas*, or "lower worlds," and six *lokas*, or "worlds," above this one, which correspond to different levels of consciousness. Each *loka* has its counterpart or corresponding *tala*, similar to two electrical poles. According to the *Mahā-bhāgavata Purāṇa*, these are the following, starting from the most elevated one:

7. *Satya-loka*
6. *Tapo-loka*
5. *Jana-loka*
4. *Mahar-loka*
3. *Svar(ga)-loka*
2. *Bhuvar-loka*
1. *Bhū(r)-loka* - earthly plane

The corresponding *talas* are:

1. *Atala*
2. *Vitala*
3. *Sutala*
4. *Talā-tala*
5. *Mahā-tala*
6. *Rasā-tala*
7. *Pātāla*

The chakras are linked to the nervous ganglia and the internal secretion glands of the endocrine system. The energy centers also have a great influence on our body, for example on the digestive, nervous, circulatory, and respiratory systems.

The asanas, or "postures of hatha yoga," directly influence the functioning of the chakras. Certain asanas work especially on the *prāṇa* movement of specific centers. Therefore, the order in which they are practiced is of great importance. The chakras not only affect us physically but also psychologically, sexually, and emotionally, as well as in our ability to communicate.

The techniques and practices of *kuṇḍalinī-yoga* require focusing our attention on each chakra's center of stimulation. However, for many beginning students, it is difficult to perceive and concentrate on these internal points. Many find it easier to concentrate on the *kṣetras*, which are the corresponding locations of each chakra in the front part of the body. The *kṣetras* are not the original points of stimulation of the chakras; they are their reflections. Concentration on the *kṣetras* creates a stimulating sensation that reaches the chakras.

The *mūlādhāra-kṣetra* is located at the base of the spine; the *svādhiṣṭhāna-kṣetra* lies at the pubic bone; the *maṇipūra-kṣetra* lies at the navel; the *anāhata-kṣetra* is at the level of the heart; the *viśuddha-kṣetra* we find at the level of the throat; the *ājñā-kṣetra*, at the level between the eyebrows; and the *sahasrāra-kṣetra*, at the crown of the head.

With regards to the characteristics of the centers, descriptions vary among the many scriptures and masters. Therefore, I have chosen to be faithful to two sources: the first is the opinion of my own eternal spiritual master, His Divine Grace Śrī Śrī Bābā Brahmānanda Mahārāja, and the second is my own experience, but only when it is in perfect agreement with the teachings of my beloved Guru Mahārāja.

The *marmas* or "vital points"

Marmas are the 107 vital points that the *nāḍīs* cross. These are *prāṇa* vortexes with great vital value, of which 57 are the most important. Damage in a *marma* can be fatal because they are vital points of great sensitivity that can cut a *nāḍī* and suppress the flow of vital energy. Ayurvedic medicine treats various diseases by applying massage, pressure, and heat to the *marma* connected to the affected organ. The asanas of hatha yoga are tremendously beneficial because they stretch the *marmas*. *Marmas* are explained in depth in the *Suśruta Saṁhitā*.

Next, we will list the principal *marmas*.

Marmas **located in the head:**

1. *Adhipati*: It is found at the crown of the head. In this *marma*, memory loss, headaches, and weakness are treated.
2. *Sīmanta*: It is found in the cranial suture. This *marma* is related to blood circulation in the head; here, migraine, epilepsy, convulsions, and amnesia are treated.
3. *Ājñā*: It is located in the space between the eyebrows. In this *marma*, loss of the sense of smell, pituitary gland problems, and colds are treated.

4. *Āvarta*: It is found above and at the ends of the eyebrows. This *marma* influences our body posture, and migraines and sinusitis are treated here.
5. *Śaṅkha*: It is located in the temples, between the eyebrows and the ears. In this *marma*, colon problems, headaches, amnesia, and dizziness are treated.
6. *Utkṣepa*: It is located above the *śaṅkha*. It is directly connected to the colon.
7. *Vidhura*: It is found below the ears. In this *marma*, the ears are stimulated.
8. *Phaṇa*: It is located on the sides of the nose. In this *marma*, flu symptoms and stress release treatments take place.
9. *Śṛṅgātaka*: It is located in the palate, under the nose and in the chin. In this *marma*, the nervous system is stimulated to alleviate headaches and dizziness.

Marmas located in the neck:

1. *Mantha*: It is located on the side of the neck. In this *marma*, difficulties in expression and paralysis are treated.
2. *Mānya*: It is on the side of the throat. In this *marma*, thyroid problems are treated, as it is related to the regulation and rhythm of the entire organism.
3. *Śira-mātṛkā*: It is located above the throat. This *marma* is related to blood circulation in the head.
4. *Nīla*: It is located in the throat. This *marma* influences the regulation of rhythms of the body.
5. *Kriya-kārika*: It is found at the base of the neck. In this *marma*, stress can be alleviated.

Marmas located on the back:

1. *Aṁśa*: It is located above the shoulder blade, between the trapezius muscle and the clavicle. In this *marma*, *viśuddha-cakra* is stimulated.
2. *Aṁśa-phalaka*: It is located on the shoulder blades. In this

marma, shoulder pain is treated and *anāhata-cakra* is stimulated.
3. *Pārśva-sandhi*: It is found above *nitamba-marma*. This *marma* regulates blood circulation.
4. *Nitamba*: It is located above the buttocks and stimulates the production of red blood cells.
5. *Kukundara*: It is located to the side of the coccyx. In this *marma*, problems in the reproductive organs are alleviated and *svādhiṣṭhāna-cakra* is stimulated.
6. *Kaṭika-taruṇa*: It is located above the buttocks. In this *marma*, fatty tissues are stimulated and muscular stiffness and pain in the legs are alleviated.

Marmas located in the thorax:

1. *Āpasthambha*: It is located below the clavicle. In this *marma*, the sympathetic and parasympathetic systems are stimulated. Asthma and breathing difficulties are treated here.
2. *Apalāpa*: It is located in the middle of the armpit. In this *marma*, breast inflammation is treated.
3. *Stanārohita*: It is located on top of the breast. In this *marma*, enflamed and obstructed breasts are treated.
4. *Hṛdaya*: It is located in the center of the thorax in the solar plexus. In this *marma*, heart diseases are treated.

Marmas located in the abdomen:

1. *Nābhi*: It is located around the navel. In this *marma*, the intestines are stimulated and constipation, diarrhea, and indigestions are treated.
2. *Vasti*: It is located in the pubic area. In this *marma*, *kapha* is stimulated and prostate and problems with the reproductive organ are treated.
3. *Guda*: It is located in the perineum. In this *marma*, constipation and hemorrhoids are treated.

Marmas located in the lower extremities:

1. *Tala-hṛdaya*: It is located in the center of the soles of the feet. This *marma* stimulates the lungs. Problems with blood circulation in the hands and feet are treated here.
2. *Kūrca*: It is located on the instep. This *marma* influences our sight, and foot pain is treated here.
3. *Kṣipra*: It is located in the upper part of the feet, between the big toe and the second toe. This *marma* is connected to the heart.
4. *Gulpha*: It is located below the ankle. In this *marma*, nervousness and stress are treated.
5. *Kūrca-śira*: It is located below the ankle. In this *marma*, muscular spasms are controlled.
6. *Indra-vasti*: It is located in the calf muscles. In this *marma*, digestive problems are treated.
7. *Jānu*: It is located behind the knees. This *marma* is connected to the liver.
8. *Ani*: It is located above the joints of the knees. This *marma* is related to muscular stiffness.
9. *Urvi*: It is located midway up the thigh. In this *marma*, muscular tension and circulatory disorders are treated.
10. *Viṭapa*: It is located below the groin. This *marma* is related to abdominal muscular tension and hernias.
11. *Lohitākṣa*: It is located in the center of the groin. In this *marma*, circulatory problems of the feet are treated.

Marmas located in the upper extremities:

1. *Tala-hṛdaya*: It is located in the center of the palm. This *marma* is associated with lung stimulation.
2. *Kṣipra*: It is located between the index finger and the thumb. This *marma* is associated with heart stimulation.
3. *Kūrca-śira*: It is located in the lower part of the wrist. This *marma* is associated with the control of the muscular spasms.

4. *Maṇi-bandha*: It is located in the wrist area. In this *marma*, tension and stress are alleviated.
5. *Indra-vasti*: It is located midway up the arm. In this *marma*, intestinal and digestive problems are treated.
6. *Kūrpāra*: It is located on the elbow. This *marma* is connected to the liver.
7. *Ani*: It is located in the elbow joint. Tension and muscles stiffness problems are treated here.
8. *Urvi*: It is located midway up the arm. In this *marma*, muscular tension and blood circulation problems are treated.
9. *Lohitākṣa*: It is located in the middle of the armpit. This *marma* is related to circulation in the lower extremities.

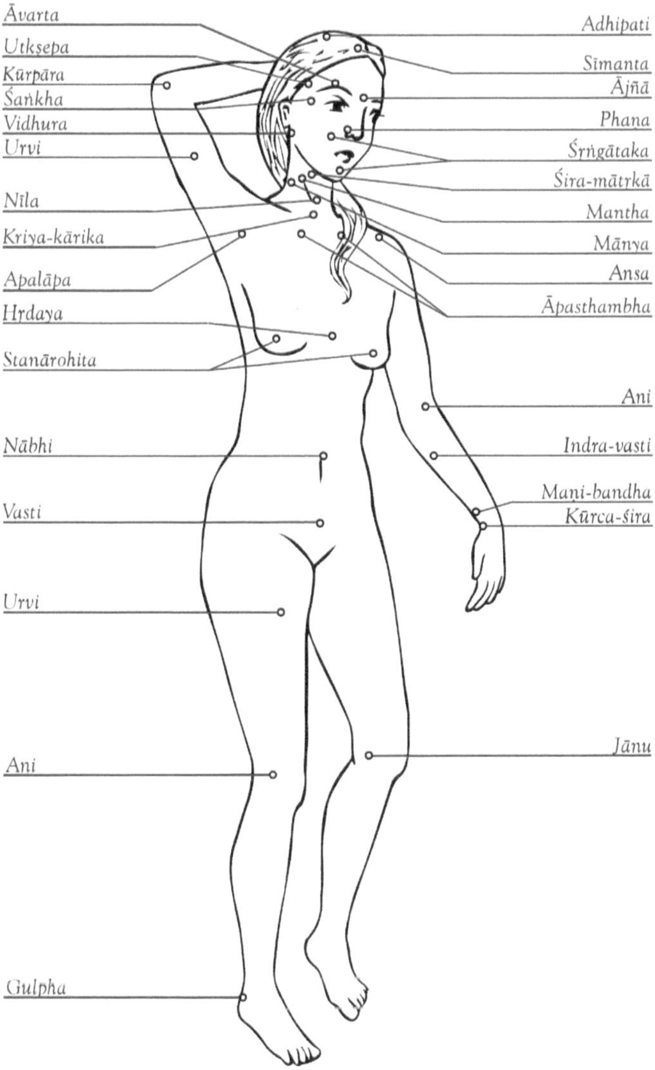

THE FRONTAL *MARMAS*

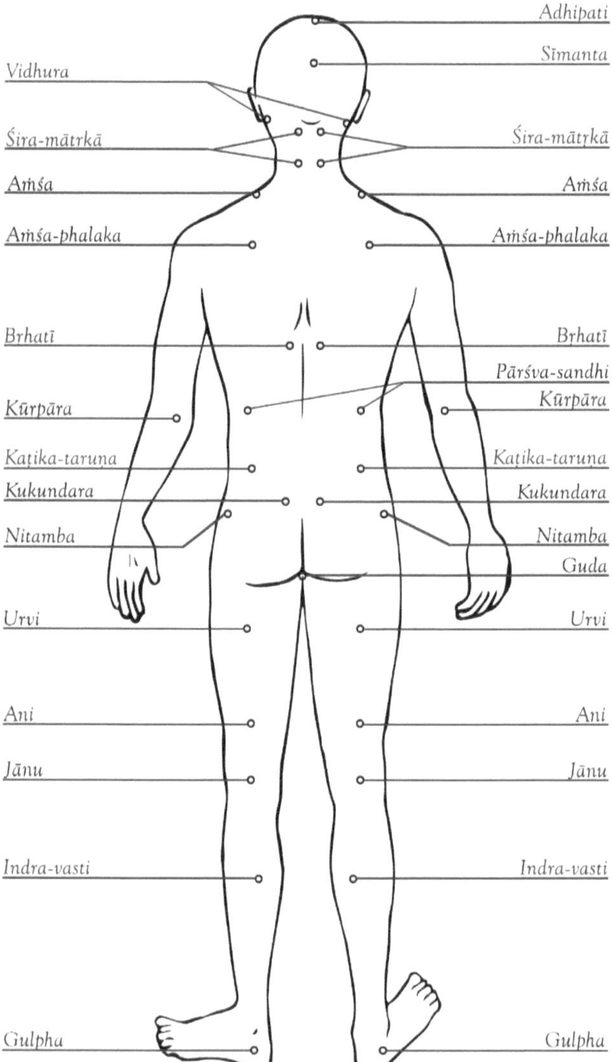

THE REAR *MARMAS*

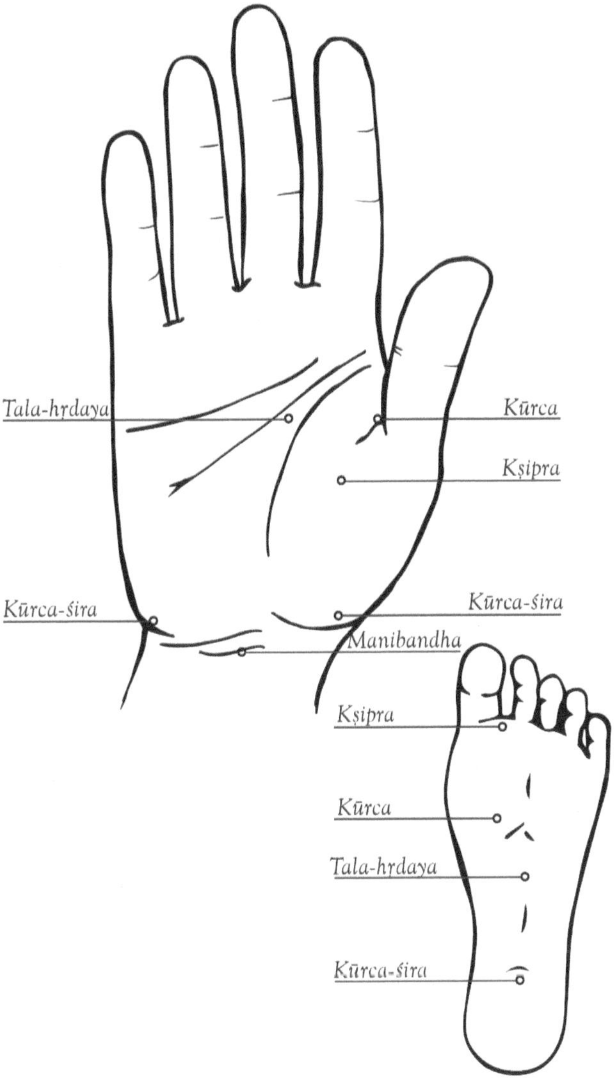

Marmas of hands and feet

The *granthis* or "knots"

The Sanskrit word *granthi* means "knot," symbolizing our earthly attachments. The *granthis* are valves whose main function is to prevent a premature elevation of *kuṇḍalinī*. They protect us, impeding the ascension of the serpentine energy during our spiritual childhood. Until these energetic valves are transcended, elevating the divine fire is impossible.

There are those who seek to gain mystical powers and others who desire particular spiritual experiences. Only few people understand that every spiritual phenomenon is intimately linked to changes in consciousness and is nothing more than a sign of internal development. In the same way, the opening of the *granthis* is a sign of spiritual evolution which is directly related to renunciation and surrender. The three main *granthis* are called Brahmā, Viṣṇu, and Śiva.

Brahma-granthi: It is found in *mūlādhāra-cakra* and corresponds to the tamasic qualities of ignorance and laziness. It rests upon various smaller *granthis* called *bhairavī*, *viśālā*, *cāmundā*, and *śīrṣā*, which remain closed while we continue to be submerged in illusion. This *granthi* is intimately related to our earthly or mundane attachments and is connected to enjoyment of the senses, egoism, and our affinity for storing, accumulating, and hoarding. Without transcending these obstacles, *brahma-granthi* will remain closed. *Sādhakas* must develop wisdom, devotion, and trust in a spiritual master. Only the enthusiastic and determined aspirant will manage to rise above the temptations of *māyā*, or "illusion."

Viṣṇu-granthi: It is found in the pectoral area, obstructing the rising of the serpentine power at *anāhata-cakra*. It corresponds to the qualities related to the modality of passion (*raja-guṇa*). It rests upon four smaller *granthis*: *śyāmala*, *kṛṣṇa*, *nīlāñjana*, and *ṣaṇ-mukha*. It is involved in sentimental attachments to loved ones. The obstacles to transcending *viṣṇu-granthi* are emotional. The opening of this valve is more difficult, as it is simpler to renounce our attachment to money, a car, or a house, than to relinquish our affections. To go beyond this knot, it is recommended to include bhakti yoga in our *sādhana*.

Śiva-granthi* or *rudra-granthi: It is located in *ājñā-cakra*. It is connected to the modality of benevolence (*sattva-guṇa*). This *granthi* rests upon six lower *granthis*: *raudra*, *mukti*, *sānāthya*, *kāpāli*, *kāla-cūḍas*, and *kula-śrava*. It remains closed as long as we are attached to mystical powers, spiritual experiences, and the desire to attain enlightenment. As long as we hold on to our goals, however spiritual they may seem to us, this knot will remain closed. One of the main obstacles to transcending this valve is to perceive ourselves as "something" or "someone," with an existence independent of the Whole. The main impediment is the mistaken conception of ourselves as personalities separate from Totality. This idea, belief, or conception is what we are; therefore, the search for external solutions only exposes our ignorance that we ourselves are the problem. As long as this idea of "I" is present, it is impossible to transcend the *śiva-granthi*.

The serpentine energy will reach the higher centers only when the knots are transcended. *Granthis* are valves that, when open, allow *kuṇḍalinī-śakti* to flow. The functioning of these valves is essential to preserve our progress, because when they close in the opposite direction, they prevent regression. The *sādhana* recommended by the master is intended to prepare us to be an instrument in every aspect and to be appropriate receptacles for the Truth. This practice has an extremely high energetic intensity. The experience of Truth requires an instrument with the proper strength to receive such intensity without the danger of disintegration.

CHAPTER 2

QUALIFICATIONS AND STAGES FOR TANTRIC PRACTICE

Qualifications for Tantra yoga practice

The wisdom of Tantric yoga is extremely profound and complex. Those who want to know it must invest time and energy and be willing to spend a lifetime studying it.

As H.H. Swami Śivānanda Sarasvatī said, "An ounce of practice is worth a ton of theory." This Rishikesh luminary was right. Theory and understanding, no doubt, have value; however, mere speculation will not lead us to substantial changes in our life. This is especially relevant in Tantra, which is more practical than theoretical. The *sādhana* is primordial.

The term *tantra* refers to the expansion of *kuṇḍalinī-śakti*, lying dormant in the first energy center. *Sādhana* is meant to awaken internal potential. Tantra does not believe that divinity is reached only after leaving the physical body. Tantra recognizes that the body is the very place where divinity resides and is also the instrument to experience it. *Tāntrikas* do not theorize based on dreams but work with the body, which is the closest and most immediate reality. If the retroprogressive process is the search for ourselves, it is natural that it would begin with bodily purification.

Tantra is the path of acceptance par excellence. Instead of condemning the body as a tool of sin, Tantra accepts it in its entirety. Instincts and desires are not seen as causes of slavery. Even sense gratification can be a means to transcend the mind's limitations. However, Tantra warns of the dangers of this sublimating attitude without proper guidance.

The mind has the power to tie us to the mundane as well as to free us from it; therefore, Tantric *sādhana* aims not to stop the mind but to direct it positively. Thought can be sublimated on the mental plane. Human beings use only a small amount of their mental capacity; their greatest potential lies in the subconscious. Traditional Tantric *sādhana* aims at awakening this potential. Accepting a spiritual master is of vital importance, and the initiation marks the entrance into the *sādhana* world. Among the practice's internal aspects are identification (*nyāsa*), meditation (*dhyāna*), seals (*mudrās*), purification of parts of the body (*bhūta-śuddhi*), and establishment of the Self (*prāṇa-pratiṣṭhā*).

Although the Tantric tradition has a tremendously rich theology and philosophy, achieving its ideals undoubtedly requires practice. Theory helps us to identify our potential, but practice is the means of applying its metaphysical vision. Only through *sādhana* is it possible to access the Tantric revelation.

Practice is indispensable for development in any discipline. To accelerate inner evolution, training is required. Yoga is the training for all spiritual paths. All paths are accompanied by their own yoga, for example yoga of action (karma), devotion (bhakti), or meditation (*dhyāna*). Similarly, there are Tantric yogas such as hatha yoga, mantra yoga, and *kuṇḍalinī-yoga*. Tantra yoga is the practical aspect of Tantra.

Our conscious life develops within extremely narrow limits. By expanding its frontiers, we can experience life beyond the mind and senses. Tantra offers a *sādhana* rich in linguistic symbology, in the form of mantras, as well as visual elements such as yantras. This *sādhana* is meant to prepare practitioners in every way to overcome mental limitations.

Many scholars believe that the Tantric and Vedic traditions are different, because practices such as *vāmācāra* and *kaula* completely violate Brahman orthodoxy. However, scholars who do not agree with this divide the literature into pro-Vedic and non-Vedic.

Some Tantric and Vedic texts are very similar in both ideas and practices. Some of them, such as the *Kulārṇava Tantra*, even affirm that Tantra is the essence of the Vedic revelation. As in the Tantric literature, its *sādhana* can be classified into Vedic and non-Vedic.

Many Tantric practices are in total discord with Vedic orthodoxy and go against the moral foundations of the Brahmanical tradition.

The Veda is divided into *Karma-kāṇḍa*, *Upāsanā-kāṇḍa*, and *Jñāna-kāṇḍa*. *Karma-kāṇḍa* is the ritualistic section explained in the *Saṁhitās* and *Brāhmaṇas*. These sections teach rites and sacrifices that help cultivate good karma. The highest aspiration of *Karma-kāṇḍa* is a reincarnation in higher worlds. *Upāsanā-kāṇḍa* is explained in the section called *āraṇyakas*, which is about worship and meditation. The *Jñāna-kāṇḍa* section deals with the highest knowledge in pursuit of liberation, explained in the Upanishads. *Karma-kāṇḍa* is the path of *pravṛtti* (go toward), and *Jñāna-kāṇḍa* is the path of *nivṛtti* (get away from). *Pravṛtti* is the permissive attitude, while *nivṛtti* is the repressive one. *Pravṛtti* suggests seeking happiness in the world and enjoying life within the limits of dharma.

Nivṛtti, or *tyāga*, proposes renouncing the world and seeking self-realization, that is, giving up worldly pleasures in pursuit of self-realization. This path is problematic for married people who live in society and have family ties. Obviously, *pravṛtti* and *nivṛtti* advocate opposite directions, but they are harmonized in Tantra, which proposes acting in the world in pursuit of enlightenment. It suggests directing sensual pleasure toward liberation. According to the *Kulārṇava Tantra*, *bhoga* reappears as yoga:

भोगो योगवते साक्षात्पतकं सुकृतायते ।
मोक्षायते च संसारः कुलधर्मे कुलेश्वरि ॥

bhogo yogavate sākṣāt
pulakam sukṛtāyate
mokṣāyate ca saṁsāraḥ
kula-dharme kuleśvari

O Kuleśvarī, on this path of *Kula*, objective worldly enjoyment becomes the means of yoga; what is normally seen as vice becomes virtue, and the world, which is ordinarily a cause of bondage, becomes a means of liberation.

(*Kulārṇava Tantra*, 2.24)

The *Kulārṇava Tantra* states that the pursuit of enjoyment can be directed toward union with consciousness. This refers to external sensual enjoyment with an inner awareness of renunciation. Tantric practices simultaneously contain both *nivṛtti* and *pravṛtti* attitudes, including *kāma*. It is the meeting place of pleasure and renunciation.

Stages of Tantric *sādhana*

Tantric Shaktism divides its *sādhana* into three stages: *paśu* (animal), *vīra* (heroic), and *divya* (divine).

The first stage, or *paśu*, is for everyone. It requires cultivating a moral character, exemplary qualities such as honesty and truthfulness, sensual control, and devotion. It includes community service, social work, and helping those in need. One must be willing to make sacrifices for the welfare of others. *Sādhakas* rise from *paśu* to *vīra* through moral actions.

The *Kāmākhyā Tantra* lists the demands of the *vīra* stage: courage, resolution, being considerate of the needs of others, and so on. Only after entering the *vīra* stage is it possible to accept *dakṣiṇācāra* (right-hand) or *vāmācāra* (left-hand) initiation.

Dakṣiṇācāra initiation is followed by bhakti and *jñāna*. The initiate's life must be socially and morally balanced. Those who choose the *vāmācāra* direction, on the other hand, are initiated into *śakti-mantras* and *pañca-tattvas*; they are spiritually authorized to reject social morality and renounce conservative conceptions of sex. They can associate with the opposite sex free of social prejudice and abandon all prohibitions of food and drink. Through the practice of *pañca-ma-kāra*, under the guidance of a bona fide spiritual master, *sādhakas* rise to the divine stage, or *divya*.

Divya is the highest state reserved only for self-realized souls. At this stage, it is possible to accept *siddhāntācāra* and *kaulācāra* initiation. All worldly and social attachments are renounced. Those who have achieved this extremely high level do not see a woman as an ordinary human being but as a manifestation of Śakti, the universal Mother, worthy of respect and veneration. They are aware that anyone who offends or hurts a woman or allows others to offend her physically, mentally, or emotionally invokes the divine wrath of the Devī.

Those at this stage are as simple and innocent as children. Through meditation, they try to reach the potential femininity that lies within. Only by accessing this pure feminine nature can one really worship the Divine. The elevation from *paśu* to *divya* is the aspiration of every *Śākta Tāntrika*.

According to Tantric *Śākta* literature, that which is human can be transformed into divine. According to the *Kulārṇava Tantra*, this can be achieved through seven religious and spiritual paths: Vedic, *Vaiṣṇava*, *Śaiva*, *Dakṣiṇa*, *Vāma*, *Siddhānta*, and *Kaula*. These seven methods are also called *Ārambha* (beginning), *Taruṇa* (youth), *Yauvana* (adolescence), *Prauḍha* (maturity), *Prauḍhānta* (end of maturity), *Unmanaḥ* (excitement), and *Anavasthā* (attainment).

The Vedic, *Vaiṣṇava*, and *Śaiva* paths can be followed by those at the *paśu* stage, that is, by anyone. The *Dakṣiṇa* and *Vāma* are meant for *vīras*. *Siddhānta* and *Kaula* are reserved for those who are at the *divya*, or divine, stage.

The Vedic path is for corporeal and mental purification. The *Vaiṣṇava* path is meant for devotion, or bhakti. The *Śaiva* path is for knowledge. *Dakṣiṇa* coordinates the first three. *Vāma* is for detachment. *Siddhānta* is for the realization of detachment, and *Kaula* is for *mokṣa*, or "liberation."

CHAPTER 3

ESSENTIAL ELEMENTS OF TANTRIC *SĀDHANA*

Here we will only discuss the essential aspects of Tantric *sādhana*, since detailing all aspects would require its own book. *Sādhana* is meant for both purification and worship. Aspirants purify what they think they are and worship what they really are. The different Tantric *sādhana*s include an immense variety of elements. Those mentioned here are common to all traditions and schools.

Accepting a guru

नास्ति गुर्वधिकं तत्त्वं न शिवाधिकदैवतम् ।
न हि वेदाधिका विद्या न कौलसमदर्शनम् ॥

nāsti gurvadhikaṁ tattvaṁ
na śivādhika-daivatam
na hi vedādhikā vidyā
na kaula-sama-darśanam

There is no principle superior to the guru, there is no God superior to Śiva, there is no knowledge superior to the Veda, and there is no *darśana* equal to the *Kaula*.

(*Kulārṇava Tantra*, 3.113)

The need for a spiritual master is a consensus among all Tantric schools. The role of the guru is essential because the Tantric path can only be walked under expert guidance. Following tradition, we see our guru as God himself. A male guru is considered Śiva and a female one Śakti.

Finding an authentic and competent guru is not an easy task nowadays. According to the *Kulārṇava Tantra*, gurus dispel ignorance of our authentic nature. Our blindness can only be cured by an enlightened guru who has experienced his or her own divine nature and, therefore, has become one with Śiva or Śakti. The *Kulārṇava Tantra* (chapter 13) details the characteristics and meaning of a bona fide guru. It also explains that giving lectures about sex is not enough to be recognized as a Tantric master. According to the scriptures, only a fully enlightened being can be accepted as a Tantric guru; he or she must know the wisdom of mantra and yantra perfectly and be able to eradicate the impurities of disciples, as the *Gautamīya Tantra* clearly states.

ॐ अज्ञानतिमिरान्धस्य ज्ञानाञ्जनशलाकया ॥
चक्षुरुन्मीलितं येन तस्मै श्रीगुरवे नमः ।

oṁ ajñāna-timirāndhasya
jñānāñjana-śalākayā
cakṣur unmīlitaṁ yena
tasmai śrī-gurave namaḥ

Salutations unto that holy guru who, applying the ointment [medicine] of [spiritual] knowledge, removes the darkness of ignorance of the blinded [unenlightened] and opens their eyes.

(*Gautamīya Tantra*, 7.11b–12a)

Initiation or *dīkṣā*

Initiation is one of the fundamental elements of Tantric *sādhana*. The *Viśva-sāra Tantra* defines it as that which eliminates sin and bestows divine knowledge:

दिव्यज्ञानं यतो दद्यात्कुर्यात्पापस्य सन्क्षयम् ।
तस्माद्दीक्षेति स प्रोक्त सर्वतन्त्रसमन्विता ॥

divya-jñānaṁ yato dadyāt
kuryāt pāpasya sankṣayam
tasmād dīkṣeti sa prokta
sarva-tantra-samanvitā

The process that bestows *divya-jñāna* (transcendental spiritual knowledge) and destroys sin is called *dīkṣā* by the spiritual masters.

(*Viśva-sāra Tantra*, Paṭala 2)

Only a genuine guru can perform a proper initiation. There is no point in practicing without first accepting a master and being initiated. Tantric initiation is available to all adepts who are willing to accept the implications of being a disciple. It is considered the main step toward liberation. The *Kulārṇava Tantra* emphatically states that one cannot attain *mokṣa* without *dīkṣā*.

Grace descends from its highest origins through the spiritual master. This initiation is called *śakti-pāta-dīkṣā*. *Śakti-pāta* is a Sanskrit word composed of the terms *śakti*, or "divine energy," and *pāta*, or "descent." Grace descends through the guru and is assimilated according to the disciple's capacity. Aspirants must first purify themselves to become adequate recipients. Initiation occurs as an interaction between the guru and the disciple. *Śakti-pāta-dīkṣā* awakens *puruṣa-jñāna*, or "transcendental wisdom," and removes the chains that bind us to the relative world. It is not an intellectual transmission of conceptual knowledge, or *vaikalpika*. Rather, it is an awakening at the level of consciousness, so it is based on self-experience, or *pūrṇā-hantā*. Transcendental wisdom is not acquired from the outside but is unveiled from inner depths. It lies in every human being but is covered by veils of impurities.

There are three kinds of Tantric initiation: that of the bird, the fish, and the turtle. The first is through physical contact, just as the bird nourishes its brood with the warmth of its wings. The second is by sight, just as the fish feeds its young. The third is by thought, just as the turtle feeds its offspring simply by thinking about them. The bird initiation is the most powerful, with the master personally injecting *śakti* into the disciple through the third eye, or *ājñā-cakra*. Initiation can be executed in person or remotely, through an object or even through a letter, an email, or a telephone conversation.

There are a great variety of initiations, depending on the disciple's level. A simple initiation is called *kriyā-dīkṣā* and extraordinary ones are called *vedha-dīkṣā*.

Generally, initiation includes the following elements:

- Granting a mantra.
- Sacrifice, or *homa*.
- Physical postures, or asanas.
- Expansion of vital energy, or *prāṇāyāma*.
- Concentration, or *dhāraṇā*.
- Meditation, or *dhyāna*.
- Practice in symbolic diagrams, or *sādhana* yantra.
- *Kuṇḍalinī-yoga* practices, such as *ṣaṭ-cakra-bheda*.

Through the aforementioned forms of initiation, the spiritual master first purifies aspirants and then transmits divine energy to them. This transfer is intended to awaken the potential that lies deep within them. However, this will happen only if the master is an enlightened soul who has awakened and raised his or her own *kuṇḍalinī-śakti*. Only a burning candle can light another one.

Śakti-pāta initiation is usually associated with divine grace, because it is not achieved by being good or by lots of practice. Abhinavagupta says: "Both *śakti-pāta* and devotion to God are independent of family, caste, body, actions, age, practices, and money." Initiation cannot be demanded; it is an act of grace (*anugraha*) done by the master. Consciousness itself descends through the guru. Grace comes through contact with an enlightened spiritual master; however, it is not given by the master but comes from God. An enlightened master is a conduit that is pure enough to allow divine energy to flow and descend.

Enlightenment is impossible unless all ties have been completely cut. These ties are the three *malas*, or impurities: *āṇava-mala*, *māyīya-mala*, and *karma-mala*. *Mala* is a contraction of consciousness that causes the absolute totality to be seen as separate individuality. *Āṇava-mala* is the impurity of individuality and personality that causes us to perceive ourselves as "someone" separate. *Māyīya-mala* is the mental aspect that contains comparison. Finally, *karma-mala* refers to the body and its relation to *prārabdha-karma*. Initiation removes these obstacles.

Bhūta-śuddhi or "bodily purification"

The term *śuddhi* means "purification." *Bhūta-śuddhi* is the bodily purification that is essential before any ritual. Aspirants are unsuitable for any kind of worship without having first purified themselves. According to the *Kulārṇava Tantra*, purification of substance, place, mantra, deity, and Self are required.

The place of worship should be kept clean, decorated with flowers, and perfumed with incense, which facilitates concentration on the deity. Substance is purified by water. The deity is purified by installing it on its seat and performing the *prāṇa-pratiṣṭhā* ritual, or "the infusion of life." The body is considered the abode of the Self and is cleansed to create an environment of both internal and external purity.

Exterior purification is carried out with hygienic practices, such as bathing and brushing our teeth. For interior purification, *nyāsa*, *prāṇāyāma*, and other practices are used. These processes, besides eradicating lower energies that neutralize benign powers, create propitious conditions and prepare a welcoming place to cordially invoke supernatural powers.

Aspirants cannot manipulate God, but they can facilitate his revelation by creating the appropriate situation through *sādhana*. During *bhūta-śuddhi*, each bodily part is offered to the deity, and minor deities are invoked to occupy places within the body.

Our physical body is composed of the five basic elements, or *pañca-mahā-bhūtas*: earth (*pṛthivī*), water (*āpas*), fire (*agni*), air (*vāyu*), and ether (*ākāśa*). Bodily cleansing is achieved by creating harmony between these elements. Aspirants mentally visualize different parts of the body and concentrate on their predominant element. *Pṛthivī* predominates from the feet to the thighs; *āpas*, from the thighs to the navel; *agni*, from the navel to the heart; *vāyu*, from the heart to the eyebrows; *ākāśa*, above the eyebrows. Next, the absorption of grosser elements in the subtler ones is visualized: earth in water, water in fire, fire in air, air in ether, ether in the ego, the ego in nature, and nature in the Absolute.

According to Tantra, every human being exists in a state of physical and mental impurity called *pāpa-puruṣa*, or "impure human being." Through the process of *bhūta-śuddhi*, impurities gradually fade away until aspirants can be considered fit to work with spiritual power, or *śakti*. The process is performed through *bīja-mantras* of the air and fire elements, which turn the impure body into ashes. Later, with the nectar that flows from *sahasrāra-cakra*, a totally new pure body is gradually created, which manifests itself from the Lord of *prakṛti*, from *prakṛti* to the intellect, from the intellect to the ego, from the ego to ether, from ether to air, from air to fire, from fire to water, from water to earth, from earth to plants, from plants to food, from food to semen, and from semen to *puruṣa*, which is "I am." This "I am" is not the ego, but the individuality that is born from the deep experience of self-realization. Without having gone through this process, aspirants are not in a position to worship a deity. According to Tantra, worship transforms the worshippers and takes them to the heights of the Divine.

Nyāsa or "mental purification"

After purifying the body, next is mental purification, which is subtler. *Bhūta-śuddhi* includes not only eliminating impurities but also the installation or placement of the Divine. Upon dissolving the impure body and constructing a purely spiritual one, the body is charged with *prāṇa*, or Divinity. This internal creation of the deity begins with *nyāsa*. The word *nyāsa* comes from *nyas*, or "to place." The *Kulārṇava Tantra* describes various kinds of *nyāsa*: the *nyāsa* of the mantra, *mahā-ṣoḍhā-nyāsa*, *karanyāsa*, and so on.

Nyāsa is performed by placing the fingertips on different parts of the body. In *mātṛkā-nyāsa*, for example, Sanskrit letters are placed on the extremities. *Mātṛkā-nyāsa* has two components: external (*bahir*) and internal (*āntar*). In the first, the letters are placed on the extremities, and in the second, on the six chakras. The letters of the Sanskrit alphabet are considered to be manifestations of *Śabda-brahman*, and therefore, are deities.

Through *vyāpaka-nyāsa*, aspirants expand their consciousness, become divine themselves, and in this way, worship God. Since human beings are what they think, they can change their personalities through thoughts. Focusing their attention on the Divine, aspirants move away from the mundane.

After corporeal and mental purification, aspirants give life to the deity through a ritual called *prāṇa-pratiṣṭhā*, or "the installation of life."

Yantras

Initially, aspirants worship the deities Viṣṇu, Śiva, or the Devī. At more advanced levels, these images are replaced by yantras. This change from deities to yantras represents a step from the gross to the subtle.

The literal meaning of the Sanskrit term *yantra* is "machine." It is a powerful instrument or tool capable of awakening different powers and energy circuits in *sādhakas*. Both yantras and mantras are important in Tantra yoga since their combination—which intermingles form and sound—generates an expansive movement of consciousness.

Each mantra has its visual equivalent, which is the geometric shape of a certain sound. Yantras are geometric shapes that represent the essential nature of the *deva*'s energy and, therefore, must be respected and venerated as if they were the deity itself. These mystical diagrams fulfill the same function as the mantras: they serve as a stimulus for meditation and help tune into the universe. Just as there are many mantras, we have yantras of different deities that help us to meditate on specific aspects of divinity.

In rituals, it is customary to draw yantras on the ground; in installations, they are usually engraved on metal plates. Yantras are links between the gross and the subtle. Through concentration, aspirants introduce vital energy into yantras, which is essential to make them effective. In fact, they adore their own vital energy they themselves imbued into the yantra. According to *Śākta Tantra*, the universe is a manifestation or expression of energy, although an ordinary person is not aware of this. What is worshipped cannot be inferior to the worshippers; therefore, they must infuse vital energy into yantras. This process is carried out by repeating mantras (*japa* and *puraś-caraṇa*).

Mantras

Mantras are essential to Tantric *sādhana* and are required for all rituals. A mantra is a sound that contains a powerful mystical energy; it is a transcendental vibration that encapsulates a power capable of freeing our minds from the clutches of *māyā*. First of all, it should be clarified that Tantric mantras are only in Sanskrit. A mantra is received through initiation and is never used from a book. The *Nirukta* (7.12.1) defines it as *mantra mananāt*, that is, it is called mantra because one reflects or meditates on it. Pāṇini, in his *Dhātu-pāṭha* (1.199), explains it as *matri gupta-paribāṣaṇe*: the grammatical root is *mantr* used in the sense of "speaking in secret" (*mantrī* is the secret conversation between the king and his advisors or between masters and disciples).

Mantra is a very important means of liberation from the mind, as stated in the *Kulārṇava Tantra*:

मननात्तत्त्वरूपस्य देवस्यामिततेजसः ।
त्रायते सर्वभयतस्तस्मान्मन्त्र इतीरितः ॥

mananāt tattva-rūpasya
devasyāmita-tejasaḥ
trāyate sarva-bhayatas
tasmān mantra itīritaḥ

> Through contemplation (*manana*) on the deity, whose form is reality and who has unlimited radiance, the mantra saves (*trāyate*) one from all fear, therefore it is known as *mantra*.
> (*Kulārṇava Tantra*, 17.54)

Mantras are like genes or mystical DNA that allow us to directly connect with the essence of yoga. They are transcendental and come from the spiritual plane. Since they are the names of God collected by the millennial Vedic literature, it is of utmost importance that they are pronounced and repeated with deep devotion. Mantras are sounds or sacred vibrations that have the ability to affect our energy centers (chakras) and generate serenity, peace, tranquility, and states of consciousness conducive to meditation. Hence repeating mantras is an invitation for the transcendental to manifest within us.

There are a great variety of mantras that serve different purposes. In general, they can be divided into four groups: friendly, helpful, supportive, and destructive. Some may have certain mundane purposes (*bhoga*), while others pursue liberation (*mokṣa*).

At the time of initiation, the guru chooses a mantra based on the disciple's personality. This mantra must be repeated constantly in the practice called *japa*. Tantra offers techniques and practices that instruct the *sādhaka* how to use mantras for specific purposes. Tantra thus addresses both philosophy and practice.

Japa

Repeating a mantra is called *japa*, or "muttering." This has been a very important practice since antiquity. It is part of the royal path, or raja yoga, and one of the aspects of *svādhyāya*, or "study." *Svādhyāya* has two components: studying sacred scriptures and repeating mantras. Through repetition, it is possible to develop mastery.

Japa is considered to be one of the most effective methods for mental purification. All aspirants must be initiated in a mantra by a guru and learn how to practice *japa* correctly. Mental repetition is the most effective practice. For distracted minds, vocal or semi-vocal practice is advised with a *mala* of 108 beads while sitting in *sukhāsana* or *padmāsana*. At advanced stages, *japa* is only mental and can be practiced even while walking or working.

Many practice *japa* to get help in achieving goals: health, work, protection, money, and so on. However, those who have ulterior motives abandon the practice upon obtaining the results. The highest *japa* practice lacks expectations and is performed solely for the pleasure it bestows. Only those who practice *japa* without selfish reasons purify their minds and create conditions for enlightenment.

After bathing and sitting in a comfortable position in a peaceful and silent place, *sādhakas* repeat the mantra in which they have been initiated. There are three ways to repeat the mantra: *vācika-japa* (aloud), *upāṁśu-japa* (muttered), and *mānasika-japa* (mentally). Mechanical repetition does not provide real benefits. *Japa* must be combined with meditation and the mantra must be repeated with observation. At a certain moment, *japa* will fall away by itself and only meditation will remain, naturally and spontaneously.

Japa practice can by itself grant peace and bliss since it targets the experience of divinity within us. As stated in the last chapter of the *Kulārṇava Tantra*:

जन्मान्तरसहस्रेषु कृतपापप्रणाशनात् ।
परदेवप्रकाशाच्च जप इत्यभिधीयते ॥

janmāntara-sahasreṣu
kṛta-pāpa-praṇāśanāt
para-deva-prakāśāc ca
japa ity abhidhīyate

> *Japa* is so called because it removes the sins accumulated in thousands of lives and reveals the supreme deity.
>
> (*Kulārṇava Tantra*, 17.34)

The universe is made of sound manifestations. The repetition of a mantra, or a name of the deity, creates a specific vibration at the level of consciousness that prepares us to experience the Absolute.

Bhāva or "disposition"

Bhāva, or "disposition," is of paramount importance to Tantric *sādhana*. The *Rudra Yāmala* emphatically states that the deity does not reside in stone or clay, but in disposition, or *bhāva*.

Tantra gives great importance to the power of thought and therefore emphasizes mental worship. Tantric *sādhana* dispels the worshipper–worshipped duality as the identities of the devotee and the deity merge. The stages from duality to union are marked by the aspirant's *bhāvas*. Three kinds of dispositions are recommended: *paśu-bhāva*, *vīra-bhāva*, and *divya-bhāva*, which are tamasic, rajasic, and sattvic, respectively.

Paśu-bhāva: The root of the word *paśu* is *pas*, or "to bind." A *paśu* is a person enslaved by desires, or *vāsanās*, that is, anyone controlled by impulses to satisfy the senses. The predominant quality in this disposition is *tamas* (inertia) and its characteristics are *ālasya* (lethargy) and *jāḍya* (rigidity). Ignorance, or *ajñāna*, does not allow the *paśu* to transcend external *sādhana* and penetrate its subtle levels.

The *Kulārṇava Tantra* mentions eight different *pāśas*, or "bonds":

घृणा शङ्का भयं लज्जा जुगुप्सा चेति पञ्चमी ।
कुलं शीलं तथा जातिरष्टौ पाशाः प्रकीर्तिताः ॥

ghṛṇā śaṅkā bhayaṁ lajjā
jugupsā ceti pañcamī
kulaṁ śīlaṁ tathā jātir
aṣṭau pāśāḥ prakīrtitāḥ

> Pity (*ghṛṇā*), doubt (*śaṅkā*), fear (*bhaya*), shame (*lajjā*), disgust (*jugupsā*), family (*kula*), disposition (*śīla*), and caste (*jāti*)—these are the eight bonds.
>
> (*Kulārṇava Tantra*, 13.90)

In other Tantric scriptures, three kinds of bonds are described: impurities (*malas*), past actions (karma), and illusions (*māyā*). Impurities are the fundamental bonds that must be overcome in order to transcend *paśu-bhāva*. The only way to remove *malas* is through initiation by a spiritual master.

Vīra-bhāva: *Rajas* is the predominating mode in this disposition. Those who are in this *bhāva* can discriminate between suffering and true happiness. As they control their senses, greed, and lust, they can participate in advanced practices such as *pañca-ma-kāra* without leaving spiritual life.

Divya-bhāva: *Sattva* is the predominant *guṇa* in this disposition. *Divya-bhāva* is "oneness with the chosen deity" and anyone situated in this oneness enjoys the bliss of the divine *bhāva*. As pointed out by the *Mahānirvāṇa Tantra*, the *sādhaka* in this *bhāva* transcends the worshipper–worshipped duality.

Tantric *sādhana* is not only intended to prepare the right situation for enlightenment to occur, but is also meant to unveil the immense physical, mental, and energetic potential that human beings hold. It offers *sādhakas* various techniques to uncover and develop their inner power. For this purpose, it deals with physical, mental, and energetic purification through mantras and hatha yoga. The hatha yoga system—its asanas (postures), *prāṇāyāma* (expansion of vital energy), relaxation, and so on—is important to Tantric practice.

Tantric *sādhana* begins with a *saṅkalpa*, or "resolution," to cultivate the *sādhaka's* will.

We must remember that this path is full of dangers. It is very easy to fall into *māyā*, or "illusion." It is not recommended to walk this path without the guidance of an enlightened spiritual master, especially when aspirants enter the world of secret practices. Only the master's instructions will prevent the disciple from falling into the trap of simple sensual licentiousness. Within Tantric *sādhana*, we find practices accepted by society, secret practices, and others designed to satisfy mundane desires.

The first type of *sādhana* is accepted by society and respected by the general public. It includes the acceptance of a guru.

The second type is rejected by society and includes practices such as *pañca-ma-kāra*, which involve *madya* (wine), *māṁsa* (meat), *matsya* (fish), *mudrā* (fermented grains), and *maithuna* (sexual intercourse).

This *sādhana* also involves *cakra-sādhana*, or *cakra-pūjā*, which is a practice of the five *ma-kāras* in a meeting of at least two couples, although ideally it should be a group of 7–10 couples who meet in a secret place, usually a cemetery. This ritual includes a process of deep purification before sexual contact. Through *cakra-pūjā*, an expansion of consciousness is achieved.

This second kind of *sādhana* also includes:

- Animal sacrifices.
- *Svagātra-rudhira-māṁsa-sādhana*, or "the practice of offering blood and flesh from one's own body."
- *Citā-sādhana*, or "the practice with the help of the funeral pyre."
- *Śava-sādhana*, or "meditation on a corpse," in a secret place, usually a cemetery.
- *Muṇḍa-sādhana*, or "the practice that is performed sitting on three or five animal or human heads."
- The third type of *sādhana* includes practices such as *ṣaṭ-karma*, or "six types of hidden *sādhana*." These are the following:
- *Śānti*, or "practices for healing or to exorcise evils."
- *Vaśī-karaṇa*, or "practices for enchanting or controlling somebody."
- *Stambhana*, or "practices for preventing an event from happening."
- *Vidveṣaṇa*, or "practices for creating a hostile relationship between certain people."
- *Uccāṭana*, or "practices for unbalancing the mind of a certain person."
- *Māraṇa*, or "practices for destroying a human being."

Tantric *sādhana* of the second and third type is considered extremely delicate and even dangerous without the proper guidance of an authoritative and bona fide spiritual master.

The *Mantra-yoga Saṁhitā* refers to the *sādhana* of Tantra yoga in the following way:

उपासनाविधौ यस्तु भावो बाह्यक्रियाश्रयः ।
आचारः कथ्यते सोऽसौ तन्त्रशास्त्रप्रवर्तकैः ॥

upāsanā-vidhau yas tu
bhāvo bāhya-kriyāśrayaḥ
ācāraḥ kathyate so 'sau
tantra-śāstra-pravartakaiḥ

The external ritual, which has been incorporated in the procedure of worship (*upāsanā*), is called *ācāra* by the proponents of *Tantra Śāstras*.

विष्णुसूर्यगणेशानां शिवस्योपासनासु च ।
चतसृष्वयमाचारो भवत्येकविधः सदा ॥

viṣṇu-sūrya-gaṇeśānāṁ
śivasyopāsanāsu ca
catasṛṣvayam ācāro
bhavaty eka-vidhaḥ sadā

These *ācāras* are always identical for the worship of the following four: Viṣṇu, Sūrya (the Sun), Gaṇeśa, and Śiva.

द्विविधस्तु भवत्येव वामदक्षिणभेदतः ।
आचारः शक्तिपूजायां सर्वतन्त्रानुसारतः ॥

dvi-vidhas tu bhavaty eva
vāma-dakṣiṇa-bhedataḥ
ācāraḥ śakti-pūjāyāṁ
sarva-tantrānusārataḥ

But for the worship of Śakti, the *ācāra*, according to all *Tantra Śāstras*, is of two types only, namely, *vāma* (*vāmācāra*) and *dakṣiṇa* (*dakṣiṇācāra*).

शक्तिप्राधान्यतश्चास्मिञ्छक्तिपूजाविधौ नृणाम् ।
साधनानां सुविस्तारः क्रियते तत्त्वदर्शिभिः ॥

śakti-prādhānyataś cāsmiñ
chakti-pūjā-vidhau nṛṇām
sādhanānāṁ su-vistāraḥ
kriyate tattva-darśibhiḥ

Due to the importance of Śakti, the seers of the Truth have elaborated greatly on the procedures for worship of this Śakti.

अधिकारोऽत्र पूजायां द्विविधो दृश्यते तथा ।
तन्त्रेषु बहुविस्तारः शक्तिपूजाविधेरभूत् ॥

adhikāro 'tra pūjāyāṁ
dvi-vidho dṛśyate tathā
tantreṣu bahu-vistāraḥ
śakti-pūjā-vidher abhūt

The rights in case of this worship are also seen to be described as two-fold. There has been a great deal of elaboration of the Śakti.

दक्षिणाचारतो योऽयं विपरीतो भवेदिह ।
वामाचारः स विज्ञेयस् तन्त्रशास्त्रविशारदैः ॥

dakṣiṇācārato yo 'yaṁ
viparīto bhaved iha
vāmācāraḥ sa vijñeyas
tantra-śāstra-viśāradaiḥ

> The adepts of the *Tantra Śāstras* have given the name *vāmācāra* to that which is the opposite of *dakṣiṇācāra*.
>
> (*Mantra-yoga Saṁhitā*, 42.1–6)

Sādhana differs according to the types of Tantric followers. As stated by the *Kulārṇava Tantra*, they are divided into *vaidikācāra*, *vaiṣṇavācāra*, *śaivācāra*, *dakṣiṇācāra*, *vāmācāra*, *siddhāntācāra*, and *kaulācāra*.

While the worship of Viṣṇu, Sūrya, Gaṇeśa, and Śiva is identical, the worship of Śakti is different and is divided into two diametrically opposed types: *vāmācāra* and *dakṣiṇācāra*.

Dakṣinācāras follow "the path of the right hand" according to the *Śrī-vidyā* tradition. Their *sādhana* mainly consists in the study and interpretation of the sacred texts, celibacy, renunciation, and distancing themselves from the phenomenal realm.

Vāmācāras, who follow "the path of the left hand"—the path of the phenomenal—use elements forbidden by orthodox paths, such as sex, wine, and meat. The left-hand Tantric path manages to overcome sin and transcend even virtue. For all Hindus, the left hand is a sign of impure activities; therefore, its name indicates that it is the art of using that which is dirty to clean, what is impure to purify, what is low to elevate. Its attitude is completely contrary to repression, although it simultaneously aims at transformation. In short, it affirms nature and aims to transcend it.

Brahmanical orthodoxy emphasizes the renunciation of worldly society. Contrary to what many believe, the Tantric vision does not conflict with asceticism. Quite the contrary, it suggests transcending all attachments to the mind and its enslaving demands.

Tantra seeks freedom from everything and everyone, including from ourselves as mental beings. However, Tantra sees renunciation as a phenomenon that occurs deep within the *sādhaka* and not on the surface. Authentic renunciation happens at the very roots of our being and not in the objective world.

According to the Tantric vision, renunciation is about the one who renounces and not to what is renounced. One does not need to escape from the object but to transcend the attachment to it. That is, hiding vanilla cookies will not help transcend our attachment to them.

The Tantric interpretation of renunciation and asceticism finds its best expression in the *Cinācāra* path. For example, the *Mahā-cīnācāra-krama Tantra* describes this ritual in detail:

आनीयोच्चतमां भद्रामेकशः कुलनायिकां ।
सुन्दरींयौवनोन्मत्तां निर्लज्जां चारुहासिनीं ।
कृत्वा दिगम्बरीं तांच गन्धचन्दन कुंकुमैः ।
अनुलिप्तां मुक्तकेशीं ततस्ताद्योनिमण्डले ।
पीठपूजां विधायाय्य तन्मध्ये पूजयेच्छिवां ।
उपचारैः पूजयित्वा चार्घ्यं दत्वा ततः पुनः ।
जप्त्वालिङ्गे भैरवञ्च पूजयित्वा महेश्वरीम् ।
गन्धासवाक्षतैः पुष्पैर्होमं कुर्य्यादतः परं ।
पूजाकालं विनानैव पश्येच्छक्तिं दिगम्बरीम् ।
पूजाकालं विनानैव सुरापेये च साधकः ।
अथवा हीयते दृष्ट्वा पीत्वापि नरकं व्रजेत् ।

ānīyoccatamāṁ bhadrām
ekaśaḥ kula-nāyikāṁ
sundarīṁ yauvanonmattāṁ
nirlajjāṁ cāru-hāsinīṁ

kṛtvā dig-ambarīṁ tāṁ ca
gandha-candana-kuṁkumaiḥ
anuliptāṁ mukta-keśīṁ
tatas tād yoni-maṇḍale

pīṭha-pūjāṁ vidhāyāyya
tan madhye pūjayec chivāṁ
upacāraiḥ pūjayitvā
cārghyaṁ datvā tataḥ punaḥ
japtvā liṅge bhairavañ ca
pūjayitvā maheśvarīm

gandhāsavākṣataiḥ puṣpair
homaṁ kuryyād ataḥ paraṁ

pūjā-kālāṁ vinā naiva
paśyec chaktiṁ dig-ambarīm
pūjā-kālaṁ vinā naiva
sura-peye ca sādhakaḥ

athavā hīyate dṛṣṭvā
pītvāpi narakaṁ vrajet

In order to perform the ritual, a beautiful young woman must be procured, in the prime of her life, who is not shy and has a smiling countenance; she must undress completely, and her body should be smeared with perfumes. Next, the *sādhaka* should worship the Divine Mother in her private parts in the prescribed manner. The worshipper must then continue with *prāṇāyāma* and maintain a calm mind, thinking that the Divine Mother is there. And he should never see a naked woman or drink wine except at the time of worship; if he does, he will surely go to hell.

(*Mahā-cīnācāra-krama Tantra*, 3.13–21)

The text is very emphatic on this point. The whole process is performed in the presence of the guru, who guides the disciple. The worshipper is reminded that all deities have their place in the woman's body, and hence the worship of the woman is considered the highest.

यतो हि योषितो देहे सर्वदेवस्य संस्थितिः ।
अतः पूजासु सर्वसु तासाम् प्राधान्यमुच्य ते ॥

yato hi yoṣito dehe
sarva-devasya saṁsthitiḥ
ataḥ pūjāsu sarvasu
tāsām prādhānyam ucyate

Indeed, in the female body, all the *devas* are situated. Therefore, it is said that to worship it is the supreme type of worship.

(*Mahā-cīnācāra-krama Tantra*, 3.5)

In this context, the three *pīṭhas* are mentioned: *yonī-piṭha* (worship in the *yonī*), *Mantra-pīṭha* (worship with the help of mantras), and *manaḥpīṭha* (mental worship). The *yonī-pīṭha* is the highest of all.

The text recommends that the worshipped woman be an actress, a *Kāpālinī*, a prostitute, a washerwoman, a hairdresser, a woman belonging to the Brahmanical caste, a *śūdra*, or a milkmaid. The lady, called *kulastrī*, must know Tantric teachings well, be very attached to her spiritual master, and be versed in a variety of mantras.

The text recommends that women to be worshipped will be:

नटी कापालिनी वेश्या रजकी नापिताङ्गना ।
ब्राह्मणी शूद्रकन्या च तथा गोपालकन्यका ॥

naṭī kāpālinī veśyā
rajakī nāpitāṅganā
brāhmaṇī śūdra-kanyā ca
tathā gopāla-kanyakā

An actress, a *Kāpālinī*, a prostitute, a washerwoman, a female hairdresser, a woman from the *Brāhmaṇa* caste, a *śudra*, or a milkmaid.

(*Mahā-cīnācāra-krama Tantra*, 3.10)

विदग्धा सर्वजातीया मन्त्रयुक्ता च तत् परा ।
गुरुपादगता ग्राह्या मान्यथा वरवर्णिनी ॥

vidugdhā sarva jātīyā
mantra-yuktā ca tat parā
guru-pāda-gatā grāhyā
mānyathā vara-varṇinī

(The lady, called *kula-strī*) must know Tantric teachings well and be versed in a variety of mantras, be very attached to her spiritual master, be well respected, and be the best of women.

(*Mahā-cīnācāra-krama Tantra*, 3.18)

The *kula-strī* is not necessarily one's own wife but a woman chosen to act as the female within the ritual. There are a great variety of practices with a *kula-strī* in which her menstrual blood is essential. While every woman represents the divine *śakti*, the *kumārī* (virgin maiden) is preferred because the Devī is more pleased with the worship of virginity.

So the ritual does not take a wrong turn, both the woman and the *sādhaka* must be advanced disciples. It is suggested that after worshipping the intimate parts of the woman, the *sādhaka* worships his own sexual organ.

अनुलिप्तां मुक्तकेशीं ततस्तद्योनिमण्डले ।
पीठपूजां विधायाथ तन्मध्ये पूजयेच्छिवाम् ॥
उपचारैः पूजयित्वा चार्घ्यं दत्वा ततः पुनः ।
जप्त्वा लिङ्गे भैरवञ्च पुजयित्वा महेश्वरीम् ॥

anuliptāṁ mukta-keśīṁ
tatas tad yoni-maṇḍale
pīṭha-pūjāṁ vidhāyātha
tan madhye pūjayec chivām

upacāraiḥ pūjayitvā
cārghyaṁ datvā tataḥ punaḥ
japtvā liṅge bhairavañ ca
pujayitvā maheśvarīm

Thereupon, there, in the middle of the *yoni-maṇḍala*, the anointed limbed Maheśvarī, Mukta-keśī, Śivā (the Divine Mother), should be worshipped. After being worshipped by the ceremony, and then offered water again, and after offering prayers in a low voice, Bhairava should be worshipped in the *liṅga*.

(*Mahā-cīnācāra-krama Tantra*, 3.15–16)

In addition, scriptures such as the *Kāmākhyā Tantra* affirm that it is preferable to practice *pañca-ma-kāra* with another man's wife or with a prostitute because it is difficult to see our own partner as a mother.

Works such as the *Kāmākhyā Tantra* carry Tantric practices to such an extreme that for an ordinary human being they are almost impossible to execute. For instance, it states that the *sādhaka* must kiss the woman, place his nails on her buttocks, and finally penetrate her, but without ejaculating. While embracing her, he must be able to mutter his mantra eight thousand times. For those who are not able to execute this worship successfully, it is recommended to look at the intimate parts of the woman while resting one's attention on the Divine Mother of the Universe. This must be repeated for seven consecutive nights. Tantric enjoyment entails an authentic renunciation, as stated in the *Mahā-cīnācāra-krama*:

योगी चेन्नैव भोगी स्याद्भोगी चेन्न तु योगवान् ।
योगभोगात्मकं कौलं तस्मात्सर्वाधिकं त्विदम् ॥

yogī cen na iva bhogī syād
bhogī cen na tu yogavān
yoga-bhogātmakaṁ kaulaṁ
tasmāt sarvādhikaṁ tvidam

Whoever is a yogi cannot be a *bhogī* and whoever is a *bhogī* cannot be a yogi; but anyone who is a *Kaula* is a *yoga-bhogātmaka* (union of yoga and *bhoga*) and therefore should be considered supreme.

(*Mahā-cīnācāra-krama Tantra*, 4.42)

(The above verse also appears, with minor differences, in the *Kulārṇava Tantra*, 2.23)

Similarly, the *Kumārī Tantra* states that any worshipper who performs this *sādhana* for the sole purpose of enjoying sensual pleasure will fall into hell. The *Kulārṇava Tantra* states that if by only drinking wine one could attain enlightenment, then every drunkard would be an enlightened saint. If simply by eating meat one could achieve bliss, then every meat-eater would have attained the supreme goal.

मद्यपानेन मनुजो यदि सिद्धिं लभेत वै ।
मद्यापानरताः सर्वे सिद्धिं गच्छन्तु पामराः ॥

madya-pānena manujo
yadi siddhiṁ labheta vai
madyā-pāna-ratāḥ sarve
siddhiṁ gacchantu pāmarāḥ

If merely by drinking wine men attained fulfillment, all wicked drunkards would reach perfection.

मांसभक्षणमात्रेण यदि पुण्या गतिर्भवेत् ।
लोके मांसाशिनः सर्वे पुण्यभाजो भवन्ति हि ॥

māṁsa-bhakṣaṇa-mātreṇa
yadi puṇyā gatir bhavet
loke māṁsāśinaḥ sarve
puṇya-bhājo bhavanti hi

If merely eating meat led to a higher state, all the carnivores in the world would be eligible for immense merit.

शक्तिसम्भोगमात्रेण यदि मोक्षो भवेत वै ।
सर्वेऽपि जन्तवो लोके मुक्ताः स्युः स्त्रीनिषेवनात् ॥

śakti-sambhoga-mātreṇa
yadi mokṣo bhaveta vai
sarve 'pi jantavo loke
muktāḥ syuḥ strī-niṣevanāt

If liberation were ensured by merely living with a woman, all creatures would become liberated through female companionship.

(*Kulārṇava Tantra*, 2.117–119)

Because this work is highly accredited about the *pañca-ma-kāra*, its statements reveal the nature of this *sādhana*.

The *Gāndharva Tantra* and the *Kumarī Tantra* also seriously warn against performing this *sādhana* just for the sake of enjoyment.

अर्थाद्वा कामतो वापि सौख्यादपि च यो नरः ।
लिङ्गयोनिरतो मन्त्री रौरवं नरकं व्रजेत् ॥

arthād vā kāmato vāpi
saukhyād api ca yo naraḥ
liṅga-yoni-rato mantrī
rauravaṁ narakaṁ vrajet

If a worshipper performs this activity for the following two purposes, sense enjoyment or material benefit, he will reach a terrible hell.

(*Kumarī Tantra*, as quoted by Kṛṣṇānanda Agamavāgīśa in his *Bṛhad-tantra-sāra*)

It is obvious that this practice demands a very high degree of sincerity and honesty. This *sādhana* is not intended for sexual pleasure or enjoyment, but for examining to what extent the objects of desire dominate the mind. The *sādhaka* does not escape from the objects that may awaken instinct but remains fixed in the Absolute.

Chapter 4

Types of Tantric *Sādhana*

Sādhana according to the *guṇas*

Sādhana can also be classified as black, red, and white Tantra, which correspond to the three *guṇas*. We have already explained that the Tantric path extends from the initial level of *paśu* through *vīra* to *divya*. These correspond to the *guṇas*: *tamas*, *rajas*, and *sattva*.

Black Tantra is tamasic, related to the mode of ignorance, and its practice is called *paśu*, or *paśvācāra*.

Red Tantra is rajasic, related to passion. It developed in North India, especially in Kashmir, and follows the *sādhana* of *vīra*, or *vīrācāra*.

White Tantra corresponds to *sattva*, and its *sādhana* includes group meditations that balance feminine and masculine aspects. The *sādhana* of *divya*, or *divyācāra*, is the highest and most abstract of all.

The type of worship varies with the *sādhaka's* competence, personality, and temperament. Methods that may be appropriate for certain people are irrelevant and even harmful to others.

The vast majority of human beings are *paśus* and their attitude is earthly. This group feels attracted to external and superficial things rather than to the internal quest. This is not a criticism of these people, but it is a fact that the nature of *tamas* prevails in them and, therefore, they are not suitable for higher practices. Generally, the demands of this level do not transcend temple worship, offerings, and prayers.

Vīras are advanced Tantric *sādhakas* who have transcended worldly attachments. Although they are not fully enlightened, they have made great progress toward the sattvic level. *Vīras* are heroic, because they are not afraid to encounter *tamas* face to face. *Tamas* attacks on the basis of attachments, selfish demands, and temptations that inevitably pull us down to the *paśu* level.

Divyas are the most elevated *sādhakas*. These aspirants are wise and have completely transcended selfish worldly attachments. They are firmly established in *sattva-guṇa*.

Of course, within these three main divisions there are a great variety of subdivisions, for example an advanced *paśu* or a beginner *vīra*.

According to the Tantric scriptures, the literal practice of *pañca-ma-kāra* within *vāmācara* is reserved only for *vīras*. *Paśus* have not yet attained the level required to participate in this ritual, and *divyas* do not need it, because they have completely transcended this level.

As *sādhakas* grow and elevate themselves, their worldview undergoes a radical transformation, enabling them to see more subtle planes. This path of expansion of consciousness can lead us from the gross to the sublime.

Pañca-ma-kāra according to levels

परिसृतं झषमद्यं पलं च भक्तानि योनिः सुपरिष्कृतानि ।
निवेदयन्देवतायै महत्यै स्वात्मीकृत्य सुकृति सिद्धिमेति ॥

parisṛtaṁ jhaṣa-madyaṁ palaṁ ca
bhaktāni yoniḥ supariṣkṛtāni
nivedayan devatāyai mahatyai
svātmī-kṛtya sukṛti siddhim eti

The ritualistic offering of wine, meat, fish, cooked grains, and a uterus, has to be done properly and consumed in the stipulated order. Offering food to the great goddess, the expert performer should consume it and attain fulfilment (of the sacrifice).

(*Tri-purā Upanishad*, 12)

Pañca-tattva, or *pañca-ma-kāra*, is one of the most controversial practices. Scriptures such as the *Kulārṇava Tantra*, *Mahā-nirvāṇa Tantra*, and *Rudra Yāmala* detail every preparation necessary to rise to the *Kaula* level. These scriptures emphatically declare that there is nothing higher than the *Kaula* practice. However, before referring to rites such as *pañca-ma-kāra*, they mention a preparatory process of asanas, *prāṇāyāma*, *mudrās*, *bandhas*, and the repetition of specific mantras. These scriptures recommend keeping these practices in the strictest secrecy by stating that the *Kaula* path is very complex and impenetrable even for great yogis.

कृपाणधारागमनात्व्याघ्रकण्ठावलम्बनात् ।
भुजङ्ग धारणान्नूनमशक्यं कुलवर्तनम् ॥

kṛpāṇa-dhārā-gamanāt
vyāghra-kaṇṭhāvalambanāt
bhujaṅga dhāraṇān nūnam
aśakyaṁ kula-vartanam

> One may walk along the sharp edge of a sword, one may hold the neck of a tiger, one may even put on a serpent on his body, but rigorously following the ways of the *Kula* is considerably more difficult.
>
> (*Kulārṇava Tantra*, 2.122)

Five elements are used in this ritual: *madya* (wine), *māṁsa* (meat), *matsya* (fish), *mudrā* (wheat germ), and *maithuna* (sexual intercourse), which are called *ma-kāras* because they all start with the letter m. Each of them receives a different interpretation according to the evolutionary level of the practitioners and their predominant modality. Furthermore, only left-hand followers practice it literally, while those of the right hand practice it symbolically.

The Tantric scriptures classify the *vāmācāra* practice in the following way:

For *paśus*, it is a symbolic practice:

- Instead of wine, they consume coconut milk or honey.
- Instead of meat: salt, ginger, garlic, or beans.
- Instead of fish: eggplant or red radish.
- Instead of *mudrā*: dry grains.
- Instead of sexual contact, they offer flowers to the Devī. They can also have sex with their own spouse, although not publicly.

For *vīras*, it is a literal practice:

- Wine can be from grapes or from molasses or rice.
- Meat cannot be from a female animal, because every female living being is considered to be a manifestation of Śakti.
- Fish can only be of a certain kind; not all kinds can be consumed in the ritual. Those with fewer bones are preferable.
- Dry grains are usually rice or barley fried in ghee, or "clarified butter".
- Sex is permitted with a woman who has undertaken the proper purification rites or who has been consciously consecrated for that rite. Participants can be husband and wife, a couple whose relationship is specifically Tantric, or even strangers. It is strictly forbidden to have sex with one's mother or sister; this is considered a great offense and a spiritual mistake.

For the *divyas*, it is a symbolic practice:

- Wine represents the wisdom acquired from Para-brahman.
- Meat represents the *sādhaka's* surrender to God.
- Fish represents compassion and the level of consciousness at which others' pain and suffering is perceived as one's own.
- Dry grains represent the renunciation of any physical, mental, or emotional association with whatever is negative and leads to slavery.
- Sex represents the union of Śiva and Śakti in the seventh chakra.

According to the *Kulārṇava Tantra* and the *Viśva-sara Tantra*, the esoteric meaning of the *pañca-ma-kāra* in the *divya* stage is the following:

- *Madya* symbolizes drunkenness with the drops of divine nectar that comes from the petals of the Tantra yogi's *sahasrāra-cakra.*
- *Māṁsa* symbolizes the surrender of the body and actions to *māṁ*, that is, God. It is closely related to the control of speech.
- *Matsya* corresponds to the expansion of the sense of self and the extension of the sense of possession. It also refers to the mastery over *iḍā* and *piṅgalā nāḍīs* through the practice of *prāṇāyāma.*
- *Mudrā* is a hand gesture for abandoning all addiction and slavery to sensual pleasure.
- *Maithuna* implies the union of the two polarities. The female creative power, which resides in the lowest energy center (*mūlādhāra-cakra*), awakens and ascends until it merges with the masculine aspect of the cosmic consciousness (Śiva), which resides in the highest energy center (*sahasrāra-cakra*), located at the crown of the head. *Maithuna* is intimately connected to the awakening and elevation of *kuṇḍalinī-śakti.*

On the *dakṣiṇācāra* path, *pañca-tattvas* are very important symbols for *sādhana*:

- *Madhya* refers to the divine nectar that drips from the pituitary gland, or hypophysis, to the tip of the tongue when it touches the palate in the practice called *khecarī-mudra.* Wine is consumed as a symbol of the nectarous essence derived from the balance of Śiva and Śakti in the crown energy center called *sahasrāra-cakra.*
- *Māṁsa* symbolizes swallowing the tongue in the practice *khecarī-mudrā.*
- *Matsya* is the activation of the *nāḍīs iḍā* and *piṅgalā* along the spinal column. This symbolism is due to their shapes, which are intertwined like two fish.

- *Mudrā* refers to the different gestures the body and hands make when *kuṇḍalinī-śakti* is awakened and elevated to flow through *suṣumṇā-nāḍī*. The term *mudrā* means "seal, gesture, or attitude." *Mudrās* can be described as gestures or emotional, devotional, or psychic attitudes. A *mudrā* implies conscious bodily participation in a ritual. It is a precise gesture that has deep symbolic meaning. It not only represents an attitude but is effective on its own.
- *Maithuna* symbolizes the union of Śiva and Śakti. The sexual act itself is preceded by a long series of rituals. The *Jñānārṇāva Tantra* (22.68) states:

तयोर्योगो महेशानि योग एव न संशयः ।

tayor yogo maheśāni
yoga eva na saṁśayaḥ

Authentic yoga is the union of man and woman.
(*Jñānārṇāva Tantra*, 22.68a)

This constitutes the final stage of the *pañca ma-kāra*. This scripture explains how the goddess enjoys union with her consort in the *sahasrāra-cakra* after having pierced each and every one of the chakras. According to the *Kulārṇava Tantra*:

आनन्दं ब्रह्मणो रूपं तच्च देहे व्यवस्थितम् ।

ānandaṁ brahmaṇo rūpaṁ
tac ca dehe vyavasthitam

Enjoyment offers a glimpse of transcendental bliss, which is how, it is said, the Absolute expresses itself in the human body.
(*Kulārṇava Tantra*, 5.80a)

The *Devī-rahasya* expresses this by stating:

आनन्दरसपूजायां तुष्यते परमेश्वरी ।

ānanda-rasa-pūjāyāṁ
tuṣyate parameśvarī

The supreme goddess is satisfied through the worship of the taste of bliss.

(*Devī-rahasya,* 58.11a)

Types of Tantric *sādhana* in the *Śrī-vidyā* tradition

Tantric practices are classified into five groups: *samayācāra*, *dakṣiṇācāra*, *vāmācāra*, *miśra*, and *kaulācāra*.

Samayācāra sādhana

This is a mental practice that reflects the independence of Śakti. It is an internal worship in which the *homa*, or "ritual of fire," is carried out without any physical elements and articles. *Pūjā* is performed through visualization. It is based on yogic practices only, without the limitation of external rituals. *Samayācāra* includes the intention of raising *kuṇḍalinī* through meditation toward union in *sahasrāra-cakra*. *Samayācāra* includes the practice of *Śrī-vidyā*.

Dakṣiṇācāra sādhana

This type of *sādhana* is focused on a physical representation of the Divine Mother. In this practice, *Śrī-cakra* is worshipped. This is external worship (*bāhya-pūjā*) of a *vigraha*, or "physical form": a deity or a yantra. It also includes *suvāsinī-pūjā*, which is a *pūjā* performed at the feet of a woman who represents the Divine Mother. The philosophical principles of *dakṣiṇācāra* are found in the *Sanat-kumāra Saṁhitā*, *Parāśara Saṁhitā*, *Nārada Pāñca-rātra*, and other *Āgamas*. This system prohibits the practice of *pañca-ma-kāra* and includes an inner worship that purifies and strengthens the internal world of the aspirant.

Within *Śākta* Tantrism, there are ten main practices known as *mahā-vidyās*. The aspirant relates to the *śakti* in ten different forms starting with Kālī, then other aspects such as Tārā, culminating in Kamala.

Vāmācara sādhana

The first two traditions are based on the protective and benevolent aspects of God. *Vāmācāra sādhana*, on the other hand, worships the fiercest aspects of divinity. The practitioner is oriented toward dissolution in every aspect. *Laya-pradhāna*, or "dissolution," is central to these practices. Dissolution is a means to rebirth. Rituals are performed in cremation grounds, where complete renunciation and detachment are found. It includes practices such as *śava-sādhana*, or "meditation on a corpse." *Vāmācāra* helps transcend fears and elevate *kuṇḍalinī* to the higher chakras, but it can be dangerous without the proper guidance of a true master. Within *Vāmācāra*, one does not relate to God's friendly and tender aspects, but to devastating and destructive ones.

Miśra sādhana

The meaning of the term *miśra* is "mixed." It is a synthesis of the *vāmācāra* and *dakṣiṇācāra* traditions. It proposes that followers first gratify the senses and then completely renounce all searching for sensual enjoyment. This attitude reflects the tradition of Śiva–Śakti, or feminine–masculine.

Miśra practice includes a mixture of internal and external rituals. Practice focuses on *anāhata-cakra*, or "the heart chakra." It cultivates devotion to divine femininity, the Mother of the Universe. This *sādhana* is *antar-yāga*, "internal sacrifice," since it internalizes attention. Much of the worship is mental, or *mānasa-pūjā*. *Kuṇḍalinī* rises to *anāhata-cakra* and cultivates a devotional relationship with the Devī.

Miśra is not limited to sexual desire; it sees desire as the original cause that drives all motivation for worldly pleasure and enjoyment. Its *sādhana* combines *bhoga*, or "enjoyment," and *tyāga*, or "renunciation."

Kaulācāra sādhana

This *sādhana* focuses on physical and mental practices. Unlike *samayācāra* and *dakṣiṇācāra*, which do not present major problems for organized religion, *kaulācāra* is criticized. Its practices are controversial because they focus on the human body as a microcosm of the entire universe. These practices provoke social problems and cause scandals between gurus and ex-practitioners that often appear in the press in the West. However, it is a very old tradition that has been present in Hinduism and Buddhism since ancestral times.

Tantra is not focused on alcohol, sex, or sensual gratification, but it uses ritualism that involves the body in order to experience the original union of the superficial polarity. It utilizes the body as a microcosm to experience cosmic realities. *Kaulācāra* includes rituals such as *pañca-ma-kāra* and *pūjā-yonī*. However, only an exclusive group of advanced *sādhakas* is allowed to perform such rituals in certain circumstances.

All religions have bodily rituals, or *nyāsas*, such as obeisance in Jewish and Muslim prayer and the sign of the cross in Catholicism. These are physical movements that reflect cosmic truths. In *kaulācāra*, the deity of the Mother is replaced by a woman, and the union of Śiva and Śakti by a couple. Rituals such as bathing a woman or a man imply a transcendental relationship with the deity, female or male. In these *kaulācāra* practices, the concept of a personal "I" is completely annulled in order to see the other person as a manifestation of divinity. One assumes the role of the deity in these Tantric practices. Great enlightened masters of Hinduism have guided in this type of *sādhana*.

Kaulācāra is divided into two types: *pūrva-kaula* and *uttara-kula*. *Pūrva-kaula's sādhana* includes the five *ma-kāras*, but only for spiritually elevated aspirants. Practices like this are strictly limited to beings that are in no danger of falling into illusion. Beginners are excluded. *Uttara-kula*, on the other hand, is purely internal and dispenses with all external worship. The fundamental principle that governs this tradition is *viṣam viṣasya auṣadham*, or "the medicine of poison is poison." The idea is that, if the dosage is correct, poison can act as an antidote against poisoning. This expresses the conviction that the thing in itself is not good or bad, but it is our attitude that transforms it into negative or positive. Just like poison, even our desires and passions constitute an energy that can be used to pursue enlightenment.

Aspirants are considered heroes, or *vīras*, because they practice *sādhana-śmaśāna*, or "the practice of cremation," which symbolizes cremating the corpses of our desires. Even if aspirants have already eliminated their *vāsanās*, their corpses must be symbolically cremated because otherwise they can resuscitate. Although there is a great deal of literature about *Kaula* practices, there is even more that has not yet been written about them.

Even though Truth is for everyone and everyone has a right to it, not everyone is equally prepared for the Truth. Even in India, *kaulācāra* has always been an esoteric path accessible only to serious aspirants who are sufficiently prepared and qualified for initiation.

In many of the most important texts, we find clear warnings that the sacred Tantric practices should not be revealed to those who have not been initiated, for these teachings not to be used inappropriately or misunderstood by the ignorant.

As we approach this wisdom, we understand more clearly the spirit of Lord Kṛṣṇa's words in the Bhagavad Gita:

इदं ते नातपस्काय नाभक्ताय कदाचन ।
न चाशुश्रूषवे वाच्यं न च मां योऽभ्यसूयति ॥

idaṁ te nātapaskāya
nābhaktāya kadācana
na cāśuśrūṣave vācyaṁ
na ca māṁ yo 'bhyasūyati

This confidential knowledge may never be explained to those who are not austere, or devoted, or engaged in devotional service, nor to anyone who is envious of me.

(Bhagavad Gita, 18.67)

Nowadays, it is extremely difficult to find a true Tantric master whose teachings are reliable and who is willing to impart this sacred wisdom. Much of what is currently offered under the name of Tantra comes from a lack of understanding on the subject. Whoever guides others along this path must necessarily have many years of experience and a high level of direct and personal realization, as it is not a mere theoretical and intellectual knowledge. Since this way of realization is not sexology but an integral part of a religion, any authority in this field must necessarily be religious and spiritual. In the words of H.H. Swami Śivānanda Sarasvatī:

Tantra is, in some of its aspects, a secret doctrine. It is a *gupta-vidyā*. You cannot learn it from the study of books. You will have to get the knowledge and practice from the practical *Tāntrikas*, the Tantric *ācāryas* and gurus who hold the key to it. The Tantric student must be endowed with purity, faith, devotion, dedication to the guru, dispassion, humility, courage, cosmic love, truthfulness, non-covetousness, and contentment. Absence of these qualities in the practitioner is a gross abuse of Shaktism.

CHAPTER 5

TANTRIC RITUALISM

A ritual is a series of actions, gestures, or words that follows a set order and has symbolic value. Rituals are physical expressions of conscious intentions, although to the eyes of a stranger, they may seem irrational or illogical.

The Tantric tradition abounds in diverse and complex rituals. The essential features of Tantric rituals are images, body engagement, and mantras. That is to say, they involve the human being in its totality. Because Tantra sees the universe as a manifestation of the dynamic aspect of the Absolute, its rituals aim to manipulate this aspect; in other words, rituals are human actions that attempt to influence divine power. For example, through sexual rites, *Kāpālikas* attempted to receive gnosis from *yoginīs*.

Unlike Vedic rituals, Tantric rituals are not limited to actions and mantras but also include visualizations. They use the imagination in pursuit of concrete inner transformation. To the complex mechanism of the mind, perceived reality is as real as envisioned reality. The mind reacts based on sensual perception, but also on the imagination.

The *dhyāna-ślokas* scriptures, or "stanzas of visual meditation," describe the deities in detail so they can be visualized. During the rites, *pūjārīs* should visualize these deities within their own body. Tantric ritual transcends the limits of a ceremony and becomes an authentic experience.

The Tantric cult has two aspects: external (*bāhya-varivasyā*) and internal (*āntara-varivasyā*). External worship focuses on icons, *mudrās*, offerings, and worship of the Divine. Internal or mental worship is related to the deity and the body. To install a deity in the yantra, one first meditates on the chosen aspect of the Divine Mother of the Universe. Then, one proceeds to invoke the deity in question.

Next, the divine presence of the chosen goddess is transmitted to the yantra, and she is invoked by her mantra. The vital energy of the goddess is infused by the *prāṇa-pratiṣṭhā* ceremony.

Pūjā or "devotional ritual"

In the *pūjā*, or "devotional ritual," respect and devotion are offered to God by worshipping one or several deities. In Tantric *pūjā*, the worshipper and the worshipped are one and the same; it consists of two aspects, internal and external. Internally, the body becomes divine through visualization. First the worshipper's body is purified and then the worshipper is deified to perform the ritual. This transformation is a requirement to worship the Divine. This external ritual is followed by an internal one with powerful visualizations.

Rituals involving fearful deities such as Bhairava are especially peculiar. His icon is a human skull; his offerings include transgressive elements like alcohol, human flesh, sex, and on certain occasions, even human waste. The greater the transgression, the more powerful the energy that the ritual will unleash.

Dīkṣā or "initiation"

विना दीक्षां न मोक्षः स्यात्तदुक्तं शिवशासने ।
सा च न स्याद्विनाचार्यमित्याचार्य परम्परा ॥

vinā dīkṣāṁ na mokṣaḥ syāt
tad uktaṁ śiva-śāsane
sā ca na syād vinācāryam
ity ācārya paramparā

It has been set down by Lord Śiva that there can be no liberation without *dīkṣā* and this initiation cannot take place without a bona fide *ācārya* (master).

(*Kulārṇava Tantra*, 14.3)

Dīkṣā is a Sanskrit term that combines *dī* (to shine forth) and *kṣa* (destruction) and is usually translated as "initiation."

ज्ञानं दिव्यं यतो दद्यात्कुर्य्यात्पापस्य संक्षयः ।
तस्माद्दीक्षेति संप्रोक्ता देशिकैस्तन्त्रवेदिभिः ॥

jñānaṁ divyaṁ yato dadyāt
kuryyāt pāpasya saṁkṣayaḥ
tasmād dīkṣeti saṁproktā
deśikais tantra-vedibhiḥ

Since it sheds light on wisdom and destroys sins, it is called *dīkṣā* by the Tantric scholarly masters.

(*Sāradā-tilaka Tantra*, 4.2)

There are a great variety of Tantric initiations, which symbolize a mutual commitment between the master and the disciple. The master formally accepts the disciple and the disciple accepts the master. The ritual celebrates this relationship and the initiate's awakening. More than a ceremony, it is a change at the level of consciousness.

The drive to be initiated comes not from the guru but from the *sādhaka*. Initiation implies a profound change in the spiritual seeker; it not only transforms but perfects. It spiritualizes the very ontology of the practitioner.

Aspirants' longing to accept a guru is a reflection of their aspiration to be disciples. The emphasis is on the quality of discipleship and not on the guru. When the grace of this desire is born in aspirants' hearts, they should seek a spiritual master who inspires and elevates them.

First, it is important for aspirants to study the sacred scriptures to learn the requirements and qualities of a true guru. The scriptures explain the nature of a bona fide guru, the character of a true disciple, and the relationship between the two. Knowing this can prevent many misunderstandings that may arise from ignoring the delicate nature of this relationship. A basic requirement is that the guru must belong to a line of disciplic succession, or *paramparā*. In regards to this, the *Kulārṇava Tantra* affirms the following:

देवास्तं एव शंसन्ति पारम्पर्यप्रवर्त्तकम् ।
गुरुं मन्त्रागमाभिज्ञं समयाचारपालकम् ॥

devās taṁ eva śaṁsanti
pāramparya-pravarttakam
guruṁ mantrāgamābhijñaṁ
samayācāra-pālakam

Devatās only provide protection to gurus who promote tradition, who know the mantras and *Āgamas*, and who follow *samayācāra*.

(*Kulārṇava Tantra*, 14.5)

तस्मात्सर्वप्रयत्नेन साक्षात्परशिवोदितम् ।
सम्प्रदायमविच्छिन्नं सदा कुर्यात्गुरुः प्रिये ॥

tasmāt sarva-prayatnena
sākṣāt para-śivoditam
sampradāyam aviccinnaṁ
sadā kuryāt guruḥ priye

Therefore, O my beloved, one should strive to find a guru of unbroken tradition originating from Para-śiva himself.

(*Kulārṇava Tantra*, 14.8)

The master must have walked the path of discipleship and fulfilled the requirements that are explained in the revealed scriptures. It is a matter that requires a lot of seriousness because it is an eternal commitment. Aspirants request initiation from the master with great respect and humility. The *Mahā-nirvāṇa Tantra* indicates how this petition should be worded:

करुणामय दीनेश तवाहं शरणागतः ।
त्वत्पदाम्भोरुहच्छायां देहि मूर्ध्नि यशोधन ॥

karuṇā-maya dīneśa
tavāhaṁ śaraṇāgataḥ
tvat padāmbho-ruhac chāyāṁ
dehi mūrdhni yaśodhana

O merciful one! Lord of the distressed! To you I have come for protection: cast the shadows of your lotus-like feet over my head, o you whose wealth is fame.

(*Mahā-nirvāṇa Tantra*, 3.130)

इति प्रार्थ्य गुरुं पश्चात्पूजयित्वा स्वशक्तितः ।
कृताञ्जलिपुटो भूत्वा तूष्णीं तिष्ठेद्गुरोः पुरः ॥

iti prārthya guruṁ paścāt
pūjayitvā sva-śaktitaḥ
kṛtāñjaliputo bhūtvā
tūṣṇīṁ tiṣṭhed guroḥ puraḥ

Having prayed to and worshipped the guru with all might, the disciple may remain before the guru with folded hands in silence.

(*Mahā-nirvāṇa Tantra*, 3.131)

Initiation is the most important step in the life of a *sādhaka*. The master will evaluate aspirants' determination and seriousness before deciding whether to accept them. Examining their character can take months or even years. Accepting a disciple is a great responsibility. An applicant can be rejected repeatedly before being accepted. The master examines the *sādhaka's* perseverance and seriousness. The *sādhaka* must be willing to follow the master's training and even accept his or her coldness without reservations of any kind.

It must be understood that the master interferes with our illusions and fantasies. Instead of being a convenience for the ego, the guru is a nuisance and an obstacle. Like an alarm clock, the master can be very unpleasant for those who are not determined to give up their dreams. If we do not clearly understand this, we may become disappointed. The master's intention is not to meet our expectations but to eliminate them. Only a charlatan meets followers' expectations.

While the initiation ritual varies from one sect to another, its meaning does not. *Dīkṣā* is simultaneously a death and a birth. Its central idea is rebirth: the old being dies to give birth to a new one.

After initiation, disciples continue with daily rituals to their spiritual master and chosen deity.

Other rituals

Tantric rituals are not limited to *pūjā* and *dīkṣā*, although these are the most important. An extensive variety of Tantric rites has permeated Hinduism. For instance, *naimittika* (occasional) rites happen on specific dates. In days called *parvan* (changes of the moon), there are meetings with *yoginīs*, in which couples of disciples meet with their guru and sometimes perform sexual rituals.

Among many other rites, there are funerary and expiatory ones, rituals for the prosperity of the monarch and the kingdom, and so on. Finally, there are magic rites that use mystical powers.

Tantric rituals include the following 16 *upacāras*:

1. Asana: Offering a seat to the deity.
2. *Svāgata*: Welcoming the deity.
3. *Padya*: Water to wash feet.
4. *Arghya*: Water for ablution.
5. *Ācamana*: Water to sip.
6. *Madhu-parka*: A mixture of honey, ghee, milk, and curd.
7. *Snāna*: Bath.
8. *Vastra*: Cloth.
9. *Ābharaṇa*: Jewels.
10. *Gandha*: Perfume.
11. *Puṣpa*: Flowers.

12. *Dhūpa*: Incense.
13. *Dīpa*: Light.
14. *Naivedya* and *tāmbūla*: Food and betel leaves.
15. *Nīrājana*, or *āratī*: Waving lights in front of the deity.
16. *Vandanā*: Obeisance and prayers.

Worship of the *liṅga* and the *yonī*

The *liṅga* and the *yonī* are the most characteristic and revered Tantric symbols. The original description of the *liṅga* is found in the *Śiva Purāṇa* in the first section, the *Vidyeśvara Saṁhitā*, chapters 5–11.

Liṅga means "symbol, sign, or characteristic." The Bhagavad Gita provides an example and general meaning of the word:

अर्जुन उवाच-
कैर्लिङ्गैस्त्रीन्गुणानेतानतीतो भवति प्रभो ।
किमाचारः कथं चैतांस्त्रीन्गुणानति वर्तते ॥

arjuna uvāca
kair liṅgais trīn guṇān etān
atīto bhavati prabho
kim-ācāraḥ kathaṁ caitāṁs
trīn guṇān ati vartate

> Arjuna inquired: O my dear Lord, by which signs are those known who are transcendental to these three modes? What is their behavior? And how do they transcend the modes of nature?
>
> (Bhagavad Gita, 14.21)

In this verse of the Gita, we can clearly see that the term *liṅgaiḥ* — the plural instrumental form of the word *liṅga* —means "signs or characteristics." Similarly, there are visible signs of the Divine awakening in a human being.

A *liṅga* marks the presence of something, for example, the *Śiva-liṅga*, which invokes the presence of Śiva in the world. It reminds us that the Self lies in the depths of every living entity. Anytime we perceive signs of sanctity in human beings: these are *liṅgas* (signs) that accredit the presence of the Lord on the earthly plane.

The *yonī*, for its part, symbolizes the womb, femininity, and divine creative energy.

तत्तत्सुखानुरागेण शिवपूजां विदुर्बुधाः ।
पीठमंबामयं सर्वं शिवलिंगं च चिन्मयम् ॥

tat tat sukhānurāgeṇa
śiva-pūjāṁ vidur budhāḥ
pīṭham aṁbā-mayaṁ sarvaṁ
śiva-liṅgaṁ ca cin-mayam

Śiva-pūjā shall be performed with a love for the happiness of different beings—so say the wise men. The pedestal represents Śiva's consort, Pārvatī, and his *liṅga* represents sentient beings.

यथा देवीमुमामंके धृत्वा तिष्ठति शंकरः ।
तथा लिंगमिदं पीठं धृत्वा तिष्ठति संततम् ॥

yathā devīm umām aṅke
dhṛtvā tiṣṭhati śaṅkaraḥ
tathā liṅgam idaṁ pīṭhaṁ
dhṛtvā tiṣṭhati santatam

Just as Lord Śiva remains ever in the close embrace of the goddess Pārvatī, so the phallic emblem grasps the pedestal forever.

(*Śiva Purāṇa*, *Vidyeśvara Saṁhitā*, 11.22–23)

In Tantric texts, the *Śiva-liṅga* is the symbol of the male sexual organ embedded in the female one. The *yonī* represents the creative power of the universe. The male reproductive organ within the female one represents the creative union that generates life on a cosmic scale.

रूपित्वात्सकलस्तद्वत्तस्मात्सकलनिष्कलः ।
निष्कलत्वान्निराकारं लिंगं तस्य समागतम् ॥

rūpitvāt sakalas tad vat
tasmāt sakala-niṣkalaḥ
niṣkalatvān nirākāraṁ
liṅgaṁ tasya samāgatam

He is also *sakala* (with division) since he has an embodied form. He is both *sakala* and *niṣkala* (without division). It is in his *niṣkala* aspect that the *liṅga* is appropriate.
(*Śiva Purāṇa*, *Vidyeśvara Saṁhitā*, 5.11)

The *Śiva-liṅga* is the *nirguṇa* aspect (without qualities) of Śiva and, therefore, is worshipped as Lord Śiva himself. In general, Śiva devotees, or *Śiva-bhaktas*, carry out the *pañcāyatana-pūjā*, a rite that also reveres Gaṇeśa, Pārvatī, Sūrya, Nārāyaṇa, and Śālagrāma.

The *Śiva-liṅga* also symbolizes Śiva's phallus. Just as semen is hidden within the phallus, Śiva is always present, even if he is not visible.

Another explanation states that the *Śiva-liṅga* represents *prakṛti*, or *pradhāna*, which is "the cosmic substance." It is Śiva's subtle body, or *prakṛti*, which is absolute reality.

The *Śiva-liṅga* has three parts. The lowest is called *Brahma-pīṭha*, the middle *Viṣṇu-pīṭha*, and the upper *Śiva-pīṭha*. The twelve main *jyotir-liṅgas* that are worshipped in India are in the sanctuaries Kedāra-nātha, Kāśī-viśva-nātha, Soma-nātha, Baija-nātha, Rāmeśvara, Ghṛṣṇeśvara, Bhīmā-śaṅkara, Mahā-kāla, Mallikārjuna, Mamaleśvara, Nāgeśvara, and Tryambakeśvara, and the five *pañca-bhūta-liṅgas* are in Kāla-hastīsvara, Jambūkesvara, Aruṇācaleśvara, Ekāmbareśvara in Kāñci-pura, and Naṭarāja in Cidāmbara.

Those who focus their worship on the *Śiva-liṅga* are called *liṅgāyatas* and can be identified by the miniature *liṅga* that they wear on a necklace for life. They are a religious group within Hinduism known for tolerance and acceptance of all human beings. This community does not accept the modern caste system.

In the Puranic literature, there is a story of Mārkaṇḍeya, a boy destined to die at age sixteen. When the night of his death arrived, he sat down to meditate on Śiva in front of a *Śiva-liṅga*. When death came to take him away, Śiva manifested out of the *liṅga*. Addressing death, he said: "You cannot touch my devotee." Mārkaṇḍeya was very devout and sincere. Sincere devotion to the *liṅga* attracts the blessings of Śiva, which help us free ourselves from worldly attachments.

The *liṅga* has three different levels: gross (*iṣṭa-liṅga*), subtle (*prāna-liṅga*), and transcendental (*jyotir-liṅga* or *bhāva-liṅga*). The gross *liṅga* is worshipped in the temple.

The subtle *liṅga* is the next level. It is the *liṅga* of vital energy (*prāṇa*) that resides in our body. According to the Agamic literature, these subtle *liṅgas* reside in our energy centers, or chakras. They are of three types: black (*itarakhya-liṅga*), smoky (*dhūmra-liṅga*), and luminous (*jyotir-liṅga*). The black *liṅga* can be perceived in *mūlādhāra-cakra* in states of deep meditation. In deep meditation, the dormant *śakti*, called *kuṇḍalinī-śakti*, awakens and we experience *dhūmra-liṅga* in the heart energy center, or *anahata-cakra*. The smoky *liṅga* is perceived as something less substantial than the black one. The black *liṅga* is perceived with certain solidity, but *dhūmra-liṅga* resembles smoke. *Jyotir-liṅga* resides in the seventh energy center, or *sahasrāra-cakra*. This *liṅga* is effulgent because it reflects the nature of Śiva. *Jyotir-liṅga* is infinite, unlimited, and the foundation of the universe; it is also called *bhāva-liṅga, tattva-liṅga*, or *parātpara*. According to the Tantric vision, when *kuṇḍalinī* reaches Sadā-śiva, illusion is transcended and enlightenment is reached. Repeating the mantra *Oṁ namaḥ sivāya* manifests *tattva-liṅga*, or *parātpara*, the last *liṅga*. At this level, the duality of the relative platform is transcended and *śiva-sāyujya*, or "fusion with Śiva," is realized.

Śiva and Śakti are not different but one and the same. Like water and moisture, Śiva includes Śakti. Within every human being there rests a power that manifests when the time comes. The pedestal on which the *liṅga* rests is called *pīṭha* and symbolizes Śakti; it has the shape of the female reproductive organ. The *Śiva-liṅga* represents the nature of both Śiva and Śakti.

The term *liṅga* is derived from the word *laya*, or "dissolution." At the end of each cycle, the cosmos merges into the *liṅga*. Thus, the *liṅga* symbolizes Parama-śiva, and *pīṭha* represents Parama-śakti. The *Śiva-liṅga* symbolizes consciousness that is oriented upward and tends to rise. *Pīṭha* is the form of Śakti that has enveloped the past, present, and future within itself. The *liṅga*'s shape expresses the aspiration to know oneself, transcend, and evolve. The shape of *pīṭha* expresses the energy that expands in the three temporal dimensions. The *Śiva-liṅga* comprises both forms. It is situated in the *yonī* because masculinity and femininity come together in this *liṅga*. This union is the origin of all creation.

ब्रह्ममुरारिसुरार्चितलिङ्गं निर्मलभासितशोभितलिङ्गम् ।
जन्मजदुःखविनाशकलिङ्गं तत् प्रणमामि सदाशिवलिङ्गम् ॥

brahma-murāri-surārcita-liṅgaṁ
nirmala-bhāsita-śobhita-liṅgam
janmaja-duḥkha-vināśaka-liṅgaṁ
tat praṇamāmi sadā-śiva-liṅgam

I bow before Sadā-śiva-liṅga (the symbol of the supreme Being), which is worshipped by Brahmā, Viṣṇu, and the other gods, which is praised by pure and holy words, and which destroys the cycle of birth and death.

देवमुनिप्रवरार्चितलिङ्गं कामदहम् करुणाकर लिङ्गम् ।
रावणदर्पविनाशनलिङ्गं तत् प्रणमामि सदाशिव लिङ्गम् ॥

deva-muni-pravarārcita-liṅgaṁ
kāma-dahaṁ karuṇā-kara liṅgam
ravaṇa-darpa-vināśana-liṅgaṁ
tat praṇamāmi sadā-śiva-liṅgam

Reverence to Sadā-śiva-liṅga, the destroyer of Cupid, which is adored by *devas* and sages, which is infinitely compassionate, and which subjugated the pride of Rāvaṇa.

सर्वसुगन्धिसुलेपितलिङ्गं बुद्धिविवर्धनकारणलिङ्गम् ।
सिद्धसुरासुरवन्दितलिङ्गं तत् प्रणमामि सदाशिव लिङ्गम् ॥

sarva-sugandhi-sulepita-liṅgaṁ
buddhi-vivardhana-kāraṇa-liṅgam
siddha-surāsura-vandita-liṅgaṁ
tat praṇamāmi sadā-śiva-liṅgam

I bow to Sadā-śiva-liṅga, which is lavished with abundant and varied perfumes and aromas, which raises the power of thought and illuminates discernment, and before which *siddhas*, *suras*, and *āsuras* bow.

कनकमहामणिभूषितलिङ्गं फणिपतिवेष्टित शोभित लिङ्गम् ।
दक्षसुयज्ञ विनाशन लिङ्गं तत् प्रणमामि सदाशिव लिङ्गम् ॥

kanaka-mahāmaṇi-bhūṣita-liṅgaṁ
phaṇipati-veṣṭita-śobhita liṅgam
dakṣa-suyajña-vināśana-liṅgaṁ
tat praṇamāmi sadā-śiva-liṅgam

Prostrations before Sadā-śiva-liṅga, the destroyer of the sacrifice of Dakṣa, which is adorned with various ornaments, precious stones, and rubies, and which shines with the king of the serpents coiled upon it.

कुङ्कुमचन्दनलेपितलिङ्गं पङ्कजहारसुशोभितलिङ्गम् ।
सञ्चितपापविनाशनलिङ्गं तत् प्रणमामि सदाशिव लिङ्गम् ॥

kuṅkuma-candana-lepita-liṅgaṁ
paṅkaja-hāra-suśobhita-liṅgam
sañcita-pāpa-vināśana-liṅgaṁ
tat praṇamāmi sadā-śiva-liṅgam

I bow to Sadā-śiva-liṅga, to which saffron and sandalwood paste are offered, which looks beautiful with garlands of lotuses, and which removes all accumulated evil deeds.

देवगणार्चित सेवितलिङ्गं भावैर्भक्तिभिरेव च लिङ्गम् ।
दिनकरकोटिप्रभाकरलिङ्गं तत् प्रणमामि सदाशिव लिङ्गम् ॥

deva-gaṇārcita-sevita liṅgaṁ
bhāvair-bhaktibhir eva ca liṅgam
dinakara-koṭi-prabhākara-liṅgaṁ
tat praṇamāmi sadā-śiva-liṅgam

Reverences to Sadā-śiva-liṅga, which is worshipped by the *devas* with genuine thoughts full of faith and devotion and which has the brilliance of millions of suns.

अष्टदलोपरिवेष्टितलिङ्गं सर्वसमुद्भवकारणलिङ्गम् ।
अष्टदरिद्रविनाशितलिङ्गं तत् प्रणमामि सदाशिव लिङ्गम् ॥

aṣṭa-dalopari veṣṭita-liṅgaṁ
sarva-samudbhava-kāraṇa-liṅgam
aṣṭa-daridra-vināśita-liṅgaṁ
tat praṇamāmi sadā-śiva-liṅgam

Prostrations before Sadā-śiva-liṅga, which destroys the eight kinds of poverty (*aṣṭadaridra*), which is the cause of all creation, and which sits on an eight-petalled lotus.

सुरगुरुसुरवरपूजित लिङ्गं सुरवनपुष्प सदार्चित लिङ्गम् ।
परात्परं परमात्मक लिङ्गं तत् प्रणमामि सदाशिव लिङ्गम् ॥

sura-guru-sura-vara-pūjita-liṅgaṁ
sura-vana-puṣpa-sadārcita-liṅgam
parātparaṁ paramātmaka-liṅgaṁ
tat praṇamāmi sadā-śiva-liṅgam

I prostrate before Sadā-śiva-liṅga, which is the transcendental and supreme Self, worshipped with countless flowers from the celestial gardens by all *suras*, preceded by their gurus.

लिङ्गाष्टकमिदं पुण्यं यः पठेत् शिवसन्निधौ ।
शिवलोकमवाप्नोति शिवेन सह मोदते ॥

liṅgāṣṭkam idaṁ puṇyaṁ
yaḥ paṭhec chiva-sannidhau
śiva-lokaṁ avāpnoti
śivena saha modate

Whoever repeats these eight *ślokas* and worships the *Śiva-liṅga* in the presence of Lord Śiva reaches the supreme abode of Śiva and enjoys eternal happiness and bliss with him.

(*Lingāṣṭaka* by Ādi Śaṅkarācārya)

The worship of the *Śiva-liṅga* precedes the veneration of Śiva's form. Before the cosmos manifested, the lack of form manifested in the form of the *Śiva-liṅga*. Hence, the *Śiva-liṅga* is the first symbol of Parama-śiva, of God. In the *Śiva Purāṇa*, Lord Śiva reveals his *liṅga* form to Viṣṇu and Brahmā and then explains its importance:

तस्मादज्ञातमीशत्वं व्यक्तं द्योतयितुं हि वाम् ।
सकलोऽहमतो जातः साक्षादीशस्तु तत्क्षणात् ॥
सकलत्वमतो ज्ञेयमीशत्वं मयि सत्वरम् ।
यदिदं निष्कलं स्तंभं मम ब्रह्मत्व बोधकम् ॥

tasmād ajñātam īśatvaṁ
vyaktaṁ dyotayituṁ hi vām
sakalo 'ham ato jātaḥ
sākṣād īśastu tat kṣaṇāt

sakalatvam ato jñeyam
īśatvaṁ mayi satvaram
yad idaṁ niṣkalaṁ staṁbhaṁ
mama brahmatva bodhakam

> In order to clarify my *Īśatva* (supreme ruler aspect), which is unknown [up to now], I have manifested myself immediately in the embodied form of Īśa. The Īśatva in me is to be known as my embodied form, and this *liṅga* is indicative of my Brahmatva (formless aspect).

लिङ्गलक्षण युक्तत्वान्मम लिङ्गं भवेदिदम् ।
तदिदं नित्यमभ्यर्च्यं युवाभ्यामत्र पुत्रकौ ॥

liṅga-lakṣaṇa yuktatvān
mama liṅgaṁ bhaved idam
tad idaṁ nityam abhyarcyaṁ
yuvābhyām atra putrakau

> Since it has all the characteristic features of a *liṅga* (a formless sign, evidence of my existence), it is my symbol. O children!, you should worship it every day.
>
> (*Śiva Purāṇa*, "*Vidyeśvara Saṁhitā*," 9.40–42)

Once Lord Śiva finishes speaking, he disappears, and the *devas* ask the sage Sūta what will be the proper way to worship of the Śiva-*liṅga*. Sūta then explains them in detail how to install Śiva-*liṅgas* and how to worship them.

Tantra refers to the creative capacity of human beings as *yonī-liṅga*; it manifests as sexual desire and is capable of creating a new life. If this energy is sublimated, it can create a melody, a poem, a dance, a painting, or a song. However, if repressed, it can lead to a fight, a battle, or a war. There is only one thing we can be sure of: it is impossible to annihilate this power.

According to Tantra, indiscriminate repression of our instincts suffocates creativity at all levels of reality. It may be surprising to learn that in Tantra, repressing sexual desire without understanding is much more dangerous than permissiveness. Conscious permissiveness, guided by understanding, can be far superior to blind and repressive celibacy.

Epilogue

Tantra and Sexuality

According to the Tantric vision, we *are* conditioning. We live based on accumulated information. The egoic phenomenon has been created and developed by society. Since birth, we have been programmed by our parents, family, neighbors, teachers, classmates, colleagues, friends, television, newspapers, religious institutions, politicians, and so on. They have taught us how to react, act, speak, think, feel, and laugh. Therefore, it is not that we are conditioned, but that we *are* conditioning. Many of the transgressive Tantric practices attempt to transcend this conditioning.

It is important to point out that the sexual aspect is a relatively small part of the ocean of Tantric wisdom. Sexual rites are not intended for all aspirants, and only certain *sādhakas* deal with these practices. Tantric sex is not limited to a physical act. Constraining sexuality to physical contact is a kind of reductionism: sexuality is not synonymous with "genitality." According to Tantra, sex is not only for procreation, but all of life is essentially sexual.

Sex is unifying; it is the creative force of divinity and the manifestation of an extremely elevated and pure power through flesh. It is a divine force that expresses itself physically. The divine power itself descends from its origin and passes through different planes of existence: astral, mental, and physical. If we ignorantly try to control or repress sexual desires, they will become an invincible enemy. But if we treat them wisely, even at the lowest levels, we will discover that sex is an important key in our evolutionary process toward freedom.

We can use the stairs to descend from a higher floor to a lower one and we can also ascend again by the same stairs: it is our choice. In any practice related to sexual energy, we must be extremely cautious and remain very alert. Our search for comfort can tempt us to go down and degrade ourselves. Like on stairs, going up is always harder than going down.

In the Bhagavad Gita, Kṛṣṇa talks about the higher taste. When the highest state is manifested, the desire for mediocre and low things naturally disappears.

विषया विनिवर्तन्ते निराहारस्य देहिनः ।
रसवर्जं रसोऽप्यस्य परं दृष्ट्वा निवर्तते ॥

viṣayā vinivartante
nirāhārasya dehinaḥ
rasa-varjaṁ raso 'py asya
paraṁ dṛṣṭvā nivartate

Though the embodied soul may be restricted from sense enjoyment, the taste for sense objects remains. But, ceasing such engagements by experiencing a higher taste, one is fixed in consciousness.

(Bhagavad Gita, 2.59)

If repression is devoid of discernment and understanding, it is only a type of violence. Fighting, even against ourselves, is a kind of aggression. The process of Tantric sublimation, on the other hand, always promotes love, harmony, and peace. It does not require violence and never conflicts with the principle of ahimsa.

Lord Kṛṣṇa affirms the following:

बलं बलवतां चाहं कामरागविवर्जितम् ।
धर्माविरुद्धो भूतेषु कामोऽस्मि भरतर्षभ ॥

balaṁ balavatāṁ cāhaṁ
kāma-rāga-vivarjitam
dharmāviruddho bhūteṣu
kāmo 'smi bharatarṣabha

> I am the strength of the strong, devoid of passion and desire. I am the sex life which is not contrary to religious principles, O lord of the Bhāratas (Arjuna).
>
> (Bhagavad Gita, 7.11)

In other words, just like strength and power, sex can be divine once worldly lust and selfish desire are transcended. Although Tantra yoga pursues transcendence, it does not deny this world. Tantra is a path that leads to the knowledge and application of dharma, to the experience and sublimation of *artha* (wealth) and kama (sensual desire), and finally, to the realization of *mokṣa* (liberation).

In the Vedic religion, fire symbolizes the ego's cremation because it consumes corpses, a symbol of the dead. However, in Tantra, fire is the life that teaches us to live in the heat of passion. The color of *sannyāsa* is orange, like flames, because *sannyāsa* means full renunciation of the earthly, the death of the mundane. At the same time, it symbolizes rebirth among the flames that consume everything that can be consumed: dreams, ideas, hopes, fantasies, and illusions. It allows us to wake up to a more authentic life.

Celibacy means transcending the need for and an addiction to the physical sexual act; this occurs naturally and effortlessly when we expand our sexuality in a movement that is always inclusive and never exclusive. By inclusive I mean transforming ourselves into Tantric beings. Although they may have completely transcended sex as a physical experience, enlightened masters are Tantric beings. Since they have merged with the Whole, they express an orgasmic state through their gaze, movements, words, way of walking, and presence.

Tāntrikas control their desires, but without suffocating or atrophying their passion, just as the lion tamer does not kill the lion but tames it. The Sanskrit word *paśu* means "beast or animal" and *pati* means "master." Paśu-pati is one of Lord Śiva's holy names that refers to the master of animal or bestial instincts. In fact, *Tāntrikas* sublimate their animal energy and ultimately transcend it.

According to Tantra, physical sex should not be repressed, but elevated and sublimated. Then, as it rises, it transforms. At first, it will manifest as sexuality, which will even increase after giving up physical sex. From that seed, love flourishes, which is then expressed as meditation and finally as prayer. Everything depends on how far we get in our purification and elevation process. Just as physical sex belongs to the instinctive or animal level, that is, to the world of the beast, attachment is born from the mind and belongs to the mental level. So, when attachment is transcended, there is a blooming of meditation… love… prayer… God. According to Tantra, it is God who sleeps deeply within minerals, dreams in plants, trees, and vegetables, moves in the beast, and awakens in the human being.

Yogis overcome desire and attachment by increasing passion because they see it as an essential element for the spiritual search. Desire is an emotion that binds, enslaves, attaches, and creates addiction. Passion, on the other hand, is an intense state, a way of being. For *Tantra-yogīs*, religion is not a creed or a faith, but an intense passion to be lived.

Tantra sees an orgasm as a mystical phenomenon and hence has deep respect for it. It considers an orgasm to be much more than a simple carnal experience or a mundane sensual pleasure. During an orgasm, all mental activity ceases. That is what really attracts so many people to sex, even if they are not aware of it. It is no coincidence that many Tantric masters refer to enlightenment as an "orgasmic" state or a cosmic orgasm.

Tantric wisdom aspires to be a decisive process of removing inhibitions and becoming more open, which necessarily leads us to see ourselves as a whole. Any experience that includes all aspects of our being will necessarily lead us to perceive the presence of our sexuality; it will make us throb in unison with the universe and with life. We will not only feel it, but be it. It is not a physical sexual experience, but, as many define it, an orgasmic experience where mental activity decreases and one feels more body, more Self. Meditation only flourishes in a heart that burns with the fire of passion for life, existence, Truth, and God.

Sanskrit
Pronunciation Guide

Vowels

अ *a*   आ *ā*   इ *i*   ई *ī*   उ *u*   ऊ *ū*
ऋ *ṛ*   ॠ *ṝ*   ऌ *ḷ*   ए *e*   ऐ *ai*   ओ *o*   औ *au*   अं *aṁ*   अः *aḥ*

Consonants

Gutturals	क *ka*	ख *kha*	ग *ga*	घ *gha*	ङ *ṅa*
Palatals	च *ca*	छ *cha*	ज *ja*	झ *jha*	ञ *ña*
Cerebrals	ट *ṭa*	ठ *ṭha*	ड *ḍa*	ढ *ḍha*	ण *ṇa*
Dentals	त *ta*	थ *tha*	द *da*	ध *dha*	न *na*
Labials	प *pa*	फ *pha*	ब *ba*	भ *bha*	म *ma*
Semivowels	य *ya*	र *ra*	ल *la*	व *va*	
Sibilants	श *śa*	ष *ṣa*	स *sa*		
Aspirates	ह *ha*				

Pronunciation

Vowels

Sanskrit letter	Transliteration	Sounds like
अ	*a*	but
आ	*ā*	father
इ	*i*	fit, if, lily
ई	*ī*	fee, police
उ	*u*	put
ऊ	*ū*	boot, rule, rude
ऋ	*ṛ*	(between ri and ru,
		as in the name Krishna)
ॠ	*ṝ*	(between ri and ru)
		crucial
ऌ	*ḷ*	(similar to lr)
ए	*e*	made
ऐ	*ai*	bite, aisle
ओ	*o*	oh
औ	*au*	found, house

Consonants

Gutturals

(back of the throat)

Sanskrit letter	Transliteration	Sounds like
क	*ka*	kill, seek, kite
ख	*kha*	Eckhart
ग	*ga*	get, dog, give
घ	*gha*	log-hut
ङ	*ṅa*	sing, king, sink

Palatals

(tip of the tongue touches the roof of the mouth)

Sanskrit letter	Transliteration	Sounds like
च	*ca*	chicken
छ	*cha*	catch him
ज	*ja*	joy, jump
झ	*jha*	hedgehog
ञ	*ña*	canyon

Cerebrals

(tip of the tongue against the front part of the roof of the mouth)

Sanskrit letter	Transliteration	Sounds like
ट	*ṭa*	true, tub
ठ	*ṭha*	anthill
ड	*ḍa*	dove, drum, doctor
ढ	*ḍha*	red-hot
ण	*ṇa*	under

Dentals

(tip of the tongue against the teeth)

Sanskrit letter	Transliteration	Sounds like
त	*ta*	(between t and th) water
थ	*tha*	lighthearted
द	*da*	(between d and th) dice, then
ध	*dha*	adhere
न	*na*	not, nut

Labials

(lips together, the tongue is not used)

Sanskrit letter	Transliteration	Sounds like
प	*pa*	pine, put, sip
फ	*pha*	uphill
ब	*ba*	bird, bear, rub
भ	*bha*	abhor
म	*ma*	mother, map

Semivowels

Sanskrit letter	Transliteration	Sounds like
य	*ya*	yet, loyal, yes
र	*ra*	red, year
ल	*la*	lull, lead
व	*va*	(between v and w)
		ivy, vine

Sibilants

Sanskrit letter	Transliteration	Sounds like
श	*śa*	sure
ष	*ṣa*	shrink, bush, show
स	*sa*	saint, sin, hiss

Aspirate

Sanskrit letter	Transliteration	Sounds like
ह	*ha*	hear, hit, home

Additional Sounds

Anusvāra

A nasal sound, written as a dot above and to the right of a Sanskrit letter.

Sanskrit letter	Transliteration	Sounds like
ं	*ṁ*	hum, tempt, pump

Visarga

A final aspirate sound, written as two dots after a Sanskrit letter.

Sanskrit letter	Transliteration	Sounds like
ः	*ḥ*	ha or hi
तः	*taḥ*	'ta-ha'
तीः	*tīḥ*	'tee-hi'

Prabhuji

H.H. Avadhūta Śrī Bhaktivedānta Yogācārya
Ramakrishnananda Bābājī Mahārāja

About Prabhuji

Prabhuji is a writer, painter, an *avadhūta*, the creator of Retroprogressive Yoga, and a realized spiritual master. In 2011, he chose to retire from society and lead the life of a hermit. Since then, his days have been spent in solitude, praying, writing, painting, and meditating in silence and contemplation.

Prabhuji is the sole disciple of H.D.G. Avadhūta Śrī Brahmānanda Bābājī Mahārāja, who in turn is one of the closest and most intimate disciples of H.D.G. Avadhūta Śrī Mastarāma Bābājī Mahārāja.

Prabhuji was appointed as the successor of the lineage by his master, who conferred upon him the responsibility of continuing the sacred *paramparā* of *avadhūtas*, officially appointing him as guru and ordering him to serve as Ācārya successor under the name H.H. Avadhūta Śrī Bhaktivedānta Yogācārya Ramakrishnananda Bābājī Mahārāja.

Prabhuji is also a disciple of H.D.G. Bhakti-kavi Atulānanda Ācārya Mahārāja, who is a direct disciple of H.D.G. A.C. Bhaktivedānta Swami Prabhupāda.

Prabhuji's Hinduism is so broad, universal, and pluralistic that at times, while living up to his title of *avadhūta*, his lively and fresh teachings transcend the boundaries of all philosophies and religions, even his own. His teachings promote critical thinking and lead us to question statements that are usually accepted as true. They do not defend absolute truths but invite us to evaluate and question our own convictions. The essence of his syncretic vision, Retroprogressive Yoga, is self-awareness and the recognition of consciousness. For him, awakening at the level of consciousness, or the transcendence of the egoic phenomenon, is the next step in humanity's evolution.

Prabhuji was born on March 21, 1958, in Santiago, the capital of the Republic of Chile. When he was eight years old, he had a mystical experience that motivated his search for the Truth, or the Ultimate Reality. This transformed his life into an authentic inner and outer pilgrimage. He has completely devoted his life to deepening the early transformative experience that marked the beginning of his process of retroevolution. He has dedicated more than fifty years to the exploration and practice of different religions, philosophies, paths of liberation, and spiritual disciplines. He has absorbed the teachings of great yogis, pastors, rabbis, monks, gurus, philosophers, sages, and saints whom he personally visited during years of searching. He has lived in many places and traveled the world thirsting for Truth.

From an early age, Prabhuji noticed that the educational system prevented him from devoting himself to what was really important: learning about himself. Despite his parents' insistence, he stopped attending conventional school at the age of 11 and engaged in autodidactic formation. Over time, he would become a serious critic of the current educational system.

Prabhuji is a recognized authority on Eastern wisdom. He is known for his erudition in the *Vaidika* and *Tāntrika* aspects of Hinduism and all branches of yoga (*jñāna*, *karma*, *bhakti*, *haṭha*, *rāja*, *kuṇḍalinī*, *tantra*, *mantra*, and others). He has an inclusive attitude toward all religions and is intimately familiar with Judaism, Christianity, Buddhism, Sufism, Taoism, Sikhism, Jainism, Shintoism, Bahaism, and the Mapuche religion, among others. He learned about the Druze religion directly from the scholars Salach Abbas and Kamil Shchadi.

Prabhuji studied Christian theology in depth with H.H. Monsignor Iván Larraín Eyzaguirre at the Veracruz Church in Santiago de Chile and with Mr. Héctor Muñoz, who holds a degree in theology from the Universidad Católica de la Santísima Concepción.

His curiosity for Western thought led him to venture into the field of philosophy in all its different branches. He specialized in Transcendental Phenomenology and the Phenomenology of Religion. He had the privilege of studying intensively for several years with his uncle Jorge Balazs, philosopher, researcher, writer, and author of *The Golden Deer*. He studied privately for a few years with Dr. Jonathan Ramos, a renowned philosopher, historian, and university professor graduated from the Catholic University of Salta, Argentina. He also studied with Dr. Alejandro Cavallazzi Sánchez, who holds an undergraduate degree in philosophy from the Universidad Panamericana, a master's degree in philosophy from the Universidad Iberoamericana, and a doctorate in philosophy from the Universidad Nacional Autónoma de México (UNAM).

Prabhuji holds a doctorate in Vaishnava philosophy from the respected Jiva Institute in Vrindavan, India, and a doctorate in yogic philosophy from the Yoga Samskrutum University.

Prabhuji holds a doctorate in Vaishnava philosophy from the respected Jiva Institute in Vrindavana, India, and a doctorate in yogic philosophy from the Yoga Samskrutum University.

His profound studies, his masters' blessings, his research into the sacred scriptures, and his vast teaching experience have earned him international recognition in the field of religion and spirituality.

His spiritual search led him to study with masters of diverse traditions and travel far from his native Chile to places as distant as Israel, India, and the USA. Prabhuji studied Hebrew and Sanskrit to deepen his understanding of the holy scriptures. He also studied Pali at the Oxford Centre for Buddhist Studies. Furthermore, he learned ancient Latin and Greek from Javier Álvarez, who holds a degree in Classical Philology from the Sevilla University.

His father, Yosef Har-Zion ZT"L, grew up under strict discipline because he was the son of a senior police sergeant. As a reaction to this upbringing, Yosef decided to raise his own children with complete freedom and unconditional love. Prabhuji grew up without any pressure. During his early years, his father showed his son the same love regardless of his successes or failures at school. When Prabhuji decided to drop out of school to devote himself to his inner quest, his family accepted his decision with deep respect. From the time his son was ten years old, Yosef talked to him about Hebrew spirituality and Western philosophy. They engaged in conversations about philosophy and religion for days on end and late into the night.

Yosef supported him in whatever he wanted to do in his life and his search for Truth. Prabhuji was the authentic project of freedom and unconditional love of his father.

At an early age and on his own initiative, Prabhuji began to practice karate and study philosophy and religion. During his adolescence, no one interfered with his decisions. At the age of 15, he established a deep, intimate, and long friendship with the famous Uruguayan writer and poet Blanca Luz Brum, who was his neighbor on Merced Street in Santiago de Chile. He traveled throughout Chile in search of wise and interesting people to learn from. In southern Chile, he met machis who taught him about the rich Mapuche spirituality and shamanism.

Two great masters contributed to Prabhuji's retroprogressive process. In 1976, he met his first guru, H.D.G Bhakti-kavi Atulānanda Ācārya Swami, whom he would call Gurudeva. In those days, Gurudeva was a young *brahmacārī* who held the position of president of the ISKCON temple at Eyzaguirre 2404, Puente Alto, Santiago, Chile. Years later, he gave Prabhuji first initiation, Brahminical initiation, and, finally, he initiated Prabhuji into the sacred order of renunciation called *sannyāsa* within the Brahma Gauḍīya Saṁpradāya. Gurudeva connected him to the devotion to Kṛṣṇa. He imparted to him the wisdom of bhakti yoga and instructed him in the practice of the *māhā-mantra* and the study of the holy scriptures.

In 1996, Prabhuji met his second guru, H.D.G. Avadhūta Śrī Brahmānanda Bābājī Mahārāja, in Rishikesh, India. Guru Mahārāja, as Prabhuji called him, revealed that his own master, H.D.G. Avadhūta Śrī Mastarāma Bābājī Mahārāja, had told him years before he died that a person would come from the West and request to be his disciple. He commanded him to accept only that particular seeker. When he asked how he would identify this person, Mastarāma Bābājī replied, "You will recognize him by his eyes. You must accept him because he will be the continuation of the lineage."

From his first meeting with young Prabhuji, Guru Mahārāja recognized him and officially initiated him into the *māhā-mantra*. For Prabhuji, this initiation marked the beginning of the most intense and mature stage of his retroprogressive process. Under the guidance of Guru Mahārāja, he studied Advaita Vedanta and deepened his meditation.

Guru Mahārāja guided Prabhuji on his first steps toward the sacred level of *avadhūta*. In March 2011, H.D.G. Avadhūta Śrī Brahmānanda Bābājī Mahārāja ordered Prabhuji, on behalf of his own master, to accept the responsibility of continuing the lineage of *avadhūtas*. With this title, Prabhuji is the official representative of the line of this disciplic succession for the present generation. Besides his *dikṣā-gurus*, Prabhuji studied with important spiritual and religious personalities, such as H.H. Swami Dayananda Sarasvatī, H.H. Swami Viṣṇu Devānanda Sarasvatī, H.H. Swami Jyotirmayānanda Sarasvatī, H.H. Swami Pratyagbodhānanda, H.H. Swami Swahananda of the Ramakrishna Mission, and H.H. Swami Viditātmānanda of the Arsha Vidya Gurukulam. The wisdom of tantra was awakened in Prabhuji by H.G. Mātājī Rīnā Śarmā in India.

Prabhuji wanted to confirm his *sannyāsa* initiation in an Advaita Vedanta lineage. His *sannyāsa-dīkṣā* was confirmed by H.H. Swami Jyotirmayānanda Sarasvatī, founder of the Yoga Research Foundation and disciple of H.H. Swami Śivānanda Sarasvatī of Rishikesh.

In 1984, he learned and began to practice Maharishi Mahesh Yogi's Transcendental Meditation technique. In 1988, he took the *kriyā-yoga* course on Paramahaṁsa Yogananda. After two years, he was officially initiated into the technique of *kriyā-yoga* by the Self-Realization Fellowship.

In Vrindavana, studied the bhakti yoga path in depth with H.H. Narahari Dāsa Bābājī Mahārāja, disciple of H.H. Nityananda Dāsa Bābājī Mahārāja of Vraja.

He also studied bhakti yoga with various disciples of His Divine Grace A.C. Bhaktivedānta Swami Prabhupāda: H.H. Kapīndra Swami, H.H. Paramadvaiti Mahārāja, H.H. Jagajīvana Dāsa, H.H. Tamāla Kṛṣṇa Gosvāmī, H.H. Bhagavān Dāsa Mahārāja, and H.H. Kīrtanānanda Swami, among others.

Prabhuji has been honored with various titles and diplomas by many leaders of prestigious religious and spiritual institutions in India. He was given the honorable title *Kṛṣṇa Bhakta* by H.H. Swami Viṣṇu Devānanda (the only title of Bhakti Yoga given by Swami Viṣṇu), disciple of H.H. Swami Śivānanda Sarasvatī and the founder of the Sivananda Organization. He was given the title *Bhaktivedānta* by H.H. B.A. Paramadvaiti Mahārāja, the founder of Vrinda. He was given the title *Yogācārya* by H.H. Swami Viṣṇu Devānanda, the Paramanand Institute of Yoga Sciences and Research of Indore, India, the International Yoga Federation, the Indian Association of Yoga, and the Shri Shankarananda Yogashram of Mysore, India. He received the respectable title *Śrī Śrī Rādhā Śyam Sunder Pāda-Padma Bhakta Śiromaṇi* directly from H.H. Satyanārāyaṇa Dāsa Bābājī Mahant of the Chatu Vaiṣṇava Saṁpradāya.

Prabhuji spent more than forty years studying hatha yoga with prestigious masters in classical and traditional yoga, such as H.H. Bapuji, H.H. Swami Viṣṇu Devānanda Sarasvatī, H.H. Swami Jyotirmayānanda Sarasvatī, H.H. Swami Satchidananda Sarasvatī, H.H. Swami Vignanananda Sarasvatī, and Śrī Madana-mohana.

He attended several systematic hatha yoga teacher training courses at prestigious institutions until he achieved the level of Master Ācārya. He has completed studies at the following institutions: the Sivananda Yoga Vedanta, the Ananda Ashram, the Yoga Research Foundation, the Integral Yoga Academy, the Patanjala Yoga Kendra, the Ma Yoga Shakti International Mission, the Prana Yoga Organization, the Rishikesh Yoga Peeth, the Swami Sivananda Yoga Research Center, and the Swami Sivananda Yogasana Research Center.

Prabhuji is a member of the Indian Association of Yoga, Yoga Alliance ERYT 500 and YACEP, the International Association of Yoga Therapists, and the International Yoga Federation. In 2014, the International Yoga Federation honored him with the position of Honorary Member of the World Yoga Council.

His interest in the complex anatomy of the human body led him to study chiropractic at the prestigious Institute of Health of the Back and Extremities in Tel Aviv, Israel. In 1993, he received a diploma from Dr. Sheinerman, the founder and director of the institute. Later, he earned a massage therapy diploma at the Academy of Western Galilee. The knowledge he acquired in this field deepened his understanding of hatha yoga and contributed to the creation of his own method.

Retroprogressive Hatha Yoga is the result of Prabhuji's efforts to improve his practice and teaching methods. It is a system based especially on the teachings of his gurus and the sacred scriptures. Prabhuji has systematized various traditional yoga techniques to create a methodology suitable for Western audiences. Retroprogressive Yoga aims to experience our true nature. It promotes balance, health, and flexibility through proper diet, cleansing techniques, preparations (*āyojanas*), sequences (*vinyāsas*), postures (*asanas*), breathing exercises (*prāṇayama*), relaxation (*śavāsana*), meditation (*dhyāna*), and exercises with locks (*bandhas*) and seals (*mudras*) to direct and empower *prāṇa*.

Since his childhood and throughout his life, Prabhuji has been an enthusiastic admirer, student, and practitioner of classic karate-do. From the age of 13, he studied different styles in Chile, such as kenpo and kung-fu, but specialized in the most traditional Japanese style of shotokan. He received the rank of black belt (third dan) from Shihan Kenneth Funakoshi (ninth dan). He also learned from Sensei Takahashi (seventh dan) and practiced Shorin Ryu style with Sensei Enrique Daniel Welcher (seventh dan), who granted him the rank of black belt (second dan). Through karate-do, he delved into Buddhism and gained additional knowledge about the physics of motion. Prabhuji is a member of Funakoshi's Shotokan Karate Association.

Prabhuji grew up in an artistic environment and his love of painting began to develop in his childhood. His father, the renowned Chilean painter Yosef Har-Zion ZT"L, motivated him to devote himself to art. He learned with the famous Chilean painter Marcelo Cuevas. Prabhuji's abstract paintings reflect the depths of the spirit.

Since he was a young boy, Prabhuji has been especially drawn to postal stamps, postcards, mailboxes, postal transportation systems, and all mail-related activities. He has taken every opportunity to visit post offices in different cities and countries. He has delved into the study of philately, the field of collecting, sorting, and studying postage stamps. This passion led him to become a professional philatelist, a stamp distributor authorized by the American Philatelic Society, and a member of the following societies: the Royal Philatelic Society London, the Royal Philatelic Society of Victoria, the United States Stamp Society, the Great Britain Philatelic Society, the American Philatelic Society, the Society of Israel Philatelists, the Society for Hungarian Philately, the National Philatelic Society UK, the Fort Orange Stamp Club, the American Stamp Dealers Association, the US Philatelic Classics Society, Filabras – Associação dos Filatelistas Brasileiros, and the Collectors Club of NYC.

Based on his extensive knowledge of philately, theology, and Eastern philosophy, Prabhuji created "Meditative Philately" or "Philatelic Yoga," a spiritual practice that uses philately as the basis for practicing attention, concentration, observation, and meditation. Meditative Philately is inspired by the ancient Hindu *maṇḍala* meditation and it can lead the practitioner to elevated states of consciousness, deep relaxation, and concentration that fosters the recognition of consciousness. Prabhuji wrote his thesis on this new type of yoga, "Meditative Philately," attracting the interest of the Indian academic community due to its innovative way of connecting meditation with different hobbies and activities. For this thesis, he was honored with a PhD in Yogic Philosophy from Yoga-Samskrutum University.

Prabhuji lived in Israel for many years, where he furthered his studies of Judaism. One of his main teachers and sources of inspiration was Rabbi Shalom Dov Lifshitz ZT"L, whom he met in 1997. This great saint guided him for several years on the intricate paths of the Torah and Chassidism. The two developed a very intimate relationship. Prabhuji studied the Talmud with Rabbi Raphael Rapaport Shlit"a (Ponovich), Chassidism with Rabbi Israel Lifshitz Shlit"a, and the Torah with Rabbi Daniel Sandler Shlit"a. Prabhuji is a great devotee of Rabbi Mordechai Eliyahu ZT"L, who personally blessed him.

Prabhuji visited the United States in 2000 and during his stay in New York, he realized that it was the most appropriate place to found a religious organization. He was particularly attracted by the pluralism and respectful attitude of American society toward freedom of religion. He was impressed by the deep respect of both the public and the government for religious minorities. After consulting his masters and requesting their blessings, Prabhuji relocated to the United States. In 2003, the Prabhuji Mission was born, a Hindu church aimed at preserving Prabhuji's universal and pluralistic vision of Hinduism and his Retroprogressive Yoga.

Although he did not seek to attract followers, for 15 years (1995–2010), Prabhuji considered the requests of a few people who approached him asking to become his monastic disciples. Those who chose to see Prabhuji as their spiritual master voluntarily accepted vows of poverty and life-long dedication to spiritual practice (*sadhāna*), religious devotion (*bhakti*), and selfless service (*seva*). Although Prabhuji no longer accepts new disciples, he continues to guide the small group of monastic disciples of the Ramakrishnananda Monastic Order that he founded.

In 2011, Prabhuji founded the Avadhutashram (monastery) in the Catskills Mountains in upstate New York, USA. The Avadhutashram is the headquarters of the Prabhuji Mission, his hermitage, and the residence of the monastic disciples of the Ramakrishnananda Monastic Order. The ashram organizes humanitarian projects such as the Prabhuji Food Distribution Program and the Prabhuji Toy Distribution Program. Prabhuji operates various humanitarian projects, inspired in his experience that serving the part is serving the Whole.

In January 2012, Prabhuji's health forced him to officially renounce managing the mission. Since then, he has lived in solitude, completely away from the public, writing and absorbed in contemplation. His message does not promote collective spirituality, but individual inner search.

Prabhuji has delegated the choice to his disciples between keeping his teachings exclusively within the monastic order or spreading his message for the public benefit. Upon the explicit request of his disciples, Prabhuji has agreed to have his books published and his lectures disseminated, as long as this does not compromise his privacy and his life as a hermit.

In 2022, Prabhuji founded the Institute of Retroprogressive Yoga. Here, his most senior disciples can systematically share Prabhuji's teachings and message through video conferences. The institute offers support and help for a deeper understanding of Prabhuji's teachings.

Prabhuji is a respected member of the American Philosophical Association, the American Association of Philosophy Teachers, the American Association of University Professors, the Southwestern Philosophical Society, the Authors Guild, the National Writers Union, PEN America, the International Writers Association, the National Association of Independent Writers and Editors, the National Writers Association, the Alliance Independent Authors, and the Independent Book Publishers Association.

Prabhuji's vast literary contribution includes books in Spanish, English, and Hebrew, for example, *Kundalini Yoga: The Power is in you*, *What is, as it is*, *Bhakti-Yoga: The Path of Love*, *Tantra: Liberation in the World*, *Experimenting with the Truth*, *Advaita Vedanta: Be the Self*, commentaries on the *Īśāvāsya Upanishad* and the *Diamond Sūtra*.

About the Prabhuji Mission

Prabhuji, H.H. Avadhūta Śrī Bhaktivedānta Yogācārya Ramakrishnananda Bābājī Mahārāja, founded the Prabhuji Mission in 2003, a Hindu church aimed at preserving his universal and pluralistic vision of Hinduism.

The main purpose of the mission is to preserve Prabhuji's teachings of Pūrvavyāpi-pragatiśīlaḥ Yoga, or Retroprogressive Yoga, which advocates for a global awakening of consciousness as the radical solution to humanity's problems.

The Prabhuji Mission operates a Hindu temple called Śrī Śrī Radha-Śyāmasundara Mandir, which offers worship and religious ceremonies to parishioners. The extensive library of the Retroprogressive Yoga Institute provides its teachers with abundant study materials to research the various theologies and philosophies explored by Prabhuji in his books and lectures. The Avadhutashram monastery educates monastic disciples on various aspects of Prabhuji's approach to Hinduism and offers them the opportunity to express devotion to God through devotional service by selflessly contributing their skills and training to the Mission's programs, such as the Prabhuji Food Distribution program, a weekly event in which dozens of families in need from Upstate New York receive fresh and nutritious food.

Service and glorification of the guru are fundamental spiritual principles in Hinduism. The Prabhuji Mission, as a traditional Hindu church, practices the millenary *guru-bhakti* tradition of reverence to the master. Some disciples and friends of the Prabhuji Mission, on their own initiative, help to preserve Prabhuji's legacy and his interfaith teachings for future generations by disseminating his books, videos of his internal talks, and websites.

About the Avadhutashram

The Avadhutashram (monastery) was founded by Prabhuji in the Catskills Mountains in upstate New York, USA. It is the headquarters of the Prabhuji Mission and the hermitage of H.H. Avadhūta Śrī Bhaktivedānta Yogācārya Ramakrishnananda Bābājī Mahārāja and his monastic disciples of the Ramakrishnananda Monastic Order.

The ideals of the Avadhutashram are love and selfless service, based on the universal vision that God is in everything and everyone. Its mission is to distribute spiritual books and organize humanitarian projects such as the Prabhuji Food Distribution Program and the Prabhuji Toy Distribution Program.

The Avadhutashram is not commercial and operates without soliciting donations. Its activities are funded by Prabhuji's Gifts, a non-profit company founded by Prabhuji, which sells esoteric items from different traditions that Prabhuji himself has used for spiritual practices during his evolutionary process. Its mission is to preserve and disseminate traditional religious, mystical, and ancestral crafts.

Avadhutashram
Round Top, NY, USA

The Retroprogressive Path

The Retroprogressive Path does not require you to be part of a group or a member of an organization, institution, society, congregation, club, or exclusive community. Living in a temple, monastery, or *āśram* is not mandatory, because it is not about a change of residence, but of consciousness. It does not urge you to believe, but to doubt. It does not demand you to accept something, but to explore, investigate, examine, inquire, and question everything. It does not suggest being what you should be but being what you really are.

The Retroprogressive Path supports freedom of expression but not proselytizing. This route does not promise answers to our questions but induces us to question our answers. It does not promise to be what we are not or to attain what we have not already achieved. It is a retro-evolutionary path of self-discovery that leads us from what we think we are to what we really are. It is not the only way, nor the best, the simplest, or the most direct. It is an involutionary process par excellence that shows what is obvious and undeniable but usually goes unnoticed: that which is simple, innocent, and natural. It is a path that begins and ends in you.

The Retroprogressive Path is a continuous revelation that expands eternally. It delves into consciousness from an ontological perspective, transcending all religion and spiritual paths. It is the discovery of diversity as a unique and inclusive reality. It is the encounter of consciousness with itself, aware of itself and its own reality. In fact, this path is a simple invitation to dance in the now, to love the present moment, and to celebrate our authenticity. It is an unconditional proposal to stop living as a victim of circumstance and to live as a passionate adventurer. It is a call to return to the place we have never left, without offering us anything we do not already possess or teaching us anything we do not already know. It is a call for an inner revolution and to enter the fire of life that only consumes dreams, illusions, and fantasies but does not touch what we are. It does not help us reach our desired goal, but instead prepares us for the unexpected miracle.

This path was nurtured over a lifetime dedicated to the search for Truth. It is a grateful offering to existence for what I have received. But remember, do not look for me. Look for yourself. It is not me you need, because you are the only one who really matters.This life is just a wonderful parenthesis in eternity to know and love. What you yearn for lies in you, here and now, as what you really are.

Your unconditional well-wisher,
Prabhuji

Prabhuji today

Prabhuji is retired from public life

Prabhuji is the sole disciple of H.D.G. Avadhūta Śrī Brahmānanda Bābājī Mahārāja, who is himself one of the closest and most intimate disciples of H.D.G. Avadhūta Śrī Mastarāma Bābājī Mahārāja.

Prabhuji was appointed as the successor of the lineage by his master, who conferred upon him the responsibility of continuing the sacred *paramparā* of *avadhūtas*, officially appointing him as guru and ordering him to serve as Ācārya successor under the name H.H. Avadhūta Śrī Bhaktivedānta Yogācārya Ramakrishnananda Bābājī Mahārāja.

Prabhuji is also a disciple of H.D.G. Bhakti-kavi Atulānanda Ācārya Mahārāja, who is a direct disciple of H.D.G. A.C. Bhaktivedānta Swami Prabhupāda.

In 2011, he chose to retire from society and lead the life of a hermit. Since then, his days have been spent in solitude, praying, writing, painting, and meditating in silence and contemplation. He no longer participates in *sat-saṅgs*, lectures, gatherings, meetings, retreats, seminars, study groups, or courses. We ask everyone to respect his privacy and do not try to contact him by any means for gatherings, meetings, interviews, blessings, *śaktipāta*, initiations, or personal visits.

Prabhuji's teachings

As an *avadhūta* and a realized master, Prabhuji has always appreciated the essence and wisdom of a wide variety of religious practices from around the world. He does not consider himself a member or representative of any particular religion. Although many see him as an enlightened being, Prabhuji has no intention of presenting himself as a preacher, guide, coach, content creator, influencer, preceptor, mentor, counselor, consultant, monitor, tutor, teacher, instructor, educator, enlightener, pedagogue, evangelist, rabbi, *posek halacha*, healer, therapist, satsangist, pointer, psychic, leader, medium, savior, or guru. In fact, Prabhuji believes that the quest for the Self is individual, solitary, personal, private, and intimate. It is not a collective endeavor to be undertaken through social, organized, institutional, or community religiosity.

To that end, Prabhuji does not proselytize or preach, nor does he try to persuade, convince, or make anyone change their perspective, philosophy, or religion. Others may find his insights valuable and apply them wholly or in part to their own development, but Prabhuji's teachings should not be interpreted as personal advice, counseling, guidance, self-help methods, or techniques for spiritual, physical, emotional, or psychological development. The proposed teachings do not aspire to be definitive solutions for life's spiritual, material, financial, psychological, emotional, romantic, family, social, or physical problems. Prabhuji does not offer miracles, mystical experiences, astral journeys, healings, connections with spirits, supernatural powers, or spiritual salvation.

Although he did not seek to attract followers, for 15 years (1995–2010), Prabhuji considered the requests of a few people who approached him asking to become his monastic disciples. Those who chose to see Prabhuji as their spiritual master voluntarily accepted vows of poverty and life-long dedication to spiritual practice (*sādhanā*), religious devotion (*bhakti*), and selfless service (*seva*). Prabhuji no longer accepts new disciples, but he continues to guide the small group of veteran disciples of the Ramakrishnananda Monastic Order that he founded.

Public services

Even though the monastery does not accept new residents, volunteers, donations, collaborations, or sponsorships, the public is invited to participate in daily religious services and devotional festivals at the Śrī Śrī Radha-Śyāmasundara temple.

Titles by Prabhuji

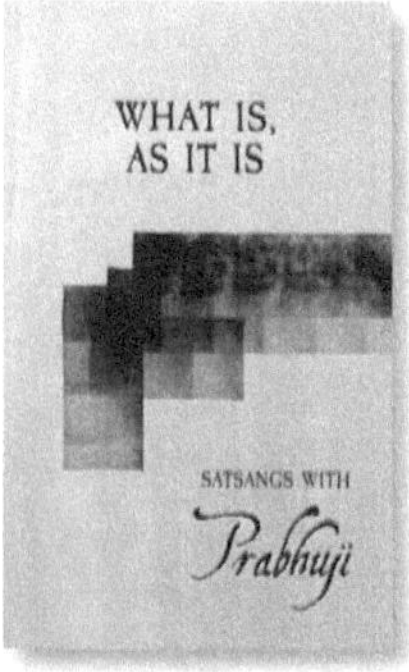

What is, as it is: Satsangs with Prabhuji (English)
ISBN-13: 978-1-945894-26-8
Lo que es, tal como es: Satsangas con Prabhuji (Spanish)
ISBN-13: 978-1-945894-27-5
Russian: ISBN-13: 978-1-945894-18-3

Kundalini yoga: The power is in you (English)
ISBN-13:978-1-945894-30-5
Kundalini yoga: El poder está en ti (Spanish)
ISBN-13:978-1-945894-31-2

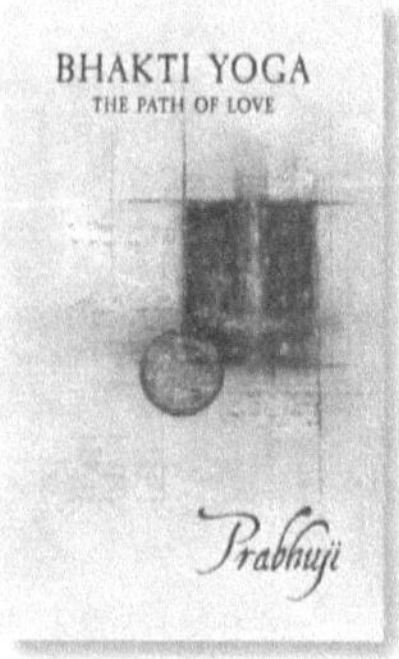

Bhakti yoga: The path of love (English)
ISBN-13: 978-1-945894-28-2
Bhakti-yoga: El sendero del amor (Spanish)
ISBN-13: 978-1-945894-29-9

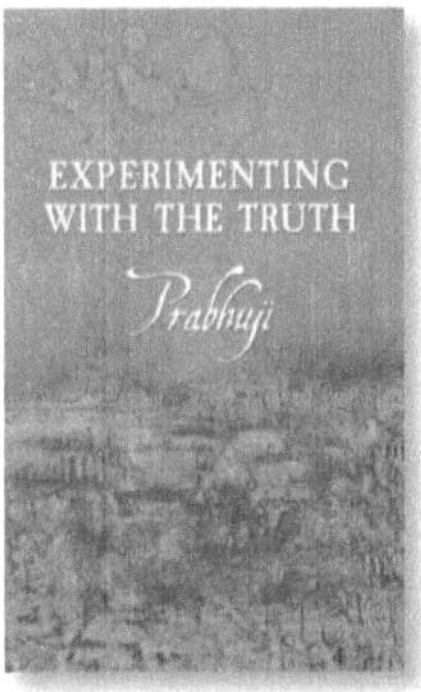

Experimenting with the Truth (English)
ISBN-13: 978-1-945894-32-9
Experimentando con la Verdad (Spanish)
ISBN-13: 978-1-945894-33-6

Tantra: Liberation in the world (English)
ISBN-13: 978-1-945894-36-7
Tantra: La liberación en el mundo (Spanish)
ISBN-13: 978-1-945894-37-4

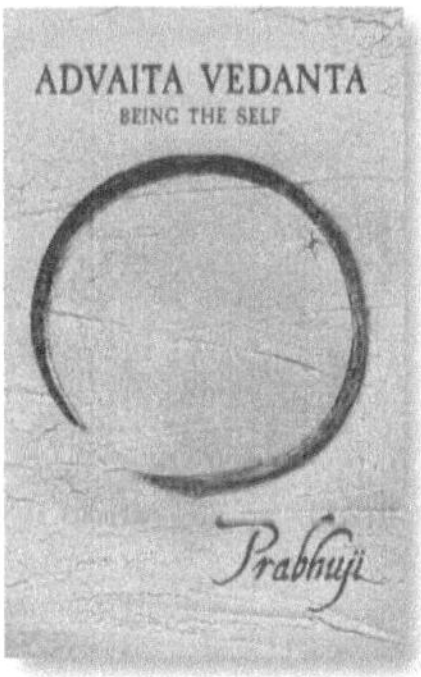

Advaita Vedanta: Being the Self (English)
ISBN-13: 978-1-945894-34-3
Advaita Vedanta: Ser el Ser (Spanish)
ISBN-13: 978-1-945894-35-0

Īśāvāsya Upanishad
commented by Prabhuji
(English)
ISBN-13: 978-1-945894-38-1
Īśāvāsya Upaniṣad
comentado por Prabhuji
(Spanish)
ISBN-13: 978-1-945894-40-4

The Diamond Sūtra
commented by Prabhuji
(English)
ISBN-13: 978-1-945894-51-0
El Sūtra del Diamante
comentado por Prabhuji
(Spanish)
ISBN-13: 978-1-945894-54-1

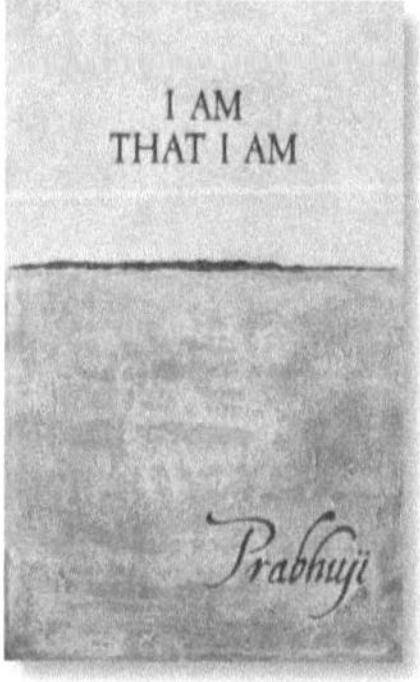

I am that I am
(English)
ISBN-13: 978-1-945894-45-9
Soy el que soy
(Spanish)
ISBN-13: 978-1-945894-48-0

www.ingramcontent.com/pod-product-compliance
Lightning Source LLC
Chambersburg PA
CBHW030106240426
43661CB00001B/34
9781945894367